SOCIETAL DYNAMICS

SOCIETAL DYNAMICS
Exploring Macrosociology

MARVIN E. OLSEN
Michigan State University

PRENTICE HALL, Englewood Cliffs, New Jersey 07632

Library of Congress Cataloging-in-Publication Data

Olsen, Marvin Elliott.
    Societal dynamics : exploring macrosociology/Marvin E. Olsen.
      p. cm.
    Includes bibliographical references and index.
    ISBN 0-13-817586-1
    1. Macrosociology. I. Title.
HM51.046   1991
301—dc20   90-7713

Editorial/production supervision: *Edith Riker/Jeanne Sillay Jacobson*
Cover design: *Marianne Frasco*
Prepress buyer: *Debra Kesar*
Manufacturing buyer: *Mary Ann Gloriande*

Printed in the United States of America

10 9 8 7 6 5 4 3 2 1

ISBN   0-13-817586-1

Prentice-Hall International (UK) Limited, *London*
Prentice-Hall of Australia Pty. Limited, *Sydney*
Prentice-Hall Canada Inc., *Toronto*
Prentice-Hall Hispanoamericana, S.A., *Mexico*
Prentice-Hall of India Private Limited, *New Delhi*
Prentice-Hall of Japan, Inc., *Tokyo*
Simon & Schuster Asia Pte. Ltd., *Singapore*
Editora Prentice-Hall do Brasil, Ltda., *Rio de Janeiro*

CONTENTS

Chapter 4
CULTURE

Chapter 5
ORGANIZATIONAL UNITS

Chapter 6
SOCIAL PROCESSES

CONCEPTUAL INTERLUDE: THE PROCESS OF SOCIAL ORGANIZATION

PART II
PREINDUSTRIAL SOCIETIES

Chapter 7
ECOLOGY AND ECONOMIES OF PREINDUSTRIAL SOCIETIES

Chapter 8
SOCIAL ORGANIZATION OF PREINDUSTRIAL SOCIETIES

Chapter 9
TRANSITION TO INDUSTRIALISM

Chapter 10
CONTEMPORARY INDUSTRIALIZING SOCIETIES

PART III
INDUSTRIAL SOCIETIES

Chapter 11
ECOLOGY OF INDUSTRIAL SOCIETIES

Chapter 12
INDUSTRIAL ECONOMIES

258

Chapter 13
MODERN POLITIES

288

Chapter 14
URBAN COMMUNITIES

318

Chapter 15
BUREAUCRATIZED ORGANIZATIONS

347

Chapter 16
SOCIOECONOMIC STRATIFICATION

Chapter 17
SOCIOCULTURAL INEQUALITY

Chapter 18
FAMILIES

Chapter 19
SOCIOCULTURAL INSTITUTIONS

PREFACE TO INSTRUCTORS

This introductory sociology textbook is designed for instructors who want to teach an intellectually challenging and stimulating course. My experience in teaching this course over the past 25 years has convinced me that most students can handle a much more intellectually demanding course than is commonly taught. Moreover, better students are frequently disappointed and disillusioned with the introductory course as it is frequently taught, and they consequently lose interest in taking additional sociology courses. I hope that this text will attract students to sociology rather than repel them—as the introductory course almost did to me many years ago.

To meet that challenge, the book contains more material than most other introductory texts. In writing the book, I have followed the strategy of including as many ideas and topics as might be appropriate for a variety of introductory courses, since material that one instructor feels is unnecessary may be crucial for another instructor. When preparing reading assignments for students, I have always found it much easier to tell them to skip certain topics or pages rather than having to locate and assign supplementary readings to cover material I thought was crucial but was omitted from the basic textbook. Quite likely, therefore, you may decide not to deal with all of the concepts and topics presented here on the grounds that some of the material is not necessary for beginning students. In my own teaching, I often omit some of the material contained in whatever text I am using, and I strongly encourage you to use this book in whatever selective manner best suits your particular course.

This text is written from a particular perspective and makes no attempt to be totally eclectic—which I believe makes introductory textbooks either bland or confusing for students. If you are familiar with the "Michigan perspective" in introductory texts—as expressed in *Principles of Sociology* by Ronald Freedman, Amos Hawley, Werner Landecker, Gerhard Lenski, and Horace Miner; *The Organization of Society* by Paul Mott; and *Human Societies* by Gerhard Lenski and Jean Lenski—you will quickly identify this book as following in that tradition. Three principal features characterize this perspective: (1) A primary focus on macrosociology, or social organization, rather than on microsociology, or social psychology; (2) A pervasive concern with societal evolution and the way in which the transition from an agricultural to an industrial economy affects virtually all aspects of societies; and (3) The use of a social ecology framework to explain the evolution of social organization.

To that "Michigan perspective" I have added three additional themes: (4) The fundamental importance of the economy as the institutional realm through which ecological forces affect human societies, as well as the social inequalities that commonly result from the functioning of the ecological and economic systems; (5) The central role of social power throughout all social organization, and particularly its concentration and use by the state; and (6) The pervasive nature and effects of belief systems and values in shaping and perpetuating human social life. In short, the dominant themes in this book are *social organization, political economy,* and *ecological evolution.*

The first two "Michigan texts" are no longer in print, but the Lenski's *Human Societies* is. This book differs from theirs in four main ways: (1) My treatment of basic sociological concepts, perspectives, and theories is much more extensive than theirs, comprising six rather than just two chapters. (2) I give somewhat less detailed attention to preindustrial societies than do the Lenskis, and I focus on developmental trends running throughout all preindustrial societies. (3) My treatment of industrial societies is considerably more extensive than theirs, with much more attention to the political economy of modern states and a more critical stance toward socioeconomic inequality. (4) I include two chapters dealing with postindustrial societies, compared to the one brief chapter on this topic in the Lenski's book.

If you are familiar with either the first or second edition of my book, *The Process of Social Organization,* you will recognize many ideas from it in this text, especially in Part I, but they have been considerably reworked to be appropriate to an introductory course.

The book is divided into four major parts. Part I, Conceptual Tools, presents the basic concepts, theoretical perspectives, and social processes used throughout the book. Part II, Preindustrial Societies, discusses those societies from both ecological/economic and social organizational perspectives, as well as the transition from agriculture to industrialism in the past and present. Part III, Industrial Societies, begins with the ecological base of industrialized societies and then covers all of the major facets and dimensions of modern societies. Part IV, Postindustrial Societies, sketches a number of emerging crises in contemporary societies and the current process of societal transformation into a postindustrial society. For consistency, each chapter is divided into five major sections, plus a comprehensive summary.

I want to thank sincerely all of my intellectual mentors—including Ed Swanson, Gerry Lenski, Al Reiss, Bill Gamson, Amos Hawley, Morris Janowitz, Ted Newcomb, Tom Lasswell, and John Burma—for initiating the process of intellectual exploration that has resulted in this book. They are obviously not responsible for anything in it, but I hope they will recognize some of their thinking in these pages. In particular, I am deeply indebted to Gerry Lenski for many of the ideas concerning ecological evolution and patterns of stratification that are central to this book. I also want to thank Michael Micklin for all his assistance in planning and editing this book, as well as his substantive contributions to Chapter 11. And I deeply appreciate the countless hours that Tammy Dennany spent typing this lengthy manuscript.

Marvin E. Olsen

PREFACE TO STUDENTS

Welcome to the world of sociology! The purpose of studying sociology is to increase our understanding of the nature and dynamics of organized social life, beyond the common sense we all acquire as members of our society. I hope that this text will expand your vision of society in two crucial ways: (1) offering a new perspective on the social world in which you live, which is sometimes called a "sociological perspective," and which may be quite different from the way in which you presently view social life; and (2) providing a deeper and more sophisticated understanding of the processes and forces that have created the kind of industrialized-urbanized society in which we live today, and that are presently transforming our society in fundamental ways that we are now only beginning to discern.

This text is intended to be intellectually challenging and demanding, but if you are serious about exploring the world of sociology, you can master it. By the time you finish this course, I trust that you will have learned a great deal, that you will have gained a sociological perspective on the world, and that you will have a better understanding of contemporary societies in the process of ecological evolution.

The book is divided into four major parts. Part I, Conceptual Tools, presents the basic concepts, theoretical perspectives, and social processes used throughout the book. Part II, Preindustrial Societies, discusses those earlier forms of societies as well as the transition from agriculture to industrialism in the past and present. Part III, Industrial Societies, includes chapters on all of the major aspects of modern societies, which are the central concerns of sociology. Part IV, Postindustrial Societies, sketches a number of emerging crises in contemporary societies and the process of societal transformation that is moving us into a postindustrial society. For consistency, each chapter is divided into five major sections, plus a comprehensive summary.

The study of sociology can be fascinating and deeply satisfying, both as an intellectual challenge and as a means of understanding the social world in which we live. I have always been thrilled with sociology, and I sincerely hope you will be also.

Marvin E. Olsen

To understand the social structure we must therefore view it in the historical process, seeking continuity, relating time-differences to time-likeness. We must, in other words, discover the direction of change, or all is meaningless. That is why the principle of evolution becomes of supreme significance. . . .

Moreover, social phenomena are historical phenomena in a profounder sense than any other. . . . Society exists only as a time-sequence. It is a becoming, not a being; a process, not a product.

Robert M. MacIver, *Society: A Textbook of Sociology,* 1937, pp. 391, 394.

1

THE SOCIOLOGICAL PERSPECTIVE

What does sociology deal with, and how is it different from psychology?
What do we mean by "social organization," and why is it called a process?
What concerns did Karl Marx, Max Weber, and Émile Durkheim share?
How do sociologists go about studying social life in a scientific manner?
Is it possible for sociologists to be both objective and value-involved?

HUMAN EXISTENCE

Human beings are always and inexorably social creatures. We must interact with one another if we are to survive as individuals or as a species. And through that interaction we create social organization. Thus human survival is a collective or organizational process (Hawley, 1986). There are no records of even the most primitive people ever living without some kind of social organization, and contemporary social life is very complexly organized.

People must create social organization if they are to attain the goals they seek. Regardless of whether we desire material comfort, personal growth, a happy marriage, community improvement, reduction of socioeconomic inequality, national prosperity, or international peace, we cannot realize these goals without participating in various forms of social organization. Throughout our lives we take part in many different kinds of organizations, ranging in size from our family and friendship groups to our society and the entire world system.

Another fundamental feature of human life is that we all seek meaning or purpose in our existence and activities. As self-conscious thinking beings we constantly search for knowledge, beliefs, and values that give meaning to life. That search necessitates our communicating with others and sharing common cultural ideas with them.

The Quest

Although most of humanity throughout history has struggled to cope with the practical demands of surviving, achieving goals, and finding meaning in life, in all eras some people have undertaken the demanding quest of understanding the nature and dynamics of organized human life. In the past, these inquirers were often called social philosophers, while today they are likely to be social scientists. Their methods of inquiry have changed through time, but the quest remains the same: to understand the process and forms of human social organization.

This book introduces you to that intellectual quest by presenting a set of concepts and theoretical ideas for understanding social organization, sketching the course of sociocultural evolution, exploring ways in which the transition from agricultural to industrial societies has altered virtually every aspect of human social life, and raising some questions about the directions of possible future trends in human societies.

Before we embark on that quest, however, we must be clear about one fundamental feature of existence as we know it. *All reality is process, and process is reality.*

The universe is continually expanding; stars go through a cycle from birth to death; subatomic particles are forever in motion; life is relentlessly evolving from simple to complex forms; the human mind continues to learn and develop throughout life; and societies are never the same from one generation to the next. As expressed by the philosopher Alfred North Whitehead (1928:317), "The flux of things is one ultimate generalization around which we must weave our philosophical system." Consequently, the many varieties of social organization that people create to ensure survival, attain goals, and give meaning to life are all dynamic processes. *Human social organization is always an ongoing process,* never a static condition.

Levels of Ordering

The components of human life ultimately form a unified whole, since all aspects of the ongoing process of reality are interrelated.

Within this totality of human life, however, we can identify four relatively distinct levels of ordering, or sets of dynamic processes: organic, personal, social, and symbolic. Each successively higher level of ordering is based on all lower levels, but also displays characteristics that do not occur at lower levels and which give it a reality of its own. These levels of ordering are shown in Figure 1-1 and described as follows.

Organic ordering is distinguished from all levels of physical existence by the presence of life. The principal type of organic system is the organism, either plant or animal; but parts of organisms (such as organs) are also ordered, as are relationships among organisms (such as food chains). Human beings are first of all biological organisms that must continually satisfy basic needs for oxygen, water, food, warmth, reproduction, and other necessities of biological life.

Personal ordering is distinguished from the organic level by the presence of a mind that is capable of intellectual, emotional, and evaluative activities. The principal type of personal system is the personality. All mammals appear to have at least rudimentary personalities, but the capabilities of the human mind are so much more extensive and complex than in most other mammals that we usually think of this level of ordering as applying only to people. Each individual possesses a distinct personality with drives for security, affection, acceptance, recognition, personal growth, and other psychological requirements.

Social ordering is distinguished from the personal level by the existence of relationships among minds or personalities. Al-

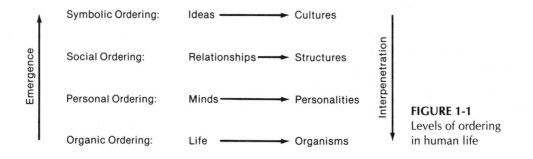

Symbolic Ordering: Ideas ⟶ Cultures

Social Ordering: Relationships ⟶ Structures

Personal Ordering: Minds ⟶ Personalities

Organic Ordering: Life ⟶ Organisms

Emergence

Interpenetration

FIGURE 1-1
Levels of ordering
in human life

though individuals create social ordering through their interaction, it consists of stable patterns of social structure. There are many different types of social ordering, or collectivities, but the most basic is the family and the most encompassing is the society. From the moment of birth we all live as members of many collectivities, and we could not exist without them.

Symbolic ordering is distinguished from the social level by the existence of ideas that are encoded into abstract symbols. There are many types of symbolic systems, or cultures, throughout the world that are associated with societies and other collectivities but are not identical to them. Throughout our lives we are constantly seeking to expand and enrich our symbolic systems as we communicate with others about our experiences, feelings, expectations, values, and beliefs.

To the extent that these levels of ordering are identifiable in human life, each is characterized by the three qualities of *emergence, independence,* and *interpenetration.* A level of ordering emerges from, or develops out of, the levels below it and is always dependent on them for its existence.

Personalities develop in conjunction with organic bodies and do not survive when the organism dies; a group is created only when two or more personalities interact and ceases to exist when all of its members withdraw; and cultures grow out of shared social experiences and become museum relics when their societies disappear. At the same time, each level of ordering possesses some independence, or autonomy, from lower levels by virtue of its distinctive characteristics. Consequently, no level is fully determined by lower levels. A personality is more than just an animated body; a group is more than just a collection of individuals; and a belief system is more than just a literal description of social life. Finally, each level of ordering interpenetrates all lower levels in the sense that it frequently influences them as well as being influenced by them. Personality tensions can result in stomach ulcers, while poor nutrition can cause emotional problems. One's work group can influence one's self-image, while a neurotic supervisor can limit the productivity of the entire group. Religious convictions can lead to collective warfare or individual martyrdom, while the complexity of a society's social structure can affect the kind of deity in which its people believe.

Perspectives and Disciplines

Although human existence incorporates all four levels of ordering, when we attempt to describe or explain human activities we often do so from the perspective of a single level (either entirely or predominantly). Associated with each of these perspectives are a number of scientific and applied disciplines. With a biological perspective, we focus on the organic features of human life, as practiced in biology, physiology, and medicine. With a psychological perspective, we focus on the mental or personality characteristics of human life, as practiced in psychology, psychiatry, and education. With a sociological perspective, we focus on the social or collective aspects of human life, as practiced in sociology, economics, political science, anthropology, social work, and public administration. With a cultural perspective, we focus on sets of symbolic ideas or meanings in human life, as practiced in philosophy, literature, linguistics, law, and religion.

Most disciplines are not very tightly contained within a single perspective, however, and tend to incorporate other perspectives to some extent. Thus psychology takes account of physiological and social influences on the personality, and sociology examines the ways in which personality characteristics and cultural values shape social life. There are also many interdisciplinary fields that bridge adjacent perspectives, such as physiological psychology, social psychology, the sociology of law, and the sociology of religion. The linkages between levels of ordering and disciplines of study make clear, however, that all of the social sciences share a common analytical perspective. They all focus primarily on patterns of relationships among people, although they commonly emphasize different kinds of relationships. In addition, they all incorporate aspects of the psychological and cultural perspectives. Because of these similarities, sociologists, economists, anthropologists, and political scientists are finding it increasingly difficult to distinguish one field from another as their disciplines become more sophisticated.

If all the social sciences primarily employ a social perspective, what distinguishes sociology from the other social scientific disciplines, other than tradition? This question may be answered in several ways, including the cynical observation that sociologists study whatever other social scientists don't deal with—such as families, race relations, and crime. Contemporary sociologists are increasingly realizing, however, that their discipline has a unique task that encompasses all the specialized subfields of sociology and cuts across all the other social sciences. This task is to explain theoretically and analyze empirically the process of social organization wherever it occurs. In this book, therefore, *sociology is considered to be the scientific study of the process of social organization and all of its forms.* Sociology is thus the most encompassing of the social sciences, and partially overlaps with all of them.

In addition to its scientific goals of describing, explaining, and predicting the process of social organization, sociology also has a humanistic concern with broadening the intellectual horizons of its students and giving them a different perspective on human life. C. Wright Mills (1959:15) termed this perspective "the sociological imagination" and described it as "not merely one quality of mind among the contemporary range of cultural sensibilities—it is the quality whose wider and more adroit use offers the promise that all such sensibilities—and in fact, human reason itself—will come to play a greater role in human affairs."

SOCIAL ORGANIZATION

Since the central concern of sociology is with the process of social organization, we shall use this concept throughout the book. Before progressing further, therefore, let us look briefly at some fundamental aspects of social organization in its most general sense.

Nature of Social Organization

The sociological quest to understand the process of social organization focuses primarily on the levels of social and symbolic ordering. How do human beings, with all their individual idiosyncrasies, manage to cooperate to create relatively stable and beneficial patterns of social ordering and to construct relatively satisfying and enduring sets of cultural meanings? As the philosopher Thomas Hobbes (1881:91–96) asked three hundred years ago, what prevents human life from inevitably being "solitary, poor, nasty, brutish, and short"? The answer to Hobbes's question provided by contemporary social science is that human beings bring order and meaning into their collective social life by establishing and maintaining social organization that can take countless specific forms. In short, *social organization is the process of creating social ordering and cultural meaning in human life.*

As an example of the everyday occurrence of organization in social life, imagine a typical city street corner. Cars speed by on one of the streets, but at the change of a light stop to allow traffic to move along the cross street. A group of people on the sidewalk are engaged in conversation. A line of pickets marches back and forth in front of a store. A number of strangers patiently wait in line to board a bus. And a crew of construction workers renovates a building. This commonplace scene actually illustrates many different forms of social organization.

Any instance of social organization is created as individuals engage in social interaction that over time becomes patterned into stable and predictable forms that become infused with symbolic meanings. As diagramed in Figure 1-2, *all social organization thus has three components: recurrent interpersonal interaction* (the topic of Chapter 2), *stable patterns of social ordering* (the topic of Chapter

FIGURE 1-2 Components of the process of social organization

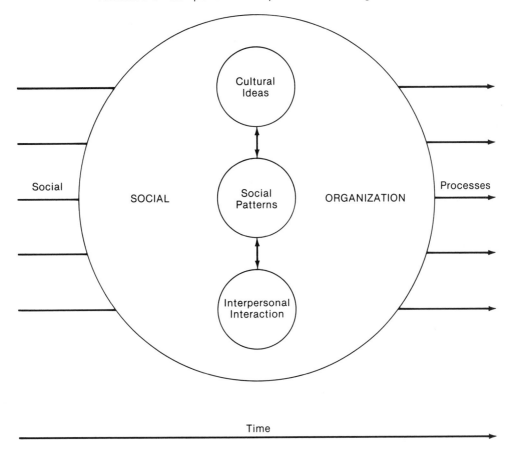

3), *and shared cultural ideas* (the topic of Chapter 4). These three components of all social organization can be seen in your own family. To create a functioning family unit, each individual must (at least part of the time) interact with other family members in ways that are relatively recurrent and predictable, so that the relationships comprising the family remain stable through time. Each person enacts a number of roles—such as income earner, cook, yard tender, or vacation planner—that are coordinated with the roles of the other family members. The resulting patterns of social ordering ensure that desired family functions—such as providing an income, performing household chores, and enjoying leisure activities—are performed adequately. Social ordering also

enables individual family members to relate to each other in relatively stable ways, rather than having to devise a new set of actions each time they interact. All this activity, meanwhile, is guided and regulated by family values, traditions, norms, rules, role expectations, and other shared ideas that comprise your family's unique culture. *Social organization thus always involves the merging of interpersonal interaction, social ordering, and symbolic meanings into a unified whole.*

Comprehending Social Organization

The street corner scene previously described suggests two difficulties that are often encountered when attempting to observe and comprehend social organization.

The first of these is that we cannot directly observe social organization in the same way that we perceive individuals and their actions. In the example we could observe some people talking together in front of a building, but not the bonds of friendship that link them into a close-knit group. Nor could we directly observe the patterns of job specialization and coordination that enable the construction workers to interact smoothly as they go about their tasks. *The existence of social organization must be inferred from its effects on the actions of the people involved,* just as the existence of gravity must be inferred from its effects on falling objects.

A second difficulty in observing social organization is that we cannot directly perceive the flow of time. The example portrays only a single slice of time, isolated from everything that led up to those specific events and everything that will follow them. It tells us nothing about the additional organized activities in which those people may engage in different situations. Nor does it say anything about the other events that may transpire at that street corner during the course of a day. *To become fully aware of the ongoing nature of social organization, we must look beyond momentary events to examine the social processes they represent.*

The idea of perceiving social organization as an ongoing process rather than as static forms can be illustrated with a simple analogy. Imagine that your mind is like a motion picture film. Suppose that you are presently observing a specific instance of social interaction, such as a man and a woman in conversation, with the woman reaching out her hand to the man. Your mind perceives a continuous stream of static observations of the interaction, no one of which tells you much about the nature of the dynamic relationship being enacted. Whatever social ordering they are creating—whether it be a marriage, a sales transaction, or a play production—existed as an ongoing process before you observed them, and will continue into the future. Each observation you make of this situation "freezes" the ongoing process into a static picture that is isolated in

time and does not fully represent what is really occurring. From a succession of these observations made through time, however, you can construct an image of the dynamic social process that is actually occurring. You then perceive the enactment of a work relationship in which the woman is giving the man instructions for the day's activities. The pattern of social ordering they are enacting now becomes visible and meaningful. Note, however, that this social organization must be inferred by you from a series of static observations. To draw accurate inferences about dynamic social processes and to determine how these processes form patterns of ordered and meaningful social organization, your perceptions of social life must constantly be attuned to the dynamic nature of all social life.

Conceiving of social organization as a continual process raises two additional questions. First, how do we manage to create stable patterns of social ordering and shared cultural ideas that endure through time? The answer to this question lies in the nature of social and cultural stability. Stability does not imply lack of change or a static condition. Quite the opposite. Stability is itself a dynamic process that is maintained through continual modification and alteration in response to changing conditions. Although some social practices and cultural ideas may be perpetuated for long periods of time, sooner or later they become useless and meaningless. In fact, traditions survive precisely because they can be adapted to changing conditions. In short, social and cultural stability are obtained through constant change. *Order and change are thus two sides of the same process.*

The second question is how can social organization be simultaneously a dynamic activity and an identifiable entity? The dictionary defines "organization" as both "an act or process of organizing" and "a body of persons organized for some end." We might therefore speak first of "organizing a new political party," and then refer to this entity as a "political organization." This dual meaning of the word "organization" is not a semantic accident. It reflects the fact that process and form are inseparable in reality. *The organizational entities that we create as we bring order and meaning into human activities are specific manifestations at particular time periods of the ongoing process of social organization.* Moreover, stable organizational forms are themselves continually changing through time as we maintain and operate them. Using the term "social organization" to mean both processes and entities thus reminds us that social reality, no matter how it may appear at any given instance, is always a dynamic process of becoming something different.

Positivism and Wholism

Ever since the French philosopher Auguste Comte coined the term "sociology" in his six-volume *Course of Positive Philosophy* that was published during the 1830s and 1840s, the concept of social organization has been characterized by two fundamental but seemingly incompatible themes that subsequent sociologists have struggled to integrate. The first of these themes is *positivism,* which is the belief that *social organization is a natural phenomenon that can be studied scientifically through research.* The route to knowledge, according to positivism, lies in the scientific collection and analysis of observations about human life. The second theme is *wholism,* which is the belief that *social organization is always a unified and meaningful process* that cannot be understood by merely observing the behavior of individuals. Because every instance of social organization is an interrelated and meaningful whole—or "system" in contemporary terminology—to understand it we must comprehend both its patterns of social ordering and its cultural meanings.

The apparent incompatibility between these two themes lies in the fact that positivism stresses objective observation, while wholism emphasizes subjective interpretation. Since the discipline of sociology (and all the other social sciences) incorporates both of these themes, many sociologists since Comte have attempted to reconcile or integrate them in various ways. Some sociologists favor one or the other of the two themes, while others assign them equal importance, but sociology always takes account of both positivism and wholism.

FOUNDERS OF SOCIOLOGY

Since antiquity, social philosophers and critics have been examining, describing, and analyzing organized human life. Hence it is impossible to say precisely when sociology emerged as an intellectual discipline. During the era of the Enlightment in Western Europe during the eighteenth century, however, scholars and intellectuals began to realize that human social organization could be studied scientifically. Although few social philosophers of that century made any attempt to test their ideas through empirical research, many of them did insist that the scientific study of society was not only possible but necessary. Without scientific research, they argued, ideas about the nature of social organization remain merely speculations or ideologies. Only as they are tested through systematic observations and analysis do those ideas become scientific knowledge.

The challenge of creating a scientific sociology was first systematically attempted by three late-nineteenth and early-twentieth century scholars whose works continue to be widely read today. These three people—Karl Marx, Max Weber, and Émile Durkheim—are therefore recognized as the major intellectual founders of modern sociology. Brief sketches of their careers are given in the following paragraphs, and their names and ideas appear often throughout this book.

Karl Marx

Karl Marx (1818–83) regarded himself as a philosopher, economist, and political activist, not as a sociologist, but his work has profoundly affected contemporary sociology. Born in the Rhine region of Prussia, Marx studied at the University of Berlin and completed his doctorate in 1841. His first job was as editor of the *Rhenish Gazette,* which he used as a platform for calling attention to the plight of the peasants and the poor. As a result, the government closed the paper in 1843, and Marx moved to Paris where he became editor of the *German-French Journal.* Two important events in Marx's life occurred during his two years in Paris: he became acquainted with many of the leading French radical intellectuals of that period, and he began working with the British textile manufacturer and radical writer Friedrich Engels. This proved to be a very fruitful partnership, and Marx collaborated with Engels throughout the rest of his life.

As a result of his radical ideas, Marx was expelled from France in 1845. He moved to Brussels, where he quickly became involved in international socialist activities. With Engels, he wrote *The Communist Manifesto,* which was intended to be a political platform to unite the developing Communist League. Pressure from the Prussian government led to his expulsion from Belgium in 1848, after which he returned to Paris and then went to Cologne to edit the *New Rhenish Gazette.* In 1849, however, Marx was again forced out of Germany because of his support for the socialist movement. After a brief stay in Paris he went into exile in London, where he spent most of the rest of his life.

Marx's years in London were plagued not by political harassment, but by continual poverty and poor health, with the result that three of his children died and he was unable to work for long periods of time. For several years, however, he sent weekly articles to the *New York Daily Tribune,* which were enthusiastically acclaimed by, among others, Abraham Lincoln. In 1850, Marx was given the privilege of doing research in the library of the British Museum in London, and whenever his health permitted he spent long periods of time there reading works on history and economics and systematizing his thinking. He published several books during the 1850s, but they were all preliminary to his major work, *Capital,* the first volume of which appeared in 1867 (although its final

version was not published until after his death in 1883, with Engels as editor).

Karl Marx dedicated his life to answering one critical question: With all of the new wealth being produced by the rapidly developing industries, why were the masses of industrial workers becoming increasingly impoverished and degraded to the point where they were virtually slaves of the emerging industrial system? He rejected traditional laissez-faire economic theory, which held that the wealth of the industrialists and the poverty of the workers were consequences of their individual actions in the economic marketplace. The extreme inequality in wealth and power that he observed throughout all industrializing societies was far too pervasive, he argued, to be attributed to individual actions. The cause of this situation, therefore, must lie in the basic nature of industrial capitalism as an economic system.

All of Marx's mature work was directed toward understanding and analyzing the dynamics of capitalism, as well as proposing an alternative type of economy that would permanently eliminate the inequalities that seem to be inherent in capitalism. Although these analyses of capitalism were essentially technical economics, *Marx became increasingly aware that all economic systems are rooted in and supported by the political systems and social structures of the societies in which they exist.* To eliminate the inequalities of capitalism, therefore, the entire society must be radically transformed into a totally new form. Marx hoped that this transformation could be carried out through peaceful democratic means, but his reading of history led him to conclude that such efforts were usually thwarted by entrenched powerful groups in the society. Therefore revolution was usually the only viable means of transforming the entire political economy and social structure to achieve social equality for all people. Marx's vision of an ideal society based on the principle of "from each according to his ability, to each according to his need" is far from being realized anywhere on earth today, but his concern for human betterment through social transformation continues to ignite hopes and political action among repressed and exploited people around the globe.

Max Weber

Max Weber (1864–1920) grew up in Berlin, studied law at the University of Heidelberg, and completed his doctoral degree in 1889. He taught first at the University of Berlin, and then in 1894 became professor of economics at Freiburg University. Two years later he returned to the University of Heidelberg as professor of economics.

Weber's relationship with his parents—especially his father—had always been strained, and in 1897 father and son had a violent quarrel. Weber accused his father of mistreating his mother and ordered him out of the house. A month later, the senior Weber died. Weber was so overcome with grief and guilt that he became severely mentally ill. He was admitted to mental hospitals several times, travelled extensively, and often attempted to bury himself in scholarly work, but not until 1918 was he again able to carry a full teaching load. In 1919 he accepted a position in Munich, but died a year later.

Although Weber did not construct a general theory of society, as did Marx, he wrote brilliant theoretical and analytical works on a variety of sociological topics. These included (1) the concept of modern bureaucratic organization, which is designed to function as rationally and efficiently as possible; (2) the nature of social stratification in modern societies; (3) the role of religious values and beliefs in promoting the early development of economic capitalism; and (4) the manner in which authority is exercised in social organization. In those and several other areas of sociological inquiry, Weber is still considered a fundamental theorist. He did attempt to write a general theoretical treatise, but only the first two volumes of it—*Economy and Society*—were completed at the time of his death.

Weber's formal education, similar to that of Marx, was steeped in traditional German historicism and idealism. Historicism took a wholistic view of human societies and argued that each society is characterized by a unique *geist* or ethos. Idealism complemented this perspective with its insistence that ideas are the essence of reality. Both Marx and Weber rebelled against this traditional worldview, but in different ways. Marx retained its wholistic perspective on total societies, but completely rejected idealism in favor of realism (which he called "materialism"). His principle argument was that societies are shaped by human efforts to deal with concrete economic and other concerns. Weber, meanwhile, rejected wholism as an analytical approach and insisted on analytical individualism. He contended that sociologists must focus on the interactions of individuals, inferring patterns of social ordering from regularities in those interactions. At the same time, he retained a wholistic theoretical perspective by accepting the belief of the idealists that all human activities are infused with meanings, so that to understand organized social life we must search for the subjective meanings that are shared by the participants. On one major thesis, however, Marx and Weber were in complete agreement: Economic activities constitute the foundation of all human societies, from which is derived political and other forms of social power that is used by dominant groups to shape and control their societies. Moreover, both of these scholars were passionately devoted to improving human society.

In their contrasting ways, both Marx and Weber strongly embraced wholism, but they only moderately accepted positivism. Although both of them understood the importance of empirical research in testing theoretical explanations and both used historical analyses to illustrate and support their theories, neither of these writers was fully committed to positivism. That side of sociology was first emphasized by Durkheim.

Émile Durkheim

Émile Durkheim (1858–1917) was born and raised in the Lorraine region of France, and at the age of 21 went to Paris to study history and philosophy at the Superior Normal School. After completing his education in 1885, he taught at three secondary schools in the Paris region before being appointed to the faculties of education and social science at the University of Bordeaux. In 1896, Durkheim became the first full professor of social science in France, and in 1898 he founded the first scholarly sociology journal, *The Sociological Annual (L'Année Sociologique).* Three years later he realized his primary life's ambition of being called to the faculty of the Sorbonne at the University of Paris. He became a full professor there in 1906, and in 1913 his appointment in education was expanded to include sociology, making him the first person to hold the title of Professor of Sociology.

Durkheim's sociology was based on two fundamental assumptions:

(1) Social phenomena are real and exert influence on individual actions apart from biological and psychological factors; and

(2) Social phenomena can be studied empirically using the scientific method.

These twin perspectives pervade his 1893 book, *The Division of Labor in Society,* which examined the bases of social solidarity in primitive and modern societies, and were stated explicitly in *The Rules of Sociological Method,* published in 1895. In taking this stance, he broke with the prevailing perspective of individualistic utilitarianism that was being espoused by British social philosophers and sociologists such as Herbert Spencer, as well as Weber's emphasis on analytical individualism. *To understand social life,* Durkheim insisted, *we must search for the social facts and conditions that shape individuals' actions and examine those facts and conditions as real phenomena that display their own unique characteristics.* At the same time, he introduced into sociology the prevailing French emphasis on positivism as an analytical procedure for testing theoretical ideas. In his study of suicide (perhaps the most individualistic action possible) he demonstrated that the rate of suicide in a society is clearly related to the extent and type of social solidarity.

Durkheim never lost sight of the wholism of all social organization. Underlying every society and other forms of organization, he argued, is a set of common beliefs and values shared by the members and viewed by them as a moral order that transcends their individual lives. In earlier societies, this moral order was frequently provided by an established religion (such as Catholicism in medieval Europe), but as societies become more complex through industrialization and urbanization the old sacred moral order is replaced by a new secular set of beliefs, values, and codified laws. As a result of his many years of teaching the philosophy and techniques of education, he became convinced that in modern societies the schools are the principal vehicles for formulating and transmitting the new secular moral order.

Durkheim was more successful than either Marx or Weber in weaving together the two fundamental themes of positivism and wholism within sociology, although he failed to integrate them fully. He shared with the other two major founders of sociology a lifelong concern with evolutionary social change and the development of modern industrial societies. He did not place as much emphasis as the other two writers on processes of power exertion by ruling classes or political authorities, but like them he was a social activist who devoted considerable energy to causes such as improving the conditions of ordinary citizens in modern societies.

SOCIOLOGICAL RESEARCH

Within all fields of science, research is the systematic search for knowledge which distinguishes the sciences from the arts. Whereas artists strive to give expression to ideas, experiences, and feelings, scientists seek to increase their knowledge and understanding of physical, biological, psychological, social, and cultural existence. Scientific research can take many different forms, including empirical observation and experimentation, information compilation and systemization, concept formation and analysis, and theory construction and revision. Sociologists engage in all those activities as they continually attempt to acquire knowledge about social activities and organizations. The following paragraphs briefly describe and illustrate the major components of scientific sociological research.

Concepts and Theories

To make sense of any phenomenon we must first devise concepts that enable us to identify and describe whatever we are observing. *A concept is a label that is applied to a particular phenomenon and is generally accepted by the members of a discipline.* In our daily lives we all use countless social concepts—such as "community" or "society" or "family"—but sociologists attempt to give each concept as precise a meaning as possible. For example, although everyone has some notion of what a family is, sociologists commonly define a family as "two or more individuals who are related by kinship, marriage, or intimate commitments." This is not a very precise definition, since it does not clearly delineate the boundaries of many families. For instance, if your parents have divorced and remarried, are your stepfather's parents now your grandparents? Nevertheless, the definition is at least a first step toward specifying what we mean by a "family."

Several aspects of sociological concepts frequently confuse sociology students—as well as professional sociologists.

(1) Many sociological concepts are not very precisely defined, as seen in the example of the family.

(2) Concepts can have two or more different meanings, depending on the context in which they are used, such as "social class," "institution," and "group."

(3) Some concepts have very different meanings in sociology than in everyday speech. Sociologists use the concept of "bureaucracy" to refer to an organization that has been designed to operate as efficiently as possible, whereas this same concept generally connotes gross inefficiency to nonsociologists.

(4) Many sociological concepts are not widely known outside the discipline, even though they refer to common situations. For instance, "relative deprivation" refers to the belief by a set of people that they are worse off than others in some critical manner, even though they may actually be well above average in that characteristic.

Whenever important sociological concepts are introduced in this book, they are italicized for emphasis and described as clearly as possible, but the semantic difficulties described here must always be kept in mind.

When two or more concepts are linked together in some manner, the result is either a generalization or a proposition. *A generalization states a frequently observed relationship between two or more concepts.* For example, "The higher one's socioeconomic status, the more politically active one is likely to be." This relationship between socioeconomic status and political activity has been observed by many social scientists, so that we are fairly confident of its validity as a generalization. Notice, however, the qualification of "likely," indicating that this is only a general tendency. No sociological generalizations are invariant laws; there are always individual or historical exceptions to every generalization in sociology.

A proposition states a theoretically presumed relationship between two or more concepts. For example, Durkheim argued that "the more fully assimilated one is into society, the less likely one is to commit suicide." Although not a direct quote from Durkheim, this proposition was part of his theoretical explanation of variations in suicide rates. It has not yet, however, been adequately substantiated to qualify as an established generalization. As propositions are repeatedly verified through empirical observation they tend to become widely accepted as generalizations, although there is no exact point at which that transition occurs. Moreover, even the best verified generalization may later be found to be incomplete or inaccurate. If that happens, the generalization is either modified and the new version viewed as a tentative proposition, or else it is totally rejected in favor of a new proposition. Scientific "truths" are always open to question and refutation, no matter how well accepted they may be at the present time.

The principal goal of all science is to construct theories that explain and therefore predict whatever is being studied. Such explanation usually implies the notion of influence or causation among factors or conditions or processes. Therefore, *a theory is a set of interrelated generalizations and/or propositions that explains how one phenomenon is related to or affects another phenomenon.* To continue the example of political activity, sociologists have constructed what is called the "social mobilization theory of political participation" (Olsen, 1982). It includes the following generalizations and propositions:

(1) The higher one's socioeconomic status, the more social resources one is likely to possess, such as communication skills, awareness of social and political issues, discretionary time and money, and contacts with diverse kinds of people.
(2) The greater one's social resources, the more likely one is to take part in a variety of social relationships and organizations, many of which involve decision-making processes that are linked to the broader society and its political system.
(3) The more extensive one's involvement in all kinds of social relationships and organizations, the more likely such activities are to mobilize one to participate in public affairs and politics.

This social mobilization theory is far from complete, and requires considerable refinement and elaboration. Nor is it the only existing theory of political participation, since there is an alternative theory that stresses the learning of political orientations in childhood and one's current political feelings such an alienation or efficacy. The social mobilization theory does, however, offer a relatively coherent and meaningful causal explanation of how people become involved in political activities. As sociology develops theories such as this that causally explain all kinds of social phenomena, our understanding of human social life gradually increases.

Observations and Analyses

Science cannot stop with theory construction, or it remains merely philosophy, speculation, or ideology. Generalizations, propositions, and theories must always be tested through empirical observation and data analysis. A considerable amount of sociological observation is done for purely descriptive purposes, by sociologists and by others such as journalists, public opinion pollsters, and social critics. They may be attempting to answer such questions as, "What are the principal conflicts in this community?" or "What trends are occurring in marriage and divorce rates?" or "What persons are making the major decisions in this organization?" Although the findings of these descriptive observations may be quite interesting and informative, they do not normally contribute to the systematic development of sociological theories.

To be theoretically relevant, empirical observations must address research hypotheses. *An hypotheses is a statement of an expected relationship (or lack of relationship) between two variables.* It is usually based on an established generalization that one wishes to examine further, or on a theoretical proposition that one wishes to test empirically. Either of those may exist as a separate statement or be part of a more encompassing theory. Sometimes hypotheses seem to occur spontaneously to scientists—but this usually happens only after they have given a great deal of thought to a problem.

The variables contained within an hypothesis are concepts that have been operationalized so that they can be measured in some manner. For instance, the concept of socioeconomic status cannot be measured directly, but must be operationalized with indicators such as years of education, type of occupation, and amount of income—which might then be combined to form an index of socioeconomic status. Many sociologists prefer to work with relatively objective measures such as education, occupation, and income, but it is also possible to operationalize many concepts in more subjective ways, such as asking people which social class they belong to or where they place themselves on a scale of socioeconomic status. Similarly, political participation can be measured objectively by determining how frequently people vote or attend political meetings, or subjectively by asking how involved they are in politics or how closely they identify with a political party. A relatively straightforward research hypothesis using objective measures that could be derived from the social mobilization theory of political participation would be that "frequency of voting increases directly with amount of education."

Data with which to test hypotheses can be obtained in many different ways from countless sources, depending on the purpose and nature of the research. The most commonly used data sources in sociology include sample surveys, personal interviews, participant observation, government records and publications, historical documents, laboratory experiments, and field experiments. We shall not attempt here to describe these different methodological procedures, since that discussion would necessarily become rather technical in nature. The serious student of sociology must, however, become familiar with these various methodologies in order to understand the kinds of empirical research conducted by sociologists.

After observational data have been gathered in some manner, *they must be analyzed to determine what they mean and the extent to which they support (or fail to support) the research hypotheses being tested.* Raw data—such as responses to survey questions or figures taken from a census report—are relatively meaningless. They must be categorized in a manner that is relevant to the research project, examined and analyzed in various ways, and reported in ways that are meaningful to others. If the data are quantitative, sociologists usually employ statistical procedures to analyze the data. Such procedures can range from simple percentage calculations to sophisticated techniques of correlation and regression analysis done with computer programs. To test the previously mentioned hypothesis concerning education and voting turnout, for example, one might calculate the correlation coefficient between these two variables and discover it to be .32, which is a moderate, but not strong, relationship. If the data are qualitative, sociologists use other analytical techniques, such as content analysis, which classify the information obtained into a set of distinct categories. If socioeconomic status and political participation had been measured subjectively, for example, the researcher might ask: "Are people who think of themselves as middle class more or less likely than those who identify with the working class to be politically apathetic?"

The final step in the research process is interpreting the results of the analyses to draw conclusions that are relevant to the hypotheses being tested and are intuitively meaningful. Such interpretation requires the sociologist to utilize insight and creativity to draw theoretical conclusions from the research results, demonstrating how those findings bear on broader theoretical arguments and perspectives. This can be a demanding task, but only as analytical results are linked back to theory does a science progress in its continual search for knowledge.

SOCIOLOGICAL ENDEAVORS

As sociologists seek to increase their understanding of social activities and social organization, they may pursue several different objectives in their work. They may also confront several critical concerns that are common to all the social sciences.

Sociological Objectives

To illustrate the different objectives that sociologists pursue, let us focus on studies of poverty and briefly examine five purposes that might guide sociological work on this topic. Any particular piece of work on poverty might address just one of these objectives, two or three of them, or all of them.

1. *Description.* With this initial objective, a sociologist might seek to determine how many people in our society are living in poverty, indicate their predominant social and economic characteristics, and describe what life is like for poor people.
2. *Explanation.* A second sociological objective that goes beyond mere description would be to discover the major causes of poverty in societal conditions that create and maintain a class of economically deprived people, as well as those individual and family factors that determine which persons fall into this impoverished class.
3. *Prediction.* Once we know the major social and personal factors that produce poverty, a sociologist might attempt to forecast developing trends that will probably affect those causes and hence influence the extent and nature of poverty in the future, and also assess the expected effects or impacts of programs intended to reduce poverty.
4. *Criticism.* A value-involved sociologist might likely critique the problem of poverty in terms of its consequences for society as a whole and for poor people, the segments of society who benefit from the existence of a deprived class, and the social changes that are being proposed to eliminate poverty.
5. *Alteration.* An action-oriented involved sociologist might focus his or her efforts on designing various programs to reduce or eliminate poverty, direct the implementation of those programs, and evaluate their effectiveness in achieving program goals.

With all of these objectives to be pursued, it is evident that even in this one area of poverty studies there is a great variety of work for sociologists and other social scientists to undertake.

Sociological Concerns

As they pursue the various objectives just mentioned, sociologists must also constantly struggle with several concerns about the nature of their work. These include such questions as the following:

1. Can We Maintain Objectivity in Our Work? The sociologist is as subjectively involved with human activities as anyone else, yet his or her work is of little use if it becomes distorted or biased. This might result from ignoring information that differs from one's own beliefs, designing research so that it will substantiate one's favorite theory, falsifying research data, or misinterpreting research results. To keep their work as objective as possible, social scientists adhere to the prescriptions of the scientific method. These normative standards for all scientific work include recording the methodological procedures employed in research, attempting to eliminate or hold constant irrelevant factors that might affect one's conclusions, examining competing explanations, publishing all of one's findings regardless of their nature, replicating research under differing conditions, subjecting theoretical arguments to rigorous scrutiny by one's colleagues, and critiquing one another's work in public communications. Although no sociologist is ever totally objective in his or her work, these established scientific practices enable others in the discipline eventually to discover and correct whatever lapses of objectivity may unintentionally or intentionally slip into our work.

2. How Do We Handle Our Personal Values in Our Work? Throughout the first half of this century, young sociologists were usually told that as scientists they must put aside all their personal values and beliefs and maintain an ethically and morally neutral stance toward whatever they studied. The purpose of sociology, they were told, was to study social life, not to judge or change it. Admittedly, we all hold many personal values and beliefs, so that value-free sociology always remained something of an unobtainable ideal, but researchers strove to keep their work as value-free as possible. More recently, however, many sociologists have taken the stance that values and beliefs so thoroughly pervade our work that it is hypocritical to pretend that sociology can ever be value-neutral. Moreover, the mantle of value-neutrality may sometimes be used to hide values and beliefs that one doesn't want to acknowledge openly. This newer stance of value-involvement argues that it is more intellectually honest to state clearly the values and beliefs that underlie and guide our work, so that others can take them into account when evaluating that work. Being open about one's values and beliefs should eliminate "hidden agendas" and subtle "manipulative strategies," as well as expose the full scope and depth of our thinking. Rejecting the myth of value-free sociology does not mean, however, that we discard the cannons of scientific objectivity. Value-involvement pertains to the goals we seek in our professional work, while objectivity refers to the methods of research and analysis that we employ in pursuing those objectives. It is quite possible to make an objective, professional analysis about a situation toward which we hold strong personal values. We may, for instance, believe that poverty is a socially undesirable and ethically abhorrent condition, and yet analyze its causes with relative objectivity and then invite others to critique and replicate our research.

3. Can We Do Both Basic and Applied Work? Traditionally, sociology has been viewed by most of its practitioners as a basic science dedicated to the pursuit of knowledge for its own sake. Beginning in the 1960s, however, the field has been subjected to increasing demands from public officials, funding agencies, students, and the public to demonstrate its usefulness in helping to solve practical problems of human life. As a result, interest in applied sociology has become quite widespread in the discipline. Typically, basic research and applied practice have been seen as essentially incompatible roles. A sociologist was expected to do one or the other, but not both simultaneously. A number of sociologists, however, have argued that (a) pursuing pure science without any concern for its applied relevance is intellectually and morally indefensi-

ble, while (b) much applied work in sociology is quite atheoretical and makes no lasting contribution to our understanding of social life. These critics have therefore suggested that it is possible and desirable to merge the two roles of basic scientist and applied practitioner into a new conception of involved sociology. Sociological research then becomes oriented toward answering questions and solving problems that are important to people outside the discipline and that affect the quality of human life. Sociological practice, meanwhile, becomes intellectually challenging and rewarding and contributes to our understanding of social organization. In short, the fully involved sociologist contributes both scientific knowledge and practical expertise through his or her professional work.

4. Can We Retain a Sense of Skepticism and Humility in Our Work? Skepticism has been described by the sociologist Robert Bierstedt (1963:21) as "a willingness, if not indeed an eagerness, to question everything before accepting it, and especially those things for which there is insufficient evidence." This spirit of skepticism distinguishes a scholar from a spectator. Although both may be curious about why something happens and both may propose theories to explain that event, the true scholar will not accept any explanation until it has been adequately substantiated by empirical evidence and rigorous analysis. Humility, meanwhile, has only recently become prevalent within many disciplines. Not too many centuries ago an educated person could possess virtually all existing scientific knowledge, which often resulted in a marked sense of self-pride. As late as the middle of the nineteenth century, the social philosopher Auguste Comte believed that the scientific pinnacle had been attained with the creation of sociology, of which he believed he knew virtually all there was to know. What wiser persons have long known, and what more of us discover every day, is that as knowledge slowly expands, so does our awareness of all that we do not know. In the words of historian Will

Durant (1965), "Education is the progressive discovery of our own ignorance."

SUMMARY

The quest of sociology is to understand the dynamic process of social organization that creates ordering and meaning in human life. The totality of human life can be divided into four distinct but highly interrelated levels of ordering: organic, personal, social, and symbolic. Sociologists commonly make numerous assumptions about individuals as biological and psychological beings who are capable of participating in organized social and cultural life. Primarily, however, the discipline of sociology—as well as the other social sciences—focuses on social and cultural processes and conditions.

Social organization has three components: interpersonal interactions, stable patterns of social ordering, and shared cultural ideas. In seeking to understand the process of social organization, sociologists commonly encounter several observational and conceptual difficulties. Social organization cannot be perceived directly, but must be inferred from its effects on individuals and collectivities. We tend to see and conceive of social organization as static forms rather than as a dynamic process flowing through time. Stability in social organization is achieved through constant change, so that order and change are two sides of the same process. Consequently, the concept of social organization refers to both an ongoing process and the entities that are manifestations of that process at particular times.

The principle founders of sociology as a discipline distinct from social philosophy were Karl Marx, Max Weber, and Émile Durkheim. All three lived in Western Europe during the latter part of the nineteenth century, when their societies were undergoing rapid social change as a result of industrialization and urbanization. Marx, Weber, and Durkheim spent their lives seeking to understand this process of change and to explain it in general theoretical terms. In this effort, they also—in differing ways—sought to combine a wholistic view of social organization with a positivistic approach to scientific observation and analysis. Moreover, all three of these early sociologists held strong views concerning the nature of a "good society," and sought to put their beliefs into practice through social and political action.

The essence of all science, including sociology, is research. This process involves formulating concepts to identify phenomena; combining concepts into generalizations and propositions; developing theories that explain how causal influences occur; specifying testable hypotheses that reflect generalizations, propositions, and theories; conducting rigorous observations to collect data pertaining to those hypotheses; analyzing the resulting data in appropriate ways; and then drawing meaningful conclusions that shed light on the initial generalizations, propositions, and theories.

Sociological efforts to understand organized social life must constantly deal with basic concerns about maintaining objectivity, acknowledging our personal values and beliefs, combining basic and applied work into an integrated whole, and retaining a sense of skepticism and humility. While carrying out our sociological endeavors, we may pursue one or more of the various objectives of describing, explaining, predicting, critiquing, or altering social life.

2

SOCIAL INTERACTION

What is social interaction, and how does it produce social relationships?
How do people acquire social roles and go about enacting them?
In social exchange, how do actors interact and maintain their relationship?
In symbolic interaction, how do actors communicate meanings and guide
   their actions?
In what ways does social power pervade all interaction, and what forms
   does it commonly take?

NATURE OF SOCIAL INTERACTION

To create any kind of social organization, two or more actors must interact with one another with some regularity and stability. Thus all organzied social life is an outgrowth of social interaction. At the same time, most social interaction occurs within, and is influenced by, existing social organization. Social life is thus analogous to the paradox of the chicken and the egg—which came first? In this chapter we somewhat arbitrarily begin with social interaction, primarily because it is generally less complex than are patterns of social ordering and shared culture—which are discussed in the following two chapters. We shall examine here the basic nature of social interaction, the enactment of social roles within social life, exchange and symbolic interaction as two ways in which people commonly interact, and power exertion as a process that pervades all instances of social interaction.

Concepts of Interaction

Sociologists use a number of concepts to describe the nature of social interaction more precisely than is possible with everyday language.

Social Actors. The *participants in any social interaction are called social actors.* We commonly think of actors as individuals, but organizations of all kinds can also interact as social actors. If a government agency negotiates with a construction firm to build a new highway, the agency officials and the company executives who sign the contract are acting as representatives of their respective units, not as autonomous individuals. Hence those two organizational units are the interacting actors in that case. Sociologists assume that individuals—whether acting on their own or as representatives of organizations—possess the psychological and communication skills necessary to engage in social interaction.

Social Action. Psychologists commonly speak of human behavior, referring to the internally motivated activities of individuals. Sociologists, in contrast, use the term *social action whenever one social actor (individual or organization) acts toward another actor in a meaningful way.* Action thus differs from behavior in three important ways:

(1) It may be carried out by an organization as well as an individual;

(2) The actor attaches some kind of meaning to it, so that it is more than just a response to internal stimuli; and

(3) It is always oriented toward another actor, usually with the intention of affecting the recipient in some manner.

The intended recipient is normally present to observe the action, but an isolated actor might be rehearsing for a future encounter or writing for an unseen audience. In all these cases, however, actors shape their actions in terms of whatever is known about the intended recipients, with the hope that those recipients will attach the same meanings to the actions as do the actors.

Social Interaction. *Whenever the actions of one actor affect the actions or ideas of another actor in any way, social interaction is occurring.* Actions do not become interactions if they never have a recipient or if the recipient totally ignores them. But once the action of an initiator has some effect on a recipient, social interaction has begun. If the recipient attaches the same meaning to the action as intended by the initiating actor, there is a sharing of meanings and we can say that communication has occurred. If the recipient attaches some other meaning to the action, the result will be confusion. A woman kissing her date goodnight might mean either "thank you for a nice time" or "come in and stay a while," and depending on how he interprets her meaning there may be accurate communication or embarassment or disappointment.

A recipient of social action will normally respond to the initial actor in some way, depending on the meaning that the recipient thinks the initiator intended to convey (regardless of the accuracy of that interpretation), on the recipient's reaction to that presumed meaning, and on the recipient's own objective in the interaction. Response is not always given, nor expected, nor even possible in some situations, however. If a television commercial implores you to try a new brand of soap, the interaction is entirely one-way—although if you eventually purchase the soap that is a response to the message. If you are listening to a lecture in an auditorium full of people, you could shout back at the speaker when you disagreed with what was being said, but such action is not expected and might not be tolerated by others. In the examples thus far, the social interaction has involved just two actors, but interaction often involves complex networks of many actors, as when representatives of all nations meet together to negotiate international banking arrangements.

Instrumental and Expressive Interaction. Instrumental interactions are means to the attainment of some goal, as when a store clerk sells merchandise to a customer or several community agencies join forces in a fundraising drive. Most of our daily transitory interactions are relatively instrumental in nature, but considerable instrumental interaction also occurs within more recurrent and enduring social relationships. Expressive interaction, in contrast, is valued for its own sake regardless of its outcome, as in a casual conversation among coworkers during a coffee break, or in a religious ceremony. Transitory interactions rarely have much expressive meaning for the participants, but this kind of interaction is a vital part of most ongoing social relationships.

Formal and Informal Interaction. Social interaction is formal to the extent that it is guided by relatively well-defined expectations, rules, laws or social norms. The actors typically deal with each other as impersonal functionaries who are carrying out a prescribed course of action, and aren't concerned about each other's personalities or feelings. More informal interaction, in contrast, is less specified, so that the participants have more opportunities for creativity and self-expression. They also tend to view one another as total persons and to respond to each other on that basis. Instrumental social interaction is often relatively formal in nature, although it can become quite informal when the actors know each other well. Expressive interaction is frequently informal and personal, but some expressive rituals can be highly formal, such as a traditional wedding ceremony.

Social Relationships. Some interactions are one-time events, as when you briefly interact with a store clerk or a bus driver. Quite often, however, two or more actors will interact regularly with one another over a period of time. Occasional dates grow into a steady involvement; several people who enjoy bowling together agree to do so on a weekly basis; or two business firms establish a reciprocal exchange of services. *As social interactions become relatively stable and enduring, we commonly say that a social relationship is developing between the actors.* As a result of their frequent interaction, the actors create a reciprocal bond that usually involves mutual interdependence, expectations about one another's actions, and common identification with each other and the shared relationship.

There is no particular point at which repeated interaction becomes a social bond that the participants recognize as a stable relationship, but at some point in this process both the participants and other observers will commonly begin referring to that social bond as a recognized relationship. If you are dating someone on a regular basis, for example, at some point both of you will likely begin thinking of yourselves as having a relationship and will talk about it in those terms. And as a relationship increases in depth and intensity, the participants will often discover that their interactions become more meaningful and predictable to one another, which gives the relationship further stability. These social bonds between interacting actors that constitute enduring rela-

tionships are the core of all social organization.

In sum, social actors, who may be either individuals or social units, can act toward one another, engage in social interaction, or establish an ongoing social relationship. Those fundamental concepts are illustrated in Figure 2-1.

Establishing Relationships

We noted earlier that social relationships develop as actors interact through time and create social bonds that are relatively stable and enduring. The participating actors tend to become increasingly interdependent in various ways, they often hold expectations about one another's actions, and they usually identify with one another and their relationships. In addition, the process of establishing and perpetuating a social relationship involves a critical shift in the manner in which the participants act and interact. This shift is fundamental to the entire process of social organization.

At least some of the time, *the participants in a social relationship shift from acting as autonomous social entities to acting as involved social parts of their relationships.* When two actors first begin interacting, they are always acting as autonomous entities with regard to one another in that situation. Very likely, of course, they are already participating as involved parts of several other relationships, but they enter this new interaction as autonomous social actors as far as it is concerned. Their actions are therefore shaped largely by their own interests, concerns, and goals.

Once an ongoing social relationship begins to develop between actors, however, their interactions in that relationship will inevitably begin to change at least some of the time and to some degree. To maintain their relationship as a viable social bond, they must begin to view themselves as participants in the relationship and to act as socially responsible parts of it. This will involve taking account of the expectations of the other person or people involved, shaping one's

FIGURE 2-1 Social actors, social actions, social interactions, and social relationships

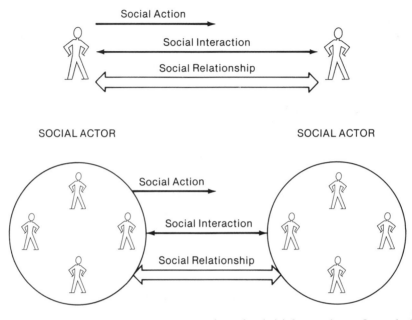

own actions in light of those expectations, and carrying out whatever activities are necessary for the survival of the relationship. The essential point is that when social actors are participating as involved parts of an ongoing relationship, they act differently than when they are acting solely as autonomous social entities.

Perhaps the clearest example of this shift of social actors from autonomous entities to involved parts of a social relationship occurs with marriage. Each person must, as an autonomous individual, independently pledge that "I will" form this social bond. Once that commitment is made, however, each person expects the other to act as a responsible partner in the marriage. Other people will also treat them as a committed couple, and will expect them to respond in a similar manner. As a consequence, as long as the marriage is viable both participants will act toward one another and other people in ways that they did not before the marriage.

Although this shift from acting as a social entity to participating as an involved part of a social relationship is most clearly seen dur-

ing the initial creation of a relationship, it continues throughout the duration of that social bond. Moreover, this shift occurs with both individual and organizational actors. On the individual level, a person is acting as an entity when he or she says, "I'd appreciate your help in carrying out this task," but as a part of a relationship or social unit when he or she says, "I'll get the information we need so that we can finish our task." On the organizational level, two airlines exploring the possibility of a corporate merger are acting as autonomous units, but when they agree to coordinate their respective time schedules they are acting as responsible parts of a business relationship. As these examples suggest, any social actor can act as either an entity or a part, depending on the situation, and may frequently shift back and forth from one mode of action to the other.

SOCIAL ROLES

As individuals create stable social relationships and act as involved parts of those relationships or more encompassing social organizations, they frequently enact social roles. Expressed differently, we participate in relationships and organizations by enacting roles that are parts of social units. Role enactment is therefore the process through which individual action becomes integrated into social life and that links individuals with society and other forms of social organization.

Role Concepts

A role is the smallest part of any social relationship or organization. Individuals enact roles and thereby become involved in organized social activities, but those roles always remain parts of established social units. It is quite possible for a person to act as a relatively autonomous entity within a relationship or organization, pursuing one's own personal interests and goals, so all social interaction is not role enactment. But to act as an involved part of that relationship or organization, one must enact a role which is relevant to it. When a person is enacting a social role, his or her actions are at least partially guided by social expectations and demands, so that those actions are defined by other participants as being socially responsible. In short, *a social role is a set of expectations and corresponding actions that is part of an established relationship or organization and is defined as appropriate for that setting.*

Social roles occur in all kinds of social relationships and organizations. As one example, consider the role of quarterback on a football team. The person enacting this role is expected by his teammates, his coach, the officials, and the fans to carry out certain kinds of actions to the best of his ability. These include calling signals, handing off the call to running backs, and passing the ball. He is not, however, expected to tackle opposing team members (except in case of an interception), and he is is definitely not expected to describe his team's plays to the other team. If he decided to temporarily step out of his quarterback role and try to make a date with one of the cheerleaders,

that would be viewed as inappropriate action on the football field. After the game was over and he was no longer enacting the quarterback role, however, the cheerleader might be quite pleased if he asked her for a date, since that action would then be appropriate.

As this example suggests, roles are dynamic sets of expectations and actions that individuals enact in relevant situations. Frequently, however, we want to locate a particular role or set of roles within an established relationship or organization. To do this, we specify the position, or structural location, of that role in relation to other roles. In other words, *a social position is a location within a social unit with which one or more roles are associated.* To continue our discussion of the quarterback, we can designate this as one of eleven offensive positions on the football team, draw a diagram to indicate the physical location of that position in relation to other team positions, and write down the duties of whoever fills that position.

There are three important distinctions between a position and a role.

(1) Since a position is a structural location, it exists regardless of whether or not anyone is filling it at the present time, whereas a dynamic role exists only when someone is enacting it.

(2) A position must be formally specified as part of a relationship or organization, whereas roles may or may not be so specified. The quarterback role is formally specified, but the role of "team sparkplug" is not.

(3) A given position may be the location of several roles, so that the quarterback position might contain the roles of offensive playmaker, team captain, and spokesperson of the team to the local press.

The concept of social position thus provides a convenient way of locating one or more roles within the structure of a relationship or organization, but to understand the interaction that is actually occurring in that situation we must examine the social roles being enacted.

Acquiring Roles

The various roles that we enact are acquired in two basic ways: through ascription and through achievement.

Ascribed roles are assigned to you because of your particular biological or social characteristics. Common bases for assigning roles to people are their sex, age, race, physical appearance, religion, family background, and marital status. It is usually quite difficult or impossible for a person to acquire an ascribed role without possessing the requisite characteristics. A male cannot become "Miss America" no matter how much be might desire that role; one must be of a certain age to enact the role of voter; and one is very unlikely to make the basketball team if one is only five feet tall. If one does possess a characteristic that is considered important in a society, meanwhile, it is often very difficult or impossible to escape the accompanying ascribed role. The son of a peasant in a feudal society did not have much choice except to continue working the family's plot of land, while in an industrial society the son of a wealthy businessman would probably have considerable difficulty escaping his upper-class background. And many people today still believe that the only proper roles for a married woman are keeping house and rearing children.

Achieved roles are acquired by you on the basis of your demonstrated capability or performance. If you want to enact a particular achieved role, you must demonstrate to others that you meet whatever criteria have been established for that role, and that you can potentially or actually enact it satisfactorily. Sometimes these role criteria and requirements are clearly defined, as in becoming a college professor or a physician, but at other times the role criteria and requirements are only vaguely specified, as in the case of being a "top influential" in the community or the "office wit." The other side of achieved roles is that you will likely lose them if you cannot continue to fulfill them adequately because of illness, lack of skills, insufficient effort, or other reasons. Thus achieved roles are open to people with talent and ambition in a way

that ascribed roles never are, but there is a built-in security with ascribed roles that does not occur with achieved roles.

The more important roles in most societies throughout human history have normally been ascribed rather than achieved. This practice assured that these vital roles were always filled and that open competition for roles was kept to a minimum, both of which tended to give stability to social life. A monarchy does not face the succession crises that periodically occur in societies with elected governments. In modern societies, however, ascribed roles are continually declining in number and importance, while more and more roles are being opened to achievement. As one illustration, women are today demanding that virtually all occupational roles be open to them on the basis of achievement, rather than being ascribed "for men only." Shifting important roles from ascription to achievement often places new demands on people and organizations for role preparation, skillful role enactment, increased sophistication in role management, and ability to handle role losses. In the long run, however, open role achievement increases personal freedom by allowing individuals to acquire and enact roles that they personally desire and are qualified for. It can also benefit organized social life by channelling the most competent people available into crucial roles and encouraging them to perform those roles to the best of their ability.

Role Enactment

The first step in role enactment is role selection, or choosing a role that is appropriate for the situation, the other people involved, and oneself. Each of us possesses a repertoire of roles—like a closet of clothes—that we have learned to wear or enact on different occasions. As we enter a social situation, we consciously or unconsciously decide which role to enact at that time, and temporarily put aside all other roles in our repertoire. As long as the situation is clearly defined, this selection process is usually not too difficult.

When you are at work, you enact your employee role. When you go to lunch with some friends, you put aside the employee role and enact the friend role. When you go home at night you enact family roles with your spouse and children. Role selection can become quite ambiguous or puzzling, however, if a situation is not clearly defined or two different situations overlap. If you go to lunch with your boss rather than with your friends, do you continue to act the employee role or do you relax and enact a more casual role? As another example, what role do you select if your instructor gives a take-home exam that is to be written without consulting anyone, but your roommate, who is also in the course, says "please be a friend and help me with this exam or I'll never pass it"?

Possessing a large repertoire of roles from which to choose can be very helpful for an individual. If one role isn't quite appropriate for a given situation, you can easily switch to another one that is. If you do not perform well in one role, you can take on another role in which you are more skilled. Resources acquired in one role—such as contacts with certain people—can often be drawn upon when enacting another role. As you learn to move smoothly from one role to another, your self-confidence and social sophistication will likely increase. And the more roles you have to choose from, the more flexible your life will become and the more freedom of choice you will enjoy.

The second step in role enactment is determining the expectations of the role one has chosen to enact in a given situation. This can be a bit demanding at times, since role expectations come from three different sources: (1) Normative expectations from the norms and rules of the culture or subculture in which we live; (2) Situational expectations from the other people with whom we are interacting at the time; and (3) personal expectations we hold about how the role should be enacted. Thus a physician treating a patient is guided by general societal norms concerning interpersonal interaction, as well as by the specific norms of the medical profession; she must also take account of the expectations of this particular patient, her nurse, and anyone else who might be involved; and she will pay attention to her own conceptions of herself as a physician. If these various role expectations are all fairly compatible, the role actor should have little difficulty determining what action is expected in this situation. But she might experience considerable role anxiety if the law says that abortions are legal, her professional oath requires her to preserve life at all times, her patient demands an abortion, and her personal ethics are opposed to that action.

The more precise and encompassing the normative expectations pertaining to a particular role, the more predictable the ensuing role actions, but the less opportunity an individual has to shape his or her role enactment to situational and personal expectations. For example, the Roman Catholic Church defines precisely most of the actions that priests carry out when celebrating a Mass. In contrast, the norm of academic freedom gives university professors great leeway—but not unrestricted license—to say whatever they think is appropriate in the classroom. When normative role expectations provide only broad guidelines rather than precise prescriptions, role actors have much more latitude to take account of situational contingencies and the expectations of the other participants, as well as their own role expectations. The resulting role actions lose some predictability, but they gain flexibility and adaptability.

The third step in role enactment is devising a role performance based on the expectations for the chosen role, situational conditions, and one's role partners. Roles are performed with role partners, or the other people in a situation with whom one is interacting. When a man is performing the role of father, his actions are directed toward his children as his role partners; the role partners of a lawyer in the courtroom are the judge and jury; and a tennis player performs her role in interaction with her opponent.

In some situations, role acting involves little more than carrying out an assigned script to the best of one's ability. In most cases, however, the actor must devise a unique role performance that is specifically adapted to that situation and one's role partners, so that role performance becomes much more than merely conforming to preordained role expectations (Turner, 1962). Because established role expectations rarely specify actions for all possible contingencies, the actor must normally translate those expectations into actions that are suitable to the situation, the other participants, and himself or herself.

Consequently, role performance is often a highly creative process, calling for considerable skill. As a result, we often feel unsure about how well we are carrying out our role performances. We frequently look to others for feedback concerning our performances, and modify them in "mid-act" to take account of the responses of our role partners. Skill in "taking the role of the other" is especially valuable in this process, since it enables

us to put ourselves in the place of a role partner, observe our role performance through his or her eyes, and then adjust our role performance in light of our perception of how our role partner is perceiving our actions and their intended meanings. Various roles differ greatly in the opportunities they give individuals to devise their own performances, but considerable skill in social interaction and role performance is necessary to enact virtually any social role. Shakespeare observed long ago that "All the world's a stage, and all the men and women merely players," but some people are much better role actors than others.

The three steps in role enactment are diagrammed in Figure 2-2.

Successful role enactment has two major benefits for individuals. First, *roles provide guidelines for our social actions*. If you are well acquainted with the expectations of a particular role and are experienced in performing

FIGURE 2-2 Steps in role enactment

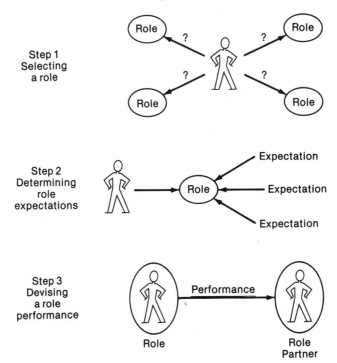

it, when the situation calls for that role you can easily step into it and enact it. Much demanding and possible embarrassing trial-and-error searching for appropriate action is thereby avoided. Although you may never before have eaten in a particular restaurant, you are able to order a meal, eat it, pay your bill, and leave without any hesitancy about what to do. The setting may be novel, but the role is not, and it provides guidelines for appropriate actions.

Second, *roles give regularity and predictability to our social interactions.* Social roles enable us to anticipate and interpret the actions of others with considerable accuracy, as long as we share similar expectations for those roles, so that we can adapt our own actions to the expectations and meanings of our role partners. The salesman in a clothing store may be a total stranger to you when you go in to buy a new coat, but as long as he enacts his role in an appropriate manner you can fairly well predict what he will do and say, and thus can interact with him quite smoothly. For all the participants in social interaction, role enactment is a continual process of interweaving one's own expectations and performances with those of one's role partners, so as to carry out meaningful and rewarding social interaction.

Role Conflict

Because all of us continuously enact many different roles with diverse role partners in widely varying situations, we inevitably experience *role conflict, or incongruencies in our role expectations and performances.* Life is full of role conflicts, as the following examples illustrate:

(1) A professional woman is torn between continuing her career and having children.
(2) A man is pressured by friends at his club to drink with them, and by members of his church to abstain from drinking.
(3) We are taught that killing is morally wrong, but as a soldier one is told to kill the enemy.
(4) A good student is asked by her best friend to pass crib notes during a forthcoming exam.

(5) A business expects its executives to participate in community civic activities regardless of their personal preferences.
(6) A wife insists that her husband help clean the house, which he does not consider to be his responsibility.

A listing of all instances of role conflict would be endless, but most sources of such conflict fall into one of two categories. Intrarole conflict, or *role inconsistency,* occurs when the conflict centers on just one role. Various role partners may hold differing expectations for the role you are enacting. Your own expectations for that role may not be the same as your partners' expectations. Or your role performance may diverge considerably from established normative expectations for that role. Interrole conflict, or *role incompatibility,* occurs when the conflict involves two or more roles. After selecting one role, you may discover that several other roles you don't want are attached to it as a role set. You may be expected to enact two incompatible roles at the same time. Or while performing one role you may discover that your partner is performing a quite different role in relation to you.

If role conflict is so prevalent in our lives, why are we not all nervous wrecks from trying to deal with impossible role expectations and performance demands? The answer is that we all learn a variety of "coping mechanisms" for managing or resolving role conflicts. Five typical role conflict coping techniques are the following:

(1) Role segregation, or separating conflicting roles into different time and places.
(2) Role sacrifice, or selecting one set of role expectations or one particular role and putting aside inconsistent expectations or incompatible roles.
(3) Role compromise, or only partially fulfilling the expectations of divergent roles.
(4) Role redefinition, in which we persuade our role partners to change their expectations for our role.
(5) Role substitution, in which we abandon a role we cannot handle and substitute a more suitable one.

We all employ such techniques in many different ways, singly and in combination, so that most of the time we avoid being overwhelmed by role inconsistencies and incompatibilities. If our coping mechanisms break down or are inadequate, however, we are likely to experience serious distress.

EXCHANGE INTERACTION

Two ways in which sociologists often describe social interaction are as social exchanges and as symbolic communications. These are not antithetical kinds of social interaction, but rather two alternative ways of viewing and understanding interaction and relationships. Moreover, these two perspectives on social interaction complement each other in several ways (Singlemann, 1972). Exchange interaction is discussed in this section, and symbolic communication in the next section.

Principles of Exchange Interaction

Much of the interaction in which we participate every day can be viewed as a process of social exchange. *Exchange interaction occurs when actors give and receive benefits from one another in a reciprocal manner.* At the beginning of any exchange process, the actors come together as autonomous elements, each seeking his or her own objectives. Each actor may be enacting a socially defined role that is part of some organization (such as a business or a government agency), or each may be acting entirely on his or her own. In either case, however, they are not at first enacting roles within a shared relationship. But this situation changes as the actors begin to enact exchange transactions. Through time they are likely to create a social relationship based on mutual interdependence and trust, in which each of them enacts one or more well-defined social roles.

To understand the process of social exchange, we must make several assumptions about social actors and actions.

(1) Actors will seek to interact with others who can satisfy their needs or facilitate attainment of their goals.
(2) All actions entail costs to the actor, such as resources, effort, and time.
(3) Social actors generally attempt to keep the costs of their actions equal to or less than the benefits they receive from those actions.
(4) When choosing among alternative courses of action, actors tend to select actions that are most favorable in terms of costs and benefits.
(5) Actors will eventually terminate interactions whose costs consistently exceed their benefits.

These assumptions do not apply to all actors or all actions, and other considerations such as loyalty, love, fear, anxiety, or ignorance may induce an actor to violate any or all of the assumptions. Nevertheless, it is surprising how extensively they do apply within many realms of social life.

Exchange interaction can be initiated in either of two ways. One way is for you to say to someone: "If you'll do this for me, I'll do that for you in return." The recipient can then respond as requested, bargain for better terms, or turn you down. This is a fairly safe opening, since it doesn't cost you anything, but you may or may not get what you want. Alternatively, you can say to someone: "I will do this for you, since I know you want it." This is a more risky opening, since it entails an initial cost to you without any guarantee of a return. But in the long run it can benefit you more, since you have obligated the other person to you. At some time in the future when you want something from that person, you can then remind him or her of that obligation and ask that it be repaid. Moreover, this approach is not as risky as it might appear, since the other person is usually quite aware that failure to reciprocate your gift would undoubtedly preclude any further exchanges with you. *The self-interested need to reciprocate for benefits received in order to obtain further benefits in the future therefore serves as a basic starting mechanism for much social exchange.*

Once reciprocal exchanges between actors have begun, the resulting transactions will follow a fundamental principle of social exchange: "If both individuals value what they receive from the other, both are prone to supply more of their own services to provide incentives for the other to increase his supply and to avoid becoming indebted to him" (Blau, 1964:88–90). In short, *mutually beneficial exchange transaction tend to be perpetuated.* They will likely continue as long as three conditions prevail:

(1) Each actor needs or wants something that the other can provide;
(2) Each actor's benefits from the exchanges equal or exceed his or her costs, at least in the long run; and
(3) No alternatives are available to either actor that offer greater benefits at less cost.

Failure to meet those three conditions may not immediately end an exchange relationship, since the actors may feel a sense of responsibility and loyalty to each other, they may be emotionally attached to one another, or they may simply keep hoping that the relationship will improve. Eventually, however, unrewarding relationships—whether they be friendships or business partnerships—are generally dissolved.

The social exchanges that occur in these transactions differ in several ways from economic exchanges. First, there is no standard quantitative medium of exchange, such as money, in the social realm. We may keep an informal tally in our mind of our obligations to others and their social debts to us, but social exchanges are usually not defined very precisely. Second, in most social exchanges the actors are not attempting to maximize their profits by obtaining the greatest benefits for the least costs, but rather they are usually satisfied to obtain something they want or need at an acceptable cost. Consequently, there can be considerably more latitude in the nature and conduct of social transactions than is usually tolerated in economic exchanges. Third, whereas we do not typically feel emotionally attached to the mechanic who fixes our car, we are quite likely to experience feelings such as gratitude,

trust, loyalty, friendship, or affection for those with whom we regularly exchange social benefits. Fourth, repayment of a social debt need not be exactly equal to the initial benefit, as long as the participants view it as appropriate and fair. Thus, fairness is much more important in social exchanges than is precise equivalency. All of these factors tend to make social exchanges considerable less precise, more complex, and more interesting than economic exchanges.

Balancing and Stabilizing Social Exchanges

For exchange relationships to endure, they must remain relatively balanced in two ways. As we have already seen, each actor's own costs and benefits must be approximately equal. In addition, *the obligations and interdependence between the actors must remain in approximate balance.* Imbalance between the participants can develop if one actor contributes much more than the other, so that the second person becomes increasingly indebted or obligated to the first one. Interpersonal imbalance can also develop if one actor becomes much more dependent on the relationship than is the other actor. The first situation might be illustrated by a father who says to his son: "I've supported you through four years of college, and now I expect you to help me run the family business." The second condition occurs whenever one member of a couple is much more emotionally involved than the other one. In both types of interpersonal imbalance, one participant is in a position to exercise considerable influence or power over the other, on the basis of obligations owed or the threat of ending the relationship. The more unbalanced the relationship becomes, the less it remains a process of reciprocal social exchange and the more it becomes unilateral social control.

Sitting on the high end of an unbalanced relationship can be quite rewarding. As long as the relationship can be maintained, the dominant person can usually obtain whatever he or she wants from it at little or no cost, by controlling the other person. Consequently, actors often purposely attempt to unbalance exchange relationships by giving more than they are receiving or by minimizing their dependence on the relationship. Sitting on the low end of such a relationship, meanwhile, is usually a rather unpleasant experience. One's costs may begin to far exceed the benefits being received, and one is likely to feel manipulated and controlled. Fortunately for this person, there are several ways of attempting to rebalance an exchange relationship: (1) minimize one's need or desire for whatever the other person is supplying in the transactions; (2) find alternative and cheaper ways of satisfying that need or desire; (3) begin giving the other participant more than he or she is contributing; or (4) persuade the other participant to alter the terms of the exchange process (Emerson, 1962). If none of these strategies is successful, the less powerful actor is forced to offer obedience and/or subservience to the more powerful actor. The result is social control and perhaps social conflict.

Relative balance is a critical, but not the only, requirement for keeping social exchange relationships stable through time. *The participants must also develop some shared norms about the exchange process and some mutual trust in each other.* Two norms that appear to be vital for stability in exchange relationships are (1) a "norm of reciprocity," which says that an actor who receives something from another is morally obligated to reciprocate that action in some manner (Gouldner, 1960); and (2) a "norm of distributive justice," which says that over time all the participants in an exchange relationship should receive benefits that are proportional to their costs (Homans, 1961:75). The consequence of such norms is to minimize or prevent actions that would enable one actor to gain a serious advantage over the other, thus keeping the relationship relatively balanced.

The creation of *a climate of mutual trust* among the participants in exchange relationships is an absolute requirement if those relationships are to endure for any period of time. Exchange transactions typically begin with small exchanges that require little trust because they involve little risk. As those exchanges are reciprocated through time, however, the participants usually come to trust one another more and more, and hence become willing to commit themselves more fully to the relationship. This expands the depth and scope of the relationship, makes the participants more interdependent, gives them confidence to risk more in the transactions, and ensures that the process of social exchange will continue between them.

SYMBOLIC INTERACTION

Whereas exchange interaction involves overt transactions of services, goods, or other benefits among actors, *symbolic interaction occurs when actors reciprocally communicate common ideas and meanings.* Virtually all social interaction is symbolic to some extent.

Principles of Symbolic Interaction

As we noted in the initial discussion of social interaction, human beings almost always assign meanings to their own and others' actions. We want others to understand our actions in the way we mean them, so that if you wave at a friend you want that gesture to be interpreted as a symbol of friendliness, not hostility. Similarly, we want to understand correctly the meanings behind the actions of others, so that if your boss says, "You did a nice job today," you can be assured that the remark was intended as praise rather than sarcasm.

In symbolic interaction we are constantly striving to communicate our ideas and meanings to others through our words and actions. We are also attempting to interpret correctly the ideas and meanings that others are conveying to us. Much symbolic communication is obviously verbal in nature, as we put our thoughts into spoken or written language. We also convey a great many ideas through our actions, however. The plea to "do as I say, not as I do" indicates that one's actions are speaking quite loudly. And our facial expressions, posture, gestures, and other "body language" also convey much meaning to others.

In social interaction, we rarely respond directly to what we hear other people saying or see them doing. Instead, we usually respond to the interpretations that we give to the meanings and ideas behind the observed words and actions. Hence my response to you is based on my interpretation of the meaning of your initial action to you, your response to me is then based on your understanding of my interpretation of the meaning of your action, and so on. Consequently, in any interaction each participant has his or her own *definition of the situation* that may be quite similar to those of others, or it may be totally different from their definitions of that same situation.

As a general principle, the longer and more intensely two people interact, the more adept they will likely become at correctly interpreting each other's intended meanings and thus communicating clearly with one another. There are many exceptions to that generalization, however. Some individuals seem to be especially adept at "reading" other people's thoughts or emphathizing with their feelings. Sociologists refer to this ability as *taking the role of the other, or viewing a situation from the perspective of a role partner.* Conversely, some individuals almost invariably seem to misinterpret messages and actions or define situations differently from others, no matter with whom they are interacting. Sometimes this limitation is merely amusing, and sometimes the person is tolerated as "weird" or eccentric, but if the problem becomes too serious the person may be labeled mentally ill. Symbolic interaction can also be particularly difficult if one or more of the participants is speaking in a foreign language in which he or she is not completely fluent, or if the participants come from different cultural backgrounds that give conflicting meanings to particular actions.

The Social Self

Symbolic interaction not only enables us to understand the meanings and ideas being expressed in the words and actions of others, but it also has a direct consequence for oneself. Each of us has a *self-concept,* or conception of ourself as a person, which affects our self-esteem and our actions toward others. As pointed out by the social psychologist George Herbert Mead (1934), *our self-concept is a direct result of our symbolic interaction with others.* As you interact with another person, you frequently "take the role of the other," or imagine yourself to be in the other's place, receiving the messages or actions that you are sending. You then view yourself through the eyes of that other person and ask yourself: "How would I interpret my own actions if I were this person?" and "How would I respond to my actions if I were him or her?" As you thus take the role of the other in symbolic interaction, you learn to see yourself as others do, from a partially objective rather than a wholly subjective viewpoint. That is, you see yourself from outside as well as inside your own perspective. By doing this, you gain a conception of yourself as others see you, rather than merely as you see yourself. Over time, your conception of yourself as a person—your *social identity—* becomes an integrated sum of all the "external" perceptions you have glimpsed of yourself through the eyes of others, combined with your own views of yourself in different social situations. In the words of Charles Horton Cooley (1956:Ch. 5), Mead's contemporary, each of us possesses a "looking glass self" that is acquired by using other people as mirrors to view ourself as they see us.

You also gain another benefit from this process. If you can take the role of another person and look at your actions through his or her eyes, you can then anticipate how that person is likely to respond to your actions. With practice, we all learn to do this prior to acting overtly. The young child reminds herself that if she hits her baby brother, "Mommy will be angry and spank me." Later on, the adult tells himself, "If I do that, he's likely to think I'm being aggressive rather than just friendly, and to be offended by my action." The more skilled we become at this process, the more able we are to modify our intended actions prior to acting, so that we are more likely to evoke the responses that we desire from others. In this manner, we learn to practice *internal social control by shaping our actions on the basis of expected responses from others*. As we do this, we avoid having others control our actions through external sanctions.

POWER EXERTION

Numerous social philosophers, from Plato to Thomas Hobbes, have argued that the exercise of social power pervades all social life, so that to understand social interaction and organization we must understand the nature of social power. Not until the 1950s, however, did most sociologists begin to give serious attention to power exertion. As expressed by Amos Hawley (1963): "Every social act is an exercise of power, every social relationship is a power equation, and every social group or system is an organization of power." In this book, we take the position that *every occurrence of social interaction and every enduring social relationship involves the exercise of power to some degree, so that power exertion is a fundamental aspect of all social organization*.

Nature of Social Power

Power in social life is analogous to energy in the physical world. Wherever we look we observe its effects, and all activities are an expression of it. Perhaps there is a sociological equivalent of Einstein's famous equation that $E = MC^2$ (energy = mass times the speed of light squared), although so far we have not discovered it. In general terms, *social power is the ability to affect the actions or ideas of others despite resistance*. Five important features of social power are included in this definition, as elaborated in the following paragraphs.

First, *social power always exists within social interactions or relationships, never within single actors*. Sitting alone on a desert island, you have no power over anyone else, no matter how much wealth or other resources you may control. Similarly, the chairperson of a committee wields power in the committee only as long as he or she holds that position and can enact the role of chair. Consequently, there are always at least two actors involved in any exercise of power, and the actions of the recipient are as crucial as those of the power wielder in determining the outcome of that power exertion.

Second, *the social actors who exert or receive power may be either individuals or organizations*. When one person persuades another to vote for a particular candidate, the power exerted is interpersonal. When representatives of a labor union and a business firm meet to bargain on a new labor contract, however, power is being exerted by organizational units through those representatives, and we speak of this as interorganizational power. It is also possible for an individual to attempt to influence an organization, and for an organization to control an individual. Social life exhibits countless combinations of interpersonal and interorganizational power exertion. For example, Senator Jones may wield interpersonal power over the other members of the legislative committee he chairs, while the legislature as a whole exercises interorganizational power over the activities of that committee, as well as many other organizations throughout the nation.

Third, *at any given time the ability of an actor to affect social life may be either potential or active*. To continue the example of Senator Jones, if he were viewed by other Senators as being potentially able to block any bill in his committee that he disliked, they might likely check with him before introducing a new bill. That potential power would become active when Senator Jones took some action that affected a bill under discussion. Potential power can be quite effective if other actors allow it to affect their actions, but sooner or later it must be actively exercised if it is to remain viable.

Fourth, *power exertion is purposeful action that is oriented toward having some kind of effect on its recipient*. A casual remark that is not meant to have any effect on the recipient—such as "it looks like it's going to rain"—would not usually be considered power exertion, even if the recipient did put up an umbrella. The desired objective of power exertion may not be readily apparent, however, if one actor is attempting to manipulate others in an indirect or subtle manner. In other situations, the exercise of power may produce effects that were not intended, as when a minimum wage law deprives teenagers of summer jobs because employers cannot afford to pay them those wages. Quite frequently, moreover, it will have both intended and unintended consequences, as when a union strike gains higher wages for its members but seriously disrupts the economy of the community. In short, power exertion is purposeful action, but its outcomes may be intended or unintended.

Fifth, *social power can either promote or prevent action by others.* The exercise of power can enable or cause actors to do things they would not otherwise do, or it can hinder or prevent them from doing things they would otherwise do. In other words, power can operate in either a positive or a negative direction. If we wish to emphasize the positive side of power, we may speak of it as exercising power *with* others in a cooperative effort to attain common goals. If we wish to emphasize the negative side of power, we may speak of it as exercising power *over* others to control them. In either case, however, one actor is purposefully affecting the actions of another actor.

Exercise of Social Power

To exert power in a social relationship, an actor must be able to draw upon some kind of resource. Resources thus provide the basis for exercising social power. Almost anything can function as a power resource, including a friend's respect for you, a bank account, military armaments, or knowledge of computer programming. It is often useful to distinguish between limited and unlimited resources, however. Limited resources are restricted in supply, so that every use of them diminishes

the amount remaining available to an actor. All tangible resources—including wealth and all material goods—are inherently limited in supply, but so are many intangible resources such as organizational positions, social privileges (which lose all meaning if everyone has them), and social obligations (which end when they are paid back). Unlimited resources, in contrast, are not diminished by use as long as they are not abused or overextended, and may in fact develop and expand with use—as in the case of learned skills. Other common examples of unlimited resources include knowledge, trust, legitimacy, friendship, reputation, and role enactment ability.

In general, it is more desirable to draw upon unlimited rather than limited resources if at all possible, since once they have been acquired they are not usually diminished through use. Your knowledge of accounting procedures is not depleted when you share it with someone else, for instance. This is not always possible, however, for unlimited resources such as special knowledge or political legitimacy are often restricted in use to particular situations or activities, and are worthless in other circumstances. Your knowledge of computer programming might be an extremely valuable resource on the job, but it is of no use in your religious activities. Limited resources also have restricted ranges of applicability, but these are often somewhat broader than those of unlimited resources. For instance, a United States $100 bill "speaks" almost anywhere in the world, and a person who occupies an important position, such as Secretary General of the United Nations, is listened to almost everywhere.

The amount and kind of resources available to an actor provide a basis for power exertion, but resources do not automatically constitute power. Three steps are necessary to transform resources into social power. The first step involves *committing some or all of one's available resources to a particular power relationship.* The actor must decide how important this particular situation is to him or her, and how many and what kind of resources to commit to it. Even if your supply of resources is quite small, if you commit all of them to a particular situation you may be able to exert more power than someone who only commits a small portion of their numerous resources to this situation. Bluffing frequently occurs at this stage of resource commitment. You can't bluff very far if other people know that your supply of resources is quite small, but if you have substantial resources you may be able to bluff others into believing that you are committing more of them than you really intend to do. The exercise of potential power stops at this point of resource commitment.

To exercise power actively in social interaction, you must carry out the second step of *converting your committed resources into some kind of action,* or convincingly threaten to do so. You might use your knowledge of computer programming to solve a critical problem and gain a job promotion, you might contribute your money to a political campaign and subsequently be appointed to public office, or you might draw on your friendship with a public official to obtain a waiver of a zoning ordinance. Considerable skill and finess is often involved in converting resources into various forms of power, and no amount of committed resources will result in power exertion unless one knows how to convert them. An outright offer of a million dollars to a public official for a political favor will likely result in a jail sentence for attempted bribery, whereas much less money invested in a political action organization might produce the desired outcome. Knowing when, where, and how to use one's resources is a critical component of effective power exertion. A power attempt, therefore, consists of committing available resources (or pretending to do so), and then effectively converting those resources into action (or threatening to do so).

The third step in effectively exercising social power is *to overcome, to at least some degree, whatever resistance is offered to a power attempt.* Power attempts are not always resisted, since the recipients sometimes willingly comply with the desires of the power wielder. Resis-

STEPS IN EXERCISING SOCIAL POWER
1. Commit some available resources.
2. Convert those resources into actions.
3. Overcome any resistance encountered.
4. Influence or control another's actions.

tance is quite common, however, since recipients often do not want to do what the power wielder wishes. Resistance can take many forms, such as passive avoidance or noncompliance, or active opposition or rejection. Depending on the kind and amount of resistance offered by the recipients, the power attempt might be totally neutralized and no power would be exercised. More commonly, however, the power attempt is altered or restricted in some manner by the resistance. In other cases, the power wielder may be able to overcome or crush completely whatever resistance is offered and to do whatever he or she wishes.

When a social actor effectively uses social power to alter the actions of another actor, the outcome is *social influence* or *social control.* When the interaction is relatively balanced (as in an exchange transaction) and the resulting changes are limited in scope or somewhat uncertain, we usually say that the power user has influenced the recipient. When the interaction is relatively unbalanced and the resulting changes are rather extensive in scope or quite certain, we usually say that the power user has controlled the recipient.

Types of Social Power

Four fairly distinct types of social power are often distinguished by sociologists on the basis of the kinds of resources they employ. These are force, dominance, authority, and attraction.

Force is the application of pressures by one actor on another. To exert force, an actor must convert some of his or her available resources into some kind of pressure that can be brought to bear on the recipient—or at least convincingly threaten to do so. The exercise of force therefore consumes resources, either permanently if they are of a limited nature, or temporarily if they are of an unlimited nature, or if the actor is bluffing. Three frequently identified forms of force in social life are persuasion, inducements, and coercion. When trying to persuade another actor to do something, one draws on such resources as attitudes, values, information, loyalties, and commitments. The use of inducements involves offering the recipient some benefit for complying with one's desires. Coercion involves applying punishments (physical, economic, symbolic, etc.) to obtain compliance. Persuasion can be difficult and uncertain, yet very stable and reliable if it is successful. Inducements often produce desired outcomes, but require continual expenditure of resources. Responses to coercion are relatively swift and predictable, but at the price of constant surveillance, minimal compliance, and resentment.

Dominance occurs when one actor affects another actor through the normal performance of social roles or functions. To the extent that actors are interdependent, their actions tend to affect one another. And the more dependent others are on one particular actor, the more that actor's actions will affect them. The resource for exercising dominance is therefore dependence by others and the ability to perform actions that satisfy their dependency. Thus the person who edits the newsletter of a special interest organization exercises dominance over the flow of communications in that organization, while a major bank may exercise dominance over the flow of money throughout many business firms within a large region. Dominance is therefore an outcome of routine, interdependent social activities.

Authority is the legitimate right to issue commands with which others are expected to comply. To exercise authority, an actor must be granted the legitimate right by others to make decisions for them and direct their activities. This voluntary grant of legitimacy is the resource base for exercising authority. Once an actor has acquired legitimacy, he or she can draw upon it to influence or control the actions of others, who will comply because they view that exercise of authority as legitimate and proper. Legitimacy is sometimes granted through formal procedures such as elections, but more commonly it is expressed through formal or informal agreements or simply through the act of voluntary compliance. Three grounds on which legitimate authority often rests, as identified by Max Weber (1947:328), are traditional values and beliefs, legal or formally agreed-upon procedures, and special knowledge or skills. To the extent that an actor draws on all three sources—as when he or she is particularly well-qualified for a role, obtains it through established procedures, and adheres to traditional role expectations—his or her legitimacy for exercising authority is likely to be particularly strong. In addition, legitimacy can also be acquired through the effective performance of vital organizational functions or even the successful employment of force, especially over long periods of time. Because authority is a highly stable and reliable form of social power, organizational leaders almost invariably seek to gain, protect, and enhance their legitimacy, no matter how they initially gain their positions or how extensively they utilize force or exert dominance in particular situations.

Attraction is power exertion based on the personal appeal that an actor has for others. That is, the others value some characteristic or ability of that actor, and consequently they are willing to follow his or her lead. This personal appeal becomes the actor's resource for exerting power over others. Attraction to others is sometimes purposefully cultivated, but in many situations it is not intended or even known by the actor. Three common sources of attraction are

(1) Identification with a person or organization ("we belong together"),

(2) Positive feelings toward a person or organization ("I respect her"), and

(3) Charisma, or the attribution of "superhuman" qualities to a person or organization ("he is our savior").

TYPES OF SOCIAL POWER

1. Force, or applying direct pressures.
2. Dominance, or performing normal functions.
3. Authority, or issuing legitimate commands.
4. Attraction, or being appealing to others.

Thus the members of a political party might follow the dictates of its leader because they identify with the party and its goals, because they trust the judgment of the leader, or because they believe that the party and its leaders are carrying out an "ultimate mission." Attraction can vary greatly in strength, from nominal party identification to total dedication to a charismatic leader. In some cases, it can provide a basis for granting legitimate authority to the attractive actor. In most cases, however, it tends to be relatively unpredictable and rather unstable.

All four types of social power occur throughout all realms of social life, on both the interpersonal and interorganizational levels, and they can range from weak influence to total control. In use, they commonly become highly interwoven, as actors convert one type to another or use one to supplement another.

SUMMARY

Social interaction involves two or more actors, either individuals or organizations, acting toward one another in a meaningful way. Interaction occurs when the actions of one actor affect the actions or ideas of another actor in some manner. If the recipient attaches the same meaning to the action as intended by the initiator, we can also say that communication has occurred. Most social interaction becomes reciprocal, as the recipient responds to the initiator.

Social relationships develop among two or more actors as their interactions persist through time in a relatively predictable and stable manner, as they become mutually interdependent, as they develop expectations about one another's actions, and as they

identify with each other and with their relationship. These social bonds constitute the essence of all social organization.

As actors establish enduring social relationships, their actions tend to shift from those of autonomous entities to those of involved parts of their relationships. At least part of the time they take account of the expectations of others and carry out activities that are necessary for the continuation of their social relationship.

As actors participate in social life they enact social roles, or sets of expectations and corresponding actions that are part of social relationships and organizations. Roles are acquired through either ascription or achievement, and they are often associated with positions located within established social settings. The process of role enactment involves selecting a role appropriate to the situation; determining the relevant normative, situational, and personal expectations relevant to that role; and devising a role performance in collaboration with one's role partners that is appropriate to the given situation. Intrarole and interrole conflict pervade social life, but most individuals learn many techniques for minimizing or resolving role conflicts.

Much social interaction can be described as social exchange, in which actors exchange desired benefits with one another. Exchange relationships tend to persist as long as the participants feel that their benefits are proportional to their costs and that the transactions are fair. This requires that the exchange transactions remain in relative balance, are regulated by common norms, and are supported by a climate of mutual trust among the actors. An unbalanced exchange relationship often results in social control.

Most interaction also involves symbols, with which the actors attempt to transmit ideas or meanings to one another. Actors are continually interpreting social actions, and their responses to the actions of others are based largely on their interpretations of intended meanings. Skill in taking the role of the other in symbolic interaction contributes to the development of one's self-identity and enables us to exercise internal social control over our actions.

A fundamental aspect of all social interaction and social relationships is the exercise of social power, which is the ability of social actors to purposely affect other actors despite resistance. Social power always exists within social relationships and can be exercised by either individual or organizational actors. It occurs in both potential and active forms, it is purposefully oriented toward affecting others, and it can either promote or prevent action.

To exert social power, an actor must commit (or pretend to commit) some available resources to that relationship, convert those resources into action (or threaten to do so), and then overcome resistance to some degree. When social power is effectively exercised, it results in either social influence or social control over others. Social power can take the forms of force, dominance, authority, and attraction, each of which utilizes a different kind of resource and each of which has different consequences for social life.

3

SOCIAL ORDERING

How do social interactions form stable patterns of social ordering?
Why is social ordering more than just the actions of individuals?
How does human social ordering follow the laws of ecology?
What are economic and political systems, and how do they form a political economy?
How and why is social ordering constantly changing?

NATURE OF SOCIAL ORDERING

As we have seen, the social relationships that comprise social organization rarely occur in isolation. Most relationships occur within complex interwoven patterns of social activity. The process of weaving together social relationships of various hues and textures to create the flowing material of social organization is called social ordering. This process of ordering occurs in varying degrees and takes many different forms; but it is always dynamic rather than static, and it always involves both power extertion and social change.

Concept of Social Ordering

Social ordering emerges as social relationships become interwoven into patterns that are relatively stable and enduring. Through this process, social activities become increasingly interre-

lated, regularized, and predictable. Patterns of social ordering may be as simple as a set of friendships among a group of people who enjoy doing things together, or as complex as the web of financial arrangements that comprise the U.S. stock market. As a result of social ordering, actors are able to cooperate in attaining common goals that might otherwise be unobtainable—ranging from operating a household to putting a person on the moon. Social ordering thus magnifies the total capabilities of a set of actors, transforming those capabilities from individual actions into collective efforts and stable organizational units.

Illustrations of social ordering can be drawn from all areas of human life:

(1) Most adults live together in pairs consisting of one member of each sex, and year after year share countless daily activities with their partner.

(2) A lecture audience remains quietly seated during a lecture, rather than milling about or engaging in private conversations.

(3) Persons who violate legal statutes are judged and punished through established legal procedures, rather than by the persons whom they have harmed.

(4) College classes meet on certain days of the week at a specified time, with one person enacting the role of instructor and the other people fulfilling the role of students.

(5) In a factory, each individual performs a specific set of tasks, which are combined to produce an automobile or television set.

(6) A group of friends gathers weekly to discuss and act on current political issues.

(7) A letter travels from one mailbox to another on the opposite side of the country, passing through many people's hands.

(8) Millions of people participate in a national Social Security program, some paying in money and some receiving money every month.

Through empirical research and theory construction, sociologists seek to describe and explain the diverse patterns of social ordering that we observe throughout social life. The two classical studies summarized in the following paragraphs illustrate typical sociological analyses of social ordering. The first one is a relatively simple and informal type of ordering, while the second is more complex and formal.

Group Leadership Roles. In a series of laboratory studies, Robert Bales (1949) and his colleagues created small discussion groups, gave them a task to perform, and then observed how they organized themselves to accomplish this task. The observers (watching from behind one-way windows) kept precise counts of the number of times each individual participated in the discussion, the person or persons to whom each communication was directed, the length of each communication, and its content. One of the findings of this research was that two different kinds of leadership roles emerge in most task groups. "Task leaders" are concerned with moving the group toward achieving its goal, while "socioemotional leaders" focus on the interpersonal relationships among participants. These two roles are quite different in their actions and expectations, and hence are usually performed by different people. They complement each other nicely, however, and both are vital for effective group functioning. Consequently, the two leaders frequently alternate in guiding the group discussion. Each period of task-oriented discussion tends to be followed by a period of person-oriented interaction that resolves conflicts, relieves tensions, and promotes group cohesion. In this manner, the group achieves its task goals and also maintains itself as a viable social entity. This study is considered a classic example of social ordering because it demonstrated the way in which stable leadership roles arise spontaneously in small task groups.

Community Power Structure. The purpose of Floyd Hunter's (1953) study of Atlanta, Georgia, was to explore the way in which social power was ordered in that community. He first compiled a lengthy list of prominent people in many realms of community life, and then asked a panel of judges who were knowledgable about community affairs to select the top influentials who made crucial decisions affecting the community. A small set of persons—Hunter limited the number to forty—were repeatedly nominated by the judges as dominant power wielders, while many other prominent people were described as merely symbolic figureheads or powerless socialites. Furthermore, these power wielders formed a relatively closed class. They interacted frequently, they tended to name each other as top influentials, and they shared a common set of beliefs about community affairs. The majority of them were businessmen, not public officials, and they exercised their power primarily through interpersonal contacts and committees, rather than by official decision making. Their power in the community was very extensive and highly effective. This study is considered a classic example of social ordering because it demonstrated that social power is quite unequally arranged in hierarchies within large communities.

Pattern Stabilization

Social ordering is always a dynamic process of becoming, characterized by continual fluctuation and variation through time. *Patterns of social ordering become relevant and meaningful to their participants, however, only as they endure with some degree of stability through time.* How can social ordering be simultaneously dynamic and stable? For example, how can a community experience continual change as a result of people coming and going, the economy growing or declining, and governments being elected or ousted, and nevertheless persist through time as a stable set of ordered social patterns?

The answer to this apparent paradox lies in the fact that social ordering that endures through time must be relatively stable, but not static. Totally static social ordering would never change in either its component parts or its overall patterns. In contrast, *stable social ordering is attained through change*, not in spite of it. To the extent that any organization is interrelated with other organizations, it must continuously deal with forces impinging upon it from its external social environment, as well as the natural environment. To cope with the resulting tensions and keep its central patterns of social ordering relatively stable, the organization must constantly change in many ways. In actuality, patterns of social ordering display all degrees of stability, depending on the external stresses and internal strains acting upon them. Nor is any particular pattern of social ordering ever inevitable or permanent, since disruptive forces and tensions may upset or destroy existing patterns of ordering at any time. As long as some dynamic stability is maintained through time, however, patterns of social ordering will continue to exist. In short, change produces stability that enhances endurance, so that stable and enduring patterns of social ordering are constantly changing.

Sometimes the changes necessary to maintain social stability are resisted by the participants, which renders their patterns of social ordering rigid and easily susceptible to disruption. The organization that says, "We've operated this way for the past fifty years and will continue to do so for the next fifty years," is undoubtedly distorting its past and will probably never last another fifty years in its present form. Sometimes necessary changes creep in unexpectedly, without anyone anticipating or initiating them, but those changes may be too little or too late to respond adequately to new conditions. A country that allows its population to grow far beyond its food supply will discover too late that there is no simple solution to overpopulation—except mass death. The most effective way of dealing with the necessity of continual change is to remain flexible and intentionally look for changes that can be introduced to keep one's organization viable and stable in the face of shifting conditions. If a community anticipates an influx of new residents as a result of a new factory that is being constructed, it can prepare for that influx in advance by building new housing, increasing the school budget, and making other changes necessary to keep the community relatively stable as it grows.

Social Structure

Observing and describing dynamic processes of social ordering can be quite difficult, because of our limited ability to perceive ongoing processes and our learned tendency to conceptualize reality in static terms. For example, we think of a stone as a static object because we cannot perceive its slow rate of creation and decay over the centuries. Our memories, aided by photographs, enable us to remember that the tall oak tree in front of our house was once a small seedling, but we still tend to think of it as relatively unchanging. Personalities are somewhat easier to perceive as developing processes, but we nevertheless expect people to remain essentially the same from day to day, and we label as mentally ill those who do not. In short, although all reality is an ongoing process, we often tend to perceive it and think about it in static terms. There is no harm in this as long as we remember that all static representations are abstractions from reality that we have constructed for our own conceptual convenience, and hence do not confuse them with social reality.

A static representation of dynamic patterns of social ordering is called a social structure. We construct these conceptual abstractions all the time in social life because it is easier to observe and describe social ordering in terms of static rather than dynamic patterns. To construct a conception of social structure, we temporarily "freeze" ongoing social activities and depict the resulting observations as a motionless configuration of roles and relationships. Thus a company president may have an "organizational chart" on his wall which shows, with boxes and lines, all the positions in the company and who reports to whom in their work roles. He knows that this isn't really the way the company operates on a day-to-day basis, but the chart is nevertheless useful as an abstract and idealized description of the structure of the firm. A sociologist studying that company, meanwhile, might construct a model of its actual influence or communication structure as a means of reporting the results of her research. Because this model would represent actual rather than ideal relationships, it would undoubtedly be considerably more complex than the president's chart.

In much sociological writing, the terms "social order" and "social structure" are used interchangeably, without regard to the distinction made here between dynamic patterns and static representations of those patterns. This common usage need not create any conceptual difficulties as long as we keep in mind the fundamental principle that all social life is an ongoing process, regardless of how we describe it.

Social Systems

Patterns of social ordering are frequently described by social scientists as social systems, as when they speak of "economic systems" and "political systems." A social system is not a particular kind of social ordering, however. Rather, *a social system is an analytical model that can be used to describe and analyze any occurrence of social ordering.* The principal reason for using this model is to emphasize the wholeness and dynamic nature of the phenomenon being examined.

A social system, as an analytical model, always displays four principal features: boundaries, interrelationships, functions, and unity. First, a system must be delineated by *boundaries* so that it can be distinguished from other activities or systems. These boundaries are defined by the observer or analyst who is creating the model. They may be quite artificial—as in a laboratory experiment in which the participants are asked to pretend that they are a functioning social group—or they may be based on real social conditions—such as a distinction between actors who do and do not make legitimate political decisions for a society. In all cases, however, those specified system boundaries delineate the actors and actions that constitute that system.

Second, the component parts of a system are linked together through a complex web of *interrelationships.* Those component parts—which may be either individuals or collectivities—are relatively highly interdependent and consequently share numerous relationships. It is not necessary that every part of the system be linked directly to every other part, but all the parts are interrelated to some degree through at least indirect relationships. In an economy, for instance, every consumer need not have a direct tie with every manufacturing firm, but all consumers purchase goods and services that are produced by various firms that are interrelated through purchasing contracts, financial ties, and legal obligations. Together, that web of interrelationships among the parts of a system constitutes its social structure.

Third, a system performs a set of related and identifiable *functions* or activities. These functions are often used to delineate the boundaries of the system, and they usually shape the relationships among the system parts. The functions of an educational system, for example, pertain to discovering, preserving, and transmitting knowledge. The particular functions of a system therefore determine the nature or content of its dynamic activities and give it meaning. Some of the functions performed by a system are usually intended, but other functions may be unintended and even unrecognized.

In combination, the boundaries, interrelationships, and functions of a system give it wholeness or *unity*. A system is a single entity that is distinct from any or all of its component parts. When social scientists use a system model to analyze social ordering, therefore, the primary emphasis is always on the structure and activities of the whole system as a single unified entity. Although the nature and actions of its parts are important, they are always examined in relation to the entire system. Use of the social system model therefore enables sociologists to describe and analyze organizational units and processes that have their own unique properties and dynamics that are distinct from those of their members or component parts.

REALITY OF SOCIAL ORDERING

Social ordering emerges from the actions and interactions of actors, as their relationships become interrelated, patterned, stable, and enduring. In other words, the social level of ordering emerges from the personal level of ordering through social interaction and relationships. The resulting patterns of social ordering acquire an existence or reality of their own, and cannot be described or explained soley in terms of personal factors.

The Social Level

Patterns of social ordering are created by individual actors (acting either on their own or as representatives of some larger entity), but those patterns are never just the sum of all the individual actions. *Social ordering constitutes a separate level of existence that is as real as its component parts.* To borrow an analogy from chemistry, when sodium and chlorine interact chemically they become salt, which is quite different from either chemical element. Similarly, when Bill and Mary interact as spouses and parents, the family they create is something different from and more than Bill and Mary as individuals.

The reality of social ordering is sometimes expressed by saying that an emergent level of existence possesses a wholeness or unity that is distinct from the sum of its separate components. That concept was expressed eloquently by Émile Durkheim (1933:102–03):

A whole is not identical with the sum of its parts. It is something different, and its properties differ from those of its component parts. . . . By reason of this principle, society is not a mere sum of individuals. Rather, the system formed by their association represents a specific reality which has its own characteristics. . . . We must seek the explanation of social life in the nature of society itself.

Supporting Arguments

Sociologists offer three principal arguments to demonstrate the reality of social ordering. These may be termed the theses of social properties, social exteriority, and social constraints.

Social Properties. Any occurrence of social ordering displays properties that pertain only to that patterning, not to its individual members. These include its size, formality, complexity, power structure, communication channels, decision-making procedures, rate of change, goal-attainment capability, and overall cohesion. All of these social properties are quite distinct from the personal characteristics of the individuals who create that social ordering. Knowing the personality profiles of Tom, Dick, Harry, Jim, and Bob tells us nothing about the basketball team they comprise—nothing about the duties of the various positions on the team, the coordination of their ball handling, their defensive strategies, their stability as a team under pressure, or their ability to win games. Those are properties of the team as a whole. If any phenomenon exhibits properties that are distinctly its own, then it must have an existence of its own apart from its component parts.

Social Exteriority. As Durkheim pointed out, individuals think about and act toward patterns of social ordering as if they are exterior to oneself. Although you may be part of the university in your role of student, you experience the university as a social entity that exists outside of yourself. The exteriority of social ordering to individuals is clearly seen in the fact that those patterns continue to exist over time despite changes in their membership. Anything short of total simultaneous withdrawal by all the members will not necessarily destroy a group, a community, a business firm, or a society. In fact, many organizations—such as the university—establish ordered procedures for the departure of old members and the acquistion and training of new members on a regular basis. The social ordering constituting the university existed long before any of us became part of it, and it will continue to exist long after we depart.

Social Constraints. Social ordering, like gravity, cannot be directly observed, but we can perceive its effects, as in the case of a falling apple. From those observed effects, we infer the existence of the underlying phenomenon. The effects of social ordering, Durkheim observed, are seen in the ways in which it influences the actions and ideas of individuals. Patterned social ordering limits or prevents some kinds of action, while providing opportunities and encouragement for other kinds of action. Most members of

an agrarian society cannot obtain a college education no matter how intelligent or ambitious they may be, because their society does not have adequate resources to build colleges, train teachers, or free students from productive labor for four years. Those people are not, however, forced to adhere to rigid work schedules or file income tax returns. In an industrial society, in contrast, it is extremely difficult to "live off the land" no matter how much one wishes to avoid regular employment. In return for performing a job, however, we receive money that we can use to purchase an endless variety of goods and services. In a more direct manner, individuals are punished for doing some things (such as stealing) and for not doing other things (such as failing to file a tax return). They are also rewarded for doing some things (such as carrying out their job) and for not doing other things (such as not taking a holiday when a report is due). Finally, the whole process of role enactment also illustrates the influence of constraining social expectations on the actions and thoughts of individuals.

These arguments for the reality of social ordering indicate that it exists not within individuals, but in the patterns of social relationships that are created among actors. As a consequence, psychological principles and insights are not adequate to explain ordered social life. Social ordering can and must be understood as an objective social reality with its own existence, properties, principles, and effects. At the same time, we must remember that the emergence of social ordering from its individual members is always partial, never total. Individual personalities and patterns of social ordering are both real, and neither could exist without the other. Social ordering must constantly be created by, and expressed through, the actions of individuals.

SOCIAL ECOLOGY

Ecology originated as the branch of the biological sciences that examines the ways in which living organisms relate to and survive in the natural environment. It is concerned with such questions as how plants and animals obtain food and other necessary resources from the environment, how different species compete for resources and become interdependent through these activities, and how these processes affect their chances for species survival and expansion. Since human beings are inescapably part of the total ecological web of life on earth, *the process of social organization is always constrained and influenced by ecological conditions.* Social ecology is the theoretical perspective within the social sciences that explores how ecological conditions affect organized social life. The principal formulator of this perspective has been the contemporary sociologist Amos H. Hawley (1986). Throughout this book, a social ecological perspective is used as part of the framework for understanding social organization and its development through the ages.

Ecosystems

All living organisms, plant and animal, exist within dynamic ecosystems. *An ecosystem is an interdependent web of relationships among all the organisms within a geographic area and between them and the natural environment.* An ecosystem may be as limited as a small pond, it may include a broad geographic area containing many different kinds of topography, or it may encompass a total human society. And at the present time, the entire earth is rapidly becoming a single ecosystem for human beings as we all become increasingly interdependent. All of the organisms living within a particular ecosystem depend on the resources available in their natural environment, and they are also dependent upon each other for survival. An example of this "web of life" is a food chain. The plants within an ecosystem draw nutrients from the soil, water, and air, and through photosynthesis using solar energy they convert those nutrients into living matter. Microscopic organisms, insects, and other tiny animals eat those plants for sustenance.

Larger herbivore animals also eat those plants, but many larger animals are partially or entirely carnivorous, eating the smaller animals. Humans exist at the apex of this food chain, eating many kinds of plants and other animals, and we could not exist without the underlying food chain to support us. Finally, when living organisms die, their bodies decay into basic elements that enrich the soil and keep the entire process going in a continual cycle.

Several natural ecological processes occur within ecosystems. All species of organisms struggle to survive in the natural environment through *adaptation,* which involves modifying their form (shape, coloring, etc.) and/or actions (food sources, reproductive practices, etc.) to fit their ecosystem. Each species thus develops a unique *niche,* or ecological role, within its ecosystem in which it can survive. If a species fails to discover or create a viable niche for itself, it is sooner or later eliminated by other species that have found a niche. The development and protection of a niche by a species is thus a fundamental requirement of all life. Sometimes two different species occupy the same niche through *symbiosis,* in which they maintain a close interdependent relationship that is mutually beneficial for both species. For example, a species of small bird exists by eating lice and other insects on the skin of rhinoceroses. The birds depend on this food supply, while the rhinos depend on the birds to keep their skin clean and healthy.

As a species carries out its particular niche activities through time, it sometimes depletes the supply of available resources that it requires, or otherwise modifies its environment so that it can no longer exist in that location. If it is a plant species it will die out, while if it is an animal species it must move to another location to survive. That in turn leaves a vacant niche that some other species may be able to occupy, resulting in a process of *succession.* For instance, if a species of foraging animals eats much of the shrubbery that has been covering an area, wild grasses may then thrive in that area because they are no longer denied sunlight, which may in turn lead to an *invasion* of rabbits into the area since they need grasses for food and protection.

Human beings are not exempt from any of these natural ecological processes, and all of the concepts noted in the preceeding paragraphs are used by social ecologists to describe human activities.

Social Ecological Factors

Social ecology goes beyond biological ecology to ask how human populations organize themselves to survive within the constraints of a limited and changing environment. *The goal of social ecology is to explain basic patterns of social ordering that human populations create as they adapt to the natural environment and utilize environmental resources and opportunities* (Hawley, 1986:26). Social ordering can therefore be viewed as part of the process through which human beings deal with environmental conditions. Early social ecologists tended to focus primarily on problems of physical survival—and those problems are still crucially important—but recently we have come to realize that an ecological perspective can help us to understand many aspects of social life, from community conflicts to international relations.

Social ecology emphasizes three sets of factors that are always fundamentally important in shaping social ordering: environmental resources, technological knowledge, and population characteristics.

Environmental Resources. Human life is of course utterly dependent on basic environmental conditions such as breathable air, drinkable water, and a limited range of temperatures. At the same time, the flow of human activities is shaped temporally by the rotation and tilt of the earth, and spatially by topographical features such as bodies of water and mountain ranges. More directly, however, the environment is the source of all the natural resources that we utilize to satisfy our biological needs and to produce material goods. These vital natural resources, upon which all human societies depend, include fuels for energy, a favorable climate, fertile soil, building materials, and minerals and chemicals. Some resources are consumed directly, but most are used to produce other items that people need or desire.

In general, the more abundant and diverse the natural resources available in the natural environment, the greater the wealth produced by a society, the larger its population, and the more elaborate or complex its patterns of social ordering. Many other factors also affect those developments, however. Conversely, shortage or exhaustion of necessary resources can severely limit what people are able to do.

Technological Knowledge. In their efforts to cope with the natural environment, humans have a tremendous advantage over all other species. Rather than having to take resources as we find them, we are capable of creating and employing knowledge and tools that greatly increase our ability to extract, transform, distribute, and employ natural resources in the pursuit of our goals. In general, technology refers to all knowledge about how to carry out specific tasks. Such knowledge ranges from primitive fire making and stone scrapers to modern computers and nuclear reactors. It includes both basic scientific knowledge about the world and practical engineering skills. Some technologies are applied directly to the environment, such as fertilizers to stimulate plant growth, while others are used to transform resources into desired items from safety pins to airplanes.

Technology is sometimes divided into the two categories of *material technology*, which pertains to the physical world, and *social technology*, which pertains to social activities. Examples of social technology include writing, monetary systems, teaching techniques, and parliamentary governmental procedures. This distinction oversimplifies reality, however, since material technology is important for human life only to the extent that it is incorporated within established patterns of social ordering, while social technology often involves some material items or procedures. In all cases, the amount and kind of technological knowledge available to people has tremendous consequences for the social ordering they create. Revolutionary transformations in human societies have been introduced, for instance, by the development of knowledge about grain cultivation and the plow, which made possible settled communities, and about factory production and the steam engine, which led to industrialization. At the same time, expanding technological knowledge can also create serious problems of resource depletion and environmental pollution, as we have discovered in recent years.

Population Characteristics. As a general principle (ignoring many other relevant factors), the more favorable the environmental resources and the more sophisticated the existing technological knowledge, the larger the size of the human population that can be supported in an ecosystem. In a fundamental sense, a population of people is the raw material for the creation of social ordering, and social ordering is always a collective property of its population. Consequently, the size and other characteristics of a population will have a multitude of consequences for whatever social ordering that population creates. A city of a million people, for instance, will of necessity contain much more complex social ordering than will a village of a hundred people. In addition to size, the rate at which a population is growing or declining can create numerous social problems, from housing availability to deviant behavior.

Other characteristics of a population can also be quite important for social ordering. These include the density with which people are distributed in space, which has direct effects on the amount and frequency of social interaction that occurs; the age distribution of the population, which determines how many adults are available for productive work in relation to dependent young and old people; and its sex ratio, which is crucial for reproduction and family life. All of these population characteristics—but

---

> **SOCIAL ECOLOGICAL FACTORS**
> 1. Environmental resources.
> 2. Technological knowledge.
> 3. Population characteristics.

---

especially size and rate of growth—can also have serious ecological consequences, as when the number of people exceeds the ability of the environment to provide needed resources.

These three sets of ecological factors—environmental resources, technological knowledge, and population characteristics—never totally determine the nature of the social ordering that people create to ensure their survival and attain their goals. Many other kinds of factors also influence the process of social organization, as we shall see throughout this book. But an ecological perspective alerts us to the crucial importance of the environment, technology, and population in making possible and limiting all social ordering. As a convenient way of remembering the fundamental ecological factors, you might associate social ecology with having a PET (population, environment, technology). To remind yourself that ecological factors provide the framework for all social ordering and organization, think of this perspective as being the concern of a POET (population, organization, environment, technology).

Ecological Carrying Capacity

The population and activities of any given species are always limited by the carrying capacity of its ecosystem. *The carrying capacity of an ecosystem for a particular species is the maximum population and standard of living that the environment can support indefinitely.* As long as the resource demands and environmental pollution of a species do not exceed the carrying capacity of its environment, it lives in balance with nature. In a hospitable environment, however, a species will often begin to multiply rapidly and make increasing resource demands on its ecosystem. Unless some kind of natural check limits its population growth or alters its manner of living, the species will eventually *overshoot* the carrying capacity of its ecosystem (Catton, 1980). When that happens, large numbers of the species will die from starvation, exposure, or other causes. Ecologists refer to this natural rebalancing process as a *population crash*. If such a crash merely reduces the population of the species to the carrying capacity of the ecosystem, that system regains ecological balance. Quite frequently, however, a population crash will often continue until a large proportion of that species—and sometimes the entire species—has been wiped out. The concept of ecological carrying capacity is illustrated in Figure 3-1.

As human populations have expanded and made increasing demands on the natural environment, they have often pushed against the carrying capacities of their ecosystems. As long as an expanding society is restricted by primitive technology, lack of food and other resources usually results in disease, famine, and other natural checks that keep its population within the environmental carrying capacity. As our technological knowledge increases, however, we invariably attempt to use it to increase our resources so as to expand our population and improve our standard of living. *Human societies over the ages have devised many ecological enhancement techniques for increasing their resources, thus raising the carrying capacity of their ecosystems at least temporarily.* Five of these techniques identified by William

Catton (1980) are takeover, tool-making, expropriation, conquest, and drawdown. Most societies use several or all of these techniques in combination.

Takeover is the simplest of these techniques, and has been used by humans since antiquity. It involves taking over resources that have previously been used primarily or entirely by other species. Early settlers in the Great Plains of the United States, for example, plowed up the wild grasses that had sustained large herds of bison and planted wheat and other grains that provided food for humans. As a consequence, many of the bison died from starvation, and most of those that did not starve to death were killed by the settlers.

Tool-making, as the name implies, involves discovering or borrowing technological knowledge that enables people to make more effective tools for extracting resources from the environment. As a result, resources that were once inaccessible become available for human use. A simple example of this was the invention of the metal plow blade to replace the traditional wooden plow, which enabled farmers to plow much deeper and more even furrows, which in turn greatly increased their crop yields.

Expropriation does not increase the total amount of resources available. Instead, it involves the redistribution of available resources among various segments of the population. If a society has reached the effective carrying capacity of its environment and can find no way of significantly increasing its

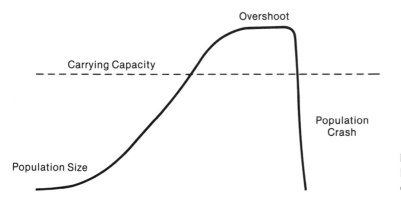

FIGURE 3-1
Ecological carrying capacity

available resources, the more powerful segments of the society may decide to continue improving their standard of living by expropriating a large portion of the resources in their society. The rest of the population may be kept at a bare subsistence level or be eliminated through starvation, war, religious sacrifices, or other practices. In the feudal societies of medieval Europe, for instance, small sets of powerful elites—often no more than two or three percent of the total population—kept most of the rest of the people in a condition of bonded serfdom, often allowing them to retain just enough of the food they produced to remain alive and working.

Conquest is an alternative to expropriation that is often practiced by societies that have developed sufficient military technology and strength to conquer other societies. The most straightforward means of increasing one's own resources is to kill or enslave most or all of the conquered people and take their land and other resources. A more sophisticated, but, in the long run, more effective way of accomplishing the same goal is to allow the conquered society to continue to exist while forcing it—through economic and military pressures—to provide the dominant society with as many resources as possible. Nineteenth-century Western colonialism illustrates this practice.

Drawdown is the newest of these techniques for increasing available resources to permit population growth and an improved standard of living. It involves using modern technology to extract nonrenewable resources from the earth, such as coal, petroleum, natural gas, and mineral ores. As long as those vital resources remain in abundant supply, a society possessing modern technology can continue to raise the carrying capacity of its ecosystem without expropriating resources from its own members or conquering resources from other societies. Because such resources are nonrenewable and hence inherently limited, however, this technique is essentially taking from the past and denying resources to future generations. Ultimately, then, drawdown is simply a temporal form of expropriation and conquest.

Although all of these ecological enhancement techniques have been used by societies throughout human history, it should be obvious that they are only temporary means of expanding the ecological carrying capacity of the earth. We cannot go on forever taking resources from other species, from each other, or from future generations. Nor will more effective technology forever enable us to create better tools for extracting natural resources that are invariably limited. *Sooner or later—and many environmentalists are convinced that it will be relatively soon—human beings may reach the ultimate carrying capacity of the earth.* If such a worldwide overshoot does occur, ecological balance will inevitably be restored through a population crash that could be the end of human civilization as we know it. The clear and only resolution of this dilemma is to find ways of keeping the total human population and its resource demands within the earth's natural carrying capacity.

POLITICAL ECONOMY

Natural resources, the technology that is used to obtain them, and the populations they sustain, are the basic building blocks of all social organization. These ecological factors always constrain and influence patterns of social ordering, but they do not directly determine the kinds of social ordering that exist in any society, community, or other organization. As a human population employs technology to obtain resources, it must create an economic system that can transform those resources into needed and usable goods and services. It must also create a political system that can coordinate and regulate the functioning of the economy and many other social activities. These two realms of social ordering—the economy and the polity—are thus fundamental components of all societies, communities, and many other kinds of social organization.

Economic Systems

All social organizations—from families to total societies—contain a set of procedures for acquiring needed resources, transforming them into necessary or desired goods and services, and distributing those products among the members of the organization. In small and relatively simple organizations such as families, those economic activities constitute roles that are enacted by individual members along with many other social roles. In larger and more complex organizations such as communities and societies, economic functions are usually conducted by specialized extraction, production, distribution, sales, consumption, financial, and other units. To identify and analyze that whole network of economically-oriented units, relationships, and functions, social scientists conceptualize them as the economy—or economic system—of the larger organization.

Endless variations can be observed among the economic systems of different societies. In some societies, the principal economic activities center around gathering edible plants and hunting wild animals. In other societies, the economy is based primarily on agriculture, including farming, herding, and/or fishing. In contemporary industrial societies, the major thrust of the economy is manufacturing and related functions. Future societies, in the judgment of many sociologists, will be increasingly oriented toward providing human services and handling information. Regardless of its nature, however, *the economy of any society, community, or other large organization is a major factor shaping the entire organization and many of its noneconomic activities.*

Sociologists hold differing views concerning the extent and nature of the influences that the economic system exerts within various organizations, ranging from theories of virtual economic determinism to the argument that the economy is only one of many organizational components. Nevertheless, it is quite apparent that within societies and communities the prevailing modes and patterns of economic ordering are a vital

component that cannot be ignored. The economic system is a key link between underlying ecological conditions and many other forms of social ordering. The structure and functioning of the economy influences the kinds and amounts of goods and services that are available to a society or community, as well as how those goods and services are distributed throughout the population. If the economy is flourishing, many other kinds of social activities become possible, from education to recreation. If the economy is floundering, there will be severe limitations on all other activities in the society. Sociologists usually leave detailed studies of economic systems to economists, but we do attempt to take account of the structure and functioning of the economy as a foundation for analyzing broader processes of social ordering.

Political Systems

All social organizations also contain a set of procedures for coordinating and regulating economic and other kinds of activities, formulating basic operating policies, and making decisions that are binding on their members. Again, in small and relatively simple organizations such as families, those political activities are only roles carried out by individual members. In larger and more complex organizations, political functions are commonly performed by specialized governmental, administrative, and legal units. Such networks of politically-oriented units, relationships, and functions are conceptualized as the polity—or political system—of the larger organization.

As with economies, political systems display countless variations among societies. The polity may consist of merely a headman (rarely a headwoman) or chief, and perhaps an informal council of elders. In other societies, military elites or hereditary monarchs control the polity and rule in a more or less autocratic manner. In some contemporary societies, the citizens select their political leaders through elections, although most of the political system still operates on the basis of appointments and delegated authority. Future societies may devise still other forms of political systems, although what they might be like is not evident at the present time. Regardless of its form, however, *the polity of any society or other organization is a second major factor—together with the economy—in shaping its overall organization and many of its activities.*

Sociologists also hold different views concerning the kinds of influences that the political system exerts within various organizations, ranging from theories of almost complete political determinism to the argument that the polity is merely a servant of the economy. At the same time, it is obvious that whoever controls the political system of a society or community is in a position to exercise considerable political and social power. The political system commonly operates as a link between the economy and most other forms of social ordering. Its structure and functioning can influence the performance of the economy, the manner in which goods and services are distributed, how collective decisions are made and who benefits from those decisions, the nature and success of military operations, and the activities of other systems such as religion and education. A strong and effective polity can ensure that other realms of a society are functioning smoothly and satisfactorily, while a weak or ineffective polity can lead to disintegration or collapse of a society. Most sociologists leave intensive studies of political systems to political scientists, but we generally take account of the structure and functioning of the polity as a crucial component of broader processes of social ordering.

Political Economy

Thus far, we have discussed the economy and the polity as separate systems, but in reality they are always interrelated. Although they can be studied separately—as commonly done by economists and political scientists—this is a somewhat artificial distinction. Many contemporary social scientists therefore argue that *it is more realistic and useful to examine the economy and the polity together as a single integrated system composed of two partially distinct but highly interwoven parts.* They use the concept of *political economy* to designate this single integrated system.

The principal arguments for employing the concept of political economy center on the many ways in which the economy and the polity of any society support and reinforce each other. Some common examples of these interrelationships are the following.

(1) The economy provides the resources— including goods and services and surplus wealth—that the polity requires to operate. A strong economy makes possible a strong government, while a weak economy leaves the government unable to perform many of its functions. The polity is thus always dependent on the functioning of the economy.

(2) The polity can adopt many kinds of policies and programs that support and promote the economy. These include taxes, tariffs, regulations, capital accumulation practices, personnel training, and price limits. The strength of the economy is therefore greatly influenced by what the polity does or does not do.

(3) In modern societies, the government is often the largest customer of the economy, so that many business firms rely heavily on government contracts. This purchasing dependence is most evident with military equipment, but it also includes everything from paper clips to computers.

(4) In most contemporary societies, the government employs a sizable proportion of the labor force.

(5) In many societies, the economic and political elites are in fact the same people, with heads of major businesses or wealthy individuals also serving in top political positions. Even if these two sets of elites are somewhat distinct, it is quite common for individual economic and political elites to move back and forth between the two realms during their careers.

(6) Top leaders in both the economy and the polity frequently share a common set of beliefs, values, and goals for their society. The most fundamental of these shared orientations is keeping the society operating smoothly and avoiding any serious disruptions or upheavals—and consequently

protecting their privileged positions in the society.

In subsequent chapters of this book, a modified political economy perspective provides part of the framework for understanding social organization. The economy and the polity are treated as partially separate subsystems of a society, each of which commonly displays distinctive structures and functions. As a result, these two subsystems may sometimes reinforce each other, while at other times they may conflict or impede one another. At all times, however, the economy and the polity of any society are necessarily interlocked in numerous ways, so that the activities of one subsystem always have critical consequences for the other subsystem.

SOCIAL CHANGE

Change is inherent in social ordering, and patterns of ordering are stable through time to the extent that they are able to adjust to or cope with changing conditions. Consequently, to reiterate a point made earlier, order and change are but two aspects of the same process. Nevertheless, we frequently observe that existing patterns of social ordering are noticeably and permanently altered in some manner. These critical turning points in organized social life—which may occur either gradually or suddenly–can be identified as significant changes *of* social ordering, rather than just ongoing changes *in* social ordering.

Nature of Social Change

Social change can be described as identified significant alterations in patterns of social ordering. What constitutes identification and significance in regard to social change?

Identification of Change. There is no sharp distinction between "routine" changes in social ordering and "nonroutine" changes of social ordering, so that the decision to label a particular alteration as a "social change" is always arbitrary. To make that decision, an observer must first be able to identify the alteration. This is done by comparing the social conditions or activities that exist at two or more points in time and then determining how much and in what ways they differ. Consequently, any identified instance of social change is actually a conceptual abstraction from social reality. It is derived from objective observations of social life, but subjectively identified and conceptualized as social change by observers. *Social changes are thus real historical processes, but to describe and understand them we must abstract them from ongoing social reality.*

Significance of Change. Any identified modification in social life could be labeled a "social change," but many of those modifications might be quite trivial. When studying social change, we usually want to focus on major events and trends that significantly alter patterns of social ordering. Two useful criteria for determining the significance of a social change are whether it has extensive effects on the distribution and exercise of social power or on activities of numerous organizational units.

As a first general principle, *changes in the distribution and use of power in a society or other organization are usually quite significant for social life.* This normally involves not just a shift in the individuals occupying power-wielding roles, but rather the development of new power relationships and the elimination of old ones. This might occur in a community, for instance, if several large corporations located there and put smaller local firms out of business. As a second general principle, *changes that stimulate further changes in many other organizational units are also quite significant for social life.* To the extent that several organizational units are functionally interdependent, an alteration in any one of them can set off a chain reaction of alterations in all the rest of them. For example, the introduction of new production procedures into a factory might require modifications in job descriptions and work group assignments, which could, in turn, lead to worker demands for greater union control over job assignments, which would result in the union growing in size and strength, which might lead management to revise many of its organizational policies, which ultimately would change the entire structure and functioning of the business.

Sources of Social Change

To understand any particular occurrence of social change, we must determine its underlying sources or causes. *Most sources of social change can be categorized as either stresses originating outside patterns of social ordering or strains originating inside those patterns.* Stresses and strains impinging on patterns of social ordering produce social tensions or conflicts that must be dealt with in some manner. Many tensions and conflicts in social life are repressed or resolved without altering the patterns of social ordering in any significant way. Others are just ignored and eventually fade away in the normal course of events. In some cases, however, social tensions and conflicts produced by stresses and strains do lead to identified significant social change. There are many different sources of social stresses and strains, several of which are described in the following paragraphs.

External Stresses. The most readily apparent source of stresses on social life is *new technology.* Technological knowledge can be acquired either through invention or discovery of something new or by borrowing from another culture. Every major technological development, from firemaking to nuclear fission, has disrupted established patterns of social life in some way. The invention of the plow led to settled agriculture and stable communities, while the steam engine ushered in industrialization and urban living. Technologies that at first appear to be purely material, such as the computer, can have social ramifications throughout many realms of society, as we are presently discovering. At the same time, new ideas that at first appear to be social in nature, such as credit purchasing, can have direct effects on economic production and the natural environment.

Any major modifications in the *natural environment* will also create stresses for social life. Climatic alterations, depletion of vital natural resources, natural disasters, disease epidemics, genetic mutations in plants or animals, and severe droughts are only a few examples of the kinds of environmental situations that will certainly have direct and serious consequences for human life. Our current concern with the impending exhaustion of finite fossil fuels clearly illustrates the many social stresses that can be generated by the natural environment.

Continuing with this ecological perspective, another critical source of stresses for social ordering is *population change,* especially when it occurs rapidly. Such changes may involve extensive population growth as a result of a "baby boom" or foreign immigration or domestic migration to "boomtowns." They may involve population decline caused by epidemics, out-migration, or mass starvation. They may also involve serious imbalances in the sex ratio or the age distribution of a population. Most common in today's world, however, is the "demographic transition" that is occuring in many developing countries. Traditionally, these countries have had very high birth and death rates, but modern sanitation, public health programs, and better diets are drastically reducing their death rates. Their birth rates often remain high, however, due to a number of factors. The result is a population explosion that can double a country's population in a single generation. Such growth obviously causes almost insurmountable problems in food production, education, employment, housing, and many other areas.

Finally, the *social environment* within which any organization is located can also exert pressures, demands, limitations, and restrictions on its patterns of social ordering. To the extent that these external social impingements involve the exercise of social power, they will create all kinds of stresses for the organization. Moreover, as modern communication and transportation continually increase the extent of interdependence among organizations, the scope and complexity of the social environment constantly expands. For example, communities within modern societies are no longer self-sufficient, but are continually influenced by stresses from other communities, governmental units, and national organizations advancing causes of one kind or another.

Internal Strains. All social ordering is subject to a wide array of inconsistencies, disjunctures, and cleavages that produce internal social strains. Even in the absence of serious external stresses, therefore, tensions and conflicts are endemic within social ordering, leading to social change.

One common source of social strains is *disjunctures between individual actions and established patterns of social ordering.* All individuals at least sometimes act as relatively independent actors seeking their own personal goals, rather than as committed members of a collectivity enacting social roles. If those actions are incompatible with the expectations and actions of the other people with whom they are interacting, strains will result. In the previous chapter, we examined the many ways in which inconsistencies and incompatabilities can occur when people are enacting social roles. Even more disruptive are actions that are socially defined as deviant, ranging from simple violations of prevailing customs to major crimes. To the extent that an organization is incapable of handling deviant actions—as when a factory cannot prevent substandard work or a police force cannot contain a riot—severe strains will be experienced. Most organizations, moreover, make no attempt to enforce total conformity to established norms and rules. By allowing individuals to exercise a certain amount of independence and creativity in their actions, the organization gains flexibility and stability, but at the price of a certain amount of internal strain.

Another important source of social strains in patterns of social ordering is *inadequate organizational functioning*, which can take several forms. An organization may not be able to fulfill satisfactorily all its functional requirements, such as acquiring vital resources, training new members, or making collective decisions. An organization may not be able to control its own subunits, so that they compete with one another or seek their own particular goals rather than working for the common welfare of the entire collectivity. An organization may be dominated by a small set of powerful elites who impose their interests and goals on everyone else and manipulate and exploit other members. An organization may not be able to establish and operate communication and coordination procedures that are needed to conduct its activities, with the result that it does not attain its goals. Finally, the distribution of benefits—such as incomes, privileges, or prestige—among the members of an organization may be quite unequal and hence unacceptable to those members who receive less than what they consider to be their "fair share" of the benefits. These various kinds of functional problems inevitably occur at one time or another, with the result that all patterns of social ordering are continually subject to internal strains, which often produce social change.

Types of Social Change

Social change can take many different forms, depending on the nature of the underlying stresses and strains, the kinds of tensions or conflicts they generate, the patterns of social ordering that are affected, the power and status of the people involved, whether the process occurs slowly through many gradual modifications or rapidly through drastic upheavals, and whether change is desired and intentional or undesired and unintentional.

Sociologists often examine social change in terms of two basic dimensions. *The first basic dimension of social change is its scope,* which can be divided into the two categories of moderate and fundamental. *Moderate social changes are relatively limited in scope or depth, so that they alter only some parts of a society or other organization.* Such changes are extensive enough to be identifiable and significant, but do not alter the entire organization. Moderate changes usually occur fairly gradually over time through a series of small but incremental steps, rather than suddenly through drastic social upheavals. As an example, the median educational attainment of the United States population rose from 8.6 years in 1940 to 12.5 years in 1980. In just one generation, the population shifted, on the average, from having just a primary education to having completed a secondary education. Needless to say, this rising level of education has affected many areas of life, but because it has occurred quite gradually, its effects have been relatively moderate—at least thus far.

Fundamental social changes are quite broad in scope and depth, so that they alter most or all parts of a society or other organization. Fundamental social changes occur much less frequently than moderate changes, but they are very evident and extremely significant when they do happen. A "boomtown" community that grows from a small village of 1,000 people to a bustling city of 20,000 in the space of two years, as a result of a huge construction project, has undergone a fundamental transformation. When the French people stormed the Bastille and overthrew the monarchy in 1789, that revolution produced a fundamentally new society. As these examples suggest, fundamental social change often occurs quite rapidly through sudden shifts in ecological conditions or drastic economic and political events.

The second basic dimension of social change is its purposefulness, which can be divided into the two categories of intentional and unintentional. *Intentional changes are instigated by individuals or organizations who seek to alter social conditions in desired ways.* This is often a complex and lengthy process, involving formulating goals to be obtained, planning strategies of action, mobilizing resources and support, conducting programs of various kinds, resolving conflicts, overcoming resistance, and finally—if successful—implementing the intended changes. Many intentional attempts at social change collapse or are defeated before achieving any of their goals. Nevertheless, some intentional change efforts do succeed over time, as illustrated by the civil rights movement in the United States since the 1950s.

Unintentional changes are not planned in advance, but occur in response to stresses and strains impinging on a society or other organization. In an effort to deal with the problems created by those tensions, various patterns of social ordering or social practices are gradually modified, or new patterns and activities are adopted. Because this process is continually occurring in all modern societies, it is often difficult to identify. Over time, however, the effects of the process can create profound changes in a society. No one intentionally adopted a national policy in the United States of promoting suburban growth, for instance. Nevertheless, as a result of a variety of causal forces—especially economic affluence, use of the automobile, and widespread desire for single-family homes—suburbs have been the fastest growing kind of community for the past fifty years in this country.

If the two basic dimensions of scope and purposefulness of social change are cross-classified, as shown in Figure 3-2, they produce a table containing four important kinds of social change. Moderate intended changes are often called *social reforms.* In this case, innovative individuals or organizations deliberately seek to introduce limited changes to achieve goals they desire or to cope with social problems. A society that establishes an unemployment benefits program to ease the financial hardships of loss of work is practicing social reform, for example. When such efforts are intended to create new social conditions, they are usually labeled "liberal," and when they are intended to preserve existing conditions that

FIGURE 3-2 Types of social change

Purposefulness of Change	Scope of Change	
	Moderate	Fundamental
Intended	Reforms	Revolutions
Unintended	Adjustments	Transformations

are being threatened, they are usually labeled "conservative".

Moderate unintended changes can be called *social adjustments*. They are usually unexpected outcomes of efforts to cope with unavoidable stresses or strains in social life. If there is a rise in the birth rate, school systems will discover that they must expand to handle the increased load, which necessitates raising school taxes and training more teachers, which in turn have other consequences for the community. As a general rule, this is the most common form of social change, although the process is often not recognized as social change until it is well underway.

Fundamental intended changes are usually called *social revolutions*. The leaders of a revolution are dedicated to creating a totally different kind of society or other organization. Revolutions are often thought of as political in nature, but there are also economic and social revolutions, which occurred in Europe during the seventeenth and eighteenth centuries as merchants deliberately sought to wrest economic and social dominance from the established landed nobility. Revolutions are labeled as "radical" if they seek to establish an entirely new set of social conditions, and as "reactionary" if they seek to restore a set of conditions that are believed to have existed at some time in the past.

Fundamental unintended changes are called *social transformations*. Most fundamental social changes are probably unintentional, at least at first. The participants often initially seek to introduce limited reforms to cope with stresses and strains that are creating social problems, but their reform efforts

may eventually transform the entire society. The social legislation introduced by President Franklin Roosevelt in 1933 was designed to end the depression by strengthening the capitalist economic system of the United States, but the eventual outcome of that process has been a fundamental transformation in the nature of modern capitalism, as well as the creation of a more welfare-oriented society. A more current example of a social transformation presently occurring in all industrial societies is a gradual shift away from high energy-consuming lifestyles toward living patterns that are more energy-conserving and utilize renewable, rather than nonrenewable, energy sources.

In reality, of course, there are no clear divisions between moderate and fundamental change, or between intended and unintended change. Moreover, through time, any change process can shift from one category to another. A process that begins as a moderate reform may stimulate a whole series of unintended adjustments, it may escalate into a social revolution, and it may eventually transform the society.

SUMMARY

Social ordering emerges as social relationships become interwoven into complex patterns that are relatively stable and enduring. As a result, social activities become increasingly interrelated, regularized, and predictable, and actors are able to cooperate in attaining common goals. Patterns of social ordering endure through time by becoming stabilized, but not static. Stability in social life is attained through constant change, which enables social organizations to deal with ever-present stresses, strains, tensions, and conflicts. Thus social ordering and social change are always inseparable social processes.

A social structure is a static representation of dynamic patterns of social ordering. Structural representations of social ordering are useful tools for both practical and analytical purposes, as long as they do not blind one to the fact that social ordering is continually being created and re-created.

A social system is an analytical model that can be applied to any occurrence of social ordering. All social systems are characterized by designated boundaries, complex webs of interrelationships, identifiable functions or activities, and overall unity.

Social ordering is always more than the sum of its individual components. It has an existence of its own as a separate level of reality. That contention is supported by the arguments of social properties that are not inherent in individuals, the exteriority of social ordering to individuals, and the constraints that social ordering exerts on individuals.

Human beings, like all other organisms, exist within complex ecosystems, or webs of relationships among organisms and between them and the natural environment. Human social ordering is always shaped and constrained by the fundamental ecological conditions of environmental resources, technological knowledge, and population characteristics. As human beings have used technology to extract resources from the environment, population size has increased until it now approaches the carrying capacity of the earth. A fundamental principal of ecology is that if the population size of a species is not controlled in some manner, it will tend to overshoot the carrying capacity of its environment and eventually crash. Human beings have devised many ecological enhancement techniques for increasing the carrying capacity of their ecosystems, including takeover, tool-making, expropriation, conquest, and drawdown.

To utilize the natural resources they obtain from the environment with the use of technology, human populations create economic and political systems. Although the economic systems of different societies vary in countless ways, the nature and performance of the economy is always a crucial factor in shaping social ordering. It constitutes a fundamental link between ecological conditions and the rest of any society or other organization. Political systems also differ greatly among societies, but the structure and functioning of the polity is a second vital factor shaping all social ordering. The polity is directly influenced by the economy, and in turn influences many other dimensions of social life.

The economy and the polity of a society or other organization are partially distinct systems, but at the same time they are always highly interwoven in countless ways. In particular, the economy provides necessary resources for the polity, while the polity protects and promotes the economy. To describe this mutual interdependence, social scientists often use the concept of political economy.

Although change is inherent in social ordering, some instances of social change can be identified as significant alterations of patterns of social ordering. Any identified change is a conceptual abstraction from ongoing reality that is thought to be significant because of its consequences for organized social life.

The many sources of social change can be classified as either external stresses or internal strains. The former are often caused by new technologies, the natural environment, population changes, or pressures from the social environment. The latter may be caused by many kinds of disjunctures between individual actions and patterns of social ordering, or by many forms of inadequate organizational functioning. Using the two basic dimensions of the scope and purposefulness of change, most instances of social change can be classified into one of four types: social reforms, social adjustments, social revolutions, and social transformations.

CULTURE

How does culture differ from social ordering, and how is culture created?
How do cultural beliefs, values, norms, and technologies each affect social
    life?
In what ways are all cultures different, and in what ways are they all the
    same?
How do individuals learn and internalize cultural ideas?
What conditions cause technologies, norms, values, and beliefs to change
    through time?

NATURE OF CULTURE

Human beings not only create patterns of
social ordering through their interactions,
but they also give meanings to their activities
and communicate those meanings to others.
These shared meanings in turn influence
and shape all of our social interactions and
patterns of social ordering. Consequently,
the process of social organization always involves the creation of both order and meaning in social life, and these two aspects of
social organization are inexorably intertwined. The set of ideas, symbols, and meanings that is shared by a population of people is called its culture. Like social ordering,
culture is a dynamic process with many components that is continually being both created and changed.

Concept of Culture

Originating in nineteenth-century anthropological studies of primitive societies,
the concept of culture initially referred to
the total "way of life" of a group of people. It
included the tools they used, the food they
ate, the clothes they wore, their family patterns, their governmental practices, their religion, and all other aspects of their social
life. Early sociologists borrowed this anthropological conception of culture as a convenient way of referring to all nonbiological
aspects of social life. As a consequence, the
terms "social organization," "social ordering," and "culture" were used almost inter-
changably for some time.

Ideas, Actions, and Objects. In recent
years, many social scientists have restricted
the meaning of culture to give it more precision (White, 1975). The contemporary sociological concept of culture refers only to
sets of shared ideas, so that its meaning is
clearly distinct from social ordering composed of patterns of relationships. The more
general concept of social organization,
meanwhile, incorporates both social order-

ing and culture. In this usage, *a culture is a set of ideas about human life that is shared by the members of a society or other social organization.* Culture gives meaning to human activities and consequently guides and maintains our collective social life.

An idea that is part of a society's culture may be closely associated with particular social actions and/or physical objects. For example, the idea of giving gifts to a person on her birthday is often expressed through the ritual of wrapping various objects in brightly colored paper, singing "Happy Birthday," and handing those objects to that person, who removes the wrappings and accepts the objects with expressions of appreciation. Two principal meanings are being expressed through this ritual: that the gift giver cares for the gift receiver and wishes her well in the coming year, and that ownership of those objects has been transferred from one person to another. In addition, other more subtle messages may also be communicated through this ritul, such as "the fact that I spent a lot of money on this present means that I really care deeply for you," or "now you owe me a gift and you'd better remember that on my birthday." Because the actions and objects involved in this social ritual are so closely associated with the idea of birthday gift giving, we often refer to them as part of the overall cultural trait of giving birthday gifts. Nevertheless, it is the cultural idea of gift giving that assigns meaning to the social action of exchanging gifts and symbolically transforms an ordinary consumer object such as a new sweater into an expression of emotional caring.

Because cultural ideas so thoroughly define the meaning and use of material objects, some sociologists speak of "material culture" as well as "nonmaterial culture." A gold wedding ring, for example, might be cited as an instance of the "material culture" of the United States. It is obvious, however, that the significance of a ring of gold worn on the left index finger lies entirely in the fact that it symbolizes the idea of a marriage commitment. The physical object itself may have some intrinsic economic or aesthetic value,

but if worn on the right hand rather than the left hand it totally loses its meaning in this culture and becomes just another piece of jewelry. We go to archeological museums to view the material artifacts of ancient civilizations (or to museums of science and industry to view the artifacts of our own society), but the pottery and tools (or computers and rockets) we see in the museum have no meaning to us unless we understand the cultural ideas imbedded in those objects.

All social actions are also thoroughly infused with cultural ideas that make them meaningful to the participants. A simple act like shaking hands, for instance, is defined by American culture as a relatively formal greeting that is generally done only with strangers or on formal occasions. This same act is defined by Swedish culture as a very warm form of greeting that is done whenever friends meet and also when they part. Within a culture, moreover, a particular act may be given quite different meanings under various circumstances. For example, if a person kills someone while conducting a robbery, that act is culturally defined as murder and the killer is severely punished. But if that same act of killing someone is performed on the battlefield by a person in uniform, it is culturally defined as fulfilling one's duty and the killer may be honored as a war hero. Because all social actions are infused with cultural meanings, sociologists sometimes use the compound term "sociocultural" to refer to both aspects of social life taken together.

Culture and Social Organization. The creation and transmission of culture depends on the human ability to use and communicate abstract symbols to represent ideas and to give meanings to actions and objects. As we saw earlier in the discussion of symbolic interaction, we constantly assign meanings to our own actions and to those of others, as well as the objects that are part of our daily lives, and we express those ideas with abstract symbols that we use in thinking and communicating. Participants in social activities continually express those symbolized ideas to one another to convey their expectations, attitudes, values, and beliefs regarding the activities taking place. As those ideas and meanings become shared and perpetuated among the members of a society or other organization, they form a common culture. This does not mean that the members of an organization necessarily all think alike, for we each have a unique mind and a history of life experiences that enable us to think individually. At the same time, however, the members of any group, organization, or society will share many ideas in common, which constitute their common culture. Thus *the process of social organization always involves both the establishment of social ordering and the creation of a shared culture,* and every instance of social organization possesses its own distinct culture.

Creation of Culture

In a fundamental sense, culture rests on an ecological foundation, since the basic requirements of all social life are survival and the satisfaction of individual and collective needs within a demanding and often limited environment. To survive, individuals must devise shared activities that meet their personal needs. And societies and other organizations must establish collective procedures to deal with such demands as procuring resources from the environment, regulating population size, producing and distributing necessary goods and services, and governing themselves.

Culture as Environmental Adaptation. Human culture can be thought of as humanity's principal survival and adaptive mechanism. Whereas other species survive in the natural environment primarily through biological mutation and genetic evolution, for at least the last 25,000 years human beings have adapted to their environment entirely through cultural development. Our species of Homo sapiens sapiens has not changed biologically throughout that time period, yet humanity's knowledge about itself and the world in which we live has constantly been

accumulating, with relatively few losses of information, through all those ages. *This process of increasing humanity's capacity to adapt to and utilize the natural environment through the gradual accummulation of cultural knowledge is called sociocultural evolution.* As a consequence of sociocultural evolution, human patterns of living have undergone several major transformations and have become increasingly diverse and complex.

Cultural Emergence. Through a long process of trial and error, some kinds of collective activities prove to be beneficial for people, while others do not. As people discover beneficial patterns of acting and satisfactory solutions to recurrent problems, they tend to describe those actions in symbolic terms and to express them as general principles of social life. Some of those generalizations are formulated as customs and traditions, some take the form of moral guidelines or norms, and some are viewed as basic values and fundamental beliefs. All cultural ideas, however, are symbolic reflections and expressions of people's collective struggles for survival and goal attainment. Thus *culture emerges from collective activities, gives meaning to those activities, and ensures their perpetuation and stability through time.*

As an example of this process of cultural emergence from ordered social life, consider the changes that have occurred in Western thinking as a result of industrialization. We have come to believe that the earth and its resources are to be utilized as fully as possible to improve our standard of living, rather than being carefully protected or even worshiped. We value economic productivity and growth above all other goals of collective life, in contrast to the older idea of producing only what was needed for continued survival. We have created a "success ethic," which holds that work is a moral virtue and that we should constantly strive to increase our income and material benefits. That success ethic has almost entirely replaced the idea that one should accept one's station in life and dutifully fulfill the roles associated with that status. And we have virtually come to worship technological innovation, rather than seeking to preserve established customs and traditions.

Over time, the cultural norms, values, beliefs, and other ideas that emerge from collective social activities tend to become disassociated from the particular situations that generated them, and are generalized to cover broad areas of social life. They take on the character of autonomous forces that direct and regulate our lives as accepted traditions and moral imperatives. The norm "thou shalt not steal" probably originated among primitive people in reference to food, which was crucial for their survival, but it has since become a generalized moral imperative that is applied to all kinds of situations and is experienced by individuals as an external cultural force. Acceptance of, and adherence to, these generalized cultural ideas are no longer matters of individual choice, but have become social obligations that people are expected to abide by and that are enforced by collective social sanctions when necessary.

In modern societies, for instance, most people firmly believe that each adult or nuclear family is responsible for supporting himself/herself or itself economically, unless incapacitated by factors beyond their control. We frequently label persons who refuse to meet this responsibility as shiftless or worthless. The idea of individual economic responsibility is so thoroughly entrenched in the cultures of modern societies that it is generally accepted without question, and few people are aware of its origin. In fact, this belief was developed only within the past few hundred years in Western societies as a direct consequence of the growth of business and industry that requires a large, readily available, and easily manipulable labor force of individuals seeking paid employment. Throughout most human history, in contrast, the prevailing belief has been that the extended family, tribe, clan, community, or other larger grouping was responsible for the economic welfare of all its members. Individuals were expected to contribute to collective economic efforts to the best of their ability, but economic activity was viewed as a cooperative effort of the entire group. Ultimately, the group—not the individual—provided for everyone's economic necessities. Moreover, this traditional belief is still widespread in most nonindustrial parts of the world, which creates severe conflicts when attempts are made to introduce Western work practices. As one illustration of this, the practice of nepotism—or hiring one's relatives regardless of their qualifications for the job—is considered a moral obligation in many parts of the world as a means of ensuring the economic welfare of the extended family.

Cultural Autonomy. Once cultural ideas have been dissociated from their original social bases, they become partially independent of patterns of social ordering. This partial autonomy of culture can be illustrated in several ways. Cultural ideas can survive—at least in libraries and museums—long after the society that generated them has ceased to exist, as with the culture of ancient Greece. Cultural ideas may also remain relatively unchanged over long periods of time, despite drastic alterations in underlying patterns of social life. The idea of monogamous marriage is as viable today as it was a thousand years ago, despite the countless changes that have occurred in family living in response to industrialization and urbanization. Finally, cultural ideas developed in one society may spread to all corners of the world, as seen in Roman legal principles or English and French concepts of political democracy.

Cultural and Social Interpenetration. Despite this partial autonomy of culture, patterns of social ordering and sets of cultural ideas always thoroughly interpenetrate each other. As a consequence, cultural beliefs, values, norms, and other ideas continually influence social ordering and interpersonal interaction. The cultural goal of achieving greater racial equality has sparked a revolution in interracial practices in the United States during the past thirty years. The norm of personal honesty leads most Americans to pay their full income taxes even though the probability of being caught cheating by a government audit are quite slim. And the custom of men opening doors for women continues to be widely observed regardless of the increasing social equality of women with men. In short, *the social and cultural realms of human life constantly influence and shape each other.*

COMPONENTS OF CULTURE

Any idea, from simple techniques of fire-making to abstract philosophies, can be included within a culture. Some kinds of ideas are more directly relevant to social life than others, however, and hence become crucial for the process of social organization. Socially relevant cultural ideas can be classified into the four broad categories of beliefs, values, norms, and technologies, as shown in Table 4–1.

Beliefs

All societal cultures contain one or more fundamental sets of ideas about the nature of the world and human life than are accepted as truth with little or no questioning. These cultural *beliefs are statements that are assumed to express fundamental truths about reality and human life.* They provide the cognitive framework within which all other cultural ideas are integrated into a relatively unified whole. Several different terms are used by social scientists to describe cultural beliefs, but they all refer to widely held assumptions or axioms about "the way things are" or "the nature of human existence."

Specific beliefs are relatively narrow in scope, pertaining to particular phenomena. Of critical importance in contemporary societies, for instance, are the beliefs that most individuals are capable of judging right from wrong and can therefore be held accountable for their actions, that the family provides the best social setting for rearing children, that individuals have the right to own and use goods as private possessions, and that the political state has the authority to issue legal directives. Beliefs such as these may be logical or illogical, sophisticated or naïve, scientifically valid or divinely proclaimed. In all cases, however, to the extent

TABLE 4-1   Four Principal Components of all Cultures

Component	Content	Example
Beliefs	What is	Extensive racial inequality is caused by exploitation and coercion
Values	What should be	Racial discrimination is wrong, and equal opportunities for all people is right
Norms	What to do	All forms of racial discrimination are intolerable, and employment opportunities will be open to racial minorities
Technologies	How to do it	Enact antidiscrimination laws, establish agencies to promote opportunities for minorities, and develop Affirmative Action programs

that such beliefs are widely accepted, they influence many aspects of social life.

Belief systems are sets of interrelated beliefs that cover broad areas of human existence. An older term for these sets of generalized beliefs was "moral philosophies," as formulated by theologians, philosophers, and other intellectuals. These often elaborate philosophies were rarely understood by the masses of ordinary people, but they shaped the thinking of the dominant classes and were translated into prevailing patterns of social life. Typical examples would be medieval scholasticism, which explained the feudal social order as God's divine scheme for coping with "worldly evils" and preparing individuals to enter the paradise of heaven, or the nineteenth-century philosophy of social Darwinism, which argued that life is a constant competitive struggle for survival in which those who work the hardest will achieve worldly success and thus further the cause of social progress.

A belief system that is held by most of the members of a society and that pertains to most aspects of social life is often referred to as a *worldview*, which is a rough translation of the German term of *Weltanschauung*. The worldview of a relatively traditional society, for example, might hold that the structure of society is preordained by the gods in a fixed pattern, and that the duty of all human beings is to maintain this pattern as faithfully as possible. A more scientifically-oriented society, meanwhile, might view social life as a dynamic process of humanly created activities that is open to continual modification.

Two conflicting belief systems are particularly crucial in today's world and are presently vying for popular acceptance in modern societies. The older, traditional perspective can be called the "technological belief system." It holds that technologies for proving natural resources can be continually improved, that the earth's resources should be used to the fullest possible extent, and that the outcome of that endeavor will be continual economic growth and human betterment. The newer, emerging perspective is an "ecological belief system." It asserts that humans are part of the earth's ecosystem and must act as stewards of the earth's resources, that technology should be used judiciously in ways that are appropriate to the tasks at hand, and that the goal of economic and political activities should be enrichment of human life rather than perpetual economic growth.

Values

Whereas beliefs and belief systems are assumptions about the fundamental nature of the world and human life, *culture values are shared conceptions of what is desirable and undesirable in social life*. Values are not simply accepted as self-evident axioms, but rather are chosen by people as commendable or despicable moral conditions to be pursued or avoided. Some of the values held by a person may be idiosyncratic to that individual, but most of our values are derived from the culture of our society or various subcultures within it. Cultural values are therefore not just individual preferences, but rather are an integral part of a total culture that is shared by all or most of the members of a society or other organization.

Sociologists frequently categorize cultural values as either *ideological* or *utopian* in nature, as first distinguished by Karl Mannheim (1936). Ideological values explain, justify, and support existing social arrangements, such as the idea of separation of church and state, or the American creed of "rugged individualism." Utopian values evaluate, criticize, and challenge existing patterns of social ordering, such as the ideas of racial equality or women's rights. Over time, a value that once served as a utopian ideal for social change frequently becomes an established ideology supporting the status quo. Political democracy, for example, was once a utopian idea that challenged the political power of the hereditary nobility, but it has since become an ideology that is widely used to justify all kinds of political practices.

Many cultural values are based on prevailing beliefs and belief systems and express evaluations concerning desirable and undesirable consequences of those beliefs. The dominant technological belief system of contemporary American society, for instance, holds the following values to be extremely important (Williams, 1970):

(1) Economic growth,
(2) Material success,
(3) Hard work,
(4) Economic and political rationality,
(5) Social progress, and
(6) Representative democracy.

Because these values all support the technological belief system that has pervaded the culture of the United States for the past two centuries, they might be called the dominant ideology of this society.

As a new belief system emerges in a society, however, it will create a partially or wholly different set of utopian values that challenge the prevailing ideology. The ecological belief system, for instance, rejects many of the established values previously listed, and espouses values such as these:

(1) Environmental preservation,
(2) Sustainable economies,
(3) Meaningful and satisfying work,
(4) Socioeconomic equality,
(5) Individual fulfillment, and
(6) Participatory democracy.

To the extent that these newer values are seen as incompatible with currently prevailing values, cultural and social conflict will inevitably occur between their opposing proponents.

By themselves, values are typically rather abstract ideas. To realize the values they cherish, societies and other organizations (as well as individuals) must translate those values into more pragmatic and attainable goals. *A cultural goal is a shared objective for collective social action.* A public school system expresses the value of universal education in terms of the goal of providing twelve years of free education to all children in the community. A business firm seeks to attain the value of economic success by achieving the goal of doubling its sales every five years. And a society that values social equity decides to seek the goal of eliminating all racial segregation.

Operational goals are extremely useful to organizations, since they provide concrete objectives for collective activities and enable organizations to determine how well they are doing in realizing their basic values. However, few organizations manage to attain all of their goals completely, and the goal of one organization may directly conflict with that of another. Because it is often easier to achieve compromises or other resolutions among specific goals than among general values, however, goal conflicts tend to be less divisive within and between organizations than are basic value conflicts. If two political parties value political democracy they are usually willing to accept periodic defeat by the other party. But if a party values victory at any cost, it may provoke a revolution rather than accept defeat at the polls.

Norms

This third category of cultural ideas with direct relevance for social organization consists of prescriptions and proscriptions concerning the means of attaining cultural values and goals. *Cultural norms are shared standards regarding acceptable and unacceptable social actions.* Individuals and organizations are normally expected to abide by them, and they may likely be sanctioned if they do not. These cultural standards for social action can be classified as moral norms, rules, customs, or traditions, although sociologists often use the single term "norm" to include all of them.

Cultural standards that carry some kind of moral or ethical imperative are called *moral norms.* They are thought of as "the right thing to do," and are complied with because of this ethical or moral injunction. A person who violates an established moral norm is usually defined as "deviant" and will likely be punished by persons acting as representatives of the society. The norms of middle-class America, for example, hold that it is wrong to steal or intentionally insult people or cheat on examinations, and that it is right to carry out one's responsibilities, thank a person who does you a favor, and respect private property belonging to others. To emphasize the moral imperative that is inherent in such norms, Durkheim referred to the body of norms contained in a societal culture as the "collective conscience" of that society.

Cultural standards that have no moral or ethical connotations are called *operational rules.* They are more or less purposefully established by some authority as a means of coordinating and regulating collective activities, and they are followed for expedient rather than moral reasons. To obtain a driver's license one must demonstrate knowledge of the rules of the road. To graduate from college a student must maintain at least a "C" average. To vote in elections one must be a citizen. And to play chess one must abide by the rules of that game. Rules are commonly enforced through rewards and punishments of various kinds, from a mild compliment or criticism to a formal commendation or jail sentence. Over time, some rules tend to shift into norms as they are accepted as the morally right thing to do, and hence require less formal sanctioning. Conversely, both norms and rules may be codified into laws and formally enforced by the state.

All cultures contain numerous *customs* and *traditions,* or established ways of carrying out particular activities or observing special occasions. A custom or tradition is a set of norms that is applicable to a specially defined situation. They are usually considered to be appropriate but not mandatory social guidelines, so that the person who ignores them may be viewed as insensitive or odd, but is not normally labeled as deviant and formally sanctioned. Practices that are viewed as tra-ditions are generally viewed as more established and important than simple customs, although there is no precise distinction between these two concepts.

William Graham Sumner, an early twentieth-century sociologist, coined the term "folkways" to refer to all of the norms that are contained within—and hence characterize—the culture of a society, as well as the shared practices resulting from those norms (Sumner, 1940). He divided folkways into the two broad categories of "customs," which carry few or no moral imperatives, and "mores," which are strong moral imperatives because they are thought to be crucial for societal existence. Gift giving is thus a custom in modern societies, while the right to protect one's private property is one of the mores of these societies.

Technologies

This fourth category of cultural ideas that influence social life consists of all the technical information contained within a culture. Technology may be as simple as knowledge about how to make a fire or find edible roots, or as complex as building a computer or a space rocket. Technology also includes knowledge of social skills and techniques that range in complexity from chairing a committee meeting to operating a huge bureaucratic organization such as a modern corporation. Regardless of its form or complexity, all *technology consists of knowledge about techniques using material objects or social actions to achieve desired objectives.* Objects and actions are not themselves technology, but rather embody technological knowledge.

As mentioned in Chapter 3, it is often convenient to distinguish between *material technology* and *social technology.* The importance of material technology for human societies hardly needs emphasizing to anyone living in the latter part of the twentieth century. During the past hundred years a constant stream of scientific discoveries and engineering inventions has extensively transformed countless realms of social life. Because of this recent inundation of new material technology, we sometimes lose sight of the vital significance of earlier technological innovations, such as the iron plow or public sewer systems, that have made modern societies possible.

The significance of developments in social technology is often less appreciated, however. Examples of social technologies upon which modern societies depend include knowledge of how to operate a monetary system based on credits and debts rather than precious metals, techniques for operating a judicial system composed of courts of law, the idea of a corporation which functions as an autonomous entity apart from the people who work for it at any given time, and procedures for managing a university composed of thousands of individuals and perhaps a hundred separate departments and institutes.

Most of humanity's present store of social technology has been acquired over the ages through a long process of trial and error, but very slowly we are learning how to transform the knowledge of the social sciences into applied social action. At the present time, however, numerous social problems are being caused by the fact that our stockpile of material technology is growing considerably faster than our technology for organizing social life. We know how to build military weapons that could destroy the entire earth, but not how to create international organizations capable of preventing nuclear war. This kind of disjunction between material and social technology was described as "cultural lag" by the early American sociologist William Ogburn (Ogburn and Nimkoff, 1950).

The problem of how to deal with nuclear weapons also illustrates the fact that material and social technology tend to become highly interwoven. To employ material technology in ways that are useful to humans, it is always necessary to develop social procedures for handling that technology. For this reason, some sociologists, prefer to use the single term "sociotechnical systems" to encompass integrated sets of material and social technologies.

ORGANIZATION OF CULTURE

Every instance of social organization—from small groups to total societies—possesses a distinctive set of cultural ideas. Many of these ideas are shared with other organizations, as a result of interrelated activities, common members, and communication networks. Nevertheless, each organizational unit has some beliefs, values, norms, or technologies that are unique to it. Moreover, the set of cultural ideas associated with any particular instance of social organization is always organized to form an integrated entity.

Cultures and Subcultures

Societal Culture. The single term *"culture" refers to the dominant, encompassing cultural of an entire society.* A societal culture normally shapes or influences the cultural ideas held by all other organizations and most individuals within its borders. The major values and norms of American culture, for example, pervade all communities, businesses, schools, churches, and even most families and small groups throughout the society. Virtually nowhere in this society can one escape the dominant cultural ideas of material success or romantic love, to mention only two obvious features of contemporary American culture. Moreover, modern mass communications are rapidly obliterating what were once relatively distinct regional and local cultures within this society, so that the whole society is tending to become more and more culturally homogeneous. In recent years, many people have become concerned about this cultural leveling process and have sought to preserve their unique cultural heritages by stressing cultural pluralism. Ethnic populations such as African-Americans, Hispanics, and Native Americans have been in the forefront of this movement, but cultural pluralism takes many diverse forms.

Subcultures. *The specific cultures associated with particular organizational units or sets of people within a society are referred to as subcultures.*

Subcultures usually include many ideas derived from the encompassing societal culture, but they also contain ideas that differ from that culture and identify them as distinct subcultures. Within the United States we can identify various ethnic, class, occupational, generational, community, and other subcultures that have so far resisted the homogenization of American culture. Each of these subcultures is unique in some way. Adolescents in this society, for example, have created a youth subculture with its own specific ideas of proper dress, modes of speech, musical tastes, and recreational preferences.

Despite the distinctive features of any subculture, it will usually be heavily influenced by the encompassing societal culture. At first glance, the values of a juvenile gang practicing car theft might appear to be in direct contradiction to societal norms concerning private property. But closer inspection will likely reveal that the gang members are stealing as a means of attaining the goal of monetary success that has been learned from the societal culture. Subcultures containing norms such as stealing, which are disapproved by the societal culture, are frequently labeled as *deviant subcultures*. Actions will likely be taken to discourage or prevent people from putting those norms into practice.

A subculture that rejects the basic beliefs and values of the dominate societal culture is called a *counterculture*. It may provide the basis for a radical social movement aimed at creating fundamental social change, as in the counterculture youth movement of the late 1960s.

Comparing Cultures

Cultural Differences. Although all subcultures exhibit some unique ideas, *fundamental cultural differences in beliefs, values, norms, and traditions are generally most evident at the societal level.* When we visit another society we may be struck by the "quaint," "odd," or "weird" ideas held by those people, as evidenced in many aspects of their daily patterns of living. On a mundane level, a Frenchman's idea of a proper breakfast is a cup of thick coffee and a hard roll, which may leave the typical American tourist longing for bacon and eggs. On a more fundamental level, an American tourist might be astonished by the extent to which the French believe in centralized political administration, so that municipal governments have relatively little autonomy in directing their own local affairs. These countless cultural differences between societies are especially vexing to people who move permanently to a new society. They often experience severe culture shock which can last for years, and many immigrants never do adjust fully to the new culture. In fact, it often requires two or three generations for the descendants of immigants to become fully acculturated to their new society.

Cultural Relativity. Because of the almost unlimited diversity among the cultures of the world's many societies, it has become fashionable in the twentieth century to espouse the idea of cultural relativity. This assertion holds that *all cultural ideas are meaningful only within their own culture*, and can only be adequately understood in relation to the total culture that comprises them. Taken out of their cultural context, they lose part or all of their meaning. Infantacide, which has been practiced in a number of societies, may seem abhorent to us until we understand that it has been their only effective way of keeping their population size in balance with their limited food supply. If they did not kill excess babies, the entire society might starve, so that infantacide was a meaningful and necessary part of their culture.

Cultural relativity also asserts that if a particular idea is accepted in a given culture, it is morally right within that culture. "When in Rome, do as the Romans do," regardless of what they are doing, for it is appropriate for that setting. This belief, which grew out of the work of early cultural anthropologists, was a direct reaction to the nineteenth-century European notion of cultural superiority and the "white man's burden" to enlighten and civilize (and dominate) the rest of the world. When the idea of cultural relativity is carried to extremes, however, it creates serious problems, since it rejects all ethical standards and leaves one with no guidelines for thinking or acting except to conform to whatever cultural ideas are prevelant among whatever group of people one is with at that time.

Cultural Universals. In the 1930s and 1940s, a number of anthropologists attempted to refute the idea of cultural relativity by searching for cultural universals that existed in all societies. They argued that because human beings everywhere face essentially the same challenges—such as obtaining food and other resources, cooperating with one another, rearing children, sanctioning people who perform undesired actions, making collective decisions, and accepting inevitable death—all cultures must contain some common traits. What they discovered was that *there are many universal themes throughout the world's cultures, but these general themes are expressed in countless different ways in specific societies.* All cultures contain the idea of the family as a basic social unit, for example, but every culture has its own particular conception of what kinds of social relationships constitute a family and what roles family members are expected to enact. George Murdock (1945) complied a lengthy list of cultural universals covering such themes as sexual relations and marriage, work, recreation, property ownership, crime and other forms of deviant behavior, art and music, education and training of children, care of the ill, group leadership, and religion. At the same time, a particular idea that one culture considers the highest moral virtue—such as sacrificing one's children to the gods—may be another culture's worst sin.

Awareness of universal cultural themes reminds us that the human endeavor to survive and cope with the problems of social living is basically the same everywhere, despite endless specific variations. Consequently, as social scientists we can attempt to evaluate various cultural ideas and their resulting social practices against universal criteria of functional effectiveness in coping with environmental conditions and enhancing the quality of human life. For instance, if the population of a society clearly exceeds the carrying capacity of its natural environment, we can describe this ecosystem as being severely out of balance, regardless of its cultural values and norms concerning birth and death.

When we make such evaluations about other societies and their cultures, however, we must always be sensitive to the pitfall of *ethnocentrism,* or judging the ideas and practices of another society by the particular values and norms of our own culture. We all tend to make ethnocentric value judgments of many kinds, ranging from a complaint that the French don't know how to prepare a proper breakfast to a condemnation of the People's Republic of China's one-party state as undemocratic or totalitarian. Nevertheless, such ethnocentric judgments of other cultures inevitably reveal our lack of understanding of those other cultures. A more sophisticated observer of other cultures will therefore attempt to keep an open mind and learn as much as possible about them as integrated systems of ideas, and will attempt to evaluate them only on the basis of universal criteria that can be applied equitably to all cultures.

TRANSMISSION OF CULTURE

If the thousands or millions of ideas and bits of knowledge that comprise a culture are to remain viable and not become museum relics, they must be continually communicated among the current members of a society and taught to the next generation of members. The transmission of culture therefore involves the two interrelated processes of communication through language and socialization of children and adults. Because these topics of language and socialization incorporate both psychological and sociological phenomena, they fall within the interdisciplinary field of social psychology. Since the focus of this book is on the process of social organization, this section merely indicates the significance of language and socialization for the transmission and perpetuation of culture and does not attempt to examine these processes in detail.

Language

To be communicated, cultural ideas must be expressed in a manner that is understood by all the people involved. For this purpose, human beings throughout all known history have used symbolic language.

Signs and Symbols. Rudimentary communication occurs among many species of animals, in several different ways. Bees use body movements to indicate the direction in which honey has been found. Wolves use their urine to give a distinctive odor to the territory they have claimed. Chimpanzees can produce a variety of sounds and gestures to express feelings and simple commands. All these forms of communication, however, rely entirely on *signs* that directly represent information.

Humans can also use signs, as one quickly discovers when in a foreign country where the language isn't known. Pointing to one's mouth indicates hunger in any society. Most human communication, however, utilizes abstract *symbols* to express ideas. Symbols are sounds, marks, or actions that have been arbitrarily chosen by a population to represent particular ideas. The spoken or written word "water" refers to the chemical compound H_2O. But to understand the meaning of this symbol one must speak the English language, since there is nothing inherent in the word "water" to indicate H_2O. The word *l'eau* is an equally adequate symbol for H_2O among French-speaking people. A language consists of thousands or millions of these abstract symbols, together with a set of equally arbitrary gramatical rules for combining those symbols into meaningful expressions.

The richness and complexity of all cultures clearly depend on the human ability to create abstract symbols and use them to communicate ideas. Symbolic language enables people to share technological information, express norms and rules that direct their activities, agree upon common values, and develop elaborate belief systems. Without language and the communication it makes possible, there would be no human culture.

Linguistic Construction of Reality. When first studying a foreign language, students often assume that it is merely a task of learning new words that are the equivalents of words in their native language, plus some different gramatical rules. As you become fluent in the new language, however, you begin to discover that to speak it adequately you must think in it, for a language shapes the way in which we think and even the way in which we perceive the world. In English there is only one word for "snow," but Eskimos have over twenty words for different kinds of snow, because of its importance for their survival. To understand their culture and appreciate their view of the world, one must learn to be sensitive to the distinction between "dry-packed-suitable-for-building-igloo snow" and "ice-crust-surface-snow."

Equally striking linguistic differences exist among cultures in regard to interpersonal relations. The language of the Navajo Indians, for instance, contains no active verbs. All actions are expressed in a passive voice, which is probably a reflection of the passive nature of their way of life. You cannot say the equivalent of "I am studying sociology" in Navajo, but rather must say something to the effect that "sociology is being studied by me." Alternatively, if you are visiting in France you must be careful to address social superiors or public officials as *vous* rather than *tu* to indicate proper respect for their position, lest you appear to be insensitive or boorish. Consequently, French-speaking people must quickly establish the nature of their relationship as soon as they begin talking, while English-speaking people can avoid this by using "you."

In short, language is not merely a symbolic medium for expressing ideas, but it also shapes our perceptions of physical and social reality and our styles of social interaction. Consequently, understanding the language of a society is an absolute prerequisite for fully comprehending its patterns of social ordering and its culture.

Written Language. Modern societies are highly dependent on written communications, and the invention of writing about six thousand years ago marked a major turning point in sociocultural evolution. With written language, a culture no longer depends on individual memories to preserve accumulated knowledge and ideas or on interpersonal interaction to convey information throughout a society. Early writing is thought to have been developed by rulers and priests to enable them to record and keep track of business transactions such as an exchange of land or a loan of grain. These protolanguages generally consisted of pictographs, or stylized pictures of the objects or actions involved. Over time, the pictures were increasingly simplified and abstracted until they bore no resemblance to physical reality, but rather represented ideas, individual words, or just single sounds. The more abstract this writing became, the greater its flexibility in expressing numerous complex ideas, thus making possible modern written communication. We can observe that process of expanding symbolic abstraction occurring even today, as mathematics—which is the most abstract and content-free form of writing—becomes increasingly important in the age of computers.

Socialization

There are two sides to the process of *socialization*, or *learning to be a functioning human being.* Psychologists generally focus on the dynamics of *personality formation,* in which children develop autonomous personalities through interaction with others. Sociologists, in contrast, are more likely to be concerned with *sociocultural learning,* in which individuals of all ages learn the social skills and cultural ideas necessary to participate in their society or other organizations. Because the sociocultural aspect of socialization is more directly relevant to the transmission and perpetuation of culture, this discussion deals only with it.

Setting of Sociocultural Learning. The process of learning social skills and cultural ideas is often thought to occur primarily in childhood, but this is an oversimplification. Certainly childhood, and especially the first few years, is an especially critical period in a person's life, and a great deal of fundamental learning occurs then. *Sociocultural learning continues throughout life,* however, although the extent to which it occurs varies widely among individuals depending on the circumstances of their lives. Every time we interact with new people, take on a new role, join a new group, or even read a serious book we inevitably learn something more about our social world and our culture—or those of others.

Social skills and cultural ideas can be learned in many different ways, including formal instruction, informal imitation, trial and error experimentation, reading, and just observing and listening. Social-psychological research has repeatedly demonstrated, however, that *sociocultural learning is most effective when its occurs through face-to-face interaction.* The family is therefore by far the most important setting for sociocultural learning for most people. A series of studies about factors that influence academic learning, for instance, demonstrated that the social and intellectual climate of the home has far more effects on most children's academic attainments than any characteristics or activities of the schools (Jencks, 1972). Other settings in which interpersonal interaction produce extensive sociocultural learning include friendship and other peer groups, work teams, and close-knit neighborhoods. Charles Horton Cooley (1956) first referred to these social settings as *primary groups* because they are of such primary importance in all sociocultural learning. That term is often used today to describe all social relationships and groups in which the interaction is direct and personal, and which therefore provide individuals with much of their sociocultural learning.

Dynamics of Sociocultural Learning. Although one can acquire information through passive observing, listening, and reading, *the process of sociocultural learning is much more intense and effective when it occurs through active involvement.* When we first begin interacting with someone, enacting a new role, or participating in a new organization, we tend to be unfamiliar with what is going on and uncertain of what is expected of us. Our initial communications and actions may be quite hesitant and tentative, trying first one approach and then another. Once we begin to receive responses from others, however, we acquire a basis for evaluating our actions and learning the social skills and cultural ideas appropriate to that situation. Some of the things we say and do will likely be disapproved by others, and we will be discouraged from repeating them. Other things we say and do will be tolerated by others, giving us leeway to decide whether or not to repeat them. Still other messages and actions will be approved by others, which encourages us to repeat and learn them. This learning process is further reinforced as we "take the role of the other" so that we anticipate in advance how others are likely to respond to what we intend to say or do. On the basis of this anticipation, we can then modify our thinking and acting, which intensifies the learning process.

Internalization. As stressed by normative theorists, internalization of norms is a crucial aspect of all socialization. *When cultural norms are internalized they are accepted as integral parts of one's personality and as one's own standards of action.* The individual then abides by those norms because he or she feels that "this is the right way for me to act." Norm internalization is largely an unconscious process. We are not usually aware of doing it and hence rarely realize the extent to which our "own" standards are actually learned from the culture and subcultures in which we participate.

For instance, many of us probably feel quite strongly that honesty is ethically desirable, and pride ourselves on being truthful. The fact that our moral inhibition against lying is actually an internalized cultural norm can be easily demonstrated, however. If we should be placed in a situation in which lying is socially expected or required—such as a "liars club" in which the members compete to see who can tell the biggest and most convincing lie—we would likely feel that lying is desirable in that setting.

The social philosopher George Herbert Mead (1934) described the process of norm internalization with the concepts of *play, games,* and the *generalized other.* As an individual temporarily "takes the role of the other" and sees himself or herself through another person's eyes, the individual develops conceptions of what that person expects. At first, these conceptions are closely tied to particular individuals, as the young child becomes aware of "what Mother expects of me" or "what Teacher expects of me." Mead called this the "play" stage, since the child is largely playing at the roles of specific others as they relate to himself or herself. Over time, though, the expectations of all those persons with whom one interacts in a given situation become fused into a single conception of what is expected in that social setting. Mead referred to this as the "game" stage, since the child is now learning to participate in organized games or group activities. Eventually, as the individual matures, these various situationally relevant standards of action tend to merge into a more general conception of what all other people expect one to do. Mead used the term "the generalized other" to describe this third stage of norm internalization. At each stage of this process, the individual not only learns the expectations of others, but also incorporates them into his or her own self-concept. Those norms become not just what others—another person, other participants in a game, or an amorphous they—expect, but what one expects of oneself because of one's own self-images and self-identity. In this manner, cultural norms become thoroughly internalized within individuals and they become socially responsible members of society.

CULTURAL CHANGE

Living cultures that are associated with ongoing societies and other organizations are always dynamic processes. The ideas and knowledge constituting a culture are continually changing, sometimes rapidly and sometimes imperceptibly. Only dead cultures of the past, preserved in libraries and museums, are totally static, although some elements of those cultures may persist in contemporary societies. *When the contents of a culture or subculture change in identifiable and significant ways, we refer to this process as cultural change.*

Because of the close interweaving of social ordering and culture in all social organization, it is often difficult to distinguish clearly between social and cultural change, and many of the features of social change discussed in Chapter 3 also apply to cultural change. There are some distinctive aspects of cultural change, however, which are most easily observed by examining the four types of cultural components: beliefs, values, norms, and technologies. The primary sources of cultural change differ among these categories, as do typical rates of change. Technological knowledge usually changes the most rapidly, followed in order by norms and customs, values and goals, and then beliefs and belief systems.

Sources of Technological Change

New technological knowledge—both material and social technology—is acquired by a culture in one of three ways: invention, discovery, and diffusion. The term *cultural innovation* refers to this overall process of acquiring new cultural knowledge.

Invention is the creation of new knowledge—or objects or actions embodying that knowledge. Any invention is essentially a synthesis of previously existing information, combined or integrated in a new fashion. Until all the necessary component information is available, it is impossible to create a particular invention. The classic example of this was Leonardo da Vinci's efforts to design an airplane in the early sixteenth century. His notebooks demonstrate that he understood the basic principles of aerodynamics and knew how to construct an airfoil, but at that time there was no engine light and powerful enough to propel a plane. Hence this effort at invention never left his notebook.

On the other hand, once all the necessary information for an invention is available in a culture, it appears to be only a matter of time until that invention is made. William Ogburn (Ogburn and Nimhoff, 1950) demonstrated this phenomenon by studying many cases of simultaneous invention, in which two or more people have independently made the same invention within a few years of each other, without knowledge of each other's work. To cite a few examples: the printing press was invented by Costner in 1423 and by Gutenberg in 1443; photography was developed by both Daguerre and Talbot in 1839; the telegraph was invented by Henry in 1831, and separately by Morse, Cooke-Wheatston, and Steinheil in 1837.

Discovery involves finding something that already existed but was not known about or recognized. When we speak of discovery we often think of finding new lands, as when Columbus "discovered" North America in 1492—except that the Vikings had "discovered" it at least 500 years earlier, and migrants from Asia had been here for at least fifteen thousand years. A discovery, in other words, may be new only in the eyes of some people.

Two other forms of discovery are especially important in contemporary societies. One is the discovery of natural resource deposits of which we were previously unaware. Geologists are searching the earth these days for additional deposits of petroleum and many scarce metals and minerals. The other form is scientific research in both the natural and social sciences, although this often involves a combination of both discovery and invention. The critical aspect of all discoveries, however, is not just finding something new, but determining how to use it. Petroleum was long considered just a curiosity or a nuisance in bogs and other places where it seeped to the surface, until we learned how to refine it into burnable fuel.

Diffusion is the transfer of knowledge, especially material and social technology, from one culture to another. Most cultures obtain most of their technological knowledge in this manner, as a consequence of trade, military conquest, immigration, or mass communications. A striking illustration of the pervasiveness of cultural diffusion was provided by the anthropologist Ralph Linton (1933) in a fascinating essay titled "The One Hundred Percent American." His essay describes the routine activities of an American man getting up in the morning and preparing to go to work, and this concluding paragraph sketches the scene as he leaves his home:

He places upon his head a molded piece of felt, invented by the nomads of Eastern Asia, and if it looks like rain, puts on outer shoes of rubber, discovered by the ancient Mexicans, and takes an umbrella, invented in India. He then sprints for his train—the train not the sprinting—being an English invention. At the station he pauses for a moment to buy a newspaper, paying for it with coins invented in ancient Lydia. Once on board he settles back to inhale the fumes of a cigarette invented in Mexico, or a cigar invented in Brazil. Meanwhile, he reads the news of the day, imprinted in characters invented by the ancient Semites by a process invented in Germany upon a material invented in China. As he scans the latest editorial pointing out the dire results to our institutions of accepting foreign ideas, he will not fail to thank a Hebrew God in an Indo-European language that he is a one hundred percent (decimal system invented by the Greeks) American (from Americus Vespucci, Italian geographer).

The aspect of diffusion that is omitted from this essay is that it is rarely a smooth process of simply adopting new technology and putting it into use. A large proportion of the ideas that diffuse from one culture to another are never widely adopted. The most frequent reason for this is that the new information does not fit into the culture, or conflicts with existing ideas and practices. This is particularly common with social technology, but it also occurs with material technology. Another common reason is that political leaders or other powerful interests block the new knowledge for fear that it will disrupt the established social order and perhaps threaten their power. As a general rule, new ideas tend to be accepted from another culture only if one of three conditions prevail:

(1) Its usefulness is readily apparent to the recipients, which is most likely with material objects;
(2) The society from which the knowledge comes is politically, economically, or militarily dominant over the recipient society, as in the case of military conquest; or
(3) Powerful leaders or organizations within the recipient society decide to adopt the new knowledge and support its acceptance in their society.

Sources of Norm Changes

New norms and customs can diffuse into a culture from other societies, although they are even more likely to be viewed with suspicion or hostility than in the case of new technological knowledge. Because existing norms are viewed as "the way things ought to be done," people are usually reluctant to abandon those norms and adopt new ones that come from foreigners. Only if those outsiders can exert enough political, economic, or military power to compel the adoption of their norms and customs is there likely to be extensive normative change through diffusion.

Most normative change originates not in external diffusion, but from internal cultural or social conflicts within a society. One way in which this occurs is when *the norms and customs being observed are in conflict with the basic values of that culture.* As an illustration, the values of a community might hold that drinking, gambling, and other such "vices" are morally wrong, while at the same time many residents might covertly accept the norm that these activities are perfectly acceptable as long as they are done in private. Alternatively, a society might value individual freedom and yet abide by the norm that every person is subject to military duty regardless of how he or she views the morality of war.

The norms and customs of a society or other organization may also contain internal inconsistencies that place strains on the culture. The by-laws of a labor union, for example, might state that no discrimination will be practiced against persons because of race, religion, nationality, or gender, but also stipulate that all new applicants for union membership must be personally recommended by a present member—almost all of whom are white, Anglo-Saxon, Protestant males. Or consider the case of a family whose norms simultaneously prescribe joint decision making on all major issues, but proscribe the wife from having any say about what job her husband takes.

A third internal source of normative strain occurs whenever *people's actions are markedly divergent from the prevailing norms.* The political norms of the United States specify that all adults are entitled to vote, but until recently blacks were often prevented from voting in many communities. In schools, the norm may be "equal education for all," while in reality children from higher-income families receive preferential attention and encouragement from teachers. On a more personal level, the norm of marital sexual fidelity is in fact violated by the majority of people in the United States.

These kinds of internal normative conflict are often ignored or endured for long periods of time within a society, but eventually they are likely to create demands for change. Those demands will typically be ignored or actively opposed for a period of time, but sooner or later the norms are likely to change.

Sources of Value Changes

Values are even more resistant to change than norms, since they are expressions of people's deepest feelings about social life.

Consequently, basic values tend to shift very gradually and only after long periods of resistance and opposition. Nevertheless, they do change with time. If we were able to travel back through time to Elizabethan England, for instance, we would probably be appalled by the callous indifference to human suffering and inequality that was accepted as natural and even appropriate at that time. If people were starving in the streets of London that was too bad, but obviously they were of the "lower classes," and society was better off without them.

The principal source of most long-term value changes is not intellectual or moral criticism, but rather fundamental shifts in underlying conditions such as environmental limitations or opportunities, demographic trends, economic productivity or decline, material standards of living, political regimes, military activities, and working conditions. As these kinds of fundamental social changes sweep through a society, individuals will slowly shift their personal values to take account of the new conditions. And as those personal values are shared among widening circles of people, old cultural values will be forgotten and new ones will arise to give meaning to social reality.

Because cultural values are so important to people, most individuals are not very likely to make radical value changes during their lifetime. It appears that many of our basic values are largely formed during adolescence and early adulthood, and are strongly influenced by the social conditions at that time. Once those values are formed, most people hold them for life. Consequently, *most value shifts occur only through time, as older generations die and are replaced by younger ones.* Sociologists use the term "cohort" to describe a population of individuals who are born and hence mature at about the same time, who experience the same social conditions during their youth and early adulthood, and whose basic values are therefore likely to be fairly similar. The "depression cohort" can thus be distinguished from the "World War II cohort," who in turn differ from the "post-war cohort," who are distinct from the "sixties cohort," and so on. Each of these cohorts holds a somewhat different set of cultural as well as personal values, so that the passage of cohorts through the life cycle seems to account for a considerable amount of value change.

Sources of Belief Changes

We do not understand very well how or why fundamental beliefs and belief systems change, since they tend to be extremely resistant to any modification. Kuhn's (1970) analysis of paradigm shifts in science offers some insights into this process, however, (A scientific paradigm is a set of beliefs that guides scientific research.)

Paradigms and other belief systems are clearly shaped by the conditions and knowledge existing at the time they are created. *Through time, as conditions and knowledge change, prevailing paradigms may become increasingly incongruent with reality as it is presently experienced.* As reality is discovered to violate the existing paradigm in more and more ways, we experience considerable confusion. At first, our reaction to this situation is likely to be denial that there is any incongruence. Next comes a period of resistance, in which we attribute the incongruency to our observations and experiences rather than to the paradigm we believe in, and hence reinterpret our observations to fit that paradigm. Then we may begin making small adjustments in the paradigm in an effort to bring it more into alignment with reality, while steadfastly holding onto the essence of the paradigm. In this manner, old paradigms may be retained long after they are "rationally" obsolete.

Sooner or later, however, the incongruencies between our present paradigm and the real world will create problems of knowledge and action that are so glaring they can no longer be denied, evaded, or just tinkered with. Intellectual crises erupt with which the old paradigm simply cannot cope. It becomes obvious to more and more people that it is time to discard the old paradigm and create a new one that is appropriate to reality as it is now being experienced. Such a paradigm shift will not occur, however, until a new paradigm is available to replace the discarded one. In some situations, the new paradigm may have already been created by a few innovative thinkers and be waiting in the wings for its turn on the cultural stage. In other situations, no alternative paradigm may be available, which leads to a frantic search for beliefs with which to construct a new paradigm. When the shift to a new paradigm does eventually occur, it results in a total transformation in the way people view and think about the world. "When paradigms change, the world changes with them" (Kuhn, 1970:111).

SUMMARY

Social organization is the process of bringing order and meaning into human social life. The meaning dimension of this process is provided by culture, or shared sets of ideas about human life. Many material objects and all social actions and interactions are thoroughly infused with cultural ideas that make them meaningful to human beings. Every instance of social organization possesses its own distinct culture, although the term "culture" is generally applied only to societies. The sets of cultural ideas associated with other organizations within a society are commonly called "subcultures".

Culture emerges from patterns of social ordering as individuals communicate their shared experiences and give symbolic meanings to their collective activities. The creation of culture is the principal mechanism through which human beings adapt to their environment and ensure their survival. Although a culture therefore reflects its underlying social base, it tends to become partially autonomous through time. Nevertheless, the social and cultural realms of human life constantly influence and shape one another.

The major components of any culture are beliefs, values, norms, and technologies. Beliefs are assumptions about fundamental truths of reality and human life, and are often combined into complex belief systems called worldviews or paradigms. Values are shared conceptions of what is desirable and undesirable in social life, they may be either ideological or utopian in nature, and they are sometimes expressed as specific goals for social action. Norms are shared standards for social action that often involve some amount of morality but can also be formulated as pragmatic rules. Norms are frequently combined into customs and traditions applicable to specific situations. Technologies consist of knowledge about procedures for achieving desired ends and can pertain to both material objects and social activities.

Because societal cultures differ widely, many people argue that all cultural ideas are relative and can be understood only within the context of their own society. At the same time, societal cultures contain ideas about numerous universal themes of human life.

Cultural ideas are expressed through symbolic language, which enables people to communicate those ideas and perpetuate them through time. In addition, language shapes our perceptions of reality and the ways in which we think. Written language is especially critical in the communication of culture. New generations learn their culture and subcultures through socialization, which enables them to develop autonomous personalities and to become competent participants in social life. Sociocultural learning occurs throughout one's lifetime, especially in small primary groups such as the family. Such learning involves a process of social reinforcement as we interact with others and take the roles of others. To the extent that norms and other cultural ideas are internalized by individuals, they can guide people's actions in socially responsible ways without external sanctioning.

Living cultures are continually changing and evolving, although the various components of a culture often change at greatly different rates. Technological change results from invention, discovery, and especially diffusion of knowledge. Norms can change as a result of conflicts with basic values, inconsistencies among norms, and incongruencies between norms and actions. Values usually change quite slowly in response to new social conditions, as new generations or age cohorts reach maturity. Beliefs are extremely resistant to change, but belief systems occasionally undergo radical transformations through total paradigm shifts.

5

ORGANIZATIONAL UNITS

How are the boundaries and membership of organizations determined?
What are the major characteristics of all organizations?
What are organizational functions and functional analysis
How do sociologists differentiate among various types of organizations?
How are organizations linked together, and why do those linkages produce
tensions?

DELINEATION OF ORGANIZATIONS

We have described the process of social organization as the merging of social interactions into patterns of social ordering that are infused with cultural meanings. As this process occurs though time, it is shaped by its participants into various kinds of units that we call social organizations. Any social organization is therefore a specific instance of a flowing process, and also a distinct social entity. Organizational units are delineated or distinguished from one another primarily in terms of their boundaries and their memberships. These two kinds of organizational delineation are interrelated, since membership is often a basic means of identifying organizational boundaries, while boundaries in turn define who is and is not a member of an organization.

Establishing Boundaries

All organizations have boundaries of some kind that distinguish them from their environments.

Boundaries therefore enable us to determine what is included within the organization and what is not. Although many organizational boundaries are rather vague and/or arbitrary, they nevertheless exist throughout social life and are recognized by organizational participants. Often those boundaries are based on recognizable "breaks" or "barriers" in ongoing social and cultural processes, such as "Who interacts with whom?" or "Who shares these basic values?"

Vagueness of Organizational Boundaries. The boundaries of many social organizations are frequently quite vague and difficult to identify, with the result that people often disagree sharply over what constitutes a particular social unit. For instance, what are the boundaries of your family? Does it consist of just one generation of yourself and perhaps a spouse? Does it include two generations of parents and their children (with you as either parent or child)? Does it extend to three generations of grandparents, parents, and their children? Does it also include any uncles, aunts, cousins, nephews, nieces, or other relatives? What about a foster child living in the home, or a person one lives with but is not married to? The actual social boundaries of a community—in contrast to its arbitrary legal boundaries—are especially difficult to locate. People who live outside a city's legal boundaries but work and shop within the city are clearly functional members of the total urban community, even if they reside within a legally separate municipality. The functional boundaries of large metropolises may extend out fifty or a hundred miles from the city center, although there are no lines on any map showing the scope of the city's influence over its surrounding hinterland. And on the societal level, nations frequently go to war over disputed pieces of land or ocean rights.

Arbitrariness of Organizational Boundaries. To clarify organizational boundaries, we often draw arbitrary lines on a map or establish arbitrary criteria that everyone can (or is forced to) agree upon. An imaginary line running down the middle of a street divides a city from its adjoining suburb. In the latter part of the nineteenth century, the major European powers divided the continent of Africa into colonial territories for themselves without any regard for the actual societal boundaries of the people living there. And even a small friendship group may arbitrarily exclude a person who is not liked. Once such arbitrary organizational boundaries have been established and accepted, however, they become just as "real" as boundaries that have emerged through "natural" social processes.

Types of Organizational Boundaries. Regardless of how they are established, most organizational boundaries fall into the following four types:

Geographical boundaries often take advantage of existing topographical features as a basis for social divisions. Oceans, rivers, mountain ranges, highways, and other physical features of the land frequently become the boundaries of societies and communities.

Interactional boundaries are based on interaction linkages among individuals or organizations. On the individual level, friendship groups are usually determined by who interacts with whom in a friendly manner on a regular basis. With organizations, functional networks are commonly defined in terms of exchange bonds among interdependent units.

Structural boundaries can take several different forms, such as membership lists, political jurisdictions, trade areas, transportation systems, and legal citizenship. In all such cases, established patterns of social ordering include some people and activities and exclude others, which provides a basis for determining the boundaries of the organization.

Cultural boundaries can rest on people's language homogeneity, shared beliefs and values, common interests and goals, customs and traditions, or arbitrary decisions about "who belongs with us and who doesn't." Even when there is an apparent "real" difference among people, however, it must be culturally defined as a social boundary if it is to serve as one. As an example, some people with quite light skins are defined as "blacks" and placed into one racial category, while other people with similar or even darker skins are defined as "whites" and placed into a different racial category.

These various kinds of organizational boundaries are not mutually exclusive, and many organizations use several of them simultaneously or under different conditions. But all of them serve to delineate an organization from its social environment.

Determining Membership

Any organization must have people who are considered to be members of it. Hence a second way in which a specific organizational unit is distinguished from other units is in terms of its membership. At the same time, organizations are rarely (with the exception of the nuclear family) dependent on having any particular individuals as members. Most organizations can experience a complete turnover of members through time and yet remain the same entity, and if an organization is to survive for long it must create procedures for at least periodically obtaining new members.

Specifying the membership of an organization is closely linked with establishing organizational boundaries, since boundaries often define who is a member and who is not. In some organizations, the membership is explicitly defined by a formal roster, as in a company's payroll list. Many organizations, however, have only an informal understanding of who is and who is not a member, as in friendship groups. Still other organizations have no clear identification of their members, as is the case with communities. Most nations, meanwhile, periodically conduct a census to identify and count their members. Even the best census always misses a portion of the population, nevertheless, and it is obsolete as soon as it is completed since the population is constantly changing. In short, even a simple enumeration of the members of an organization can often be quite difficult and less than fully accurate.

Beyond that problem of counting the members of an organization, three additional aspects of organizational membership are criteria, identification, and commitment.

Criteria for membership are requirements established by an organization or some higher authority such as the government. Sometimes these criteria are stated explicitly, as with the requirement that one must have a law degree to be a member of the American Bar Association. In less formally organized groups, the criteria are often understood without being specified, as with friendship cliques or social classes. Even when the criteria are stated explicitly, there may be confusion over membership status, as occasionally happens with national citizenship. The United States automatically grants citizenship to all children born within the geographic boundaries of the nation, regardless of their parents' citizenship. If foreign visitors have a child while in this country, that

infant may have dual citizenship in both its parents' country and in the United States. In other cases, for various legal reasons a person may find himself or herself without recognized citizenship in any country.

Biological, personal, social, economic, legal, or other characteristics may be used as membership criteria by organizations. Sometimes these criteria are intended to be rational, as in educational and experiential requirements for many jobs. At other times, the criteria are frankly established to limit membership to certain kinds of people, such as whites or males or Gentiles or the wealthy. Highly demanding criteria may also be erected by an organization as a means of maintaining the power and prestige of its members, as is done by many professional associations. Conversely, other organizations may have no membership requirements beyond expressing interest and signing a membership application, in order to attract as many members as possible and develop organizational size as a power resource. Even organizations that coerce people into membership, such as the military operating with a draft, normally set negative criteria for individuals they do not want.

Identification by individuals with an organization is not necessary for the organization to exist, but if the members are aware of and identify with that organization, this will greatly strengthen its ability to function effectively. For instance, if several hundred people live in close proximity to one another and interact frequently in the course of their work and other daily activities, they may constitute a small community even if they do not recognize it as such. If they begin thinking of themselves as the residents of "Crossroads Junction," however, they are much more likely to cooperate in shared community activities, such as operating a volunteer fire department or building a new school. In a different context, Karl Marx argued that awareness of and identification with one's social class is vital if oppressed workers are to act together to improve their status in society. He distinguished between a working class that exists only "in itself" because of the similar but unrecognized positions and interests of its members, and a working class that exists "for itself" because its members have developed class consciousness and are therefore more ready to take collective action.

Identification with an organization will often have observable effects on a person's actions. A college freshman who joins and identifies with a sorority may likely modify her appearance, study habits, or values so as to be more like her sorority sisters. A store proprietor who begins to identify with the local business community will likely adopt and express conservative political views and vote Republican. A third example would be the recent immigrant to a society who conspicuously adopts all the customs and traditions of his or her neighbors because "this is the way we live in my new country." Over time, strong identification with an organization can lead to internalization of its norms, which can further influence one's actions.

People may also identify with organizations of which they are not members but would like to or expect to join. This is particularly evident when a person is attempting to raise his or her socioeconomic status by acquiring more education or obtaining a better job. As part of the process of becoming socialized into the desired status, the individual may drop old friends and make new ones with higher statuses, develop new speech patterns, alter his or her attitudes on a variety of issues, and perhaps even begin attending a different church. Sociologists use the concept of *reference group* to describe any organizational unit with which an individual identifies strongly, regardless of formal membership. For example, a manual worker might adopt the business community as a reference group, and then conform more rigorously to middle-class norms than do most persons working in business occupations.

Commitment by members to the values and norms of an organization is a key determinant of the cohesion and strength of that unit. The "Crossroads Junction Community Improvement Association" is not likely to ac-

complish much community improvement if the members merely give lip service to its importance and refuse to become involved in it. That organization may be quite effective, however, if many community residents are personally committed to it, attend its meetings regularly, contribute money to it, serve on various task forces, and urge their neighbors also to become involved. Without strong commitment to an organization, individuals may participate in it and enact organizational roles because they are coerced into doing so (as in a prison) or because they expect to receive financial or other utilitarian benefits from their actions (as in a job one doesn't like but needs for income). Neither of those bases for compliance with organizational demands and role expectations are nearly as effective as compliance based on personal commitment to organizational values and norms. With such commitment, the individual will often go far beyond the minimal requirements and expectations of a role and be willing to do whatever is necessary to ensure the success of organizational activities.

CHARACTERISTICS OF ORGANIZATIONS

Knowledge about organizational boundaries and members can tell sociologists a good deal about organizational units, but through further observations and analyses we can learn much more about any organization. A number of important organizational characteristics are discussed in this section, under the headings of demographic, interactional, structural, and cultural characteristics.

Demographic Characteristics

The most important demographic characteristic of any organization is its size. The addition of even one person to a couple can change its entire nature—"two's company, but three's a crowd"—and a small family or friendship group is an entirely different kind of organization from a large corporation or university or government. As the size of an organization increases, there are likely to be corresponding changes in the ways in which members interact and enact their roles, the patterns of relationships they form, the manner in which activities are performed and decisions are made, the norms that are observed, and the values that are cherished within the organization.

Determining the size of an organization is not always a simple task, however. The most common meaning of size is number of members, which assumes that the organizational membership has been accurately delineated. Counting the number of members in a small group is not difficult, but this process can become exceedingly demanding in large organizations, as evidenced by the enormous amount of work and expense required to conduct a census of the United States every ten years. Moreover, in many cases a measure of size more sophisticated than sheer membership is needed. When studying a voluntary association such as a community service organization, for instance, we often measure degrees of participation. Some persons will be listed as members of the association but have virtually nothing to do with it; others will attend meetings occasionally; others will be actively involved in all activities of the association; and a few persons will occupy positions of leadership in the association. Other criteria of size beyond number of members or participants are also used by organizations. Businesses, for example, are frequently compared in terms of their total financial assets or annual sales figures. Hospitals and other service organizations might be described in terms of the number of patients or clients served. In short, *the criteria used to determine organizational size depend on the nature of the organization and the reasons for measuring its size.*

Several other demographic characteristic are sometimes used by sociologists to describe organizations, including their age and sex distributions, racial or ethnic compositions, and rate of growth or decline. Such characteristics can be quite important with particular organizations, but size is generally the most critical demographic feature of any organization.

Interactional Characteristics

A direct outgrowth of organizational size is expansion of the number of roles and positions existing within an organization. As a general principle, *the larger an organization, the more roles it will encompass, the greater the differentiation and specialization among those roles, and the more likely the roles are to become formal organizational positions.* Consequently, the most important interactional characteristics of any organization are the number and nature of its social roles.

In small organizations, such as families, friendship cliques, and work teams, the number of roles available for any individual to enact is restricted by the limited number of alternative role partners with whom to interact. In addition, with limited role partners there is often not much opportunity to try out new roles. Because of this limited availability of different roles and role partners, the roles that are enacted tend to be relatively unspecialized and not sharply differentiated from one another. Consequently, these roles tend to remain quite fluid and diffuse, so that they are not likely to be crystallized into formally established organizational positions.

The situation is quite different in larger organizations such as corporations, government agencies, schools, or medical facilities. Consider a business firm with several hundred employees. It will contain hundreds of different roles from president to janitor, and an individual may enact many alternative roles with various role partners. Moreover, these diverse roles will tend to be narrowly defined in terms of specified activities. The role of division manager will not include scrubbing the floors, in contrast to the familial role of husband, which might include that task. To clarify and perpetuate this network of numerous specialized roles, particular sets of roles are commonly defined as established organizational positions that carry prescribed power, privileges, and prestige.

The greater the role proliferation and specification within an organization, the more extensive is its division of labor, or differentiation and specialization of tasks, activities, and roles. Although there is some division of labor in almost all groups and organizations, this process is especially evident in large bureaucratically structured organizations within modern industrial societies. One of the most critical consequences of an extensive division of labor is functional interdependence among roles. The more narrowly defined and specialized a role, the more dependent it becomes on other complementary roles with which it is closely linked. A classic example of this situation is modern medicine. An old-style general practitioner might have done his best to treat whatever was wrong with a patient. In contrast, a contemporary medical specialist will deal with only a few kinds of ailments and depends heavily on many other specialized physicians, medical technicians, nurses, and other medical personnel to carry out his or her role as a physician. Role specialization and its resulting division of labor can lead to greater competence in performing one's roles, but it also creates numerous problems of communication and coordination among specialists, all of whom are highly interdependent on one another because of their task specialization.

Structural Characteristics

The greater the size and role diversity within an organization, the more likely it is to develop a complex structure. An organization can be described as complex in two different ways. In terms of social interaction, complexity involves extensive role differentiation, specialization, and interdependence, with resulting intense division of labor among roles. In terms of social ordering or structure, complexity involves the creation of numerous subunits, each of which performs its own specialized activities, and hence is highly interdependent with other subunits within a structural division of labor.

A one-room school, for example, has virtually no structural complexity. It probably contains just two main roles—teacher and student—and has no established subunits. Students at different grade levels may study various topics, but they are not arranged into separate classes. Nor are there likely to be specialized organizational units such as hobby clubs or sports teams. In total contrast, a large university is an extremely complex organization. Roles are generally divided into the four broad categories of administrators, faculty, support personnel, and students, each of which contains countless specialized roles. Structurally, the university is arranged into several colleges, each of which contains numerous academic departments, research institutes and centers, and specialized degree programs. Within every department, moreover, there are a number of committees dealing with such topics as the curriculum or degree requirements or student advising. And students usually create a wide array of their own governmental associations, interest groups, and living units.

Communities and total societies also display great variation in structural complexity. A small agricultural village or a town such as Crossroads Junction is nowhere nearly as complex as a giant metropolis such as New York City or Tokyo. One of the most striking features of societal evolution is the development of complex systems of functionally specialized and interdependent organizations of all kinds, throughout all realms of social life.

Another major structural characteristic of all organizations is the distribution of social power, especially legitimate authority. *The greater the complexity of a society or other organization, the more likely its power structure will be centralized in a few elite roles or subunits, and the more likely it is to contain several levels of hierarchically arranged power-wielding positions.* Positions and units at the center or top of a complex organizational structure will usually exercise extensive influence and control throughout the entire organization. In contrast, positions and roles located toward the periphery or bottom of the organizational structure will often exercise little or no power over organizational activities. The board of directors and the president of a business corporation clearly exercise a great deal more social power than the secretaries or machine operators. This power imbalance can be partially offset through the creation of groups such as labor unions, which enable low-level personnel to speak with a collective voice, and many complex organizations are currently experimenting with ways of decentralizing authority structures in order to improve their functional effectiveness. Nevertheless, organizational complexity always shapes the distribution of social power.

Cultural Characteristics

Among the many ways in which the culture of a society or other organization can be characterized, three pairs of features are especially useful for sociological analysis: sacred versus secular, formal versus informal, and rational versus nonrational. Each of these is actually a continuum along which cultures can be placed, but for convenience each continuum is often described in terms of its polar extremes.

Sacred versus Secular Beliefs and Values. Totally sacred beliefs and values are thought to originate outside human experience—from a diety, the supernatural, or some other realm of existence. As a result of their origin, such beliefs and values are held to be eternal and immutable. Criticizing them is blasphemous, rejecting them is heretical, and changing them is impossible. Everyone is therefore expected to accept and abide by the existing beliefs and values, and anyone who does not is severely punished. At the opposite extreme of this continuum, totally secular beliefs and values are recognized as being created entirely by humans for human purposes. As a result, they are continually subject to criticism, change, or rejection. People may accept and abide by them, but this is an intentional choice rather than a mandatory obligation. Actual beliefs and values may range anywhere between these two extremes, although secular beliefs

and values tend to be predominant in the cultures of modern societies.

Formal versus Informal Norms and Role Expectations. Highly formalized norms, customs, and role expectations are specified in great detail and are rigidly applied without exception to all relevant situations. Social actors are expected to comply completely with those norms and expectations and are given few or no opportunities to modify the norms or devise novel role performances. Those who do not comply are labeled as "deviant" and receive various kinds of sanctions in an effort to control their actions. In contrast, highly informal norms, customs, and role expectations are not specified in a great detail and are viewed as merely appropriate guides to action. Actors are encouraged to modify the norms to fit specific situations and to perform their roles with considerable spontaneity and individuality. Emphasis is placed on adaptability rather than conformity, and a wide latitude of actions is permissible before a person is viewed as deviant. In reality, most cultures include some relatively formal norms and some relatively informal ones, with different norms being evoked under varying circumstances.

Rational versus Nonrational Rules and Social Technologies. Cultural rationality emphasizes the attainment of organizational goals in the most effective and efficient manner possible. Accordingly, operating rules and social technologies are formulated to be as appropriate and pragmatic as possible. If a particular rule or procedure does not contribute to the effective and efficient attainment of desired goals, it is altered or replaced. Consequently, innovation is strongly encouraged and highly praised. Cultural nonrationality, meanwhile, emphasizes the perpetuation of traditional ways of doing things, regardless of their consequences for goal attainment. The focus is on the rules and procedures as ends in themselves, rather than on the goals they are—or were once intended—to achieve. Innovation is strongly discouraged and resisted. Most cultures contain elements of both rationality

TYPES OF ORGANIZATIONAL CHARAC-
TERISTICS

1. Demographic: population size and composition.
2. Interactional: number and specification of
   roles.
3. Structural: number and interrelationships of
   parts.
4. Cultural: prevailing beliefs, values, norms
   and technologies.

and nonrationality in varying degrees, which
can create considerable cultural conflict.

Sociologists frequently characterize modern cultures as moving toward ever-
increasing secularization, formality, and rationality. The extremes of all three of these
characteristics would undoubtedly be totally
unrealistic and quite unworkable, however.
Hence the real challenge in contemporary
societies appears to be finding ways of
blending or integrating secular with sacred
beliefs and values, formal norms and expectations within informal ones, and rational
rules and procedures with respect for traditional patterns of living.

FUNCTIONS OF ORGANIZATIONS

In addition to describing the major characteristics of organizations, sociologists often
investigate their dynamic functions. This
concept of organizational functions is used
in several somewhat different ways by sociologists, but essentially *functions are activities
performed by an organization that serve or accomplish some social purpose.* When sociologists investigate organizational functions,
therefore, they commonly examine the consequences of organizational activities for the
attainment of various outcomes.

Types of Functions

It would seem obvious that social organizations are created for various purposes,
such as educating children (schools), making
laws (legislatures), manufacturing goods

(factories), providing a stable settlement
(communities), worshiping (churches), waging war (armies), and so on. Indeed, we often label organizations in terms of these purposes which they serve. The main reason for
speaking of organizational functions rather
than purposes is that the latter term implies
that each organization does just one thing
that is evident to all observers. In reality,
organizational functions often change
through time, are multiple in nature, may be
implicit and not recognized by most people,
or may be completely unintended by the
members of the organization. Several ways
of categorizing organizational functions are
discussed in the following paragraphs.

Original versus Current Functions. An organization is often originally created to perform one kind of purpose, but over time it
may minimize or completely discard that initial purpose and adopt a new one. An example of this kind of goal replacement is the
March of Dimes, which was originally established to raise money for medical research
on polio. After the Salk vaccine virtually
eliminated polio as a major disease, the organization decided to shift its focus to the fight
against birth defects and today functions as
the major source of funding for medical research in that area (Sills, 1958).

Single versus Multiple Functions. Most organizations serve more than one purpose.
Even a small group such as a bridge club,
whose apparent purpose is to give its members an opportunity to play bridge together,
has the secondary functions of providing
recreation for its members and giving them a
chance to interact informally and make new
friends. Larger and more complex organizations often perform many different functions. A company that manufactures household appliances, for instance, not only
produces refrigerators and washing machines for households, but also provides jobs
for its employees, tax revenues to the local
community, and profits for its owners.

Explicit versus Implicit Functions. All of
the examples given thus far involve rela-

tively explicit purposes, but the functions of some organizations are only implicit and hence much more vague. For example, what is the purpose of a community such as Crossroads Junction? Is it to provide public services such as police and fire protection and to maintain roads and utilities? Is it to give its residents a place they can call their home town as well as a sense of community with which they can identify? Is it to function as a marketplace for the exchange of goods and services among the residents? The community undoubtedly serves all these functions and many others, but none of them will likely be stated explicitly as the purpose of Crossroads Junction. All these functions will simply be understood by the residents and carried out with more or less agreement.

Intended versus Unintended Functions. In addition to the purposes that are intended (either explicitly or implicitly) by the members of an organization, its activities may also serve other functions that are not intended and may not even be recognized. A classic study of urban political machines by Robert Merton (1957) discovered that these organizations perform the intended or *manifest* functions of supporting candidates for city offices and coordinating city governmental activities. At the same time, political machines also perform many unintended or *latent* functions, including organizing neighborhoods to deal with local problems, helping immigrants from rural areas or foreign countries adjust to urban life, providing financial aid to needly families, resolving community conflicts, and offering career opportunities for ambitious young political activists. Political leaders often view these additional unintended functions as merely expedient techniques for gaining political support and winning elections, not as organizational purposes, but for the community as a whole they are valuable functions of the political machine.

Functional Analysis

As a consequence of all the preceding factors, organizational functions are often quite difficult to identify and anlayze accurately. An important kind of sociological investigation, therefore, is *functional analysis*, or *studying the functions performed by social organizations and the outcomes of those functions for them, their members, and other organizations*. In addition to identifying the various functions—explicit and implicit, intended and unintended—that are being performed by a particular organization, sociologists may also ask several other kinds of functional questions. For example: What members of the organization are benefiting most from those functions, how are they benefiting, and why are they, rather than others, receiving those benefits? How efficiently and effectively is the organization performing its functions, and can those performances be improved? What basic organizational requirements—such as obtaining new members, making collective decisions, or resolving conflicts—are being fulfilled by the functions of the organization? What basic organizational requirements are being ignored or inadequately fulfilled? What are the consequences of organizational functions for other organizations or categories of individuals? Are those social impacts beneficial or harmful for others, and in what ways? Functional analyses of social organizations can thus lead investigators in many intriguing directions.

TYPES OF ORGANIZATIONS

At the present time, sociology does not have a rigorous taxonomy for classifying and describing different types of social organizations. Nevertheless, sociologists commonly divide organizations into several broad categories, eight of which are listed in Table 5-1 and sketched in this section: groups, families, communities, associations, aggregates, classes, institutions, and societies. First, however, populations are discussed as a category that underlies all types of organizations, although a population is not itself a social organization.

TABLE 5-1 Types of Social Organizations

Population	A set of individuals who are defined as having one or more common characteristics
Group	A small organization whose members identify and interact with one another personally
Family	An organization whose members are linked by kinship ties
Community	An organization that is territorially located and is the setting for most daily activities
Association	An organization that is purposefully created and operated to attain specific goals
Aggregate	A temporary organization that develops spontaneously as an expression of shared feelings or concerns
Class	A loosely structured organization composed of people with relatively similar power, privileges, and prestige
Institution	A network of interrelated organizations that all deal with a common functional requirement and share similar activities
Society	The most inclusive type of organization that exercises functional and cultural dominance overall other social units within it

Populations

A population is a set of individuals who are defined as having one or more common characteristics. There are endless possibilities for defining populations. We often think of populations in terms of political units such as cities or nations. Other criteria commonly used by demographers and sociologists include sex, age, race, marital status, religion, education, occupation, and income. Additional criteria might also be used for particular purposes, such as all handicapped people or all the readers of a particular newspaper. These criteria can also be combined in various ways to define a more limited population, such as "black females with a college education who live in California."

Although all the members of an identified population rarely interact with one another, create patterns of social ordering, or share a culture, populations are important social phenomena. As a result of their common characteristics, the members of a population may share a number of interests or problems and they may act in similar ways, even though they are not aware of their similarities. Over time, moreover, they may begin to identify with one another and act in unison, thus creating social organization. By identifying populations that share several common characteristics, therefore, sociologists can discover potential or developing organizations. Marxian theory, for instance, predicts that as workers in modern societies become aware of their shared plight as powerless pawns of industrial systems, they can create an organized social class that could transform an entire society. In recent years, blacks and women have begun to recognize their common concerns and have created social movements to improve their positions in society.

Groups

A group is a small organization whose members identify and interact with one another in a relatively personal manner. The small size of a group is its most basic characteristic. There is no agreed-upon upper limit for the size of a group, but most contain fewer than about 15 people, and 20 to 30 people would constitute a rather large group. The important point is that the small size of a group enables its members to know each other personally and interact with one another on a fairly regular basis. As a result, individual members often feel strong social bonds with one another and with the group as a whole. There are countless varieties of groups in modern societies, including friendship cliques, work crews, teenage gangs, sports teams, juries, rap groups, and committees of all kinds. Some groups are very loosely organized, such as a set of casual friends, while others are tightly organized, such as a sports team. They may exist either as relatively autonomous units, such as a group of neighbors, or as subunits of larger organizations, such as work crews.

Groups in which the interaction is especially personal and the social bonds are quite close are often called *primary groups*, as suggested by Charles Horton Cooley (1956), because of their primary importance in the socialization process. Typical examples of primary groups are friendship cliques and youth gangs, as well as the family. Close primary relationships develop in all kinds of groups, however, and also to some extent in larger and more complex types of organizations. Wherever they occur, primary relationships can provide individuals with many personal satisfactions and strengthen their ties to the groups and organizations to which they belong.

Families

A family is an organization whose members are linked by kinship ties. Most families can be described as groups, since family members generally interact on a regular basis in a personal manner, but they have an additional characteristic. Beyond the ties of friendship or shared interests and tasks that link the members of other groups, family members are bound together by biological, emotional, or marital kinship. These kinship bonds are often so strong that family commitments and responsibilities override all other social relationships. "The family comes first" in many situations, sometimes regardless of how we personally feel toward individual family members.

The family is so basic to human social life that all societies have some kind of family structure, although the cultural definition of what constitutes a family varies widely among societies. In modern societies, the *nuclear family*—normally consisting of a couple and their minor children who live together as a household—is the dominant family form. Two variations of the nuclear family are also becoming quite common today: single parents with children, and unmarried couples who live together in a shared commitment (and perhaps with children from former marriages).

Throughout most of human history, however, the *extended family* has been at least as important as the nuclear family, if not the dominant family form. An extended family can encompass all kinds of relatives, including uncles and aunts, nephews and nieces, first and second cousins, and so on. Some societies even have provisions for incorporating totally unrelated individuals into an extended family or clan as socially defined kin. An extended family can thus become quite large, so that it does not fit the criteria of a small group. All the members of an extended family rarely, if ever, live together as a single household, but many of them may live in close proximity to each other.

Communities

A community is an organization that is territorially located and is the setting for most daily activities. For many reasons, ranging from economic interdependence to shared cultural values, families and other groups that live in close proximity usually form communities. The community then becomes the geographic and social setting for most daily economic, political, educational, religious, recreational, and other shared activities. As communities grow, other types of organizations are often established within them to perform specific functions, but the community as a whole remains the setting within which those activities occur. Communities obviously vary widely in size and complexity, from Gnawbone, Indiana (a gas station, a general store, and a few houses), to New York City. All communities nevertheless have some ordered procedures for carrying out daily activities and for making collective decisions about those activities.

Because of the importance of collective decision making in all communities, they are often thought of in terms of their government, but that is only one part of the total community organization. The sociological concept of community is also more encompassing than a legally defined city, since in reality most community functions extend beyond their legal boundaries to include suburbs and other surrounding areas. In some cases, however, a functional community may be smaller than the legal city in which it exists, as in a relatively self-contained immigrant or ethnic settlement.

A major trend in all large communities in modern societies throughout the twentieth century has been outward expansion. Families, businesses, schools, and other organizations have constantly been moving out of central cities into suburbs and other outlying areas. There are many reasons for this trend, including available transportation into the central city, cultural and financial emphasis on single-family homes, availability of land for new housing, lower taxes, and desires to escape the congestion of city life and to find adequate schools and other community services.

Associations

An association is an organization that is purposefully created and operated to attain one or more specific goals. In other words, it is a goal-oriented organization. As societies become increasingly complex, many organizations tend to focus on limited and explicit functions or goals. Whereas communities encompass all aspects of daily living, associations perform only a few activities or seek to attain quite specific goals. The functions performed and the goals sought by particular associations vary almost infinitely in modern societies. Some common kinds of associations include government departments and agencies, businesses and industries, retail and wholesale stores, schools and colleges, churches and synagogues, labor unions and professional associations, fraternal and service associations, civic and charitable associations, political parties and lobbies, social and recreational associations, military services and units, hospitals and clinics, libraries and museums, civil rights and ethnic associations, police and fire departments, and special interest associations from antique collectors to zoology enthusiasts.

One way of dividing this array of different associations into meaningful subcategories, as suggested by Peter Blau and Richard Scott (1963:46–67), is to focus on who benefits from the attainment of association goals. Business associations include all those whose dominant goal is to benefit their owners financially. Mutual benefit associations operate to serve their members in some way, ranging from labor unions to recreational clubs to churches. Service associations are those whose major goal is to provide services to clients, ranging from schools to hospitals. Commonwealth associations include all those whose dominant goal is to serve an entire community or society, such as government agencies and museums. All such classification schemes are rather arbitrary, but they serve to indicate the wide diversity of goal-oriented associations that exist in modern societies.

Aggregates

An aggregate is a temporary organization that develops spontaneously as an expression of shared feelings or concerns. Common examples of aggregates are crowds, mobs, demonstrations, riots, and audiences. As with associations, aggregates tend to focus on a specific concern, but they are basically expressive rather than instrumental in nature. In other words, rather than purposefully establishing formal procedures to attain desired goals, aggregates arise spontaneously or are created temporarily to express shared feelings or interests or to respond to a specific situation. They usually form quite quickly, display minimal patterns of ordering, share only a few cultural ideas, and disband as soon as their members become satiated or the situation changes. Aggregates are thus the least stable type of social organization, but they can stimulate either repressive actions or extensive social change.

Observers of these activities often refer to them as "collective behavior." To the extent that those observers are concerned with the behaviors of individuals within aggregates, this term is appropriate. The participants in a riot behave very differently from their normal daily routines. When we consider an aggregate as a whole, however, we can observe that, despite its ephemeral nature, it temporarily functions as an organizational entity. Even a lynch mob is not just a collection of separate individuals, but rather a collectivity that acts in a relatively predictable manner with emergent leadership, patterns of relationships, and shared norms.

Classes

A class is a loosely structured organization composed of people with relatively similar power, privileges, or prestige. In some situations, a class is little more than a population of people who have similar occupational, income or other statuses in society, while in other situations a class may be a relatively close-knit organization that actively promotes its common interests and shared concerns. An example of the former kind of class might be all manual workers in an industrial society, while the latter kind of class would be illustrated by the "best families" in a community. We usually associate the idea of class with socioeconomic stratification, which is discussed in greater deal in the following chapter. To the extent that socioeconomic power dominates a society, wealth or control of the economy will likely provide the basis for most classes. But as other forms of social power and inequality—such as political authority or technical knowledge—gain importance within a society, they provide new foundations for different kinds of social classes.

This broad conception of social class can include the various classes within a feudal society (such as serfs, peasants, artisans, and nobility); the established castes of India; the three legally defined estates of prerevolutionary France (nobility, clergy, and everyone else); the Marxian conception of two fundamental classes in industrial societies (the bourgeoise and the proletariat); and whatever classes exist in contemporary societies (such as a power elite, the middle class, and the working class). To qualify as classes, however, such categories of people must not only evidence similar amounts of social power, privileges, or prestige, but also create at least some minimal patterns of social ordering and shared cultural ideas.

Institutions

Before defining this type of social organization, we must introduce the idea of societal *functional requirements.* These are basic operational necessities that must be fulfilled in some manner within a society if it is to survive for long and function effectively. Numerous social theorists have offered various lists of these requirements, but all of them include such activities as maintaining the population, training new members, providing channels of communication, procuring necessary resources from the natural environment, coordinating diverse activities, making collective decisions, establishing operating rules and procedures, controlling deviant actions, distributing benefits to members, and defending the society against threats. In all societies, networks of groups, families, associations, classes, and other organizations tend to become established around each of these functional requirements, sharing a concern with meeting that need and developing interdependent relationships. Over time, they also come to share many cultural values and norms.

An institution is a network of interrelated organizational units that all deal with a common functional requirement and hence share similar activities and norms. Within modern societies, the major institutions include

(1) The economy (all businesses, industries, stores, banks, etc.);
(2) The polity (all local, state, and federal governmental units, political parties, etc.);
(3) The educational system (all public and private schools, colleges, training programs, etc.);
(4) The legal system (courts, police departments, law firms, etc.);
(5) The military (the various armed services and the local militia);
(6) Mass communications (television and radio stations, newspapers, magazine, etc.);
(7) Labor (unions, technical and professional associations, etc.);
(8) Religion (churches, synagogues, religious order, etc.);

(9) The socialization system (families, youth groups, preschools, etc.); and

(10) Medicine (hospitals, clinics, medical laboratories, etc.).

Any given institution often includes several different kinds of organizational units. Concurrently, one particular kind of organization may fit into two or more different institutions. Thus schools are part of both the socialization and educational institutions; government agencies may become involved in economic, legal, and educational activities, as well as the political system; and the mass media frequently take part in many institutional spheres. The unifying feature of any institution, however, is its focus on a particular kind of activity or set of related activities, plus its shared norms. Since most institutions engage in activities that extend throughout a society, they are often described as the major subunits or subsystems of society.

Societies

A society is generally the most inclusive type of organization, exercising functional and cultural dominance over all other social units within it. With the exception of multinational and international organizations, all social units exist within a society, all aspects of human life are encompassed by a society, and the way in which a society is organized tends to influence all the patterns of social ordering and cultural ideas that occur within it. In the contemporary world we often think of societies as identical with nation-states, since national political boundaries commonly coincide with societies and the national government exercises political authority throughout the entire society. Technically, however, a state is a political unit centering around a national government, while a nation is a society in which the political system possesses supreme legal sovereignty. Historically, societies have not always been nations, nor are all of today's nations true societies. Prior to the development of the modern nation-state, dominant political units ranged in scope from local

fiefdoms to vast empires and bore little resemblence to societies as sociocultural entities. In Africa today, many of the recognized nations were created by colonial powers without regard to native societal boundaries, with the result that a single political unit may include two or more traditionally distinct societies. The situation becomes even more complex as nations around the world are beginning to create international federations—such as the European Economic Community—which may eventually unify their component societies into broader economic and political entities. Nevertheless, for the foreseeable future, societies will undoubtedly remain the dominant social units within which almost all other forms of organization exist.

The dominance of societies over other organizations is both functional and cultural in nature. Societies exercise functional dominance in several ways. First, most social relationships and other types of social organizations exist within the boundaries of a society, with only a small minority of all relationships and organizations involving participants from two or more societies. Second, societies attempt to become as self-sufficient as possible by establishing procedures for securing whatever resources they require and satisfying the needs of their members. Third, a society is the ultimate decision-making unit for its members and exerts influence over most spheres of social life. The cultural dominance of societies over other organizations results from the fact that all the members and parts of a society share a common societal culture. Although various subcultures may deviate from the societal culture in some ways, they are always shaped by the prevailing societal beliefs, values, norms, technologies, and other cultural ideas.

ORGANIZATIONAL LINKAGES

Thus far, organizational units have been discussed as if they were separate entities, unrelated to one another. In reality, most organizations are linked to other organizations, both vertically and horizontally. As a result, we might think of social organizations as comprising a huge interwoven web, with interorganizational relationships running in all directions. To a considerable extent, these webs of social organizations occur within societies, but total societies are also linked together in many ways to form what sociologists call the "world system."

Vertical and Horizontal Linkages

Vertical linkages among organizations result from the fact that *smaller social units are almost always either parts of larger units or are strongly influenced by larger units, while at the same time most organizations are composed of a number of subordinate units.* Small groups, for instance, are usually either a subpart of an association or operate within a community. In either case, the larger social unit exercises considerable influence or control over the group. Families exist within communities and classes that shape many of their activities. Associations and classes—as well as groups and families—are generally parts of one or more social institutions. And all these types of organizations are located within societies that extensively influence the social ordering and cultural ideas of all units within their boundaries. Moreover, as any particular organization becomes increasingly complex in structure, it will include numerous divisions, departments, branches, offices, and other subordinate units.

At the same time, *most organizations are also interlocked horizontally with many other organizations through both functional and cultural ties.* These are not superordinate and subordinate linkages, but rather bonds based on functional and cultural similarities or interdependence. Horizontal linkages can occur among all types of organizations, regardless of their size or complexity. These interorganizational ties occur at two levels. First, individuals are almost invariably members of more than one organization. The typical person in a contemporary society probably belongs to a family, several small groups, a church or other religious body, a labor union or professional association, a community, one or more classes, sometimes an aggregate, several institutional spheres, and the encompassing society. Through such overlapping memberships, the activities of all these organizational units become interrelated. Second, most organizational units crosscut and overlap other organizations in their activities. As a common example, a business firm influences many families through the work schedules and pay rates of its employees; many friendship cliques form within the firm; the firm must deal with a labor union, a chamber of commerce, and other associations; it pays taxes to the community in which it is located as well as to the federal government; the manner in which it is organized may contribute to the formation of various social classes; it plays an active role in the economic institution of its society; and it may rely heavily on contracts with national government agencies.

Vertical and horizontal linkages within and between organizations are illustrated in Figure 5-1.

Organizational Pressures

Any specific organization will likely have countless vertical and horizontal linkages with many other units, all of which can become highly interwoven. Consequently, *all social organizations experience constant pressures resulting from their simultaneous efforts to avoid and establish relationships with other social units.* On the one hand, an organization will normally seek to maintain as much functional autonomy, or control over its own activities, as possible under the prevailing circumstances. Relative functional autonomy enables an organization to direct its activities without undue influence from superordinate units or other organizations with which it interacts. It is also better able to obtain the resources it needs through balanced exchange transactions, to control the actions of its subordinate parts, to attain its goals in an efficient manner, and to maintain operational flexibility and stability.

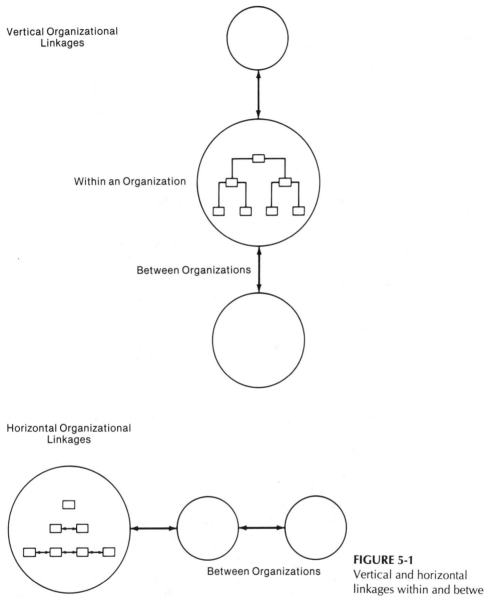

Vertical Organizational Linkages

Within an Organization

Between Organizations

Horizontal Organizational Linkages

Between Organizations

Within an Organization

FIGURE 5-1
Vertical and horizontal linkages within and between organizations

On the other hand, an organization will normally seek to establish and maintain relationships with other organizations with which it is functionally interdependent. It will depend on other kinds of organizations for the resources it needs and for the at- tainment of its goals; it will operate effec- tively only to the extent that all of its subparts perform their various specialized functions; and it will be influenced or regulated by higher-level organizations such as govern- mental units. Since these pressures for greater functional autonomy and increased functional interdependence push in opposite directions, all organizations are constantly subject to social tensions. There is rarely an ideal way of resolving those contradictory tensions, so that organizations must continually strive to maintain a workable balance between functional autonomy and interdependence.

The World System

Historically, societies—especially nation-states—have attempted to maximize their functional autonomy in relation to other societies. They have accomplished this by controlling their international trade relationships, asserting their political sovereignty, and maintaining military forces to protect their interests from foreign interference. Nations cannot escape ties of social, economic, political, and military interdependence with other societies, however. Recent research (Wallerstein, 1974 and 1980) has clearly demonstrated that as early as the fifteenth century, the emerging nations of Europe were constantly forging interdependent linkages with one another.

Consequently, to understand the historical development of any particular nation we must examine its numerous relationships with other nations, as well as its continuing struggles to gain functional and cultural ascendancy over those other nations so as to increase its power on the world scene. To emphasize the critical importance of these international linkages among societies, contemporary theorists often use the concept of a world system. *A world system perspective views all societies as constituting a single functional system of economic and political interdependences.* Within this system, core societies dominate all critical international relationships, periphery societies are largely controlled by other societies, and semiperiphery societies are partially controlling and partially controlled. Quite clearly, this world system of nations has become increasingly complex and interdependent in the latter part of the twentieth century.

SUMMARY

Specific organizational units that are created through the process of social organization are delineated from one another in terms of their boundaries and members. All organizations have boundaries that may be geographical, interactional, structural, or cultural in nature, although such boundaries are often rather vague or arbitrary in nature. All organizations also have members who are defined in terms of various criteria, who are likely to identify with the organization, and who may be committed to the values and norms of the organization.

Any social organization will display many different characteristics that can be described and analyzed. The most important demographic characteristic pertaining to any organization is its size, measured in terms of the number of members or some other indicator. Major interactional characteristics involve the number of roles contained within an organization, the degree to which those roles are differentiated and specialized to form a division of labor, and the extent to which the roles constitute established organizational positions. One structural characteristic that is crucial in most organizations is its amount of complexity, in terms of both social roles and organizational subunits. A second critical structural characteristic is the distribution of social power throughout an organization. Some important cultural characteristics include the contrasts between sacred versus secular beliefs and values, formal versus informal norms and role expectations, and rational versus nonrational rules and technologies.

As units, all organizations perform many different kinds of functions. These functions are frequently thought of as the purpose(s) of an organization, although in reality an organization may change its purposes through time, may have several different purposes at any one time, may enact implicit functions that are unexpressed or unrecognized by its members, and may perform functions that are unintended by most or all of its members. Functional analysis examines the various functions performed by organizations, how adequately those functions are being conducted, and the consequences or impacts of those functional activities.

Sociologists frequently classify social organizations into several broad categories: groups whose members identify and interact with one another in a personal manner; families whose members are bound together by ties of kinship; associations that are established to attain specific goals; aggregates that temporarily give expression to shared emotions and concerns; classes based on similar amounts of power, privileges, or prestige among their members; institutions consisting of networks of organizations which are all concerned with a common functional requirement and that share similar activities and norms; and societies that incorporate most other organizational units and dominate them functionally and culturally. In addition, sociologists often analyze populations of people who are defined in terms of common characteristics.

All social organizations are linked together in many different ways, both vertically and horizontally. Many organizations contain subordinate units, and most organizations are part of or are influenced by more inclusive organizations. Organizational units are also linked through overlapping memberships and interdependent activities. As a result of all these interorganizational linkages, most organizational units experience two opposing kinds of pressures. They seek to maintain as much functional autonomy as possible, and at the same time they seek to establish functionally interdependent relationships with other organizations on which they depend. Organizational linkages occur among all types of organizations, so that even nations are interwoven within the world system.

CHAPTER
6

SOCIAL PROCESSES

Why and how are the actions of individuals and organizations controlled in
   social life?
In what ways can organizations become unified into cohesive entities?
Why does conflict pervade all social life, and how can it be managed to
   produce beneficial consequences?
What forms of social inequality, or stratification, occur throughout
   organized social life?
What is meant by the ecological evolution of societies?

SOCIAL CONTROL

In a utopian society, individuals would always interact without friction or misun-
derstandings, all social roles would be clearly
defined and competently enacted, there
would be no deviant or socially undesirable
activities, the component parts of any organization would cooperate smoothly to attain
their collective goals, organizations would
relate to one another in ways that adequately
satisfied their mutual interdependent needs,
basic cultural beliefs and values would be
accepted by all members of the society, and
the prevailing norms and rules would be totally congruent with those beliefs and values.
In real societies, of course, none of those
conditions are ever fully realized. This is
probably quite fortunate, since—as pointed
out by Ralf Dahrendorf (1958)—a perfectly
organized utopian society would undoubtedly be an extremely dull and unstimulating
place in which to live. Because of all the "im-

perfections" that occur throughout organized social life, the exercise of social control
is asolutely necessary for the survival of all
social organization.

Nature of Social Control

The process of social control is a fundamental aspect of all social life and was a major concern of most early social theorists. As
expressed by Morris Janowitz (1975), social
control "focuses on the capacity of a social
organization to regulate itself." This concept
of self-regulation can be applied to the actions of individuals and organizational units.
In either case, the crucial question is how
patterns of social ordering and shared cultural ideas are created and maintained
through time. Without social control, even
the best-intentioned efforts at cooperative
endeavors would quickly dissolve into un-
coordinated separate actions by the various
participants.

Following Janowitz, we can conceptualize *social control as the process through which an organization regulates itself to attain its goals.* By exercising control over its individual participants, its subunits, and other interrelated units, an organization is able to achieve stability through time and to function more or less effectively. The actual exercise of social control is of course carried out by individuals, and at times their actions may be self-serving efforts to protect or promote their personal interests. Much of the time, however, those individuals are acting as agents of an organizational unit such as a group, a family, a community, an association, or the total society. Their control efforts therefore reflect shared cultural values and norms and are conducted through established organizational procedures.

The necessity of exercising social control throughout organized social life does not mean that individuals and organizations must totally conform to arbitrarily imposed norms and role expectations. Some organizations—such as prisons, concentration camps, or totalitarian societies—may attempt to enforce extreme conformity, but the vast majority of organizations do not. Most organizations exercise only enough control over vital activities to ensure that the organization can function in a relatively ordered and predictable manner. Consequently, *effective social control can allow considerable leeway for individual choice of action.* There are several reasons for this.

First, the norms, rules, laws, and role expectations of an organization need not be arbitrarily formulated or imposed. To the extent that an organization operates in a rational manner, its activities can enable the participants to obtain many of their personal goals as well as contribute to the attainment of collective organizational goals. Moreover, the organizational standards that are being enforced can be modified or completely changed when they prove to be ineffective. This is especially likely if democratic decision-making procedures are followed, if individuals and subunits retain some amount of functional autonomy, and if the organizational standards are viewed as secular rather than sacred.

Second, total conformity of all actions to established social standards is never necessary for the creation or maintenance of social organization. In fact, despite the predictions of George Orwell's book *1984*, absolute control could never be imposed on people for very long. Since most organizations attempt to control only those activities that are vital for their existence and welfare, social control is usually applied only to a limited portion of any individual's life. An employer may require all his employees to be on the job from 8:00 A.M. to 5:00 P.M. on Monday through Friday, but he will not attempt to tell them what time they must go to bed or what they must do on weekends. In addition, different organizations exercise control over different aspects of people's lives. A family may be quite concerned about the manner in which its members express their emotions to one another in private, while a community is primarily concerned that individuals act as law-abiding and responsible citizens in public.

Third, standards for social control need not be minutely or rigidly prescribed. Many cultural norms and role expectations, for instance, provide only broad guidelines for action, leaving considerable latitude for individual modification and elaboration to fit specific situations. Organizations also frequently provide alternative standards for a given activity or situation, from which individuals and subunits are free to select the one that is most appropriate for a given situation. In addition, organizations can encourage innovation among their members in developing entirely new standards of action.

In short, *effective social control is rarely an end in itself, but rather a means of ensuring that individuals and organizational units act in a socially responsible manner.* To the extent that this occurs, the resulting social organization can provide its participants with opportunities and benefits—and hence freedom—that would be unattainable outside of organized social life. For example, social control in some areas of life—such as the prevention of crime or the enforcement of public health measure—increases the total amount of freedom available to all the members of a community or society.

Control of Individual Actions

To encourage desired actions and discourage undesired actions by individuals, all organizations utilize various kinds of social control mechanisms. There are no absolute definitions of what constitutes either commendable or deviant actions, however. The specific actions that an organization rewards or punishes will depend on its cultural beliefs, values, and norms, on the role expectations of its members, on the functional requirements of the organization and its subunits, on whatever external pressures the organization is experiencing from its natural and social environments, and on the specific activities of the organization at any given time.

Compliance and deviance are always socially defined within particular sociocultural settings. In the United States we would react with horror if someone butchered a visitor from another community and then called in friends for a ritual feast. Yet there have been tribes in New Guinea that considered such actions quite proper. Gambling may be a crime in one community but not in a neighboring one. A middle-class man who deserts his family is likely to be severely criticized by his friends, but in a poor neighborhood this action might be viewed as a sacrifice by the man to enable his family to obtain Aid to Families with Dependent Children. In all such situations, some individuals may disagree with the prevailing sociocultural definition of the action in question. Nevertheless, that sociocultural definition will largely determine the kind and amount of social control exerted upon the individuals involved.

Internal Control. In most situations, individuals control their own actions by complying with cultural norms and role expectations. Such internal control is primarily a result of previous socialization and role learning. These processes teach individuals to internalize norms and to enact roles in socially expected ways. Although no external pressures are exerted on the individual, his or her actions are nevertheless being socially controlled by the sociocultural environment. Thus, *internal social control is the process of voluntarily abiding by the norms and expectations we have learned from our society.* Most of the time, this form of social control is highly effective.

Social Sanctioning. In some situations, however, it is necessary to apply external pressures or sanctions on individuals to control their actions. Thus, *social sanctioning is the application of rewards or punishments to encourage desired or discourage undesired actions by individuals.* All kinds of rewards and punishments are employed as social sanctions, ranging from the simplest and most informal compliments and criticisms to the most elaborate and formalized rituals of awarding a Nobel Prize or executing a death penalty. Social sanctions may be interpersonal in nature, such as welcoming or ostracizing an individual; they may involve organizational actions such as promotions or demotions to new positions; they may involve money, as with fines or bonuses; they may be physical actions such as spanking or hugging a child; or they may be entirely symbolic in nature, such as awarding a citation or labeling a person as a criminal.

Despite the widespread use of all kinds of sanctions throughout social life, this form of social control has several serious limitations, especially when it involves formal rewards and punishments. One of these limitation is surveillance. It is obviously impossible to watch everyone all the time to determine when sanctions are required. A second limitation is administration. Punishments are often difficult to impose and tend to produce only minimally acceptable actions, while rewards must be dispersed sparingly or they will become defined as rights due to everyone. A third limitation is social reinforcement. Unless sanctions are reinforced by the larger social environment they lose their effectiveness, as with an imprisoned terrorist who is viewed as a political martyr or an entertainment celebrity who is ridiculed by the public as lacking any talent.

Social Management. Another form of social control that reinforces individuals' social control through own internal controls and avoids the problems of external sanctioning is through social management. Since social actions are always affected by the setting in which they occur, social control can be exerted by arranging or modifying that context in various ways. *Social management is the manipulation of social situations to influence actions in desired ways.* For example, middleclass parents send their children to "good" schools and colleges so that they will interact with the "right" people and thus enhance their opportunities for a successful career or marriage. Conversely, one of the principal reasons why so many black Americans are undereducated, underemployed, and poor is because the white majority has for generations denied them opportunities to acquire adequate education, secure better jobs, and earn sufficient income to improve their standard of living.

In addition to providing or denying opportunities for various kinds of action, social management can also be accomplished by altering the structure or activities of a social organization. For example, the managers of a factory might attempt to increase worker productivity by improving the physical work setting, by eliminating unpopular rules and regulations, by cutting back on supervision and giving workers more latitude to determine their own work routines, and by including workers' representatives in company decision-making sessions. Another illustration would be a community master plan that sought to contain urban sprawl by refusing to extend utilities and other public services any further into surrounding farmlands.

Control of Organizational Actions

Within any social organization, the people who are enacting leadership roles must be able to direct and control the activities of the organization as a whole and of its component parts. Without such direction and control, the organization is unlikely to attain whatever goals it is seeking and may not even survive for long. In addition to exercising social control over the actions of individual members, therefore, organizations ranging from small groups to societies must also exercise control over their collective activities. Just as there are countless ways of imposing sanctions on individuals and managing social situations, there are also numerous procedures for controlling organizational activities. Many of these fall within the two broad categories of regulation and decision making.

Organizational Regulation. *If an organization is to perform tasks adequately or achieve its goals, the activities of its component subunits must be coordinated and controlled* so that all those activities mesh together in a relatively smooth and effective manner. The central problem here is that the activities of one subunit often produce uncertainties for other subunits. For instance, the production department of a manufacturing firm may have to contend with uncertainties concerning the ability of the purchasing department to have raw materials on hand when needed, of the personnel department to provide qualified workers, of the maintenance department to keep the machinery operating, and of the sales department to market the finished products. Because these kinds of functional uncertainties will normally occur among all the parts of any organization, they can never be entirely eliminated. In the words of James

---

FORMS OF INDIVIDUAL
SOCIAL CONTROL

1. Internal control through socialization and role learning.
2. Social sanctioning through punishments and rewards.
3. Social management through manipulating social settings.

Thompson (1967), "The central problem for complex organizations is one of coping with uncertainty."

However, organizational leaders can establish various regulatory procedures for coping with functional uncertainties. Some commonly used regulatory procedures include the following:

(1) Adopting overall plans and time schedules to guide organizational activities;

(2) Specifying the tasks and responsibilities of each position and subunit;

(3) Formulating standardized rules and operating procedures to be followed whenever applicable;

(4) Creating extensive communication channels among all parts of the organization; and

(5) Providing feedback to operating units about how their activities are affecting other parts and the organization as a whole.

To accomplish these regulatory functions organizations often create a special role, unit, or agency with responsibility for coordinating internal organizational activities and administering organizational regulations. In small groups or families this may be simply a designated role enacted by one person; in more complex associations it may be a separate administrative department; and in communities and societies it usually consists of a whole set of governmental agencies. In all cases, however, these actors are given authority to regulate the activities of all other parts of the organization so that organizational goals can be achieved.

Organizational Decision Making. *If an organization is to function effectively as a unified entity, it must continually make decisions* about its goals, activities, participants, relationships with other organizations, and countless other collective matters. Any member or subunit of the organization could conceivably make those decisions, but if they are to be binding on the organization they must either be viewed as the exercise of legitimate authority or be backed by the ability to exert force. In either case, whoever makes deci-

sions for an organization will be able to exert considerable control over its functioning.

Organizations differ greatly in their decision-making procedures, ranging between the extremes of unitary versus polyarchic decision making.

In *unitary decision making,* a single leader or small group of elites makes all major decisions for the organization. Authority to carry out those decisions is delegated downward from the top of the organization through a graded hierarchy of subordinate units and offices. Each position in this hierarchy derives its authority from the level immediately above it and is always responsible to that superior level. Furthermore, each successively lower level generally contains more positions than the level above it, which gives the organization a pyramidal structure. The principle arguments supporting this form of decision making are that it is fast, efficient, easily understood, and unambiguous.

Unitary decision making tends to produce many serious problems for organizations, however. One of these is the stifling of initiative and creativity among members. They are expected to do exactly as they are told, without question, and never to try new ways of doing things. A related problem is organizational rigidity. Because the component parts have no functional autonomy to make decisions for themselves, the organization as a whole is incapable of adjusting quickly to new conditions. A third problem is member apathy. Members tend to become uncommitted and uninvolved in the organization, doing as little as they can get away with.

In *polyarchic decision making,* all the component parts of an organization have their own spheres of responsibility and competence and make their own decisions within those spheres. Decisions affecting the organization as a whole may be arrived at through a process of discussion and negotiation, but no single subunit makes decisions for the entire organization. Structurally, the organization resembles a set of loosely-linked circles rather than a pyramid, and some of those linkages may be quite tenuous. The arguments supporting this form of decision making are that it encourages initiative and creativity, gives the organization great flexibility, and can produce strong commitment among members. However, polyarchic decision making is slow, inefficient, ambiguous, frustrating, and often breaks down before any general consensus can be reached.

SOCIAL COHESION

The exercise of social control at the individual and organizational levels enables social organizations to maintain some degree of ordering, predictability, and activity. It does not, however, ensure that organizational units will be able to preserve their unity and viability through time, especially as they encounter external stresses or internal strains that threaten their stability or existence. For that kind of toughness and durability in the face of adverse conditions, organizations must also have strong cohesion.

Nature of Social Cohesion

Most of us have an intuitive sense of what it means to say that a group or community or society is tightly unified or displays strong solidarity. Yet this concept of social cohesion becomes rather elusive when we attempt to examine it.

As an organization gains cohesiveness, its members and component parts become tightly linked together so that the organization as a whole operates as a single unit. More precisely, *social cohesion is the process though which the members and parts of an organization become bound together into a unified entity.* All organizations possess some amount of cohesion, but the strength of that cohesion can vary greatly among organizations and within an organization through time.

Some organizations can be maintained with very little cohesiveness, as in units such as prisons, which depend heavily on the exercise of coercive control. As cohesiveness develops within an organization, however, it acquires greater internal strength and unity, stability through time, and functional effectiveness.

Forms of Social Cohesion

Social organizations gain cohesion in either of two ways. These contrasting but complementary forms of social cohesion were labeled by Durkheim (1893) as mechanical and organic solidarity, but today they are more commonly called normative and functional cohesion.

Normative cohesion centers on shared culture. This process rests on a set of basic values that is shared among the members and parts of an organization as a result of a common cultural heritage. These values are applied to specific social situations in the form of moral norms that direct social actions. As people create various kinds of organizations to attain collective goals, those units become infused with their shared values and operate in accordance with the prevailing norms. This process of building values and norms into organizational units is sometimes called "institutionalization". Organizations, in turn, shape individuals, through socialization and role enactment, into social actors who internalize the shared values and norms and seek to perpetuate them through their actions as responsible members of the organization. In short, *an organization gains normative cohesion as moral norms based on shared values become imbedded within its parts and members.* Social ecology theory refers to this kind of cohesion as "commensalism," or social relations based on common interests among actors (Hawley, 1986:30).

The amount of normative cohesion in any organizational unit will depend on a variety of factors, including:

(1) The extent of consensus on basic values and the absence of any strong competing values;
(2) The development of an adequate and internally consistent set of norms, the lack of which Durkheim (1897) called "anomie";
(3) The degree of congruence between the values and the norms, so that adherence to

the norms enables people to realize their values;

(4) The effectiveness with which norms are infused into organizations, so that organizational activites reflect underlying basic values; and

(5) The adequacy of socialization and role learning among individuals, so that they fully internalize the shared values and common norms.

Functional cohesion centers on social relationships. This process begins as the members or parts of an organization become specialized in their activities or functions. Task specialization, or division of labor, makes these actors increasingly interdependent. Their mutual interdependence, in turn, necessitates the formation of numerous exchange transactions, which bind the members together in networks of functional relationships. To protect and enhance those relationships, the participants must create operational rules and establish administrative procedures to coordinate and regulate their exchange activities. In short, *an organization gains functional cohesion as complementary exchange relationships are established among its parts and members.* Social ecology theory refers to this kind of cohesion as "symbiosis," or social relations based on complementary differences among actors (Hawley, 1986:30).

The amount of functional cohesion in any organizational unit will depend on the following factors:

(1) The degree of task specialization or division of labor among its parts and members;

(2) The extent to which complementary exchange relationships are established among those interdependent components;

(3) The creation of adequate and consistent procedural rules to direct those exchange transactions, the lack of which may be termed "discordance" (Olsen, 1965);

(4) The effectiveness of administrative units in providing overall coordination and regulation of exchange networks; and

(5) The effectiveness of reciprocal information flows so that operational rules are understood

---

> **FORMS OF SOCIAL COHESION**
>
> 1. Normative cohesion, based on shared cultural values and norms.
> 2. Functional cohesion, based on social interdependence and exchange.

by all and operational problems are handled expeditiously.

Evolution of Social Cohesion

Durkheim (1893) argued that normative cohesion tends to predominate in the more simply organized societies that existed throughout the world prior to industrialization. Such societies are characterized by traditional values, strong norms, and relatively little division of labor. As societies grow in size and density of social relationships, however, the division of labor increases and functional cohesion based on mutual interdependence and exchange relationships becomes increasingly prevalent. Durkheim did not say that functional cohesion replaces normative cohesion as societies become larger and more complex, since he carefully pointed out that agreement on moral norms and operating rules is still vital in modern societies for the establishment and enactment of contractual relationships. Rather, Durkheim's evolutionary thesis was that *in modern societies, functional cohesion is increasingly expanding and becoming the dominant form of organizational unity, while normative cohesion supports and complements the creation of networks of interdependent exchange relationships.*

Contemporary sociologists have come to realize that these two forms of social cohesion are highly complementary. As pointed out by Robert Angell (1968), neither form of social cohesion can develop very far without corresponding developments in the other form. At the most fundamental level, for example, individuals and subunits are unlikely to become highly specialized and thus relinquish their functional self-sufficiency unless they trust others to interact with them in ways that will satisfy all of their other needs. The creation of mutual trust, in turn, depends on the actors sharing a set of basic values and norms. Hence the entire process of functional specialization, interdependence, and exchange rests on a foundation of common values and norms. At the same time, individuals and subunits tend to develop common values and norms as they engage in shared activities in which they enact interrelated roles. Hence the process of normative cohesion requires a foundation of mutually beneficial functional relationships.

Because the creation of normative and functional cohesion is such an intertwined process, *as growing size, technology, and other factors increase the complexity of societies and other organizations, they tend to develop more extensive processes of both functional and normative cohesion that are mutually complementary.* Failure to do this will leave a society vulnerable to all kinds of disruptive stresses and strains, and may eventually result in a breakdown of the whole process of social organization. As that occurs, the government or some other unit may attempt to preserve the society by exercising increasing power and social control. Such efforts may or may not succeed, but in any case the society will suffer a loss of stability, vitality, unity, and functional effectiveness.

Examples of this situation can be observed in many developing countries today. If a society simultaneously experiences rapid industrialization and a breakdown of its traditional values as a result of contact with the Western world, its normative cohesion will not evolve at the same rate as its developing functional specialization and interdependence. It may likely begin to display various signs of social disruption and disintegration. A frequent response to this situation is a coup d'etat by the military, which promises to restore order and stability. The military may be able to do that, but it is usually incapable of generating a new set of values and norms that are compatible with industrialization and acceptable to the people. That process requires time, and it is best accomplished by schools, churches, families, youth groups, and other organizations. Conse-

quently, the society is likely to undergo a long series of social and political upheavals before it regains a complementary balance of adequate functional and normative cohesion.

Social Cohesion in Modern Societies

Strong normative cohesion is most effectively created and maintained in societies that are relatively small, homogeneous, and simply organized. In such settings, common values and norms are more easily developed, shared, and imbedded within units and individuals. In societies that are large, heterogeneous, and complexly organized, it is much more difficult to maintain strong normative cohesion. They commonly attempt to create some consensus on basic values through a variety of techniques such as mass communication, standardized school curricula and educational systems, national youth organizations, state religions, adult discussion and study groups, and national political parties. However, the effectiveness of such efforts is often limited by social cleavages that divide people into diverse and often conflicting groups on the basis of socioeconomic class, ethnicity, lifestyles, interests, and other characteristics. Such cultural diversity can prevent the development of common societal values and severely hinder the process of creating normative cohesion.

That problem need not occur, however, if the various components of the society are willing to operate within a common set of political, economic, legal, and social rules, despite their value differences. In other words, *complete value consensus throughout a society is not necessary for normative cohesion, as long as people are willing to "play the game" of organized social life according to a common set of procedural rules.* This is the essence of political democracy based on acceptance of electoral procedures and a respect for value differences. However, if many people reject those procedures—such as refusing to abide by the outcome of an election or the decision of a court—the normative cohesion of society will certainly break down.

Viable functional cohesion is more suitable for large, heterogeneous, complexly organized societies that contain extensive division of labor. However, the attainment of functional cohesion also requires a network of complementary exchange relationships, effective operating rules, and overall coordination and regulation to handle operating problems and prevent exploitation of weaker actors by stronger ones. All of these requirements for viable functional cohesion tend to push modern societies in the direction of centralized administration and decision making by the national government. The tendency toward increased centralization of administration and decision making in all modern societies is so pervasive that social theorists often argue that growing functional specialization within an organization demands increased centralized control if the unit is to remain functionally cohesive.

Totally centralized control is not necessary for effective functional cohesion in modern societies, however. Although there must be centralized administrative coordination and regulation of the economy, polity, and other parts of the society, decision making on fundamental policies and issues need not be highly centralized. In other words, legislative functions must be kept separate from administrative functions. Moreover, it appears that decision making remains most responsive to the needs and interests of the people when it is relatively decentralized. In short, *a partially decentralized structure of power and decision making, in which the component parts of the society retain considerable operational autonomy, can promote viable functional cohesion as long as adequate procedures are present for societal-wide regulation and coordination of interdependent activities.*

SOCIAL CONFLICT

The processes of social control and social cohesion, if effectively conducted, might seem capable of ensuring that organized social life is characterized by complete harmony and cooperation. For a variety of reasons, however, that never happens. All social organizations also experience social conflict within themselves and with other social units. Such conflict can have numerous beneficial consequences for social organization if it is adequately managed.

Nature of Social Conflict

Social conflict is not social disorganization, although protracted and unresolved conflict may eventually produce a breakdown in the process of social organization. War, for example, can either enhance or destroy a society, depending on how it is conducted and resolved. In either case, a war or any other kind of social conflict is a highly organized process in which interactions form ordered patterns that have considerable meaning to their participants. Within communities, for instance, James Coleman (1957) identified several distinct stages through which controversies normally pass before they are resolved.

Conflict always involves two or more interacting actors (either individuals or organizational units) who are seeking a common goal that is scarce or limited, or else different goals that are incompatible. Two thirsty individuals drinking from a stream are not likely to come into conflict, since there is plenty of water for both to satisfy their thirst. However, if those two people are farmers who want to divert the stream to irrigate their land, they will likely conflict over this limited resource. Or, if one person wants to drink from the stream and the other wants to dump waste material into it, their goals are incompatible and they will almost certainly come into conflict.

When actors oppose one another in social conflict, each one attempts to exert some kind of social power toward their opponents in an effort to influence or control the situation. If the power exerted by one actor is considerably greater than that of the others, the dispute may quickly end in complete domination or even elimination of the other parties. If the power exertion is relatively balanced, however, the resulting conflict may become quite protracted. In sum, *social conflict occurs when two or more actors oppose one another in social interaction, exerting social power in an effort to attain a common limited goal or incompatible goals.*

Types of Social Conflict. Sociologists frequently classify social conflicts into four pairs of contrasting types. Each of these pairs is actually a continuum, or fundamental dimension of conflict, but for clarity only the polar opposites of each dimension are described here.

Latent conflict exists when two or more actors have opposing interests or goals but do not interact over them. For instance, the management of a business firm may want to keep wages low to increase profits, while the workers want higher wages to raise their standard of living. As long as those incompatible goals are not overtly expressed, the conflict remains latent. Latent conflicts are important in social life because they create social tensions that can easily erupt into *overt conflict,* which is expressed in interaction and the exertion of social power.

Verbal conflict involves only an exchange of words in an effort to persuade, discredit, demean, threaten, or intimidate other actors. Much social conflict is conducted in this manner, including interpersonal arguments, political campaigns, and scholarly debates. This kind of conflict is often preferred by the participants, since it involves little or no expenditure of scarce resources. *Action conflict,* in contrast, involves taking actions that may be physical, economic, social, or legal in nature. When conflict involves such activities, it frequently becomes very costly to the participants.

Pragmatic conflict involves specific objectives, such as winning an argument, scoring points in a sports event, or obtaining higher wages. As a consequence, the conflict is usually fairly limited in scope and is relatively amenable to resolution. *Ideological conflict* is quite different, since it involves fundamental beliefs or values that are deeply held. The participants seek not merely specific objectives, but rather total supremacy over, or

> **TYPES OF SOCIAL CONFLICT**
> 1. Latent versus overt conflicts.
> 2. Verbal versus action conflicts.
> 3. Pragmatic versus ideological conflicts.
> 4. Regulated versus unregulated conflicts.

complete elimination of, their opponents. Hence their conflict may be very broad in scope and not easily resolved.

Regulated conflict is conducted according to moral norms or operating rules that are accepted by all the participants. Examples are games, elections, and trials. To the extent that conflicts are regulated, there is an established set of procedures that guides the expression and resolution of the conflict. *Unregulated conflict,* on the other hand, follows few or no norms or rules. Although it is not entirely true that "All's fair in love and war," this may be true in the case of political assassinations and riots. Obviously, such conflict tend to be highly unpredictable and difficult to manage constructively.

Ecological and Economic Conflict

All forms of social conflict can and do occur in every realm of organized social life, from small groups to societies within the world system. Sociologists therefore study family conflict, community conflict, class conflict, institutional conflict, and many other kinds of conflicting social relationships. The most fundamental conflicts in social life, however, often occur within ecological and economic systems. Conflicts originating in those realms can have ramifications throughout an entire society or the whole world.

Ecological Conflict. In nature, conflict is endemic within ecological processes. Different species of organisms are constantly competing with one another for scarce resources. Although symbiotic relationships sometimes occur, these are relatively rare. The struggle for survival among the various species within an ecosystem is normally unrelenting. Sometimes this struggle results in the elimination of a species from an ecosystem, but many ecological conflicts are resolved in less drastic ways. One of these is niche differentiation, in which each species finds a unique niche or role in the ecosystem that does not directly compete with the niches of other species. Another way of resolving ecological competition is territoriality, in which each species demarks a specific geographic territory which other species respect.

Human beings, as members of ecosystems, also engage in ecological conflict with other species. When societies have rather low levels of technology, this competition may be direct and intensive. Do the humans or the wild pigs, for instance, obtain the edible roots of plants in the forests of New Guinea? However, *as human societies have developed more sophisticated and effective technology, they have become increasingly dominant over other species in ecological competition for scarce resources,* often taking over resources that were once used by other species.

In high technology societies, ecological struggles are often transformed into two kinds of social conflict. First, as we consume large amount of finite natural resources such as petroleum, we are in effect *in conflict with future generations* for the use of those resources. Since those future generations are not present to defend their interests, however, the present generation has a tremendous advantage in this conflict. Second, *existing societies conflict with one another* for scarce resources through colonialism, international trade, war, and other forms of conquest. In these conflicts, the victors are usually those societies that have higher levels of technology and extensive resources at their disposal, while less developed and weaker societies are the losers.

Economic Conflict. At the same time that societies are competing with one another and with future generations for scarce resources, relentless economic conflict is also occurring among various segments within societies for desired benefits. We commonly think of such conflict as occurring within an economic marketplace, in which individual and organizational consumers vie for available commodities through economic exchanges. This *consumption side* of economic conflict has enormous consequences for the standards of living enjoyed by different individuals and families, as well as the activities that various organizations are able to perform. It largely determines which people live affluently and which live in poverty. It also affects the economic welfare of organizations ranging from communities to universities.

To engage in consumer competition, however, actors must possess financial, political, legal, social, or other kinds of resources with which to bargain. How do they obtain those resources, and what factors determine how they are distributed among the members and parts of a society? The fundamental insight of Karl Marx concerning the dynamics of all societies with market economies was that to understand the economic system we must also examine the *production side* of economic conflict. Economic production is the major source of wealth and other resources in human societies (unless they exist largely or entirely through conquest of other societies), and producer competition is the major determinant of the distribution of resources within a society. Marx's principal thesis was that in *every society there is a fundamental mode of economic production that shapes its entire economy.* In agricultural societies the dominant mode of production is farming, while in industrial societies it is manufacturing. *Whatever segment of the society controls its major mode of production, therefore, dominates the creation of wealth and other resources.* That segment, consequently, has enormous advantages in consumer competition for goods and services. In agricultural societies the key economic resource is ownership of arable land, while in industrial societies it is ownership of factories and related businesses.

Benefits of Social Conflict

Any specific instance of social conflict will frequently harm one or more of the participants, at least in the short run, to the extent that they are prevented from obtaining some or all of the goals they seek. Even the apparent winners of the conflict may be harmed to the extent that they expend vital resources to gain victory. Nevertheless, sociologists have discovered that social conflict can also benefit some or all of the participants in various ways. These beneficial consequences of social conflict are never inevitable, but rather depend on how the conflict is conducted and resolved. Among the many potential benefits of social conflict that have been identified by Lewis Coser (1956a), three are particularly important.

First, strains and tensions will almost inevitably occur among the various members and/or parts of any organization. If these difficulties are not adequately resolved, they may continue to build up until they explode in rebellions or revolts that can destroy the entire organization. However, *if strains and tensions are expressed and resolved through periodic limited conflicts, they can be dissipated before they do irreparable harm.* A frequent outgrowth of this process, moreover, is the creation or revitalization of norms and rules that will aid the organization in coping with such difficulties in the future. As a result, the organization gains stability through time.

Second, if any organizational unit is to engage effectively in social conflict, it must be able to act in a concerted and unified manner. Therefore, *conflict with other units can be an effective means of drawing together and solidifying the members and parts of an organization, as well as delineating its boundaries in relation to other units.* A potential or actual external conflict will commonly push an organization to tighten up and increase its capability for unified action. An additional result of this process is that the organization may establish new relationships with its allies and/or opponents that may endure long after the immediate conflict is resolved and that may develop into beneficial cooperative arrangements.

Third, *social conflict can provide a strong stimulus to social change within an organization.* It can point out structural weaknesses and

inadequate operating procedures, challenge established modes of action, give rise to new and more capable leaders, and suggest alternative and more effective ways of dealing with organizational problems. Conflict does not always produce change, of course, and not all changes are beneficial to an organization. However, if conflict is continually suppressed, the organization will undoubtedly lose its ability to remain flexible in the face of emerging internal strains and impinging external stresses.

Management of Social Conflict

If social conflict is to produce the kinds of benefits just described, it must be effectively managed and resolved. Conflict management is therefore a crucial social skill for all organizations. Conflicts are most easily managed and resolved when they are limited in the scope of the issues involved, when they are pragmatic rather than ideological in nature, when they involve nonviolent rather than violent actions, and especially when they are regulated by shared norms or rules. Common conflict management techniques include:

(1) Bringing the opponents into a neutral setting such as a conference or court;

(2) Promoting open communication among them;

(3) Establishing negotiating and bargaining procedures;

(4) Searching for solutions that provide some benefits to all the participants; and

(5) Providing compensation for losses suffered in the conflict.

Labor-management negotiations illustrate the application of such techniques to one kind of conflict common in modern societies. Mediation and arbitration are two other procedures that are frequently used to manage and resolve conflicts. These conflict management procedures can enable the conflicting parties to resolve their differences peacefully and to achieve solutions that benefit all of them to at least some degree. Civil court trials are another procedure for settling conflicts, but because they result in an explicitly identified winner and loser, they are often less desirable.

The extent and success of these management procedures largely determine the form that conflict will take in any organization. *If an organization manages conflict through resistance and suppression, it will likely occur only sporadically.* Conflict can never be eliminated entirely, however, since external stresses and internal strains never cease acting upon an organization. If the pressures they generate are not dealt with in some manner, tensions will continue to build up within the organization. Eventually they may become uncontainable and erupt into sharp and often violent conflicts that can be highly disruptive and destructive. Divorces, strikes, race riots, and political revolutions are expressions of this kind of drastic conflict. In contrast, *if an organization manages conflict through established regulative procedures, it will likely occur rather continuously.* No single conflict will become too intense or extensive, but over time the cumulative outcomes of many small conflicts may produce extensive social change and organizational stability. Such organizations are spared the throes of violent and disruptive conflicts, because stresses and strains are resolved as they arise rather than mounting up over time.

Organizations falling at the beginning end of this continuum can be described as rigid, whereas those at the latter end are called flexible (Coser, 1956b). A relatively *rigid organization* resists and suppresses conflict as much as possible. Such tactics may enable it to survive for some time; but because it does not resolve stresses and strains, it will in the long run become increasingly inflexible and incapable of adapting to changing conditions. A relatively *flexible organization* promotes and encourages conflict through established procedures. Because conflicts frequently occur, such an organization may appear to be rather unstable. But because it resolves stresses and strains as they develop, the organization is able to adapt to changing conditions and thus maintain stability through time.

SOCIAL STRATIFICATION

Throughout all realms of social life, we distinguish among individuals, families, and other social units on the basis of many diverse characteristics. These include gender, age, race, nationality, education, occupation, income, residency location, possession, lifestyles, and many other factors. This process is called *social differentiation,* and it is important because the members of different categories—men versus women, young versus old, etc.—are usually viewed and treated differently in social life. Sometimes these differences are essentially equivalent, so that one category of people is not seen or treated as better or worse than another category—just differently.

As a general principle, however, when categories of people are differentiated, they are usually also viewed and treated unequally. All known societies throughout history have contained ordered patterns of social inequality, and this is also true of most other kinds of organizations such as communities, associations, and even small groups. As patterns of inequality are perpetuated through time—via such practices as inheritance of occupations and wealth, differential socialization and education, and selective recruitment to organizational positions—social stratification develops.

Nature of Social Stratification

Social stratification is the process though which social benefits are distributed unequally among social actors and those patterns of inequality are perpetuated across generations. Social benefits can include anything that people value and desire, but they are frequently classified into the three broad categories of power, privilege, and prestige, which Gerhard Lenski (1966) identified as the major components of all social stratification.

Social power has already been described as the ability of social actors to affect others, despite resistance. The ability to exercise power rests on the possession of resources and one's skill in employing them in interaction. *Social privilege* is access to desired goods, services, activities, or positions that is granted to an actor by others. The most obvious privilege in modern societies is money, which enables the holder to acquire a wide variety of goods and services. Privileges also include admission to certain activities or organizations, perogatives to act in distinctive ways or to receive services from others, and the right to wear distinctive clothing or symbols of rank. *Social prestige* is favorable evaluation that an actor receives from others. It takes many forms, including recognition, esteem, honor, and fame. Prestige is often expressed through deference by others, such as compliments or praise, use of titles, actions such as saluting or remaining standing in the presence of another person, and formal citations and awards.

Power, privilege, and prestige are distinct kinds of social benefits, but they usually become highly interrelated. In fact, it is often possible for an actor to transform one kind of benefit into another, as when a person uses his or her "good name" to acquire special privileges or to influence a decision, or when membership on the executive committee of an organization gives a person honor and control over organizational policy. And money can serve alternatively as a resource for power (when it is used to influence ac-

tions or decisions), as a means of acquiring privileges (when it is spent for goods and services), or as a prestige symbol (when it is displayed or given away).

Forms of Stratification

As pointed out by Max Weber (1958), there are many different dimensions of inequality, each of which constitutes a distinct form of social stratification. The most important forms of stratification in contemporary societies—as illustrated in Figure 6-1—are:

(1) Economic production stratification, based on one's relation to, or control over, the major means of economic production (as emphasized by Marx);

(2) Socioeconomic stratification, based on one's educational attainment, occupation, income, possessions, and related factors (or as Weber expressed it, one's "life chances" in the marketplace);

(3) Ethnic stratification, based on one's race, national origins, or religion;

(4) Gender stratification, based on one's sex and gender-determined roles;

(5) Age stratification, based on one's chronological age and age-determined roles;

(6) Political stratification, based on one's involvement and influence in political affairs; and

FIGURE 6-1   Major forms and bases of social stratification

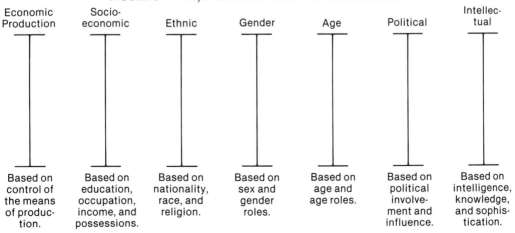

Economic Production	Socio-economic	Ethnic	Gender	Age	Political	Intellectual
Based on control of the means of production.	Based on education, occupation, income, and possessions.	Based on nationality, race, and religion.	Based on sex and gender roles.	Based on age and age roles.	Based on political involvement and influence.	Based on intelligence, knowledge, and sophistication.

(7) Intellectual stratification, based on one's level of intelligence, knowledge, sophistication, and intellectual accomplishments.

Relationships among these different forms of social stratification may vary considerably from one society to another. For example, a person's race and gender might have considerable effects on his or her socioeconomic position in one society, but not in another. At the same time, each of these stratification dimensions displays its own particular patterns of inequality.

All forms of stratification contain two or more unequal statuses. *A social status is an identified position or rank within a dimension of stratification.* Gender stratification is the simplest, since it contains just two statuses. Socioeconomic stratification, in contrast, may contain numerous occupational and income statuses. With the exception of gender stratification, the precision with which distinctions are drawn between statuses often varies from one situation to another. With ethnic stratification, for instance, we sometimes categorize people into numerous racial and nationality statuses, while at other times we simply distinguish between "whites" and "nonwhites."

Most people hold statuses on all of the preceding dimensions of stratification, so that any individual's overall social standing is a combination of many different statuses. Some amount of congruence usually exists among a person's various statuses, since power, privileges, and prestige on one dimension of stratification can often be transferred to other dimensions. For instance, being a middle-aged white male may assist a person in achieving relatively high socioeconomic status, while being a young black female may make it difficult for a person to achieve a comparable socioeconomic status.

Nevertheless, a considerable amount of disparity can occur among a person's statuses on the various stratification dimensions. A person might, for example, have high socioeconomic status as a wealthy physician, low ethnic status as a person of Chinese ancestry, modest political status as an ordinary citizen, high intellectual status as the author of a well-known book on health care, and low status in the realm of economic production as a result of not holding stock or an executive position in a major business corporation. Sociologists use the terms *status consistency* or *status crystallization* (they are synonymous) to describe the degree to which the diverse statuses of an individual are similar or disparate (Lenski, 1954). In general, the more complex a society and the faster the rate of social change, the more likely it is that many people will experience status inconsistency. A person with several inconsistence statuses, such as the physician just described, might experience numerous psychological and social tensions in his or her life. However, the effects of status inconsistency are frequently minimized if a person holds at least one important high status, since that status tends to influence how others relate to him or her in all realms of life. Thus the high educational, occupational, and income status of the physician might largely override her lower ethnic status.

Social Strata and Classes

Social Strata. Within each form of stratification, it is usually possible to identify numerous individuals or families who hold approximately similar statuses. On the socioeconomic dimension, for instance, some people have quite high statuses, some have above-average statuses, some have below-average statuses, and some have relatively low statuses. When such distinctions are drawn arbitrarily, the resulting clusters of people are called *social strata*. In other words, *a social stratum is an arbitrarily defined set of individuals who hold similar statuses on a dimension of stratification*. With income, for instance, we might classify a population into several levels ranging from "poor" (perhaps less than $10,000 annual income) to "rich" (perhaps more than $100,000 annual income). The income figures used to define those levels are obviously quite arbitrary, since a contemporary American family with an income of $10,001 is still quite poor even if it is not placed in that income category. Or consider age stratification. At age 64 a person might be employed and called "late middle-aged," but when that person becomes 65 and retires he or she might then be categorized as a "senior citizen." Such distinctions are frequently made for administrative and legal purposes, and they are also made by sociologists as a convenient way of classifying people, but they do not necessarily correspond to any real social categories within a stratification system.

Social Classes. Whereas the distinctions between social strata are arbitrarily defined at convenient points along a stratification dimension, the divisions separating social classes are real social cleavages. In addition to sharing similar social statuses, the members of a class typically interact with one another to establish class boundaries, create patterns of social ordering, and share a common class subculture. In other words, *a social class is an organization of people holding similar statuses on one or more dimensions of stratification that displays boundaries, internal ordering, and a unique subculture.*

For example, in many societies the dimension of economic production contains at least four distinct social classes: a very small elite or controlling class composed of those who own the major means of production; another fairly small class of subelites who perform supporting administrative and professional activities for the elites; a quite large class of people who sell their labor within labor markets; and a relatively small dispossessed class at the bottom composed of people who are more-or-less excluded from the labor market. A very similar class structure is often observed on the dimension of political stratification: a ruling class of political elites who dominate the government; a class of subelites who operate the political system; the mass of ordinary citizens; and a bottom class of people who are excluded from all political activity.

As indicated by these examples, a set of classes is often identified in terms of one dimension of stratification. Because the various types of stratification are commonly interrelated, however, in reality we often find that the members of any particular class also tend to hold similar statuses on several other dimensions of stratification. For instance, many members of the controlling economic production class are also likely to be part of the ruling class of political elites, to have very high socioeconomic statuses, to belong to the dominant ethnic class, and to be middle-aged or older males.

As social classes develop within a society, several trends are likely to occur that further separate the various classes.

(1) The members of a class come to identify with one another and with their class on the basis of their common interests and concerns and thus develop a sense of class consciousness.

(2) They strengthen the boundaries separating their class from others above and below them, so as to increase their class cohesion.

(3) They create associations such as interest groups and political parties to protect and promote their class position and interests.

(4) They share a unique set of cultural beliefs, values, and norms that shape their ways of thinking and their lifestyles.

(5) They come into conflict with other classes over the distribution of power, privileges, and prestige in the society, seeking either to perpetuate the existing distribution of social benefits or to change it.

As a consequence of all these trends, stratification systems are frequently fraught with internal tensions.

Status Attainment and Mobility

Status Attainment. As with social roles, statuses within any dimension of stratification are acquired through either ascription or achievement. *Ascribed statuses* are gained on the basis of one's family background, ethnicity, sex, age, or race, and obviously cannot be altered by one's actions. *Achieved statuses*, in contrast, are acquired on the basis of one's activities and accomplishments, such as acquiring an education, obtaining a desirable job, earning money, becoming active in politics, or making intellectual contributions. Historically, most important statuses have been assigned to individuals through ascription, which tends to make stratification systems rather inflexible. Ascriptive status attainment also occurs in many realms of modern societies, especially in regard to ethnicity and gender. One of the most striking features of many modern societies, however, is *the opening of more and more statuses to personal achievement,* which often involves competition with others. There are many reasons for this trend, including rapidly expanding public education, the creation of considerable wealth that can be distributed among a large proportion of the population, and slowly developing norms of rational efficiency and social equality.

In recent years, sociologists have conducted considerable research on the process through which individuals attain occupational statuses. In industrial societies, critical factors influencing occupational status attainment are the educational and occupational statuses of one's parents, the amount of one's education, and the status of one's first job, (Blau and Duncan, 1967). Among women and blacks, however, their ascribed gender and/or racial status can have important effects on their occupational status attainment. Many additional factors are also critical in this process, including one's intelligence, ambition, job opportunities, and interpersonal contacts. The principal point, however, is that a person's occupational attainment is a result of numerous interacting social and psychological factors, and is rarely due to simple chance or good luck.

Social Mobility. Although patterns of social stratification commonly display considerable stability through time, in most societies and other organizations at least some individuals alter their statuses by gaining or losing power, privileges, and prestige. That is, they are socially mobile, in either an upward or downward direction. *Social mobility occurs when a social actor acquires a higher or lower status on one or more dimensions of stratification.*

Some amount of social mobility is inevitable in any organization, as old members leave and others take their places. Several other social conditions also contribute to upward and downward mobility, however. First, as the practice of status achievement becomes increasingly prevalent in an organization, opportunities for mobility expand. Open competition for statuses enables people to be upwardly mobile to the limit of their abilities and desires, which often forces other, less competent or competitive people to move downward. Second, broad changes in overall patterns of stratification often produce considerable social mobility. If the major resource for power exertion in a society shifts from control of money to possession of technical knowledge, for instance, many individuals will find themselves either gaining or losing privileges and prestige. Third, extensive expansion or contraction in the size or activities of an organization often leads to widespread mobility. If an organization is growing, new roles and statuses are continually being created, thus allowing many members to be upwardly mobile. However, if an organization is declining, numerous members may be pushed downward.

Social mobility is often described as either career or generational in nature, especially in regard to people's occupational and other socioeconomic statuses. *Career mobility occurs when a person significantly changes his or her status during the course of their lifetime.* For example, if a woman begins working as a sales clerk at a rather low wage but eventually attains the position of marketing manager with a substantial salary, she has been quite upwardly mobile during her career. *Generational mobility occurs when a person attains a significantly different status from his or her parents.* If a man's father had a high school education and was a blue-collar worker in a factory, but the son completes college and becomes a business executive, he has been quite upwardly mobile across generations.

SOCIAL EVOLUTION

Our previous discussions of social and cultural change did not take into account the fact that broad patterns of change in societies are often developmental or evolutionary in nature. Not all social change is developmental, of course. Norms concerning proper social etiquette seem to vary almost randomly, while styles of political intrigue often appear to be cyclical in nature. From a broader perspective, nevertheless, the process of societal change can often be described as evolutionary. *Social evolution is a process of long-term social change that moves in an identifiable direction and develops in a cumulative manner.*

Nature of Social Evolution

Early sociological thinking was thoroughly infused with crude notions of social evolution, which were often coupled with ideas of either social progress or social degeneration. Auguste Comte believed that all societies evolve through three stages, which he called theological, metaphysical, and positive (or scientific). Herbert Spencer, the first major English sociologist, wrote that sociology is "the study of evolution in its most complex form" (Spencer, 1873:350). The German theorist Ferdinand Tönnies saw social evolution as movement from *gemeinschaft* communities based on personal, communal relationships, to modern *gesellschaft* societies in which social relationships are impersonal and contractual. Durkheim's thesis of the growing dominance of organic (functional) over mechanical (normative) solidarity in contemporary societies also expressed an evolutionary perspective. William Graham Sumner tried to apply Darwin's theory of biological evolution through natural selection and survival of the fittest to organized social life. Most important, Marx's contention that social change will ultimately move all humanity from feudalism through capitalism to socialism was thoroughly evolutionary.

Today, the process of societal evolution is often called modernization or development. Regardless of the term used, social evolution results from social change that is directional and cumulative in the long run. *Social change is directional if nonrepetitive trends run throughout many diverse events and alterations in social life.* The steady decline in the death rate that has been occurring around the world during the past century is an example of directional change, as is the continual growth in white-collar occupations. *Social change is cumulative if it builds upon itself, so that prior changes are not only retained but also influence future changes.* Although cumulative change can occur in a downward direction of increasing disintegration of social organization, most such change during the past several hundred years has been upward growth or development of social organization. The process of societal industrialization, for instance, tends to be relatively cumulative, as well as directional in nature. The more industrialized a society becomes, the more extensively its economy can expand to promote further industrial growth. The growth of large urban communities is another example of cumulative social change.

To avoid the biases that were inherent in earlier notions of social evolution, contemporary sociologists attempt to avoid several assumptions that are sometimes associated with the concepts of social evolution and modernization. These include the ideas of:

(1) Progress, or increasing improvements in human happiness or quality of life;
(2) Determinism, or the thesis that evolution is somehow inherent in all social life and hence beyond human control;
(3) Ethnocentrism, or the assumption that modern Western nations represent the most advanced type of society; and
(4) Teleology, or the belief that some kind of ultimate plan or purpose underlies all social evolution.

By rejecting notions such as these, sociologists hope to keep the study of social evolution as objective as possible and to find answers to the question, "How has social organization changed through history, and where is it likely to go in the future?"

Ecological and Political Economy Evolutionary Theory

Part of the theoretical perspective on social evolution used throughout this book—especially in Part II—is called *ecological evolutionary theory*. As formulated by Gerhard and Jean Lenski (1982), the essence of the ecological evolutionary perspective is that *evolutionary development of human societies is always shaped and influenced—but never fully determined—by the ecological conditions within which they exist*. More specifically, the fundamental ecological factors of population characteristics, technological innovation and diffusion, and natural resource availability constitute the framework for all social evolution and heavily influence the nature and course of social change. They never fully determine the evolutionary process, however, since a number of key social organizational factors also play critical roles in societal development. These include the economic system, the political system, stratification patterns, settlement patterns, family patterns, and cultural beliefs and values. Although these social organizational factors are broadly shaped by prevailing ecological conditions, they also continually affect the manner in which a society responds to its ecological conditions and hence the ways in which social change occurs through time.

Another way of expressing the fundamental idea of ecological evolution is that *societies tend to develop in an evolutionary manner as they become more ecological effective* (Hawley, 1986:52). As populations utilize technological knowledge to obtain needed resources, societies tend to become increasingly effective in coping with the natural environment. As a result, societies are able to extract more and more resources from the environment, transform those resources into desired goods and services, accumulate increasing amounts of surplus wealth, raise their standards of living, create more complex forms of social ordering, and expand their cultures. None of these steps is inevitable, so that a particular society might concentrate most of its wealth in the hands of a small ruling class and keep the rest of the population living at a subsistence level. Moreover, as we are becoming aware, when this process is stretched beyond the carrying capacity of the natural environment, it will inevitably result in environmental degradation or destruction. As a general trend, however, increasing ecological effectiveness has provided the foundation for all societal evolution.

The ecological evolutionary perspective is extremely useful in explaining fundamental changes between the basic types of societies discussed in this book: foraging, horticultural, agrarian, industrial, and postindustrial. It does not tell us very much, however, about the numerous developmental trends in social organization that have occurred and are presently occurring within each of those types of societies. Consequently, that perspective must be supplemented with a second theoretical perspective on societal evolution, known as *political economy evolutionary theory*. As sketched in Chapter 2, the political economy perspective on societal evolution argues that *the nature and functioning of the economic and political systems in a society tend to influence—but again never fully determine—all of its other forms of social organization*. These two core subsystems, or social institutions, are shaped by ecological conditions within a society, and, in turn, direct the flow of resources, energy, and power that are used by all other institutions and organizations in that society.

The ecological and political economy perspectives are not alternative theories of societal evolution, but rather highly complementary and frequently interwoven ways of viewing this process. In this book, therefore, both perspectives are used quite extensively and are integrated as fully as possible. Since no single sociological term combines both perspectives, however, the orientation of the book toward societal evolution is best de-

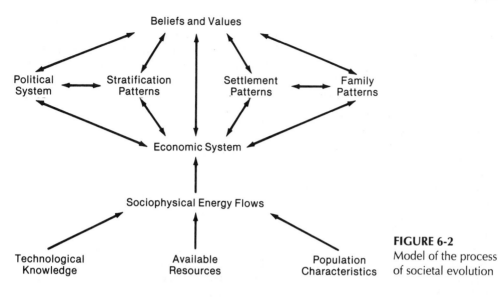

Beliefs and Values

Political System · Stratification Patterns · Settlement Patterns · Family Patterns

Economic System

Sociophysical Energy Flows

Technological Knowledge · Available Resources · Population Characteristics

FIGURE 6-2
Model of the process of societal evolution

scribed by the compound phrase *ecological and political economy evolutionary theory.*

Figure 6-2 gives a model of the process of societal evolution as conceptualized in this book. It begins with changes in the ecological factors of technological knowledge, available resources, and population characteristics, which together shape the flows of sociophysical energy through the society. Those flows of sociophysical energy, which include all forms of animate and inanimate energy and social power, are the lifeblood of social evolution. The extent and forms of these flows heavily influence the economic system of the society, including its basic nature (e.g., agriculture or manufacturing), the level of its economic productivity, and the amount of surplus wealth (beyond that needed for survival) that is available. The economic system of a society, in turn, strongly influences other parts of that society such as its political system, stratification patterns, settlement arrangements, and family forms. These exertions of influence among all the component forms of social ordering within a society are normally reciprocal (as indicated by the double-headed arrows in the model). Finally, all forms of social ordering interact with cultural beliefs and values. Although many other sociocultural characteristics can

also affect the process of ecological evolution, the factors included in this model are generally the most central and influential.

Dimensions of Sociocultural Evolution

To describe and analyze the process of sociocultural evolution, sociologists frequently identify several major dimensions along which societies tend to move as they develop. Four of these basic dimensions of societal evolution are organizational growth, functional specialization, structural complexity, and cultural secularization.

Organizational Growth. As a general principle, increasing energy flows and surplus wealth enable societies and other organizations to grow in a variety of ways. On the societal level, growth can occur in the size of its population, the land area it encompasses, the extensiveness of its national government, or the strength of its military forces, to mention a few examples. Within a society, there can be an increase in the total number of organizations, or in the number of units of various particular types of organizations such as churches or schools. There may also be growth in the diversity of organizations, such as special-interest associations ranging from antique collectors to zoology enthusiasts. In addition, growth can be expressed in terms of the number of transactions occurring, such as car sales or marriages. In short, *organizational growth refers to increases in the number or size of the components of a society.*

Functional Specialization. As a society or other organization grows in size, the activities or functions performed by its members often become increasingly specialized. In a retail store, for instance, one person no longer orders goods, stocks the shelves, waits on customers, keep the books, and sweeps the floor. Instead, different people perform each of these activities as a specialized task. In this example, specialization is taking place at the individual level. As an organization continues to grow in size and scope of activities, specialization may also occur among its component subunits, so that eventually a store contains separate departments for purchasing, advertising, accounting, and so forth. In addition, many of the social institutions in a society also become increasingly specialized, so that each one—schools, hospitals, the mass media, etc.—performs a particular social activity or function. Even total societies may become specialized within the world economy, as some countries function primarily as suppliers of food or other raw materials, while other countries emphasize such functions as manufacturing, trade, or finance. In short, *functional specialization refers to an increase in the number of specialized roles and activities in a society.*

Structural Complexity. As functional specialization progresses among the roles and activities of an organization, increasing structural complexity is almost inevitable if the organization is to continue operating. More and more subunits are created within the organization and become interwoven into complex networks of exchange and power relationships. To continue the example of the retail store, each department might be further divided into several sections, and each section might be composed of a number of smaller work teams. All of these teams, sections, and departments would be highly interdependent and hence have to interact with one another on a regular basis. To maintain all of those relationships among units and keep the entire organization operating smoothly, an extensive set of operating procedures and rules would have to be created and enforced. This process of increasing structural complexity occurs within all kinds of organization, so that the total society contains extremely complex patterns of social ordering. In short, *structural complexity refers to an increase in the number of subunits and their interrelationships within a society.*

Cultural Secularization. Traditionally, cultural values, norms, rules, and other ideas have reflected long-established ways of thinking and acting. They are perpetuated and enforced because "that is the way we do things" or "that is what we believe is right." As the pace and scope of societal evolution intensify, however, old cultural ideas are frequently no longer relevant to the new conditions, and people begin to question them or propose new ways of thinking. It is quite possible, of course, for one set of traditional or sacred ideas simply to replace another. With growth, specialization, and complexity, however, societies and other organizations often begin to develop entirely new values, norms, and rules that are derived from deliberate experimentation, rational analysis, pragmatic considerations, or future planning. These secularized cultural ideas, unlike traditional or sacred ones, are continually open to revision as conditions change. They may or may not be more adequate than traditional ideas, but they are decidedly

---

DIMENSIONS OF SOCIOCULTURAL EVOLUTION

1. Organizational growth.
2. Functional specialization.
3. Structural complexity.
4. Cultural secularization.

more flexible. In short, *cultural secularization refers to an increase in the number and influence of nontraditional beliefs and values in a society.*

SUMMARY

Social control is the process of regulating the actions of individuals and organizational units so as to maintain and perpetuate organized social life. It normally involves the exercise of power in some form by one or more persons acting as representatives of an organization, directed toward others whose actions are culturally defined as deviant or undesirable. Effective control is intended to influence and shape social actions, but it need not entail total conformity to established norms and rules. People's actions are most commonly controlled through the three procedures of socialization, social sanctioning, and social management. Activities of organizational units are commonly controlled by establishing regulatory procedures for coping with functional uncertainties, or by making and enforcing organizational decisions in either a unitary or polyarchic manner.

Social cohesion is the process of binding the members and parts of an organization together into a unified entity. Normative cohesion occurs as moral norms based on shared values become imbedded within the component parts and members of an organization. Functional cohesion occurs as complementary exchange relationships are established among the component parts and members. These two kinds of social cohesion are highly complementary, so that neither form can develop very far without corresponding developments in the other. Although functional cohesion is becoming increasingly prevelant in modern societies, this process always rests on a foundation of shared cultural values and norms. Normative cohesion in complex societies can be attained if people and units agree to abide by a common set of procedural rules. Increasing functional cohesion in contemporary societies necessitates the creation of overall coordination and regulation by administrative units, but does not require total centralization of decision making.

Social conflict is not social disorganization, but rather a type of ordered social relationship. It occurs when two or more actors oppose one another in social interaction and exert power in an effort to attain a common goal or mutually exclusive goals. Conflicts can usually be characterized as latent or overt, verbal or action, pragmatic or ideological, and regulated or unregulated. Ecological conflict over scarce resources occurs among all species, although as humans have developed increasingly effective technology they have become dominant over all other species. Human societies tend to transform ecological conflict for scarce resources into social conflict with other societies and with future generations. Within societies, humans also engage in economic conflict within both the production and consumption sides of the economy. Whatever segment of a society controls the major means of economic production tends to wield considerable power throughout that society, while competition in the marketplace determines the distribution of desired goods and services. At the same time, social conflict can have numerous beneficial consequences for social organization, the most important of which is encouraging social change. For this to occur, conflict must be adequately managed through regulative procedures that permit continual conflict and promote organizational flexibility.

Social stratification is the process through which social power, privileges, and prestige are distributed unequally among social actors, resulting in patterns of inequality that are perpetuated through time. The most common types of social stratification in modern societies involve economic production, socioeconomic status, ethnicity, gender, age, political influence, and intellectual attainment. Individuals normally hold a status on each of these dimensions of stratification, and those various statuses may be relatively congruent or quite inconsistent. Each dimension of stratification may be arbitrarily divided into two or more social strata consisting of people with approximately similar statuses. At the same time, each dimension usually contains two or more social classes that are distinguished by social cleavages and boundaries, internal ordering, and unique subcultures. Social statuses can be attained through either ascription or achievement, although the latter process is becoming increasingly common in modern societies. Quite frequently, individuals are socially mobile as they move up or down various dimension of stratification, which may result from either their own efforts or from changes in the stratification system.

Social evolution occurs as broad processes of social and cultural change are directional and cumulative over time. This process, especially contemporary efforts toward societal modernization, is a fundamental concern of sociology. The theory of ecological evolution argues that sociocultural development is shaped and influenced by the basic ecological factors of population characteristics, technological knowledge, and available resources, which together affect the flows of sociotechnical energy through a society. Those flows, in turn, influence critical structural components of the society, especially its economic system, political system, stratification patterns, settlement patterns, and family patterns. The theory of political economy evolution emphasizes the critical importance of the economic and political systems in shaping all other instituions and organizations within that society. All of these forms of social ordering interact with one another and with cultural beliefs and values, as well as many other aspects of social organization. The major dimensions of sociocultural evolution as it has occurred during the past few hundred years are organizational growth, functional specialization, structural complexity, and cultural secularization.

Conceptual Interlude
THE PROCESS OF
SOCIAL ORGANIZATION

The preceding six chapters have presented a diverse array of basic sociological concepts for understanding the various components, dynamics, characteristics, and forms of social organization. Thus far, however, all of these concepts have been discussed separately and have not been brought together into a holistic overview of the total process of social organization. This short interlude sketches a model of that total process, as a means of integrating a number of these basic sociological concepts and providing a conceptual framework for the rest of the text. Since this interlude is quite brief and introduces no new concepts, it does not constitute a normal chapter. It is, rather, a transition from Part I to the remaining parts of the book.

The conceptual model of the process of social organization given in Figure A includes only the most crucial features of this total process. For simplicity, moreover, it depicts only the most critical linkages

among those features and omits many additional interrelationships that often occur among them. It also omits numerous other aspects of social organization that are discussed in subsequent chapters. Despite the simplicity of this model, however, it should provide a useful overview of the process of social organization.

The model begins at the bottom, with social action and interaction among social actors (who may be either individuals or organizational units). Many of these actions/interactions can be described as social exchanges, and most of them involve symbolic meanings and interchanges. The topic of action change, indicated by the horizontal arrow, was not specifically discussed in Chapter 2. Because actions and interactions are ongoing processes, however, they are continually being modified and altered as actors respond to shifting situational conditions and to the actions of other actors.

FIGURE A   Conceptual model of the process of social organization

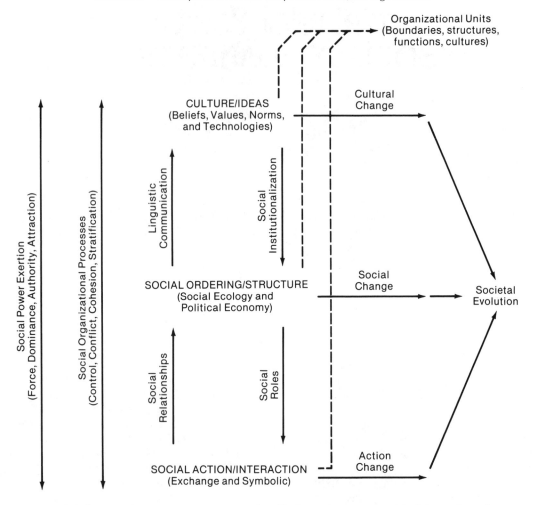

As social interactions are perpetuated through time, the actors establish and maintain social relationships among themselves, as depicted by the upward arrow. When a number of social relationships become interwoven to form stable and enduring patterns, social ordering or structure is created. Ecological conditions and processes underlie and affect all social ordering to some extent, and the most central component of most social ordering is its political economy, or interrelated economic and political systems. As individuals participate in established social ordering, they enact social roles.

(Role actions are guided by cultural norms and role expectations and are usually creatively devised by individual role players, so that role enactment actually involves all three levels of the model. The model depicts social roles only as a downward arrow from social ordering to social action/interaction, however, since roles are essentially properties of social ordering.) All social ordering/structure is constantly changing through time in countless ways, as suggested by the horizontal arrow.

As the participants in any instance of social ordering use language to communicate with one another about their shared activities, they create a culture composed of ideas that are relevant to their common experiences, as indicated by the upward arrow. (This may be a societal culture or a subculture that is specific to a more limited set of people or an organizational unit.) A culture is composed of beliefs, values, norms, and technologies. An established culture, in turn, influences patterns of social ordering/structure to the extent that those ideas become imbedded, or institutionalized, within social life, as depicted by the downward arrow. (Cultural ideas also influence individual personalities and social actions/interactions through socialization, although that downward arrow is omitted from the model for simplicity, since this process is primarily social-psychological rather than sociological in nature.) All cultures gradually change through time, as shown by the horizontal arrow.

Social power, which is exercised through social interaction, is constantly being exerted throughout the entire process of social organization, as depicted by the double-headed arrow running from social interaction through social ordering to culture, and back again. Social power can be expressed as force, dominance, authority, or attraction. Several other specific social processes—social control, social conflict, social cohesion, and social stratification—also occur throughout all social organization, involving interaction, ordering, and culture. For simplicity, they are shown in the model as one double-headed arrow, although they are distinct processes that occur within all social organization and thus might well be indicated by separate arrows.

If the model could be three-dimensional, the third dimension (extending outward from the paper) would contain all of the various types of organizational units that are created through the general process of social organization. As described in Chapter 5, these units range from small groups to entire societies. All of these different types of social units display boundaries, structural characteristics, dynamic functions, and unique cultures. Since the model is limited to two dimensions, however, this aspect is crudely suggested by the broken arrows extending upward.

Finally, to the extent that action, social, and cultural changes are directional and cumulative through time, they can result in social evolution. At the societal level, this evolutionary or developmental process is described very broadly—throughout the remainder of the book—as movement from preindustrial to industrial to postindustrial societies.

ECOLOGY AND ECONOMIES OF PREINDUSTRIAL SOCIETIES

What factors shape the process of ecological evolution in all types of
preindustrial societies?

Since the human race has lived in foraging societies for most of its existence,
what was the ecological basis for it?

What ecological conditions pushed foraging societies into practicing
horticulture?

How did the practice of gardening alter the ecological and economic
conditions of horticultural societies?

How did the practice of settled agriculture change the ecological conditions of
agrarian societies and lead to the creation of dual command economies?

SOCIETAL EVOLUTION

Humanlike beings, or hominids, have prob-ably existed on earth for at least four million years, and the species Homo sapiens—or "thinking man"—is now believed to have de-veloped close to a half million years ago. However, our own subspecies of Homo sapi-ens probably did not appear until approxi-mately 35,000 years ago, hardly more than a brief "blip" in archeological time. Since then, there have been no significant genetic changes among human beings. During this time span over a thousand generations of people have come and gone, however. Al-though we do not know very much about how most of those people lived, one general-ization about them is virtually certain. Throughout most of its existence, humanity has had to struggle continually to survive and maintain itself in the natural environ-ment. Consequently, *until rather recently, hu-man social organization has been quite minimal in scope and complexity and relatively unchanging*

through time. Human societies have been lim-ited to very small and simply organized fami-lies and communities, and the heavy hand of tradition has determined most aspects of peoples' lives.

Roughly 10,000 years ago, however, orga-nized human life began to change in a direc-tional and cumulative manner, so that soci-eties and other forms of social organization started to evolve toward greater environ-mental adaptation and control, with result-ing growth in size and complexity. *To under-stand this process of societal evolution, we must view it within the ecological contexts in which it has occurred and which have made it possible.* This chapter explores those ecological con-ditions of human life, from the appearance of Homo sapiens sapiens until the beginning of industrialization about two hundred years ago, and describes the types of societal econ-omies that emerged from those ecological conditions. Chapter 8 examines the pre-vailing patterns of social organization within those various types of preindustrial societies.

Chapters 9 and 10 discuss the process of industrialization in Western societies since the eighteenth century and in developing societies today. Throughout these chapters, we focus on broad patterns of societal organization and evolution, not on any specific societies.

As mentioned in the Chapter 6, our theoretical framework for understanding this process of societal change and development is called *ecological and political economy evolution,* because of its fundamental emphasis on the role of ecological conditions in shaping and altering social organization (Lenski and Lenski, 1982), coupled with the central role of economic and political systems in all societies. We must remember, however, that ecological and political economy conditions never operate in a social vacuum; they are always highly interrelated with numerous social and cultural characteristics within societies.

Ecological Factors

The most fundamental ecological factors affecting societal evolution—as mentioned in Chapters 3 and 6—are resources, knowledge, and population, as well as sociophysical energy flows.

Resources. All living organisms must obtain the resources they require for life from the natural environment. With all other animal species, those necessary resources are limited to food, water, air, and warmth, which they take directly from the environment in one way or another. The resource needs of early hominids were probably not much more extensive, and they were normally obtained in the same manner. At some distant time in the past, however, hominids took a radically new step that forever distinguished them and their ancestors from all other species. They began using their minds and their agile hands to create tools to facilitate the process of obtaining necessary resources from the environment. The first tools were, of course, extremely crude— clubs, stone scrapers, digging sticks, and sim-

ilar natural objects they could pick up and use with little or no modification. Over the centuries, however, those tools were gradually improved and elaborated. *Each improvement of an existing tool or invention of a new one enabled our ancestors to obtain more and better resources from the environment,* thus making life somewhat easier. Until a few thousand years ago, this process of innovation and its consequent expansion of usable resources progressed extremely slowly. As humanity's accumulated store of technological knowledge began to grow more rapidly, however, so did its available resources and therefore its capacity to create more complex forms of social organization.

Two critical conditions, in addition to tools, also affect the ability of human beings and societies to obtain resources from the biophysical environment. One of these factors is *the nature of the environment and the kinds and amounts of resources that it contains.* People who are located in relatively warm and hospitable environments with plenty of water, lush vegetation, and extensive animal life obviously have a much larger store of natural resources to draw upon than do people living in harsher environments. Those who live on a grassy plain have quite a different resource base than do those who live in a forest or beside an ocean. More recently, societies whose land contains rich deposits of minerals, coal, and oil have found it much easier to industrialize than nations lacking such resources.

The second additional factor is *the extent to which societies deplete their resources or degrade the environment*—their land or water supplies, plant and animal life, minerals and other deposits, or air quality. As long as human populations were small and widely scattered, this was not a serious problem. Such societies rarely exhausted the available resources or degraded the environment in serious or permanent ways. And if the nearby supply of game animals should be killed off or the soil became too poor through constant farming, new and undepleted resources were likely to be available not far away. As populations grew and improved technology enabled people to exploit the environment to an ever-increasing extent, however, resource exhaustion and environmental degradation started to become a serious limitation on societal evolution.

Knowledge. From an ecological perspective, accumulated knowledge is the principal factor that sets human ecosystems apart from biological ecosystems. *Human beings and societies utilize all kinds of technological knowledge—both material technology pertaining to the physical world and social technology relevant to social organization—to facilitate their adaptation to the natural environment.* As we saw in Chapter 4, societies acquire technological knowledge through innovation, which may take the form of invention, discovery, or diffusion from another society. The rate of innovation in any society is determined by numerous factors, including its existing store of knowledge, the nature of its biophysical environment, functional requirements of the society, its population size, the manner in which it is organized, its contacts with other cultures, and its values regarding new ideas.

Not all innovations are readily—or ever—accepted by a society. A selection process occurs in all societies that results in some new knowledge being immediately rejected, some being tried provisionally for a period of time before it is either adopted or rejected, and some being adopted rather quickly. This selection process is governed by several relevant factors, including the perceived usefulness and benefits of the new knowledge, how well it fits in with existing knowledge and practices in the society, the costs (economic, political, social, and environmental) of adopting it, and the stance of powerful groups in the society toward that knowledge. Very frequently, this process of adopting or rejecting new knowledge is quite prolonged, since all of the benefits and costs of an innovation may not be recognized until it has been tried out by some members of the society for a considerable period of time.

The communication techniques possessed by a society greatly affect its capability to acquire new knowledge. If a society lacks writing—which was not invented until about 6,000 years ago—all new knowledge must be retained in people's memories and transmitted orally. In preliterate societies—some of which have existed as late as the twentieth century—much new knowledge is lost before its benefits become generally recognized, and new ideas spread very slowly if the population is at all large. Moreover, as long as literacy is restricted to a small upper class of scholars, priests, and other elites, limitations on the retention and transmission of knowledge continue to pose severe barriers to innovation. With the spread of mass education and communications during the last century in developed societies, the rate and extent of innovation has obviously been greatly accelerated.

Population. The size, structure, and distribution of the population of a society influence its organization and evolution in numerous ways. *Population size can have either beneficial or harmful effects for a society.* On the positive side, the larger the population, the greater the possibilities for technological innovation, the larger the work force engaged in extracting resources from the environment, and the more extensive the role and structural specialization within the society. On the negative side, however, the larger the population, the more resources are required to provide for people's needs, the more likely the environment is to become depleted or degraded, and the greater the demand for overall coordination and regulation within the society.

The distribution of a population over its land area directly affects the ecological conditions of that society. In general, the sparser the population distribution, the less competition there is for scarce natural resources, but also the slower the rate of knowledge innovation and societal evolution. Denser populations tend to experience more intense ecological demands and competition, but this frequently stimulates innovation and societal development. Extreme population density can be devastating for a society with limited natural resources, however.

Sociophysical Energy Flows. The preceding ecological factors of knowledge, resources, and population are relevant for societal evolution primarily to the extent that they contribute to energy flows within a society. Energy is the capacity to perform work of all kinds, so that in a broad sense, all human activities require the expenditure of some amount of energy. Although energy is commonly thought of in physical terms, it is also a biological and social phenomenon that is crucial for all life and a fundamental factor in human social organization (Adams, 1975). The term "sociophysical energy" is used throughout this book as a reminder that energy is social as well as physical in nature. *Sociophysical energy includes all the inanimate and animate energy used in a society, as well as all the social power exercised by its members.*

Sociophysical energy can be conceptualized as a common denominator for all resources used by societies. Whatever those resources may be—food, water, climate, minerals, domesticated animals, human labor, craft skills, or communication media—they are relevant for social life only to the extent that they enable people to carry out organized activities. In other words, all resources must in one way or another be transformed into sociophysical energy in order to be used directly in human social life.

The amount and flows of sociophysical energy in a society have enormous influences on the structure and dynamics of that society at any given time, as well as the manner in which it changes and evolves through time. The concept of energy flows includes the distribution of energy in a society, the purposes for which it is used, and the manner in which it is employed. As a general principle, *the larger the amount and the more diverse the flows of sociophysical energy in a society, the greater its potential for developing effective economies and complex social organization.* A simple organized society with little technological knowledge, few available resources, and a small population typically generates relatively little energy beyond that required for survival, and whatever surplus it does produce is likely to be poorly organized and inefficiently used. In contrast, a modern industrial society generates enormous amounts of energy and organizes that energy into complex social structures to attain collective goals.

Types of Economies and Preindustrial Societies

Societal evolution is a continual process with countless gradations of development that shift almost imperceptibly from one to another. Any typology that divides societies into broad categories is therefore arbitrary, depending on what criteria are used to define those categories and place various societies into them. Nevertheless, typologies are useful analytical tools, because they enable us to focus on fundmental differences among societies that may take hundreds or thousands of years to become fully evident.

The typology of societies used in this book is based on fundamental differences among economic systems, since *the economy of a society is the principal channel through which ecological factors influence its patterns of social organization.* Numerous other components of a society—including its political system, its stratification system, and its cultural beliefs and values—also directly influence the process of social evolution, but they are all shaped to some degree by the economic system of that society.

From this ecological-economic perspective, *there have been four broad types of societies throughout human history: foraging, horticultural, agrarian, and industrial* (Lenski and Lenski, 1982). There have been, of course, numerous sybtypes and levels of development within each of these categories, but none of those variations are as fundamental as the differences among the four categories. This part of the book deals with the first three types of preindustrial societies, while the following part deals entirely with modern industrial societies.

We often think of the three types of preindustrial societies as developing in sequential order from foraging to horticultural to agrarian societies—all of which

---

FUNDAMENTAL TYPES OF SOCIETIES

1. Foraging societies.
2. Horticultural societies.
3. Agrarian societies.
4. Industrial societies.

---

precede industrial societies. This sequence is partially correct in several respects.

(1) Originally, all human societies had foraging economies.
(2) The first horticultural economies were established about 10,000 years ago, or around 8,000 B.C. (Clark and Piggot, 1965).
(3) Agrarian economies did not appear until about 5,000 years ago, or around 3,000 B.C. (Struever, 1971).
(4) Societies did not begin to industrialize until the eighteenth century.

We misinterpret this sequence, however, if we assume that each earlier type of economy disappeared when the next type appeared, since *societies with all three types of preindustrial economies continue to exist at the present time.* Although it is true that foraging societies have become steadily less prevelent ever since the development of horticultural and agrarian economic systems and are now virtually extinct, a few of them still remain in isolated parts of the world. Similarly, horticultural societies began diminishing after the advent of agrarian economies, but quite a number of them survive today. Finally, a large majority of all currently existing societies are still based primarily on agriculture, since less than one-fourth of all societies have reached the stage of full industrialization.

We also misinterpret this sequence if we assume that all societies must necessarily go through all four stages. The United States, for example, was never a foraging society (although the original native inhabitants were). Today, many of the remaining horticultural societies in the world are attempting to move directly into industrialization, without going through an agrarian phase (Lenski and Nolan, 1984).

Foraging Societies. To forage means to search for food. *The economy of a foraging society—also called a hunting and gathering society—is based on hunting wild animals and gathering wild plants.* This simplest type of economic system thus depends entirely on finding food and other resources that occur naturally in the environment. It has no domesticated livestock and practices no agriculture. Consequently, it is entirely at the mercy of the immediate environment, and if those natural resources are not sufficient to meet the needs of the population, the society must either move or perish. Foraging societies that exist in bountiful environments—such as rain forests full of game and edible plants—may live fairly comfortably as long as their population remains fairly small. For many of these societies, however, existence is often rather precarious. Perhaps the most fortunate hunting and gathering societies are those that live near rivers or oceans containing abundant fish. Those people can count on a continual supply of easily obtainable food.

Horticultural Societies. *The economy of a horticultural society rests on small-scale gardening.* Food and fibers are grown on a more or less continual basis, but with limited use of tools. Depending on the level of technological development in a society (as well as soil quality and rainfall), horticulture may range from crude slash-and-burn techniques to semisettled gardening. Most horticultural societies sooner or later find it necessary to move on to new land, however. The level of agricultural productivity varies widely among horticultural societies, but in all cases the people have some control over the availability of the resources they require. Many horticultural societies also maintain limited amounts of livestock, and some of them depend largely or entirely on herding rather than farming. (Some social scientists classify nomadic herding societies as a separate type, but they are generally at about the same level of economic development as societies based on horticulture.) A distinction can be made between simple and advanced horticultural societies, depending on whether or not they have discovered metallurgy and are able to make simple metal tools, but that discovery does not alter the basic form of their economy.

Agrarian Societies. This type of economy, like horticulture, is based on agriculture (usually combined with some amount of livestock maintenance). The basic difference between the two types lies in the manner in which agriculture is practiced. *The economy of an agrarian society is based on settled agriculture.* These societies are able to farm the same land on a permanent basis because they have acquired plows pulled by domesticated animals, which enables them to turn and cultivate the soil and thus preserve its nutrients. Other soil management techniques, such as natural fertilization and crop rotation, also facilitate permanent settled farming. These agricultural techniques generally result in much higher levels of productivity than in horticultural societies. Extensive and dependable agricultural surpluses, combined with permanent settlements, enable agrarian societies to become much larger and more complexly organized than is possible in those based on horticulture. A distinction is often made between simple and advanced agrarian societies, depending on whether or not they have learned how to smelt and manufacture iron tools, but again this innovation does not alter the basic nature of the economy. Maritime societies, whose economies rest primarily on shipping, are sometimes treated as a separate type, but those societies are similar to, and highly dependent on, agrarian societies.

The following sections of this chapter discuss the ecological and economic characteristics of the three major types of preindustrial societies in greater detail.

FORAGING SOCIETIES

Living in this era of high technology, we easily forget that throughout most of humanity's existence our ancestors have survived with very little technological knowledge and have been totally dependent on hunting and gathering to satisfy their material needs. Considering the physical demands and economic uncertainty of this kind of existence, the fact that Homo sapiens sapiens managed to persist through all those thousands of years is a tribute to the ingenuity and adaptability of our species. How did early humans living in foraging societies manage to survive?

Simple Tools

Much of the answer to this question lies in the ability of humans to create tools to supplement our rather puny physical capabilities. Although the tools developed in early societies were extremely crude by modern standards, they nevertheless gave human beings a tremendous advantage over all other creatures—none of whom systematically used tools of any kind. *Since the economies of foraging societies were based almost entirely on hunting animals and gathering plants, most of their tools were associated with those activities.* For example, while simple spears have been used by humanlike beings for hundreds of thousands of years, somewhere around 35,000 years ago hunters discovered how to attach bone and stone to their spears to increase their penetration, and they created the spear thrower, which doubles the distance and force with which a spear can be hurled. Even more dramatic was the somewhat later invention of the bow and arrow, which greatly extended the range, speed, and accuracy with which a weapon could be propelled toward an animal (Semenov, 1964). To facilitate gathering and preparing plants, meanwhile, a variety of different tools were created, including stone axes and mattocks, stone and bone knives and scrapers, wood and bone sickles, wooden digging sticks and shovels, stone pestles and grinding slabs, and reed and clay bowls and baskets. Fishing societies, meanwhile, developed hooks, nets, and traps to catch fish. With the invention of bone pins, awls, and needles with eyes, these people were able to sew clothing to fit their bodies. Knowledge of building techniques permitted them to construct shelters, sledges enabled them to move heavy loads, oil lamps gave them light at night, and brushes and mixed pigments were used to draw animal and human figures on cave walls.

As these and many other tools made of stone, bone, wood, clay, and other natural materials were developed and adopted, the tasks of hunting animals, gathering plants, preparing food, building shelters, and making clothing became increasingly easier and more efficient. As a result, the struggle to survive became much less precarious and demanding, so that the members of twentieth-century hunting and gathering societies that have been studied by anthropologists were frequently able to satisfy all of their material requirements with four or five hours of work per day. In short, *the invention and use of tools that facilitate work tasks has been one of the key factors in societal evolution since Homo sapiens sapiens first appeared on earth.* In all foraging societies, nevertheless, the tools used were generally rather crude and inefficient. As a result, these people were rarely able to accumulate much surplus wealth beyond their subsistence requirements.

Environmental Conditions

Despite the advantages of tools, they facilitate survival for hunting and gathering societies only if the natural environment provides sufficient plant and animal resources. These societies have existed in all kinds of environments, ranging from forests to grasslands to deserts, from the slopes of mountains to river valleys, from cold northern climates to hot tropical lands. Some of those environments may have been "Gardens of Eden" that provided bountiful resources of all kinds, but most of them were undoubtedly far from ideal, so that *foraging societies were continually challenged to obtain the food and other resources they needed from the environment.* They also had to cope with environmental crises such as droughts, floods, advancing glaciers, and climatic shifts.

In addition, human beings inevitably affect the environment in which they live. Extensive hunting kills off or drives away game animals, and prolonged gathering activities can seriously deplete plant life. As a consequence, *most foraging societies were necessarily nomadic,* periodically moving from one campsite to another to find new animal and plant life. Depending on the surrounding environmental conditions, these moves might have been as frequent as every few weeks or might only have been necessary every few years. Sometimes the entire community moved together, while at other times it temporarily or permanently split into smaller groups of families that went off in different directions looking for food. Because these were group rather than individual moves, they did not normally disrupt the social bonds among people and families. And since these moves ensured a continuing food supply, they were probably viewed as quite desirable.

Regardless of how frequently they moved, *foraging societies normally restricted their wanderings to relatively small territories,* often no more than about 20 or 30 square miles in area. There were several reasons for this territoriality, including the desire to remain in land that was familiar, to make use of former campsites, and to avoid conflicts with other societies over land rights. In addition, the traditional territory was often viewed as sacred land to which the people felt a strong spiritual attachment. Moving to an entirely new territory would have meant abandoning ancient traditions associated with their land and losing the assistance of the spirits that they believed kept their land fertile and protected them from enemies.

Population Limits

Our knowledge about the populations of foraging societies is derived largely from studies of those groups that survived into the twentieth century, but there is no reason to think that these societies have been much different throughout their existence. Since these societies were totally dependent on whatever food and other resources they could take from their local territory and carry back to their campsite, and since they could rarely accumulate surpluses beyond their immediate consumption needs, *their populations remained quite small.* A typical hunting and gathering community in this century contained between 25 and 50 people, or about 2 or 3 persons per square mile of territory (Birdsell, 1968:235). Since these communities were usually relatively autonomous, *each community constituted a separate society.* If the population of a community/society grew much beyond 50 people, it typically split into two separate communities, each of which would then claim its own separate territory.

Population growth beyond the number of people who could survive within the established territory appears to have been rather infrequent, since birth and death rates tended to remain in balance. Although birth rates were much higher than in modern societies, they were limited by two factors:

(1) Female ovulation tended to be irregular, due to fluctuating food supplies; and
(2) Mothers nursed their children for two or three years after birth, which ususaly prevented too-frequent pregnancies.

In addition, rates of infant and child mortality were usually quite high due to inadequate nutrition and disease. Lack of sufficient food, hunting accidents, diseases, and the physically demanding nature of their existence also took heavy tolls among adults. The average lifespan was therefore probably no more than 35 to 40 years, and few people lived past age 50.

If those natural checks on population growth failed to keep the number of people in balance with the environment, *foraging societies often took intentional actions to limit their population* (Dumond, 1975). Almost all of these societies that have been studied by anthropologists practiced abortion and infanticide at least occasionally. It was also common for elderly or physically handicapped people who could no longer contribute to the continual search for food to leave the camp—

either voluntarily or involuntarily—and go off to die. Those practices do not mean that hunting and gathering societies did not care about their children or old people. Such practices do indicate, however, that these people understood the absolute necessity of keeping their population size in balance with environmental resources if the community as a whole was to survive.

Low Energy Level

The ecological conditions of foraging societies virtually assured that their flows of sociophysical energy would be quite minimal. Even with a variety of hand tools, they were rarely able to obtain any significant amount of surplus food beyond their immediate sustenance needs. Since they had to carry all their possessions with them when they changed campsites, their tools were small and limited in number, and they rarely built any permanent shelters. (The term "cave men" is rather misleading, since they were much more likely to live in huts made of brush or skins, although a dry cave was a welcome shelter in cold weather.) Other kinds of natural resources such as timber or minerals were of little or no use to them, since they lacked both knowledge of how to turn such resources into usable goods and any source of inanimate energy other than fire. In short, *because foraging societies possessed virtually no surplus natural resources and very few nonutilitarian goods, they could not accumulate much economic wealth that might be transformed into social power.* They did sometimes collect attractive stones or shells, but these were valued for their aesthetic qualities, not as symbols of wealth or power.

Every able-bodied member of a foraging society, from young children to surviving elders, normally participated in the essential tasks of either gathering plants or hunting animals. With a tiny population and the continual demands of obtaining enough food, they could not exempt any individuals from sustenance-producing work to engage in more specialized activities on a full-time basis. Consequently, they did not have an extensive division of labor that might constitute a basis for a permanent power structure. This situation, combined with their low level of material resources, meant that the exercise of organized social power was generally quite restricted in these societies.

For all the preceeding reasons, *foraging societies generally functioned with very low levels of sociophysical energy.* They actively used their environment to satisfy their sustenance needs, and were certainly not just passive inhabitants of that environment. However, they did not attempt to change the environment to any great extent. They lived largely at the mercy of the natural environment, but in balance with it.

Subsistence Economy

Hunting and gathering societies operated with a subsistence economy in which virtually all economic activities were directed toward meeting immediate needs (Coon, 1971). Most of the food they killed or gathered was usually eaten within a few days, since preserving it for an extended period was quite difficult. Meat might be dried in summer or frozen in winter, and nuts and tuberous roots might keep for some time, but these were exceptions to the standard practice of direct consumption. The hand tools they made and the clothing they fashioned from animal skins were put to immediate use. And the shelters they constructed were inhabited only as long as they remained at a campsite before moving on in their constant search for food. Depending on the abundance of resources in the environment, these people might live fairly comfortably at times. But at other times— especially during the winter months or periods of drought—they might experience severe hardships or even starvation.

In these subsistence economies, exchanges of goods or services were not economic transactions. Whatever plants were gathered—wild grains, berries, nuts, roots, etc.—usually belonged to the family unit that found them. Small game—such as rabbits, squirrels, and birds—was also eaten by the hunter's family. Meat from larger animals was generally shared with the entire community (after the hunters had first choice of the most desirable parts), since it was difficult to preserve. However, no payment was made for that meat, apart from the expectation that when someone else brought in meat at another time they would also share it. An individual who was especially skilled at making stone tools or sewing skins might make such items for people outside his or her immediate family, which were then given as gifts without payment. Again, there was merely an informal expectation that the recipients would give or do something in return at a later time. As a result, goods and services had no exchange value based on market transactions; their value lay entirely in their functional use to whoever possessed them. Tools, weapons, clothing, and similar items might be "owned" by individuals or families, although many of these societies operated on the principle that ownership lasted only as long as an item was being used. If the last owner of a spear or scrapper was no longer using it, someone else might acquire it simply by making use of it. Land, however, was never privately owned; it belonged collectively to the entire community.

As previously mentioned, *there was very minimal task specialization, or division of labor, in foraging societies.* Children began participating in the search for food as soon as they are able to follow instructions, and at puberty they underwent rites of passage—often elaborate ceremonies—after which they were defined as adults and were expected to carry out adult work roles. A few individuals might perform special roles such as headman, shaman, medicine man, or artist, but these were in addition to their normal activities of bringing in food.

The only kind of task specialization that was clearly defined in hunting and gathering societies was between men's and women's work. Normally, only men and older boys hunted, while women and girls (and boys too young to hunt) were entirely responsible for gathering plants. This division of food-acquiring roles was often so strict that females were not permitted even to touch hunting weapons, while males would not touch plants until they were ready to eat. Rather interestingly, although plants generally constituted a much larger proportion of the total food supply than did meat, hunting was almost always a more highly valued activity than plant gathering. While hunting entailed excitement, skills, challenge, and sometimes danger, plant gathering was viewed as a much more routine, unskilled, and undemanding activity. Even in these very early societies, therefore, women were assigned work tasks that were very arduous but not highly valued, while men performed the more highly skilled and valued work. Other activities were also gender-defined. Women generally prepared the food, made the clothing, and cared for young children, while men made tools, conducted religious ceremonies, produced art, and made war. The only activity that appears to have been commonly shared by men and women was constructing shelters.

Each foraging community/society was largely economically self-sufficient. Consequently, *there was little trade between societies.* When these societies did come into contact, whatever items they exchanged—shells, feathers, stones, etc.—were ususally not for economic purposes. Instead, these were social transactions to express friendship, establish alliances, and obtain marriage partners. The latter function was particularly important, since a society of 30 or 40 people often did not contain enough single persons to provide marriage partners for its young people. Periodically (perhaps every few years) all of the societies within a large area would likely gather together for several days of feasting, contests and games, exchanging news and tales, and arranging marriages.

TRANSITION TO AGRICULTURE

A hunting and gathering economy and its resulting way of life apparently served humanity fairly well, since all societies lived in this manner for hundreds of thousands of years. Nevertheless, when people began to practice simple horticulture, the result was an economic and social revolution that forever transformed human life.

Beginning of Horticulture

Archeological evidence indicates that at least some hunting and gathering people possessed rudimentary knowledge of plant cultivation and intentionally began growing some crops more than 20,000 years ago (Wendorf and others, 1979). For a number of ecological reasons, however, *the practice of horticulture, or gardening, did not become common until roughly 10,000 years ago* (about 8000 B.C.). By then, people had acquired considerable knowledge about collecting seeds from plants, preparing the ground for planting, caring for growing plants, and harvesting crops. For people to begin using that technological knowledge on a sustained basis, they also required a hospitable environment with fertile soil, plenty of water, and a long growing season. Such conditions existed in the Middle East and a few other places at that time, with the result that people in those regions began growing crops year after year on the same land.

The practice of horticulture was undoubtedly spurred by a genetic mutation that apparently occurred among wild grasses about 10,000 years ago. Although the seeds of most wild grasses are edible by humans, they are not very nutritious. For unknown reasons, at about that time some grasses began to produce larger seeds that contained considerably greater amounts of nutrients. This was a period of warming climate, as the remnants of the last ice age retreated to the far North, and this may have facilitated the emergence of the larger seeds. Whatever other factors contributed to this mutation—a change in the sun's radiation, a shift in the earth's tilt, chemical changes in the soil, etc.—remain a mystery. The consequences of the mutation are quite evident in fossilized remains, however. Larger seeds had the dual benefits of (1) facilitating the growth of new plants and (2) providing a more nutritious diet for humans. Consequently, there was a remarkable increase in both the quantity and quality of the crops that early farmers were attempting to grow.

Gardening requires land that is relatively flat, clear, adequately watered, and contains sufficient plant nutrients. Such land is most abundant in the flood plains of rivers that overflow their banks each year and spread a layer of new soil over the land. Consequently, *plant cultivation first developed in the valleys and plains surrounding major rivers*— the Tigris and Euphrates Rivers in what is now Iraq, the Nile in Egypt, the Indus in India, and the Hwang Ho in China. As the practice of growing food crops expanded, however, it was often necessary to clear the land of trees and brush before it could be planted. This was usually done by slashing and burning—cutting down the vegetation and burning it to add the ashes to the soil. Since this soil was not replenished annually by a flood, it typically became depleted after several years of use and had to be abandoned for a number of years until a new growth of natural vegetation had grown back and could again be slashed and burned.

The plow was not invented until sometime in the 4th century B.C. Consequently, for about 5,000 years, all the work of preparing land for planting was done entirely by hand with digging sticks of various designs. In addition to being arduous labor, this technique did not expose much of the soil to the air and sunlight, from which it obtains necessary nutrients, and it did not facilitate the absorption of rainwater. In flood plains, nature largely prepares the soil without much human effort, but elsewhere the preparation was usually quite crude. Depending on the soil, climate, and other factors, slash-and-burn gardeners were sometimes able to rotate among several fields without moving to a new residence, but usually they had to move to new land every few years.

As crops grew more abundant, enough surplus food was produced to feed animals as well as humans. As a result, people began domesticating cattle, sheep, pigs, and other livestock. These animals gave them a dependable supply of meat, milk, and other foods, which meant that it was no longer necessary to hunt wild animals.

The most direct consequence of growing crops and managing livestock was that *these early horticulturists were generally able to establish semi-permanent villages where they lived for a number of years*—and to which they would eventually return after the soil had replenished itself. Consequently, from about 8,000 B.C. to 3,000 B.C., increasing proportions of humanity gradually made the transition from nomadic foraging to semi-settled horticultural societies.

Another fairly obvious consequence of the larger and more stable food supply provided by horticulture was that many more people could be fed and otherwise supported. *Populations therefore increased rapidly.* Horticulture and population growth in turn necessitated more developed forms of social organization.

The Ecological Crisis

New grain seeds, climatic changes, knowledge about planting techniques, and other factors combined to make horticulture possible, but that did not mean that people everywhere immediately abandoned hunting and gathering and settled down to plant crops. Hunting and gathering was the only kind of life that humanity had ever known, and it had served people fairly well. Why should they discard a way of life that was known to provide adequate—if not abundant— resources for survival and adopt an entirely new kind of economy and way of life that was quite unknown and fraught with potential peril?

It is highly unlikely that most hunting-and-gathering people abandoned their traditional way of life and created a totally different kind of economy and society on a purely voluntary basis. *Something had to force the shift to horticulture upon people so imperatively that no real choice was possible.* They had to be faced with a situation in which their very survival depended on making the first fundamental revolution in human existence. What caused this imperative for change?

We have no written records from that time to tell us what happened, since writing was not invented until about 6,000 years ago and was not widely practiced for a long time after that. However, our knowledge of the ecological problems that have occurred in contemporary foraging societies suggests what very likely may have occurred. As argued by several recent writers (e.g., Cohen, 1977) the critical factor was likely population increases. Figure 7-1 diagrams this presumed process, which represents a potentially overwhelming ecological crisis. The figure is divided into upper and lower sections. The top section depicts the en-

abling conditions—discussed in the preceding section—that made possible the emergence of horticulture. The bottom section depicts the imperative conditions—the ecological crisis—that may have pushed humanity from hunting and gathering into horticulture.

We have seen that, over time, foraging societies gradually created new weapons and techniques that considerably improved the efficiency and effectiveness of their hunting. Consequently, they became capable of killing more and larger game animals. With more meat to eat, their populations invariably began to grow. With more people to feed, they had to increase their food supplies even further through more hunting and

FIGURE 7-1 The agricultural revolution

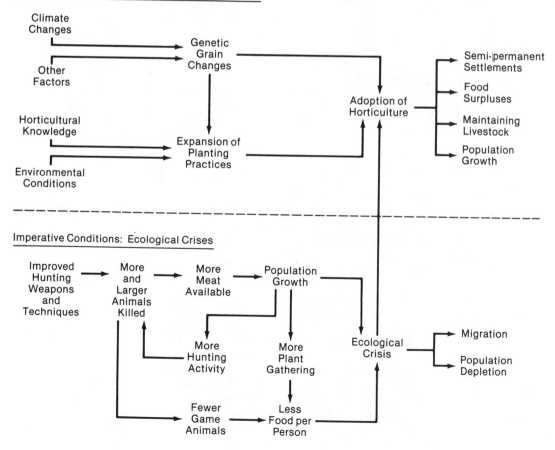

gathering. That, of course, gradually depleted the supply of game animals and edible plants in the surrounding region. Over time, the outcome was that less food could be obtained. *This combination of more people and less food inevitably produces an ecological crisis.*

Foraging societies generally responded to this ecological crisis in either of two ways.

(1) If vacant land was available that contained more animal and plant resources, part or all of the community moved to it. Normally, those moves were of relatively short distance. Sometimes, however, they led to long migrations that might take several hundred or thousands of years to complete. Perhaps the longest of those treks was the slow movement of Asian people more than 15,000 years ago across the then-existing land bridge from Siberia to Alaska, down the west coast of North America and inland for hundreds of miles, through Central America, and eventually clear to the tip of South America.

(2) If no additional land was available, the populations of hunting and gathering communities were reduced through natural processes—malnutrition, disease, starvation, and lower birth rates—until their numbers were again in balance with environmental resources (or sometimes until the entire community/society died off).

By about 10,000 years ago, many regions in the Middle East had become as densely settled as the land could sustain with a hunting and gathering economy. As populations continued to grow, natural food supplies relentlessly shrank as people hunted all available game animals and gathered all available edible plants. They could not migrate elsewhere, since by that time their entire part of the world was occupied by foraging societies. The option of movement was therefore no longer possible. Unless they could find new food supplies, they would experience the natural ecological processes that inevitably reduce surplus populations of all species down to the carrying capacity of the environment. *Horticulture—planting of crops and herding of animals—offered the additional food source they desperately needed.*

It is doubtful if any hunting and gathering people rationally discussed the fact that they were experiencing an ecological crisis and deliberately decided to begin planting crops. Rather, their concern was undoubtedly simply how to adapt to a changing environment to ensure their continued survival. Nevertheless, over time hunting and gathering people did alter their whole economy and way of life. In doing so, *they initiated the agricultural revolution that gradually, but permanently and radically, transformed human existence.*

This fundamental transformation of human societies certainly did not occur all at once. While it began about 10,000 years ago in some locations, elsewhere it was not initiated until several thousand years later, and in a few places foraging societies persisted until the twentieth century. The time at which this transformation began in any particular location was undoubtedly a result of many converging factors, the most important of which was probably the ecological crisis previously described. Moreover, the transformation process undoubtedly occurred quite slowly in most societies, as they gradually reduced their reliance on hunting and gathering and became increasingly dependent on planting and herding.

HORTICULTURAL SOCIETIES

Horticulture is small-scale gardening, or growing plants on a semi-permanent basis using simple hand tools. By necessity, the amount of land cultivated by any one person or family is rather limited. In other words, horticulture is garden farming. Horticulture may also involve keeping small herds of domesticated livestock, and in some of these societies herding is the primary economic activity. Horticultural societies were considerably more settled than foraging communities, but at first most of them still moved occasionally from one location to another to obtain more fertile land.

Horticultural societies first appeared about 10,000 years ago, as we have seen.

Evidence of them dating from that period has been found throughout most of the Old World, but not until sometime later in North and South America. There have probably been thousands of horticultural societies over the centuries, although they began declining in frequency about 5,000 years ago with the introduction of permanently settled agriculture. A number of horticultural societies still exist today, primarily in Africa and Southeast Asia, although all of them are now in the process of shifting to industrial economies.

Horticultural societies have varied widely in their economic development, size, and organizational complexity. At first, they resembled small hunting-and-gathering communities, except that they practiced slash-and-burn gardening in addition to hunting wild animals and gathering wild plants. Later on, as their gardening practices became more advanced, these societies often increased greatly in size and complexity. To indicate such development among horticultural societies, some writers (Lenski and Lenski, 1982) divide them into the two subcategories of simple and advanced horticultural societies. The basis for that distinction is whether or not a society had discovered metallurgy and made metal tools and weapons. Although the discovery of metal had major consequences for these societies—as we shall see more fully in the following chapter—it did not alter their fundamental dependence on a horticulture economy. Moreover, the introduction and use of metal objects was undoubtedly a rather gradual process in most of these societies. For those reasons, it seems most realistic to describe horticultural societies as existing along a continuum from very simple to quite advanced levels of ecological and organizational development.

Technological Knowledge

The shift from hunting and gathering to horticultural economies became possible only after people acquired a considerable body of technical knowledge about soil preparation, weather, seeds, cultivation, harvest-ing, and food preservation. Initially, however, it did not depend on the invention of any new tools. Simple wooden digging sticks, hoes, and similar tools had undoubtedly been used for a long time for digging and gathering wild plants, and they were easily converted to use with cultivated crops. The slash-and-burn method of cleaning fields that was commonly used by early horticultural societies required heavier stone axes for falling trees than had been used previously, but again this was probably a fairly simple matter of enlarging existing hunting axes. In short, *while new technology was extremely crucial for the agricultural revolution, this was knowledge about gardening techniques, not material tools.*

The adoption of plant cultivation sooner or later—but apparently inevitably—led to several other important technological developments in horticultural societies. One of these was clay *pottery.* Hunting and gathering societies frequently made simple bowls and other utensils on a small scale, but they had no need for many of them. And since all their possessions had to be constantly carried about, these utensils were usually light (made of wood or grasses) and small. Farmers, in contrast, needed to be able to store their seeds and harvests for long periods of time. For this, they needed many containers of fairly large size that were waterproof, so that the contents would not spoil or be eaten by animals. Consequently, they developed pottery making to a high level of expertise, which necessitated learning how to make hot fires in kilns to harden the pottery.

Weaving of *fabrics* was another outgrowth of early gardening, although it was not a necessity, such as pottery. Although simple weaving techniques were likely discovered by foraging people as they worked with rushes and other grasses, they rarely had a sufficient supply of fabrics to perfect this craft. With horticulture, however, it became possible to grow plants that provided large amounts of fibers that could be woven. And with the domestication and herding of sheep, wool also became available for fabrics. The principal purpose of weaving, of course, was to produce materials that could be fashioned into clothing. People therefore began wearing cloth garments rather than animal skins, and clothing became a major concern of human beings.

Sometime toward the end of the horticultural era—although we do not know exactly when—the *wheel* was invented. This discovery enabled people to begin building simple hand-pulled carts for transporting goods. The first goods carried on these carts may likely have been the heavy pots and jars containing harvested grains. Since early horticultural societies that practiced slash-and-burn gardening still had to move every few years to a new location, they needed to transport their stored grains, which were too heavy to be carried by hand. Carts enabled them to be mobile, so that when their fields became infertile they were able to move on and begin farming in another location.

By far the most significant technological discovery made by more advanced horticultural societies was *metallurgy*. This is the process of extracting metals from their ores, refining them, and forming them into useful objects. Although stones can be flaked and chipped into many forms, the tools that can be made from them are inherently limited and crude. With metallurgy, it became possible to fashion all kinds of objects with much greater precision than was possible with stone. The first metal to be worked in this manner appears to have been copper, since archeologists have unearthed objects made of copper that are believed to be about 6,000 years old. This is not surprising, since copper ores can be found in exposed rocks without excavation, and the resulting metal can quite easily be formed into all kinds of useful objects. However, a very hot fire is needed to separate the ore and melt the copper. The kilns that had been built for pottery making provided such heat, so it is likely that pottery making was a necessary precondition for metallurgy. The first objects made of copper may have been simple domestic tools, but it probably did not take people long to discover that copper could also be used to make many kinds of weapons such as knives and

spear heads. This had direct consequences for the conduct of warfare, which—as we shall see in the next chapter—greatly altered the activities and organization of more advanced horticultural societies.

Sometime later, advanced horticultural people discovered the process of *alloying metals*, combining tin with copper to produce bronze. Copper is a rather soft metal that is easily dented and does not hold a sharp blade. Bronze is much harder and hence considerably more desirable for all kinds of tools and weapons. As the techniques of metal alloying became known, therefore, copper was largely relegated to the production of ornamental objects, and bronze became the preferred metal for tools and weapons. Recent excavations of burial sites in China over three thousand years old have yielded remains of elaborate bronze armor, spears, knives, swords, hatchets, and other artifacts of warfare.

One additional innovation that first appeared in advanced horticultural societies also deserves mention, although it did not have extensive consequences for societies until much later. This was the creation of *proto-writing*, or the use of simple signs to record information. These signs, often drawn on soft clay tablets, were literal representations of objects and did not constitute an abstract written language. They might, for example, represent a certain number of vessels of grain owned by a particular family. Horticultural people were not literate, however, and written communication played a very minor part in their daily activities.

Environmental Relationships

Horticultural societies were as dependent on environmental conditions as were foraging societies, but in a somewhat different manner. Whereas hunters and gathers were largely at the mercy of whatever food and other resources happened to be available in the surrounding environment, horticulturists began to manipulate that environment for their own purposes. Instead of just taking whatever resources they could find, they produced food through their own efforts. Their ability to do this was of course severely restricted by their limited knowledge of agricultural processes and crude tools. Nevertheless, *horticultural people began to alter the natural environment to satisfy their needs* to a much greater extent than done by hunting and gathering people.

Probably the major environmental limitation experienced by horticultural societies was soil infertility. Unless they happened to be located on the plain of a river that flooded the land and deposited a new layer of rich soil every year, *their simple gardening techniques could easily deplete essential nutrients from the soil within a few years.* When that happened, as already mentioned, they were forced to move on and look for new land. A typical practice among slash-and-burn horticulturists was to have several plots of land among which they rotated in a regular pattern. By the time they returned to a previously used location, it would have become overgrown with wild vegetation that they could again cut down and burn, thus adding a new layer of nutrients to the soil.

Other environmental conditions with which horticulturists had to cope were rainfall (either not enough or too much), climatic variations (either too hot or too cold for their crops), and wild animals (which might eat their crops before they could be harvested). To the extent that they kept domesticated animals, this practice gave them a relatively assured source of milk and meat that was not available to hunters. To keep their animals alive and healthy during the winter, however, they had to grow enough food for them as well as themselves, and they also had to devise ways of keeping them from wandering off or being eaten by wild predators.

Population Size

As a general principle, as the economic productivity of a society increases, so does its population size. *In simple slash-and-burn horticultural societies, productivity was usually not far above the subsistence level, so that their popula-*tions *remained relatively small.* One to two hundred people may have constituted a good-sized village at that stage of development—not greatly larger than a typical foraging community. The high birth rate common in these societies was balanced by an equally high death rate, so that population size remained fairly stable. And since villages were still largely autonomous social units, each community constituted a separate society.

The better tools that could be produced with metallurgy in more advanced horticultural societies, together with their steadily expanding knowledge of agricultural techniques, considerably increased their level of economic productivity. With larger surpluses of food and other resources came population growth. *Advanced horticultural societies often contained several thousand people,* rather than just a few hundred. And rather than all living in one community, these people were likely to be distributed among several medium-sized villages located within close proximity to one another. With that development, societies were no longer limited to single communities, but they began to encompass a number of interlinked villages.

Frequency of migration also influenced population size. If a village had to move every few years because of poor soil or other factors, its population was likely to remain small. In addition to the logistic difficulties of transporting many young children and old people, the irregular food supply associated with frequent migration also tended to restrict population growth. As horticulturists became more skilled and productive, and especially as they discovered simple methods of crop rotation and fertilization with animal and human wastes, they were able to remain for long periods of time in one location. This geographical stability, combined with a more abundant and regular food supply, contributed to steady population growth.

Energy Flows

Sociophysical energy flows within a society are generated by the availability of resources that can be utilized to carry out activities. The primary resource in horticultural societies is, of course, food. Consequently, the larger the abundance of plants grown and animals herded, the greater the potential for generating energy flows that might be transformed into social organization. In simple slash-and-burn horticultural societies, those energy flows often remained at about the same minimal level that was typical of foraging societies. However, *as agricultural productivity increased in horticultural societies, the expanding surplus resources made it possible to begin creating a more diversified economy, as well as other kinds of organizational structures.*

Surplus resources create sociophysical energy flows only when two conditions exist, however. The first necessary condition is that the society's population size must grow more slowly than its available resources. With rapid population growth, the increasing resources are entirely consumed by the additional people, so that surpluses cannot accumulate. For this reason, horticultural societies that grew too rapidly could lose the struggle to remain in balance with the ecosystem in which they lived, and thus experience a declining standard of living. The second condition is that the society must establish some procedure for allocating the surplus resources to various activities and members. This is partially a political process, which meant that advanced horticultural societies had to develop simple political systems, as we shall examine more fully in the next chapter.

Expanding Economy

The most critical feature of horticultural economies was that they gradually progressed beyond the subsistence level. By growing crops and herding animals, these people began to produce relatively stable and dependable economic surpluses above their survival needs. The amount of this surplus varied widely among horticultural societies, depending on the level of their technological development and the quality of the natural environment in which they were located. That surplus ranged from quite minimal in very simple horticultural societies to rather large in the most advanced ones. But regardless of the size of the surplus, *all horticultural societies were fundamentally different from foraging societies, because they controlled the production of their food and other resources and could normally count on living above the subsistence level.*

A society can do several different things with surplus resources. It can increase its population and use all those resources to support the additional people. It can keep its population stable and raise its standard of living by consuming the surplus resources. It can free some of its members from agricultural work to engage in crafts and other activities. It can create new kinds of organizations such as political or religious bodies. It can trade its surpluses with neighboring societies for goods it needs. Or it can make war on its neighbors. Horticultural societies with growing surpluses did all of these things—sometimes singularly, but often in various combinations at different times. The larger the surplus, the more options a society has among those possible courses of action. Hence the more advanced the level of economic development in horticultural societies, the more of those options they were likely to undertake. The fundamental point, nevertheless, is that *expanding surplus resources enable a society to develop in many new directions*—none of which were possible in foraging societies living at the subsistence level.

One of the preceding options that was almost universally chosen by even the simplest horticultural societies was to exempt a few of their members from agricultural work—often on a full-time basis—to engage in such crafts as pottery making, weaving, and metallurgy. Because these craft products were so useful to horticultural societies, craftspeople were encouraged to develop their skills and in exchange were supported by the community's agricultural surplus. Thus the process of *occupational specialization* began in simple horticultural societies.

Along with occupational specialization came further *task specialization based on gen-*

der. Clearing fields and planting seeds were most commonly defined as men's work, while cultivating and otherwise tending the growing plants were usually done by women and children. Depending on the nature of the crop, harvesting might be done by either men or women or both together. Herding of animals was almost always done by men or older boys. Most domestic tasks were assigned to women. Weaving and constructing clothing were also commonly thought of as women's work. Pottery making might be done by either a man or a woman, perhaps with a man handling the hot kiln while a woman shaped the clay into objects. When people began practicing metallurgy, however, this high-status craft was exclusively controlled by men.

Occupational specialization requires the establishment of procedures for exchanging goods and services. In horticultural societies these were *barter exchanges,* not monetary transactions. Nevertheless, they represented the beginnings of markets in which goods and services are exchanged on the basis of negotiations.

Another option often chosen by horticultural societies with surplus resources was *trade with other communities or societies.* Initially, most trade probably involved foodstuffs or animals. If one village had surplus oats and another had extra pigs, they might arrange an exchange that benefited them both. Later, as crafts were developed, those items often became highly desired trade goods. Thus a particularly skillful pottery maker in one village might trade his pots for other craft objects or surplus food from several surrounding communities. Consequently, market processes gradually expanded beyond single communities to encompass much larger areas.

AGRARIAN SOCIETIES

Agriculture is large-scale farming on a permanent basis using complex tools. The transition from gardening to farming occurred very gradually, and at different times in various parts of

the world. The earliest evidence of permanently settled agriculture comes from Mesopotamia and Egypt about 5,000 years ago, or 3000 B.C., and over the following two thousand years it spread throughout most of the Old World. It did not penetrate to sub-Sahara Africa or the New World until much later, however. For the last three thousand years, agriculture has provided the principal economic base of most societies.

Throughout the ages, *agrarian societies have displayed even greater variation in level of development, size, and complexity than occurred within horticultural societies.* Early agrarian societies were probably not greatly different from the advanced horticultural societies from which they evolved. By the sixteenth and seventeenth centuries A.D., however, Western European agrarian nations such as Holland, Spain, and England had become world powers. And at the present time, agrarian societies such as China, India, and Indonesia are among the most populous countries in the world. There is considerable justification, therefore, for dividing countries based on agriculture into the two broad categories of simple and advanced agrarian societies (Lenski and Lenski, 1982). This distinction—as with horticultural societies—is based on developments in metallurgy, although with agrarian societies this was iron smelting. Widespread use of iron tools and weapons created innumerable changes in the organization and functioning of agrarian societies. Nevertheless, the economies of all agrarian societies—no matter how advanced they have become—continue to rest on agriculture. Consequently, it again seems most realistic to treat all of these societies as a single fundamental type that varies tremendously along a continuum of economic and social development.

Technological Advancements

Of all the technological advances that appeared in advanced horticultural societies beginning about 6,000 years ago, by far *the most crucial innovation for the practice of settled agriculture was the invention of the plow.* Because plows turned over the soil to a much greater depth than was possible with hoes, weeds were buried and thus added humus to the ground, and nutrient-rich lower soil was brought to the surface where it could sustain new crops. The plow thus enabled farmers to till the same land on a permanent basis (Farmer, 1968).

The first plows were undoubtedly made entirely of wood and pulled by humans. It apparently did not take the first agriculturalists long to add two further improvements to this technology, however. Bronze blades provided a much sharper and more durable cutting edge to the plowshare, and cattle or oxen were harnassed to the plow to move it much deeper and faster through the ground. Drawings from Egypt made around 2700 B.C. show men handling a metal-bladed plow being pulled by a team of oxen. With that new technique of cultivation, gardeners became farmers.

At about the same time, several other innovations also contributed greatly to agricultural productivity in advanced horticultural and early agrarian societies (Child, 1964). The cattle and oxen that pulled the plows were also hitched to *carts and wagons* to carry harvested crops back to the village or between communities for trade. Since those cattle or oxen were usually kept in stalls, their manure could easily be gathered and spread on the ground as *fertilizer*. Canals and ditches were dug to provide *irrigation* to the fields, so that farmers did not have to depend on intermittent rains or hand-carried buckets of water to keep their crops growing in the heat of the summer. With the development of *sailboats*, large and bulky cargoes of agricultural products could easily be transported long distances by water. And *orchard husbandry* was discovered, so that fruits could be grown as crops in the same manner as grains and vegetables.

Another area of rapid technological advancement during this period around 5,000 years ago was *building construction.* Prior to this time, buildings were made of natural materials such as logs, stones, or skins. Eco-

nomic surpluses resulting from improved agricultural productivity enabled people to begin experimenting with manufactured building products such as cut lumber and clay bricks, and increasingly buildings were made of those materials. Glazing techniques for making rough glass for windows were also invented, as was the arch for spanning wide openings.

Several major nonmaterial technological advancements also began to occur at about this time. The literal drawings of objects that had been used in earlier forms of protowriting became increasingly abstract and stylized, until they bore little or no resemblence to the objects they represented. The eventual outcome was *pictographic writing,* in which arbitrary pictorial symbols stand for objects, actions, and other ideas. Along with that development came *written numbers and simple mathematics,* although the ability to calculate was limited for a long time by lack of the concept of zero. Nevertheless, these people developed *solar calendars* based on observations of the moon and the sun, and could thus keep track of months and years. The earliest known *metal money* also dates from this period, indicating that people were beginning to use money in economic exchanges. It consisted of irregularly sized and shaped bars of bronze or silver, and was probably restricted to major transactions, since all metal was extremely scarce and expensive. Most economic exchanges were still conducted by barter, although in Mesopotamia and Egypt it became common to use specified quantities of barley or wheat as acceptable payment for all debts.

After this relative flurry of technological advancements between roughly 4000 and 2500 B.C., there was a period of more than a thousand years during which humanity made virtually no important technological innovations of which we are aware. Instead, as we will discuss in the following chapter, this was an era of extensive development in social organization, which was made possible by the economic surplus provided by settled agriculture and the other technological advances associated with it.

The next major technological innovation was techniques for *smelting iron,* which were developed around 1500 to 1400 B.C. People had probably known of iron—at least from meteors—for thousands of years, but they had not been able to use it. This requires techniques for extracting iron ore from the ground, separating the iron from the ore in a very hot fire, mixing carbon with it to harden it, and then quenching it in cold water. At first, iron was extremely expensive—five times more expensive than gold and forty times more expensive than silver. Its use was therefore limited largely to the ruling class of Egypt and other dominant societies, who primarily made weapons and decorative items with it. Not until the century between 900 and 800 B.C. did iron smelting processes become developed to the point where iron could be used to make ordinary farming and other tools at affordable prices. During the following few hundred years, iron production and tool manufacturing spread rapidly throughout the Middle East, around the Mediterranean, into Europe, throughout India and Southeast Asia, and into China. This dispersion process did not reach into sub-Saharan African or to the Americas for another 1,500 years, however.

One other notable technological innovation occurred around 1300 B.C. This was the invention of *alphabetic writing* by the Greeks, although it had earlier Semetic origins. In an alphabet, each abstract symbolic identifies only one sound, rather than an entire word. The primary advantage of alphabetic writing over pictorial writing is that it is much easier to learn and use, since all words can be written with various combinations of between 20 and 30 symbols.

During the last thousand or more years of the agrarian era, prior to the industrial revolution in the nineteenth century, technological innovation occurred at an ever-increasing rate. Although it is impossible here even to list all of the major material and nonmaterial technological advancements of that period, we can mention just a few discoveries that had endless ramifications for agrarian societies:

(1) Iron and later steel casting, which enabled these materials to be formed into every imaginable form;

(2) Horse harnesses and later stirrups, which made possible the era of armored knights;

(3) Gunpower, which enabled foot soldiers to defeat knights in battle;

(4) The screw, which had endless applications from augers to windmills;

(5) The magnetic compass, which made possible cross-ocean voyages of discovery and then commerce and conquest;

(6) The clock, so that time could be accurately measured;

(7) The printing press, which eventually enabled everyone to read; and

(8) The steam engine, which led to the industrialization of manufacturing.

As a result of these and countless other technological advancements in all realms of life, advanced eighteenth-century agrarian societies were vastly more complex and highly developed than the simple agrarian societies that began farming with a plow about 5,000 years ago.

Environmental Control

The key to economic success in agrarian societies is learning how to acquire as much control as possible over all aspects of the natural environment relevant to agriculture, in order to increase its productivity. Although many aspects of nature cannot be controlled, agriculturalists have discovered through the ages how to apply technology (both material and nonmaterial) to most phases of farming. These include soil preparation, seed planting, weed and insect control, crop harvesting, storage and transportation of agricultural products, animal breeding and care, and food preparation. With each small improvement in these various agricultural activities, productivity tended to increase and the life of agriculturalists became somewhat more secure.

This process of slowly gaining control over the natural environment does not imply that farmers have ceased being dependent on the environment. Quite the contrary. *Each new development in agricultural techniques tends to increase the interdependence between farmers and environmental processes as they strive to maintain and raise their production of plant and animal products.* Foraging societies simply moved on whenever the environment failed to satisfy all their needs, and horticultural societies could also resort to migration if necessary. Agrarian societies, however, are bound to their land. It is impossible for them to move for four main reasons.

(1) Because their fields are much larger than horticultural gardens, most or all of the nearby arable land is already being cultivated, and there is nowhere else to go.
(2) Their much larger populations cannot all migrate at once.
(3) Their villages, towns, and cities consist of permanent buildings that are not transportable.
(4) Complex economic and political arrangements of land ownership and tenancy cannot easily be altered or disregarded.

Consequently, agriculturalists must farm their land on a permanent basis, learning how to cope with such problems as loss of soil nutrients, drought, flooding, weed growth, plant diseases and pests, loss of livestock, and severe weather. Their gradually expanding knowledge of farming practices enables them to cope more effectively with those environmental problems, so that they live in active interdependence with the natural environment.

Population Growth

One of the most predictable outcomes of increasing economic productivity is population growth. Even the most advanced horticultural societies were usually limited to populations of a few thousand people at most, and their communities typically contained no more than a few hundred persons. In sharp contrast, *early agrarian societies often had populations of several hundred thousand.* And while they continued to contain numerous small villages and towns, they were also able—for the first time in history—to support a few large cities. A number of those cities, mainly in Mesopotamia and Egypt, probably had populations of 50,000 or more people, and one or more of them may have reached the 100,000 level (Hammond, 1972).

As advancements in agricultural technology and techniques continued to be discovered and implemented, the constantly growing surplus of food and other resources enabled the populations of more advanced agrarian societies to expand even further. Egypt, which was the largest of the simpler agrarian societies, probably reached a population of about 15 million around 1500 to 1000 B.C. Somewhat later, the Roman Empire contained at least 70 million people, although that was due more to military conquest than greatly improved agricultural productivity. Cities also continued to grow rapidly, so that Rome at the height of its power may have had close to a million inhabitants, and a number of other Mediterranean and near Eastern cities contained several hundred thousand people for periods of time (Davis, 1955). Today, India has a total population of about 700 million and China's population numbers over a billion. In short, settled agriculture enables the population of a society to become thousands of times larger than was ever possible in horticultural societies. As India and China indicate, however, the population of an agrarian society can grow faster than the food supply, producing a population surplus.

The surprising fact about many agrarian societies in the past is that their populations did not expand even more rapidly than actually occurred. *Birth rates in agrarian societies at all levels of development are typically extremely high,* often reaching 40 births per 1,000 population per year. That birth rate can potentially double the population of a society in a single generation. There are several reasons for these high birth rates, beyond the fact that modern methods of birth control are often unknown.

(1) Families in agrarian societies usually desire many children (especially sons) as a source of labor to help with all the work involved in operating a farm.

(2) With more food available, pregnancies are more likely to result in live births.

(3) Since people become unable to perform many of the tasks of farming as they grow older, they need a number of children to support them in their old age.

(4) Whatever reluctance wives may feel about bearing large numbers of children is ignored because of their subordination to their husbands.

Excessive population growth in agrarian societies is limited not by a low birth rate, but by an almost equally high death rate. These deaths result from several causes.

(1) If the crops fail and adequate reserves have not been stored from previous years, many people may starve to death before the following year's crops became available. Several successive years of bad crops will certainly result in mass famine.

(2) As we shall see in the following chapter, warfare became extremely frequent in more advanced agrarian societies. This resulted in numerous direct deaths from battles—without much knowledge of medicine, most people with serious wounds died—and perhaps even more indirect deaths from crops being ignored or destroyed.

(3) Increasingly complex technology exposes people to more opportunities for accidents, many of which are fatal because of limited safety and medical knowledge.

(4) Until recently, however, disease has probably been the most prevalent cause of death. High population densities almost invariably breed contagious diseases, and when the people know little or nothing about containing them, epidemics can decimate an entire population.

Epidemics have been particularly common in rapidly growing urban communities, where thousands of people are often crowded together in totally unsanitary conditions. Animal and human sewerage often contaminate water and food supplies, and disease-carrying insects breed everywhere. Streams flowing through cities often serve as both sewerage systems and sources of drinking water. And entire families—or several families—often live in one room without any kind of sanitation facilities. By the Middle Ages, urban living conditions had become so unhealthy that the Black Plague, which swept through Europe at the middle of the fourteenth century, killed a third of the population in England and France and half of Italy's population. Two thousand years ago, average life expectancy in Rome was probably no more than 20 years, and in seventeenth-century London, it was still only about 25 years. As late as the first half of the eighteenth century, there were an estimated 500,000 more deaths than live births per year in London. Under these conditions, it is perhaps surprising that the populations of most agrarian societies grew at all.

Energy Diversion

The primary source of surplus resources in agrarian societies is the ability of farmers to produce more food and other agricultural products than they consume. The extent of these surplus resources has varied tremendously among agrarian societies, but has tended to increase through time as these societies developed from relatively simple to relatively advanced forms. *The larger the agricultural surpluses, the greater the flows of sociophysical energy through agrarian societies and the greater their potential for creating more diversified economies and more complex forms of social organization.*

As we saw in the preceding discussion of energy flows in horticultural societies, surplus resources create sociophysical energy only under two conditions. The first of these is that the population of a society must grow more slowly than the available resources. In most agrarian societies, their extremely high death rates have tended to keep population growth below the increases in agricultural productivity. Consequently, the overall trend has been for the volume of sociophysical energy flowing through agrarian societies to expand fairly steadily through time.

The second necessary condition is that the surplus resources being produced in a society must be distributed in some manner throughout the population. Since this is partially a political process, the expanding economic surpluses produced in agrarian societies have necessitated a more-or-less continual growth in the functions and power of their political systems. As a consequence, sociophysical energy flows in agrarian societies—especially those that are more highly developed—are diverted by political elites for their own purposes. In horticultural societies, most of the sociophysical energy flows that resulted from food surpluses tended to remain within the communities where they were generated, and hence were never very far removed from the people who produced them. In agrarian societies, in marked contrast, powerful elites and dominant social classes use a variety of techniques to extract a large proportion—often half or more—of the surplus resources from those who produce them. Consequently, *energy flows are diverted from the contexts in which they are generated, and are taken over by small sets of elites who do not contribute to their creation.* To the extent that elites are successful in doing this, they are able to live lavishly, control political systems, and wage war to whatever magnitude they desire. Meanwhile, the vast bulk of the population that is producing these surpluses receive few of their benefits, so that their level of living is typically no better than in horticultural societies—if not worse.

Simple Agrarian Economies

The economies of relatively simple agrarian societies were somewhat more elaborate than those of advanced horticultural societies, but not fundamentally different from them. However, several economic trends that first appeared in highly developed horticultural societies became more evident in early agricultural societies because their larger economic surpluses provided the resources necessary to pursue new kinds of economic activities.

One of those expanding economic trends was *occupational specialization by a small proportion of the population in handicrafts* such as tool making, carpentry, masonry, weaving, pottery making, and metal working. Although early agrarian households undoubtedly made most of goods they needed themselves, growing surpluses freed a few people in each community to devote part or all of their efforts to skilled crafts. They then exchanged those objects with farmers for the food and other agricultural products they needed. As this form of task specialization increased, the members of agrarian communities became more interdependent on one another.

A second economic trend was *the development of trade in grains and other bulk goods among communities.* A community with an abundance of wheat, for instance, might trade its surplus for another community's excess cattle. These large-volume and long-distance trades were made possible by improved means of transportation, such as horse-drawn wagons and sailing ships. Initially, most of this trade was still conducted through bartering, in which one commodity would be directly exchanged for another. Gradually, however, crude metallic money began to be used as a medium of exchange. These trade arrangements had the consequence of linking communities into interdependent economic networks.

The rise of trade—especially when conducted with money—spurred a third economic trend, the *emergence of merchants operating in markets.* These middlemen purchased surplus goods from farmers and artisans not for their own consumption, but in anticipation of selling them to others at a profit. The merchant role often involved transporting goods from one location to another, but it also required skills in locating potential purchasers and convincing them that they needed or wanted the goods being offered for sale. Merchants must therefore take financial risks, but if they are successful they can make large profits from their work.

This is particularly true if they can generate new demands among people for goods they have not previously possessed. Trade activities by merchants create economic markets that stimulate the flow of goods throughout a society and thus raise its overall level of economic activity.

Although these and related expanding economic trends laid a foundation for eventual major changes in economic systems, *nonagricultural economic activities constituted only a minor part of simple agrarian economies.* The vast majority of the people in those societies spent their lives tending their fields and herds, and were not greatly influenced by specialized artisans, trade agreements, or merchants operating in markets. For the bulk of farmers in early agrarian societies, agricultural and household work continued in much the same manner as it had for centuries.

Advanced Agrarian Economies

When we shift our focus from rather simple to relatively advanced agrarian societies, the economic scene becomes markedly different. In making this abrupt shift, we are ignoring many hundreds of years of gradual economic modifications and transitions during the intervening period. We are also ignoring the fact that societies accomplished this shift at greatly different rates and times. The resulting economic contrasts nevertheless strikingly demonstrate the effects that growing economic surpluses have on societies through time.

Two features of advanced agrarian economic systems are especially crucial for understanding their functioning. The first feature is that these societies no longer contain just a single agricultural economy that may be enriched by a small amount of handicraft production and limited trading. *Advanced agrarian societies contain two distinct, though highly interrelated, economies: a rural economy based on agriculture and an urban economy based on commerce that manipulates the surplus resources produced by the rural sector.* These societies can therefore be described as having a *dual economy,* although the urban component is essentially a parasite on the rural component.

The second feature is that neither of those economies operate on the traditional principle of production-for-use, in which the goods being produced are intended for relatively direct and immediate consumption. *Both of the economies in advanced agrarian societies operate primarily on the principle of production-by-command, in which goods are produced or traded at the commands (and for the benefit) of persons outside the economic system.* These societies can therefore be described as having primarily *command economies.* This is particularly evident in the rural economy, but it also occurs among urban merchants and artisans who are heavily controlled by the dominant noneconomic elites.

The rural agricultural economy constitutes the economic foundation of all advanced agrarian societies. It typically encompasses 80 or 90 percent of the total population, and produces most of the surplus wealth. As a general principle, however, this economy is not controlled by the serfs, tenants, peasants, and other farmers who operate it. Much of the land—which is the ultimate source of wealth and power in these agrarian societies—is owned by a very tiny class of nobles or other elites who typically comprise no more than one or two percent of the society's population. Through this land ownership, plus other financial practices, *the elites effectively control almost the entire rural economy.* And since they usually also dominate the political, military, religious, and educational systems in agrarian societies, these elites are extremely powerful.

The prevailing belief among elites in most advanced agrarian societies is that they are entitled to extract as much wealth from the rural economy as possible, short of totally destroying it. Very often, this has amounted to more than half of all the agricultural goods produced. This expropriation is accomplished in a variety of ways. Many of the people who till the land in these societies are serfs. Serfs are legally bound to the land they farm, and hence to the noble who owns that land. They are not quite slaves, since the noble owns the land to which they are bound, but does not legally own them as persons. Nevertheless, serfs must produce whatever the landowner commands and are obligated to turn over to him whatever portion of those products he demands. A serf is not free to leave the land or to refuse to work, and the noble who owns the land is legally entitled to take whatever actions may be necessary to keep his serfs on the land and working. Tenant farmers are not bound to the land in the same manner, but the rents they pay for the fields they farm are set by the landowners at whatever level they desire. These rents, which are typically expressed as a proportion of the total amount of goods produced by the farmer, are invariably very high. Peasants who own their own plots of land rarely fare much better. The elites usually impose all kinds of exorbitant taxes, fines, obligatory "gift" requirements, tithes, and compulsory labor demands on them.

With such a large proportion of their products taken from them by the landowning elites, *most farmers in advanced agrarian societies throughout history have lived very impoverished lives.* They have typically existed at or barely above the basic subsistence level, living with entire families in a single room; eating mainly bread, cheese, and soup; wearing rags and often having no shoes; and sleeping on piles of straw on the floor. When the crops have failed, large numbers of them have often starved to death. In other words, although the agricultural economies of advanced agrarian societies normally produce much greater surpluses of food and other resources than are ever grown in horticultural or simpler agrarian societies, most of the people in these more highly developed societies have lived at a much lower standard of living than ever before in human history.

One major cause of this condition has been that *the peasants and serfs in advanced agrarian societies typically have few legal or political rights,* and hence are largely at the mercy of the ruling elite class. These elites, meanwhile, have frequently looked upon the peasants and serfs as subhuman creatures whose only reason for being is to work and produce wealth for them. And if the peasants and serfs are not considered to be fully human, they are not entitled to many more rights or privileges than cattle. Throughout history, agrarian peasants and serfs have expressed angry resentment at their condition, contrived to hide part of their harvest and otherwise escape the heavy hand of the tax or rent collector, and staged uprisings and rebellions. All of this has been to no real avail, however. The elites in these societies have always been so powerful that they could easily squelch all attempts by the masses of people to change the economy or other patterns of social organization.

The urban economies of advanced agrarian societies typically produce no more than about 10 or 15 percent of all the wealth created in these societies. Most of that production occurs within two kinds of commercial activities that began expanding in simpler agrarian societies: handicrafts and trade. By this stage of development, however, *occupational specialization among artisans and other urban workers has proliferated extensively,* so that there may be several hundred distinct kinds of jobs within larger cities. Each of these craft trades, moreover, is usually organized as a guild that tightly controls all the work performed within its sphere. In each guild, the artisans are divided into three categories: master craftsmen who have been practicing their skill for many years and now own their own shops; journeymen who work for a master and actually carry out most of the production under his supervision; and apprentices who are older boys and young men who work in the shop for board and lodging while learning the craft. Outside of the crafts, urban dwellers may work in a variety of jobs ranging from innkeeping to street sweeping.

Economic specialization also becomes quite common among cities, regions, and countries, with resulting developments in trade and transportation. The major merchants who conduct these trade activities no longer function as single individuals, but are usually organized as family owned firms or partnerships with considerable capital investment in inventories, warehouses, and ships. Commercial trade thus becomes an established business that may operate over large areas within and between societies, and may even be organized as multinational commercial leagues. These trading firms provide many kinds of jobs, such as cargo handlers, sailors, teamsters, bookkeepers, and clerks. Large-scale commercial trade also gives rise to numerous small retail stores that provide additional jobs for urban dwellers.

Although both artisans and merchants sell their goods within markets, these are not the kind of free competitive markets that exist in the contemporary western world (and in many developing agrarian societies today). They are, rather, largely *command markets in which most of the objects produced by artisans and most of the goods handled by merchants are intended for the dominant elite class.* Since most of the surplus wealth in these societies is controlled by the elites, they largely determine what is produced and sold. A small proportion of those items go out to rural villages to be sold to the peasants, and some of them are bought by urban workers. Apart from the master artisans and the major merchants, however, agrarian societies do not contain the large middle class or the financially stable working class that provide the bulk of consumers in modern societies. Consequently, the urban economies of most advanced agrarian societies are largely dominated by landowning and political elites. This pattern typically continues until the final stages of the agrarian era when the merchants become wealthy and powerful enough to begin controlling markets for their own purposes.

Because the urban economies of advanced agrarian societies are so different from the horticultural and agricultural economies that prevailed throughout the preceding several thousand years, and because the histories of these societies have been written by educated members of the elite classes, we often think of these societies largely in terms of urban artisans, merchants, courts, and churches. This view overlooks the fundamental fact that the urban economies within agrarian societies—again until the final stages of the agrarian era—have been essentially parasites on their underlying rural agricultural economies. Most of the surplus wealth produced in even the most developed agrarian societies comes from the land, and only a very small portion of it is generated by urban artisans and merchants. *The urban economy appears to be much more crucial for the society than it actually is because so much of the agricultural surplus is extracted from the serfs and peasants who produce it and appropriated by the dominant urban elites.* They consume much of that wealth themselves, and funnel the rest of it into the urban economy to support their desires for goods and services. Expressed differently, the rural agricultural economy of an advanced agrarian society is self-sustaining and could function very well—probably even much better—if the urban commercial economy did not exist. In sharp contrast, the urban economy could never exist if the underlying rural economy was destroyed.

SUMMARY

Ecological and political economy evolutionary theory provides a framework for understanding how human societies have evolved over the ages. This perspective emphasizes the fundamental factors of resources, knowledge, population, and sociophysical energy flows, together with economic systems.

Societies use technological knowledge to obtain the resources they need from the surrounding natural and social environments. The size, distribution, and other characteristics of a society's population are influenced by its technological development and its available resources. The flow, distribution, and use of sociophysical energy throughout a society influence its patterns and complexity of organizational development. The economic system of a society provides a crucial link between those ecological factors and the rest of its social organization.

The three fundamental types of preindustrial societies—foraging, horticultural, and agrarian—are defined primarily by the nature of their economies, in combination with their underlying ecological conditions.

Foraging societies possessed only very crude tools that severely limited their ability to obtain food and other resources from the environment. Except in extremely abundant environments, they were forced to be more or less continually nomadic as they searched for edible plants and game animals. Because of their limited resources and nomadic existence, their populations were usually quite small. These ecological conditions resulted in very low amounts of sociophysical energy within hunting and gathering societies, so that most of the time they possessed little or no wealth beyond the basic subsistence level. Virtually, all their economic activities were directed toward meeting immediate needs, and there were generally no economic exchanges within or between communities. There was also almost no task specialization beyond simple divisions of labor based on sex and age.

As techniques of hunting animals and gathering plants improved, populations began to grow, which depleted available food supplies. If that imbalance between people and food was not resolved through either increased migration or natural population depletion, societies had to begin gardening and herding to sustain their populations. Consequently, about 10,000 years ago, people began to grow food crops on a regular basis.

Horticulture is small-scale, semi-permanent, gardening using simple hand tools, and may also include keeping herds of livestock. Initially, the development of horticultural gardening depended primarily on knowledge of planting techniques. Simple horticultural societies did make a number of important technological innovations, however, including pottery making, weaving, and the wheel. About 6,000 years ago, metallurgy was discovered, which enabled these societies to begin making objects of copper, and later of bronze.

Although horticultural societies generally remained in one location for a number of years, their simple gardening techniques tended to depelete soil nutrients. They were then forced to move in search of new fertile lands. In simple slash-and-burn horticultural societies, productivity was usually not far above the subsistence level, so that their populations remained relatively small. As gardening techniques and productivity improved, populations began to number several thousand people. Increased productivity also expanded the amount of sociophysical energy in these societies, which enabled advanced horticultural people to begin creating a more diversified economy.

The most critical feature of the economies of horticultural societies was that they gradually progressed beyond the subsistence level. In addition to enabling their populations to grow, surplus resources led to the beginning of occupational specialization as a few people were freed from farming to develop other skills. That led to the establishment of barter exchanges and some limited trade.

Agrarian societies practice large-scale farming on a permanent basis, using complex tools. Early agrarian societies were not greatly different from advanced horticultural societies, but later advanced agrarian societies became quite highly and complexly organized. The plow, especially when pulled by draft animals, was the principle technological innovation that made possible settled agriculture. Knowledge of fertilizers and irrigation were also important. Later development of techniques for smelting and manufacturing iron greatly facilitated the development of more effective tools and weapons. Cultural innovations such as pictorial and later alphabetic writing, mathematics, calendars, and money were also crucial for agrarian societies.

The greatly increased agricultural productivity that resulted from settled agriculture led to rapid population growth, so that these societies contained hundreds of thousands and eventually millions of people and were able to sustain the first true cities. With extremely high birth rates, agrarian populations would have grown very rapidly if they had not also experienced almost equally high death rates. The larger the agricultural surplus in agrarian societies, the greater the flows of sociophysical energy they contain and the greater their potential for creating complex forms of social organization.

Three important economic developments in earlier agrarian societies were increased occupational specialization in handicrafts, intercommunity trade in agricultural commodities, and the emergence of merchants operating in economic markets. The economies of more advanced agrarian societies become much more complex, containing distinct but interrelated rural and urban economic systems. The rural agricultural economy constitutes the economic foundation of these societies and produces most of their wealth. However, a large proportion of the arable land is usually owned by small numbers of elites, who typically extract as much wealth as possible from the peasants and serfs, who often live very impoverished lives. The urban economy in an agrarian society rests on extensive occupational specialization among artisans and other urban workers, plus commercial activities by larger merchants and small businesspeople. Most of these urban economic activities are oriented toward and highly influenced by the dominant elite class. The economies of advanced agrarian societies can therefore be described as dual command economic systems.

8

SOCIAL ORGANIZATION OF PREINDUSTRIAL SOCIETIES

How did kinship ties influence social life in foraging societies?

What new patterns of social organization appeared in simple horticultural societies?

Why were political and military activities so crucial in transforming the social organization of advanced horticultural societies?

What social trends from advanced horticultural societies became greatly intensified in simple agrarian societies?

In what ways do the ruling class in advanced agrarian societies dominate all aspects of these societies?

FORAGING SOCIETIES

As we saw in the preceding chapter, Homo sapiens sapiens have existed on earth for at least 35,000 years. From the first appearance of our species until about 10,000 years ago, all humans lived in foraging societies, and a few of these societies still exist today. In short, *hunting and gathering has been the prevailing basis of social organization in most human societies*. Given the simple technology and subsistence economic level of most of these societies, what kinds of social ordering and cultural ideas did they create?

There is a common tendency among members of twentieth century industrial societies to view hunters and gatherers as primitive people because of their simple technology and way of life. Unfortunately, that ethnocentric perspective overlooks several vital aspects of foraging societies. Although their way of life was vastly different from ours, it was not necessarily any less desirable or satisfying than contemporary life-

styles. *Their lack of modern technology and complex organizational structures was compensated by other features of their social life.* As discussed in this section, their societies were generally communal and egalitarian, which normally gave all individuals a strong sense of belonging to a meaningful and caring community in which all persons were valued more or less equally. In addition, these people typically enjoyed an extremely rich social life in terms of interpersonal relationships and shared cultural activities such as storytelling, music, rituals, and celebrations. Their collective way of life was therefore far from primitive.

Kinship

Ties of kinship based on marriage and birth were the main links among individuals in all foraging societies, so that kinship was usually the basic organizing principle in these societies. Individuals defined almost all of their relationships with others in terms of kinship, which largely determined how they interacted with every other person. The family was the basic economic unit for hunting and gathering, with the males hunting game and the females (and preadolescent boys) gathering edible plants. Most other kinds of social activities—such as education, religion, collective decision making, and recreation—also took place within the family. *The hunting and gathering family was thus the original all-purpose social unit, and was the core of social organization in foraging societies.*

In daily activities, the *nuclear family* typically acted as a unit in obtaining, preparing, and eating food, in making clothing and other personal possessions, and often—though not always—in sharing a dwelling. Since most of the members of a community were usually related in one way or another, however, the entire community was essentially one *extended family,* and these extended kinship relationships influenced all collective social activities.

Kinship ties promoted the practice of sharing, which was quite prevalent within foraging communities. If a nuclear family was low on food, relatives would usually share whatever was available with them. Child-rearing tasks were also commonly shared among relatives, as was care of the ill or injured. And when the community moved, families commonly helped each other in erecting new shelters. This cooperation was functionally necessary if the community as a whole was to survive, but it was facilitated and legitimated by extended kinship relationships.

The majority of these societies probably had a *patriarchal* form of family organization, in which the oldest male dominated (Service, 1962:61). Polygyny, in which older men have more than one wife, was also fairly common, since hunting accidents tended to result in a shortage of males. Consequently, kinship ties were frequently defined in terms of the dominant males. Nevertheless, since the plant-gathering activities of women provided the bulk of the food supply most of the time, this function gave them a basis for exerting influence within the nuclear family.

And some foraging societies had a matriarchal form of family organization, in which the women were dominant and defined kinship ties.

Community

A typical foraging community consisted of no more than 25 to 50 people, since that was the largest number of persons who could usually be supported by food-gathering activities within a day's walking distance from the settlement. If the population grew larger than that, part of the group would usually split off to find a new area and create a separate community. In special environmental conditions, however, a community might be able to sustain two or three times that number of people—as in the case of a predominantly fishing community located near an abundant supply of marine life.

Each community was self-sufficient economically. The land—and all the food it contained—belonged to the entire community, so that there was no private ownership of land. Food belonged to a particular nuclear family only after it was brought in, and even then it was frequently shared, especially in the case of a large animal that was killed by a hunting party of several men. In some foraging societies, each nuclear family lived in a separate hut made of branches or skins or other natural materials, which was its personal property. In other societies, the entire community lived together in a large cave or a lodge made of logs, so that the dwelling belonged to everyone collectively.

Because each foraging community was economically and politically autonomous, it also constituted a separate society. At the same time, several nearby communities/societies might be loosely linked by kinship and cultural bonds that tied them together as a tribe or clan (Hoebel, 1966). When communities split apart—because of population growth or internal conflict—they continued to share kinship ties and a common culture and language. They might also have a common name for themselves, which often meant simply "the people." Exchanges of adolescents among communities as marriage partners also created kinship and cultural links. Communities/societies sharing these bonds would periodically gather together for a few days—typically once a year—to visit, feast, conduct religious rituals, engage in games, and arrange marriages. Although food and decorative objects were exchanged at these times, these were sociocultural transactions, not economic trade. Nor were these gatherings any kind of political conclave, since each society considered itself an independent political unit.

Government

All of the able-bodied members of a hunting and gathering society had to take part in food-gathering activities if the community was to survive. There were rarely enough surplus resources to exempt anyone from sustenance-obtaining work. Consequently, these societies had no kind of formal government. Because they were so small and closely knit through kinship bonds, *important collective decisions were generally made either through discussion and consensus among all adults in the community, or by an informal council of elders.* Typically consisting of the older (i.e., perhaps over 30) men who were heads of households, these councils also operated largely through extensive discussion and consensus building. "Primitive" societies thus operated in a more completely democratic manner than any subsequent, more complex, societies.

Most (although not all) hunting and gathering societies had a *headman* who conducted council meetings and provided informal leadership for the community on a day-to-day basis. This person—almost invariably one of the older men—was chosen by his peers because he was seen as having special hunting skills, knowledge of community history and traditions, interpersonal abilities in resolving conflicts and building consensus, and wisdom. A strong headman might be able to exert considerable influence over other members of the community, but normally he could not issue authoritative commands to anyone. The fundamental power resource in the community—the ability to provide for one's material needs through hunting and gathering—was possessed more or less equally by all nuclear family units. Consequently, *the headman's influence rested largely on his ability to assist or persuade or inspire others* (Schapera, 1956). And although he might remain in this role for several years, when he failed to fulfill it adequately because of incompetence or advancing age, he would usually be replaced by a new headman. The political/stratification structure that typically existed in foraging societies is illustrated in Figure 8-1.

Stratification

Differences in status among the members of a society can be based on power, possessions, or prestige. We have just seen, however, that no formal power structures existed in foraging societies, and participation in collective decision making was usually shared fairly broadly. Although council members and the headman did exercise informal influence over community activities, their power was severely limited. Thus *power differences provided only a very minimal basis for stratification.*

There was even less basis for inequality based on possessions in these societies. Their simple technology, limited resources, collective ownership of land, sharing practices, and nonmaterial way of life made it virtually impossible for any individual or family unit to acquire many more possessions than anyone else. Individuals might own some hunting weapons, household tools, simple clothing, and a few other items, but everyone else also possessed essentially the same things. And while one person might be more skilled than others at making particular objects such as bows and arrows or pottery, there was no point in amassing more of such items than he or she could use at one time. Moreover, since the community constantly moved about the people had to carry all their possessions on their backs, it was impossible for anyone to accumulate

FIGURE 8-1 Political and stratification structure in foraging societies

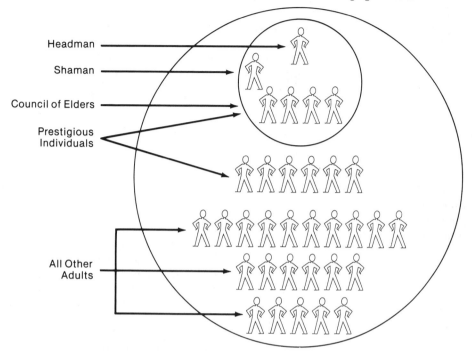

many objects beyond what they used every day.

The only significant basis for inequality in hunting and gathering societies was personal prestige (Lenski, 1966). Most commonly, such prestige resulted from hunting skills among men and homemaking abilities among women, but it might also be based on knowledge of traditional customs, wisdom in decision making, or admired personality characteristics. Because the society contained no formal social structure with designated positions, authority roles, or distinct social classes, there were no organizational barriers—except for age and gender—to a person's attaining whatever prestige was warranted by their actions. Therefore, *foraging societies were typically more egalitarian than any subsequent kind of society.*

Religion

All humans grapple with ultimate questions about the meaning and conduct of life and also with more pragmatic questions about the functioning of both the natural and social worlds. When people lack factual answers to such questions, they are likely to create beliefs that provide suitable answers. Whenever those beliefs involve forces or beings that lie outside the normal realm of existence—in the supernatural—the belief system is viewed as sacred and becomes a religion. All recent hunting and gathering societies have contained relatively elaborate supernatural or sacred belief systems, and presumably this has been true since humans first become capable of thinking abstractly and communicating symbolically.

The exquisite cave paintings of animals that have been discovered around western Europe are believed to be from 20,000 to 30,000 years old. They may have served several purposes, including recording important events or legends, providing a setting for social rituals, expressing aesthetic feelings, or inspiring religious rituals. In addition, clear evidence that these early people believed in some kind of life after death is provided by the numerous graves found throughout Europe that are 20,000 or more years old. The skeletons they contain are frequently adorned with ivory beads, polished shells, and necklaces of bears' teeth. The deceased were unmistakenly being prepared for an afterlife, a very basic religious belief.

The most common type of religion in recent hunting and gathering societies has been animism (Service, 1966:68–70). This is the belief that spirits inhabit all living creatures—plants, animals, and humans—and also many nonliving objects, such as mountains, lakes, or even stones. The spirits are constantly intervening in human affairs, sometimes assisting and sometimes hindering people's activities. One spirit may guide a hunter's arrow that kills a deer, while another spirit causes him to trip over a rock and fall down a cliff. Spirits may heal a wound or bring a fatal disease. Fortunately, however, these spirits can be influenced by humans if they perform the proper chants, rituals, or sacrifices.

Each community typically contained one person who was particularly knowledgeable and skillful in such matters, known as a *shaman* or *medicine man*. When hunters wanted to ask the spirits to give them success, or when a parent needed assistance in caring for a sick child, the shaman was called upon to perform the proper ceremony. As these examples suggest, *the shaman role combined both religious and medical functions*, so that those two realms were thoroughly interwoven in foraging societies. Shamans expected to be compensated for their services through gifts of food or other goods, so that this role represented the earliest form of nonproductive task specialization. And if a shaman felt that he (they were almost always men) had not been adequately compensated or had been harmed by someone, he might use his special influence with the spirits to punish the offender. A shaman could therefore exercise considerable influence over other people.

Social Conflict

Conflict between nuclear families or other groups in the community was minimized by the strong traditional norms that pervaded all social life, by the necessity for cooperation if the community was to survive, and by the practice of talking through differences until consensus was achieved. If a conflict could not be resolved informally, it might be settled through a ritualized contest of skill or chance in which each party to the conflict was represented by one or a few people. Because of their limited resources and precarious existence, these societies could not allow major internal conflicts to remain unresolved for long. If all else failed, the society would likely split into two factions, each going its separate way to create a new community. Serious conflicts between societies, meanwhile, were relatively infrequent, because they had little contact with one another. If one society infringed on the territory of another or failed to fulfill an agreement to exchange young people for marriage, such disputes were usually settled through negotiations conducted by the elders of both communities. Gifts might also be given to appease the community that had been wronged. Occasionally, two societies might engage in highly ritualized warfare accompanied by a great deal of posturing and threats and a brief skirmish. With such small populations, however, they could not afford to lose many people, so that after one or a few individuals were wounded a victor would be declared—often the side that drew "first blood"—and the war would be over. Generally, war was a very minor part of the life of foraging societies.

Leisure

If the natural environment was at all abundant, people in foraging societies could often satisfy all of their physical needs with four or five hours of work a day (Service, 1966:13). They thus had considerable free time for leisure activities. These typically included singing and dancing, artistic activities such as drawing and ornament making, games of chance and skill, religious rituals, feasting, and gossiping with friends. Probably the most important leisure activity among these people was *storytelling* by the elders of the community. Since all hunters and gathers were nonliterate, their entire cultural heritage—important past events, values and norms, legends and myths, family lineages, and religious beliefs—had to be preserved and transmitted through stories and other narratives. Remembering and recounting these tales in complete detail was a highly valued ability, and it was one of the major functions performed by older people, both men and women.

Sociocultural Change

Change was almost nonexistent in foraging societies throughout the thousands of years that they existed. Nineteenth-century hunters and gatherers lived in essentially the same manner as did their ancestors 30,000 years ago. These were highly static societies, for several reasons. They rarely developed new technologies through innovation, and their isolation from other societies prevented much diffusion of new knowledge. Because their populations remained so small, they did not normally have to cope with the problems created by excess people. And as long as their environmental conditions did not shift drastically, there were no external pressures to change their traditional way of life. As we have seen, however, when foraging societies began experiencing severe ecological crises about 10,000 years ago, many of them gradually evolved into horticultural societies or else perished. And in the twentieth century, as new technologies and overwhelming social pressures have been imposed on the last remaining hunting and gathering societies by the outside world, almost all of them have been destroyed or incorporated into modern nations.

SIMPLE HORTICULTURAL SOCIETIES

Relatively simply organized horticultural societies were a transition stage between foraging and large-scale gardening economies. They planted small plots of crops, often herded a few animals, and usually remained in one location for several years. At the same time, they frequently continued to do some hunting of game and gathering of wild fruits and vegetables. Their patterns of social organization displayed numerous continuities from the past, although some new activities were gradually initiated. These early horticultural societies first appeared in the Middle East, and then spread slowly eastward into Asia Minor and eventually to China. In more recent times, they were found primarily in the Pacific islands and in North and South America.

Kinship

The major organizational continuity from a hunting and gathering way of life was the primary importance of kinship in simple horticultural societies. *Kinship links remained the basis of most social organization,* and individuals continued to interact with one another primarily in terms of how they were related. Nevertheless, an important shift slowly occurred in the nature of those kinship bonds. Although the nuclear family still provided the setting for most daily activities, extended family ties became more important as a determinant of social organization.

Clans and tribes based on extensive networks of extended kinship relationships played a major role in simple horticultural societies (Hoebel, 1966). Clans were usually somewhat smaller than tribes and were based largely or entirely on kinship, whereas tribes frequently included some unrelated individuals and two or more kinship groups. Clan and tribe networks commonly extended across several adjacent communities, creating larger organization units than had existed in isolated foraging societies. They performed a number of vital functions for their members, including economic support in hard times and mutual protection against external enemies. They also regulated marriages through intricate rules that defined acceptable sources of spouses and determined the religious beliefs and practices of their members. The clan or tribe to which one belonged was typically the most important social fact in people's lives.

Another feature of families in many of these societies was the *critical economic role of women*. Because women often did most of the work of cultivating the gardens, they controlled a crucial resource for exercising social power. In hunting and gathering societies, power within the family rested largely with the men who did all the hunting. As gardening became the principle economic activity, however, men gradually came to play a subordinate economic role to women. Women typically owned the garden plots and often the dwellings. Men commonly enacted noneconomic religious, political, warfare, ceremonial, and leisure roles that were functionally less important than gardening—although these tended to be higher-status activities than tending gardens. Their only significant economic role was clearing the ground in preparation for planting. Most known matriarchal and matrilineal societies (in which females are relatively powerful and lineage is traced through the maternal line) have had horticultural economies (Schneider and Gough, 1961). In these societies, the women largely ruled the nuclear family, even to the extent that a women's brothers replaced her husband as the social father of her children. Nevertheless, men continued to dominate broader community affairs.

Community and Society

Probably the most striking effect of horticultural gardening on social life was that it made possible, for the first time in human existence, the establishment of *semi-permanent settlements* (Childe, 1964). Communities no longer had to be continually moving about in search of game and wild plants,

since their gardens produced most of the plants they needed, and herding provided them with a relatively stable source of meat and dairy products. They might still have to relocate every few years as the soil lost nutrients through repeated plantings, but these were deliberate moves—often to a familiar location they had left several years ago. And in the Middle East, where simple horticulture first became firmly established, the soil was rich enough that settlements could be inhabited continuously for many generations.

A direct consequence of this settling down was that dwellings and other buildings became larger and more substantial. In the Old World, they were frequently constructed of sun-dried clay blocks (the Middle East) or timber (southern Europe). Instead of being one-room huts, they commonly consisted of several rooms, plus amenities such as courtyards or porches. In addition, these villages sometimes contained collective facilities, such as public squares, religious shrines, stone-paved streets, and protective walls. Buildings in the New World and throughout the Pacific Islands were not usually so elaborate, however.

Early horticultural villages, like foraging communities, were still *largely self-sufficient economically and therefore also constituted relatively autonomous social and political units*. Most social relationships were confined to the local community, and each village was usually self-governing in most matters. Unlike foraging communities, however, each of these horticultural settlements was not necessarily a separate society. The relative permanence of villages frequently enabled people to develop and maintain *loose sociocultural ties with several adjacent settlements* (Lenski, 1966:119–20). These ties were commonly based on clan or tribal affiliation, as well as a common language, cultural heritage, and religion. Communities were sometimes also consolidated by war. A single clan might thus have "branches" in a number of villages located within walking distance of one another. In a sense, therefore, some—though not all—

horticultural societies could be described as multicommunity networks. A more appropriate term for them, however, might be "clan-based alliances."

Government

Politically, simple horticultural societies were generally not markedly different from hunting and gathering communities. There were no formal governmental structures with established offices or laws. Community leadership was provided by a *headman,* even when the social structure was matriarchal. He usually exercised influence informally through persuasion and respect, not by issuing authoritative commands. Because of the greater economic resources available in horticultural societies, however, the headman might be exempted—either part-time or full-time—from farming. In addition, he might have one or more informally designated "lieutenants" who assisted him in overseeing community activities and extended the scope of his influence.

Although the headman might be chosen because of his special knowledge or skills, as in hunting and gathering societies, a more common basis for holding this role was occupying a respected status in the clan network. Consequently, it was easier for the headman role to be passed on from father to son. Moreover, because of the prestige associated with his status within the clan, *a skillful horticultural headman could often exercise considerably more influence than in foraging societies.* There was generally less emphasis, therefore, on reaching collective decisions through discussion and consensus.

As a consequence of the political alliances among villages based on clan or tribal linkages, there was likely to be a *clan or tribal chief* who served as both a symbolic and functional leader of the entire kin network. In matters involving more than one village, the various headmen would be subordinate to that chief in both status and influence and would be guided by his decisions. Figure 8-2 illustrates the political/stratification structure typically found in simple horticultural societies.

Stratification

Because village headmen and tribal chiefs typically exerted considerable influence in early horticultural societies, there was some basis for inequality based on power differentials. Nevertheless, since these leadership roles were not formal positions with authority to issue binding commands, they did not provide a power basis for extensive stratification.

Increasing productivity and semipermanent residence did, however, enable families and individuals to acquire material possessions. The most important possession was land, since garden plots were commonly private property, as were dwellings. People were also able to acquire numerous tools, animals, weapons, household goods, and ornaments. Although the distribution of these items among the members of a community was not grossly unequal, some people came to own more possessions than others. And since those possessions were commonly passed on from one generation to the next within the family, *stratification based on accumulated wealth gradually developed* (Steward and Faron, 1959).

Differences in prestige accorded to individuals, families, and clans still provided the most important basis for inequality, nevertheless. The headman and the shaman usually enjoyed the greatest prestige in a village, while other individuals might be admired because of their skill in oratory, reputation for wisdom, or braveness in battle. In addition, a person's kinship lineage was often quite important.

Warfare

Although it was rare or absent in most foraging societies, *warfare became fairly common in a large majority of simple horticultural societies* (Lenski and Lenski, 1982:156). One likely cause of this development was land ownership. Since the amount and quality of

FIGURE 8-2 Political and stratification structure in simple horticultural societies

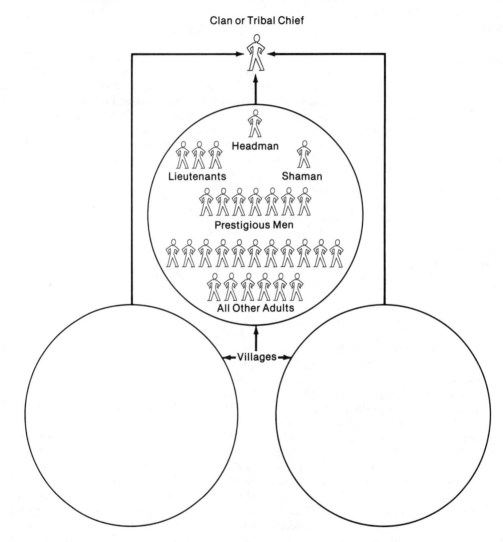

land owned by the members of a village was the primary determinant of its gardening productivity and wealth, villages with less or poorer land than their neighbors were often tempted to wage war to gain more land. Another probable cause was the fact that men were relatively unoccupied in horticultural societies, since most of the gardening was commonly done by the women. Combat gave them something to do, and it offered a sub-stitute for the challenges and rewards that hunting had previously provided.

The practice of frequent warfare had three consequences for these societies. First, it constituted a recognized route through which men might gain *prestige and influence*. Headmen commonly achieved their status through achievements in battle, and other men who demonstrated bravery in battle were greatly respected. As a result, warrior cults were often established. Second, to demonstrate and record their accomplishments in battle, warriors frequently brought home *war trophies* such as prisoners, scalps, or heads. Prisoners might be kept alive for some period of time, but sooner or later they were usually killed in an elaborate ritual. In many New World and Pacific horticultural societies, the body would be roasted and eaten by all the members of the village as ceremonial cannibalism. Heads of enemies killed in war, meanwhile, might be impaled on stakes or shrunken and displayed at the residences of the warriors who had taken these trophies. Third, warfare served as a means of *limiting population growth,* since warring horticultural societies sought to kill as many of their enemies as possible rather than just achieve a symbolic victory on the battlefield. In addition, female infanticide was quite common, which also kept the population in check (Harris, 1974). This practice enabled a society to field the largest possible number of warriors without wasting vital resources on surplus females.

Religion

Animism continued to prevail in many early horticultural societies, in which spirits were thought to dwell in all important objects and creatures. Since the livelihood of these people depended on the success of their gardening, they were particularly likely to be concerned about spirits associated with the soil, the weather, seeds, and their crops. And given the importance of warfare in their lives, they were also concerned about the spirits that inhabited their weapons. Elaborate rituals and ceremonies lasting several days were frequently conducted to influence the appropriate spirits when crops were being planted or warfare was imminent.

At the same time, a new kind of religious belief was gradually grafted onto animism. As clans and tribes based on extended kinship linkages became increasingly prevalent forms of social organization, and as one's lineage became a major determinant of one's social status, people often became highly preoccupied with their ancestors. Each clan or tribe created lengthy and elaborate narratives—usually part fact and part fiction—about its important ancestors. These tales were remembered and related by the elders, especially on ceremonial occasions, in order to preserve the cultural heritage of the community. Over time, the deeds of ancient ancestors tended to become so magnified that these people acquired a sacred image. They were then worshiped as well as remembered, which gave rise to cults of *ancestor worship*. Rituals were performed in their honor, and sacrifices were made to them. Worship of ancestors did not replace animism in most cases, but added another dimension to the religious beliefs and practices of horticultural societies.

With the advent of ancestor worship, shamans gained a second religious function. In addition to knowing the secrets for influencing living spirits, they also conducted the rituals that honored revered ancestors. *Shamans thus became increasingly powerful in guiding the affairs of the community*. In some of these societies, the shaman also served as the headman of the community or as chief of the entire clan or tribe, which made him quite powerful. In other societies, secular headmen took over the role of shaman in order to strengthen their influence. Consequently, religious and political leadership were closely linked or completely integrated in simple horticultural societies (Lowie, 1948).

Sociocultural Change

Change was not entirely absent within simple horticultural societies. They had, after all, undergone a profound shift from a hunting and gathering to a gardening economy. This new way of life posed numerous problems to be coped with, such as bad weather, poor yields, stray livestock, and food shortages. Relatively permanent settlements, extended kinship linkages, and other features of their mode of living also posed new challenges. To some extent, therefore, these people had to be innovative and develop new technologies and patterns of social organization. Nevertheless, *the rate of innovation and change was glacially slow.* Even a simple new tool, such as an improved digging stick, might require decades to be widely adopted. And the rate of sociocultural change was often much slower. Traditional ways of acting and thinking were extremely ingrained and powerful, and they posed formidable barriers to all innovation. When changes did occur, therefore, they were usually necessitated by a crisis—ecological, economic, political, or war—rather than by any intentional effort to improve social life.

ADVANCED HORTICULTURAL SOCIETIES

As discussed in the preceding chapter, the concepts of simple and advanced horticultural societies refer to the contrasting poles of a continuum of societal development, not to two distinct kinds of societies. Some authors (Lenski and Lenski, 1982) use the discovery of metallurgy—first copper, and later bronze—as a dividing point between the simple and advanced ends of this continuum, but that was only one of several kinds of development that occurred in horticultural societies over time. There were also numerous major changes in patterns of social organization within these societies as they evolved.

This section focuses on those aspects of social organization that most sharply differentiated more advanced horticultural societies from their earlier predecessors described in the previous section. Although several of these social developments were quite profound, all horticultural societies nevertheless shared the common ecological/economic base of gardening. Consequently, *all of the social organizational developments that occurred in more advanced horticultural societies were direct or indirect outgrowths of improvements in gardening practices that gradually increased* the level of productivity and provided an increasing supply of surplus resources.

Kinship and Community

Kinship ties—within both the nuclear and the extended family—continued to be quite important in more advanced horticultural society. Nevertheless, one of the most fundamental changes that differentiated these societies from simpler horticultural societies was that *kinship was no longer the primary basis of social organization.* Three other forms of social organization became increasingly important in advanced horticultural societies and were gradually superimposed on top of immediate kinship and extended clan and tribal bonds. The first of these organizational forms was communities with a distinct economic base. The second form was politically organized societies, and the third form was two-class stratification systems. Community organization is discussed in this section, while the other two forms are examined in subsequent sections.

Many communities in advanced horticultural societies were much larger than had ever before existed, often containing from several hundred to a few thousand residents (Lenski and Lenski, 1982:91). This growth in the size of communities was a direct consequence of the increasing productivity of horticultural gardening, which enabled more and more people—although still a small minority of the total population—to engage in other kinds of work. And for the same reason, these societies typically contained many more towns than could ever be supported in simpler horticultural societies. Although advanced horticultural societies were in no sense highly urbanized, town living became an established way of life for a portion of their population.

Although many town dwellers undoubtedly continued to plant gardens in plots of land within or immediately outside the community and to keep livestock, some of them were full-time craftsmen. Although occupational specialization had been quite limited in simpler horticultural societies, it now became an important feature of the urban economy. Examples of craft specialties that were fairly widespread in many of these societies included metalworking, weaving, basket making, leather working, pottery making, and building construction (Lenski and Lenski, 1982:94). However, almost all of these specialized craft workers were men, since women's work was still confined largely to the garden and the home. Another urban occupation that grew in importance was trading, both within and between communities.

As considerable numbers of people settled in towns and became craftsmen and traders, these communities could no longer be organized entirely around clan or tribal relationships. Those organizational forms continued to be extremely important in rural areas and small villages, and they were normally also carried into larger towns. At the same time, those towns also contained numerous people who shared no clan or tribal bonds. *Community organization was increasingly built around economic interdependencies among households rather than kinship ties.* As a direct consequence, marriage came to be viewed as primarily an economic bond between families. Marriageable daughters were considered valuable property for whom a "bride price" must be paid in goods or services.

To ensure that economic relationships among households functioned smoothly, towns also had to establish more elaborate governments. These were typically semiformal in nature, since political leadership roles were often full-time occupations for several people within the community, although most of their power still rested on informal influence rather than formal authority. The town headman often had several subordinates who assisted him in overseeing community activities, resolving conflicts, and carrying out other governmental functions.

Government and Warfare

In more advanced horticultural societies, communities were rarely autonomous. All of the villages and towns within a geographic region were usually tied into a larger political system that constituted a moderately unified society. *Politically organized societies were a second new form of social organization that emerged in advanced horticultural societies* (Service, 1975). The process through which these societies developed is often called state-building, although the resulting societal political systems were rarely as complex or strong as the more highly developed states that were created in agrarian societies.

The populations and geographical sizes of these politically organized societies varied greatly. In some cases, they comprised only a few thousand people located within less than a hundred miles of each other. At the opposite extreme, some advanced horticultural societies in Africa and South America were large empires containing tens of thousands of people spread over several hundred miles.

The political systems that united these societies were hierarchical in structure, and they sometimes contained three or four separate levels of government. Several nearby communities might be linked together under a clan or tribal chief, as in simple horticultural societies, but he was then often subordinate to a higher-level societal ruler. Larger kingdoms or empires might also establish an intermediate level of government between the tribal chief and the ruling king or emperor. The political ruler of an entire society was often the chief of its dominant tribe, or he might have risen to power through military conquest.

Since there were no formal limits on the power of the societal ruler, his influence could pervade not only the entire political system, but also the military, the economy, and the religion. In practice, however, there were usually many limitations on the exercise of that influence. These included the necessity of keeping the peasants working and adequately satisfied; the difficulty of locating and expropriating surplus resources; the demands of keeping subordinate political officials committed to his regime, which meant that he had to share some power with them; enormous difficulties of communication and transportation over any distances; the continual requirements of resources to maintain military forces; frequent conflicts with his own kin and other nobility; and the fact that the political system was quite loosely organized, so that local officials retained considerable political autonomy.

To administer his kingdom or empire, the ruler frequently assembled a set of retainers who were personally committed to him. To ensure their total loyalty to the ruler, they could not be recruited from established clans or tribes to which they owed allegiance. Most commonly, therefore, they were individuals who had been expelled from their kinship networks for misconduct, who had lost their kin ties through warfare or natural disasters, or who were members of ethnic minorities. In other words, this process of creating a political state on top of the established kinship structure was carried out largely by people without strong kinship ties who could devote themselves to creating an entirely new form of sociopolitical organization (Mair, 1962).

Warfare, as we have seen, was fairly prevalent in simple horticultural societies. However, *as these societies became more highly developed, so did their propensity to make war*. To the extent that societies produced surplus resources, two conditions became obvious to them.

(1) They could afford to expend some of those resources (including surplus population) in war without threatening the survival of the society.
(2) Taking additional resources from another society could be much faster and simpler than producing them gradually through the hard work of gardening.

In short, conquering other people appeared to be much easier than conquering nature.

Growing surpluses of economic and population resources was one of the two key developments that made possible extensive warfare among advanced agrarian societies. The other crucial factor was metal weapons, first made of bronze, and later of iron. As expressed by Lenski and Lenski (1982:145), "One might say that bronze was to the conquest of people what plant cultivation was to the conquest of nature. Both were decisive turning points." As mentioned in the previous chapter, advanced horticultural societies produced metal spearheads, axes, knives, hatchets, and bows, as well as personal armor such as helmets, shields, and metal-plated chariots. An army equipped with such formidable offensive and defensive weapons could easily overpower soldiers using cruder weapons.

The process of state-building, or creating societal political systems, was closely linked with warfare (Mair, 1962). Previously independent clans and tribes were not likely to submit voluntarily to the dictates of a would-be political ruler. By and large, these larger political systems were formed through warfare, as a militarily strong tribe conquered and subjugated weaker kinship networks. Moreover, a few military successes were often sufficient to set in motion a cumulative process of power accumulation. The leaders of a victorious tribe instantaneously acquired four significant conquests:

(1) Land already under cultivation;
(2) Weapons, stored food, and other material resources;
(3) Servants, slaves, retainers and craftsmen, and
(4) Women to produce additional warriors.

In addition, political leaders who were successful in warfare acquired a reputation for exercising preponderant military and political power. This frequently led less powerful communities, tribes, and societies to place themselves "voluntarily" under the protection of the dominant society's protection to avoid being decimated by it or some other invader. When this occurred, the subordinated unit was often allowed to retain its land and local leaders, in return for payment of tribute to the dominant ruler, which further increased the ruler's wealth and power. In peaceful times, that tribute largely consisted of agricultural products, but in time of war it might also have included warriors to serve the king or emperor.

As might be expected during times when political systems were being forged and constantly challenged by warfare, *the governments of advanced horticultural societies were often quite unstable.* Although large-scale political systems could be knit together through success in battle, defeat often resulted in the destruction of those systems. When that occurred, the land and communities of the defeated society were taken over by the victorious leader and incorporated into his kingdom or empire—at least until the next war. Another common source of political instability was internal political revolt, either in outlying areas or within the ruling government. These were rarely mass revolts by the ordinary people, however. Most revolts were instigated by members of the ruler's own family—often his brothers or other immediate kin—who coveted his power and believed that the easiest way of acquiring it was to kill him and take over his role as ruler of the society.

The considerably more complex governmental and stratification structure that characterized advanced horticultural societies is illustrated in Figure 8-3.

Stratification

Distinct social classes was a third new form of social organization established in advanced horticultural societies. This stratification system was not complex by modern standards, since it usually consisted of only two classes — the rulers and the ordinary people—but the differences between these classes were often enormous (Davidson, 1966; Hsu, 1965). This stratification system was directly related to the creation of political states, so that the more highly organized and powerful the political system, the greater the social inequality.

The ruling class consisted of the societal ruler, his lieutenants and retainers, the subordinate clan and tribal chiefs, descendants of past rulers, elite warriors, and priests. This political-military aristocracy usually constituted no more than one or two percent of the total population of the society, but it controlled much of the surplus wealth and virtually all of the political and military power. Through techniques ranging from conquest and expropriation to taxes and religious offerings, the dominant class generally managed to acquire a considerable proportion of the agricultural goods and other economic resources produced within the society. It used this wealth for several purposes, including political administration, warfare, construction of public buildings and private residences, feasts and other elaborate celebrations, and ensuring itself a comfortable lifestyle. *Membership in the ruling class was normally determined almost entirely by heredity, so that ordinary people had no opportunity to join it.* Assignments of individuals to political and military leadership roles were based on kinship ties, not personal ability, to ensure that the boundaries of the dominant class remained closed to all outsiders. These elites usually lived in the largest towns, which further contributed to urban growth. These towns—or the portions of them where the elite lived—were often surrounded by walls or other barriers that were built partly for military protection and partly to symbolize their status in society.

The mass of ordinary people, meanwhile, went about their usual routines of planting and tending gardens, herding livestock, managing households, practicing crafts, and engaging in trading. They were not normally serfs, since they were not bound to the land or to a particular noble family, as occurred in later agrarian societies, but most of them were peasants. That is, *the material level of living of most ordinary people was not far above the subsistence level,* since a great deal of whatever surplus wealth they produced ended up in the hands of the ruling class. They did all of the work necessary to keep the society functioning, since the members of the ruling class did no productive labor. Town-dwelling craftsmen often did manage to live somewhat more comfortably, however, since much of their output was bought by the dominant class. The rulers depended on

FIGURE 8-3 Governmental and stratification structure in advanced horticultural societies

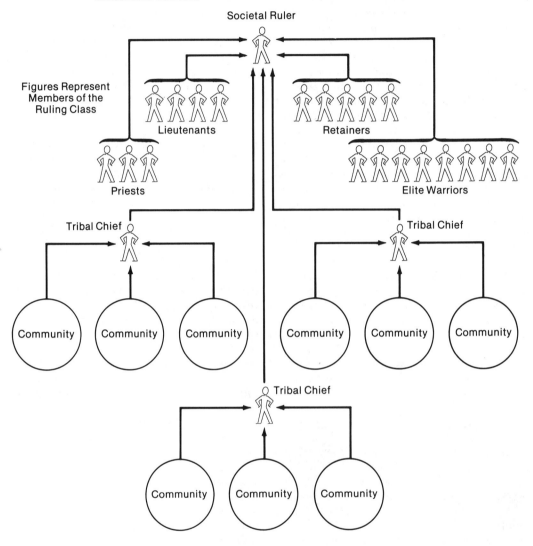

these craftsmen for most of the goods they consumed, from military weapons to household furnishings, so that the craft shops were assured of steady customers.

Some advanced horticultural societies also contained a slave class located below the common people. Slaves were usually war captives who served the members of the dominant class and were permitted to live only as long as they were useful to the rulers.

When they were no longer useful or became too numerous, they were usually killed in public rituals, games, or religious ceremonies.

Religion

Religion and politics were thoroughly interwoven in most advanced horticultural societies. Earlier forms of animism were largely replaced by more elaborate religious belief systems centering on worship of ancestors and kings and emperers. Religion was an important aspect of most people's lives, but *all religious activities and ceremonies were controlled by the ruling class.* The rulers either appointed priests to operate the church or acted as priests themselves, so that church and state became essentially a single entity. In some societies, the ruler was considered to be divine or at least to have direct access to divine powers (Murdock, 1985; Watson, 1961).

To emphasize and enhance the role of religion in advanced horticultural societies, their rulers often built elaborate temples and religious centers. These monuments also served, of course, to increase the prestige and legitimacy of the political/religious leaders.

Because of this interweaving of religion with politics, rebellion by ordinary people against their rulers—or even questioning their power—was inconceivable. Any proposed change in the political system was viewed as heretical, or blasphemy against the divine, and would quickly be suppressed—usually by death. This religious mantle of the ruler did not protect him against overthrow by his kin, however. The entire heredity-based ruling class shared this special religious status, so that all (male) members of it were viewed by the public as religiously qualified to control the political system—if they could seize it from the current ruler.

Sociocultural Change

Perhaps the most remarkable overall feature of advanced horticultural societies was the extent of change that they experienced. The rate of change was still extremely slow by contemporary standards, so that most inhabitants of these societies were probably entirely unaware that any changes were occurring. From an historical perspective, nevertheless, *these societies underwent a remarkable process of social transformation.* Patterns of social organization in simpler horticultural societies were not greatly different from those that had existed for thousands of years in foraging societies. In advanced horticultural societies, in contrast, expanding economic surpluses and metal tools and weapons enabled people to alter fundamentally and permanently several basic patterns of social organization. The primary forces producing these changes were political and military, and to a large extent they were forced upon the masses of ordinary people by their leaders. Nevertheless, these societies initiated processes of organizational development that have continued into the present.

SIMPLE AGRARIAN SOCIETIES

Even the most simply organized agrarian societies were fundamentally different from horticultural societies in their ecological/economic base. Invention of the plow, improved agricultural practices, and the many other technological innovations that occurred in these societies gave them an economy that was considerably more productive than horticultural gardening. Their expanding supply of surplus resources ensured that eventually these settled agrarian societies would far surpass all horticultural societies in the complexity of their organizational patterns.

Those new developments appeared very slowly, however. *Most of the creative efforts of simple agrarian societies went into gradually establishing a superior ecological/economic base, not to creating new organizational structures.* Consequently, all of the fundamental organizational developments described in the preceding discussion of advanced horticultural societies continued into the early stages of the agrarian era with only minor modifications. For the most part, simple agrarian societies simply intensified and expanded those earlier patterns. Most of the significant modifications in social organization that characterized agrarian societies came later, after the ecological/economic base of permanent agriculture was fully established.

A basic principle of the process of societal

evolution should be evident at this point. *So-cieties do not usually make major changes in both their ecological/economic and their social organizational patterns at the same time. Instead, this process has tended to progress through alternate stages.* For some time after a major technological breakthrough has occurred that fundamentally alters the manner in which societies relate to their ecological environment, most of their efforts focus on the application of that technology to economic activities, in order to increase productivity and support a growing population. Only after the amount and stability of their economic resources have greatly expanded do they begin to transform those resources into new organizational forms. They then enter a period—often rather prolonged—during which the ecological/economic base remains essentially unchanged but the extent of social organizational change is quite far-reaching.

More specifically, simple horticultural societies established a radically new ecological/economic base that was no longer dependent on hunting and gathering, but their organizational patterns continued to center on traditional kinship bonds. Advanced horticultural societies retained that gardening economy, but created several crucial new forms of social organization. Simple agrarian societies then transformed hand gardening into much more productive large-scale agriculture, but they retained most of the organizational patterns of advanced horticultural societies. In advanced agrarian societies—which will be described in the following section—organizational change again came to dominate social life.

Because the social organization of early agrarian societies was typically quite similar to that of advanced horticultural societies, this section focuses on just four realms of social life in which previous social trends were intensified. These were government, warfare, stratification, and religion. Much of our knowledge of this kind of society comes from Mesopotamia and Egypt during the period from roughly 3000 B.C. to 1000 B.C.

Government

Those early agrarian societies were considerably larger than any horticultural society in terms of both population and territory. Politically, they were commonly organized as empires in which the central society ruled vast surrounding areas. *The governments of those societies were usually highly centralized in a single ruler who was all powerful and totally autocratic, plus a small ruling class that served and supported the supreme ruler.* In one sense, this was merely a continuation of the process of state-building that began in advanced horticultural societies, in which the political state came to dominate all the communities and clan or tribal units within its boundaries.

In another sense, however, the governments of simple agrarian societies were considerably more developed than earlier political systems. In these large and far-flung empires, the supreme ruler could no longer control the government through his own decisions and actions. If the government was to rule effectively, it had to become more formalized in two important ways: establish complex administrative structures and create legal systems.

As the administrative problems and tasks of these governments continually multiplied, *rulers found it increasingly necessary to establish formal administrative structures comprised of numerous officials, subordinate rulers, and scribes* (McNeill, 1963). In his immediate court, the ruler appointed large staffs with specified responsibilities for operating the royal household and various branches of government. These persons were usually selected on the basis of their demonstrated loyalty to the ruler rather than on any objective criteria of competence, and they were commonly his relatives or personal friends. To ensure their continued loyalty, they were paid directly from the immense royal coffers and were expected to carry out the dictates of the ruler without question. Consequently, these administrative courts were not bureaucracies in the modern sense of organizations that function impersonally on the basis of detailed procedural rules.

To maintain control over his vast empire, the supreme ruler also had to appoint subordinate rulers in the outlying areas, each of whom also appointed his own administrative staff. These subordinate rulers were expected to follow and enforce the dictates of the emperor or king, and they could be replaced if they failed to do so. Nevertheless, because of extremely limited communication and transportation capabilities, the local rulers generally enjoyed considerable autonomy in running their district or region however they pleased. As long as they defended their territory against external treats, maintained internal order, and kept sufficient wealth flowing into the royal treasury, the king or emperor was usually content to leave them largely alone.

To maintain adequate administrative records, both the supreme and local rulers began employing full-time scribes whose services were greatly in demand (Childe, 1964). Writing was a highly skilled craft at that time, since early systems of pictorial writing—such as cuneiform or hieroglyphic scripts—contained hundreds of different characters that had to be carefully memorized and precisely drawn. Because only the male members of the ruling class were literate, most scribes were younger sons of the nobility who had no hope of inheriting their fathers' titles or lands. Their limited numbers and the political importance of their skills nevertheless ensured that they would remain at least marginal members of the ruling class.

As a direct outgrowth of the establishment of vast political empires controlled by a hierarchy of officials and subordinate rulers, *kings and emperors also found it necessary to begin creating standardized laws and legal systems.* In simpler types of societies, headmen or chiefs typically made decisions and issued proclamations on an ad hoc basis as the need arose and then enforced those rules through direct sanctions. As a result, each community or local area contained its own unique set of regulations. Centralized political rulers seeking to maintain control over vast areas could not tolerate such legal diversity, however. To establish some degree of legal uniformity throughout their realm, they began issuing sets of relatively systematic and codified laws with prescribed penalties for violations. The most famous of these was the Code of Hammurabi, formulated by the most powerful emperor of Babylonia during the second millenium.

By modern standards, these first formal legal systems were not very elaborate in scope or uniform in application. Nevertheless, they were a critical advancement in the development of legal systems, and they performed several crucial functions. For the king or emperor, they ensured that all subordinate rulers operated within a common legal framework, which greatly enhanced his control over them. For those local rulers, a standardized legal system enabled them to ignore or abolish local customs and traditions of justice and demand that everyone obey the royal edicts. They had to do this to establish and enforce their rule, since they were not usually natives of the areas they ruled. For scribes, the task of recording and disseminating these legal codes greatly enhanced their functional necessity and social status, and it also made writing an increasingly important component of social organization.

Warfare

Warfare was a frequent—and sometimes almost perpetual—activity among advanced horticultural societies, and that practice continued in early agrarian societies. The nature of warfare changed in two important ways with the emergence of agrarian empires, however.

The first change was in the composition and organization of armies. In horticultural societies, all able-bodied males were expected to be warriors and to participate in wars whenever they occurred. The army of a society was therefore a loosely organized militia of volunteers for whom fighting was only a part-time activity. In contrast, *agrarian kings and emperors needed a standing full-time army to fight for the state against other societies and to maintain internal order* (Turner, 1941). Consequently, just as political administration became more formally and hierarchically organized, so did armies. Volunteer militia were replaced by permanent, trained armies that were tightly organized under the command of the rulers. And just as administrative officials and subrulers owed personal allegiance to the supreme ruler, so did the military forces. In other words, these were not national armies that defended their society, but rather royal armies that served the emperor or king. They were supplied and paid from the personal treasury of the supreme ruler, directly commanded by him or his immediate subordinates, and fought for whatever purposes he wished.

The second change was in the purpose for engaging in warfare. In horticultural societies, battles were fought primarily to defend the society against external enemies or rebellious clans or tribes within the society. In agrarian societies, in contrast, *kings and emperors frequently initiated wars to acquire more territory, resources, or slaves, so as to increase and consolidate their power and wealth.* War thus became highly politicized and served primarily the interests of the supreme ruler rather than the society as a whole. Indeed, these empires were largely created and maintained through military force. The "cult of the warrior," which had been so important to most men in horticultural societies, was no longer appealing to anyone other than professional soldiers, now that large-scale farming demanded all of the efforts of most peasants. They could not, however, avoid paying for the "king's wars," since he obtained most of the necessary resources for his permanent army by extracting them from the peasants.

Stratification

Distinct social classes—and thus organized stratification systems—first appeared in advanced horticultural societies and continued into simple agrarian societies. As discussed previously, this was basically a two-class system, composed of a tiny ruling class and the mass of ordinary farmers, peasants, artisans, and other workers—although in some societies there was also a slave class. In horticultural societies, the ruling class enjoyed considerably more power, wealth, and prestige than ordinary people, and those class differences became even more pronounced in early agrarian societies. In addition, the elites in these societies were strictly urban dwellers. The structure of the ruling class in simple agrarian societies is shown in Figure 8-4.

Whereas the two classes in horticultural societies continued to share essentially a common culture, *in agrarian societies the ruling class gradually created a distinct subculture that was not shared by the masses* (Turner, 1941). Because most male members of the elite class were at least semiliterate, they began developing the rudiments of abstract knowledge that define "civilization". This knowledge included ideas about philosophy, science, history, literature, and art—as well as more practical technological and administrative information.

As a consequence, the elites came to view themselves as intellectually and morally superior beings. While they were concerned about the "better" and "finer" things in life, ordinary people were seen as little more than ignorant brutes. There was undoubtedly some validity to this view, since most peasants were not only illiterate but also extremely limited in knowledge and parochial in outlook. They usually knew nothing about abstract ideas or ways of life beyond their immediate circle of acquaintances, and their lives were totally dominated by traditional belief systems. The result of this cultural bifurcation between the two classes was that elites came to view the masses of people as subhuman. In their eyes, this justified their practice of expropriating as many surplus resources as possible from the peasants and leaving them to survive at a bare subsistence level.

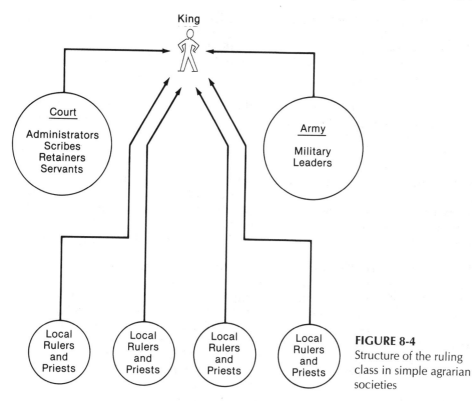

FIGURE 8-4
Structure of the ruling class in simple agrarian societies

Religion

In advanced horticultural societies, religion was often a mixture of ancestor worship and reverence for current rulers. In early agrarian societies, ancestors were gradually forgotten in favor of multiple dieties who were seen as controlling everything that occurred. Mesopotamia and Egypt created two contrasting kinds of polytheistic religion, but in both societies *religion became highly pervasive throughout all realms of social life.*

Because Mesopotamia was not as highly centralized as Egypt, each local area retained its own particular religious structure and worshiped its own special diety. Within each region, its particular diety was all-powerful, and his priests constituted his royal court. The presumed purpose of the local priests was to mediate between the area's god and the people, expressing his will and carrying out his dictates. To perform those functions,

the local temple and its attendant priests had to be supplied with a continual flow of tribute from the peasants. Temples were continually enlarged, and their priests became managers of large businesses (Childe, 1951). Consequently, priests were the sacred rulers of their areas, while the societal king and his local officials were only secular landlords.

In contrast, the Egyptian Pharaoh was seen as a living diety who dominated all local gods. Although each temple might be dedicated to a local diety, it also contained reliefs of the Pharaoh. Whenever he visited an area, he was viewed as the living embodiment of the true god (Murray, 1944). In principle, he owned all the land and the crops produced from it, and he could demand whatever portion of them he desired. The priests, therefore, were under his direct control to a much greater extent than in Mesopotamia.

Despite these differences between the religious systems of Mesopotamia and Egypt, they shared one fundamental feature in common. In both societies, *established religion—which by this time had become exceedingly powerful—served to legitimize the established political/religious structure and its economic practices.* No ordinary person would dare question or criticize the dictates of the priests or rulers, for that would be tantamount to challenging the power of the gods. Therefore, if the priests or the Pharaoh demanded that they turn over half of their crops to the temple or to the Pharaoh's representative, they complied without resistance since this was necessary to appease the gods. Established religion was therefore a crucial factor in concentrating the wealth of the society into the hands of the ruling class of priests and/or political rulers. In the words of Lenski and Lenski (1984:173): "Technological advance creates the possibility of a surplus, but to transform that possibility into a reality requires an ideology that motivates farmers to produce more than they need to stay alive and productive, and persuades them to turn that surplus over to someone else."

Sociocultural Change

Change was gradual but cumulative within simple agrarian societies. The four organizational trends that became so evident in these societies—government centralization, professional warfare, class bifurcation, and religious pervasiveness—were outgrowths of changes that began in advanced horticultural societies. With a more secure ecological base and a much larger economic surplus, however, early agrarian societies were able to expand those trends greatly and thus create much more complex patterns of social organization.

ADVANCED AGRARIAN SOCIETIES

Although the era of advanced agrarian societies—roughly the last two thousand years—has been no longer than any of the previous stages in process of societal evolu-

tion, it has been by far the most complex. During this period so many diverse forms of fully developed agrarian societies appeared around the world that it is impossible to describe the social organization of all of them in any composite sketch, no matter how elaborate it might be. Fourth-century China, for example, was radically different from fifteenth-century England, which in turn was quite unlike twentieth-century Argentina.

There has been much more variation in the organizational patterns of advanced agrarian societies than in any other stage of human history, primarily because the considerable economic surplus produced in most of these societies has not been needed for capital investment in the economic system. Ownership of agricultural land—which is the basic factor in their economies—is largely determined by traditional heredity principles or by warfare, and it does not require huge capital investments in factories. The agricultural technology used in these societies has not changed greatly throughout the intervening two thousand years, so that it has not necessitated substantial capital investments. And until the twentieth century, there has been little effective demand to raise the standard of living of the bulk of the population, so that surplus wealth has not gone into public services or other efforts to benefit the masses of people. Consequently, *the elites of most advanced agrarian societies have controlled huge amounts of surplus wealth to use essentially as they pleased.* The most common uses of that wealth have been to enhance their own standards of living far beyond those of ordinary people, to create elaborate political states and governing courts, to sustain permanent armies and navies and wage extensive warfare, and to support social institutions such as state churches that directly benefited them.

Given the tremendous diversity that has existed and continues to exist among advanced agrarian societies, the generalizations about patterns of social organization sketched in this section must be viewed with considerable caution. Although these generalizations apply in broad terms to many fully developed agrarian societies, numerous exceptions to each of them could be found throughout the last two thousand years of human history.

The Family

Kinship ties ceased being the primary basis of social organization in advanced horticultural societies, and by the time advanced agrarian societies developed, kinship had become simply one of many interwoven organizational patterns. This does not mean, however, that families are unimportant, since they continue to perform four critical functions for these societies.

Most important, *the family is still the primary unit of economic production* in both rural and urban areas. Most farms in agrarian societies are operated by families who own or rent their land or are bound to it as serfs. Regardless of these legal arrangements, the actual work of growing crops and tending animals is normally performed by families that work together as productive units. Moreover, families generally remain on the same piece of land through successive generations, inheriting ownership or tenant rights or feudal obligations to that land. In towns and cities, meanwhile, most businesses are owned and operated by family units. Small businesses such as craft shops and stores are normally run by a single family, often with its members (including the children) participating in the work. Larger businesses, such as trading firms, are also often owned by a single family, although they frequently employ additional workers.

Second, *the family also commonly plays a critical role in the political system*. Royal status—including the ruling position of king or emperor—is almost always inherited, so that control of the government remains within a single family through several generations. The right to occupy powerful administrative and military positions within the ruling class is also frequently handed down from one generation to the next within families. These offices are, in effect, family possessions that are retained as long as some family member is capable of occupying them. Even when a high office is open to competition, it is often restricted to members of the nobility, and family influences and wealth largely determine who obtains it.

Third, *the family unit—either nuclear or extended—performs most social welfare functions*. Prior to the twentieth century, agrarian societies have not had public programs to assist the unemployed, the handicapped, the mentally and physically ill, or the elderly. Whatever care these dependent individuals received generally came from their family, not the state. (Among urban artisans, however, their guilds have often provided some of those services for their members.) This dependence on one's kin is one of the primary reasons for the high birth rates that have traditionally occurred in most agrarian societies, since parents needed to have children who could care for them in old age. If a dependent person did not have a family to provide the necessary care (or was rejected by his or her family), that individual was often forced to turn to begging, stealing, or prostitution in an effort to stay alive.

Finally, *much basic education and vocational training continues to occur within the family*. Although advanced agrarian societies generally contain some formal schools—at least at the primary level to teach basic literacy—only a small portion of all education and training usually occurs there. Most children are fortunate to obtain even a few years of formal schooling, since (until the twentieth century) schools were normally private rather than public, which meant that they were largely limited to the middle and upper classes. In addition, they were often restricted to boys, so that whatever education most girls received came from their parents. And almost all training for specific jobs—whether farming, the crafts, business, or homemaking—was traditionally acquired by participating directly in family work activities.

Communities

A large majority of the people in all advanced agrarian societies continue to be rural dwellers. As long as the economy of a society is based primarily on nonmechanized agriculture, most people will be farmers living on or near their land. Scattered throughout those rural areas are numerous small villages ranging in size from a few families to one or two thousand people. The residents of these villages are primarily artisans, such as blacksmiths and potters, or shopkeepers who serve the needs of the farmers.

A few larger towns and small cities had existed in advanced horticultural and simple agrarian societies, but they contained only a tiny proportion of the total population. Advanced agrarian societies, in contrast, are generally wealthy enough to support numerous towns of several thousand people. They also generally contain at least a few cities that attain a size of a hundred thousand or more people, or occasionally a half million or more (Chandler and Fox, 1974). And contemporary agrarian societies have even much larger cities. *As a major societal trend, urbanization began in fully developed agrarian societies.* Nevertheless, no agrarian society, past or present, can be described as an urbanized country. Their towns and cities rarely contain more than about one-fourth of the population, and frequently a much small proportion. Moreover, those urban communities are always highly dependent economically on the agricultural base of the society. In other words, these are still essentially rural societies, but they produce enough surplus wealth to support some urban development.

The towns and cities that arise in agrarian societies frequently display a diverse array of economic activities. There are artisans of all kinds who produce goods for the elites, other urban residents, and the more well-to-do farmers. There are countless small shops, taverns, inns, and other kinds of retail and services businesses. There are traders and merchants who buy, transport, and sell both surplus agricultural commodities and luxury items. If the community is located on a river or ocean, there are sailors, dock hands, and shipping firms. There are also many kinds of noneconomic activities, including governmental offices, churches and other religious organizations, military barracks, schools, independent professionals such as lawyers and physicians, entertainers, and providers of personal services from barbers to prostitutes. In addition, there is also likely to be a palace housing the local nobility or a ruler's court. In short, there is an established urban political economy that is quite distinct from—but still highly dependent upon—the rural agricultural economy (Sjoberg, 1960).

Another feature of urban life in these towns and cities is the creation of special-interest associations. The most extensive of these are typically artisan guilds. The practitioners of each craft specialty—bakers, weavers, glass makers, silversmiths, etc.—are commonly organized as a guild to protect and promote their particular interests. These guilds control entry into the craft through the apprentice system of training, set wages for journeymen, establish standards of quality, regulate the sale of the goods produced, control competition, settle conflicts, and sometimes even set prices. In addition, guilds often function as social welfare agencies for their members, providing such services as help in rebuilding a shop destroyed by fire or financial assistance to the widow and children of a deceased member. As trade and commerce become extensive in these societies, merchants also frequently form associations to look after their common interests, from enforcing contracts to insuring themselves against business losses.

The Polity

The process of national state-building that began in advanced horticultural societies and continued through early agrarian societies typically reaches its peak in fully developed agrarian countries. *The political state becomes unified—usually through warfare or other use of coercive power—into a single en-*

tity with a national government (Sorokin, 1962:196–98). This government is almost invariably a heredity monarchy or empire headed by a single supreme ruler who wields absolute power.

The degree of political centralization, and hence the amount of power exercised by the ruler, has varied widely among these societies, however. In some of them, particularly in the Near and Far East, all political power has typically been centralized in the central government, and the supreme ruler has totally dominated all subordinate political leaders. In medieval Europe, in contrast, the local landed nobility retained sovereign control over their vast estates and ruled them as semiautonomous fiefdoms. The national political system was therefore relatively decentralized, and the power of the king was severely limited until late in the agrarian era. Consequently, there was a continual power struggle—often expressed in open conflict—between the crown and the nobility for control of the land, which was the primary basis of most wealth in the society. Legally, landed estates were granted to members of the nobility by royal charter, in exchange for pledges of political, military, and financial support to the king. In practice, however, the monarch frequently lacked the power to enforce those pledges. He thus had to bargain continually with the nobility for their support in order to keep the national government functioning, maintain his court, and wage war with other societies.

The national governments that were created through this process of state building have typically been based on a quite different political philosophy than prevails in the modern world. Contemporary governments—regardless of whether they rest on a capitalist or a socialist economy—are viewed as public organizations that are intended to serve the common interest and promote the welfare of the entire society (however that is defined). In contrast, *until recent times the political systems of most agrarian societies—and especially the more developed ones—have been based on a proprietary conception of the state* (Weber, 1947:341–48). From

this viewpoint, the government is a private rather than a public organization, much like a private business. Whoever acquires ownership or control of the government, regardless of how that is done, is entitled to use it (within very broad and vaguely defined limits) for their own personal benefit. The terms "state" and "estate" clearly come from the same root, and under the proprietary conception of the state it is essentially no different from a private estate.

In governments based on this principle, *minor offices are often bought and sold like pieces of property, and the purchasers are entitled to use their office to make as much profit as possible.* Since these offices usually carry no salary, incumbents must use the powers and privileges of their positions to obtain whatever benefits they can for themselves. If one wants to obtain "justice" in a local court, for example, one must first pay an appropriate amount of money to the judge and other court officials for their services. Beyond maximizing their own personal gain, the obligations of these officeholders are primarily to serve the rulers who appoint them, not the public.

Higher political positions, meanwhile, are viewed as prizes to be obtained through power struggles, and the position of king or emperor is the supreme prize in the political system. Members of the elite class therefore employ intrigue, bribery, assassination, or war to gain ruling governmental positions. And once in office, they have few or no responsibilities to serve the public. The government belongs to them personally, to be operated in whatever manner they desire in order to protect and expand their own power and privileges. If they want to add more territory to their domain, they conscript an army and go to war. If they want to increase the wealth of the royal treasury, they arbitrarily raise taxes. And if they want to live more lavishly, they draw upon the treasury to build a bigger court or hire more servants. As a consequence, the ruling class commonly controls half or more of the total wealth in the society (Lenski, 1966:219, 228). The personal incomes of the higher nobility are customarily hundreds of times larger than those of ordinary people, while the wealth of the king or emperor may be thousands of times greater than anyone else. Even more critical is the fact that there are no limits on the amount of power exercised by the political rulers, other than those imposed by their ability to organize and operate the government to their own advantage.

Gerhard Lenski (1966:210–11) summarized the proprietory conception of the state in advanced agrarian societies in this manner:

The state was not merely an organization which defined and enforced the rules in the struggle for power and privilege. It was itself one of the objects of the struggle. In fact, because of the great powers vested in it, it was the supreme prize for all who coveted power, privilege, and prestige. To win control of the state was to win control of the most powerful instrument of self-aggrandizement found in agrarian societies. By the skillful exercise of the powers of the state, a man or group could gain control over much of the economic surplus, and with it at his disposal, could go on to achieve honor and prestige as well. As a consequence, the one who controlled the state would usually fight to preserve his control, while others would strive either to curry his favor and thus share in his good fortune, or would seek to displace him.

Under these conditions, it is not surprising that *all kinds of political violence—both interpersonal and collective—are rampant in most advanced agrarian societies.* Internally, rulers often use the power of the state rather ruthlessly to squelch peasant revolts or other popular uprisings. They also use their power to control or eliminate rival contenders for their governmental positions, as well as dispose of current office holders. Externally, these governments are frequently engaged in almost continual warfare with other societies over land, valuable resources, trade routes, religion, or other causes.

Stratification

A *direct consequence of the much greater surplus wealth produced in advance agrarian societies is the creation of a more complex stratification system than existed in simpler agrarian societies.* Instead of containing just two or three classes, advanced agrarian societies often include six or eight distinct classes. In addition, there may be considerable variation in power and wealth within each class, so that they overlap with one another to some extent. For example, while the ruling class is, on the average, much wealthier than the merchant class, some members of the nobility are quite poor, despite owning large amounts of inherited land; while some merchants who own large trading companies may become quite wealthy. As a result of this overlapping, a limited amount of social mobility tends to occur among adjacent classes.

It is also important to remember that all of the intermediate classes located between the rulers and the masses of peasants owe their existence primarily to the ruling class. The flow of wealth within the society is largely from the peasants to the elites, who then dispense some of that wealth to the merchants, artisans, and other intermediate classes in exchange for desired goods and services. Consequently, the members of those classes derive most of their incomes from the ruling class, not from the peasants, so that they are economically and socially dependent on the elites.

The fact that these stratification systems become quite complex does not mean that there is any movement toward greater socioeconomic equality. The vast majority of the population—often two-thirds or more—consists of peasants who exist at or near a bare subsistence level. The intermediate classes are typically quite small in size, so that none of them usually contain more than roughly five percent of the population. And the differences in power and wealth between all of these classes and the tiny set of elites is normally immense. In short, *there is extreme economic and social inequality within most advanced agrarian societies.*

The following paragraphs briefly describe nine social classes that may exist in these societies. No particular society has necessarily contained all of these classes, but most of them have been fairly common in advanced agrarian societies prior to the beginning of industrialization (Lenski, 1966:Chs. 8 and 9). This class structure that commonly exists in advanced agrarian societies is illustrated in Figure 8-5.

Ruling Class. This elite class consists of the supreme political ruler, high government officials, top military leaders, the landed nobility, and their relatives. Although it effectively controls the entire society, it rarely comprises more than one percent of the total population. Its immense wealth and power are derived from ownership of the land, control of the state, and military conquest. It frequently expropriates for itself more than half the total wealth being produced in the society through such techniques as taxes, land rents, fines, fealty

FIGURE 8-5 Social class structure in advanced agrarian societies

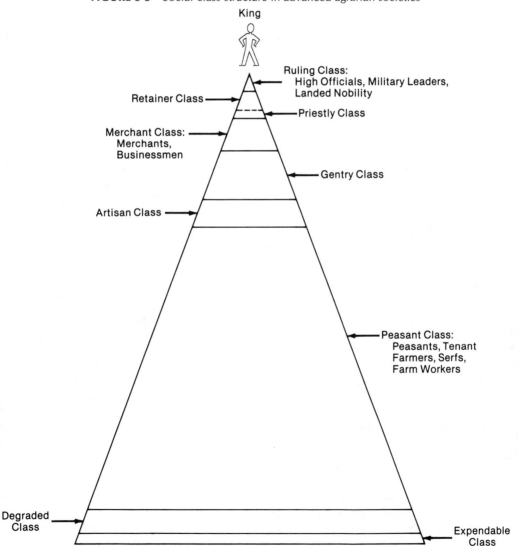

payments from peasants, direct confiscation from serfs, sale of titles and offices, graft, and military coercion. In return for supporting the authority of the ruling political regime, the rest of the ruling class shares in the wealth of the state, so that most members of this class live lavishly in large courts and palaces with countless servants and attendants. At the same time, a continual struggle for power goes on between the supreme ruler and the local nobility for land ownership, control of the state, and surplus wealth. In general, the advantage in this struggle tends to lie with the supreme ruler, because of his more unified forces and greater resources, as well as a lack of organization among the landed nobility. Because that ruler is ultimately dependent on the nobility to extract agricultural surpluses from the peasants and serfs, however, if the nobility unite against the king, they can sometimes force him to make political concessions to them—as occurred in the English Magna Carta in 1215.

Retainer Class. This class, which exists to serve the elites, includes lower-level government administrators, scribes and clerks, local officials such as sheriffs and tax collectors, professional soldiers, and household and personal servants. In return for the services they render to the elites, they receive privileges and prestige (but very limited power) that are not available to common people. Consequently, they are totally dependent on the ruling class. Collectively, they are invaluable to the elites because of the necessary services they perform, but individually they are almost totally dispensable.

Priestly Class. In some agrarian societies, high-level priests are considered part of the ruling class, and lower-level clergy might be placed in the retainer class. Frequently, however, religious leaders form a distinct class of their own. High-level priests, who are commonly recruited from the landed nobility, perform two important functions in addition to administering the established church. They formulate and propound a religious ideology that supports the existing social and political orders, and thus confers legitimacy upon them. Kings, for instance, almost always have themselves crowned by the head of the church. And since the high priests are generally the best educated people in the society, they also perform many useful intellectual and scholarly activities. As a result, some of these church leaders may become quite powerful and wealthy. Because the lower-level clergy generally identify with the existing social structure and encourage the ordinary people to accept and support it, they, too, serve the ruling class.

Gentry Class. When this class exists in an agrarian society, it consists of independent farmers who own moderate amounts of land but are not titled and do not belong to the landed nobility. They own enough land, which they farm with the assistance of tenants and hired workers, to live fairly comfortably, and hence they are not peasants. But since they are not nobility, they exercise little or no political power. If they are successful in acquiring more land, buying a title, or marrying their daughters into titled families, however, they may eventually join the landed nobility.

Merchant Class. In simple agrarian societies, most merchants have essentially the same status as artisans. As the wealth of the society increases and their businesses expand, however, merchants tend to grow steadily in numbers, wealth, and power. They operate trading companies, wholesale businesses, transportation facilities, banks, retail firms, and many other kinds of commercial enterprises, all of which have the potential of generating considerable wealth that is not directly dependent on agriculture. They serve the ruling class by providing it with luxury goods and services, helping to extract surplus wealth from the peasants, and loaning money to courts. The rulers cannot easily control them, however, because of their independent sources of wealth. Consequently, supreme rulers often form alliances with leading merchants, exchanging royal charters, titles, and military protection for political and economic support. Through time, the merchant class in a society can rise from near the bottom of the stratification system to become so wealthy and powerful that they are able to challenge—and eventually replace—the landed nobility within the dominant class.

Artisan Class. Artisans are skilled craftsmen who produce goods of all kinds through handicraft techniques. Initially, most of their products are bought by members of the ruling class, so that the artisans are economically dependent on those elites. As merchants (and sometimes gentry) become more wealthy, however, artisans are able to expand their sales and increase their incomes. Nevertheless, they rarely become wealthy and hence do not experience the upward mobility that occurs among some merchants. Members of the artisan class are usually drawn from the peasants, and their standard of living is generally only marginally better than those of peasants. Their guild organizations function to protect their particular roles in the economy, but they are not normally powerful enough to increase their status substantially.

Peasant Class. In addition to peasants, who own their own small plots of land, this class includes tenant farmers who rent their land, serfs who belong to the estates of the landed nobility, and hired farm workers. They constitute a large majority of the population and provide most of the economic base of all agrarian societies. Although their productivity is much greater in advanced than in a simple agrarian society, most of that surplus is taken from them by the ruling class, and to a lesser extent by the merchant and artisan classes. Most of them therefore live at or near a bare subsistence level, and they have few or no opportunities to improve their lot in life. Generation after generation of peasants continue to perform the same menial agricultural labor, with virtually no changes in their life conditions. The only significant variation in their living patterns occurs when the local nobility or the

king conscripts them to fight his wars. And while peasants uprisings or revolts have been quite common throughout this entire era, the ruling class has almost always been able to suppress those protests very quickly. Consequently, the most effective defense of the peasantry against even greater exploitation by the elites is passive evasion, such as not working any harder than necessary to survive or hiding part of one's crops from the tax or rent collector.

Degraded Class. These are manual workers who are outside the agricultural system and perform tasks that no one else will do. Examples including hauling garbage, burying the dead, maintaining roads, loading ships, and performing as street entertainers. Very frequently, they are foreigners or ethnic minorities who cannot acquire any land, or slaves taken through military conquest. When they find work, they may be able to sustain themselves at a subsistence level, but quite frequently jobs are not available or wages are so low that they cannot support themselves. They then either die or fall into the expendable class.

Expendable Class. Most advanced agrarian societies face a continual threat of overpopulation because of the confiscation of wealth by the elites and the high birth rate among the peasants. They must, therefore, have some mechanism for "squeezing" people out of the society. Sometimes this is accomplished through religious rituals or sports contests in which excess people are intentionally slaughtered. More commonly, however, the excess population is simply forced off the land and out of other kinds of work, so that they die from starvation or disease. Some of those individuals— probably the brightest and most capable— do manage to survive, however, by engaging in such activities as theft, robbery, begging, and prostitution. This expendable class is even worse off than the degraded class, since they receive no support from society and are often intentionally killed. They live miserable, brutal, and short lives.

Religion

Whereas simple agrarian societies typically accepted some version of polytheism that incorporated numerous gods peculiar to each society, more advanced agrarian societies developed a very different kind of religious belief system. They have given rise to three major (and several minor) monotheistic and universalistic religions: Judaism, Christianity, and Islam. Each of these religions is monotheistic because it proclaims that there is only one diety, rather than a number of gods, although they differ considerably in their concepts of that diety. They are universalistic because they hold that their god rules the entire world, not just the society that gave birth to that religion. As people became more aware of other societies through trade and improved transportation, they came to believe that their tribal or societal god was not unique to them, but was concerned about all humanity.

A second important religious development in advanced agrarian societies has been a gradual separation between the church and the state (Bellah, 1964). In simple agrarian societies, these two social institutions were so thoroughly intertwined that they often functioned as a single unit. As the rulers of advanced agrarian societies become more involved in creating and operating a unified political state that encompasses many diverse cultures and continually seeks to increase its wealth and power, they find it expedient to make the state a more secular institution. Consequently, they began allowing the church to have more autonomy as a distinct sacred organization. Although these kings and emperors still claim to rule "by the Grace of God" which gives them a "divine right" to issue authoritative proclamations, they no longer claim to be gods themselves or to function as high priests of the established church. Those clerical tasks are increasingly turned over to separate religious leaders whose total concern is the maintenance and operation of the church. This structural separation of church and state enables the political leaders to devote their full attention to matters of government and politics.

All of this depends, obviously, on the willingness of the church leaders to support and cooperate with the state. To ensure this loyalty, the ruler frequently gives large grants of land and special tax privileges to the established church. And since land ownership is the principal source of wealth in these societies, such gifts often enable the church as an organization—and its leaders as individuals—to become quite wealthy and powerful. In medieval Europe, the Catholic Church often owned as much as one-fourth to one-third of all the land, and was second only to the state as a seat of power in society.

The established church in advanced agrarian societies also acquires power through its ability to shape the beliefs and thinking of the ordinary people. Most of them are illiterate or barely able to read, and (prior to the modern era of newspapers and radios) they have few sources of information about the world other than through the church. As a church becomes highly organized throughout a whole region, it comes to serve as the major media of mass communication.

Leisure and Fine Arts

No matter how harsh their life, people always invent ways of amusing themselves. The peasants, artisans, and other ordinary people in advanced agrarian societies have been no exception (Bennett, 1960). They frequently gather together for all kinds of collective events, from religious ceremonies and weddings to public games and hangings. Singing, dancing, gossiping, storytelling, gambling, courting, fighting, and a great deal of drinking make these gatherings quite lively. In the towns and cities there may also be professional entertainers—acrobats, jugglers, jesters, actors, dancers, and singers—who earn a precarious living by amusing people in the streets or in taverns and then passing the hat. For the most part, all these forms of popular amusement are generally crude, raucous, and often violent by contemporary standards. Yet we must not judge them too severely, since they merely reflect the hard lives and lack of sophistication among the ordinary people of those societies.

In sharp contrast, the amusements of the elites are often highly sophisticated pursuits of the fine arts. With wealth to burn and an intense desire to demonstrate their personal and intellectual superiority to themselves and others, they vigorously support the arts and letters. In the past, they have erected spectacular palaces, temples, cathedrals, government buildings and other structures. They have commissioned the best artists and sculptors to fill those buildings with magnificent works of art. They have employed writers and poets to produce literature for their leisure hours. They have subsidized composers to create both secular and sacred music. Most of these architects, artists, writers, and performers have been supported through patronage, in which political and religious elites guarantee them a fixed income in return for output on demand. The marvelous artistic accomplishments of advanced agrarian societies are thus ultimately an outcome of the extreme concentration of wealth and the leisure it affords to the ruling class.

Sociocultural Change

Sociocultural change is pervasive and extensive within advanced agrarian societies, although from the perspective of modern industrial societies, it is still quite slow. As a result of the large economic surpluses provided primarily by agriculture and, to a lesser extent, by trade and military conquest, fully developed agrarian societies enjoy much greater disposal wealth to invest in social and political development than any previous societies. Because the ruling class is generally so effective in extracting and consolidating that wealth, it is able to channel its use into many new realms of societal development and to create quite complex patterns of social ordering. These include growing urban communities, unified political states

with effective national governments, complex stratification systems, and established national churches.

At the peak of this era in seventeenth– and eighteenth-century Europe, the dominant societies were not only highly developed internally, but they had also expanded their spheres of economic and political influence throughout much of the rest of the world. Their patterns of agrarian-based social organization might have continued indefinitely, if an entirely new mode of economic production based on manufacturing had not emerged.

SUMMARY

Kinship was the primary basis of social organization in all foraging societies. Most social functions were performed by the family unit, which typically was patriarchal in form. Both nuclear and extended families placed great emphasis on sharing among their members, which was often necessary for collective survival. Hunting and gathering communities were quite small, and most of their members were linked by kinship bonds. Each community was economically self-sufficient and politically autonomous, and thus constituted a society in itself. Collective decisions were reached through discussion and consensus, either among all the people or by an informal council of elders. The headman was chosen because of his skills or knowledge.

Stratification was very minimal, and what inequality did exist was based largely on hunting or other personal skills that gave an individual prestige, but not power or wealth. The most common type of religious belief system was animism. The shaman or medicine man performed religious and medical functions as he sought to influence the all-pervasive spirits through sacred rituals. The cultural heritage of the society was transmitted largely through storytelling. Social change was virtually nonexistent, since the primary value was perpetuating traditional patterns of living.

In simple horticultural societies, kinship remained the primary basis of social organization, but the dominant unit was the clan or tribe that linked together several neighboring communities. These kinship networks provided economic support and mutual protection for the members, regulated marriages, and determined religious beliefs and practices. Women enacted a vital economic role, since they did most of the work of tending the gardens, and these societies were frequently matriarchal and matrilineal in structure. Men performed a variety of noneconomic but higher-status roles.

Horticultural gardening necessitated the establishment of semipermanent settlements with larger and more substantial buildings. As the soil became depleted through continual gardening, entire communities sometimes moved to a new location. Villages typically contained no more than two or three hundred people and were largely self-sufficient economically. Clan and tribal affiliations, as well as linguistic and cultural similarities, often extended across several neighboring villages.

The political systems of these societies were quite informal, although the village headman and his subordinates exercised considerable influence. The clan or tribal chief served as a symbolic and functional leader of the entire kin network. The influence exercised by headmen and chiefs created some power inequality, and stratification based on wealth developed as families acquired land, houses, and other material possessions. Personal prestige and clan or tribal lineage were the most crucial determinant of status, however. Warfare over land ownership and tribal boundaries was fairly common. It had the social consequences of providing prestige and influence, creating war trophies, and limiting population growth.

Animism, celebrated through elaborate rituals, continued as the prevailing form of religious belief. It was often supplemented by ancestor worship, in which the village shaman enacted a very influential role. Some social change did occur, but at an extremely slow pace, since traditional ways of acting and thinking were strongly ingrained in the culture.

In more advanced horticultural societies, the primacy of kinship was replaced by three new forms of social organization. One of these was larger communities composed of craft specialists and traders who were linked by economic interdependencies. As a result, marriage came to be viewed as an economic bond between families. These towns also established semiformal governments composed of several full-time positions.

A second new form of organization was politically unified states containing three or four hierarchical levels of government. The rulers of these political systems attempted to control many aspects of the society, utilizing a set of subordinate retainers who were personally committed to them, but their power was limited by a number of structural conditions. The surplus resources and metal weapons available to them enabled them to engage in frequent wars with other societies, so that the process of state-building was closely linked with warfare.

The third new form of social organization was formal stratification systems with two distinct and highly unequal social classes. The tiny hereditary-based class of ruling political-military elites controlled much of the surplus wealth and most of the power in the society. The masses of peasants and craftsmen did all of the productive work, but much of what they produced was extracted from them by the elites, so that they lived at or near a subsistence level. Some of these societies also contained a slave class.

The predominant form of religion was worship of ancestors, kings, and emperors. The religious system was closely interwoven with politics, and the rulers used it to support and legitimate their power. They either appointed the church leaders, or they assumed the role of priests or gods themselves. Social change was more extensive than in the past, as these societies gradually developed more complex forms of social organization.

Early agrarian societies were much larger than any horticultural societies, and they were often organized as vast empires. Their governments were highly centralized in a powerful autocratic ruler and a small ruling class. The rulers established elaborate formal administrative structures of officials, subordinates, and scribes to control their empires, and they also created the first standardized laws and legal systems. Warfare continued to be a frequent or perpetual activity, but it was increasingly conducted by permanent royal armies of professional soldiers. Kings and emperors intentionally engaged in war to acquire more territory, resources, slaves, and wealth, so that war became highly politicized.

A two-class stratification systems of elites and peasants became even more pronounced in simple agrarian societies. The ruling class controlled most of the political power and economic wealth of the society, enjoyed urban living, and began creating a distinct subculture based on literacy that was not shared by the ordinary people. Elites came to view themselves as intellectually and morally superior to the "subhuman" masses of people.

Polytheistic religion was highly pervasive throughout all realms of social life. Priests became extremely powerful and constructed elaborate temples supported by tribute from the peasants. These highly organized religious systems served to legitimize the existing political and economic systems and to justify their expropriation of economic surpluses from the peasants. Social change was gradual but cumulative, with societies becoming increasingly complex and more tightly organized.

In advanced agrarian societies, the tremendous surplus wealth generated through settled agriculture and expanding commerce makes possible much more extensive and diverse patterns of social organization than in any previous societies.

The family performs four critical functions in these societies: it is the primary unit of economic production, it plays a critical role in the political system, it performs most social welfare functions, and it carries out a great deal of education and vocational training. In addition to villages and towns, these societies contain a few medium-sized cities, so that about one-fourth of their population commonly lives in urban settings. These towns and cities display a diverse array of economic activities that constitute a political economy distinct from the rural agricultural economy. A number of special-interest associations exist within these cities.

The political state becomes unified into a single entity with a national government. The government is almost always a heredity monarchy or empire, but the degree to which political power is centralized in the national government varies widely. These political systems are usually based on a proprietary conception of the state, which views the government as essentially a private, rather than a public, organization. The government may be used by whoever controls it for their own personal benefit, offices are bought and sold, and there is a continual struggle for control of the state.

The stratification system contains a number of distinct but overlapping social classes, and there is tremendous inequality of power and wealth between the tiny ruling class and most of the rest of the population. Classes commonly found in advanced agrarian societies include the governing class of political rulers and the landed nobility, a retainer class of persons who serve the rulers, a priestly class who support the rulers, a gentry class of independent farm owners, an upwardly mobile merchant class, an artisan class of craftsmen, a peasant class of farmers and serfs, a degraded class of itinerant workers, and an expendable class of individuals outside the economic system.

The religion of these societies is generally monotheistic and universalistic. The church becomes an autonomous institution separate from the state, but it supports and legitimizes the existing political and economic systems. It strongly influences peoples' belief systems, because of its control of information and communication. Ordinary people entertain themselves in a variety of ways, while the elites support and promote literature and the fine arts.

Sociocultural change is more extensive in advanced agrarian societies than ever before in history, although it is still quite gradual by contemporary standards. Large economic surpluses that are confiscated and used by the ruling class enable these societies to develop elaborate forms of social organization and to become quite structurally complex and culturally diverse.

9

TRANSITION TO INDUSTRIALISM

How did the development of commercial trade lay a foundation for industrialization?

What role did the merchant class play in the creation of modern nation-states?

Why did industrialization depend on changes in agriculture, population, technology, and values?

How did capital accumulation, energy exploitation, and economic reorganization contribute to industrialization?

In what ways does industrialization transform an entire society?

COMMERCIAL TRADE

Until about two hundred years ago, all societies rested on an agricultural base—either foraging, gardening, or farming—that shaped most other aspects of their social organization. One of the most fundamental and far-reaching changes in human life, therefore, has been the industrial revolution that began in Western Europe during the latter part of the eighteenth century and is continuing today around the world. The approximately 35 nations that have thus far undergone this revolution are totally different from the agriculturally-based societies they were in the past and the more than 100 agricultural societies that still exist today.

Although the industrial revolution is often said to have begun about two hundred years ago, it did not suddenly emerge within societies that were entirely based on agriculture prior to that time. A variety of underlying technological, economic, political, and social trends began occurring in Western societies long before the eighteenth century. These gradual changes in social organization laid the foundation for industrialization and contributed to its development. The first two sections of this chapter examine two critical societal trends—the expansion of commercial trade and the creation of national states—that began three hundred years earlier and provided a basis for the later emergence of industrial economies. The third section sketches a number of other processes that slowly developed during the period preceding the industrial revolution and contributed to its occurrence. The last two sections pertain more directly to the process of industrialization. All of the changes discussed in this chapter occurred first in Europe, but they subsequently affected industrialization in the United States.

Growth of Trade

People have always traded with one another for things they needed, but most trade throughout history has been conducted on a direct, interpersonal basis. "I'll give you 100 bushels of my wheat for three of your cows." Beginning in the latter half of the fifteenth century, however, trade in the Western world began to take on a different character. People started specializing in the economic role of trader. They were not peasants or farmers exchanging their surplus goods, but merchants who bought, transported, and sold goods for others as a full-time occupational role. They sought not to obtain items that they themselves needed, but rather to make a profit by facilitating the exchange of goods among others. Throughout the Middle Ages there had been wandering peddlers who bought and sold goods, but they dealt primarily with either rare luxuries (for the nobility) or trinkets (for the masses), and their role in the economy was negligible. The activities of traders, in contrast, began to transform societal economies.

Early traders were commonly financed by governments and other elites, who commissioned them to obtain luxury items or gold and silver. Columbus, for example, was sent to bring back spices, silks, and precious metals from the Orient. It became evident fairly early, however, that much greater profits were to be made by commercializing trade and dealing in everyday necessities. Commercial traders therefore began to handle such goods as foodstuffs from the land and sea, fibers and fabrics, wood for fuel and building, and similar items. These kinds of goods were much easier to obtain than luxuries, and the market for them was considerably larger. As commercial trade expanded, merchants also began to form trading leagues or guilds that enabled them to regulate and finance their own activities and to retain the profits themselves rather than turning them over to a sponsoring monarch. *By the seventeenth century, organized commercial trade was well-established as a viable economic activity throughout Western Europe, and a new class of increasingly wealthy merchants had emerged.*

Commercial trade was further stimulated as the North American colonies began to grow in population and economic viability. Cotton, timber, and many other raw materials were shipped from the colonies to Europe, in exchange for manufactured goods of all kinds. Although the New and Old Worlds both benefited from this trade, it was particularly desirable for European nations, since it provided them with urgently needed natural resources that were unobtainable or very expensive on the continent. Large profits were also made by merchants who shipped human slaves from Africa to North America.

Development of Shipping

If substantial profits were to be made from buying and selling everyday necessities within growing markets, merchants had to handle relatively large quantities of goods. Land transportation was still limited to horse-drawn wagons traveling over incredibly poor roads, however, and it was constantly threatened by tax collectors and robbers. Therefore, *commercial trade in bulk goods was almost entirely dependent on water transportation,* since ships could carry large cargoes quite rapidly and inexpensively. The magnetic compass, which enabled ships to sail beyond the sight of land, had been invented in the twelfth century, and as maps and other navigational aids became increasingly sophisticated, shipping became a much more reliable mode of transport. In addition, during the following several centuries numerous technological improvements were made in ship design and construction—such as the stern rudder, multiple masts with numerous sails, and an increase in the length of ships relative to their width—that made vessels more dependable and efficient as haulers of cargo (and also as mobile platforms for cannon).

These developments in marine engineering and navigation had two important consequences in addition to making possible large-scale commercial trade. First, many countries sent "explorers" to new lands not to trade but to conquer. Repeated expeditions to Central and South America brought back huge amounts of gold and silver to the royal coffers of Europe, followed by furs from North America and many kinds of raw materials from Africa. Although these voyages of conquest were not explicitly commercial in nature, they interjected vast amounts of new resources and wealth into Europe. Second, some governments began building large fleets of warships. Although the creation of a powerful navy was often justified on the grounds that it was needed to protect merchants, warships could just as easily be used to plunder the cargo ships of other nations. Consequently, whichever country possessed the strongest navy at any particular time controlled the seas. Over time, naval supremacy—and hence economic and political dominance over all of Europe—shifted from Spain to Holland to England.

Consequences of Trade

The growth of commercial trade from the fifteenth through the eighteenth centuries had numerous vital consequences for Western European nations. Three of those were particularly important for the process of industrialization.

One consequence of developing commercial trade was to promote the *expansion of education and communication skills*. During the feudal era, only the elite class was educated, while the large bulk of the population remained illiterate. Commercial activity, however, required merchants not only to become literate, but also to acquire such skills as bookkeeping and accounting. Formal schooling, knowledge of mathematics and science, training in engineering, and other educational opportunities therefore became available to a growing proportion of the population.

A second consequence of commercial trade was the gradual *emergence of a new type of market economy*. Under feudalism, most economic activity had been oriented to satisfying people's immediate needs. The limited trading that did occur was generally conducted through direct barter between the involved parties, and its primary concern was to make a fair exchange, not a profit. Commercial trade, in contrast, created an economic system in which goods were bought and sold in the marketplace by merchants whose primary objective was profit making. Such transactions obviously required a money economy rather than a barter procedure. They also required the development of a new orientation toward economic activity, which came to be known as entrepreneurship. Merchants had to be willing to take economic risks to create and operate their businesses and to value business and profit making as a desirable kind of work. Finally, the market system had to be freed from the heavy hand of tradition and government regulation that had prevailed under feudalism. Merchants demanded that markets were to be governed only by the economic laws of supply and demand, not by traditional values or political edicts. The desired role of government—expressed in the ideology of mercantilism—was to protect and support commercial activities in order to maximize the wealth and power of the merchant class and the state.

The third—and perhaps most crucial—consequence of the expansion of commercial trade was to *improve the basic ecological conditions of Western Europe*. Prior to that time, European societies had been largely dependent on whatever natural resources existed within their borders. Growing commercial trade, expropriation of resources from less developed areas of the world, and naval supremacy brought untold new resources and wealth into Western Europe. As a result, the economies of those societies were able to develop far beyond the limits imposed by domestic resources. The merchant class benefited immensely from this economic growth, but part of the new wealth also flowed to other sectors of the economy—including kings, bankers, shipbuilders, shopkeepers, craftsmen, and even artists. Most importantly, however, it created a pool of surplus capital that could be invested in new commercial ventures, and eventually in the construction of industries.

NATION-STATES

Traditional European feudal societies were not political states in the modern sense, since they did not contain a strong national government or a unified political system. Each local lord was legally and morally the ruler of his own fiefdom. Political and military alliances were often established among members of the nobility, and they might give pledges of loyalty to a distant king or emperor if it suited their interests. Each fiefdom, nevertheless, functioned as a relatively autonomous political unit. Consequently, the ruling lords within those feudal societies were constantly struggling among themselves for control of the land—which is the principal economic resource in an agrarian society—as well as for political and social preeminence.

Feudal Kingdoms

Sometimes the struggles among feudal nobility were only economic in nature, but very frequently they were conducted through intermittent or continual warfare and subsequent military conquest. Over time, these struggles often resulted in one lord gaining economic and military ascendancy over the others within a geographical area. As that dominant lord increased his power over other fiefdoms, he frequently forced the subordinant lords to grant him certain political and financial rights over their activities and to support his military actions. And if his power over them became great enough, he might even compel them to acknowledge him as king of the entire region. *These feudal kingdoms were the beginnings of nation-states in Europe.* Nevertheless, they were usually quite weakly unified, since the subordinate lords retained an independent economic base in their land and periodically challenged the edicts of the king. In addi-

tion, transportation and communication limitations, cultural and linguistic differences, trade barriers, and many other factors severely restricted the ability of the king to govern his kingdom effectively. In short, *the kings that existed throughout Western Europe during the feudal era were quite weak politically and were frequently embroiled in conflicts with their subordinate nobility and with other kingdoms.*

Feudal monarchs typically maintained large standing armies to protect their territory, increasingly large numbers of administrators such as clerks and tax collectors to operate the government, and elaborate courts to symbolize their political and social status. All these endeavors required huge amounts of wealth. Traditionally, this wealth came from the subordinate local lords, who in turn extracted it from their peasants. With a limited supply of arable land and rather inefficient agricultural practices, however, this source of wealth was inherently finite and often insecure. Kings were therefore perpetually in need of more wealth, and they were continually looking for new ways of obtaining it.

As commercial trade began to develop, it provided a highly lucrative new source of wealth for kings that was not dependent on land ownership or payments from subordinate nobility. Trade also offered possibilites for obtaining the luxury goods that were desired to enhance the royal lifestyle. As discussed in the preceding section, therefore, feudal kings eagerly encouraged and often financed early efforts by merchants to expand commercial trade and dispatched expeditions to exporpriate wealth from foreign lands. *As commercial trade and military conquest began to flourish, the royal coffers grew immensely, and kings increased and consolidated their political control over the subordinate landed nobility.*

The Merchant Class

Through time, the emerging merchant class gained increasing control over its own economic activities and became quite wealthy relative to other sectors of society. Nevertheless, because traditional political and social values continued to prevail in these societies, the wealthy merchants did not at first challenge the political rule of the kings. *The merchants were primarily interested in developing their businesses and making money, not acquiring political power.* The prevailing ideology of mercantilism nicely legitimated this division of labor, with the government protecting and supporting commercial trade but not attempting to control it, in return for which the merchants stayed out of politics. The merchants strongly desired, nevertheless, to gain the social status in society to which they thought their growing wealth entitled them. They therefore attempted to buy their way into the nobility by purchasing land, titles, estates, and daughters of the nobility as wives. The established landed nobility viewed these efforts as direct threats to their privileged social status, and strongly resisted them. This left the merchants in a rather ambiguous social position, to which they frequently responded by further intensifying their business efforts in order to acquire even more money with which to demonstrate their rights to high social status.

Monarchs, meanwhile, were frequently caught in a financial squeeze. On the one hand, their need for funds was virtually insatiable as a result of constantly raging land and naval wars, ever-growing state administrative demands, and the lavish courts which they felt compelled to maintain. On the other hand, there was a limit to the amount of wealth they could acquire by taxing merchants or engaging in warfare. Many merchants, in fact, became quite skillful at avoiding royal taxes by shifting their business to whatever country offered them the most advantageous conditions. Wealthy merchants were usually very willing, however, to loan large amounts of money—at interest—to financially desperate monarchs. This practice not only increased their financial profits, but it also gave them influence over the government with which to extract favorable trade and other economic concessions. As a result of this process, *developing national governments became increasingly allied with the growing merchant class in a reciprocal exchange relationship.* The merchants provided the wealth that the governments desperately needed, while governments provided military protection and legal encouragement to merchants.

Other Classes

Most other classes within later feudal societies also tended, over time, to become allied with the king and his state government. The professional military forces were almost entirely dependent on the state for their support. The ever-growing body of national government administrators—from the highest state ministers to the lowest clerks—owed their very existence and livelihood to the state. Religious leaders sometimes retained traditional linkages with the local nobility, but they usually found it increasingly advantageous to align themselves with the national state. In return for anointing the king with moral legitimacy, the church received the protection and support of the state. The gentry—small independent landowners and professionals such as lawyers—traditionally had close political and social ties with the landed nobility, not the state. However, expanding commercial activity offered them growing opportunities to sell their goods and services in the marketplace for cash rather than having to barter with the nobility. Consequently, as they became economically linked with the merchant class, their political and social allegiances also tended to shift to the state. Skilled craftsmen, finally, quickly discovered that both the royal court and the wealthy merchants were much more able to purchase their goods than were the old landed nobility. Eventually, only the peasants remained closely tied to the local lords, but the peasant class was relatively powerless politically.

The dual outcomes of all these shifting alliances were to *constantly strengthen the economic and political power of the national government while simultaneously weakening the power of the landed nobility.* Although the local lords retained their titles and land holdings, they became increasingly isolated from the mainstream of economic and social development, and hence they were relegated to minor political roles as local subordinates of the national state.

State Building

The process of state building occurred fairly early in some societies such as England and France, which developed strong national governments by the seventeenth century. In other countries, such as Germany and Italy, the landed nobility remained politically viable much longer, and the process of state unification was not completed until late in the nineteenth century. Regardless of the speed with which the process occurred, however, its fundamental dynamic was the same throughout Europe. As the economic base of a society expanded to include trade and other commercial activities in addition to agriculture, a new class of merchants emerged that generated immense economic resources that were not directly dependent on land ownership and agriculture (although they were still dealing largely with agricultural goods and other natural resources).

As a result of their independent economic base, merchants were able, through time, to challenge and slowly replace the landed nobility as the dominant economic class in society. Because a unified national state was much more advantageous to commercial activity than was the old political system of small feudal fiefdoms, the merchant class provided the financial support that enabled monarchs to expand and consolidate their political control over the entire society. The merchants did not seek to become directly involved in state politics, however. For related reasons, most other classes also tended to shift their political support from the landed nobility to the state. The national government, meanwhile, provided various military and legal benefits to the merchants and other classes. *Through this process, the political systems of European societies were transformed from local fiefdoms to relatively unified national states ruled by monarchs.*

ADDITIONAL CONTRIBUTING DEVELOPMENTS

In addition to the fundamental trends of trade expansion and state building, a number of other developments that occurred in Western Europe during the eighteenth century also contributed to, and made possible, the industrial revolution. Four of these developments—each of which was actually a complex set of interrelated changes—are described in this section: agricultural productivity, population growth and redistribution, technological innovation, and value changes.

Agricultural Productivity

The ability of an agriculturally-based society to develop economically is directly dependent on the productivity of its farming practices. If those practices are relatively inefficient—as they were throughout Europe until roughly the beginning of the eighteenth century—most of the population must be engaged in agriculture to produce enough food and other products to satisfy subsistence needs. There is relatively little surplus available to invest in new economic ventures. Farming practices did not change greatly in Europe from neolithic times until the eighteenth century. Plots of land were quite small and often widely scattered most of the work was done by hand or with a few draft animals, one-fourth of the land was left fallow each year on a rotating basis to avoid depleting nutrients in the soil, and much of the livestock was slaughtered each fall since means of feeding large numbers of animals through the winter were unknown. In addition, local landowners confiscated from one-fourth to one-half of the products of the peasants each year through taxes and rents.

During the seventeenth and eighteenth centuries, the landed nobility began to experience severe economic pressures from several sources. The importation of large amounts of gold and silver from the New World created rapid inflation that seriously hurt the nobility, who had essentially fixed incomes from their land. Monarchs, meanwhile, kept continually demanding more and more financial support from the nobility to meet military, governmental, and court expenses. And the rising class of wealthy merchants was directly challenging the landed nobility for economic dominance and social status. Consequently, *throughout the eighteenth century, land owners began searching for new ways of increasing their agricultural productivity and wealth.*

One obvious means of doing this was to bring more land into cultivation. Swamps were drained and forests were cleared, with long-term harmful ecological consequences that were not apparent at the time. The practice of crop rotation was devised, so that instead of leaving a fourth of the land fallow, different crops that restored nutrients to the soil were planted on a rotating basis, which greatly increased total productivity. And in England, Parliament passed a series of Enclosure Acts that entitled the nobility to fence off and cultivate lands—called commons—which had previously been used by the peasants as communal livestock grazing pastures. This practice immediately increased agricultural productivity for the nobility, but at the expense of many peasants who depended on use of the commons to feed their few cows and other animals.

Another way of increasing agricultural productivity was to introduce more efficient farming techniques. The peasants' small and scattered plots of land were gradually combined into large fields that could be cultivated more economically, but at the expense of the peasants' traditional way of life. Better harnesses for draft animals and better plows were invented, which enabled farmers to plow more deeply and expose more soil to cultivation. The use of fertilizers became more widespread, and new techniques for harvesting grain were devised.

Procedures were also developed for storing fodder throughout the winter so that cattle could be kept alive. Selective breeding was introduced, so that by the end of the eighteenth century the average weight of animals sold at auction in England was double what it had been at the beginning of the century. Finally, sheep raising became much more widespread, since wool was in great demand by the developing textile industry, and because sheep required less pasture than cattle per pound of meat produced.

Three general points concerning these agricultural developments are especially critical. First, it was the landed nobility—not the peasants—who introduced such developments in an effort to compete economically with the merchants and to preserve their traditional economic role and social status in society. Second, agricultural productivity increased dramatically throughout the eighteenth century in Europe. Most of the resulting new wealth, however, went to the land-owning nobility and ultimately to other classes such as merchants and political rulers. The masses of peasants who worked the fields received relatively few of those benefits. Third, many of the new farming practices introduced by the nobility were quite shortsighted in nature, and they had many detrimental ecological, economic, and social effects that in the long run hastened the transition from an agricultural to an industrial economy. *Paradoxically, the efforts of the landed nobility to preserve their traditional way of life created conditions that eventually led to their downfall.*

Population Growth and Redistribution

Although relatively little of the expanding agricultural surplus was retained by the rural peasants, the amount of food available to the society as a whole was sufficient to produce *a marked growth in population within many European societies during the eighteenth century.* In England, for instance, the total population increased only from 6.0 to 6.5 million between 1700 and 1750, but during the next 50 years it rose to over 9 million. This population growth was due almost entirely to more and better food, not to medical practices. Medical care was still very primitive at that time, and fresh air and bloodletting were common remedies for many ailments. The germ theory was unknown, so that wounds were wrapped with dirty rags; and most people who went to hospitals soon died. Diseases such as smallpox ravaged the population, with no known cures. Nevertheless, populations began to increase because people were eating more and better food.

A growing population always constitutes a potential source of social change, since it creates stresses with which the society must deal. How are the additional people to be fed and housed? What kinds of work will they find to do? Can traditional values and norms be preserved? Although such issues pose serious problems for communities and societies, the simple fact of increasing numbers of people is often less critical for social change than the related matter of how those people are distributed geographically. If the increasing population in England and other Western European countries during the latter half of the eighteenth century had remained largely in rural areas and small villages, competition for land and food might have intensified, but the basic structure of society would probably not have changed greatly.

Large numbers of those additional people migrated from rural areas to towns and cities, however. To continue the example of England, the population of London grew from about 600,000 to over 900,000 between 1750 and 1800. This urban migration was caused by two kinds of pressures, which demographers call "push" and "pull" forces. Peasants were pushed from rural to urban areas by the efforts of the landed nobility to improve agricultural efficiency and productivity. Land consolidation and enclosure of the commons deprived peasants and tenant farmers of sufficient land to make an adequate living. Technological improvements in farming practices, meanwhile, enabled the land owners to produce larger crops with fewer workers, which further increased the surplus rural population.

When people find it difficult to make an adequate living in rural areas, they tend to drift to towns and cities. Such migration is particularly likely to occur when new work opportunities emerge that pull them toward urban centers. During the latter half of the eighteenth century, increasing numbers of jobs were created in such sectors of the economy as shipping, trade, and commerce—almost all of which were located in cities. Consequently, during this period—and continuing throughout the nineteenth century—there was a steady flow of people from rural to urban areas throughout Europe. Even though the death rate from diseases associated with poor environmental and living conditions was generally much higher in urban than in rural areas, cities continued to gain population because of the continual flow of urban migrants.

The most important consequence of this urban migration was that it provided an ever-growing number of urban dwellers anxious for work and the opportunity to sell their labor in the marketplace. When industrialization began to develop in urban centers during the nineteenth century, consequently, there was already a large available pool of workers to form an industrial-urban labor force.

Technological Innovation

The heart of industrialization is the substitution of power-driven machinery for human labor in the production of goods. For those changes to occur, many new kinds of machinery had to be invented. This process of industrial innovation began in England and centered in the *textile industry,* thus enabling British textiles to dominate the world market for several decades. As described by Mott (1965) and Lenski and Lenski (1982), this process was initiated with the invention of the flying shuttle by John Kay in 1733, which permitted the weaving of broader bolts of cloth much more rapidly. As a result, spinners could not keep up with the demand for yarn, triggering a series of further inventions. In 1765, James Hargreaves developed the spinning jenny, containing eight spindles and later 120, to replace the traditional single-spindle spinning wheel. Several additional improvements in the technology of spinning were incorporated a decade later into the spinning mule, which rapidly produced fine but strong threads.

Meanwhile, weaving looms had become so large and heavy that they were almost impossible to operate manually. This led to a search for new sources of inanimate power. Waterpower was tried, but England had relatively few suitable streams and rivers, and the machinery was extremely inefficient. James Watt had invented the *steam engine* in 1767 to pump water out of coal mines, and it was not difficult to adapt it to drive looms. By the end of the eighteenth century, the textile industry in England was almost entirely powered by steam. All of these inventions increased the productivity of the textile industry many times over, which greatly enhanced the national income.

Another industry that grew rapidly in England during the latter part of the eighteenth century was *iron manufacturing*. The traditional process used charcoal, which became increasingly scarce as England's forests were cut down. Moreover, the resulting pig iron was very hard and brittle and hence unsuitable for many uses. The invention of the blast furnace by Abraham Darby and Henry Cort revolutionized the iron industry, since it produced large quantities of malleable iron at considerably less cost. In 1788, England produced only 68,000 tons of poor quality iron, whereas by 1845 it was producing over 1,600,000 tons of much higher quality iron. This rapid improvement and growth in the iron industry was particularly critical, since it made possible the production of durable machinery that was subsequently introduced into many other industries.

The development of the steam engine and the expansion of the iron industry greatly increased the demand for *coal*. Fortunately for Britain, as its forests were depleted it was able to begin utilizing its large reserves of coal as a new source of energy. Toward the end of the eighteenth century, several improvements in mining technology made it possible to extract coal with much

greater speed and efficiency. In 1760, the country mined only five million tons of coal, but by 1845 this figure had increased to nearly fifty million tons.

Less dramatic but equally important were developments in the manufacturing of *machine tools and machinery*, which had ramifications throughout countless emerging industries. With early machine tools, for example, a single tool had long been used for drilling, boring, grinding, and milling. Gradually, specialized tools were designed for each of those operations that were capable of precision work to the thousandth of an inch. In the production of machines, a major advance was the invention of interchangeable parts. A supply of spare parts could then be kept on hand for each machine, and breakdowns could easily be repaired without having to craft replacement parts by hand.

Industrial goods must be transported from the producer to the consumer. Consequently, during the eighteenth century, England and other European countries began to improve their *transportation systems*. An extensive network of toll roads, or turnpikes (so named because a toll collector had to turn a key to open a gate every few miles) was constructed by private builders throughout England around the middle of the century. By the end of the century most of those roads had permanent, all-weather surfaces. During that same time, a large number of canals were constructed throughout England, which enabled heavy and bulky goods such as coal and iron to be shipped quite inexpensively.

The importance of the canals was quickly diminished, however, by the introduction of the steam engine into the transportation industry during the nineteenth century. Wooden sailing ships were gradually replaced by steel ships propelled by steam that could carry much larger loads more inexpensively and with greater dependability. In 1831, DeWitt Clinton placed a steam engine on a wheeled platform that ran on iron tracks, attached several carriages behind it, and created the first railroad. The superiority of trains over horse-drawn wagons for transporting bulk goods was readily apparent, and by 1850 most English cities were linked by a network of rails. Railroad transportation greatly reduced the cost of shipping many commodities, which in turn lowered their market price and expanded the demand for them, leading to further industrial growth.

Value Changes

If the traditional beliefs, values, and norms that typically existed in agriculturally-based societies had continued to prevail in Western Europe during the eighteenth and nineteenth centuries, it is unlikely that the technological innovations previously described would have produced an industrial revolution. The widespread application of those inventions to manufacturing required a major change in the way people viewed work and business.

This change began with Martin Luther's insistence that all honest forms of work were Christian callings "which challenged both the medieval Christian view of work as punishment for sin and the traditional aristocratic view of work as degrading and beneath the dignity of a gentlemen" (Lenski and Lenski, 1982:239). As the Reformation progressed in Europe, the new Protestant faiths also tended to undermine the traditional fatalism of the masses and to promote a more rational view of life. For example, "Methodism" encouraged its adherents to plan a rational method for conducting their lives, rather than living on a day-to-day basis. Calvinism, preached by John Calvin and his followers, was particularly relevant to emerging industrialism. It stressed the virtues of hard work, self-denial, self-discipline, thrift, frugality, self-reliance, and individual initiative—all of which were ideally suited to the new world of entrepreneurship and industry.

Early in this century, Max Weber (1958) proposed the thesis that this set of Calvinist beliefs, values, and norms—which he termed the "Protestant Ethic"—was a key

component of the "spirt of capitalism" that made industrialization possible in Europe. Moreover, the absence of a Protestant Ethic, he argued, prevented China and India from becoming industrialized much earlier. Calvinists formulated this ethic as a purely religious doctrine, as a way of demonstrating in one's daily life that one was not damned to Hell and might even be one of the elect who was predestined for Heaven. Weber's argument was that the Protestant Ethic unintentionally justified and praised the dedication to work, individual initiative, financial risk-taking, and commitment to profit making that were necessary for early industrialists to succeed in business. To support his thesis, Weber pointed out that Protestant England, Germany, and Scandinavia industrialized earlier and more extensively than did Catholic France, Italy, or Spain.

Later critics have discovered several factual and logical errors in Weber's analysis of the linkage between Protestantism and what is now commonly called the "work ethic." For instance, the second country to industrialize after England was Belgium, which is heavily Catholic. And Catholic regions within Germany tended to industrialize just as rapidly as did Protestant regions of that country. Some critics have even argued that the work ethic was a result of industrialization, rather than a cause. Nevertheless, it is quite evident that *beliefs, values, and norms concerning work and business changed dramatically throughout Europe during the early stages of industrialization.* This was undoubtedly a reciprocal process, with developing economic and social conditions giving rise to new cultural ideas, which in turn supported and

---

DEVELOPMENTS CONTRIBUTING TO INDUSTRIALIZATION

1. Expansion of commercial trade.
2. Creation of nation-states.
3. Increased agricultural productivity.
4. Population growth and redistribution.
5. Extensive technological innovation.
6. Fundamental value changes.

legitimized further social and economic change.

SOCIETAL INDUSTRIALIZATION

All the developments described thus far in this chapter—commercial trade, nation building, agricultural productivity, population growth and redistribution, technological innovation, and cultural changes—laid a foundation for the process of societal industrialization. Some of these trends were ecological in nature, while others involved the political economics and cultures of those societies. By themselves, however, these developments were not sufficient to produce industrialization. This process also involves several major transformations in the economic and social organization of societies. Basically, *industrialization occurs as inanimate-energy-driven machinery in factories is applied to all forms of economic production,* which greatly expands the ability of a society to manufacture all kinds of goods efficiently, abundantly, and relatively inexpensively. As a consequence, the economic system of a society produces increasing amounts of surplus wealth that are not needed for sustenance requirements. Considerable resources and effort can then be redirected toward many other kinds of collective activities.

Four central features of the process of societal industrialization are examined in this section: accumulation of new sources of investment capital, exploitation of new energy sources and raw materials, reorganization of the economic system in industrializing societies, and creation of new types of economic organizations.

Sources of Capital

Technological innovations, no matter how promising they may appear, are useless unless a society possesses an adequate supply of available capital to invest in new production facilities to utilize these new technologies. Regardless of whether new technologies spur the accumulation of additional investment capital or whether the availability of surplus wealth stimulates additional technological innovation, adequate investment capital must be available if new technologies are to become incorporated into an economy. This is true regardless of whether the necessary capital is provided by private entrepreneurs or by the state. Investment capital is sometimes referred to as "surplus capital," since it consists of wealth that is not needed by a society to feed its population and satisfy other basic sustenance needs, although it is certainly not surplus from the perspective of industry. Early industrializing societies typically acquired investment capital from several sources, as illustrated in Figure 9-1.

An initial source of investment capital for several Western European societies was *foreign trade and commerce.* As we have seen, commercial trade began to develop in Europe as early as the fifteenth century, and by the nineteenth century when these countries were starting to industrialize, this was a major source of new capital. It is important, however, to distinguish between domestic and foreign trade. Internal domestic trade and commerce can extensively redistribute existing wealth among individuals and classes within a society, but it does not generate new wealth for the society. External foreign trade and commerce, in contrast, can provide large amounts of new capital for a society. This is also basically a redistribution process, but *among* countries rather than *within* a country, so that while some societies lose wealth, others acquire it. To the extent that this newly acquired wealth is not consumed by the population to raise its standard of living, it is available for investment in developing economic ventures such as industry.

A second source of investment capital that was closely linked to foreign commercial trade was *conquest and colonialization of less developed societies.* Again, this involved exploitation of weaker societies by more powerful European countries. In this case, however, instead of trading for goods, the dominant country simply took them, either through

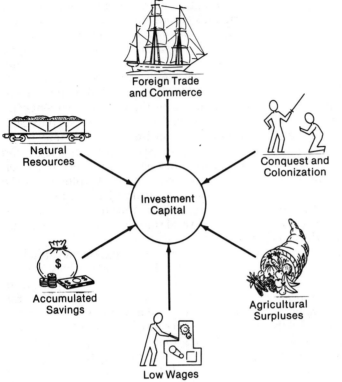

Foreign Trade
and Commerce

Natural
Resources

Conquest and
Colonization

Investment
Capital

Accumulated
Savings

Agricultural
Surpluses

Low Wages

FIGURE 9-1
Sources of capital
for industrialization

military invasion or by establishing more permanent colonial domination over the subjugated societies. With colonialization, there is a fine line between trade and expropriation, since the colonial powers did provide "protection," administration, and some manufactured goods to their colonies. This balance of trade was typically so uneven or one-sided, however, that in many situations it amounted to thinly disguised expropriation.

Growing agricultural surpluses in many European countries, as previously discussed, constituted a third source of investment capital. Since that surplus consisted of food and fibers produced by peasants and farmers, however, it had to be redistributed and transformed before it became available as wealth for investment in manufacturing. This was done in three steps. First, much of the agricultural surplus was taken from its producers by the landed nobility and the central government, through increased taxes and land rents. Second, those surpluses were sold in the marketplace for goods and services, which transformed the agricultural surpluses into wealth in the hands of merchants. Third, merchants directly invested their new wealth in fledgling industrial ventures, or else put those funds into banks, which, in turn, invested them in industry.

The fourth way of acquiring investment capital that was widely used during the early stages of industrialization was *paying low wages to factory workers*. Since there was often a large pool of unemployed people in towns and cities who were eager to work, factory owners could hire them for literally a few pennies a day. These wages were commonly so low that entire families (including children as young as six or seven) had to work long hours in factories merely to keep themselves alive. They lived in crowded hovels and faced an early death from malnutrtion and/or exhaustion. Karl Marx's major criticism of nineteenth-century industry was that factory owners paid their workers much less than the true value of their work in both human and economic terms, so that it amounted to virtual slave labor, which robbed workers of their humanity. Factory owners, meanwhile, often sold their manufactured products at prices that far exceeded the value of the materials and labor required to produce them, thus reaping huge profits. Part or all of those profits were then available for investment in industrial expansion.

Fifth, the main source of investment capital advocated by early economic theorists such as Adam Smith was *accumulated savings.* As ordinary people built up small amounts of savings, they could put their money in banks that pooled those funds and invested them in businesses. More important in this process, however, were wealthy merchants and industrialists who had sufficient savings to invest directly in new economic ventures. This is still the way in which classical economic theory proposes that capital should be accumulated for business investments. There were two serious problems with this theory in the early stages of industrialization, however. First, the vast majority of workers—both on farms and in factories—lived a hand-to-mouth existence and had no surplus savings to invest. Second, merchants and industrialists were often more interested in consuming their wealth through lavish lifestyles in an effort to compete with the nobility for social status. The fact that some merchants and industrialists did save some of their profits and invested them in new businesses gives testimony to the strength of the work ethic in emphasizing the value of self-denial and deferred gratification.

A sixth source of investment capital that is often overlooked is *extraction of natural resources* at low cost. Coal, iron ore, other minerals—and later oil—constituted vast stores of resources that required no human effort or cost to create. The only costs involved were for extracting and transporting them, and with new technologies and cheap labor, these costs were usually minimal. Consequently, these natural resources were in effect inherited capital waiting to be taken from the earth. Individuals who realized the potential of this situation and took advantage of it reaped huge fortunes. The fact that these resources are all finite in quantity did not occur to anyone until well into the twentieth century. Vast amounts of new capital were there for the taking, and we have drawn heavily on them to finance industrial development in the West.

A critical turning point in this process of capital accumulation has been identified by Walter Rostow (1964). From historical analyses of industrialization in various countries, he concluded that the annual rate of capital investment in industry must exceed 10 percent of the country's total income before it can "take off" into self-sustained industrial growth. Rostow estimated that this take-off point was achieved in Great Britain between 1780 and 1800; in Belgium and France between 1830 and 1860; in the United States between 1840 and 1860; in Sweden between 1870 and 1890; in Japan between 1880 and 1900; and in Russia between 1890 and 1910. After a country achieves economic take-off, its industrial profits are sufficient to sustain further industrialization and continued economic growth, provided those profits are reinvested in economic development and not immediately consumed as a result of a rapidly growing population or escalating standards of living.

Subsequent writers have criticzed Rostow's thesis as too rigid, because it does not take account of other factors that are unique to the economy of each country, and as too narrow because it ignores international trade. Nevertheless, the essential idea that a certain amount of capital accumulation must occur in a society—from whatever sources—before it can sustain full-scale industrialization is certainly valid.

Exploitation of Resources

The use of machinery to produce goods and services requires, above all, vast amounts of inanimate energy. As long as human and animal muscle power provided the chief sources of energy for economic production, no economy could develop beyond simple agriculture and the production of handicraft goods. *Early factories became possible only after the steam engine was invented and connected to machinery.* The first fuel burned in those steam engines was wood, which was later replaced by charcoal derived from wood. Great Britain and Western Europe were once covered with forests, but during the eighteenth century they were cut down much faster than they could be regrown, so that the available supply of wood diminished steadily. Some timber was imported from the New World, but shipping it across the Atlantic was obviously an expensive process.

Fortunately for the industrial revolution, a new source of energy was available to replace wood and charcoal. Great Britain and Western Europe contained vast deposits of coal, and throughout the nineteenth century coal mining increased very rapidly as a result of numerous technological innovations in both coal extraction and transportation. *Coal literally fired the industrial revolution until well into the the twentieth century,* providing an energy source that at the time seemed inexhaustible. Reliance on coal as the principal energy source for industrial production posed three serious problems, however. First, because it is bulky and heavy, coal is difficult to transport from mine to factory, although railroads largely solved that problem. Second, as coal deposits lying near the surface are depleted, mines must be dug deeper and deeper. Deep mining is much more expensive than surface mining, and it can also be exceedingly dangerous work for miners. To cope with this problem, mining was increasingly mechanized and safety procedures were developed, which kept the economic and human costs within tolerable limits. Third, burning coal produces large amounts of dirty smoke that is breathed by everyone in the surrounding area. The famous "London fogs" of the late nineteenth and early twentieth centuries were not natural occurrences, but a direct result of the heavy deposits of coal soot that were constantly in the air above the city. This third problem was not really solved during the era of coal, but was simply endured, despite the filth and disease it created.

Oil was first intentionally drilled in Pennsylvania in 1859, but for a long time its usefulness as an energy source was not appreciated. Oil and the natural gas found with it were used largely for such purposes as lubrication and lighting. More than anything else, the invention of the automobile brought oil to the forefront as a fuel. Unlike coal, it is relatively easy to transport, it can easily be pumped to the surface once a well has been drilled and hence is very cheap to extract, and it burns with a much hotter and cleaner flame than coal. *As techniques of refining oil were developed, it steadily replaced coal as the primary energy source in all industrial nations and remains so today.* Although factories—as well as homes and other buildings—now rely heavily on electricity to power motors of all kinds, most electricity is still generated by burning oil. And motor vehicles, trains, and planes are, of course, totally dependent on oil products as fuels. Although coal initially fired the industrial revolution, oil and natural gas have kept it going throughout the twentieth century. However, they will be largely exhausted within another hundred years.

Industrial production also requires continuing supplies of all kinds of minerals and other natural resources, in addition to coal or oil as fuels. The most basic of these is iron ore for the production of steel, but many other natural resources are also vitally important. These include copper, tin, zinc, bauxite, lead, manganese, nickel, and silver, as well as many rarer minerals. As industrialization progressed, extraction of these minerals from the earth also had to increase constantly. Thus far, supplies of these resources have been adequate to allow industrial production to keep growing. Deposits of all minerals and many other natural resources are finite, however, and sooner or later will become very scarce or prohibitively expensive.

The term "exploitation" was purposefully

used in the heading of this section, rather than the more common term "development." *From the beginning, industrialization has been exploiting the earth's existing natural resources, not developing them.* To develop something is to create it, and natural resources are not created by humans. We simply find them and extract them from the earth, drawing down limited deposits that in most instances cannot be replenished. The process of industrialization has, in effect, been continually withdrawing resource deposits from our "earth bank account" without replacing them. As with any bank account, when the balance reaches zero the account is useless.

Reorganization of the Economy

As a society begins to industrialize, its agriculturally-based economy will no longer be adequate to sustain and facilitate the new kinds of economic production that are being developed. Over time, its economic system will be forced to change in several critical ways. The eventual outcome of this transformation is an entirely new kind of economy. The most important changes that typically occurred in the economic systems of Western nations, all of which industrialized with a capitalist type of economy, are described here.

Profit-making Orientation. In a feudal type of economy, most economic activity is oriented toward satisfying immediate needs such as food, clothing, and housing. Although both peasants and landowners normally seek to improve their standard of living, they do not attempt to accumulate wealth for its own sake. In other words, they usually exchange any surplus wealth they generate for producer or consumer goods. The values of feudal societies reinforced this tendency by teaching that profit making and wealth accumulation are immoral.

In contrast, *capitalistic industrial economies are primarily oriented toward financial profit making, wealth accumulation, and capital investment as their major goals.* In other words, business owners must be willing to at least tem-

porarily defer gratifying some of their desires for consumer goods. They must also come to believe that profit making is a worthwhile activity in its own right, which necessitates the creation of a new value system emphasizing profit-making economic activities. This kind of economic orientation is absolutely vital if the society is to accumulate sufficient capital for sustained economic growth. As we have already seen, a profit-making economic orientation arose in Western Europe during the seventeenth and eighteenth centuries as a consequence of rapidly expanding commercial trade, so that when the process of industrialization began in the nineteenth century, that orientation was already well-established within the merchant class. As industrialization progressed, this orientation became increasingly dominant throughout most other sectors of those countries.

Laissez-faire Ideology. In early capitalistic-industrial societies, businessmen (businesswomen were virtually nonexistent then) seeking to maximize their profits feverently desired to be left entirely alone by the government and to operate their businesses in whatever manner they saw fit. They strongly resisted any efforts by the national government to regulate their activities, for fear that such controls would reduce their profits. To legitimize this stance, they developed a laissez-faire economic ideology to replace the earlier ideology of mercantilism. Loosely translated from French, "laissez-faire" means "allow to happen" or "leave alone." *The proper role of government in laissez faire ideology is to leave business entirely alone,* regardless of whatever practices businesses may adopt in their drive for profit maximization. The mercantile philosophy that had developed with the expansion of commercial trade provided the foundation for laissez-faire ideology, but it required one important modification. Under mercantilism, the government was expected to take actions to promote trade and other commercial activities, such as facilitating capital accumulation and investment and protecting and expanding markets, although it was not expected to regulate business activities. The laissez-faire ideology of early industrialization took the further step of rejecting all ties between business and government. In practice, businessmen were often willing to accept governmental activities that benefited them, such as issuing patents or imposing duties on foreign imports, but they did not want the government to interfere in any way with wages, working conditions, products, markets, or other factors that would affect their profits.

Commodity Markets. *Capitalist economies operate through markets in which businesses sell and buy goods and services.* We often think of these markets in terms of retail trade, but there are also markets for raw materials, component parts used in manufacturing, wholesale trade, and stocks and bonds. In all these markets, sellers and buyers negotiate over the financial worth of the commodities being exchanged until they agree on mutually acceptable prices. If the seller's asking price for an item is higher than the buyer is willing to pay, that item remains unsold until another buyer is willing to meet the asking price or the seller lowers the price. The operating principle of the market is open competition, which over time is supposed to produce a natural balance between supply and demand. In a balanced market, the going prices presumably reflect the true values of the commodities being exchanged.

A market economy is quite different from the economic exchanges that typically occurred in feudal nonmarket economies. In a feudal economy, as we have seen, many transactions are based on barter involving direct exchanges of goods or services. In addition, peasants fulfill their fealty obligations to the lord or pay their land rents to him by giving him a portion of all the goods they produce. None of these transactions involve the assignment of monetary value to commodities, but rather are governed by traditionally established norms of fairness and/or obligation. The development of an economy based on commodity markets therefore ne-

cessitates creating an entirely new kind of economic system.

Banking Systems. A commodity market economy obviously requires a monetary system to provide a medium of exchange in the marketplace. Money has been in use, on a limited basis, for thousands of years, so industrializing societies did not have to invent money. What they did have to create were *complex banking systems to handle the continually expanding flow of money in market economies.* Banks provide numerous services that are indispensable in such economies. They facilitate the accumulation of capital, make it available for investment in businesses, handle the financial transactions through which markets operate, and create money by issuing bank notes backed by the deposits they manage.

In the early stages of industrialization, banks were typically quite small in terms of their total assets and the geographic area they served. They also functioned independently of one another, even to the extent of issuing their own banknotes that were not honored by other banks. However, as business continued to grow, both financially and geographically, more complex banking systems were gradually developed to serve the needs of those enterprises. Many small local banks were forced out of business, while the surviving banks began handling ever-increasing amounts of money, operating on a national or even international scale, and establishing interdependent linkages among themselves. A critical outcome of this process in all industrial societies was the development—generally around the beginning of the twentieth century—of state-controlled or regulated central banks that coordinate all banking transactions within a country and issue a national currency that is honored throughout the country.

Labor Markets. Goods and services were not the only things that became organized into markets in industrializing societies. *Labor was also rapidly transformed from a personal relationship between a landowner or mer-*

chant and his workers into an impersonal contract between employer and employee, creating labor markets. Employers enter a labor market with an offer to hire anyone who is able and willing to perform specified tasks for given wages, while laborers enter the market by offering to work for cash wages. When employers and employees reach agreement on the jobs to be performed and the wages to be paid, employment contracts are signed and the laborers go to work for their employers.

Labor markets differ from commodity markets in a fundamental respect, however. In a commodity market, sellers and buyers both have resources (goods or money) with which to bargain. If the market is operating adequately, most exchanges should represent a relatively equal balance of market power, with the result that both parties benefit from the exchange and neither is exploited. In a labor market, in contrast, employers typically command much greater power than workers, especially in the early phases of industrialization before the creation of effective labor unions. When there was a large surplus of unskilled workers who had to find a job to survive, as was often the case when peasants are streaming into towns as a result of changes in agricultural conditions, they were forced to accept whatever working demands, conditions, and wages that employers offered. With their overriding drive to maximize profits, employers typically offered as little as possible to their workers. If one person refused a job, there were usually many others anxious to take it at any wage. The consequences of this situation throughout the nineteenth century were atrocious working conditions, 60-hour work weeks, extremely low wages for workers, frequent industrial accidents, and miserable poverty for the vast majority of workers.

Complex Economic Organizations

As more and more machinery was introduced into the production process, several problems began to arise. First, the machinery was expensive, and many individual craftsmen did not have the capital to purchase it. Second, machinery needed more space than was typically available in homes or shops. Third, machinery required a reliable source of inanimate energy that was not available in "cottage industries." Fourth, use of machinery generally required many technical and administrative skills not possessed by handicraft artisans. This set of difficulties demanded a new type of business organization, with the result that *economic production moved fairly rapidly away from homes and shops to factories.*

A large factory building solved the space problem, allowing many interrelated machines to be located together. This, in turn, eased the energy supply problem, since all those machines could be connected to a single source of power. At first, this was typically a steam engine located at the factory, but as electricity was introduced into factories, the generating plant could be located some distance away and serve many factories.

The problem of accumulating sufficient capital to purchase many expensive machines and construct and operate factories was not so easily solved. Since few individuals or families could afford the new machinery or the cost of building a factory, businessmen seeking to establish or expand an enterprise often had to combine their financial resources in a partnership. Although this legal arrangement enabled them to pool their funds and jointly own the business, it had several serious limitations. Initial investment capital was limited to whatever financial resources the partners could contribute

---

REORGANIZATION OF THE ECONOMY WITH INDUSTRIALIZATION

1. Adoption of an profit-making orientation.
2. Development of a laissez-faire ideology.
3. Expansion of commodity markets.
4. Creation of banking systems.
5. Establishment of labor markets.

from their own savings or could borrow from a bank. Each partner was legally liable for all the financial activities of the firm, so that if one partner was financially incompetent or dishonest, the other partners were all personally liable for any ensuing debts or lawsuits. If the firm went bankrupt, all of their personal possessions and wealth could be seized by the courts. Finally, the firm existed only for the lifetime of the partners.

To overcome these limitations, a new type of business organization, the joint-stock corporation, was invented. *A corporation is an organizational entity that is chartered by a government and is legally considered to exist independent of any individuals.* This type of organization has many advantages over personal ownership or partnerships. It can sell stock to raise capital from the public, which immensely expands its financial base. The stockholders are the legal owners of the corporation, but when a large number of stocks is distributed among many individuals, no single stockholder is likely to own a large enough proportion of the total stock to control the company. Consequently, the corporate managers can direct the company as if they owned it. No stockholder is financially liable for corporate losses beyond the amount of money invested in the stock, so there is less fear of bankruptcy and a greater willingness to invest in the company and take financial risks in expanding its activities. The corporate managers, meanwhile, are not financially liable for the company at all, unless they are also stockholders. And since the corporation is an independent legal entity, it continues to exist despite turnover among stockholders and managers.

The problem of acquiring the technical and administrative skills necessary to operate a factory or other business had far-reaching consequences for economic organizations and working conditions in all industrial societies. For individuals, the essential nature of work changed dramatically. Most workers could no longer master an entire craft and carry out the complete production process. *At all levels, jobs became increasingly specialized, focusing on only one or a few narrow tasks in the production process.* As a result, workers typically lost their autonomy as independent craftsmen and their sense of satisfaction that comes from creating a finished product. Instead, most workers became merely specialized and interchangeable parts in an industrial system.

As work was increasingly specialized, economic organizations inevitably became more complex. Each task in the overall production process became highly interrelated with, and dependent upon, many other specialized tasks. Economic organizations therefore became not only larger, but they also were structured into numerous separate but interdependent subunits. In a complex organization, each work unit, section, office, and department performs a particular specialized function. Within a modern factory, for instance, various component parts are each produced by a different unit, and them assembled by other workers into a finished product. Purchasing, design, accounting, advertising, sales, and other functions are also carried out by specialized units of the organization.

To keep such complex organizations functioning smoothly, procedures had to be established for overall communication, coordination, and control throughout the entire operation. The easiest way of doing this was *to arrange all the units of the organization into a hierarchy of authority in which management decisions were made at the top and enforced down the hierarchy through detailed operating procedures and rules.* Consequently, economic organizations—and subsequently many other kinds of organizations in industrial societies—became not only large and complex, but also hierarchical in structure. Thus was created the modern bureaucratic organization.

TOTAL SOCIAL CHANGE

Thus far we have been discussing industrialization primarily as a process of economic change. In reality, however, *societal industri-*

alization is a process of total social change that fundamentally transforms all aspects of a society. An industrial society is fundamentally different from an agrarian society in virtually all dimensions of human life. This section focuses on two critical aspects of this process of total social changes that are directly linked to economic industrialization.

Economic Growth

The overall outcome of the capitalistic industrial economies that developed in Western Europe and the United States during the nineteenth and twentieth centuries was continual and rapidly increasing rates of economic growth. As businesses acquired more investment capital, developed new technologies, ruthlessly exploited natural resources, sought to maximize their profits, operated without any governmental regulation, developed ever-expanding commodity markets and banking systems, manipulated labor markets to their advantage, and created new types of economic organizations, they were frequently able to increase their economic productivity—and hence their wealth—many times over within a generation or two.

To cite one example, in the United States the Gross National Product (the total monetary value of all goods and services produced by a country during a year), expressed in 1972 dollars, was only about $800 per capita in 1870 (the first year for which this figure is available). It had risen to approximately $2,000 per capita by 1920 and had reached $5,300 by 1970. During this 100-year period there was almost a seven-fold increase in total wealth per person, despite a rapidly growing population. The total Gross National Product, without standardization for population size but again expressed in 1972 dollars, rose during those 100 years from about $35 billion to $1,086 billion, an increase of 3000 percent! Most other industrializing countries also experienced similar rates of economic growth during that period. The economic growth that occurred during the early stages of industrialization in

the West was immensely beneficial to those societies, although most of the newly acquired wealth remained for a long time in the hands of a small number of economic elites. The bulk of the laboring population, meanwhile, continued to live at or near the poverty level and commonly experienced a much lower standard of living than they or their parents had known as peasants on the land.

Redistribution of Power

To enact any process of extensive social change, and particularly the transformation of an entire society, *considerable amounts of social power must be exercised in several critical realms.* With industrialization these included:

(1) Overcoming the dominance of the old land-based nobility;
(2) Unifying the national political system;
(3) Accumulating and investing large amounts of capital in emerging economic enterprises;
(4) Securing and utilizing vital natural resources; and
(5) Creating new kinds of business and other organizations.

None of these changes occurred spontaneously of their own accord, nor were they the result of altruistic intentions or feelings of goodwill toward others. Quite the opposite. Changes in all these realms were vigorously pursued by some actors because they believed that the new arrangements would benefit them, expand their organizations, or fulfill their basic values. Other actors just as vigorously resisted each new development because they believed it would harm them, threaten their organizations, or conflict with their cherished values.

Out of these opposing forces in society came social conflict, which may be expressed in economic competition, political struggles, interorganizational disputes, class conflict, religious clashes, social movements, or war. All these forms of social conflict have periodically erupted within and between societies as they industrialized. Such conflicts have sometimes involved large portions of the population, but they have been most evident among competing sets of elites struggling to exert power over one another. Established elites who held privileged positions and exercised control over the old social order—such as the landed nobility and hereditary monarchs—have fought to maintain traditional patterns of social ordering and cultural values. Newly emerging elites—such as business owners and leaders of social and political movements—have constantly attempted to acquire additional power resources and to establish different forms of social ordering and cultural values. In short, *the exercise of social power was necessary not only to initiate change, but also to overcome resistance to change and resolve the inevitably resulting conflicts.*

If wielding of extensive social power was the central dynamic in the process of total social change arising from industrialization, two questions are immediately suggested. (1) What previously unused or underused resources have been drawn upon to generate new power in social life? (2) What individuals or organizations have exercised this new power to promote radical social change?

The answer to the first question lies primarily, but not exclusively, in the generation of wealth. Since increased production and economic growth were direct outcomes of industrialization, vast amounts of new wealth were created in this process. That new wealth could be used not only to promote further industrial growth, but also to improve one's standard of living, gain social status, acquire political power, and control other organizations such as educational and religious institutions. It was no accident, therefore, that *the possession and use of great wealth became the primary source of social power in industrializing societies.*

The answer to the second question follows directly from the preceding answer. As wealth became the principal power resource in industrializing societies, whichever actors received the wealth being generated by industry largely controled the direction of social change. Over time, *most traditional elites were gradually displaced by the rising new class of industrial owners and managers.* As the wealth and power of these emerging business elites continued to expand, they were able to gain control of the economic system and later the political system in all industrializing nations.

SUMMARY

The initial foundation for the industrial revolution was the development of commercial trade that began in Western Europe during the fifteenth and sixteenth centuries. These commercial endeavors introduced the idea of engaging in business transactions to earn a profit, provided a new source of wealth, established the first large-scale economic markets, and created a rising class of merchants. A critical technological development that made possible commercial trade was improvements in ship design and navigation. The expansion of commercial trade greatly improved the ecological conditions of Western Europe, which enabled the economies of those countries to grow far beyond the limits of their domestic resources.

A second important foundation for the industrial revolution was the rise of the nation-state as a political unit. The autonomous fiefdoms that existed during the feudal era slowly gave way to more unified kingdoms ruled by monarchs. This process of political consolidation was accomplished largely through warfare, but as commercial trade increased, the dominant political elites were able to draw on the new wealth being produced to further strengthen their rule. Monarchs welcomed this new wealth, since it freed them from dependence on local lords for resources and enabled them to support their governments and courts. As merchants became increasingly wealthy, they created alliances with monarchs, supplying them with necessary funds in exchange for protection and support. These alliances strengthened both parties and gradually enabled the merchants to replace the landed nobility as a privileged class. Several other classes also sided with the monarchs in their struggles against the landed nobility, thus enabling the monarchs to consolidate their political authority and control over the state.

A number of other developments that occurred in Western Europe during the eighteenth century also contributed to the industrial revolution. As a result of numerous technological and managerial innovations, agricultural productivity rose dramatically. These agricultural improvements were largely introduced by the landed nobility in an effort to increase their resources, but they eventually hastened the transition to industrialism. As a direct result of more food being produced, populations in Western European nations increased rapidly in size. Many of those additional people migrated to urban centers, where they became a labor pool for factories.

Many technological innovations made possible the application of machinery to economic production. Machinery was first introduced into the textile industry in England in the late eighteenth century, which quickly necessitated the adaptation of the steam engine to industrial use. Other industries that benefited greatly from the early introduction of machinery were iron manufacturing, the production of machine tools, coal mining, and railroads.

The eighteenth and nineteenth centuries also witnessed the introduction of a new set of cultural beliefs and values that gradually replaced traditional medieval culture. This new view of life emphasized the dignity of secular work, rational planning, thrift, self-discipline, individual initiative, and material wealth.

The capital to finance these new economic ventures was obtained from several sources. These included foreign trade and commerce, conquest and colonialization of less developed societies, growing agricultural surpluses, payment of low wages to factory workers, accumulated savings of wealthy individuals and families, and extraction of nat-

ural resources from the earth. Resource exploitation was particularly important in this process, since it provided immense amounts of new wealth at very little immediate cost. As the supply of wood diminished in Europe, coal became the principal fuel that fired the industrial revolution. Later, petroleum and its derivatives became the primary energy source for industry.

As industrialization progressed, it led to the development of an entirely new kind of economic system, which replaced agriculturally-based economies. This emerging capitalistic industrial economy contained many novel features. It was oriented toward profit making rather than meeting immediate economic needs. It was legitimized by a laissaz-faire ideology, which said that business had the right to do whatever it wanted without governmental interference. It operated through commodity markets in which the supply of goods and services offered for sale presumably balanced the demand for them through the mechanism of unregulated prices. It necessitated the creation of extensive national banking systems. And it transformed labor into an impersonal wage market.

Industrialization also led to the creation of new kinds of economic organizations. Economic production shifted from homes and shops to factories containing large numbers of machines driven by a common source of inanimate energy. Individually-owned firms and partnerships gave way to corporations owned by stockholders and operated by business managers. Jobs at all levels became increasingly specialized and narrowly defined, with the result that workers lost control of their own labor. And industries and other businesses became steadily larger and more complex, consisting of many functionally specialized and interdependent subunits arranged in a hierarchy of authority.

As industrialization progressed, it gradually transformed entire societies. One direct consequence of developing industrial economies in Western Europe and North America was extensive economic growth. The Gross

National Products of these countries, measured on a per capita basis, typically increased many times over their preindustrial levels. A second direct consequence was the exercise of increasing amounts of power by industrialists and other business people, which led to pervasive social conflict. Drawing on the immense wealth generated by industrialization, this new class of industrial owners and managers gradually replaced traditional elites and came to dominate their societies.

CHAPTER 10

CONTEMPORARY INDUSTRIALIZING SOCIETIES

How do industrializing societies compare with industrialized societies in terms of their national wealth?

What problems do capitalist economies face in industrializing societies, and why are many of those economies partially or wholly socialist?

Why is Western-style political democracy very unlikely to occur in industrializing nations?

What are some major differences between the traditional and modern sectors of industrializing societies?

Why is it rather unlikely that many presently developing societies will achieve full industrialization in the near future?

ECONOMIC CONDITIONS

The previous chapter dealt with the process of industrialization as it occurred in Western Europe and North America during the nineteenth and early twentieth centuries, as well as prior developments that laid the foundation for the emergence of these industrial societies. In contrast, this chapter focuses on contemporary conditions in the many societies around the world that are presently struggling to make a similar transition from an agricultural to an industrial economy. In this overview of contemporary industrializing societies we must necessarily ignore the vast differences that exist among them in levels of economic development, patterns of social ordering, and cultural ideas. Our focus, instead, is on the common conditions and problems shared by these societies as they attempt to become industrialized.

Categories of Industrializing Societies

Today there are 172 independent nations in the world with populations over 150,000

that are members of the United Nations. Only 35 of those nations are generally considered to be highly industrialized. The remaining *137 nations, or 80 percent of the world's independent countries, have not become fully industrialized.* Those nonindustrialized nations contain 76 percent of the world's population.

Two objective measures and one subjective measure are commonly used to distinguish between industrialized and nonindustrialized societies. The objective measures, for which relatively accurate figures are available from most countries, are

(1) Energy consumption per capita per year; and
(2) Gross National Product (GNP) per capita.

Approximate criteria for industrialized nations on those two measures in 1987 were energy consumption per capita greater than 50 gigajoules per year and Gross National Product per capita greater than $2,000 per year. (A gigajoule is the standard measure of energy used in United Nations statistics. About 6.1 gigajoules of energy are equivalent to one barrel of oil.) The third measure—dominance of the economy by manufacturing and related nonagricultural activities—remains subjective, since adequate objective data are not presently available for many countries.

The nonindustrialized societies of the world can be divided into three broad categories, on the basis of their current economic conditions.

Advanced industrializing nations are those that nearly or entirely meet the objective criteria for energy consumption and national wealth, but whose economies are not yet considered to be fully industrialized. There are 22 such societies at the present time. These include ten oil-producing countries that contain very little other industry; the two city-states of Hong Kong and Singapore, whose economies are based primarily on commerce but which are expanding their industrial base fairly rapidly; the two Caribbean island-states of Barbados and Trinidad and Tobago, whose economies are based primarily on tourism; and eight nations whose economies will probably be considered highly industrialized within the next decade or so: Mexico, Cuba, Argentina, Venezuela, Taiwan, North and South Korea, and South Africa.

Agrarian industrializing nations are those whose energy consumption and national wealth are well below the criteria for industrialized countries, and whose economies are based primarily on settled agriculture. Approximately 70 nations fall into this category at the present time. They are located in South and Central America, the Middle East, Northern Africa, and Asia. All of these nations have begun the process of industrialization by establishing some manufacturing and related businesses.

Horticultural industrializing nations have very low levels of energy consumption and national wealth, and their economies are based largely on gardening, using hand tools rather than plows and other mechanical equipment. There are approximately 45 nations in this category, located primarily in sub-Saharan Africa and on the Pacific Islands (Lenski and Nolan, 1984). The division between horticultural and agrarian societies is somewhat arbitrary today, since mechanical farming techniques are being introduced fairly rapidly into many of the remaining horticultural societies, but on the whole these countries are unquestionably much less developed economically than contemporary agrarian societies. Nevertheless, most of these horticultural countries also contain some industry.

The term "industrializing" is included in the names of all three of these categories, since there are almost no purely agrarian or horticultural societies left in the world today. *Even the least developed countries contain some factories and are attempting to move toward more industrial-based economies, and many of them are at least partially industrialized.* Moreover, all of them import manufactured goods from industrialized nations, their people are somewhat aware of the standards of living enjoyed in those societies, and they undoubtedly desire to have some of those goods for themselves.

The discussion of contemporary industrializing societies in this chapter pertains most directly to those in the first and second of the preceding categories, although to a limited extent it can also be applied to the third category of horticultural societies. Nations in that latter category present an interesting situation, since many of them are attempting to move directly from gardening to industrial economies, bypassing the agrarian stage of development. It is still too early to know if they will be successful in this endeavor, but it is clear that they are severely disadvantaged in this process in comparison with agrarian nations (Lenski and Nolan, 1984).

Comparative Economic Conditions

All industrializing societies are quite poor in comparison with the fully industrialized societies. Table 10-1 demonstrates this tremendous disparity in wealth in some detail. It gives the Gross National Product per capita in 1985

TABLE 10-1 Gross National Product Per Capita in 1985 for for Four Sets of Societies*

Highly Industrialized Societies		*Advanced Industrializing Societies*	
	GNP/Capita		*GNP/Capita*
United States	$16,400	Singapore	$7,400
Switzerland	16,400	Hong Kong	6,200
Norway	13,900	Venezuela	3,100
Canada	13,700	South Korea	2,200
Luxembourg	13,400	Mexico	2,100
Sweden	11,900	Argentina	2,100
Japan	11,300	South Africa	2,000
Denmark	11,200		
West Germany	11,000	Average	$3,600
Finland	10,900		
Australia	10,800		
Iceland	10,700		
France	9,600		
Austria	9,200		
Netherlands	9,200		
Belgium	8,500		
United Kingdom	8,400		
New Zealand	7,700		
USSR	7,400		
East Germany	7,000+		
Average	$10,500		

Agrarian Industrializing Societies		*Horticultural Industrializing Societies*	
	GNP/Capita		*GNP/Capita*
Algeria	$2,500	Fiji	$1,700
Malaysia	2,100	Mauritius	1,100
Panama	2,000	Congo	1,000
Uruguay	1,700	Cameroon	800
Brazil	1,600	Nigeria	800
Syria	1,600	Zimbabwe	700
Jordan	1,600	Papua-New Guinea	700
Chile	1,400	Cote d'Ivoire	600
Colombia	1,300	Soloman Islands	500
Costa Rica	1,300	Liberia	500
Tunisia	1,200	Mauritania	400
Ecuador	1,200	Zambia	400
Turkey	1,100	Senegal	400
Peru	1,000	Sierra Leone	400
Thailand	800	Ghana	400
Dominican Republic	800	Kenya	300
Egypt	700	Somalia	300
Guyana	600	Sudan	300
Bolivia	500	Guinea	300
China	300	Gambia	200
Average	$1,300	Average	$600

Average GNP/capita for all 35 industrialized societies	$9,900

TABLE 10-1 *Continued*

Average GNP/capita for all 137 industrializing societies	$700
Average GNP/capita for the entire world	$2,900

* Among highly industrialized, agrarian industrializing, and horticultural industrializing societies, those with the greatest energy consumption per capita in 1985 are included. The advanced industrializing societies listed are those that are most industrialized, and they exclude the oil-producing and tourist nations with high energy consumption and GNP but little industry. Countries for which GNP data are not available are omitted from the table.

+ Estimated.

Source: Population Reference Bureau, World Population Data Sheet, 1987, Washington, D.C.

for four sets of nations: the 20 most highly industrialized societies; seven advanced industrializing societies whose economies are the most industrialized (but which are not the most wealthy since they do not include the oil producers); the 20 agrarian societies whose economies are most developed; and the 20 most developed horticultural societies. (In the latter three categories, some nations are omitted because GNP data were not available for them.) These listings (with the exception of the advanced industrializing societies) are therefore biased toward higher levels of economic development; they do not include the least developed and poorest nations within each category. If those latter agrarian and horticultural societies had been included, the disparity in national wealth between industrialized and industrializing nations would have been even greater, as seen in the summary figures at the bottom of the table.

The 20 most highly industrialized nations had Gross National Products per capita in 1985 ranging from $16,400 for the United States and Switzerland to $7,000 for East Germany. The remaining 15 industrialized nations not included in the table are less wealthy, with 1985 GNP's ranging from $6,000 for Czechoslovakia to $2,000 for Hungary, Yugoslavia, and Portugal. The

average GNP per capita for the industrialized nations listed in Table 10-1 was $10,500 in 1985, while for all 35 of these nations (weighted by population size) it was about $9,900.

The seven advanced industrializing nations listed in Table 10-1 overlap the poorer industrialized countries in wealth. Nevertheless, their average 1985 GNP per capita was only $3,600.

The 20 most developed agrarian nations in Table 10-1 are considerably poorer, with an average GNP per capita of only $1,300 in 1985. India, which is the second largest agrarian country after China, had a GNP of only $250 per capita.

For the 20 most developed horticultural nations in Table 10-1, the average per capita 1985 GNP was only $600. Many of the other horticultural societies not listed in the table are extremely poor, and in nine of them the per capita GNP was less than $200. The poorest country in the world is Ethiopia, where the 1985 GNP per capita was only $110.

The average GNP per capita for all industrializing nations (weighted by population size) was only about $700 in 1985. Residents of the highly industrialized nations thus enjoy, on the average, 14 times as much wealth as residents of industrializing nations. The average GNP per capita for the entire world (again weighted by population size) was about $2,900 in 1985.

In sum, *the world is today divided into two sets of very different societies: a relatively small number of industrialized nations, many of which are extremely wealthy, and a large number of industrializing agrarian and horticultural nations, most of which are quite poor.* This situation produces countless tensions and problems around the globe that could easily erupt into political, economic, and social conflicts or crises. Most inhabitants of nonindustrialized countries are more or less aware of the economic affluence that exists in the industrialized nations, and they want to share in those economic benefits.

Data for energy consumption per capita per year—which is the other objective measure commonly used to determine industrialization—are not included in Table 10-1. However, a brief summary of these data also demonstrates the tremendous disparity between industrialized and industrializing nations in levels of development. The highly industrialized nations in the table consumed an average of 170 gigajoules of energy per person in 1984. For the advanced industrializing nations in the table, the comparable figure was only 80 gigajoules. (Among the oil-producing countries, it is, of course, much higher.) For the agrarian nations in the table, average per capital energy consumption was just 20 gigajoules, while for the horticultural nations in the table it was merely six gigajoules. The differences in these energy consumption figures for industrialized and industrializing societies are thus as dramatic as those for national wealth.

Dual Economic Systems

An additional situation that further compounds the economic problems facing most industrializing societies today is that they commonly contain two quite disparate economic systems. *Their agricultural economy has typically not developed very significantly from what it has been for the past 2,000 years.* Most of the agricultural tools and techniques being used are still quite elementary, with animals and humans providing much energy and labor. Consequently, the standards of living prevailing within the agricultural economies of these societies are generally extremely low, and the social patterns of these people are highly traditional. Moreover, societies that have attempted to develop their agricultural economies to produce commodities to sell in the world market have typically been forced by market conditions to specialize in only one or a few export crops. For example, Cuba depends on sugar exports for over four-fifths of its foreign sales, while Colombia derives almost two-thirds of its foreign exchange from the sale of coffee. Such extreme specialization makes a country highly vulnerable to shifts in world markets. If the price of sugar drops, Cuba's economy can be devestated. If the demand for coffee declines, Colombia's economy will suffer greatly.

At the same time, *most industrializing societies also contain a modern economy based on commerce and industry.* This modern economy is located in urban centers, linked into world markets, and operated by people with Western educations and orientations. Consequently the modern business economy is usually not only distinct from the traditional agricultural economy, but it operates almost independently of it. The modern economies of these industrializing societies are not just small-scale versions of Western industrial economies, however. Many large businesses are owned largely or entirely by foreign interests, and they primarily serve markets in other countries. Other businesses are owned by the state rather than by private individuals. In addition, these developing industrial economies also tend to be highly specialized, so as to be competitive in the world market. They must find an economic niche that is not already dominated by industrial nations and exploit it to the fullest, regardless of how one-sided their economy becomes in the process. For instance, Iraq sells virtually nothing but petroleum on the world market, while Taiwan's foreign exports consist largely of electronic equipment, the component parts of which are shipped there by industrial countries for assembly by low-paid labor. As with single-crop agrarian economies, such specialization makes these developing societies dangerously dependent on shifts in world markets. Consequently, most of them lack a stable economic base for sustained industrial growth.

ECONOMIC SYSTEMS

Although almost all industrializing societies contain dual economic systems, most of their efforts toward economic development occur in the modern economy based on commerce and industry. The traditional economy based on agriculture usually remains oriented primarily toward maintaining long-established farming practices. Even when agricultural production has become focused largely on one or a few crops for sale in the world market, the large estates producing those crops are typically controlled by wealthy landowners who are not involved in the commercial and industrial economy. Only in some socialist countries, such as China, has any significant portion of agricultural activity been brought under the control of the modernizing national leaders through rural collectivization. Consequently, the following discussion of the economies of industrializing nations pertains primarily to the modern sector of their economies.

Developing Capitalist Economies

Western ideas of entrepreneurship, private ownership of business, and free markets have penetrated into most developing nations whose economies are more or less capitalist in nature. *In a capitalist economy, businesses are privately owned and operate within competitive markets.* Those private firms are of two types: domestically-owned and foreign-owned. Let us first consider the domestic businesses, since a developing nation's hopes of establishing a self-sustaining modern

economy generally rest more heavily on those enterprises. The principal factor limiting the growth of these businesses is lack of investment capital. The principal reason for this is that *they do not have access to most of the sources of capital that were utilized by developing businesses in Western nations during an earlier period.* This situation results from several related factors.

First, the *foreign trade and commerce* of these societies is sharply curtailed by the fact that they must compete in world markets that are dominated by large, powerful, and wealthy firms in industrial countries. Hence, as we have seen, developing countries must often restrict their exports to a few types of products for which there is demand in the world market. And even in those narrow economic niches, world market prices are generally outside the control of developing countries.

Second, *international conquest and colonialization* are no longer possible or profitable. Although ambitious developing nations may sometimes attempt to gain economic or political control over weaker neighbors, the major world powers usually quickly intervene to prevent or halt such imperialistic ventures. Even if an industrializing nation is successful in dominating a weaker agrarian or horticultural society, the subservient country rarely contributes much wealth to the colonizer because of its own poverty.

Third, the traditional economies within most industrializing societies rarely produce enough *agricultural surplus* to provide much investment capital for developing commercial and industrial firms. Those agrarian economies have generally not been able to adopt or afford most of the modern farming equipment that makes Western agriculture so productive. Moreover, whatever agricultural surplus is produced in these societies is often quickly consumed by their rapidly growing populations.

Fourth, much of the industrial development that has occurred in these countries has been financed with loans from industrialized nations and international banks. During recent decades, the *financial debts* of many developing nations have become so large that they cannot make regular payments even on the interest owed, let alone the principal. Consequently, even if economic growth produces a surplus beyond the survival needs of the nation, it cannot be invested in activities that will improve the social and economic welfare of the population.

Fifth, relatively little investment wealth can be obtained by drawing on the *accumulated savings* of the more affluent members of these societies. Their middle and upper classes are typically very small, these individuals are generally interested in spending whatever extra wealth they have to raise their own standard of living, and the traditional land-owning upper class often uses its surplus wealth to acquire more land.

Consequently, *most capital for domestic economic growth in developing capitalist societies has to be taken from workers by paying them very low wages.* This practice was Karl Marx's primary criticism of early industrialists in Europe, and it is equally relevant to many domestic businesses in contemporary industrializing societies. There is also a severe limitation on this source of capital, however, since many workers in developing nations are already living at or near the subsistence level and hence could not survive on even lower wages.

Because of this severe shortage of domestic capital, *large privately owned commercial and industrial firms in industrializing countries are often branches or subsidiaries of multinational corporations.* The headquarters, primary sources of capital, and leadership of these corporations are located in industrial nations. This situation has both advantages and disadvantages for developing societies. The primary advantage is that these international firms provide jobs for local workers, although the top managerial positions in such companies are usually held by foreigners brought in by the parent corporation. A secondary advantage is that these firms often provide training and experience for local employees that would not otherwise be available, enabling at least some of them

to become skilled craftspersons, clerical workers, technicians, and low-level managers.

The fact that the capital for establishing these firms is brought into the developing country from outside might appear to be another advantage of multinational corporations. That potential advantage is offset, however, by the principal disadvantage of foreign-owned firms. Most of the profits generated by these firms go back to the parent corporation and are not available as capital to be invested in developing domestic businesses. To the extent that capital is drained out of countries in this manner, the process of domestic capital accumulation for industrial growth is further curtailed. A second disadvantage is that foreign-owned firms often keep wages quite low, since their principal reason for locating in developing countries is to obtain cheaper labor than is available in their home country. A third disadvantage is that most of the products produced by these foreign-owned firms are often shipped out of the country to be sold in industrial societies. As a result, the developing countries are deprived of the opportunity to consume many of the products they are producing.

Developing Socialist Economies

As a direct consequence of the economic problems facing industrializing societies because of their lack of domestic capital and the presence of foreign-owned firms—as well as the political trends to be discussed in the next section—the economies of many of these nations have been either partially or wholly socialized. *In a socialist economy, some or all of the major businesses (usually the larger industrial firms) are owned by the state, and most or all of the commodity and financial markets are state-controlled.* Capital is as vital for economic development in socialist economies as in capitalist ones, but in socialist economies the state plays an active role in accumulating and investing capital, rather than leaving that process in the hands of private entrepreneurs.

There are many important differences between state-owned and privately owned businesses. The major operating policies of state-owned firms are set by government officials, and the firm's managers are responsible to those officials rather than to a board of directors. Wage and salary scales are also established by the government. State ownership of businesses does not mean that they are not expected to make a profit, but those profits are returned to the government to be used for whatever purposes political leaders decide are desirable for the country. State control of commodity and financial markets typically means that the kinds and amounts of goods available for domestic consumption are determined by governmental economic planning agencies, and the prices of goods are set by those agencies rather than by supply and demand in the marketplace.

The economies of some industrializing societies are largely socialist in nature, with few private businesses. In these societies, most industries, commercial firms, large stores, and other businesses are owned by the state and operate according to regulations established by governmental agencies that oversee their operations. In these highly socialized economies, much of the agricultural production is also done on collective farms that are owned and controlled by the state in the same manner as other businesses. Typically, the only privately owned businesses in these societies are small retail shops and services, plus tiny farm plots on which rural residents grow food for their own subsistence.

More commonly, *industrializing societies tend to have mixed economies that are partly socialist and partly capitalist in nature.* The typical pattern is for some or all of the major industrial and commercial businesses that comprise the core of the modern economy to be state-owned and controlled, while other businesses are privately owned. Most or all agricultural land is also privately owned, and farming practices remain highly traditional. Governmental regulation of these mixed economies is usually rather limited. State-owned firms may have considerable latitude

in establishing their own operating policies and procedures, and they may compete with privately owned firms in selling their products in markets. Some of these societies with mixed economies also contain foreign-owned private businesses, although in recent years many of those firms have been nationalized, or taken over by the government, because of the dominant role they play in the nation's economic system.

Why do so many industrializing societies have at least partially socialist economies? Simplistic answers to this question often point to ideological factors, arguing that the leaders of these countries have been heavily influenced by Marxist or communist belief systems. The implicit assumption underlying those arguments is that if the leaders of developing countries had a better understanding of Western capitalist economies and were more economically sophisticated, they would undoubtedly prefer capitalism over socialism. There is some validity to this ideological explanation, in that the ideals of socialism have thoroughly pervaded most industrializing societies.

That ideologial explanation is generally invalid on several other grounds, however. First, many of the political and economic leaders of industrializing societies have been educated in Western universities and have acquired a rather thorough understanding of modern capitalism. The conclusion they often reach is that although capitalism may work satisfactorily in highly industrialized societies, it is not appropriate or workable in their own developing economies. *In their view, developing economies are often too fragile and vulnerable to survive the continual cycles of disruption, inflation, unemployment, labor unrest, and other problems that seem to be inherent in capitalist economies.* They believe that their economies require greater stability, regulation, and pubic assistance to achieve full industrialization and prosperity, so that the government must play an active role in the economic system.

Second, there is a very compelling economic argument for developing economies to be partly or wholly socialist in nature. *Be-*

cause domestic sources of investment capital are so severely restricted in all industrializing societies, they must utilize whatever capital they have as effectively as possible. The economy must be monitored carefully to locate all available surplus capital and to ensure that it is wisely invested in businesses that will benefit the entire society. These societies cannot afford to have potential capital spent on unnecessary consumer goods or put into business ventures that will only benefit a few people. Since consumer goods are quite limited, markets must be regulated to ensure that those goods are distributed equitably at affordable prices. And foreign-owned corporations cannot be allowed to drain large amounts of capital and profits out of the country.

Third, the leaders of many—although certainly not all—industrializing societies are genuinely concerned about the economic plight of their citizens. Most of their people are desperately poor and are impatient for a better standard of living. As we have seen, the main source of investment capital for privately owned domestic firms is paying the lowest wages the labor market will bear. Consequently, those leaders are concerned that *reliance on private businesses to industrialize the country will result in the perpetuation of subsistence-level wages and continued poverty for the bulk of the population.* State ownership of many or most businesses will not automatically ensure that all workers receive adequate incomes, but it does enable governmental leaders to exercise some control over wages and prices. They believe they can achieve somewhat greater equity than is possible under capitalism by balancing the requirements of businesses for capital with the needs of the public for food, shelter, clothing, and other necessities of life.

POLITICAL SYSTEMS

No industrializing nation has the kind of democratic political system found in Western European and North American countries. Democratic political practices such as periodic contested elections, two or more strong political parties, and complete freedom of speech and assembly are rather rare in developing societies. This is at least partially explained by the fact that *Western-style political democracy is very unlikely to occur in a society until it achieves a relatively high degree of industrialization and economic affluence* (Coulter, 1975; Jackman, 1975). A number of other conditions must normally also exist in a society if political democracy is to occur, such as widespread literacy and at least primary education, a sizable middle class, the presence of numerous newspapers and other communication media, and considerable urbanization (Olsen, 1982). All of these other indicators of societal modernization are also fairly strongly related to a country's level of economic development, although each of them contributes to strengthening the socioeconomic base within a society that makes political democracy possible. Since industrializing countries generally score rather low on all of these modernization factors, we should not expect them to be able to sustain Western-style democratic political systems at the present time.

The political systems of most industrializing nations can be classified into four broad categories, as described in the following paragraphs.

One-Party-Dominant Systems

This first category most nearly approximates Western democracies. A number of these nations, such as India and Mexico, are often called democracies, despite the limitations of their political systems. The most important of those limitations is that *one political party—usually the party that led the struggle for political independence—is considerably larger and stronger than any of the other parties and hence consistently wins national elections.* Although politicans compete for public offices in free elections, those elections generally do not constitute meaningful political contests. Major political decisions are made by the leaders of the dominant party in closed meetings, and public elections primarily legitimize the right of that party's candidates to assume office. Other limitations commonly found in these political systems are restrictions on complete freedom of speech and assembly, relatively little dissemination of information about candidates and issues to the voters, and denial of the franchise to various categories of people such as ethnic and racial minorities and/or women.

Single-Party Systems

This second category is by far the most common among industrializing nations. As the name implies, *these countries contain only one political party that totally controls the political system.* Almost invariably, it is the party that organized the revolution that overthrew a previous monarchy or other traditional form of government and is attempting to lead the country toward modernization. Nations with single-party political systems may or may not hold periodic elections, but if they do occur, there is only one slate of candidates and the election serves merely to legitimize the ruling party leaders. In addition, severe restrictions are typically imposed in these countries on freedom of speech and assembly, information dissemination, and the right to vote.

Military Dictatorships

A considerable number of industrializing countries fall into this third category of political systems. Their distinguishing characteristic is that the government is controlled either by a single military leader or by a small clique of military officers. In either case, *military leaders take political power by overthrowing the previous government and rule by authoritarian decree without any pretense of holding elections.* Many of these countries periodically alternate between a military dictatorship and a single-party (or occasionally a one-party-dominant) type of political system. After military rulers have controlled the government for some length of time, they may agree to step aside and permit the election of civilian leaders. But if that regime proves (in the

eyes of the military) to be incapable of governing the nation effectively, military leaders will often retake political power and establish another dictatorship.

Heredity Monarchies

The number of nations in this fourth category of political systems in industrializing nations is rapidly diminishing, as traditional monarchies are being overthrown by revolutionary political parties or military leaders. Most of the few remaining monarchies are located in the Middle East. Traditional beliefs and values are still dominant among the majority of the people in these societies, and their monarchial systems are strongly supported by powerful land-owning elites who seek to preserve their traditional status in the society. However, *many of the remaining monarchs are attempting to develop their countries and hence preserve their political legitimacy through public actions, rather than just hereditary claims to the throne.*

Operational Problems

Regardless of the nature of the political systems in developing societies, most of these nations are burdened with three pervasive problems that severely hinder the ability of political leaders to govern effectively. The first of these problems is *lack of sufficient governmental revenues to carry out extensive public programs.* Because these countries are typically so poor, it is often impossible for the government to acquire enough revenues through taxation or other means to do very much to promote modernization of the society. This problem is often more acute in capitalist countries than in socialist nations in which the government controls the economy, but even in those cases the government is likely to be severely limited by inadequate funds.

The second problem is *lack of educated and qualified people to operate all of the bureaus and agencies required by a modern national government.* The number of people capable of performing effectively as government officials and bureaucrats is restricted primarily by the low level of education in these societies. It is also limited by the fact that to obtain governmental positions, individuals must often accept the ideology of the dominant political party and have the proper connections with people in the government.

The third problem pervading governments in developing countries is that *Western ideas of rationality and impersonality are typically quite weak.* Government officials at all levels are much more likely to be motivated by other concerns. Quite frequently they are committed either to putting ideological purity ahead of rational expediency or to advancing their own and their family's welfare at government expense. Western observers often condemn the resulting practices as gross inefficiency or blatant dishonesty and corruption. From the perspective of these government officials in developing countries, however, they are acting in accordance with the values of the revolutionary party or their traditional familistic norms.

For all the reasons discussed in this section, it is quite unrealistic to expect contemporary industrializing societies to have the kind of political systems found in Western industrial nations. *The economic, social, and political conditions prevailing in developing countries are generally not adequate to support Western-style democracy and rationally-oriented government bureaucracies.* Although Western political ideals of popular democracy and rational efficiency may serve as ultimate goals for industrializing societies, these societies lack the means of achieving these goals at the present time. Much more immediate and pressing for these societies are the overwhelming tasks of promoting economic development and societal modernization.

SOCIAL ORGANIZATION

All realms of social life within contemporary industrializing societies reflect the consequences of their ongoing efforts to become more economically developed and socially modernized. Four of those realms of social organization are examined in this section: social stratification, urbanization, kinship, and cultural beliefs.

Stratification

As a direct result of their dual economic systems, these societies typically also contain dual structures of socioeconomic stratification. On one hand, *their traditional stratification structure closely resembles that found in all agrarian societies.* At the top is a very small class of land-owning elites. These elites often own huge estates of agricultural land and are quite wealthy, even by Western standards. They use their wealth and power to defend the traditional agricultural way of life, and they fervently resist land reforms and other social movements that would deprive them of their privileged position in the society. Traditionally, they have also controlled the top ranks of the government and the military, although political and/or military revolutions in many of these countries have recently been ejecting them from these positions of power. Below the land-owning elites is a relatively small class of artisans and shopkeepers who also enact traditional economic roles in the society. The bulk of the population within the traditional stratification structure consists of small farmers and peasants who farm the land in the same manner as their ancestors have done for centuries. At the bottom of this class structure is a growing number of dispossessed peasants who have drifted into urban centers looking for work. Many of them barely survive by doing odd jobs, living in shanties or on the streets, rummaging in garbage dumps for discarded food and clothing, turning to thievery or prostitution, or begging.

On the other hand, *the modern stratification structure in industrializing societies resembles that of fully industrialized societies,* but with some important differences. The small upper class in this structure consists of a few wealthy merchants, top business mangers who typically work for foreign-owned or state-owned firms, plus high government officials and military leaders if those institutions have been separated from the old landed elites. The middle class, which is quite small in comparison with industrialized societies, is composed primarily of bureaucrats in businesses and government agencies, middle-level military officers, and professionals such as doctors, lawyers, and teachers. Members of both these upper and middle classes have frequently received a Western education and are the leaders in the struggle to modernize their society. To the extent that industry has penetrated into these societies, there is also a working class of laborers in manufacturing and other businesses. In comparison with the working class in industrial societies, however, its members are considerably less skilled and receive much lower wages. They may be better off financially than many members of the farmer/peasant class in their own society, but by Western economic standards most of them would be considered to be living in poverty.

The differences between the traditional and modern stratification structures in industrializing societies are typically at least as great as the divisions between the classes within each structure. Members of the traditional classes are usually committed to perpetuating the established agricultural-based economy and its political system, while members of the modern classes are seeking to introduce change and development into the economic, political, and social systems of their society. The traditional classes are located primarily in rural areas, whereas the modern classes reside almost entirely in urban centers. Members of the two class structures commonly hold quite distinct belief systems and values. As a consequence of all these differences between the traditional and modern classes, members of the two systems frequently come into sharp conflict over numerous issues, which can erupt into violent confrontations or revolutions.

Urbanization

Industrializing societies are not as highly urbanized as most Western nations, where 60 to 70 percent of the population typically lives in urban communities. In developing nations, from one-fourth to one-half of the people typically live in towns or cities, although there is wide variation among these countries in their degrees of urbanization. Nevertheless, *urban centers in industrializing societies are presently growing very rapidly.* Their rate of growth is often 8 to 10 percent per year, due to large numbers of people streaming into them from the rural countryside, coupled with high birth rates in the cities. This trend is occurring despite the fact that these cities often lack most of the conditions considered necessary for rapid urban growth, such as an extensive agricultural surplus, expanding job opportunities, sufficient housing, adequate transportation systems, public health and sanitation facilities, and political stability.

The continual rural-to-urban migration taking place in many developing societies is caused by two types of conditions:

(1) "Push factors," such as the inability of the land to support increasing numbers of farmers and peasants, unequal distribution of rural land, and growing social unrest among rural dwellers; and

(2) "Pull factors," such as expectations of employment in cities, hopes that their children will receive a better education there, and the lure of a more stimulating lifestyle.

Some sociologists refer to this situation as "overurbanization," suggesting that urbanization is occurring faster in these societies than the ability of their cities to employ, house, and service rural migrants.

To illustrate the fantastic rates of urban growth now occurring in many industrializing societies, the United Nations Fund for Population Activities recently estimated the probable populations of the ten largest metropolises in the world in the year 2000 if their growth rates continue at present levels (*The Futurist*, 1982). Eight of those ten cities are located in developing countries: Mexico City (expected to be 30 million), São Paulo (26 million), Shanghai (23 million), Beijing

(20 million), Rio de Janeiro (19 million), Bombay (17 million), Calcutta (17 million), and Jakarta (17 million). The only metropolises included in this list that are located in industrial societies are Tokyo (24 million) and New York (23 million). Overall, about two billion people are expected to be living in cities of all sizes within developing countries by that time.

Just as the economic and stratification systems of industrializing societies are divided into traditional and modern sectors, so are their cities. *The modern sector of these cities is typically quite Western in its organization and appearance,* with government and business office buildings, retail stores, some factories, restaurants, theatres, schools, large apartment buildings, and private residences of the well-to-do. In addition, this sector is often set off physically from the rest of the city by open spaces, rivers, boulevards, or even walls. It is largely self-contained, and the members of the modern middle and upper classes who live and work there rarely venture into other parts of the city.

The traditional sector of the city—which may contain several distinct ethnic or religious quarters—exists as a world apart from the modern sector. It is often organized around a traditional market area or a past governmental center and contains a jumbled mixture of old buildings and small shops, handicraft workplaces, churches, open-air markets, permanent living quarters, and squatter settlements. Economic transactions reflect both traditional barter and modern money systems. There may be a partially separate government with laws that pertain only to the traditional sector. Public services and facilitates are extremely limited or nonexistent. Social life follows traditional patterns of living, and the culture emphasizes ancient beliefs and values.

Perhaps the most appalling feature of most large cities in industrializing societies is the *sprawling shantytowns that typically surround their outskirts* and are sometimes interspersed among modern neighborhoods. As peasants stream into the cities looking for a better life—or survival—there is often no housing

available for them in the existing traditional sectors. Consequently, they are forced to settle as squatters on vacant land, constructing crude shacks made of scrap lumber, tin sheeting, or even cardboard, all of which are tightly crowded together on every available bit of land. A large proportion of these people are unemployed or find only occasional menial jobs, and they frequently live in abject poverty. Few or no sanitation, health, educational, transportation, and other public services are available to them. Not surprisingly, social and personal problems such as disease, illiteracy, alcoholism, crime, prostitution, gambling, drug use, family breakups, illegitimacy, malnutrition, and mental illness are often rampant in these shantytowns.

Nevertheless, the "urban peasants" living in these shantytowns are often able to organize themselves effectively and to improve the physical and social quality of their neighborhoods (Plotnicov, 1967; Roberts, 1973). Moreover, despite their difficult existence, most of these people are glad to be in the city and have no desire to return to their rural lands and villages. No matter how miserable urban life may be for them, their prospects for survival are generally more promising in the city. At least they have the hope of finding work there and slowly improving their way of life, while at home there were few job opportunities and frequent food scarcities. As a result, more and more peasants keep moving into drastically overcrowded cities that are largely unprepared for them and are incapable of meeting most of their basic needs.

Kinship

Kinship is the primary social bond in traditional societies, and the family is the most important type of social organization for most people. Although the size and composition of the family unit vary greatly among societies, the basic unit is typically an extended family consisting of a considerable number of people related by birth or marriage. Quite often, an entire village may consist of people who are related through at least distant kinship ties. Tribal bounds are also very strong in some of these societies, so that tribes function as a kind of larger kinship network even though all the members of a tribe are not related.

Within contemporary societies undergoing the transition to industrialization, family and kinship ties are often subject to severe strains. In rural areas and small villages, these bonds typically remain quite strong. As a result, when rural poverty and the allure of the city compel people to migrate from rural to urban areas, the move becomes much more than just a change of residence. It often means leaving behind the social groups that have been most fundamental in one's life. The resulting separation is not only very painful emotionally for many people, but it may also cut them off from the social support and controls that have guided them throughout their lives.

For those individuals who make a complete shift from a traditional rural existence to a modern urban industrial life, the resulting break with their family ties is especially difficult. Even though they may attempt to maintain some of those bonds through periodic visits home, over time their lifestyles and values almost invariably diverge greatly from those of their rural kin. Consequently, it becomes increasingly difficult for them to preserve close family ties. This break with the past is particularly sharp for young people who leave home to obtain a formal education and eventually become socialized into the beliefs and values of the modern middle or upper class of their society. Their worldview and lifestyle will likely become so divorced from the traditional culture of their kin that the gulf is almost insurmountable. They often have no alternative to leaving their past entirely behind them by severing all ties with their extended family.

For many rural migrants who settle in the shantytowns surrounding urban centers, however, their traditional kinship ties can be lifesaving. If they have kin who are already living there, as is often the case, those relatives can be of immense help in easing the adjustment to ur-

ban life. These kin may initially take arriving migrants into their home, help them make new friends, assist them in finding work, show them where to find space and materials to build their own shack, and otherwise provide the social support they desperately need. Consequently, life in these shantytowns is often not too different from traditional rural life. In fact, urban shantytowns are often essentially rural villages that have been transported to an urban setting.

Life in these urbanized rural villages is drastically different from life in the modern sector of the city, which greatly intensifies the social, economic, and political tensions besetting the city as a whole. These sharply divergent living patterns and the resulting tensions between the modern and the traditional sectors of the urban community can also make it extremely difficult for shantytown dwellers to find permanent jobs and otherwise become assimilated into the modern sector. Nevertheless, many rural migrants would likely not survive long in the city without a transported rural village based on traditional extended kinship ties. It is quite common for migrants without kin in a shantytown village who can give them the assistance and support they require to eventually return to their rural home. Although the dominant population flow in industrializing societies is from rural to urban areas, in all of them there is a considerable flow of people from urban back to rural areas.

Cultural Beliefs

In the areas of stratification, urbanization, and kinship, the typical situation in industrializing nations is a sharp contrast of old versus new: agricultural-based versus business-based class structures; rural versus urban communities; and extended versus nuclear family groups. The situation is not that simple in the realm of cultural beliefs, however.

In the rural-agricultural sector of these societies, there is likely to be a single dominant belief system composed of the prevailing traditional religion and its related secular ideology. This belief system is preached by religious leaders, strongly supported by the landed upper class, and accepted without question by the masses of farmers and peasants. It usually emphasizes the fixed nature of the existing social order, the desirability of agriculture as a way of life, the legitimate right of land-owners to protect and control their property, the duty of farmers and peasants to obey the dictates of the upper class, the futility of attempting to change traditional social patterns, and the rewards that await individuals in an afterlife if they dutifully accept their lot on earth and lead moral lives. The overriding message of such a belief system is clear to all: established traditions are ethically and religiously virtuous, while social change is undesirable and sinful.

In the urban-industrial sector of these societies, however, there is rarely a single modern belief system. Those people who have made the shift to urban living and wage employment often find themselves confronted by a bewildering array of conflicting belief systems, each of which claims to be the true embodiment of the modern worldview. In the political realm, the Western ideal of popular democracy is likely to be extremely widespread, although many individuals may hold quite simplistic and naïve conceptions of democratic political processes. In the economic realm, the more prosperous business owners and managers are often strongly committed to capitalism and private enterprise, while many industrial workers may fervently believe that socialism and state ownership of industry offer their only hope of a better standard of living. Regardless of which economic ideology people accept, whenever their incomes rise above the subsistence level they are likely to become ardent believers in consumerism as they strive to acquire better housing, home appliances, bicycles or automobiles, and luxuries such as television sets.

Cutting across and intermingled with all these competing ideologies and religious beliefs—traditional and modern—is the relentless appeal of nationalism. As espoused by political, military, business, and labor leaders, *nationalism is commonly the overriding belief system in developing societies.* This ideology emphasizes the importance of the nation-state and its unique social and cultural characteristics above all other forms of social organization. Initially formulated as a protest against colonialism and Western economic and political domination, nationalism comes to symbolize people's desires for a more comfortable standard of living, increased social status, national autonomy and unity, military strength, cultural identity and pride, international respect, and a modern way of life. In practice, nationalism often implies quite divergent courses of action to different people and social classes. It may mean nationalizing foreign-owned businesses, engaging in warfare with neighboring societies, establishing a single national language, or creating a national airline. Nevertheless, the symbols and rituals of nationalism can minimize these policy disputes and unite the entire population under a common banner, at least superficially.

RESTRICTED INDUSTRIALIZATION

If the economic benefits of industrialization are so ardently desired by most societies around the globe, why have only 35 nations thus far attained that goal? What is preventing the remaining nations in the world from achieving full industrialization? If Europe, North America, the Soviet Union, Japan, Australia, and New Zealand all succeeded in making the transition from an agrarian to an industrial economy by the early decades of the twentieth century, why have no other societies completed that transition during the last 50 years? However this question is expressed, it is crucial for the future of human civilization. Some partial answers to that fundamental question and some likely consequences of restricted industrialization are offered in this section.

Limitations on Industrialization

Many interrelated factors and conditions are severely limiting the further economic development of contemporary industrializing nations. Broadly speaking, the essence of the problem is that *the world no longer provides a suitable ecological base for the transition from an agricultural to an industrial economy.* There are several dimensions of this situation.

We have already examined one of the most critical of these dimensions: *lack of investment capital,* combined with the fact that most of the sources of capital exploited by the presently industrialized countries during the nineteenth and early twentieth centuries are no longer available. Without surplus capital to invest in factories, raw materials, machinery, commerce, transportation systems, and other infrastructures required for industrialization, it is virtually impossible for any society to achieve "take-off" into sustained economic development. On a world scale, there is undoubtedly enough capital available at the present time for at least the more economically advanced nations—such as Mexico and Argentina—to complete the industrialization process. Most of that available capital, however, is controlled by the industrial nations of the world. They have not shown any great willingness to share it with developing countries, except through the practices of establishing branches of multinational corporations in those countries or offering them development loans at interest.

We have also briefly noted another of these dimensions: *lack of an adequately educated and trained work force.* It is true that in the nineteenth century much of the labor force in Western industrializing nations was no better educated or trained than the populations of contemporary industrializing nations. If Western societies succeeded in industrializing with work forces consisting largely of unskilled rural migrants, why cannot presently industrializing countries repeat that process? The answer to this question lies in the nature of modern industry. In the nineteenth century, most industrial machinery and production processes were relatively simple, so that with minimal on-the-job training large numbers of workers could master whatever limited tasks they were assigned. Much contemporary industry, however, involves highly complex and sophisticated machinery and production processes that demand much greater knowledge and skills of workers.

Some experts believe that a solution to the problems of limited capital and unskilled workers lies in introducing *appropriate technology* into industrial nations (Schumacher, 1973). Appropriate technology refers to machinery and other technology that is relevant to the economic and human resources of a society. If a nation cannot afford to manage the technology required to manufacture automobiles or computers, it should be discouraged from attempting to establish such industries, these writers argue. Instead, those nations should be encouraged to produce simple hand tools or household goods that require less capital investment and less-skilled workers and that are of direct use to them. This argument has considerable logic and merit. Unfortunately, however, industries based on relatively simple technologies rarely generate the large profits that can be made with "high tech" industries. Consequently, leaders of developing countries often view the appropriate technology argument as merely a Western ploy to prevent them from generating enough capital to finance full-scale industrialization. They fear that this policy would perpetually keep them economically subservient to the industrial nations of the world, and they fervently reject that prospect.

Another dimension of the world ecological problem is *insufficient fuels and other natural resources* within developing countries, coupled with lack of funds to purchase these resources on the world market. With the exception of those few nations that contain large deposits of oil or other natural resources, most industrializing nations are extremely resource-poor. As a result, they must purchase in the world market the petroleum they need to generate energy for their factories, as well as many of the raw materials required for manufacturing. When they enter the world market to purchase these resources, however, they find that they are disadvantaged on two counts. First, supplies and prices in these markets are largely controlled by the industrial nations, so that industries in those countries generally have first choice of the available resources, and developing nations are left with only whatever resources have not already been taken by others. Second, to purchase resources in the world market a nation must usually be able to pay for them in hard currency. That is, they must have American dollars, West German deutschemarks, or other currencies that are readily accepted in international trade. Their own soft currency may be almost worthless in the world market. This creates a terrible dilemma for them. To obtain hard currencies they must sell goods in the world market, but they cannot produce and sell such goods until they have the hard currencies to pay for the resources needed to produce them.

The escape from this financial dilemma that has been used by many industrializing nations in recent years has been to borrow hard currencies from the World Bank or from banks in the United States and other industrial societies. As a consequence of this practice, *many developing countries are presently heavily in debt*—often by tens or even hundreds of billions of dollars—and have no realistic possibility of repaying their debts in the foreseeable future. As previously mentioned, even the interest on these debts is ofen more than they can afford to pay from their meager sales of goods in the world market. Hence they must continually borrow more money just to keep making their interest payments. They thus slide further and further into debt to industrial nations.

Severe as the preceding limitations on industrialization are for most developing societies, almost all of these countries are beset by an even more overwhelming problem: *rapid population growth*. Table 10-2 lists the same sets of nations included in Table 10-1, but this table gives their annual rate of population increase in 1987, plus the number of years required for their population to double in size at the current growth rate. The difference between industrialized and in-

dustrializing nations in population growth rates is quite striking. The 20 most highly industrializing societies listed in the table are growing at an average rate of just 0.3 percent per year, and all 35 industrialized societies have an average growth rate of only 0.5 percent per year. Even at that latter rate, a country's population will require more than 100 years to double.

In sharp contrast, the advanced industrializing societies listed in the table have an average growth rate of 2.1 percent, the agrarian societies have an average rate of 2.4 percent, and the horticultural societies have a rate of 2.8 percent. For all the industrializing nations of the world, the average population growth rate is 2.1 percent. Although growth rates of 2.1 or even 2.8 percent may not seem remarkably high, they can have disastrous demographic consequences for a country. With a growth rate of 2.1 percent per year, a country's population will double in a generation of about 33 years. At 2.4 percent, that doubling time drops to about 29 years. And at 2.8 percent, that time is only 25 years. In more concrete terms, a country with a population of 40 million people and an annual growth rate of 2.5 percent will add a million more people to its population every year.

The principal consequences of such rapid population growth are quite evident. Much of whatever increased productivity most of the developing countries achieve through improved farming practices or new industries is needed to sustain their additional people. *A rapidly increasing population can consume a society's wealth as fast is it is produced, leaving little or no surplus capital for investment in economic development.* And if a society's population is growing more rapidly than the rate at which it is producing additional wealth, the standard of living of at least part of its people will decline each year, despite its best efforts to raise its economic productivity. This problem is even more acute for horticultural than for agrarian societies. During the 1970s, the Gross National Product per capita for agrarian societies increased at a rate of slightly more than three percent per

TABLE 10-2 Population Growth Rate and Years Required to Double the Population in 1987 for Four Sets of Societies*

Highly Industrialized Societies			*Advanced Industrializing Societies*		
	Percentage	*Years*		*Percentage*	*Years*
United States	0.7	102	Singapore	1.1	61
Switzerland	0.2	301	Hong Kong	0.9	77
Norway	0.2	408	Venezuela	2.7	26
Canada	0.8	91	South Korea	1.4	51
Luxembourg	0.0	—	Mexico	2.5	28
Sweden	0.1	636	Argentina	1.6	44
Japan	0.6	124	South Africa	2.3	30
Denmark	−0.1	—			
West Germany	−0.2	—	Average	2.1	33
Finland	0.3	224			
Australia	0.8	86			
Iceland	0.9	76			
France	0.4	178			
Austria	0.0	—			
The Netherlands	0.4	182			
Belgium	0.1	577			
United Kingdom	0.2	462			
New Zealand	0.8	92			
USSR	0.9	79			
East Germany	0.0	—			
Average	0.3	224			

Agrarian Industrializing Societies			*Horticultural Industrializing Societies*		
	Percentage	*Years*		*Percentage*	*Years*
Algeria	3.2	22	Fiji	2.3	31
Malaysia	2.4	28	Mauritius	1.2	57
Panama	2.2	32	Congo	3.4	21
Uruguay	0.8	90	Cameroon	2.7	26
Brazil	2.1	33	Nigeria	2.8	25
Syria	3.8	18	Zimbabwe	3.5	20
Jordan	3.7	19	Papua-New Guinea	2.4	29
Chile	1.6	44	Cote d'Ivoire	3.0	23
Colombia	2.1	33	Soloman Islands	3.6	19
Costa Rica	2.7	25	Liberia	3.2	22
Tunisia	2.5	27	Mauritania	3.0	23
Ecuador	2.8	25	Zambia	3.5	20
Turkey	2.1	33	Senegal	2.8	24
Peru	2.5	28	Sierra Leone	1.8	38
Thailand	2.1	33	Ghana	2.8	25
Dominican Republic	2.5	28	Kenya	3.9	18
Egypt	2.6	26	Somalia	2.5	28
Guyana	2.0	35	Sudan	2.8	24
Bolivia	2.6	27	Guinea	2.4	29
China	1.3	53	Gambia	2.1	33
Average	2.4	29	Average	2.8	25+

	Percentage	*Years*
Average for all 35 industrialized societies	0.5	128

TABLE 10-2 *Continued*

Average for all 137 industrializing societies	2.1	33
Average for entire world	1.7	40

* Population growth rate is the annual percent rate of natural population increase. Years required to double the population is a projection based on the current growth rate. Among highly industrialized, agrarian industrializing, and horticultural industrializing societies, those with the greatest energy consumption per capita are included. The advanced industrializing societies listed are those which are the most industrialized and exclude the oil-producing and tourist nations with high energy consumption and GNP, but little industry.

⁺ The average doubling time given is the time required for the average growth rate and is not a numerical average of the years for the countries listed.

Source: Population Reference Bureau, World Population Data Sheet, 1987, Washington, D.C.

year. Because most horticultural societies are developing economically at slower rates but have higher population growth rates, their average rate of increase in Gross National Product per capita per year during that time was less than 0.5 percent (Lenski and Nolan, 1984).

Finally, the efforts of industrializing nations to develop economically have been severely hampered by their *dependent role* in the world political economy. The only items that most of these countries have to sell in the world economy are natural resources, agricultural goods, and cheap wage labor. With the exception of the oil-rich nations that have formed the Organization of Petroleum Exporting Countries (OPEC) to control their sales of oil, most of these developing nations are essentially at the economic mercy of world markets that are controlled by the in-

dustrial nations. In the language of world systems theory, they are "periphery" or at best "semiperiphery" nations that are highly dependent economically on the "core" developed nations. Those industrialized core nations frequently exploit the economies of the periphery and semiperiphery nations to obtain natural resouces, agricultural products, and wage labor at the lowest possible prices. As a result, most developing countries exercise little control over their own economies in terms of what is produced, when and for what prices their goods are sold, or the directions that their future economic development might take.

Likely Consequences

In combination, all of the limitations to industrialization previously discussed—lack of investment capital, an inadequately prepared work force, the technological sophistication of modern industry, insufficient natural resources, rapidly growing populations, international economic dependency, and lack of control over their own economies— are so overwhelming that full industrialization often appears to be an impossible goal for most developing nations. There are potential solutions to all these problems, however. The necessary investment capital

---

LIMITATIONS ON DEVELOPING COUNTRIES

1. Lack of investment capital.
2. Inadequately educated work force.
3. Insufficient natural resources.
4. Heavy international debts.
5. Rapid population growth.
6. Dependent role in the world economy.

could be given by industrial nations to developing countries as outright grants. Industrial nations could establish and fund basic educational systems and technical training programs in developing countries. Politically acceptable forms of appropriate technology could be made available to these societies. Although all natural resources are inherently limited, international programs of resource conservation and equitable distribution could ease many of the problems in that realm. And population growth can be halted through effective birth control programs, which also requires encouragement and funding from the industrial nations. At the present time, however, none of these potential solutions are being implemented on an effective world-wide scale.

Consequently, *it appears quite unlikely that no more than a handful of presently developing nations will achieve full industrialization in the near future.* As a result, the world will undoubtedly remain divided between some 35 relatively affluent industrialized nations and all of the remaining agrarian and horticultural societies. A number of likely consequences of this situation can be predicted.

The most obvious consequence is that *about three-fourths of humanity will likely remain desperately poor, with standards of living at or not far above the subsistence level.* Even worse, if the populations of those countries continue to increase at their present rates, more and more people will be forced below the subsistence level and begin starving to death—as is already occurring in parts of Africa. Mass starvation and its associated diseases will ease world population pressures, but this solution is clearly ethically intolerable.

Within developing societies there will continue to be sharp economic and political cleavages between participants in the traditional and modern economies, between the small middle and elite classes and the masses of peasants and workers, between rural and urban dwellers, between dominant and minority ethnic or religious groups, and between older and younger generations. *As*

these cleavages become increasingly pervasive and divisive within a society, they are very likely to erupt into overt social and political conflicts. Peasants and workers may rebel against their deprived status, political parties dedicated to modernization may clash with more traditionally-oriented parties, sociopolitical movements may attempt to seize the land of the traditional aristocracy and divide it among small farmers and unemployed urban dwellers, dominant ethnic or religious groups may persecute minorities, or military leaders may take over the government in an attempt to operate it more effectively. In short, there is likely to be continual turmoil and clashes among various segments within most industrializing nations.

On a world scale, *the developing nations will continue to be highly dependent on the industrialized nations, both economically and politically.* Their economies may be constantly battered and upset by shifts and pressures in world commodity and financial markets. Their governments may remain relatively powerless in world political affairs. Economic and political leaders in these countries will deeply resent their subservience to the industrial nations and may challenge them at every opportunity to provide greater equality among all nations. At the same time, these leaders of developing countries may frequently conflict with one another in their struggles to improve their economic and political conditions.

We need not end our examination of contemporary industrializing societies with these pessimistic predictions, however. As we saw earlier, there are potential solutions to all the problems that are presently limiting the economic development of these nations. All these solutions have one feature in common. They demand that *the presently industrialized nations of the world cooperate in establishing worldwide programs to assist developing societies in coping with the paralyzing problems currently besetting them.* Only with that kind of worldwide cooperative effort is there any realistic hope that the goal of economic development will be realized by all people throughout the world.

SUMMARY

Four-fifths of the nations in the world have not progressed through the transition from agricultural to industrial economies. Some of them have made moderate progress toward economic development, while many others are just beginning that process. However, even those countries that are partially industrialized are still extremely poor in comparison with the industrialized nations. As a result, the world today is sharply divided into two disparate sets of nations: the relatively wealthy industrial societies and the desperately poor agrarian and horticultural societies.

Industrializing nations typically contain two distinct economic systems. Their traditional agricultural economies remain much the same as they have been for many hundreds of years. At the same time, their modern commercial-industrial economies are striving for development and a place in twentieth-century world markets.

Within societies with primarily captialist economies, growth of domestically-owned businesses is severely limited by lack of investment capital. These societies cannot draw upon most of the sources of capital utilized by the Western nations, such as profitable foreign trade and commerce, international conquest and colonialization, large agricultural surpluses, or accumulated savings of the middle and upper class. Consequently, their major source of investment capital for economic growth is paying low wages to workers. In addition, the larger and more profitable business firms in these countries are frequently owned by foreign multinational corporations. Although those firms provide jobs and opportunities for domestic workers, most of their profits are returned to the parent corporation, they generally pay very low wages, and most of the goods they produce are not available for local consumption.

The economies of many industrializing societies have been at least partially socialized under state ownership and control. Although some industrializing nations have totally socialized economies, the majority of them contain a mixture of state-owned and private businesses. Contributing to the prevalence of socialist economies in developing nations are their beliefs that capitalism is too unstable and socially disruptive, that all available capital must be utilized for economic growth, and that domestic and foreign private businesses often exploit local workers.

Industrializing nations do not have fully developed democratic political systems because they lack the economic and social base necessary for political democracy. The politics in these countries can be described as either one-party-dominant systems, single-party systems, military dictatorships, or hereditary monarchies. Although some of these systems hold periodic elections or in other ways attempt to appear democratic, none of them fulfill the Western ideal of complete political democracy.

Governments in almost all industrializing societies are severely hampered by several operational problems. They lack adequate revenues to conduct necessary public programs, they do not have enough qualified and capable employees, and norms of rationality and impersonality are not widespread.

The stratification structures of these societies are sharply divided. There are traditional classes of land-owning elites, artisans and shopkeepers, and farmers and peasants. There are also modern classes of business elites, middle-class bureaucrats and professionals, working-class industrial and commercial laborers, and dispossessed unemployed or semiemployed urban migrants. The members of these two stratification systems are distinctly different in their beliefs and values, economic activities, political orientations, social patterns, and desires for social change.

Developing societies are not as highly urbanized as most industrial nations, but the major cities in these countries are growing very rapidly and will soon be the largest metropolises in the world. Explosive urban growth in these societies is caused by both rural "push" and urban "pull" forces. Large cities in these countries generally contain both a modern and a traditional sector. The modern sector is similar to cities in Western nations, while the traditional sector is typically still medieval in both appearance and functioning. Around or within most of these cities are shantytowns of rural migrants who have drifted to the city looking for some kind of work in order to survive. These shantytowns consist of flimsy shacks, have no legal status and few public services, and the people living in them experience all kinds of social and personal problems.

Traditional extended family and kinship systems are not well-suited to modern urban wage-labor lifestyles. As a result, family and kinship ties often undergo severe strains in industrializing societies, especially for those individuals who make the transition from traditional to more modern modes of living. However, kinship ties are extremely important for urban migrants who settle in shantytowns, since these people depend on relatives to assist them in the transition to urban life.

Whereas the traditional sector of industrializing societies may have a well-established set of cultural beliefs and values, this is rarely the case in the modern sector of these societies. Numerous competing religions and ideologies often vie for popular support, which leaves many people confused and bewildered. To some extent, nationalism serves as a unifying cultural theme within the modern sector of developing societies, but this ideology often carries vastly different meanings for various segments of the society.

Contemporary developing societies are finding it extremely difficult to complete the transition to full industrialization. The basic reason for this is that the world no longer provides an adequate ecological base for societies to become industrialized. Several dimensions of this situation are lack of investment capital, lack of an adequately educated and trained work force, the high level of technology used by many modern industries, insufficient fuels and other natural resources, and rapidly growing populations that often consume a country's wealth almost as fast as it is produced.

As a result of all these limitations, it appears rather unlikely that many presently developing nations will achieve full industrialization in the near future. The world seems destined to remain sharply divided between rich industrialized and poor agrarian and horticultural societies. Cleavages between the traditional and modern sectors of industrializing societies will deepen and may give rise to severe internal conflicts. These nations will remain economically and politically dependent on industrial nations. Only through worldwide cooperation can the developing societies of the world ever achieve full industrialization.

CHAPTER 11

ECOLOGY OF INDUSTRIAL SOCIETIES

How has technological knowledge affected modern industrial societies?
To what extent are industrial societies consuming natural resources?
In what ways have the populations of industrial societies recently been
   changing?
What trends are occurring in demographic processes around the world?
What kinds of energy flows typically occur in industrial societies?

TECHNOLOGICAL KNOWLEDGE

The ecosystem within which a society exists shapes its patterns of social organization in countless ways, providing opportunities for change and development but also setting constraints and limits on social processes and structures. Although the ecosystem never fully determines the manner in which a society is organized or operates, these influences are extremely pervasive and can never be ignored. Ecological influences operate most directly on the economic system of a society, but they also affect many other aspects of the society such as its political system, settlement patterns, socio-economic inequality, and beliefs and values.

Because the four ecological factors of knowledge, resources, population, and energy are so highly interrelated within the global ecosystem, discussing them one at a time—as is done in this chapter—introduces artificial separations into what is actually a unified dynamic system. However, since it is impossible to discuss the four factors simul-

taneously, we must continually remind ourselves that each section of this chapter is only part of the complete ecological context of modern societies. This section deals with technological knowledge, the second section focuses on natural resources, the next two sections discuss population conditions and dynamics, and the final section examines energy flows.

Technological Expansion

There can be no doubt that technological knowledge about the physical world, plus the tools and machines that embody that knowledge, have been crucial influences in the development of modern societies. Nor is there any doubt that most aspects of contemporary life are inescapably affected by material technology. Although the effects of technology are especially evident in the realm of economic production, they extend throughout all dimensions of social life, including government, communications, transportation, medicine, education, recreation, and even religion.

As technological innovation and development have transformed virtually every aspect of modern economic systems, this knowledge has become the major factor producing sustained economic growth during the twentieth century. As demonstrated in the economic theories and research of Robert Solow, who was awarded the 1987 Noble Prize in Economics for this work, most growth in real income within modern economies can be attributed to technological knowledge. Two features of this technological transformation of modern economics are particularly crucial. First, technology and machinery have greatly reduced the amount of labor required in most production processes while simultaneously demanding ever-increasing amounts of investment capital. In other words, technology provides a substitute for human labor, but it is often much more expensive than the labor it replaces. As a result, the competitive advantage within the economy shifts from firms that have large work forces to firms that can acquire new technological knowledge and have the capital necessary to utilize the machines and procedures made possible by that knowledge. Second, economic production processes that are highly mechanized are more likely to utilize human-made materials, such as plastics and chemicals (many of which are derived from petroleum) rather than natural materials, such as wood and fibers. In addition to depleting our reserves of scarce resources such as oil, the production of these new materials often pollutes the natural environment in serious ways.

The governments of all industrial societies have played a major role in promoting the development of capital-intensive technologies in economic production. As observed by Allan Schnaiberg (1980:130), these governmental policies have been based on the dominant ideological beliefs that economic growth is the solution to virtually all social problems and that technological investment is the most efficient path to economic growth. These policies are still widely prevalent today, despite two decades of growing awareness of the environmental and social costs of unrestrained technologically-based economic growth.

To appreciate more fully the impacts that technological development have had on industrial societies during this century, let us examine a few statistics for the United States in agriculture, manufacturing, communication, and transportation.

In *agriculture*, changes in productivity are commonly measured in terms of the hours of labor required to produce various commodities. Between 1910 and 1984, the number of hours of labor needed to produce 100 bushels of wheat declined from 106 to seven; to produce 100 bushels of corn the necessary number of hours dropped from 135 to three; to produce a bale of cotton the requirement went from 276 to five hours; and to produce 1,000 pounds of beef these figures declined from 46 to ten hours (U.S. Bureau of the Census, 1987:638). To a major extent, the dramatic increases in productivity experienced in these and many other agricultural commodities can be attributed directly to technological advances in farming equipment, seeds, fertilizers, pesticides, and herbicides.

In *manufacturing*, productivity can be measured with the dollar value added per hour of labor by workers. Even a short-term comparison of 1958 with 1984 reveals nearly a doubling in productivity, from approximately $22 per worker-hour to $40, with both figures expressed in 1984 dollars (U.S. Bureau of the Census, 1987:723). These figures clearly indicate the growth in manufacturing productivity that occurred in this country during recent times. Most of this increase has been due to technological development in virtually every kind of manufacturing.

In *communications*, technological innovations of the twentieth century have revolutionized the extent to which information can be disseminated throughout a society. Telephones and radios have so thoroughly pervaded the United States during this century that at the present time 92 percent of all households have a telephone, and 99 percent have at least one radio. Between 1950 and 1984, the number of television stations in this country grew from 98 to over 1,200, and the proportion of households with a television set has gone from four to 86 percent (U.S. Bureau of the Census, 1987:531).

In *transportation*, the principal technological developments of this century have been motor vehicles and airplanes. At the beginning of this century, there were only a few experimental cars and no planes. In 1985, there were about 115 millions cars in use in the United States, or approximately one car for every two persons, plus over 40 million trucks (U.S. Bureau of Census, 1987:584). In that same year, there were approximately 2,900 planes in operation in this country that carried 380 million passengers (U.S. Bureau of the Census, 1987:603).

Similar illustrative statistics could be cited for all other spheres of activity within the United States and all other industrial societies. The essential point is not the magnitude of these figures themselves, however, but rather the countless ways in which material technology has come to pervade so thoroughly every aspect of contemporary life.

Scientific Research

Much of the technology that has shaped modern societies during the twentieth century has resulted from scientific research. Science, in all its various forms, is so prominent in contemporary societies that we often forget its youth. Small numbers of people have been doing scientific research for hundreds of years, of course. But as a major professional endeavor, science is not much more than 100 years old. It has been estimated that 90 percent of all existing scientific knowledge has been acquired since 1950, and that half of all the scientists who have ever lived are alive today. In the United States in 1984, there were approximately 1.8 million persons in the labor force classified as scientists, or about 1.6 percent of the total work force. They are distributed among the various branches of science as follows:

computer sciences = 24%
life sciences = 20%
social sciences = 19%
physical sciences = 13%
behavioral sciences = 12%
environmental sciences = 6%
mathematics = 6%

(U.S. Bureau of the Census, 1987:569).

Expansion of scientific research has been especially evident during the last 20 to 30 years. This growth can be indicated by comparing the total amount of money spent for all scientific research in the United States in 1970 and 1986. (These figures are expressed in constant 1982 dollars, to eliminate the effects of inflation). For basic research, the expenditures were roughly $8 billion in 1970 and $12 billion in 1986. For applied research, the corresponding figures were $14 billion and $22 billion. Total expenditures for all scientific research were therefore approximately $22 billion in 1970 and $34 billion in 1986. During this brief period, in other words, the total amount of real wealth spent on all forms of scientific research increased by 50 percent. Of the $34 billion invested in research in 1986, about 14% was spent by the federal government, 50% by private industry, 30% by universities and colleges, and 6% by non-profit research institutes (U.S. Bureau of the Census 1987:565). This total expenditure of $34 billion on scientific research in 1986 represented only one percent of the country's Gross National Product, however. Most other industrial nations spend roughly similar proportions of their total wealth for research, but the Soviet Union is spending almost twice that proportion of its national wealth on science. Very clearly *scientific research has become the principal key to technological development in the contemporary world, and technology is the major factor creating economic growth.*

Beliefs About Technology

Prevailing beliefs about the role of technology and machinery in modern societies have shifted drastically during the past fifty years. In the 1920s and 1930s, the prevailing belief was that technology represented the great hope for humanity's future, providing the staircase that would enable all societies and all people to realize ever-higher levels of production and progress. Machines were the friends—or even the saviors—of humanity and could be intentionally and intelligently directed to improve human life. This highly optimistic view of technological progress was expressed with great vigor by Lewis Mumford, one of the most prominent writers on technology and society, in his 1934 book, *Technics and Civilization.*

By the 1960s and 1970s, however, prevailing beliefs concerning the role of technology in human affairs had been largely reversed. *Many critics and writers—as well as much of the public—became convinced that material technology and its resulting machinery were dominating society and directing its future with little or no control by human beings.* The creation of nuclear weapons in the 1940s undoubtedly contributed considerably to this ideological turnaround, but many other forms of modern technology also came to be seen as completely out of control. Mumford was one of the foremost spokespersons for this reversal in beliefs about the desirability of technology and machinery. His two-volume work, *The Myth of the Machine,* completed in 1970, railed against the "megamachine" that had gone totally out of control and was destroying human civilization.

Numerous other recent writers have addressed this problem of harnessing runaway technology, some with despair and some with cautious hope. One of the most interesting of these assessments of modern technology is offered by Witold Rybczynski (1983). His central argument is that the problem lies not in machines, but in the people who use them, since machines are really nothing more than mechanical extensions of our physical abilities. As we attempt to control technology, "we shall succeed only if we are able to accept what at first appears to be an impossible shift in our point of view. . . . Just as we have discovered that we are part of the natural environment, and not just surrounded by it, so also we will find that we are an intimate part of the environment of technology. The auxiliary 'organs' that extend our sight, our hearing, and our thinking really are an extension of our physical bodies. When we are able to accept this, we shall discover that the struggle to control technology has all along been a struggle to control ourselves."

NATURAL RESOURCES

The most important natural resources used by all societies can be placed into the five broad categories of land, water, forests, minerals, and fuels. In addition, food and other agricultural products are frequently considered in conjunction with land, even though they are the results of human labor.

Land and Food

In horticultural and agrarian societies, by far the most crucial economic resource is arable land that can be used for growing crops and grazing animals. A large majority of the population (often two-thirds to three-fourths) lives on the land and make its living from agricultural work. And most of whatever surplus wealth the society enjoys comes from agricultural production.

In industrial societies, technology and capital have replaced land as the fundamental economic resources, with the result that we often tend to forget our inescapable dependence on agriculture. Although farming now occupies only 2.4 percent of the work force in the United States and produces only 1.9 percent of the country's Gross National Product, we could not survive for long without this sector of the economy.

Historically, there has been a direct relationship between the amount of land in a country that was available for agriculture and the volume of agricultural productivity. Therefore, if a society sought to increase its production of food and fibers to support a growing population, raise its standard of living, or enhance its surplus wealth, it usually had to expand its agricultural land. This might be accomplished by cutting down forests, draining swamps, irrigating dry or desert land, settling vacant land, buying land from another society, or taking it through warfare. All these practices were employed extensively by the United States throughout the seventeenth, eighteenth, and nineteenth centuries as this society spread from the eastern seaboard across the continent. The most frequently used tactic, of course, was taking over land that had previously been the domain of Native American Indians.

Today, 17 percent of the land area in the United States is used for raising crops, and another 29 percent is pasture and grasslands (U.S. Bureau of the Census, 1987:182). Only an additional one percent of the land is classified as cropland that is not being farmed. A very significant feature of land use in this country, which is not true of most other nations, is that we have set aside large tracts of land for other uses and stipulated in law that they cannot be farmed. Forests still cover some 29 percent of our territory, and although much of this land is not suitable for agriculture, two-thirds of all forest acreage is publicly owned and protected against indiscriminate logging. In addition, another four percent of the land is being preserved as natural wildlife areas, and five percent is designated as recreational areas. *Since the middle of this century, most industrial societies have not significantly increased the proportion of their land devoted to agriculture.* In Europe (with the exception of the Soviet Union) and in Japan, this has been because almost all their arable land is already under cultivation, while in the United States this has been due to the public policy of preserving forests and other natural areas. Between 1960 and 1985, for example, agricultural land in this country expanded by only 19 million acres, from 324 to 343 million acres, which represented only a 6 percent increase

(U.S. Bureau of the Census, 1987:639). *Nevertheless, farm productivity has grown dramatically during recent years.* In the United States, total agricultural output increased by 66 percent between 1960 and 1985, and numerous other countries have experienced similar gains. This increased productivity—often called the "Green Revolution"—has been due primarily to several technological advances. Increasing knowledge about plant genetics has enabled scientists to develop new hybrid strains of many grains that are resistant to drought and insects and that yield many more bushels per acre. Chemical fertilizers have come into widespread use, as have many new kinds of pesticides and herbicides. And expanded irrigation has enabled farmers to grow crops on land that receives little rain. At the same time, these new practices have created serious environmental and health problems in many countries, while intensive cultivation is severely depleting soil nutrients and augmenting soil erosion. We are therefore paying a heavy environmental price for our increased agricultural productivity. But at the present time, at least, the industrial nations of the world are able to feed their people fairly adequately and some of them are able to export surplus food to less developed nations.

Fresh Water

Abundant fresh water is needed not only for domestic use but also for many industrial processes and for farm irrigation, which alone accounts for more than two-thirds of all water use. Thus far, North America as a whole has not suffered from acute water shortages, although some local regions (such as southern California) are experiencing this problem. Most of this continent presently has at least 10 million cubic meters of water per person (which is considered a high level of water availability), and none of the continent has less than 5 million cubic meters per person (which is considered medium water availability) (Council on Environmental Quality, 1980:24). Throughout the rest of the world, all of South America has high water availability, as does most of Southern Africa, Scandinavia, the eastern part of the Soviet Union, and most of Australia. In contrast, almost all of the European industrial nations, as well as Japan, have only one to five million cubic meters of water per person (which is considered low availability). This is also true of all of Northern Africa and almost all of Southeast Asia.

The United States, Canada, Scandinavia, Switzerland, the Soviet Union, and Australia are the only industrial countries in the world that presently have adequate supplies of fresh water. That statement is misleading for the United States, however, since in many parts of the country, especially the Midwest farm states, water availability is being maintained by drawing on underground aquifers that are being depleted much faster than they are being replenished through natural processes. Moreover, demands for fresh water are rising rapidly in the United States, as well as most other parts of the world. Consequently, by the end of this century all of this country is expected to have declined to the level of medium water availability, and the Midwest plains states will likely have fallen into the low category, along with almost all other industrial nations (except Scandinavia, the Soviet Union, and Australia) (Council on Environmental Quality, 1980:25). In short, *the vital natural resource of fresh water that has previously been readily available for all our needs is rapidly becoming an increasingly scarce resource in almost all industrial nations.*

Forests

Prior to the twentieth century, wood was the primary fuel throughout the world, as well as a principal building material. As a result, the thick forests that once covered all of Europe were steadily cleared to obtain the wood needed for fuel and building, as well as to provide more land for farming. Today, consequently, all of Europe contains only 15 billion cubic meters of growing timber, compared to 79 billion cubic meters in the Soviet Union and 58 billion cubic meters in the United States (Council on Environmental Quality, 1980:23). *Wood has thus become a scarce natural resource in most of the industrial nations of Europe.* In contrast, all of the developing countries in the world still contain over 300 billion cubic meters of standing timber, although those forests are now also being cleared at a rapid rate to provide fuel and agricultural land for their exploding populations. The Brazilian rain forest, for example, will be completely eliminated within about 20 years if the present rate of cutting continues. *Deforestation is therefore becoming a serious environmental concern throughout much of the world today.*

In the United States, wood is no longer a major fuel, and a large proportion of the remaining forests are owned and protected by the federal government. Consequently, our forest reserves—measured in terms of total amount of both forest land and standing timber—have actually increased slightly since 1950 (U.S. Bureau of the Census, 1987:654). Nevertheless, many environmental organizations are gravely concerned about the timber-harvesting practices that are being widely used today throughout the Western states where our major forests are located. Because clear-cutting large tracts of land is economically efficient for timber companies, they generally prefer this method of logging. However, clear-cutting leaves the area susceptible to soil erosion and brush fires. Even if the land is replanted with new trees, it will be many years before the new forests are fully grown. Environmentalists are therefore warning that if we do not protect our existing forests more adequately, wood will eventually become a scarce natural resource in this country as it already is in most other industrial nations.

Minerals

The heavy manufacturing industries that constitute the foundation of all industrial economies consume huge amounts of mineral ores as raw materials every year. Prior to the twentieth century, very little attention was given to the amounts of these metals existing in the earth, since those reserves were typically viewed as virtually inexhaustable at the rates they were then being mined. *During the first two-thirds of this century, however, consumption rates of most metals rose rapidly at ever-increasing rates as industrial production grew steadily.* By 1970, for example, the United States was mining 90 million tons of iron ore per year. Other minerals in high demand include bauxite for aluminum, copper, lead, manganese for magnesium, nickel, and zinc. In 1970, the total value of all mining in this country was $1.5 billion, and by 1985 it had risen to $3.4 billion (U.S. Bureau of the Census, 1987:672).

In the early 1970s, three important changes occurred in the United States and other industrial nations in regard to minerals. First, we finally began to realize that at present rates of consumption we were rapidly depleting the earth's deposits of almost all minerals and that they would not last too much longer. Many of them will be largely or totally exhausted by the end of the next century. Second, prices of most metals began to rise rather sharply, primarily because of dwindling supplies. For instance, between 1970 and 1985 the price of iron ore tripled. Third, largely as a result of those rising prices, the demand for many metals began to decline. Production of iron ore in this country, for example, declined over 40 percent between 1970 and 1985 (U.S. Bureau of the Census, 1987:690). If these lower levels of mineral consumption continue in the future, the life expectancy of our remaining reserves will, of course, be prolonged. However, prices of most minerals will undoubtedly continue to rise because of their increasing scarcity.

In short, *the minerals that are vital raw materials for industrial production in modern societies are all finite resources that are rapidly being consumed.* Without these resources—especially iron—industrial production as presently practiced will no longer be possible.

Fuels

Since the role of energy in industrial societies is examined in the final section of this chapter, the present discussion deals only with the sources of that energy. The contemporary world runs largely on three kinds of fossil fuels: coal provides 30 percent of all energy produced, petroleum provides 45 percent, and natural gas provides 21 percent (U.S. Bureau of the Census, 1987:833). All other fuels—primarily wood, hydroelectricity, and nuclear reactors—together account for only 4 percent of total world energy. *The industrial nations of the world are consuming these fossil fuels at prodigious rates to produce energy.* Although they contain only about 25 percent of the world's population, they are presently using over 75 percent of all energy produced (U.S. Bureau of the Census, 1987:550). The United States, with only five percent of the earth's people, consumes 26 percent of the world's energy. In this country, coal provides 24 percent of our energy, petroleum 42 percent, natural gas 24 percent, and all other sources 10 percent (U.S. Bureau of the Census, 1987:542).

In the early 1800s, coal began to replace wood as the principal fuel in industrializing nations and remained so for a century. Although the first oil well was drilled in Pennsylvania in 1859, for a long time petroleum was a minor fuel source used primarily to produce kerosene. Not until automobiles began to be mass produced in the 1920s did gasoline and other petroleum products come into widespread use. Only since World War II has oil been consumed on a massive scale. In 1950, world oil production was still only 3.8 billion barrels per year, whereas in 1980 this figure had risen nearly six-fold to 21.7 billion barrels a year. Oil and natural gas are much more preferable than coal as fuels for several reasons: they are easier and cheaper to extract from the earth, they are less heavy and bulky to transport and store, they are more convenient to burn, and they are less polluting. Consequently, *oil and natural gas are by far the most important sources of energy in all industrial societies today,* and coal is now used extensively only in large heating and electric-generating plants and in steel mills.

Because coal is so abundant in the earth, during the nineteenth century when it was the primary fuel there was little or no concern about its availability. It was viewed as an inexhaustible natural resource. That same mode of thinking was also applied to petroleum until after the middle of this century, since vast new reserves were being discovered at a much faster rate than oil and natural gas were being consumed. Not until the 1960s did we begin to give serious attention to the fact that all fossil fuels are finite in supply, and eventually will be largely or totally exhausted. There is still a great deal of coal remaining in the earth, and although mining it may do serious harm to the natural environment, the known reserves of coal will probably last into the twenty-second century and perhaps for another 200 years after that, depending on how rapidly we consume it. That is not the case with petroleum, however. *At our present rate of consumption, it is estimated that half of the world's total petroleum reserves will be gone before the end of this century, and 90 percent of the reserves will be used up by 2030* (Humphrey and Buttel, 1982:143). At that point, petroleum will likely have become so expensive that it will no longer be feasible to use it as a fuel. By the time that happens, we will have had to invent substitutes for petroleum products if our vehicles and furnaces are to continue operating.

POPULATION CONDITIONS

A fundamental proposition of social ecology is that population size is directly related to people's ability to adapt to and utilize the natural environment. As technological knowledge expands and is used with increasing effectiveness to obtain vital resources from the natural environment, population size almost inevitably grows. Throughout the many thousands of years in which humans lived in foraging, horticultural, and agrarian societies, the total population of the world never exceeded one billion. In fact, that point was not reached until sometime during the first quarter of the nineteenth century, after the industrial revolution had begun. However, it required only a hundred years of industrial development to double the world's population to two billion by about 1925. Since then, population growth has been staggering. Only 45 years were needed to increase the total population to three billion in 1960, just 15 years were required to raise that figure to four billion in 1975, and in merely 12 more years the world's population had grown to five billion by 1987. Quite clearly, *population growth is closely linked with economic development throughout the world.*

The population explosion of the twentieth century is creating severe social problems in most nations, and these problems will undoubtedly become even more critical in the years ahead. The most fundamental of those problems is providing enough food and other basic necessities to keep people alive. Beyond that are the countless problems of ensuring everyone a minimally adequate standard of living, educating new generations of people, providing jobs for them, and meeting all their other needs. Although those problems are presently most evident in the developing regions of the world, it is the populations of the industrial societies—with their enormous consumption of natural resources and resulting high standards of living—that are placing by far the most severe demands on the world ecosystem.

Demography

The scientific study of human populations is called demography. The central concept in demography is *a population, which is a set of individuals who have at least one common characteristic.* The world population obviously includes all beings who belong to the species Homo sapiens sapiens. Generally, however, demographers focus on more restricted populations, defined in terms of nationality, residence in a particular community or other location, biological criteria such as gender or age, social criteria such as religion or marital status, or membership in a particular organization. Although demographers are often thought of as being merely population "nose counters," their work includes studies of population structures (their size, distribution, and composition), population processes (fertility, motality, and migration rates and patterns), and population policies and programs.

The demographic study of *population structures* is concerned not only with measuring population sizes and rates of changes but also with the distributions and compositions of populations. The manner in which a population is distributed over a geographical territory can be tremendously important both ecologically and socially, since the denser the population, the greater the demands for land and other natural resources and the more frequent and intense the patterns of social interaction. And the composition of a population—in terms of its sex ratio, age structure, marital statuses, religious affiliations, income distribution, and many other characteristics—has untold consequences for its patterns of living and social organization.

Demographers who study *population processes* focus on fertility, mortality, and migration rates and their effects on populations. These rates are usually expressed as the number of specific events (such as live births) occurring within a given time period (usually a year), divided by the size of the relevant population (expressed in some base number such as thousands or millions of people). Thus the birth rate for a given country might be stated as the number of live births per year per 1,000 population. That figure would be the *crude rate* of births for the country, because it is based on the size of the entire population. Crude rates are often not very useful, however, since their base populations generally include many people for whom that event is not directly relevant. The crude birth rate, for example, is based on the total national population, in-

cluding women below and above the childbearing ages and all men. For greater precision, demographers frequently compute *refined rates* based on more precisely defined populations. The refined birth rate of a country, for instance, gives the number of live births a year per 1,000 women in the childbearing ages of 15 to 45. Demographers also frequently study social and personal factors that influence fertility, mortality, and migration rates.

Other demographers, meanwhile, are concerned primarily with *policies and programs* designed to affect or control population structures and processes in various ways. Those policies sometimes pertain to population sizes and rates of growth, such as a national policy to prevent further population expansion or a community policy to increase its size. Population policies may also pertain to particular activities, such as use of contraception or admitting foreign immigrants. To achieve these policy goals, governments and private organizations such as churches or labor unions often implement action programs of various kinds. These might range from a national movement to legalize abortion to efforts by an ethnic minority to encourage its people to move out of urban ghettos.

Population Theories

Since antiquity, social philosophers have speculated about demographic processes and proposed population policies. Plato, for example, believed that the ideal size of a city-state was 5,040 people, and that ethnic diversity should be avoided because it weakened the existing social order. The first significant population theory was proposed in 1798 by Thomas Malthus, an English clergyman and economist, in his *Essay on the Principle of Population*. He formulated a "natural law" of population growth, which stated that *all populations will increase faster than the available food supply unless they are checked in some manner*. This occurs because populations tend to grow at a geometric rate (1,2,4,8,16 . . .), since couples normally have several more children than are necessary to replace themselves. Food supplies and other subsistence necessities tend to increase at only an arithmetic rate (1,2,3,4,5 . . .), however, because of limited land and other natural resources. Therefore, *unchecked populations will always eventually outstrip the resources necessary to sustain them, leading to widespread death.* Malthus saw only two means of curbing population growth. *Intentional preventive checks* included abstinence, deferral of marriage, and "vice" (which meant prostitution, extramarital sexual relations, and contraception, since it was considered immoral in his time). If those checks proved ineffective (as he believed they generally were), *natural positive checks* such as famines, epidemics, and wars would inevitably take over and reduce the excess population to a level that could be sustained by the environment. Malthus's thesis was severely criticized and then largely forgotten for over a century, as nineteenth- and twentieth-century advances in agricultural technology kept food supplies increasing faster than populations throughout the world. In recent years, however, we have come to realize that population growth is now occurring at a faster rate than increases in food production, so that Malthus's ideas have become the basis of much current ecological thinking.

Malthus was not as totally pessimistic about population growth as his "natural law" suggests. In his later writings, he pointed out that the privileged classes in all societies have almost invariably had lower birth rates than the rest of the people, presumably because they understood the economic and social benefits of smaller families. He therefore hoped that as peasants, workers, and other ordinary people gradually improved their level of living and became aware of the benefits of small families, they would also reduce their birth rates (Peterson, 1975:154–60). That optimistic expectation is reflected in the *demographic transition model,* which has become the major theoretical explanation of population dynamics among contemporary demographers (Beavers, 1975).

This model was initially developed to explain why the populations of Western industrializing countries grew so rapidly during the century from approximately 1850 to 1950 and also why the growth rates of those nations later declined abruptly. More recently, the model has also been applied to contemporary industrializing societies, although they have not yet completed this transition process. As depicted in Figure 11-1, *the demographic transition model consists of three stages that all societies presumably go through as they develop economically and socially.*

FIGURE 11-1 Demographic transition model Source: *Environment, Energy, and Society* by Craig R. Humphrey and Frederick R. Buttel, p. 65. Copyright 1982 by Wadsworth, Inc. Reprinted by permission of the publisher.

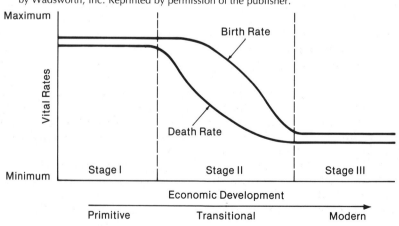

During Stage I of Primitive development, both the birth and death rates are quite high, resulting in a relatively stable population with little growth. At the beginning of the nineteenth century, the crude birth and death rates in all Western societies ranged from 30 to over 50 per 1,000 population, which meant that large numbers of babies were being born each year and almost the same number of people were dying each year. These high birth rates were due partially to the importance of having a number of children to help with the farming and to care for the parents in their old age, and partially to lack of knowledge about contraception. The corresponding high death rates were caused by such factors as inadequate food supplies and poor nutrition, filthy and unsanitary living conditions, epidemics of infectious diseases, and limited medical knowledge.

During Stage II of Transitional development, the death rate first drops quite drastically, falling to only seven to 15 deaths per 1,000 people a year. Since this occurred in the West before the discovery of modern public health measures, disease prevention through innoculations, or antibiotics such as penicillin, it must have been caused by other factors. One of these was undoubtedly more abundant food supplies and better diets. Another was a series of improvements in urban sanitation conditions, including clean water supplies, sewage disposal systems, garbage collection, and street cleaning. For a considerable period of time after a country's death rate falls, however, its birth rate continues at a high level, resulting in very rapid population growth. This condition is usually attributed to the persistence of traditional beliefs about the desirability of large families, which are usually supported by established customs, norms, laws and religious injunctions. Moreover, during that period most people know little or nothing about birth control, so that they are unable to limit their procreation even if they wanted to.

Eventually, nevertheless, the birth rate begins to decline to match the death rate, for a variety of reasons. As the economy shifts from agriculture to manufacturing and people move from rural to urban areas, large families become an economic liability rather than an asset as they are on the farm. Whereas there is always necessary work for children to do on a farm, in the city those tasks do not exist, and raising large numbers of children becomes a tremendous economic and social burden, especially when both parents are employed outside the home. In addition, better nutrition and sanitation result in more children reaching adulthood, so that having a large number of children is not necessary to ensure that there will be someone to care for the parents in their old age. Traditional and religious beliefs become weaker and are slowly replaced by more secular values stressing individual achievement and raising one's standard of living. Parents increasingly want to use their economic resources to improve their living conditions and to provide a comfortable home and educational opportunities for a few children, rather than attempting to just feed and clothe many offspring. As more and more women seek employment outside the home, they no longer want to spend their entire lifetime caring for children. Knowledge and availability of contraception methods obviously facilitates this trend toward smaller families, but it is important to realize that the Transitional Stage II was largely completed in the West before modern contraception practices became widespread.

The Modern Stage III of the demographic model is reached when the birth rate has finally declined to a level that is close to, or at, the low death rate. The population is then again in balance, and it experiences little or no further growth. All highly industrialized countries, containing about one-fourth of the world's population, are now in this stage. Overall, their average crude death rate is presently 10, and their average crude birth rate is 15, which gives them an annual growth rate of just 0.5 percent (Population Reference Bureau, 1987).

The major point to understand about this demographic transition is that until recently it has commonly been viewed as a natural and presumably inevitable consequence of industrialization and modernization. From this perspective, it has seemed reasonable to assume that as contemporary industrializing societies gradually developed economically and socially, they would also enter Stage III and complete the demographic transition process. Thus far, however, that has not happened. Although some very poorly developed countries are still in Stage I, *most developing nations are presently in the midst of Stage II and thus far have shown few signs of completing the demographic transition.* Since World War II, the death rates in almost all of these transitional societies have declined sharply, so that their overall average is only 11 deaths per 1,000 people a year, almost the same as that of the industrial nations. In addition to the factors that reduced death rates in the West, many of these countries have also benefited from assistance programs conducted by industrial nations. We have given them technological assistance to increase their food production, economic aid to promote industrialization, information about modern water and sanitation systems, and massive public health programs to eliminate contagious diseases. All this has been done with the best humanitarian intentions, but our assistance has had the unintended consequence of stimulating much faster population growth in those developing countries than ever occurred in the West during Stage II of the transition.

If the developing countries eventually succeed in lowering their birth rates, they will move into Stage III and also complete the demographic transition. At the present time, however, their overall average birth rate is still 32 per 1,000 people a year. This gives them an annual growth rate of 2.1 percent, which means that their populations are doubling every 33 years (Population Reference Bureau, 1987). Demographers do not fully understand why at least the more highly developed of these societies are not significantly lowering their birth rates. Some demographers believe that these countries have simply not yet progressed far enough through the transition, but they eventually will. Others suggest that various factors that were not present in the West are operating in these countries to keep their birth rates high, so that the transition may not be completed in the foreseeable future and their populations will continue growing rapidly. Such factors may include men's beliefs that they must produce children to prove their masculinity, strong traditional emphasis on the desirability of large families, or widespread despair about the possibility of ever achieving higher standards of living. Still other demographers argue that colonization and economic exploitation of developing societies by industrial nations have supported the continuation of high birth rates to ensure a plentiful supply of workers willing to work at low wages and thus indirectly benefit the developed countries. Whatever the reasons, much of the world is still stuck in Phase II of the demographic transition and the world's population continues to explode. By the year 2010 there will likely be at least seven billion people trying to survive on this earth, and a very conservative estimate is that we will reach eight billion no later than 2030, if not much sooner (Population Reference Bureau, 1987).

Population Sizes and Growth Rates

Although our central concern in this chapter is with industrial nations, population figures for them are not fully meaningful unless placed in the context of the entire world. Table 11-1 therefore presents an overview of the world population in 1970, 1980, and 1987, for all industrial and all industrializing nations, for broad geographical regions, and for each industrial society. The table shows population sizes in millions, the annual percentage rate of population growth in 1987, and the number of years in which the population will double in size at the 1987 rate (assuming that it and all other factors remain constant).

During this 17-year period, total world population increased by nearly one and a third billion people, from slightly over 3.7 billion to more than 5 billion inhabitants. This increase was greater

TABLE 11-1 World, Regional, and Industrialized Nations' Population Sizes in 1970, 1980, and 1987 and Growth Rates in 1987

Area	Population in Millions			Annual Percent Growth Rate in 1987*	Doubling Years from 1987**
	1970	*1980*	*1987*		
Entire World	3,721	4,473	5,026	1.7	40
Industrialized Nations+	1,063	1,140	1,195	0.5	128
Industrializing Nations	2,669	3,333	3,832	2.1	33
(% of World)	(72%)	(75%)	(76%)		
Asia	2,112	2,593	2,930	2.2	31
Africa	375	491	601	2.8	24
Europe	460	484	495	0.3	272
Latin America	286	364	421	2.2	30
Soviet Union	243	266	284	0.9	79
North America	226	252	270	0.7	101
Oceania	19	23	25	1.2	59
United States	205	228	244	0.7	102
Japan	104	117	122	0.6	124
West Germany	61	62	61	−0.2	—
United Kingdom	56	56	57	0.2	462
Italy	54	56	57	0.1	1,155
France	51	54	56	0.4	178
Spain	34	37	39	0.5	147
Poland	33	36	38	0.8	88
Canada	21	24	26	0.8	91
Romania	20	22	23	0.5	147
Yugoslovia	20	22	23	0.7	102
East Germany	17	17	17	0.0	—
Czechoslovakia	14	15	16	0.3	257
Australia	13	15	16	0.8	86
Netherlands	13	14	15	0.4	142
Hungary	10	11	11	−0.2	—
Belgium	10	10	10	0.0	—
Greece	9	10	10	0.2	289
Portugal	9	10	10	0.3	257
Bulgaria	8	9	9	0.1	578
Sweden	8	8	8	0.1	636
Austria	7	8	8	0.0	—
Switzerland	6	6	7	0.2	301
Denmark	5	5	5	−0.1	—
Finland	5	5	5	0.3	224
Norway	4	3	4	0.2	408
Israel	3	4	4	1.7	41
Ireland	3	3	4	0.8	85
New Zealand	3	3	3	0.8	92
Albania	2	3	3	2.0	34
Cyprus	0.6	0.6	0.7	1.1	63
Luxembourg	0.4	0.3	0.4	0.1	636
Malta	0.3	0.3	0.4	0.8	89
Iceland	0.2	0.2	0.2	0.9	76

* Annual percent rate of natural population increase, excluding migration.

** Projection based on the current growth rate.

+ All of Europe plus Australia, Canada, Israel, Japan, New Zealand, the Soviet Union, and the United States

Sources: U.S. Bureau of the Census, Statistical Abstract of the United States, 1987, Washington, D.C.: U.S. Government Printing Office, Table 1437. Population Reference Bureau, World Population Data Sheet, 1987, Washington, D.C.

than the total number of people in the world in 1850. However, the annual growth rate, which had been 2.0 percent in 1970, dropped to 1.7 in 1987. The expected doubling time for the world's population at that 1987 rate was 40 years, so that by 2037 it could be over 10 billion.

Very little of that world population growth occurred in the industrial nations, since their total population increased by only 132 million during this period, to about 1.2 billion in 1987. Moreover, their annual growth rate, which had been 1.0 percent in 1970, was cut in half, to 0.5 percent, by 1987. Consequently, their doubling time was expected to be 128 years. Most of the world's population growth between 1970 and 1987 obviously occurred in the developing countries. Their total population increased by nearly 1.2 billion people, to about 3.8 billion in 1987, which was 76 percent of the world's total. Their overall annual rate of growth did decline, from 2.5 percent in 1970 to 2.1 percent in 1987, but their doubling time was still only 33 years.

Major variations in population sizes and growth rates exist among the world's geographical regions. The largest population concentration is in Asia, with more than 2.9 billion people. The next most populous region is Africa, with 600 million people, followed by Europe with 495 million, Latin America with 421 million, the USSR with 284 million, North America with 270 million, and Oceania with just 25 million people. The highest rate of population growth is occurring in Africa, at 2.8 percent a year, which gives it a doubling time of just 24 years. Almost equally high growth rates are occurring in Asia and Latin America, at 2.2 percent a year and a doubling time of about 30 years. In sharp contrast, growth has been very slow in Europe, which added only 35 million people between 1970 and 1987 and is currently increasing by just 0.3 percent a year, for a doubling time of 272 years. The Soviet Union and North America are also growing relatively slowly, but at a faster rate than Europe. The USSR has a growth rate of 0.9 percent, relatively high for a developed

nation, for a doubling time of 79 years. In North America that rate is 0.7 percent, for a doubling time of 101 years. Oceania, finally, is increasing at a rate of 1.4 percent a year, which makes its doubling time 51 years.

The largest industrial society is the Soviet Union, with a population of 284 million in 1987. The second largest industrial society is the United States, whose 1987 population was 244 million. Japan ranks third with a population of 122 million. It is important to realize that these three nations, which together contain only 13 percent of the world's population, presently account for approximately half of all natural resource consumption in the world. *From a world ecological perspective, therefore, the U.S.S.R., the U.S., and Japan are the most over-populated nations in the world today.*

If an annual population growth rate of 1.0 or less is taken as an indication that a society has reached Phase III of the demographic transition, then all industrial societies (except Albania and Cyprus) are now in that stage. (Israel is in Stage III since its population growth is due mainly to immigration, not a high birth rate.) *All of these industrial nations have achieved a condition of relative population stability based on low birth and death rates.* Nevertheless, most of these nations are still growing, at least slowly, and will continue to do so for another generation or two. After the birth rate in a country drops to the replacement level—as it has in the United States—its population will keep expanding for at least a generation because of *demographic momentum*. This concept means that as long as the newly-born generation is larger than its parental generation, the birth rate will continue to exceed the death rate at least slightly. Only when the new generation is the same size as, or smaller than, the older generation will national population growth cease totally, as it has in a few countries.

United States Population

Since 1790, the United States has conducted a national census every ten years.

TABLE 11-2   United States Population Sizes, Growth Rates, and Immigration from 1790 to 1987

Year	Population Size in Millions	Increase in Millions During Past Decade	Percent Increase During Past Decade	Immigrants in Millions During Past Decade	Immigrants as Percent of Growth During Past Decade
1790	3.9	*	*	*	*
1800	5.3	1.4	35	*	*
1810	7.3	2.0	36	*	*
1820	9.6	2.6	33	*	*
1830	12.9	3.3	34	0.2	6
1840	17.0	4.1	33	0.6	15
1850	23.2	6.2	36	1.7	27
1860	31.4	8.2	36	2.6	32
1870	39.9	8.5	27	2.3	27
1880	50.2	10.3	26	2.8	27
1890	62.9	12.7	25	5.2	41
1900	76.1	13.2	21	3.7	28
1910	92.4	16.3	21	8.8	54
1920	106.5	14.1	15	5.7	40
1930	123.1	16.6	16	4.1	25
1940	132.4	9.3	8	0.5	5
1950	152.2	19.8	15	1.0	5
1960	180.7	28.5	16	2.5	9
1970	205.1	24.4	14	3.2	8
1980	227.8	22.7	11	4.5	22
1987	243.8	22.9**	9**	2.9***	*

* Not known

** Projected to 1990

*** As of 1985

Source: U.S. Bureau of the Census, *Statistical Abstract of the United States, 1987.* Washington, D.C.: U.S. Government Printing Office, Tables 1, 2, and 7.

Table 11-2 reports the population of this country at each census, plus the estimate for 1987. It shows this nation's population size in millions, the population increase during the preceding decade in millions, that increase as a percentage of the population at the previous census, the number of immigrants during the preceding decade, and the approximate percentage of the increase during the preceding decade due to immigration (not counting emigrants who left this country).

In 1790, the population of the United States was slightly under four million. By 1830, it had more than tripled, to almost 13 million, and by 1860 it was more than 31 million. During those 70 years the rate of growth was extremely high, averaging 35 percent per decade, or 3.5 percent per year.

By 1860, immigrants accounted for nearly one-third of total population growth. During the next 70 years, from 1860 to 1930, the rate of population increase slowed considerably, dropping to 16 percent by 1930. Population size continued to grow steadily during that period, however, reaching 76 million in 1900 and 123 million in 1930. These figures show that, as a country's population increases, even a relatively modest growth rate can result in large numbers of additional people. A major proportion of the nation's growth during those 70 years was due to immigration, reaching a peak of 54 percent of all growth during the 1900-1910 decade.

The decade between 1930 and 1940 saw considerably less population growth and very little immigration due to the Great Depression. During the 30-year period from

1940 to 1970, population growth regained its predepression level of about 15 percent per decade, so that by 1970 the total population was 205 million. This period (from 1946 at the end of World War II until 1965), is known as the "baby boom" era due to its high birth rates. Immigration accounted for only a very small proportion of the population growth during those years.

Since 1970, the growth rate in this country has declined to about 10 percent per decade. Nevertheless, during the 17 years from 1970 to 1987, the United States added more than 45 million new residents—more than the total size of the country in 1875. Although the birth rate declined considerably during that time, this decline was largely offset by the large number of immigrants in the same period. While immigrants accounted for nearly one-fourth of total population growth between 1970 and 1980, the flow of immigrants has slowed considerably since 1980.

Overall, *the population growth of the United States has been spectacular.* In 200 years, the country increased from less than four million to about 244 million, a growth of 63 times over the 1790 figures. This growth has been a combined result of rapidly falling death rates, high birth rates during most of those decades, and more than 50 million immigrants.

Various regions of the United States have been growing at quite different rates in recent years. In broad terms, between 1980 and 1985 the Midwest grew slightly; the Northeast experienced modest growth; the West grew extensively; and the South experienced the greatest amount of population expansion. In particular, California's population increased by 2.7 million during that period, which accounted for more than one-fifth of the entire population growth of the nation. Two other states also grew quite rapidly: Texas gained 2.1 million people, and Florida's population increased by 1.6 million. In colloquial terms, large numbers of Americans have moved from the Midwest snow belt to the Southern sun belt.

Population Distribution

In addition to measuring population size and growth rates, demographers are also concerned about how populations are distributed in space. *The two most frequently used indicators of population distribution are density, which is the number of people per square unit of land, and urbanization, which is the number or proportion of people living in urban places.* There are serious problems with both of these indicators. When population density is based on the total land area of a region or nation, in countries like the Soviet Union, Canada, and Australia, that includes vast expanses of almost useless territory. A more meaningful measure of density would be people per square unit of usable or arable land. However, definitions of what constitutes usable land change over time, thus making this a shifting measure and limiting its usefulness. The problem with all indicators of urbanization is that there is no standard worldwide definition of what constitutes an "urban place." As will be discussed in Chapter 14, this definition varies from 2,500 people in the United States to 10,000 or more in other nations. Since data on urbanization are gathered by each country, these measures are never fully comparable across nations.

With that warning in mind, Table 11-3 presents measures of population density and urbanization for the entire world, industrial and industrializing nations, major geographical regions, and each industrial society, following the format of Table 11-1. Density is measured here in number of people per square mile, while urbanization is measured in terms of each country's definition of "urban place."

For the world as a whole, there are presently 94 people per square mile of land, while 43 percent of the world's population is urbanized. The 35 industrial nations are less densely settled than the world as a whole, with only 56 people per square mile on the average. These countries are much more urbanized than the world as a whole, however,

TABLE 11-3   World, Regional, and Industrialized Nations'
Population Density and Proportion Urbanized in 1987

Area	Population Per Square Mile	Proportion Urbanized*
Entire World	94	43
Industrialized Nations	56	72
Industrializing Nations	123	34
Asia	271	32
Africa	50	30
Europe	262	73
Latin America	53	67
Soviet Union	32	65
North America	32	74
Oceania	7	71
United States	67	74
Japan	845	76
West Germany	633	85
United Kingdom	599	90
Italy	492	72
France	262	73
Spain	200	91
Poland	311	53
Canada	7	76
Romania	638	53
Yugoslovia	236	46
East Germany	400	77
Czechoslovakia	315	74
Australia	5	86
Netherlands	922	89
Hungary	296	56
Belgium	838	95
Greece	145	70
Portugal	284	30
Bulgaria	210	66
Sweden	48	83
Austria	233	55
Switzerland	405	57
Denmark	307	84
Finland	38	60
Norway	33	70
Israel	536	90
Ireland	134	56
New Zealand	32	84
Albania	272	34
Cyprus	188	53
Luxembourg	368	78
Malta	2,901	85
Iceland	6	89

* As "urban" is defined by each country.

Sources: U.S. Bureau of the Census, Statistical Abstract of the
United States, 1987. Washington, D.C.: U.S. Government Printing
Office, Table 1437. Population Reference Bureau, World Popula-
tion Data Sheet, 1987, Washington, D.C.

with 73 percent of their people living in urban communities. In contrast, the developing nations of the world are much more densely settled, having 123 people per square mile on average. They are considerably less urbanized, however, with only 34 percent of their people living in urban communities.

Among the major geographical regions of the world, Asia is not only the most populous but also has the highest population density, at 271 people per square mile. Because Asia (with the exception of Japan) is not very industrialized, however, its level of urbanization is quite low, with only 32 percent of the people residing in urban communities. Africa is even less urbanized, at just 30 percent, but its population density is a very low 50 people per square mile. Europe, meanwhile, is almost as densely settled as Asia, with 262 people per square mile. But because all European nations are industrialized, this region is quite highly urbanized, at 73 percent. Latin America, the Soviet Union, and North America all have very similar patterns of density and urbanization. None of these regions are very densely settled, with only 53, 32, and 32 people per square mile, respectively. All three have moderately high levels of urbanization, however, at 67, 65, and 74 percent, respectively. Oceania, finally, has extremely low population density (due primarily to Australia) but rather extensive urbanization.

Industrial societies are listed in Table 11-3 in the same order of decreasing population size as in Table 11-1. Inspection of both distribution measures quickly reveals two broad generalizations:

(1) *There is extremely wide variation among the industrial countries in population density and hence no relationship between population size* (as indicated by their rank ordering) *and population density.*

(2) Although all but two of these countries (Portugal and Albania) are more urbanized than the world as a whole, *there is also considerable variation in rates of urbanization among industrial countries and hence no relationship between population size and proportion urbanized.*

In regard to population density, eight of these nations have extremely high densities of 500 or more people per square mile. Tiny Malta tops the list, with a density of 2,901 people per square mile. The Netherlands and Belgium are also extremely dense, with figures of 922 and 838, respectively. (Since virtually all of their land is in use, these are "true" density measures.) The other five very densely settled industrial countries are Japan, West Germany, the United Kingdom, Romania, and Israel. At the other end of the density scale, Canada, Australia, and Iceland are extremely sparsely settled, with less than ten people per square mile, since much of their land is not usable. The Soviet Union, Sweden, Finland, Norway, and New Zealand also have relatively low densities below 50 people per square mile. The United States, with 67 people per square mile, can be described as having moderately low population density. All other industrial nations have densities between 100 and 500 people per square mile.

In regard to urbanization, a proportion of 80 percent or more is often taken as a very high level of urban settlement. Twelve countries are above that level, headed by Belgium, which is 95 percent urbanized. The next most urbanized country is Spain, at 91 percent. The remaining highly urbanized nations are West Germany, the United Kingdom, Australia, the Netherlands, Sweden, Denmark, Israel, New Zealand, Iceland, and Malta. Most of the remaining industrial nations are also moderately highly urbanized, with levels between 60 and 80 percent. The United States is currently 74 percent urbanized, while the Soviet Union is 65 percent. The only industrial countries that are less than 50 percent urbanized are Yugoslovia, Portugal, and Albania.

Population Composition

A third aspect of populations that demographers often investigate is their composition in terms of different kinds of personal characteristics. The composition of a population can be described in terms of a wide variety of factors that fall into two broad categories: ascribed characteristics such as sex, age, race, and kinship, and achieved characteristics such as nationality, language, marital status, religion, place of residence, education, occupation, and income. Although all of these ascribed and achieved characteristics are important for demographic and sociological analyses, *the two factors most commonly reported when describing the composition of a population are its sex and age structures.*

The standard indicator of sex composition is the *sex ratio, which is the number of males in a population per 100 females.* At birth, this ratio is approximately 105 in all countries, reflecting the fact that about 105 males are born for every 100 females. But since males have higher death rates than females at all ages, the sex ratio gradually declines with age. It drops to 100 in middle age, and after that females always outnumber males in a national population. The overall sex ratio in a country, as well as its age-specific sex ratios (that is, the sex ratio for all people at any given age), can be affected by several different factors. Until middle age, accidents (especially automobile accidents) tend to kill many more men than women, as do wars. Later in life, many kinds of mature illnesses such as cancer, heart attacks, and strokes strike down more men at younger ages than women. In the past, large-scale international migrations have frequently upset sex ratios, since males have been more likely to migrate than females. Today, however, women are almost as likely to migrate as males. In general, *whenever the sex ratio of a nation or other area becomes even moderately unbalanced in either direction, it can have quite serious consequences for rates of marriages, births, crimes, and other actions.*

The world sex ratio in 1980 was 100.6, indicating an even balance between males and females. There are considerable variations amount countries, however. Overall, *industrial nations tend to have lower sex ratios (fewer men than women) than do developing nations,* which is primarily a reflection of their age compositions. Industrial countries generally have somewhat older populations (for a variety of medical, nutritional, and socioeconomic reasons) in which women outnumber men. In contrast, developing countries tend to have younger populations, so that the higher birth rate of males puts them in the majority. Among the major geographical regions of the world, the lowest sex ratios are found in the Soviet Union (87.8 in 1980), North America (95.3), and Europe (95.2)—all of which are composed of industrial nations. The highest sex ratio occurs in Asia (about 104 in 1980), but in Africa it is only about 100 (United Nations, 1985, Vol. I, Table 7).

The sex ratio in the United States has declined steadily during the twentieth century as its population has gradually aged. In 1910, it was 106.0; in 1940, it was essentially balanced at 100.7; and by 1970 it was down to 94.8, where it remains today (U.S. Bureau of the Census, 1987:17).

This decline is particularly evident among people age 65 and older, as more and more elderly women are surviving many years longer than men. Among people in this age category, the sex ratio was 101.1 in 1910, but only 67.8 in 1985. A direct consequence of this trend is that the number of elderly widows in the United States is steadily increasing.

The age composition of a population can be measured in several different ways. Comprehensive data can show the number of people at each age, but this is very cumbersome. More commonly, these tabulations are reported in five-year (0-4, 5-9 . . .) or ten-year (0-9, 10-19 . . .) age categories. An alternative measure is the *median age of a population, or the age at which half of the population is younger and half is older.* Although this indicator is much less precise, its conciseness makes it quite useful. Demographers also frequently group populations into a few broad age categories representing major life stages, such as "young," "intermediate," and "elderly". The dividing points between those three categories are generally set at ages 15 and 65. This procedure enables them to calculate the *dependency ratio of a population, which is the number of young and old people per 100 people age 15 to 65.* The dependency ratio can be used as an indicator of the economic burden carried by the "productive" segment of the population in supporting "nonproductive" people. The higher this ratio, the greater the number of dependents who must be supported by employed people.

In 1985, the median age of the world's population was 23.5 years, which is rather young. In the industrial countries, that age was 32.3 years, while in the developing countries it was only 21.0 years. In other words, *the populations of industrial nations are much older, on the average, than those of developing societies.* That difference is reflected in the median ages for the various major geographical areas. For Europe, that age is 33.9 years, for North America it is 31.3 years, and for the Soviet Union it is 27.6 years. In contrast, for Asia it is only 22.3 years, for Latin America it is 20.8 years, and for Africa it is just 17.3 years. Oceania's median age is 27.6 years (United Nations, 1986: Annex II).

Dependency ratios also show wide variations among different parts of the world. For the world as a whole, this ratio was 64 in 1985. For the industrial nations, it was only 49, while for developing countries it was 69. These ratios indicate than *in industrial societies there are about two people in the "productive" years for every person in the "dependent" years, but in developing countries this ratio is only about 1.4 "productive" persons for each "dependent" person.* The dependency ratio is extremely high in Africa (92), fairly high in Latin America (72), and almost as high in Asia (64). In both Europe and North America, in contrast, it is only 47, in Europe it is 52, and in the Soviet Union it is 54 (Population Reference Bureau, 1987).

The *United States' population has been growing slowly older for a long time.* In 1820, the median age was just 16.5 years; in 1860 it was 19.4 years; in 1900 it was 22.9 years; in 1930 it was 26.4 years; and in 1950 it was 30.2 years. During the 1950s and 1960s the median age declined somewhat because of the Post-War "baby boom," so that in 1960 it was

29.5 and in 1970 it was down to 27.9 years. By 1980 the median age had begun to rise again, however, reaching 30.0 in that year and 31.5 in 1985—so that the U.S. population was then older than ever before (U.S. Bureau of the Census, 1987:17). This aging trend is also evident in the proportion of the population age 65 and older, which rose from 9.8 percent in 1970 to 12.0 percent in 1987. Unless the United States undergoes another "baby boom," its population will continue to grow steadily older in the future, with a consequent increase in its dependency ratio.

The age structure of a nation's population has important consequences for many aspects of social life. A country with a very young population (as in most developing societies) or one which experiences a rapid increase in the number of young people (as in the United States during the 1950s and 1960s) often encounters many serious problems. It must provide adequate education for its large number of children, as well as job opportunities, housing, and other services for those people as they become adults. A country with an aging population, as in all industrial nations (including the United States since 1970), faces a different set of problems. It must ensure that retired people have adequate incomes through Social Security or other pension plans, which means that employed people must support increasing numbers of elderly persons. It must provide extensive and expensive medical services for the elderly, since they are much more likely to require prolonged medical care than younger people. With better health and medical care, many people over age 65 may not want to retire, which can create problems in the job market for younger people.

POPULATION DYNAMICS

All changes in population conditions are a result of trends and variations in the three basic demographic processes of fertility, mortality, and migration. Whether a population grows or declines, becomes more or less concentrated,

DEMOGRAPHIC PROCESSES
1. Fertility
2. Mortality
3. Migration

or changes its composition depends on its net balance of births, deaths, immigration, and emigration. The study of population processes is therefore a fundamental concern of demography. In addition, knowledge about these demographic processes is essential for formulating and implementing population policies and programs.

Fertility

Demographers calculate many different indicators of fertility for various analytical purposes. As mentioned earlier, the simplest of these is the *crude birth rate,* or number of live births in a year per 1,000 population. Despite its inexactness as a measure of fertility, it is the most widely used of these rates, because it is easy to interpret and is available for most countries for the past several decades.

Another widely used fertility measure is the *total fertility rate,* or the average number of children that will be produced by each woman in a population during her lifetime, given current age-specific birth rates. This rate takes account of the age structure of the population and the fact that the birth rate varies for women in different age categories. It is therefore a fairly precise estimate of the number of children that all women in the population will likely bear. It is a very useful measure because it is easy to interpret and shows whether a population is producing more or less children than are necessary to replace itself.

The replacement level for a population is the total fertility rate at which births equal deaths. It is always somewhat more than 2.0 children per woman because not all children survive to the childbearing years. In the United States and most other industrial nations at the present time, the replacement level is about 2.1 children. This level can be as high as 2.5 in developing countries, however, because of their age structures and the fact that fewer children survive to adulthood. If a country's total fertility level is above its replacement level, the population will be growing. If its fertility level falls below its replacement level, the population will continue to increase somewhat for a generation or two because of demographic momentum, but eventually its population size will stabilize or even begin to decline.

Table 11-4 gives crude birth rates and total fertility rates in approximately 1970 and 1987 for the entire world, industrial and industrializing nations, and the major geographical areas. It also shows those two measures for each of the 35 industrial nations in 1987, indicating their current fertility rates. *In the world as a whole, fertility has declined markedly since about 1970.* The crude birth rate has dropped from 34 to 27 live births per 1,000 women, and the total fertility rate has gone from 4.9 to 3.5 children per woman. If those earlier rates had continued, the world's population would be considerably larger than it is today, and we would already be experiencing severe overpopulation. Nevertheless, because the total fertility rate of 3.5 is still far above the replacement level, the world's population will continue to grow fairly rapidly for some time to come.

Fertility rates have declined in both industrial and developing nations during the last two decades. In the industrial countries, that decline has been relatively modest, with the crude birth rate dropping from 18 to 15 and the total fertility rate going from 2.4 (slightly above the replacement level) to 2.0 (slightly below the replacement level). *Overall, the developing societies have experienced a much greater decline in fertility than the industrial societies during this time period.* Their crude birth rate has dropped from 41 to 32, and their fertility rate has shrunk from 6.0 to 4.1. Consequently, differences in fertility between these two sets of societies are not as great now as they were in 1970. Nevertheless, most developing countries are still producing far more children than are required for

TABLE 11-4 World, Regional, and Industrialized Nations' Fertility Rates in 1970 and National Rates in 1987

Area	Crude Birth Rate		Total Fertility Rate	
	*1970**	*1987*	*1970**	*1987*
Entire World	34	27	4.9	3.5
Industrialized Nations	18	15	2.4	2.0
Industrializing Nations	41	32	6.0	4.1
Asia	38	28	5.7	3.5
Africa	48	44	6.6	6.3
Europe	18	13	2.5	1.9
Latin America	38	30	5.5	4.1
Soviet Union	18	19	2.4	2.4
North America	18	15	2.5	1.8
Oceania	25	20	3.5	2.6
United States		16		1.8
Japan		12		1.8
West Germany		10		1.3
United Kingdom		13		1.8
Italy		10		1.4
France		14		1.8
Spain		13		1.8
Poland		18		2.3
Canada		15		1.7
Romania		16		2.3
Yugoslovia		16		2.1
East Germany		14		1.8
Czechoslovakia		15		2.1
Australia		16		2.0
Netherlands		12		1.5
Hungary		12		1.8
Belgium		12		1.5
Greece		12		1.8
Portugal		12		1.9
Bulgaria		13		2.0
Sweden		12		1.7
Austria		12		1.5
Switzerland		12		1.5
Denmark		11		1.4
Finland		13		1.7
Norway		12		1.7
Israel		23		3.1
Ireland		18		2.5
New Zealand		16		1.9
Albania		26		3.3
Cyprus		20		2.5
Luxembourg		11		1.4
Malta		16		2.0
Iceland		16		1.9

* Some data given for 1970 were gathered as early as 1965.

Sources: United Nations, World Population Prospects: Estimates and Projections as Assessed in 1984. New York: Department of International Economic and Social Affairs, 1986, Annex II. Population Reference Bureau, World Population Data Sheet, 1987, Washington, D.C.

replacement, which is resulting is the rapid rates for population growth reported in Table 11-1.

Europe, North America, and the Soviet Union all have rather low crude birth rates—13, 15, and 19, respectively—at the present time. Consequently, the total fertility rate is well below the replacement level in Europe (1.9) and North America (1.8), but it is still above that level in the Soviet Union (2.4). In fact, the Soviet Union is the only area of the world that has experienced an increased birth rate since 1970. Africa has by far the highest crude birth rate (44) and total fertility rate (6.3) of all the major geographical areas and hence is growing the fastest. Latin America has the second-highest rates (birth rate of 30 and fertility rate of 4.1), while Asia is not far behind it (birth rate of 28 and fertility rate of 3.5). The rates in Oceania (birth rate of 20 and fertility rate of 2.6) are slightly higher than in the Soviet Union.

With a few exceptions, *most of the industrialized nations of the world have succeeded in reducing their fertility rates to or below the replacement level.* Most present population growth in these societies with low fertility rates, therefore, is due to demographic momentum and will likely cease in a generation or two, provided their fertility rates remain at present levels. And several of these nations—West Germany, Italy, the Netherlands, Belgium, Austria, Switzerland, Denmark, and Luxembourg—already have very low fertility rates of 1.5 or fewer children per woman.

In the United States, fertility has declined fairly steadily during the twentieth century, except for the "baby boom" years of 1946–65. In 1910, the crude birth rate was 30, and in 1920 it was still 28. There was a sharp decline during the 1920s, however, so that the rate was only 21 in 1930, and was down to 19 in 1940. In both 1950 and 1960 it went up to 24, reflecting the surge of births during those postwar years. In 1970 it was down to 18, however, and in 1980 and 1987 it was only 16. A similar pattern is seen in the total fertility rate, although data are only available beginning in 1940. In that year, it was 2.5 children per woman; in 1950 and 1960 it went up to 3.3 children; in 1970 it was back down to 2.1 (the replacement level); and in 1980 and 1987 it was only 1.8 (U.S. Bureau of the Census, 1987:58).

Despite the low fertility rate in the United States, the total number of births in this country has increased somewhat during recent years. From a low of about 3.2 million births in 1973, this figure rose to about 3.8 million births in 1986. Although that was still well below the 4.3 million births that occurred at the peak of the "baby boom" in 1957, the country is presently experiencing a second "mini-baby boom" or "baby boom echo." This is occurring despite a low birth rate because the large number of women born during the first "baby boom" are now in their reproductive years. The number of women age 15 to 44 in the United States rose from 43 million in 1970 to 57 million in 1986, and will peak in 1990 at 58 million. That year should therefore also be the peak of the current second "baby boom," after which the number of births will gradually decline again and by 2000 should be even lower than in the early 1970s. Beginning about 2010, we can expect to see a third "micro-baby boom" as the women born during the second "baby boom" enter their reproductive years. However, as long as the birth rate remains at or below its present level, that third "baby boom" will be quite small in size. After that, the United States population should stop growing or even begin declining. That projection assumes, however, that there will be no significant decline in the death rate in the future or massive increase in immigration.

Mortality

As with fertility, demographers calculate many different indicators of mortality. Again, the simplest of these is the *crude death rate,* or the number of deaths in a year per 1,000 population. This measure is considered crude because it does not take into account the age structure of the population, which has considerable affect on the death rate. Nevertheless, it is the most commonly used measure of mortality for the same reasons that the crude birth rate is widely used: it is easy to interpret and the data are generally available.

Another measure that is closely related to the death rate is *life expectancy at birth,* or the number of years that a child born in a given year can expect to live, on the average. Since this measure takes account of the age in which people die, it is more precise than the crude death rate. Moreover, life expectancy is a measure that everyone understands and is interested in. In all societies today, women have a longer life expectancy than men, so that this measure is generally reported separately for men and women, as well as for the total population.

Table 11-5 reports the crude death rates and life expectancies in approximately 1970 and in 1987 for the world, industrial and industrializing nations, and the major geographical areas. It also gives those two measures for all industrial societies in 1987. *In less than two decades a remarkable decline has occurred in world death rates.* Although a decline in the world's crude death rate from 13.0 to 10.0 per thousand may not appear to be very noteworthy, it represents an eight-year increase in average life expectancy, from 55 to 63 years. During this time, the death rate in industrial societies actually increased slightly, from 9.1 to 9.6 per thousand (a reversal of a long-term downward trend). Life expectancy in these nations did increase, however, from 71 to 73 years, and in the future their death rates are expected to resume their long-time downward movement. In the developing countries, meanwhile, the overall death rate dropped from 15 to 11 per thousand, and life expectancy rose from 52 to 59 years. There is still a marked difference in mortality between these two sets of nations, however, since babies born in 1987 in industrial societies can expect to live an average of 14 years longer than babies in developing countries.

Africa has by far the highest death rate, at 16 per thousand and the shortest life expectancy, at just 51 years. All other regions of the world, however, presently have death rates that are essentially at or below the world average, ranging from 8.0 to 11.0 per thousand. Life expectancy is still shorter than average in Asia (61 years), but everywhere else it ranges from 66 to 75 years. The Soviet Union is an interesting anomaly in these data, however, since it is the only part of the world in which the death rate rose between 1970 and 1987, from 8 to 11, and in which life expectancy decreased, from 70 to 69 years. (That significant increase in the death rate in the Soviet Union is the reason why the death rate for all industrial countries rose slightly during this time period.)

Most of the industrial nations have death rates between 7.0 and the world average of 10.0, although in a number of them this rate is 11.0 or 12.0. The industrial nations thus have no monopoly on low death rates. Life expectancy at birth, meanwhile, is between 70 and 76 years in all industrial nations (except Hungary, at 69 years.) Consequently, even those industrial countries that presently have higher-than-average death rates still offer long life expectancies to babies being born today. We can therefore conclude that, *on the whole, the industrial societies are healthier places to live than most developing countries, although this difference is rapidly diminishing—except in Africa.*

In the United States, the crude death rate has declined steadily throughout this century. In 1910 it was 15.0 per thousand; in 1930 it was 11.0; in 1950 through 1970 it was 10.0; and in 1980 and 1987 it was down to 9.0 per thousand. *The corresponding increase in life expectancy at birth has been even more dramatic.* In 1920 it was only 54 years; by 1940 it was up to 63 years; in 1960 it was 70 years; in 1980 it had reached 74 years; and in 1987 it was 75 years. The current life expectancy for males is 71 years, while for females it is 78 years (U.S. Bureau of the Census, 1987:58 and 69).

TABLE 11-5 World, Regional, and Industrialized Nations' Mortality Rates in 1970 and 1987 and National Rates in 1987

Area	Crude Death Rate		Years of Life Expectancy at Birth	
	*1970**	*1987*	*1970**	*1987*
Entire World	13	10	55	63
Industrialized Nations	9	10	71	73
Industrializing Nations	15	11	52	59
Asia	14	10	53	61
Africa	21	16	44	51
Europe	10	10	71	74
Latin America	11	8	59	66
Soviet Union	8	11	70	69
North America	9	9	71	75
Oceania	10	8	64	72
United States		9		75
Japan		6		76
West Germany		12		74
United Kingdom		12		73
Italy		10		74
France		10		74
Spain		8		73
Poland		10		71
Canada		7		75
Romania		11		70
Yugoslovia		9		70
East Germany		14		72
Czechoslovakia		12		71
Australia		8		75
Netherlands		9		76
Hungary		14		69
Belgium		11		73
Greece		9		74
Portugal		10		71
Bulgaria		12		74
Sweden		11		77
Austria		12		74
Switzerland		9		76
Denmark		11		75
Finland		10		75
Norway		11		76
Israel		7		75
Ireland		9		73
New Zealand		8		74
Albania		6		71
Cyprus		9		74
Luxembourg		11		73
Malta		8		73
Iceland		7		77

* Some data given for 1970 were gathered as early as 1965.

Sources: U.S. Bureau of the Census, Statistical Abstract of the United States, 1987. Washington D.C.: U.S. Government Printing Office, Table 1441. Population Reference Bureau, World Population Data Sheet, 1987, Washington, D.C.

Migration

A country may gain or lose population not only through births and deaths but also through migration. People who migrate to a country are called immigrants, and their rate of arrival per year is called the immigration rate. Conversely, people who migrate out of a country are called emigrants, and their rate of departure per year is called the emigration rate. The rate of immigration for a country, minus its rate of emigration, is its *net migration rate*, or the total number of people it gains or loses during a year through migration.

For the world as a whole, United Nations data on migration are rather limited. Most of the developing countries do not record or report migration data at all, and the data for many industrial nations are of questionable validity. For example, France reported in 1983 that it took in over one million immigrants, but in 1985 it reported only 44,000 immigrants. Realistically, it is highly unlikely that immigration to France declined that much over just two years. And some industrial countries—most notably the Soviet Union—do not give the United Nations any figures on immigration or emigration.

With that caution in mind, we can nevertheless make the broad generalization that *the total amount of international migration has been quite high for at least the past 15 years, with a large proportion of those people going from developing to industrial nations.* Since 1975, when the United Nations began attempting to gather international migration on a yearly basis, the total number of migrants has ranged between three and four million persons a year, although there is considerable variation from one year to the next depending on economic and political conditions around the world (United Nations, Demographic Yearbook, 1985, Table 38).

The most common destinations of these migrants in recent years appear to have been the United States, France, India, and West Germany. Each of these countries reports receiving nearly or more than 500,000 immigrants most years since 1975. South Africa

reports taking in more than 300,000 a year, and about 200,000 migrants have gone to Great Britain each year. Australia and Venezuela both report receiving about 150,000 immigrants each year, and about 100,000 per year have gone to Mexico. No other country reports receiving more than 100,000 immigrants a year on a regular basis since 1975, although almost all industrial nations have some amount of immigration. In addition, many of these countries—primarily in Western Europe—admit several thousand temporary immigrants each year as "guest workers." These people, almost all of whom are from developing nations, typically remain in the "host" country for a few years until they can save enough money to go back home and start a small business or obtain a home for their family.

During the past 200 years, the United States has taken in far more immigrants than any other nation. As was seen in Table 11-2, more than 50 million people have come to live in this country, although some three million of them were brought here involuntarily as slaves. Immigration to the United States was almost completely unrestricted until the 1920s, with the vast majority of those people coming from Europe. The inscription at the base of the Statue of Liberty—"Give me your poor, your huddled masses. . . ."—was given meaning throughout the nineteenth and early twentieth centuries.

In the 1920s, however, politically influential segments of the U.S. public became greatly alarmed by the vast numbers of "poor and huddled masses" of people—20 million of them between 1900 and 1920—coming into this country, increasingly from Southern and Eastern Europe. Congress therefore passed a series of immigration laws that placed sharp limits on the total number of immigrants that would be admitted and established small quotas for all countries except those in northwestern Europe. This immigration policy was clearly extremely discriminatory, especially against non-Caucasians. Nevertheless, it was not substantially modified until the Immigration

TABLE 11-6   Sources of United States Immigration, 1961–1985

Source	Distribution			
	1961–1970		1971–1985	
	Number in Thousands	*Percent of Total*	*Number in Thousands*	*Percent of Total*
Entire World	3,322	100	7,357*	100
Europe	1,223	37	1,040	14
Central America	1,064	32	2,360	32
South and East Asia	387	12	2,696	37
Canada	287	9	171	2
South America	228	7	468	6
Middle East	58	2	315	4
Oceania	19	—	58	1
Soviet Union	16	—	83	1

* Number between 1971–80 was 4,493,000, and between 1981–85 was 2,864,000.

Source: U.S. Bureau of the Census, *Statistical Abstract of the United States, 1987.* Washington, D.C.: U.S. Government Printing Office, Table 8.

Act of 1965 eliminated those national quotas and considerably increased the total number of immigrants permitted to enter the country. During the decade of the 1970s, over 400,000 immigrants came into the United States each year, and in the early 1980s that figure increased to over a half-million each year.

Table 11-6 shows the areas of the world from which immigrants to the United States have come since 1960. During the 1960s, Europe was still the largest source of immigrants to this country, accounting for 37 percent of the total. Another 32 percent came from Mexico and other Central American countries. South and East Asia accounted from only nine percent, another seven percent came from Canada, and only two percent were from the Middle East. That pattern has changed dramatically during the 1970s and 1980s, however. *Immigration from South and East Asia has risen sharply,* to 37 percent of the total, largely because of the political and military upheavals occurring in that part of the world. The proportion of people coming here from Europe has declined sharply, to just 14 percent of the total. Central America has remained the same, at 32 percent. The flow of Canadians has dropped to just two percent; the rate from

South America has remained about the same at six percent; and four percent come from the Middle East. In addition, the number of people coming from Oceania (primarily Australia and New Zealand) and from the Soviet Union has also increased considerably, although each of those areas still accounted for just one percent of the total.

The country that has contributed by far the largest proportion of immigrants to the United States during the last two decades has been Mexico, with 13 percent of the total. (That figure represents only legal immigrants, and does not include the several million Mexicans who have entered the country illegally.) Another eight percent of the total during this period has come from the Philippines; Vietnam and Korea have each accounted for another six percent; and China (including Taiwan) and Cuba have each contributed another four percent of the total. As a result of this recent shift in sources of immigrants, *the United States population is steadily becoming less Anglo-Saxon and more ethnically and racially diverse in composition.*

Population Control

Although fertility rates around the world have been declining steadily during the last two decades, so have mortality rates. Consequently, as we have seen, world population is still growing steadily. Although the annual world growth rate dropped from 2.0 percent in 1970 to 1.7 in 1987, one and a third billion people were added to the earth's population in those 17 years. Very clearly, population growth must be halted soon if the earth's ecosystem is to continue supporting the human race. In most developing countries, population control is absolutely essential if the people are to have even minimally adequate food supplies and other basic necessities. In industrial countries, population control is necessary if the people wish to retain their present standards of living.

There is very little disagreement anywhere in the world today about the necessity for global population control. This principle is strongly supported by the United Nations, many international organizations such as the World Bank and UNESCO, the governments of almost all industrial nations and of many of the larger developing countries, and a number of major foundations. Numerous private organizations are also working to promote population control, the largest of which is the International Planned Parenthood Federation, which consists of national Planned Parenthood associations in 59 different countries. In addition, most major religious organizations—including the Catholic Church—support the principle of family planning. At the individual level, meanwhile, studies from many developing countries around the world have consistently found that large majorities of all women want to limit their families to four living children—although that is still almost two children per family above the replacement level (Brown, 1981:152). In most industrial nations, meanwhile, the commonly desired family size is now two children.

The debate that is raging around the world today concerns not the desirability of population control, but rather how to accomplish it. There are four major policy positions in this debate. One position, taken primarily by the Catholic Church and some other religious bodies, is that all "artificial" means of birth control—contraception, sterilization, and abortion—are immoral. The only means of promoting population control that they condone are *"natural" practices* such as delayed marriage, abstinence, and the rhythm method of contraception.

The second position is strongly espoused by most developing societies, as well as many neo-Marxian scholars. They insist that primary emphasis should be placed on *national economic and social development*, not family planning. They point to the demographic transition that has occurred in the West and argue that if developing countries are assisted in attaining the West's standard of living, their population growth will slow down the same way it has in all industrial societies. This policy was the emphatic conclusion reached by the World Population Conference sponsored by the United Nations in 1974 (Humphrey and Buttel, 1982:83–88). In addition to stressing the importance of overall economic development, the proponents of this approach place particular emphasis on three social development trends that are highly related to declining fertility in all nations. These are urbanization, education of women, and employment of women outside the home (Brown, 1981:155).

The third position in this debate is taken by the governments of most industrial nations, the major foundations, and private organizations such as Planned Parenthood. It places primary emphasis on *voluntary family planning programs* and argues that such programs should be supported with both public and private funds in all countries. These family planning programs include information about the importance of family planning, family planning clinics that provide contraception instruction and devices at little or no cost, and sometimes also sterilization and/or abortion services. (The latter services are often condemned by religious or political groups, however.) There are two serious limitations to this approach in many less developed societies. The more obvious limitation is that adequate funds have never been available to provide family planning information and clinics to large numbers of women in those countries, especially in rural areas. The more subtle limitation is that many men oppose family planning—at least until they have several children—because of traditional beliefs about masculinity and procreation.

The fourth policy position is that the state must implement *public incentives and pressures* if population control is to be achieved. In recent years, an increasing number of developing countries have adopted financial incentive programs to encourage families to limit their number of children. For example, the Philippine government allows tax deductions for only the first four children, while Nepal has eliminated tax deducations for children altogether. In Singapore, women employed in governmental and unionized jobs are given two months of paid maternity leave, but only for the first two children. Several other countries give priority access for public housing to families with two or fewer children (Brown, 1981:157–58). And a few countries—most notably the People's Republic of China—have adopted comprehensive public population control programs that go considerably beyond simple financial incentives.

China's national population control program is the most extensive effort in the world today to reduce fertility. In 1979, China's population was nearly one billion (it reached that point in 1980) and was increasing rapidly. Government officials realized that if they were ever to achieve their economic development goals for the country, strong measures had to be taken immediately to halt population growth. They therefore announced a One-Child Family Program for the entire country. Many different procedures were introduced to eliminate the ancient Chinese tradition of large families and to encourage one-child families (Brown, 1981:160). New values stressing the social desirability of having only one child are promoted through mass publicity campaigns, traveling information programs, and study groups organized in all communities.

Couples who pledge to have no more than one child are immediately given a 12 percent wage increase. Contraception, sterilization, and abortion services are available to everyone at no cost. Couples with one child receive better housing than those with larger families. Single children are given preferential treatment in school admissions and job assignments. And couples with only one child are eligible for a retirement pension equal to 80 percent of their last salary, whereas those with more children receive only a 70 percent pension. Westerners frequently object to the semi-coercive nature of many of these measures, but they are proving effective in coping with China's drastic population condition. In 1987, after the program had been in effect just eight years, China's crude birth rate had dropped to 21, its total fertility rate was down to 2.4 (just slightly above the replacement level), and its annual rate of population increase was a moderate 1.3 percent per year (Population Reference Bureau, 1987).

ENERGY FLOWS

As the fundamental ecological factors of knowledge, resources, and population continually interact within the ecosystem, they generate energy flows that shape human societies. We have previously used the term "sociophysical energy" to indicate that these energy flows have both physical and social aspects. Although energy by itself is the physical capability to accomplish work, the ways in which physical energy is used—its amounts, forms, and applications—are determined by social conditions and choices. This section focuses on the physical aspects of energy flows in industrial societies, while the following two chapters on the economies and polities of modern societies deal extensively with the social aspects of those flows.

Theoretical Perspective

This theoretical perspective that energy flows are a fundamental process within social organization has recently come to be called *energetics* (Adams, 1982:12). Although this idea was discussed in the 1860s by the early British sociologist Herbert Spencer (1862), it was largely ignored for almost a hundred years until social scientists began searching for a way of explaining the evolution of societies from simpler to more complex forms. The anthropologist Leslie White (1949:366) made energy utilization the core of his explanation of societal development: ". . . culture evolves as the amount of energy harnessed per capita per year is increased, or as the efficiency of the instrumental means [i.e., technology] of putting the energy to work is increased." A few years later, the sociologist Fred Cottrell (1955) developed the thesis that the amount and kind of energy available to a society limit what it can do and influence what it will do and argued that pervasive social, economic, and political changes have resulted from the transition from low-energy to high-energy societies. More recently, the social anthropologist Richard Adams (1982) has proposed that societies should be conceptualized as energy input-output systems (which he calls "dissipative systems," since they are continually dissipating energy). Social ordering is a direct result of the ways in which energy is taken into, used by, and discharged by the system.

The amount of energy available in a society is determined by the kind and extent of accessible fuels, the ease with which those fuels can be extracted from the environment with existing technologies, and the efficiency with which they can be converted into energy. *The more extensive and usable the supply of energy available in a society, the greater the ability of that society to obtain other vital natural resources, produce food, provide needed goods and services, and transport goods and people.* Those economic processes, in turn, determine the amount of surplus wealth generated by the society beyond its sustenance needs. And the greater the surplus wealth—in conjunction with many other factors—the more complex and highly developed the entire structure of the society can become.

Energy and Industrialization

Prior to the beginning of the industrial revolution in the eighteenth century, almost all energy was obtained from work animals, human labor, wind (via sails and windmills), flowing water (via waterwheels), and burning wood. All preindustrial societies were very low energy users, typically generating the equivalent of only a few horsepower of energy per person a year. They were able, nevertheless, to produce enough energy to meet their needs. When power-driven machinery was introduced into the British textile and other industries in the 1760s and 1770s, those machines demanded much more energy than had ever been needed before. This demand was met primarily by cutting down forests to provide wood for furnaces. By the end of the eighteenth century, deforestation had become so widespread throughout Great Britain and most of Western Europe that they began to experience a serious energy crisis. There was no longer enough wood available at affordable prices to keep their developing industries operating.

Fortunately for the future of industrialization, coal was available as a substitute fuel. People had known about coal since antiquity, but it had never been worth the cost and effort necessary to dig it out of the ground as long as energy demands were quite low. With energy demands rising sharply and wood supplies dwindling rapidly, however, most newly industrializing countries had begun mining and burning coal at increasing rates by the end of the eighteenth century. *By the 1840s, most industrial machinery throughout England, Europe, and the United States was operated by coal-fired steam engines.* In addition, of course, coal was vital for the rapidly growing iron industry. The age of coal was then in full swing and persisted for almost another hundred years.

Industrial development in the United States, as in all other Western nations, has been highly dependent on ever-rising levels of energy use. Table 11-7 illustrates the growth in energy use that occurred in this

TABLE 11-7 Estimated Annual Work Output per Capita in the United States Between 1850 and 1950, by Source of Energy

Energy Sources	Horsepower Hours per Capita		
	1850	*1900*	*1950*
All sources	44	103	445
Traditional sources	41	34	41
Work animals	22	23	3
Human labor	6	6	4
Fuel wood	3	*	*
Windmills and sailing vessels	6	1	*
Water wheels	4	3	*
Fossil fuel sources	3	70	404
Coal	3	69	147
Oil	0	1	166
Natural gas	0	*	91
Hydroelectric power sources	0	2	34

* Less than one horsepower hour.

Source: Otis Dudley Duncan, "Social Organization and the Ecosystem." *In* Robert E. L. Faris, ed., *Handbook of Modern Sociology*, (Chicago: Rand McNally & Co., 1964), p. 63.

country between 1850 and 1950 as industrialization progressed. These data show changes in the estimated annual work output per person from various sources, measured in horsepower hours per capita. *During the nineteenth century, the total amount of work performed per capita increased ten times, which was due largely to increased consumption of fossil fuels.* From 1850 to 1900, the fuel used was almost entirely coal, while between 1900 and 1950 oil and natural gas also became vitally important.

In recent years, total energy consumption in the United States has commonly been measured in quadrillion BTUs (or quads). As shown in Table 11-8, in 1950 that total figure was approximately 34.0 quads, or 223 million BTUs per capita. Between 1950 and 1979, energy consumption continued to increase steadily, both in total amount and per capita. In the peak year of 1979, the United States used a total of 78.8 quads, or 351 million BTUs per person. However, *beginning in 1980, energy consumption began to decline for the*

first time, dropping by 1985 to 73.8 quads, or 309 trillion BTUs per person. This current trend has been caused largely by the rapid rise in world petroleum prices that resulted from the oil crisis of the 1970s, combined with the extensive energy conservation programs and practices that have been adopted in the United States during the last 15 years. It is still too soon to tell if this decline in energy consumption will become permanent, but it is beginning to appear that the dramatic increase in energy use that has been occurring in this country since 1850 may at last be ending.

For the world as a whole, the rate of growth in energy consumption has declined recently, although it is still increasing. In this case, energy use is often measured in the equivalent of tons of coal consumed per year. In 1970, that figure was 7.0 billion tons, and by 1980 it had risen to 9.3 billion tons, an increase of 33 percent in just ten years, or 3.3 percent per year. Between 1980 and 1984, however, there was only a slight increase to

TABLE 11-8 Total and per Capita Energy Consumption in the United States, 1950–85

Year	Total Consumption (Quadrillion BTUs)	Percent Change Over Five Years	Per Capita (Million BTUs)
1950	34.0	—	223
1955	39.7	+17	239
1960	43.8	+10	247
1965	52.7	+20	274
1970	66.4	+25	325
1975	70.5	+06	327
1979	78.9		351
1980	76.0	+07	334
1985	74.0	−03	309

Source: U.S. Bureau of the Census, *Statistical Abstract of the United States*, 1987. Washington, D.C.: U.S. Government Printing Office, Table 932.

9.4 billion tons, which was an annual growth rate of only 0.35 present (U.S. Bureau of the Census, 1987:833). Of the total world energy use in 1980, about 47 percent came from oil, about 20 percent came from coal, about 17 percent came from natural gas, and the remaining 16 percent was from other sources (Council on Environmental Quality, 1980:31). The most critical point about world energy consumption, however, is that *approximately 77 percent of all energy used throughout the world in 1984 was consumed by the industrialized nations*, even though they contain only 24 percent of the earth's population (U.S. Bureau of the Census, 1987:833–44).

Across all countries in the world, the correlation between Gross National Product per capita and energy consumption per capita is .95, an almost perfect relationship. This linkage is also reflected in total figures for the Gross World Product and world energy consumption, both of which increased about 4.5 times between 1950 and 1986. Because of this relationship, the argument is frequently made that economic development is absolutely dependent on increasing energy use. The conclusion is then drawn that if modern nations want to promote further economic growth, they must necessarily use

more and more energy. There are two flaws in this argument, however.

First, while it is true that developed nations consume much more energy than developing ones, the correlation between GNP and energy use per capita is only .49 among industrialized countries (Olsen, 1990). In other words, *although a huge increase in energy consumption occurs when a country industrializes, further economic development is not linked very tightly to energy use*. In the United States, the amount of energy required for each dollar of GNP declined steadily between 1970 and 1985, from 27.5 to 20.7 BTUs (measured against constant 1982 dollars).

Second, when other indicators of societal development and quality of life are substituted for Gross National Product, many of the relationships between those indicators and energy consumption per capita are relatively weak (Mazur and Rosa, 1974; Buttel, 1979; Olsen, 1990). As stated in one recent study: ". . . there appears to be little relationship between levels of energy consumption in the advanced industrial societies and a wide range of indicators of societal well-being," (Rosa, Radzik, and Keating, 1980). In other words, *even if economic growth is somewhat dependent on energy consumption in industrial nations, the quality of life in these societies*

TABLE 11-9 Energy Consumption in the United States from 1960–1985 by Sector

Sector	1960		1970		1980		1985	
	Quads	*Percentage*	*Quads*	*Percentage*	*Quads*	*Percentage*	*Quads*	*Percentage*
Buildings	8.7	20	12.1	18	10.7	14	9.8	13
Industry	16.3	37	21.9	33	21.0	28	17.5	24
Transportation	10.6	24	16.0	24	19.7	26	20.0	27
Electricity generation	8.2	20	16.3	25	24.5	32	26.5	36
Total	43.8	100	66.3	100	75.9	100	73.8	100

Source: U.S. Bureau of the Census, Statistical Abstract of the United States, 1987. Washington, D.C.: U.S. Government Printing Office, Table 936.

can be improved in many ways without any increase in energy use. And if recent trends in the United States and other industrial countries continue, it may prove possible to sustain economic growth and improve societal well-being while simultaneously reducing the total amount of energy consumed in a society.

Energy Use Patterns

To gain an idea of how energy is used in industrial societies such as the United States, let us examine data on energy consumption by use sectors. Table 11-9 shows the distribution of energy consumption among the four sectors of building heating (residential and commercial), industry, transportation, and electricity generation from 1960 to 1985. (The first three of these sectors are final end-users, while electricity is ultimately used in both residentail and commercial buildings and in industry. About two-thirds of all electricity is consumed by the residential/commercial sector and about one-third by the industrial sector.) The table includes the amount of energy consumed (in quadrillion BTUs, or quads) and the proportion of the total used in each sector.

For buildings, the amount and proportion of energy consumed have declined steadily since the 1960s, so that this sector now accounts for about 13 percent of all energy use, exclusive of electricity. For industry, the amount of energy use peaked in 1979 at 22.8 quads (not shown in the table) and has declined somewhat since then, while the relative proportion consumed by this sector has declined sharply since 1960. It now uses 24 percent of all energy, exclusive of electricity. For transportation, in contrast, both the amount and proportion of energy use have increased steadily during these 25 years. It now accounts for 27 percent of all energy use. For electricity generation, both the amount and proportion of energy use have risen dramatically, so that 36 percent of all primary energy use in the United States now goes into producing electricity.

Because so much of this electricity is used by industry, when current electricity consumption is distributed among the other sectors, we find that *industry is the largest consumer of energy,* at 37 percent of the total. Transportation is second, at 27 percent. Residences account for 20 percent of all energy use, and commercial businesses use 15 percent (U.S. Bureau of the Census, 1987:544).

SUMMARY

The basic factors constituting all human ecosystems are knowledge, resources, population, and energy, in combination with systems of social organization. The ecosystem within which a society exists shapes its patterns of social organization in countless ways, providing opportunities for change and development but also setting constraints and limits on social processes and structures.

Technological knowledge has become the major factor producing sustained economic growth during the twentieth century in industrial societies. The governments of these societies have actively promoted the development of capital-intensive technologies in economic production. New technologies are increasingly being generated by systematic scientific research. In recent years, however, large segments of the public have begun to question whether technology is dominating social life too greatly.

Arable land is still a vital natural resource in all modern nations, even though their economies no longer rest primarily on agriculture. The dramatic growth in agricultural productivity that has occurred during the last several decades has been due to increased use of fertilizers, pesticides, herbicides, irrigation, and hybridization. Many of those practices have created serious environmental problems, however. Until recently, adequate amounts of fresh water have been available in all industrial nations, but water is rapidly becoming a scarce natural resource in these countries as well as in many developing societies. Forest land is quite limited throughout Europe, and deforestation is a serious environmental concern in much of the world. Deposits of most of the minerals on which industrial societies depend are presently being depleted at rapid rates, and many of them will be largely or totally exhausted by the end of the twenty-first century. Coal supplies are still sufficient to last at least another 200 years, but oil and natural gas are presently being consumed so rapidly that most of the world's reserves of these fuels will be used up before the middle of the next century.

Population growth throughout the world has been closely linked with economic development during the last two hundred years. Total world population was still less than one million at the beginning of the nineteenth century, but since then it has been growing at an increasingly faster rate, and in 1987 it reached five billion. A fundamental principle in demography, first noted by Malthus in 1798, is that populations often tend to grow faster than available natural resources, unless limited by intentional or natural checks.

The demographic transition model underlies much contemporary thinking about population growth in relation to socioeconomic development. In Stage I, societies have small, stable populations based on very high birth and death rates. In Stage II, the death rate first declines sharply but the birth rate remains high, resulting in very rapid population growth. Sometime later, the birth rate also declines as the society becomes more modernized. In Stage III, a much larger population regains stability based on low birth and death rates. This model fits the industrial nations quite well, virtually all of which are now in Stage III. Thus far, however, almost all of the developing societies are still in Stage II and are continuing to grow very rapidly.

In the last two decades, the world's population has increased by one and a third billion people, although the rate of growth has slowed slightly. Most of that population growth has occurred in developing societies throughout Africa, Asia, and Latin America. Because the highly industrialized countries are consuming such a large proportion of the earth's natural resources, however, from an ecological perspective they are the most overpopulated nations in the world.

The population of the United States has grown dramatically during the last 200 years, from under four million to nearly 250 million. A considerable proportion of this growth has been due to immigration, especially during the first two decades of this century and during the last two decades. In addition, the "baby boom" that occurred after World War II added large numbers of people to the population.

On the average, the industrial nations are not as densely populated as the developing countries, but their populations are much more concentrated in urban cities and towns. No relationships exist between population size and either density or urbanization.

The industrial nations generally have lower sex ratios (fewer men than women) than do the developing countries, which is primarily a consequence of their considerably older populations. Because of the large numbers of young people in most developing countries, as a result of their high birth rates, their dependency ratios are generally much higher than in industrial nations. In the United States, the sex ratio has declined steadily during this century, while the median age has steadily risen.

For the world as a whole, both the crude birth rate and the total fertility rate have declined markedly since 1970. Those declines have occurred in industrial and developing countries but have been considerably greater in the latter societies. Most of the industrial nations presently have relatively low fertility rates that are at or below the replacement level. Most developing societies have not yet dropped to that level, however, despite their declining fertility rates. Fertility in the United States has declined fairly steadily during the 20th century, except for the "baby boom" years.

There has been a remarkable decline in death rates around the world during the last two decades, raising average life expectancy from 55 to 63 years. Death rates in most industrial societies (except the Soviet Union) have gone down slightly during that period, while those in most developing countries (except in Africa) have declined sharply. The death rate in the United States has declined steadily throughout the twentieth century, with an increase in average life expectancy from 54 to 75 years.

The total amount of international migration has been quite high during the last two decades, with most of it going from less developed to more developed societies. During the last 200 years, the United States has received far more immigrants—over 50 million—than any other country. In recent years, the primary source of those migrants has shifted from European to Asian countries, as well as Mexico.

There is very little disagreement today about the necessity for global population control, but there is a great deal of debate over how to attain that objective. Four alternative policy positions in this debate are reliance on natural means of birth control, facilitation of national economic and social development, promotion of voluntary family planning programs, and implementation of public incentives and pressures for population control.

As the ecological factors of knowledge, resources, and population interact within the ecosystem, they generate flows of sociophysical energy that shape human societies. In general, the more extensive and usable the supply of energy available in a society, the greater its ability to generate surplus wealth and to support socioeconomic development. The industrial revolution was initially fueled by coal, but during the last hundred years all industrial nations have become increasingly dependent on oil and natural gas as fuels, which are presently being consumed at extremely high rates. Energy use per capita in this country peaked in 1979 and has declined somewhat since then. For the world as a whole, energy use is still increasing every year, but not as rapidly as in the past. The industrial nations use about three-fourths of all energy in the world, even though they contain less than one-fourth of the world's population. Once a country achieves full industrialization, however, further improvements in its quality of life are not highly dependent on increasing energy use.

CHAPTER 12

INDUSTRIAL ECONOMIES

What is a capitalist economy, and how does it differ from welfarism and
socialism?

Why are national and international corporate systems so important in the
modern world?

In what ways do corporations influence governments?

How has industrialization affected income levels, occupational distributions,
and education?

What effects does corporate capitalism have on individuals and societies?

ECONOMIC SYSTEMS

The economy is one of the major institutions, or component systems, within all industrial societies. It functions as a crucial link
between the ecological factors discussed in
the previous chapter and the social organization of a society, since the economy utilizes
technology to transform resources into the
goods and services required by a population
for its survival and welfare. Moreover, as
we saw in Chapter 9, change in the nature of
economic systems is one of the fundamental
causes of evolutionary development from
agriculturally-based to industrially-based societies. To understand modern societies,
therefore, we must examine the major
features of their industrial economies.

More specifically, *an economy is an interrelated network or system of beliefs* (concerning
work, property, constructs, and wealth), *activities* (extraction, production, distribution,
consumption), *organizations* (business firms,
labor unions, consumer associations, regula-

tory agencies), *and relationships* (ownership,
management, employment, sales) *that provides the goods and services consumed by the members of a society*. In this chapter, the two terms
"economy" and "economic system" are used
synonymously.

As an overview of the kinds of economies
that exist in modern societies, the first section of this chapter briefly describes five
contrasting types of economic systems:
mercantilism, market capitalism, regulated
capitalism, welfarism, and socialism. The
major goal of each of these systems is given
in Table 12-1. Some of these types of economies are more common in contemporary societies than are others, but the economic system of any particular society will often
display a mixture of several of them.

Mercantilism

This type of economy prevailed throughout Europe during the seventeenth and
eighteenth centuries, as national and inter-

TABLE 12-1   Types of Economic Systems and Their
Major Goals

Type of Economy	Major Goal
Mercantilism	Maximize the wealth and power of the state
Market capitalism	Maximize the profits of private businesses
Regulated capitalism	Maximize the stability and productivity of the economy
Welfarism	Maximize the economic well-being of the population
Socialism	Maximize economic and social equality in the society

national commerce developed and laid the foundation for industrialization. Although it is no longer the dominant type of economy in any fully industrialized society, vestiges of mercantilistic thinking and practices can still be found in many modern societies, as well as in developing societies around the world.

The essence of mercantilism is that the economy should serve the political state by maximizing its wealth and power (Smelser, 1963:55). The economy does not exist to satisfy the needs of the population but to benefit the state. The first goal of mercantilism is to maximize the total amount of wealth in a society. Unlike the contemporary concept of wealth that measures all the goods and services produced in a society, however, mercantilism has usually equated wealth with the possession of precious metals such as gold and silver, since national currencies were not well-established nor trusted in earlier items. And since the world's stock of gold and silver is inherently limited, the total amount of wealth in the world was thought to be finite. From this perspective, therefore, the only way in which a society could accumulate wealth was to take it from other societies through economic or military means.

The second goal of mercantilism is to increase the power of the state. Since mercantilism believed that power flows from the possession of wealth, accumulating national wealth directly serves this second goal. At the same time, as the state grows more powerful in economic and political terms, it is able to

take actions that will assist the economy and hence further increase state wealth and power in a reciprocal process. These government actions include:

1. Building strong military forces and engaging in military conquest;
2. Granting legal monopolies to business firms that produce goods for export;
3. Creating tax systems that promote and benefit crucial economic activities;
4. Prohibiting or restricting imports so as to maintain a surplus of exports over imports; and
5. Establishing colonies that provide precious metals or that supply raw materials for trade and manufacturing at low cost.

In short, in a mercantilist economy, wealth and power are thought to be inextricably linked, so that increasing one also increases the other, and together they strengthen the nation-state. If properly managed by the state, the economic and political systems of a society are complementary and mutually reinforcing. As both these systems are expanded and developed through government actions, the society is expected to grow and prosper.

Market Capitalism

In 1776, the Scottish moral and economic philosopher Adam Smith published *An Inquiry into the Nature and Causes of the Wealth of*

Nations (Smith, 1937). In this book—which laid the foundation for all modern economic thinking—Smith vigorously criticized the prevailing mercantilistic doctrines and outlined a very different kind of economic system. He began by demonstrating that the wealth of a society lies not in its hoard of precious metals, but rather in the strength of its economic productivity and the ability of the economy to provide "the necessaries, comforts, and conveniences of life." Money is only a medium of economic exchange.

Smith then asked what kind of economic system could maximize the productive capabilities of a society, while at the same time serve the economic needs of the entire population in an efficient and equitable manner. His answer, which came to be known as laissez-faire or free enterprise or free market capitalism, centered on the concept of the "perfectly competitive market." *In a free market capitalist economy, all economic enterprises are privately owned.* Similarly, all economic decisions concerning production, labor, prices, and sales are made by private businesspersons. *The driving force of a capitalist economy is profit making.* In an effort to maximize their profits, economic entrepreneurs establish businesses, produce goods and services, and sell them in the marketplace at the highest possible prices. The principal techniques for increasing production and sales, Smith argued, are accumulating capital and expanding the market for one's products. Production costs, meanwhile, can be minimized through task specialization, or division of labor, in the business firm, so that each worker performs only one simple task within the total production process. High productivity and sales, coupled with low costs, will maximize the profits of capitalists and keep the economy constantly growing.

All economic transactions in a market capitalist economy take place within unregulated free markets, in which goods and services (as well as labor, stocks, and other items) are bought and sold according to the law of supply and demand. Although each individual participant in a market is attempting to maximize his or her profits by buying as cheaply and selling as expensively as possible, Smith maintained that the free market nevertheless serves the public interest quite well. The "invisible hand" of competition forces sellers to keep their prices at a reasonable level, or else they will be undersold by their competitors. At the same time, the supply of goods and services available for sale will, over time, tend to balance public demand for them. Market forces will therefore eliminate inefficient or greedy producers and enable buyers to obtain the best products available at the lowest possible cost. Efficient businesspersons who understand and abide by the law of supply and demand will realize a handsome profit.

For a capitalist economic system to operate smoothly and serve the economic needs of a society, three conditions must exist. First, the society as a whole must have a common set of moral values and norms that provide consensus on the goals being sought through the economic system and which enable economic actors to trust one another. The ideology of capitalism must therefore be accepted throughout the society, and fraud and dishonesty must be culturally defined as immoral and intolerable. Second, to ensure open competition, no business should be so large or powerful that it dominates the entire supply of any product and thereby controls its price. In other words, no monopolies, oligopolies, trusts, or conspiracies must be permitted that could dominate the market. Because numerous monopolies, trusts, and similar arrangements to restrict market competition became quite extensive during the period between about 1890 and 1930, however, market capitalism also became known as "monopoly capitalism." Third, the role of the state in the economy must be limited to establishing a legal framework to ensure that contracts and sales are fulfilled. The government must not grant special financial or legal favors to any business firms, and it must not attempt to regulate the marketplace in any way. In short, state interference in the economy must be kept to an absolute minimum. For the most part, this was the situation in Western capitalist societies until the 1930s.

If these three conditions prevail, the economic system of a society will presumably be self-regulating as a result of the invisible hand of supply and demand, all buyers and sellers will benefit to the fullest possible extent, and the society as a whole will have a productive and efficient economy that will maximize real national wealth.

Regulated Capitalism

A basic assumption of market capitalism is that the marketplace operates under conditions of perfect competition, so that the law of supply and demand can serve as an invisible hand regulating economic transactions. By the early decades of the twentieth century, however, most economists had come to realize that markets are never perfectly competitive. Imperfect competition develops in economic markets for a variety of reasons:

(1) One or a few large companies often come to control the entire supply of a product, as smaller and less efficient firms are driven out of business or absorbed by larger firms.

(2) Powerful businesses often put strong pressure on the government to take actions that will protect their markets and enhance their profits. Examples include imposing import tariffs on competing foreign firms, giving businesses tax benefits such as writing off costs of new equipment against their tax liabilities, assisting them in accumulating capital, buying their goods, or preventing other firms from producing similar products.

(3) Competing businesses may conspire to establish a common minimum price for their products so that they do not undersell each other.

(4) Many businesses at least occasionally set their prices below their production costs so as to capture the market for a particular commodity, after which they can sell it for as much as "the traffic will bear."

In these and many other ways, businesses act as political rather than purely economic units, transforming the market economy into a political economy that is no longer self-regulating.

At the height of the Great Depression in 1936, the British economist John Maynard Keynes published his *General Theory of Employment, Interest, and Money*. The purpose of this book was to reformulate capitalist theory and rescue capitalist economies from the devasting problems they were experiencing at that time. Keynes's central thesis of regulated capitalism took account of the realistic conditions of imperfect competition. If the economy is to serve the public interest, he insisted, *government must impose a "visible hand" on the market by regulating (but not controlling) its operation.* Only in this manner could private ownership of businesses be preserved, ensuring that they earned an adequate profit while also serving the economic needs of society as a whole.

The focus of Keynes's analysis was the total economic system, rather than the individual business firm. He identified the key dynamics of a capitalist economy as savings, investment, and consumption and asked what actions government might take to regulate those factors to prevent the serious problems of unemployment, inflation, insufficient capital, business failures, and other conditions that periodically beset unregulated market economies. His answer to this question dealt with four fundamental kinds of government economic policies.

(1) Governmental *monetary policies* must control the supply and flow of money in the economy through interest rates and other banking practices.

(2) Governmental *fiscal policies* must regulate supply and demand in the market through the government's budget and purchases.

(3) Governmental *corporate policies* must prevent the formation of monopolies or oligopolies or other constraints on free trade through laws and court suits.

(4) Governmental *distributive policies* must regulate the distribution of income through such means as taxes, subsidies, and welfare programs.

The ultimate goal of all these policies is to increase the demand for goods and services, thus stimulating economic growth, while also ensuring that necessary commodities are available to the public at affordable prices.

Today, governmental regulation of the economic system is widely accepted in all capitalist societies as a necessary requirement for a healthy economy. Government agencies regulate or influence many aspects of the economy, from interest rates to production decisions to consumption practices. However, many present-day economists and political leaders believe that governments have carried regulation too far and are stifling economic productivity and markets. In recent years, consequently, a strong movement has arisen to deregulate many industries and permit freer market competition. Regardless of the amount or nature of government regulation in modern capitalist political economies, all such efforts are intended to strengthen capitalism, not replace it with some other kind of economic system.

Welfarism

In foraging and horticultural societies, caring for the economic needs of individuals was usually considered the responsibility of the entire community, and no one went hungry or homeless as long as the community possessed any resources. In agrarian societies this responsibility typically shifted to the extended family, and to the lord of the manor in feudal economic systems, but it remained a collective responsibility. In the early stages of industrialization, however, the importance of the extended family declined, people tended to live in small nuclear families, and workers were hired in the labor market as individuals rather than as family units. As a result, each individual worker was seen as being responsible for the economic welfare of himself and his immediate family. Business firms merely hired labor and had no responsibility beyond paying workers whatever wages they agreed to work for. Under both mercantilism and market capitalism the state had no obligation to provide for the economic welfare of individuals.

A new philosophy began to develop in the early part of the twentieth century, and it was strongly spurred by the worldwide depression of the 1930s. This idea of *welfarism asserts that society as a whole has an obligation to ensure that all its members receive at least minimal economic benefits* (Mott, 1965:179). In other words, individual economic welfare is a collective responsibility of the entire society. This philosophy was first adopted as a national policy and enacted into a set of programs by the Social Democratic Party in Sweden in the 1930s. In most other industrial societies, liberal political parties were also advocating various forms of welfarism at that time. The New Deal of the Roosevelt administration in the 1930s included a number of welfare measures, such as Social Security, but it was not nearly as comprehensive as the Swedish system.

The ideal of welfarism is accepted to at least some extent in all industrial societies today. Typical welfare programs that have been enacted in most of these societies include unemployment compensation, disability benefits, children's allowances (except in the United States), financial aid to poor people, medical insurance or services, and retirement programs.

Strictly speaking, welfarism is not a distinct type of economic system, since it always exists in conjunction with regulated capitalism or socialism. In capitalist societies, however, the acceptance of welfarism shifts the central focus of concern from economic production to the welfare of individual consumers and thus quite significantly alters the fundamental nature of the economy. In socialist societies, meanwhile, welfarism is typically viewed as a temporary means of coping with the problems of economic inequality, which presumably will be eliminated once full socialism has been achieved.

The present-day acceptance of welfarism in capitalist societies can be explained in terms of economic and cultural arguments. *From an economic perspective, welfare programs to protect disadvantaged individuals and families are quite rational.* In addition to preserving and expanding consumer demand, these programs:

(1) Assist employers to retain highly skilled employees;

(2) Help individuals and families through temporary financial crises and thus keep them available for future employment;

(3) Contribute to reducing social problems, such as family disruption and crime, that can have enormous costs for society; and

(4) Keep people committed to the existing economic and political systems, so that they do not attempt to alter them radically.

Another important factor is that the immense wealth produced by highly developed industrial economies permits the society to distribute some of this wealth to disadvantaged people without reducing the standard of living of everyone else. In fact, modern welfare systems generally provide much greater economic benefits to well-to-do people—through such provisions as tax deductions for home mortgage interest payments—than are ever received by disadvantaged people (Turner and Starnes, 1976: Ch. 6).

From a cultural perspective, welfarism represents a major change in social values that has been occurring during the past few decades. We are slowly coming to realize that most economically disadvantaged people—including children, the disabled, many unemployed persons, and the elderly—are not personally responsible for their dependency. In many instances, they are the victims of broad economic and social changes occurring in society. The economic dislocations produced by the Great Depression initially provoked this awareness in many people. More recently we have also come to see that war, shifts in the structure of the economy, employment practices, medical care that keeps alive people who would previously have died, and numerous other structural conditions can leave many people economically dependent on society. From this perspective, if economic and social conditions are rendering people incapable of providing for their own economic needs, then society as a whole has a collective obligation to care for them. At the same time, however, there is little public consensus on precisely what kinds of welfare programs and benefits are necessary or socially desirable to fulfill society's moral obligation to disadvantaged people.

Socialism

Observing Europe at the middle of the nineteenth century, Karl Marx was struck by the existence of a profound paradox. On one hand, growing capitalistic industrialization was creating more wealth than ever before in human history. On the other hand, everywhere one looked there were pitifully low wages and gross exploitation of workers, atrocious working conditions, extreme poverty, a small class of business owners becoming extraordinarily wealthy, production of goods and services that did not meet pressing human needs, and extensive waste of resources and wealth. What was wrong with the organization of societies that produced so much inequality, misery, and waste in the midst of this expanding wealth? How must the economic and social structures of society be reorganized to correct these evils and enable everyone to benefit from the productivity of industrialization? These were the questions that Marx attempted to answer in his analysis of capitalism as an economic system (Marx, 1936). We shall not attempt here to present a complete summary of Marx's answers to those questions, but will focus on his concept of socialism as an alternative to capitalism.

Pervading all of Marx's thought was the thesis that *all societies rest on an economic foundation, the most critical feature of which is its dominant "mode of production."* This is the principal process through which a society produces its goods and services. In an agrarian society the dominant mode of production is agriculture, while in an industrial society it is manufacturing and associated commerce. The dominant mode of production in any society has two components:

(1) The "forces of production" are the resources and technology used in the major means of production; while

(2) The "social relations of production" are the financial, legal, and other relationships that determine ownership and control of the major means of production.

Both these components are important in shaping the economy of a society, but Marx gave primary attention to ownership and control of the economic system because it largely determines the structure of power in that society.

All other sectors of a society, but especially its political system and its cultural belief system, rest on its economic foundation and are highly influenced by it. These other sectors—which Marx called the "superstructure" of society—therefore reflect and support the dominant mode of production, although they are never totally determined by it.

Because the dominant mode of economic production is the primary source of wealth in a society, whoever owns or controls it will be able to exercise extensive power throughout all other sectors of that society. Under feudalism these economic elites were the landed nobility; with the advent of industrialization they have become the owners of factories and related businesses. Relationship to (or control over) the major means of economic production is thus the principal factor shaping not only the economic system, but the entire society.

Why do capitalists exploit their workers? The owners of industries are not evil people, Marx insisted, but are forced by the intrinsic laws of a capitalist economy to act in that manner. Under capitalism, businesses are established and operated to make a profit. If they do not, sooner or later they go bankrupt. According to the economic thinking prevailing in the nineteenth century, labor is the main factor determining the cost of manufactured goods. To make a profit, therefore, capitalists must pay their workers less than the true value of the labor required to produce those goods. Only by paying their workers as little as possible could capitalists sell their products at competitive prices and realize a profit. This "labor theory of value" has since been shown to be incomplete, especially as sophisticated machinery and complex organizational arrangements have come to play increasingly important roles in the production process. We know now that many other factors, such as technical efficiency and organizational effectiveness, contribute greatly to profit making. Nevertheless, the argument that capitalism promotes exploitation of workers was at least partially correct in Marx's time—as well as today—and provided him with an economic rationale for condemning capitalism as inherently inhumane and as the principal cause of socioeconomic inequality in capitalist industrial societies.

If the problems created by capitalism are inherent in the nature of this kind of economic system, the way to eliminate those problems is to create a different kind of economy, according to Marxian economic theory. Such an economy should attain several goals:

(1) Serve public needs rather than private interests;

(2) Promote production for use rather than for profit;

(3) Emphasize cooperation rather than competition;

(4) Distribute power more evenly throughout society; and

(5) Create greater socioeconomic equality among all people.

These goals could best be achieved, Marx argued, with a socialist economy.

The essence of socialism is that the major means of economic production are publicly rather than privately owned. In an industrial society, this would include all business concerns that contribute to manufacturing or distributing goods, such as natural resource extractors, factories, wholesalers and retailers, banks, transportation systems, and the like. It would not include private property such as homes, nor need it include small stores and services. By making the relations of production public rather than private, no set of capitalist owners could control the economy for their own purposes and profits. Instead, the economic system would be operated to serve the collective needs of the entire society. Because such an economy would not rest on the profit motive, it would have no need to exploit workers. And because there would be no dominant economic elites, power and privileges would be much more equally distributed throughout the population. Ideally, no citizens would be economically disadvantaged under socialism, because the structure of the entire economic system would ensure that it served all people adequately.

In the initial stage of creating a socialist economy, the government must function as the representative of the public, owning and controlling the major means of production so as to shift the focus of the economy from profits to service. The government will therefore formulate long-range economic plans, direct the utilization of capital throughout the economy, determine what kinds of goods are to be produced and in what quantities, set prices and wage rates, distribute goods, and otherwise regulate the entire economic system. The Union of Soviet Socialist Republics and other socialist societies are still in this first phase of socialism.

Although Marx and his collaborators did not attempt to describe a mature socialist economy in great detail, they had a vision of *an ideal kind of society, which they called communism.* Their vision incorporated all the major ideals of the Judeo-Christian religious tradition, including equality of wealth and power among all people, an economy without markets in which people contribute according to their abilities and receive according to their needs, social relationships based on cooperation rather than exploitation and conflict, the absence of the state and other organizations that coerce people's actions, elimination of all war and other violence, material abundance for everyone, and full opportunities for people to live their lives in a self-fulfilling manner. No nation today even approximates an ideal communist society, and perhaps none ever will. It is crucial to remember, however, than an authoritarian state is the absolute antithesis of Marx's vision of a communist society in which

freedom, justice, and equality would be maximized for all.

CONTEMPORARY CORPORATIONS

Capitalism has changed dramatically since the days of Adam Smith, especially as a result of increasing government regulation during the last fifty years. Nevertheless, two basic features of capitalist economies—private owership of capital and businesses and reliance on the profit motive to drive the economy—have undergone relatively few modifications as capitalism has evolved in industrial societies. *Most of the major changes that have occurred in capitalist economies have involved the practice of market competition and the nature of business firms.*

Smith's conception of capitalism relied on continual unrestrained competition in the marketplace to ensure that the supply of goods and services balanced the demand for them, that prices were held to the lowest possible level, and that the economic system functioned adequately to satisfy the material needs of the entire society. Open market competition is an extremely risky and insecure process for private businesses struggling to maximize their profits, however, as well as for consumers and society as a whole. Consequently, business firms in capitalist economic systems have continually sought ways of reducing or controlling market competition.

In addition, the major businesses in capitalist economies have become vastly larger and more complex than in Smith's time. They have become corporate organizations, have grown immensely in size and wealth, constitute national corporate systems, and operate increasingly on a worldwide scale. As a result, market competition among large business firms has been severely curtailed.

Corporate Organizations

Until late in the nineteenth century, most manufacturing and other businesses were owned and operated by a single individual or family or by a partnership. A number of those companies still bear family names such as Ford, du Pont, or Mellon. Since then, for a variety of financial and legal reasons, almost all major businesses in industrial societies have become public corporations. Consequently, the economies of contemporary Western societies are sometimes described as "corporate capitalism."

Corporations are chartered by governments and exist as legal entities apart from their owners or members, they are owned by stockholders, and they operate under the principle of "limited liability" so that the stockholders are not financially liable for the company beyond their actual investment. The following paragraphs describe several major features of modern business corporations.

Goals. As mentioned previously, *in capitalist economies the primary goal of all private businesses is to make as much profit as possible.* All other goals that a corporate might also pursue must, of necessity, be subordinate to the "bottom line" of showing a net profit at the end of each year. Moreover, *the cultures of industrial societies generally view the profit-making goal as socially desirable and morally right.* The larger the profit, the more the company is esteemed and the more valuable its stock tends to become. At the same time, corporations may also seek additional goals such as:

(1) Maintaining the organizational strength or cohesion of the company and its operational viability;

(2) Promoting corporate growth in terms of the number and kinds of products produced and sold; and

(3) Creating a favorable public image of the corporation.

To the extent that these subsidiary goals are attained, they will, of course, contribute to corporate profits.

Wealth. Many large corporations are immensely wealthy, with total assets of billions of dollars. When a company owns this amount

of wealth, it will inevitably be able to influence many aspects of the economic, social, and political systems within its society. Moreover, *this corporate wealth is highly concentrated in the largest firms.* Of the approximately 1.7 million business corporations in the United States at the present time, the largest 1.0 percent own about 75 percent of all corporate assets, the largest 0.5 percent own about 60 percent, and the biggest 0.1 percent own about 40 percent of this wealth (Blumberg, 1975:16). Among the 500 largest American corporations in 1976 (0.3 percent of the total), the typical firm held $2 billion in assets and had sales of about $1.4 billion (Forbes, 1977:156). In 1980, the top six industrial firms—Exxon, General Motors, Mobile, International Business Machines, Ford, and Texaco—together were worth $180 billion, which was 15 percent of all industrial wealth in the United States. Table 12-2 lists the 25 largest industrial firms, banks, utilities, and insurance companies in the U.S. as of 1985, showing the total assets of each of those corporations.

Ownership. Corporations are legally owned by their stockholders, who may number in the tens or hundreds of thousands. As a result, the contemporary United States and other industrial societies are sometimes described as examples of "people's capitalism." This idea ignores the fact that *stock ownership is highly concentrated among a very small proportion of the population.* In the mid-1970s, the wealthiest five percent of all families in the United States owned 86 percent of all privately held corporate stock, and the wealthiest one percent of those families owned 62 percent of that stock (Turner and Starnes, 1976:118). That situation had not changed greatly since the 1920s (Kolko, 1962), and there is no evidence that it has changed in recent years. Even more important is the fact that *the majority of all corporate stock is owned by other corporations, especially banks.* A few years ago, for example, a U.S. Senate investigation discovered that Chase Manhattan Bank owned at least two percent of the stock (enough to wield considerable influence on a

TABLE 12-2   The Largest United States Corporations in 1985

	The 25 Largest Industries			The 25 Largest Banks	
Rank	Corporation	Assets ($ billions)	Rank	Corporation	Assets ($ billions)
1	Exxon	$62.9	1	Citicorp (New York)	$134.7
2	General Motors	45.7	2	BankAmerica Corp. (San Francisco)	121.2
3	IBM	37.2	3	Chase Manhattan Corp. (New York)	81.9
4	Mobil	35.1	4	Manufacturers Hanover Corp. (New York)	64.3
5	Texaco	27.2	5	J. P. Morgan & Co. (New York)	58.0
6	Standard Oil (Indiana)	25.8	6	Chemical New York Corp.	51.2
7	du Pont	24.4	7	First Interstate Bancorp. (Los Angeles)	44.4
8	Standard Oil of California	24.0	8	Continental Illinois Corp. (Chicago)	42.1
9	Ford Motor	23.9	9	Security Pacific Corp. (Los Angeles)	40.4
10	General Electric	23.3	10	Bankers Trust New York Corp.	40.0
11	Atlantic Richfield	23.3	11	First Chicago Corp.	36.3
12	Shell Oil	22.2	12	Wells Fargo & Co. (San Francisco)	27.0
13	Gulf Oil	21.0	13	Mellon National Corp. (Pittsburgh)	26.4
14	U.S. Steel	19.3	14	Crocker National Corp. (San Francisco)	23.4
15	Tenneco	18.0	15	Marine Midland Banks (Buffalo)	22.9
16	Standard Oil (Ohio)	16.4	16	InterFirst Corp. (Dallas)	21.7
17	ITT	14.0	17	First Bank System (Minneapolis)	20.9
18	Phillips Petroleum	13.1	18	Norwest Corp. (Minneapolis)	19.9
19	Sun	12.5	19	Bank of Boston Corp.	19.5
20	Dow Chemical	12.0	20	Texas Commerce Bancshares (Houston)	19.5
21	Occidental Petroleum	11.8	21	RepublicBank Corp. (Dallas)	19.1
22	Eastman Kodak	10.9	22	Irving Bank Corp. (New York)	18.6
23	Getty Oil	10.4	23	First City Bancorp. of Texas (Houston)	17.3
24	Union Carbide	10.3	24	NBD Bancorp. (Detroit)	13.2
25	Union Pacific	10.2	25	NCNB Corp. (Charlotte, N.C.)	12.8

TABLE 12-2 *Continued*

	The 25 Largest Utilities			The 25 Largest Insurance Companies	
Rank	Company	Assets ($ billions)	Rank	Company	Assets ($ billions)
1	AT&T	$149.5	1	Prudential (Newark)	$72.2
2	GTE	24.4	2	Metropolitan (New York)	60.6
3	Pacific Gas & Electric	14.7	3	Equitable Life Assurance (New York)	43.3
4	Commonwealth Edison	13.6	4	Aetna Life (Hartford)	31.4
5	Southern Company	13.5	5	New York Life	24.2
6	American Electric Power	12.8	6	John Hancock Mutual (Boston)	23.5
7	Middle South Utilities	11.1	7	Travelers (Hartford)	20.7
8	Southern California Edison	11.0	8	Connecticut General Life (Bloomfield)	17.4
9	Texas Utilities	8.8	9	Teachers Insurance & Annuity (New York)	16.1
10	Public Service Electric & Gas	8.6	10	Northwestern Mutual (Milwaukee)	14.5
11	Consumers Power	8.5	11	Massachusetts Mutual (Springfield)	12.3
12	Consolidated Edison	8.2	12	Bankers Life (Des Moines)	11.4
13	Detroit Edison	8.2	13	Mutual of New York	9.3
14	Philadelphia Electric	8.1	14	New England Mutual (Boston)	8.5
15	Florida Power & Light	7.7	15	Mutual Benefit (Newark)	7.9
16	Dominion Resources	7.7	16	Connecticut Mutual (Hartford)	6.7
17	Duke Power	7.4	17	State Farm Life (Bloomington, Ill.)	5.0
18	Houston Industries	6.6	18	Lincoln National Life (Fort Wayne, Ind.)	4.7
19	Long Island Lighting	6.4	19	Continental Assurance (Chicago)	4.1
20	Pennsylvania Power & Light	6.0	20	Penn Mutual (Philadelphia)	4.0
21	Ohio Edison	5.9	21	Nationwide Life (Columbus, Ohio)	3.9
22	Central & South West	5.7	22	Phoenix Mutual (Hartford)	3.8
23	Niagara Mohawk Power	5.4	23	National Life & Accident (Nashville)	3.5
24	General Public Utilities	5.3	24	Western & Southern Life (Cincinnati)	3.4
25	Carolina Power & Light	5.3	25	Variable Annuity Life (Houston)	3.4

Source: Thomas R. Dye, *Who's Running America? The Conservative Years,* 4th ed. (Englewood Cliffs, N.J.: Prentice-Hall), 1986, pp. 17–22.

company) in 46 major corporations (U.S. Senate, 1974:6). In addition, in many corporations large blocks of stock are usually owned by the top executives of that company, as a result of options that permit them to purchase stocks for less than current market prices. In short, most corporations are owned by a small number of wealthy individuals and families, by banks and other corporations, by pension and investment programs, and by top corporate executives, not by ordinary citizens.

Structure. Corporations are hierarchically organized, with all authority flowing downward from a few positions at the top of the pyramid. Basic policy for a corporation is formulated by its board of directors, typically consisting of 15 to 25 persons. Although the directors are elected by the stockholders, this is usually a mere formality. Because the board nominates individuals to fill vacancies in its membership, who are then routinely elected at stockholders' meetings, a *board of directors is actually a self-perpetuating oligarchy.* Some members of the board usually come from outside the company, but they are typically top executives of other corporations, foundations, or similar organizations. In most companies, meanwhile, several members of the board (including its chair) are chosen from among the top executives of that company. These "inside directors" are generally the ones who propose policies for the board to adopt, so that in practice they tend to dominate board decisions. Moreover, most operating decisions and day-to-day control of the corporation are delegated by the board to a small set of top executives, who in turn delegate authority and responsibility down the hierarchy to lower levels of management. There is no pretense of democracy in corporations, and it is virtually impossible for ordinary employees to challenge management decisions.

Corporate Systems

In theory, each corporation is a separate entity, competing with other corporations in the marketplace. In practice, however, business corporations in capitalist societies—especially the larger companies—are increasingly becoming interwoven into complex national corporate systems. This process occurs both formally, through mergers, and informally, through stock ownership and interlocking directorates, as well as through many operating practices.

Corporate Mergers or Acquisitions. Two corporations merge when one of them acquires ownership of the other by buying a majority of its stock and then exchanging shares of its own stock for the remaining outstanding shares of the acquired firm. Although the acquired firm may likely retain its own identity and structure, it is now legally and financially part of the corporation that bought it. Corporate mergers have been occurring at an accelerating rate throughout the twentieth century in industrial societies. If you had been shopping for an automobile in the United States at the beginning of the century, you would have been able to choose from among cars made by 181 different companies (Evans and Schneider, 1981). Today your choice is limited to four U.S. companies (unless you decide to buy an imported car), which over the years have absorbed or outlasted all of their competitors. Some of those former competitors remain as divisions of a parent company (such as Oldsmobile), while others have disappeared (such as Studebaker).

This type of merger among competing companies is called *horizontal integration.* It is continually occurring in most industries in capitalist economies. Larger and more successful companies buy out smaller and less successful firms for a variety of reasons. The purchasing company may want to:

(1) Reduce competition;
(2) Expand markets;
(3) Obtain additional capital or other resources;
(4) Realize economies of scale in production; or
(5) Gain greater market predictability and stability.

Whatever the reasons for these mergers, the result is the development of *oligopoly, or the domination of an industry by a few giant corporations.* Oligopolies pervade modern capitalist economies. For example, in the United State four or fewer corporations presently control at least three-fourths of the domestic production in such diverse industries as automobiles, breakfast cereals, cigarettes, mainframe computers, and flat glass. The list of industries in which the four largest producers control over half the domestic production is much longer. Whenever oligopoly exists within an industry, market competition is severely restricted.

A second type of corporate merger, which is also very common in capitalist economies, is *vertical integration.* In this process, a manufacturing firm buys up other companies on which it is directly dependent. It can then control the entire production process, from acquiring raw materials to distributing final products. Exxon Corporation, for instance, owns not only petroleum refineries, but also oil fields, tanker fleets, pipelines, distributors, and service stations. Similarly, a furniture manufacturer might seek to acquire forest tracts, sawmills, fabric producers, and furniture stores. These vertical corporate linkages eliminate many market uncertainties and risks for the parent corporation, such as price increases or cancelled contracts.

There is also a third type of corporate merger, which produces *conglomerates.* In this process, a powerful corporation—often merely a stockholding company—buys an array of diverse firms producing many different kinds of products. One of the largest conglomerates is International Telephone and Telegraph, which is not only in the communications business, but also owns Sheraton Hotels, Avis Rent-a-Car, Wonder Bread, the Hartford Insurance Group, and approximately 150 other companies. At first glance, such conglomerate mergers may appear senseless, but there are sound economic reasons for them. By diversifying into many different areas of business, a corporation gains greater financial stability by protecting itself against losses in any one area. Moreover, if the corporation does lose money in some of

---

> **TYPES OF CORPORATE MERGERS**
> 1. Horizontal integration.
> 2. Vertical integration.
> 3. Conglomerate integration.

---

its ventures, it can use those losses as tax write-offs against its profits in other areas, thus minimizing its total corporate taxes.

Interlocking Directorates. Even when corporations remain legally separate, they often become highly interrelated through stock ownership and interlocking directors. We have already noted that large corporations—especially banks—frequently own large amounts of stock in one another. However, stock ownership merely entitles the holder to vote in annual stockholders' meetings. A more direct and much more effective way in which one corporation can exert influence on another company is through interlocking directors. *Two corporations have interlocking directors when one or more persons (usually a top executive of one of them) sits on both boards of directors.* Almost all of the largest corporations in the United States, as well as many smaller ones, have interlocking directors (Allen, 1974).

Among the largest 1,100 firms in this country, there is an average of ten interlocking directorates per firm, and the larger the corporation, the more such linkages it tends to have. General Motors, for example, was recently found to have interlocking directorates with 29 other corporations, and each of them, in turn, had such linkages with from two to 59 other companies (Mintz and Schwartz, 1981). This study then looked for those corporations that lay at the center of the densest and most interconnected sets of major corporations, using what it called a measure of "hub centrality." Of the 20 companies constituting the hub of the United States economy, 15 were large banks and insurance companies, many of which have their home office in New York City. Moreover, those financial companies are all highly linked with one another through stock ownership and interlocking directorates. The study concluded that a few huge New York financial firms, which largely control the flow of finance capital throughout the U.S. economy, constitute the heart of a moderately well-integrated national corporate system in this country.

Operating Practices. Corporations may also attempt to minimize price competition through a variety of operating practices, especially when only a few large firms effectively control an industry. Some of these actions are illegal, though still widely practiced. These include "price fixing," in which all of the major firms in a field informally agree to charge approximately the same price for competing products, and "bid rigging," in which several firms that frequently bid on the same contracts agree to take turns submitting the lowest bid (which is set as high as they dare), while the others bid even higher to make the low bid appear acceptable. Other practices are legal, though ethically questionable. An example is "price leading," in which the largest firm in an industry sets its price at a level that will maximize its profits while ensuring adequate profits for its competitors, and the other firms then charge similar prices for their products. The result of such practices, whether legal or illegal, is to minimize or eliminate price competition for that industry. There will still be market competition among firms, but it will be on the basis of product differentiation rather than prices. That is, one company may claim that its detergent washes clothes cleaner than any other detergent, even though they all cost about the same.

Multinational Corporations

Corporate systems are rapidly expanding beyond the borders of single countries, and they are in the process of creating *a single world economy that encompasses all the capitalist industrial nations and many developing societies.* A company that operates in two or more countries—and frequently worldwide—is called a *multinational corporation.* More than one-fourth of the total world production of all goods is presently done by multinational corporations, and that proportion is expected to double by the year 2000 (Vernon, 1977). Three hundred of the world's largest multinational corporations have their headquarters in the United States, but they earn 40 percent of their net profits outside this country. Exxon operates in over 100 countries, while International Telephone and Telegraph employs over 400,000 people in 68 countries. Decisions made by a small number of corporate elites in the United States therefore often result in economic prosperity or devastation for many other societies around the world.

Many of the multinational corporations are immensely wealthy, and the total assets of a number of them are larger than the gross national products of most nations. Exxon's total wealth, for instance, is larger than that of Mexico, while General Motors is worth more than the economy of Austria. As a result of their great wealth, together with the fact that they operate to a large extent outside the authority of any national government, *the multinational corporations are becoming major world economic and political powers.* They frequently establish their own policies and operating procedures, negotiate directly with governments as equals, and often act covertly to support or undermine political parties and governments within the countries where they do business. As a result, there is no effective governmental control over many of the activities of the multinational corporations.

As examples of the political actions of multinational corporations, consider the following. ITT offered the Nixon administration $1 million to help overthrow the government of Chile in 1972. Exxon has contributed nearly $60 million to government officials in 15 countries. And Lockheed has distributed nearly $200 million in payoffs to political leaders in such countries as the Netherlands, Japan, Colombia, and Italy. The business activities of multinational corporations do, of course, promote economic growth in many societies, especially developing countries, as they introduce investment capital and new technologies, establish firms and employ workers, develop new markets, and promote international trade. But their objectives are always to expand their businesses and increase their corporate profits, not to benefit the people of the societies in which they operate.

There are many reasons why corporations become multinational in scope. These include:

(1) Obtaining raw materials at low prices from other countries;

(2) Gaining access to investment capital that is available in foreign financial markets;

(3) Reducing labor costs, since workers can often be hired in developing nations for pennies an hour rather than $15 an hour in the United States;

(4) Expanding their markets beyond their home country;

(5) Avoiding the corporate taxes levied by governments of industrial societies, often through questionable bookkeeping procedures or shifting funds among banks in various countries; and

(6) Escaping governmental regulation in their home society, such as selling pharmaceutical products in other nations that are banned by the U.S. Food and Drug Administration because they are unsafe.

Modern Dual Economies

In discussing the economies of developing societies in Chapter 10, the point was stressed that they contain two distinct economic systems: an emerging modern industrial economy (often dominated by multinational corporations) and a traditional economy of agriculture and handicraft production. *Capitalist industrial societies also contain dual economies,* but they differ from those in developing societies in two fundamental ways (Galbraith, 1967). First, both of the economic systems in industrial societies are based on manufacturing. The difference between these two systems is rather one of organizational size and scope of activities. This chapter focuses on the large corporations

that are so evident in industrial societies, which John Kenneth Galbraith called the "industrial system." However, these societies also contain thousands of medium-sized and small businesses, which Galbraith labeled the "enterpreneurial system." Because of their small size and limited scope of business activities, they are much more subject to both the competitive forces of the marketplace and government regulations. As a result, their profit margins and their continued existence are often quite perilous.

The second distinctive feature of the dual economies of industrial societies is that the few hundred mammoth corporations constituting the industrial system completely dominate the entire natural economy. The major corporations in industrial societies determine the flow of capital through the economic system, are responsible for most technological innovation, decide what products are produced and not produced, create mass markets, and—as will be elaborated in the following section—heavily influence government policies and practices. Internationally, they also dominate the emerging world economic system.

CORPORATE INFLUENCES ON GOVERNMENT

Although the economy and the polity are distinct systems within contemporary societies, they have become so highly interwoven that it is common to describe them as forming a relatively unified political economy. This section examines the ways in which corporations influence governments in contemporary capitalist industrial societies. The opposite side of this reciprocal process—government influences on the economy—is discussed in the following chapter on political systems.

In a continual effort to create and sustain conditions that are favorable to private business, the major corporations in contemporary capitalist industrial societies are constantly seeking to influence government policies and programs. Because of their immense wealth and power, these businesses generally exert much more influence on the state than do any other organizations or interest associations. This influence is particularly evident in four realms of activity: maintaining economic stability, contributing to political campaigns, exchanging executive personnel, and providing information.

Maintaining Economic Stability

Major business corporations are the primary creators and controllers of wealth in all capitalist societies. They are the major sources of investment capital, users of raw materials, producers of consumer goods and services, generators of employment and income, and providers of government tax revenues. Directly and indirectly, therefore, *all governments depend on the continued effective functioning of the national economy.* Directly, the government depends on the economy for almost all the revenues it receives to fund its activities. If the economy declines, so do both corporate and individual tax revenues, and the government becomes increasingly constricted and ineffective. Indirectly, the legitimacy and authority of the entire political system rests on continued public satisfaction with the manner in which the society, and particularly its economy, is operating. If large numbers of people are unemployed, if desired goods and services are not available, or if prices rise rapidly, many people will blame the government for those problems. They will then likely demand new political leaders or even an entirely new political system. Conversely, if the economy is prospering and expanding, people will generally be satisfied with the government and support it.

One of the principal concerns of all governments, therefore, is to keep the economy healthy and stable. As expressed by Martin Marger (1981:183): "Government cannot stray too far from the maintenance of a stable economic system. There is, in other words, a limiting framework which constrains government activity, and in American society that framework is drawn most clearly by the dominant economic institution, the corporation." If a government fails in this endeavor, it will suffer loss of revenue, public support, and legitimacy. Given this dependence of government on the economy, major corporations are able to exert considerable influence on the government. If corporations need a new employment policy or tax provision, for example, they will press government officials to adopt it and are quite likely to be successful. Indeed, the government cannot let the economy or major corporations fail, as illustrated by the United States government's financial "bail-outs" of the Lockheed Corporation in 1971 and the Chrysler Corporation in 1979. If either of these huge businesses had gone bankrupt, it would have placed too severe a strain on the entire national political economy.

This symbiotic relationship between the corporate economy and the national government does not mean that conflicts cannot occur between these two realms. Quite the contrary, as we read in the newspapers almost daily. Economic and political leaders are constantly battling over various policies and programs. At times, these conflicts may become quite vehement, as government officials reject business demands, or corporate executives find the stance of government to be intolerable on a particular issue. Nevertheless, most of the time these disputes focus entirely on short-term objectives or specific practices. *Conflicts between the economic and political systems of a society rarely question the fundamental goal of maintaining a strong economy and mutually beneficial relationships between those two realms.* The national (and increasingly worldwide) political economy has become too tightly interwoven, and too many people depend on its continued stable functioning, to tolerate divisive conflicts that would seriously threaten or destroy this system.

Contributing to Political Campaigns

In this day of televised and other mass media campaigning, running for public office has become an extremely expensive operation costing hundreds of thousands or even millions of dollars. No candidate for major political office can afford to cover all those costs from his or her own funds, so that all candidates rely heavily or entirely on campaign donations from others. Moreover, while political parties often make a great display of soliciting donations from individual citizens, *a large proportion of all campaign funds are obtained from corporations and other business organizations seeking to influence the political process.* Although labor unions, professional associations, and special-interest associations also commonly make campaign contributions, because of the immense wealth of the large corporations, their ability to provide financial support to parties and candidates often far surpasses that of any other organizations.

In the United States, business corporations are prohibited by law from contributing directly to candidates, but this restriction is easily circumvented in at least three ways:

(1) Corporate funds are channeled to individual corporate executives, who then contribute the money to candidates favored by the company.

(2) Corporations and business organizations organize political action committees (PACs), which can legally solicit corporate funds to be donated to candidates or used to support political activities.

(3) Large corporations sometimes establish "slush funds" that are not recorded in their books, so that they can be used (illegally) for whatever political purposes the company desires.

The purposes of most campaign contributions are to communicate and promote corporate views on specific issues to the public and/or to insure corporate access to public officials after they are elected. A sophisticated corporation will no longer say to a politician: "We paid for your campaign, and we want you to vote our way on this issue." But it might likely say: "The public supports our position on this issue, and we would like to explain it to you." That politician will undoubtedly give serious attention to the concerns of the corporation.

Exchanging Executive Personnel

The management skills required to administer a large, complex organization are essentially the same for business corporations and government agencies. Competent executives who possess such skills are always in short supply and high demand. It is not surprising, therefore, to discover that *top executives often move back and forth between corporate and government positions.* For individuals, such career shifting increases their knowledge, skills, experience, and contacts. At the same time, corporations frequently encourage their top executives to accept high government positions for a few years, since this interchange of personnel can greatly benefit these businesses. As with campaign financing, a sophisticated corporation would not consider saying to a former executive now working in government: "Support this policy because it will benefit our company." But it would expect to have relatively open access to that individual and to be able to present its case on relevant issues. It would also expect that person to understand business concerns and to promote policies that would generally benefit the corporate economy. Government agencies, meanwhile, are usually delighted to hire former business executives because of their managerial abilities and their experience in the business world with which the government must deal.

This practice of executive interchange has been particularly evident in the regulatory agencies of the United States government. Members of these commissions are commonly recruited from the industries they regulate, since the commissioners must have thorough knowledge of those industries if they are to be regulated effectively. Such exchanges also occur quite frequently within most departments of the executive branch, and in Presidential cabinet appointments. A study of executive exchanges between corporations and the cabinet over a 75-year period concluded that "all Cabinet posts are to a high degree interlocked with the elite business sector" (Freitag, 1975).

Providing Necessary Information

Although lobbying is by no means unique to the United States, it is a distinctive feature of the U.S. political system. *Most large corporations maintain permanent lobbying offices in Washington, D.C.,* so that there are presently estimated to be at least 5,000 full-time lobbyists in that city. In addition, broadly based business associations such as the National Association of Manufacturers and the National Chamber of Commerce maintain lobbying staffs that promote general business interests. Meanwhile, lobbyists for various industrial organizations such as the American Petroleum Association and the American Truckers Association represent the concerns of their industries.

Although some lobbyists may attempt to use high pressure techniques to influence government officials, more subtle approaches are often much more effective. Members of Congress have very small personal staffs and hence frequently find it difficult to gather the information they need to make informed decisions on all the issues confronting them. Consequently, sophisticated lobbyists function primarily as providers of background information on pending legislation, and members of Congress frequently rely heavily on them for such information. Needless to say, no matter how objective lobbyists may claim to be, the information they provide will invariably favor the business interests they represent.

Since experienced politicians know that information acquired from lobbyists is biased, *many government officials prefer to obtain information from presumably neutral research and policy advisory organizations.* These bodies—of which there are several hundred—are composed of professional researchers and policy analysts who make detailed studies of broad issues and problems and offer recommendations for dealing with them. Their reports are undoubtedly more thorough and comprehensive than the information provided by most lobbyists. Nevertheless, most of these organizations represent some particular point of view,

---

CORPORATE INFLUENCES ON GOVERNMENT

1. Maintaining economic stability.
2. Contributing to political campaigns.
3. Exchanging executive personnel.
4. Providing necessary information.

---

ranging from environmental protection to foreign trade, and their reports almost invariably reflect their perspectives.

The largest, best financed, most respected, and most influential of these policy research and advisory organizations are headed by top corporate business executives and are oriented toward corporate business concerns. They include the Business Council, the Committee for Economic Development, the Council on Foreign Relations, and the Trilateral Commission. These organizations strive to produce policy analyses and recommendations that represent the best interests of the entire society and cannot be accused of favoring any particular firm or industry. Nevertheless, all of them accept the desirability of maintaining the existing economic system and hence rarely advocate fundamental changes of that system. Their reports will likely question current policies and recommend new ones, but almost inevitably with the goal of preserving and enhancing the existing corporate-based capitalist political economy.

SOCIOECONOMIC CONSEQUENCES OF INDUSTRIALIZATION

As the process of industrialization has engulfed Western nations during the nineteenth and the twentieth centuries, it has transformed virtually all aspects of their social, economic, and political life. Highly industrialized societies are radically different from agrarian societies. This section focuses on a number of fairly direct consequences of industrialization on the socioeconomic structure of societies, including their total wealth and income levels, occupational distributions, and educational attainments. Data for the United States are used to illustrate the major trends that have occurred during the past 100 years in these areas, although similar trends can be observed in most industrial societies.

Wealth and Income Levels

The socioeconomic change most directly caused by industrialization is an immense increase in societal and personal wealth, as mentioned in Chapter 9. Total societal wealth is most commonly measured with the Gross National Product. It is usually expressed as GNP per capita, to take account of population increases, and frequently in "constant" dollars for an arbitrarily selected base year, to take account of inflation. The growth of the United States' GNP per capita as a result of industrialization is illustrated in Figure 12-1, expressed in constant 1972 dollars. In 1870, at the beginning of the industrial revolution in this country, the total GNP was $35 billion

in 1972 dollars. This amounted to about $800 per person. Thirty years later, in 1900, the total GNP was $116 billion, or $1,500 per person. In 1930, following the boom years of the 1920s and just prior to the Great Depression, it had reached $275 billion, or $2,250 per capita. The period following World War II saw even greater economic growth, so that by 1960 the GNP was $737 billion, or $4,100 per person. Finally, in the 25 years between 1960 and 1985 it rose to $1,670 billion, or nearly $7,000 per person. Expressed in current 1985 dollars, the GNP was $4,185 billion in that year, or about $17,400 per capita (U.S. Bureau of the Census, 1975 and 1987).

Personal income, meanwhile, is usually indicated by the Disposable Personal Income (DPI) per capita, which is the average amount of income available to individuals after federal taxes. Again expressed in constant 1972 dollars, the DPI per person is estimated to have been about $500 in 1870, typical of agrarian societies today. Data are not available for 1900, but by 1930 the DPI

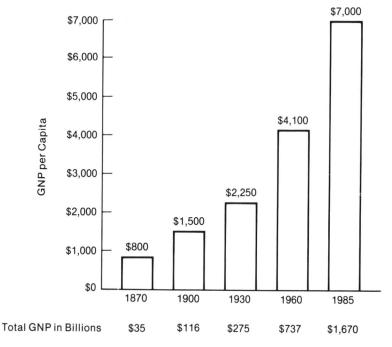

FIGURE 12-1   Growth of the gross national product per capita of the United States between 1870 and 1985 (in 1972 constant dollars)

had increased to approximately $1,700 per person. In 1960, that figure stood at $2,800, and in 1985 it was $4,200. In current 1985 dollars, it was $11,700 in that year.

Occupational Distributions

As the economic base of a society shifts from agriculture to manufacturing, a decreasing proportion of the work force is engaged in farming, and more and more people seek urban employment. Going back to 1840, nearly two-thirds (63 percent) of the total labor force in the United States consisted of farm owners or workers. In 1870, that figure had declined to 53 percent, and by 1900 it was 43 percent. Even sharper declines in farm employment have occurred during the twentieth century, so that farming accounted for only 22 percent of the total national labor force in 1930, just eight percent in 1960, and only three percent in 1985. At the present time, this tiny proportion of the work force is producing enough food for all the rest of the U.S. population (as well as producing surpluses that are shipped to many other countries around the world). However, the number of people engaged in processing, packaging, distributing, and selling agricultural products has steadily grown over the years.

Employment in manufacturing and related work has not risen as rapidly as farm work has declined, since urban residents work in many different kinds of jobs. The proportion of the labor force in manufacturing grew most rapidly in the United States during the early stages of industrialization, from nine percent in 1840 to 19 percent in 1870. It reached a high of 27 percent in 1920 and had dropped to 19 percent in 1985. In other words, the tremendous growth in manufacturing output that has occurred throughout this century has been accomplished by increasing the productivity of workers through better material technology and organizational practices, not by hiring an ever-larger proportion of the labor force.

Two other trends have pervaded the occupational scene during the twentieth century in the United States and most other industrial nations. First, *the average number of hours worked per week has declined considerably.* Although we lack accurate figures for the nineteenth century, historical accounts suggest that work weeks of 60 or more hours were quite common, especially in manufacturing. In 1900, the average work week in the U.S. was 56 hours, but it began to decline steadily after that, primarily as a result of union efforts. The average figure in 1920 was 48 hours, and by 1940 it had fallen to slightly less than 40 hours per week. The 40-hour work week still prevails today in most occupations, although some clerical jobs require only 37.5 hours per week. At the same time, a small proportion of the work force (about 3 percent) "moonlights" on second jobs, which can add ten or even 20 more hours to an individual's total work week.

Second, *the proportion of women who are gainfully employed outside the home has risen sharply*, primarily since 1940. In that year, only 28 percent of all adult women held paying jobs, but by 1960 that figure was 38 percent, and in 1987 it had risen to 56 percent. In short, women have invaded the labor market in large numbers, first in response to the demands of World War II, and later as a result of such factors as family desires for larger total incomes, the increasing education of women, the declining number of children per family, the rising divorce rate that forces many women to be financially self-sufficient, and the emphasis of the Women's Liberation Movement on the right of women to be employed.

Let us now examine trends that have occurred in various types of urban occupations. Table 12-3 shows the proportion of the civilian labor force employed in seven broad urban occupational categories defined by the U.S. Census Bureau for five points in time: 1870, 1900, 1930, 1960, and 1985. In addition to discussing the major changes that have occurred in the distribution of occupations among these broad categories, the following paragraphs also mention significant shifts that have taken place within the various categories.

TABLE 12-3 Changes in the Urban Occupational Distribution of the United States, 1870–1985

Occupational Category	Percent of the Civilian Labor Force*				
	1870	*1900*	*1930*	*1960*	*1985*
Professional and technical workers	3	4	7	11	16
Managers, proprietors, and administrators	6	6	7	11	11
Clerical and sales workers	4	7	15	21	28
Skilled craft workers and foremen	9	11	13	13	12
Semiskilled operatives	6	13	16	18	15
Service workers	10	10	11	12	12
Unskilled laborers	9	12	11	5	4

* Percentages for each time period do not equal 100, because all agricultural workers are excluded.

Sources: U.S. Bureau of the Census, Statistical Abstract of the United States, 1987. Washington, D.C.: U.S. Government Printing Office, Table 657. U.S. Bureau of the Census, Historical Statistics of the United States. Washington, D.C.: U.S. Government Printing Office, 1975, Part 1, pp. 139–40.

Beginning with the category of *professional and technical workers,* we see a constant expansion from three percent of the work force in 1870 to 16 percent in 1985. Much of this growth has occurred in the newer professions such as science, engineering, and accounting, as well as in related technical fields such as laboratory and electronic technicians. The older professions—including medicine, law, and the ministry—have grown more slowly.

The occupational category of *managers, proprietors, and administrators* has not expanded so rapidly, increasing from six percent of the work force in 1870 to 11 percent in 1985. However, these figures hide an extremely important shift within this category. A hundred years ago, most of these people were self-employed owners of small businesses such as retail stores or service establishments. Today, a large majority of them are executives and managers within business firms or government agencies. Although many of these people exercise considerably more power and enjoy much higher incomes than the typical small independent businessperson, they are nevertheless employees of large organizations, not independent entrepreneurs.

The third category of *clerical and sales workers* has experienced by far the greatest growth as a result of the industrialization and bureaucratization of society. In 1870,

just four percent of the labor force was engaged in handling paper or selling goods. As seen in Table 12-3, that proportion has risen sharply, so that more than one-fourth of all employed persons now do this kind of work. Clerical and sales work have both experienced rapid expansion, although it has been considerably greater among office clerical workers. A large proportion of the additional clerical workers have been women, since office work is the most common type of employment for them.

Skilled craft workers include such trades as carpenters, machinists, electricians, plumbers, tool and die makers, and masons, as well as all foremen. There has been some growth in this area, from nine percent in 1870 to 12 percent in 1985, but on the whole this has been a fairly stable type of employment in terms of its proportion of the total labor force. In general, craft work depends as much on personal skills as on machinery, so that it has not been too greatly affected by mechanization or the growth of large business organizations.

Semiskilled operatives are all workers whose essential task is operating machinery, whether it be in a factory, a small shop, or on the road driving a truck. This kind of work expanded fairly steadily for a long period of time, rising from only six percent of the labor force in 1870 to 18 percent in 1960. Since then, however, it has declined somewhat, to 15 percent in 1985. This recent downturn is due to such trends as plant closings and automation in many industries.

The category of *service workers* encompasses all persons who perform a service rather than operate machinery. Its share of the labor force has also remained rather stable, rising just slightly from ten percent in 1870 to 12 percent in 1985. However, some forms of service work—such as household servants—have almost disappeared. Some forms—such as barbers, waitresses, and others who provide specialized personal services—have remained fairly constant. And still other forms—primarily public service workers such as police officers and mail carriers—have grown rapidly during this time period.

Finally, *unskilled laborers* are employed as construction laborers, custodians, dishwashers, garbage collectors, stevedores, and workers doing similar kinds of tasks. During the early stages of industrialization there was a steady demand for laborers, so that such jobs increased from nine percent of the labor force in 1870 to 12 percent in 1900, and were 11 percent as recently as 1930. The need for unskilled workers has declined rapidly in recent years, however, so that these people constituted only four percent of the work force in 1985.

Educational Attainments

As the distribution of occupations has shifted constantly toward urban and more highly skilled kinds of work, employers have demanded ever-increasing levels of education among their employees. At the turn of the century, an eighth-grade education was sufficient for most kinds of jobs. By mid-century, this expectation had risen to a high school diploma, and today more and more jobs require either technical training beyond secondary school or two to four years of college education. Consequently, *the educational attainment of the United States population has risen dramatically since World War II.* This trend can be demonstrated in two different ways. Although data on median years of schooling completed (among person age 25 or older) are only available beginning in 1940, in that year the median was still only 8.6 years. By 1960 it had risen to 10.6 years, and in 1985 it was 12.6 years. In other words, median education in this country has increased from grade school to high school in little more than one generation.

Alternatively, we can examine the proportion of the population completing secondary school. In 1870, only two percent of the adult population in the United States had graduated from high school, in 1900 that figure was still just six percent, and as late as 1940 only 25 percent of the population had completed high school. By 1960, however, that figure had risen to 41 percent, and in 1985 it was 76 percent. College students, meanwhile, constituted just 5 percent of the adult population in 1940, and by 1960 that proportion was still only eight percent. Since then, however, college education has become much more prevalent, so that in 1985 nearly 20 percent of all adults in this country had a bachelor's degree.

Job requirements are not the only reason for staying in school, of course, and many other factors have contributed to this pervasive trend in all industrial societies. Farming often demands that children assist their parents at planting and harvesting times, whereas urban childen are free to attend school full-time. Rising levels of family affluence enable more and more parents to afford to send their children to secondary school and college, rather than demanding that they go to work as early as possible. Also important is the fact that a rich society has more financial resources to invest in schools and teachers, thereby providing opportunities for children to stay in school longer.

SOCIOECONOMIC CONSEQUENCES OF CAPITALISM

The wealth, occupational, and educational trends examined in the previous section generally occur in all industrial societies, regardless of the nature of their economic system. In contrast, the five conditions discussed here are often attributed more directly to capitalism—especially corporate capitalism as it has developed in Western societies in the twentieth century. Since some of these conditions are also beginning to appear in the Soviet Union and other societies with noncapitalist economies, the extent to which they are consequences of capitalism rather than the more general process of industrialization is open to debate. Nevertheless, they are certainly all very evident in societies that have industrialized under capitalism.

Economic Insecurity

Despite the extent to which landowners grossly exploit peasants and farmers in agrarian societies, most of the agricultural workers in that kind of economy have some economic security. They generally retain traditional rights to work their plots of land regardless of economic conditions, and the landowners frequently have well-defined traditional responsibilities to protect and care for "their" peasants. The landowners and peasants are thus bound together by strong ties of fealty, which are much more encompassing and deep-seated than simple employment contracts.

In most capitalist industrial societies, however, labor is bought and sold in the labor market in much the same way as goods are exchanged. Employers and employees are linked together only by a labor contract, which is strictly economic in nature. If the employer no longer needs a job performed or prefers to hire someone else to do it, the employer has no moral responsibilities and few legal obligations to the employee, so that the employment contract can be fairly easily terminated. This situation means that *employees are vulnerable to fluctuations in the economy, changes in the labor marketplace, and arbitrary decisions by employers.* Employees can be laid off or fired with relatively little notice and thus be thrown back into the labor pool

of unemployed workers seeking jobs in the labor market. As a result, many workers experience a great deal of economic insecurity throughout their lives, never knowing if or when they might lose their jobs and be left with no income to support themselves and their families. As will be discussed shortly, labor unions have made great efforts to mitigate this problem, but with only limited success.

Unemployment figures for the United States during the twentieth century illustrate the vicissitudes of the labor market in capitalist societies (U.S. Bureau of the Census, 1975 and 1987). From 1900 through the 1920s, the unemployment rate remained fairly constant between five and six percent. By the beginning of the Great Depression in 1930, however, it had risen to almost nine percent, and at the height of the depression in 1933, fully 25 percent of the total labor force was unemployed. This rate remained quite high throughout the 1930s, despite the strenuous efforts of the Roosevelt administration to stimulate the economy, and was still almost 15 percent in 1940. Realistically, it was World War II that pulled the United States out of the depression, so that in 1944 the unemployment rate was only one percent. From the end of the war until the mid-1970s, this rate repeated the pattern of the early decades of the century, remaining between four and six percent, although there were brief economic slumps when the rate rose somewhat. With the economic problems of the late 1970s, however, unemployment again began to rise. In 1980 the national rate was seven percent, but some sections of the country were experiencing as high as ten percent unemployment. By 1985, some of the worst of those local unemployment situations (such as displaced auto workers) had eased somewhat, although the national unemployment rate remained at 7 percent. In short, *unemployment and its resulting economic insecurity has been a constant threat or reality for millions of workers in the United States throughout most of this century.*

At the same time, it must be noted that

some societies give workers much more economic security than does the United States. Throughout this century, for example, Sweden has generally kept its unemployment rate below three percent, and in Japan many employees enjoy the security of knowing that if they perform their work satisfactorily, their employer will provide a job for them for their entire lifetime.

Labor Unions

As individuals, workers are extremely vulnerable in the labor market because the exchange relationship between employer and employee is so heavily one-sided or unbalanced. Almost all the bargaining power lies on the side of the employer, especially for industrial and service workers who possess relatively few skills with which to negotiate for better jobs and higher wages. Consequently, *the only effective way in which many workers can exert any significant power in the labor market is to band together in labor unions, so that they can bargain collectively with employers.*

As early as the 1860s, Marx strongly advocated the creation of labor unions as a crucial means through which workers could counter the overwhelming power and exploitative practices of early capitalists. His call went largely unheeded for a long time, however, and not until the twentieth century did the labor movement begin to gain momentum in Western societies. In 1900, less than one million workers in the United States belonged to unions, but by 1914 that figure had grown to almost three million (Vatter, 1976:300); and by 1920 it had reached five million workers. The Great Depression of the 1930s provided a strong stimulus to the growth of unions. In 1933, union membership was still only six percent of the labor force, whereas in 1940 it had reached 16 percent, and by 1950 it was 22 percent. Since then, union membership in this country has remained relatively stable at just under one-fourth of the labor force (U.S. Bureau of the Census, 1975). The United States is not nearly as highly union-ized as many Western European nations, however, with the sharpest contrast being Sweden, where over 90 percent of all employees belong to a union.

Moreover, there is a crucial difference between European unions and those in North America. Although very few unions anywhere advocate the kind of radical transformation of society called for by Marx, labor unions in all Western European societies are quite closely linked to a political party that represents their interests within the political system—such as the Labour Party in Great Britain and the Social Democratic parties in France, West Germany, and the Scandinavian countries. These labor-oriented political parties continually press for legislation to improve working conditions, wages, and other employee benefits.

In the United States, linkages between the union movement and the Democratic party have always been rather loose and tenuous. With a two-party system—in contrast to the multiparty systems existing in West European nations—if the Democratic party is to attract a majority of all voters, it must present itself as an "all-purpose party" that represents a wide array of citizens' interests and concerns, rather than just as a labor party. In general, Democratic politicians have given more attention to the problems of workers than have Republicans, but they are generally less committed to the goals of the labor movement than are the leaders of European labor-based parties. And while it is true that the majority of blue-collar workers traditionally vote Democratic in the United States, large numbers of them do not hesitate to vote for popular Republican candidates for Congress and the Presidency. As a consequence of these political conditions, the union movement in the United States has been primarily limited to the economic realm and has had much less political strength than in most European nations.

Despite the relatively restrained and nonpolitical activities of American labor unions, for a long time most employers strongly resisted all efforts by workers to organize unions. Corporate leaders often refused to permit any union activities in their firms, summarily fired workers who attempted to form unions, and did not hesitate to call in the police or National Guard to break up labor demonstrations and strikes and cart the leaders off to jail for "disturbing the peace" or "inciting to riot." Conflicts between employers and workers reached a peak in 1919, when fully 20 percent of the entire labor force in the United States went on strike during that year.

The prosperity of the 1920s diminished the proportion of workers going on strike to under ten percent during that decade. In addition, during the 1920s and 1930s, labor unions were increasingly accepted by corporate leaders. *Employers slowly began to realize that unions were not a serious threat to their businesses and that by accepting unions and meeting some of their demands for better wages, the corporation actually benefited in three important ways.*

(1) Unions guaranteed a more stable supply of disciplined workers willing to work at a predictable wage.
(2) It was often much easier for employers to bargain with a few union leaders than with masses of unorganized workers.
(3) Paying somewhat higher wages to workers kept them more committed to the company and more able to purchase the goods they were producing, thus expanding the market for those goods.

Since World War II, labor unions have become a fully accepted part of the American economy. Union-management negotiations now occur on a regular basis in most industries, with representatives from both sides negotiating labor contracts specifying hiring practices, wages, fringe benefits, working conditions, job security, retirement, and other concerns of workers. The percentage of the labor force who have gone on strike to attain their objectives has remained under five percent every year since 1950 and less than three percent since 1972.

Advertising and Consumerism

In nonindustrial societies, individuals and families directly produce many of the goods and services they require, or else they trade with other people in the local community for those items. In modern industrial societies, in contrast, most of what we need is produced by business corporations and purchased in the marketplace. Consequently, the goods and services that are available to us, the prices we pay for them, and even our conceptions of what we need or want are determined by corporations.

Long ago Marx argued that if a capitalist economy is to remain viable, it must continually grow. Most businesspersons continue to accept that belief without question. Consequently, they commonly assume that business firms cannot rely simply on supplying the current material needs of the society but must constantly expand their markets and increase their sales in order to maintain their profits in the face of competition. Growth of businesses and the total economy can be achieved in several ways.

(1) By paying higher wages to employees, more people are able to purchase more commodities, thus expanding the market.
(2) By undertaking marketing activities in new geographical areas or in foreign countries, the number of potential customers is increased.
(3) By producing goods of mediocre quality that quickly wear out, consumers are forced to keep buying new goods.
(4) Through research and development of new products, additional markets can be created.
(5) Most importantly, effective advertising can induce many people to want more and newer goods and services and to believe that items that were once considered luxuries are really necessities that they must acquire.

Mass advertising is thus a key aspect of what John Kenneth Galbraith called "demand management" of the economy, the purpose of which is "to insure that people buy what is produced," (Galbraith, 1967:203).

Business corporations in capitalist economies annually spend many billions of dollars on advertising to create consumer demands for their products. For example, soap and detergent firms spend 20 percent of all sales revenues on advertising, and Procter and Gamble (the nation's largest advertiser) alone spends almost half a billion dollars annually for advertising (Zim, 1978:54). Or consider the fact that drug firms spend four times more on advertising than they do on research to develop new drugs (Green, 1972:13). Advertising one's goods or services is unquestionably a necessary practice for all businesses—even the smallest local firms. What concerns many observers are the huge amounts of money that are poured into advertising, plus the consequences of mass corporate advertising for both individuals and society.

One of those consequences is that advertising is designed to *create perceived desires or needs for products* that are frequently frivolous or totally unnecessary. Mass corporate advertising does not simply tell consumers where or how to obtain goods and services they genuinely require. It creates their desires and demands for products and may induce them to spend their money foolishly or go deeply in debt to obtain still more consumer goods.

Second, by continually stressing the importance of possessing the newest and "most advanced" version of all products, advertising promotes the *planned artificial obsolescence of goods*, which can become extremely wasteful. Even though your present refrigerator may be totally adequate, advertising may attempt to convince you that it is obsolete because it does not have a built-in ice water dispenser, so that you should junk it and spend $1,200 for a new one with such a gadget.

Third, advertisers exert tremendous influence over the *content of the mass media*, especially television. In the printed media, advertisers merely buy space and do not sponsor particular articles. They may, of course, refuse to advertise in publications whose articles they do not like. In television,

however, advertisers sponsor particular programs and hence can directly influence what is presented or not presented to the public. A program that deals with a vital but controversial issue or that takes an unpopular stance toward such an issue may never be broadcast because no advertisers will sponsor it.

Fourth, mass corporate advertising stresses the importance of constantly *consuming goods and services* and becoming a "good consumer." The act of consumption becomes an end in itself, the role of consumer becomes of great concern to many people, and "sophisticated consumption" of everything from cars to wines becomes an important goal in people's lives. This process of "commodity fetishism" was one of Marx's strongest criticisms of capitalism, since it diverts people's attention away from more important human concerns, such as eliminating exploitation of disadvantaged groups or fulfilling one's personal capabilities. As a result, Marx argued, people become alienated from one another and from themselves.

Finally, as an outgrowth of all the preceding consequences of pervasive advertising and consumerism, *materialism has become a dominant value* within the cultures of contemporary Western societies. We have come to value the possession and use of material goods above virtually all other aspects of life, insist many social critics. Other cultures throughout human history—including contemporary non-Western societies—have placed primary emphasis on such non-material values as interpersonal relationships, religious faith, intellectual development, personal fulfillment, or family responsibilities. Contemporary Western societies, in contrast, have tended to enshrine materialism as the most important value in human life.

Concentration of Wealth and Power

As we have seen, advanced industrialization produces enormous amounts of wealth in a society. *Within capitalist economies, wealth—and the power it conveys to its owners—tends to be highly concentrated in a tiny minority of the population.* For convenience, we refer to these people as the controlling stratum of a society. The following illustrative data are for the United States, but the situation is fairly similar in most other industrialized capitalist societies.

Let us arbitrarily define the controlling stratum in American society as the wealthiest one-half percent of the population, which is about 1.2 million people. Most of the heads of these households are either top executives in major corporations or professionals. In 1975, these families had annual incomes of $85,000 or more (Dalphin, 1981:26), so that by 1985 that figure was probably over $150,000, as a result of economic growth and inflation. Although exact figures on their current total wealth are not available, in 1962 the average wealth of these families was more than $500,000, and in 1979 that figure was over $1 million. We also know that *in 1975 this one-half percent of the population owned approximately 20 percent of all private wealth in this country.* Moreover they owned 80 percent of all trusts and 50 percent of all privately owned corporate stocks and bonds (Dalphin, 1981:28). These figures vividly illustrate the extent to which great wealth is enormously concentrated in a very tiny minority of the American public.

This controlling stratum of American society effectively controls the corporate system of the country in three ways. (1) *Ownership of corporate stock.* As previously noted, the controlling stratum owns at least half of all privately owned stock. Some of these people own large blocks of stock in one or more corporations. However, because stock ownership in most corporations is widely distributed among thousands of stockholders, ownership of as little as five percent of the stock in a corporation is often adequate to control its activities. Consequently, even if an individual or family holds only a small block of stock in a particular corporation, those holdings are often sufficient to enable it to influence or control that company. (2) *Holding top cor-*

porate executive positions. Not all corporate executives belong to the controlling stratum, but those in top positions—presidents and vice-presidents—of the largest corporations generally do. In addition to their salaries (which are usually in six figures and may be as high as $1 million or more per year), top executives commonly receive extensive fringe benefits, large expense accounts, non-monetary corporate privileges (cars, use of company resorts, etc.), and options that entitle them to purchase stock in the corporation below current market prices. (3) *Membership on corporate board of directors.* Most of the board positions in major corporations are filled by top corporate executives, either from that company or from other corporations with which it does business. Most of these people belong to the controlling stratum. Moreover, most corporate boards are self-perpetuating oligarchies that select their own members (although those selections must be legitimated by the stockholders), so that they are generally able to restrict their membership to high-status individuals.

All three of these bases of corporate power are typically highly interrelated. Holders of top executive positions also sit on corporate boards of directors, and they commonly own large amounts of corporate stock. This situation recently led John Dalphin (1981:53) to conclude that: "The upper class owns and controls the economic system. . . ."

Public and Environmental Irresponsibility

The purpose of capitalism as an economic system is to make financial profits for the owners and managers of private businesses. *In principle, capitalism is totally unconcerned with providing collective public services or protecting the natural environment.* Regardless of the validity of Adam Smith's thesis that the invisible hand of the marketplace will ensure that people's needs are adequately served by private enterprise, his theory of market capitalism pertained only to goods and services whose production or distribution generates a profit for someone. When activities do not generate profits, capitalist economies are typically quite ineffective in ensuring that they are performed, regardless of how necessary or desirable they may be. This situation is most pronounced with public services such as education and sanitation and recently has become very evident with environmental problems, such as pollution and depletion of nonrenewable resources.

Actions that are totally rational from the perspective of an individual seeking to maximize profits in the marketplace can have disastrous consequences for the public welfare or the natural environment. The unanticipated linkage between individual rational economic action and public and environmental tragedy has been graphically described by ecologist Garrett Hardin (1968:1245–46) as the "Tragedy of the Commons." Although it refers to preindustrial England, it is equally applicable to all capitalist industrial societies.

Picture a pasture open to all. It is to be expected that each herdsman will try to keep as many cattle as possible on the commons. Such an arrangement may work reasonably satisfactorily for centuries because tribal wars, poaching, and disease keep the numbers of both man and beast well below the carrying capacity of the land. Finally, however, comes the day of reckoning. . . . As a rational being, each herdsman seeks to maximize his gain. . . . [He] concludes that the only sensible course for him to pursue is to add another animal to his herd. And another and another. . . . But this is the conclusion reached by each and every rational herdsman sharing a commons. . . . Each man is locked into a system that compels him to increase his herd without limit— in a world that is limited. Ruin is the destination toward which all men rush, each pursuing his own best interest in a society that believes in the freedom on the commons.

The full "tragedy of the capitalist commons" is even greater than depicted by Hardin. Rational economic self-interest not only destroys irreplaceable natural resources (e.g., petroleum), but also adds additional pollutants to the environment (e.g., toxic wastes), fails to provide many kinds of public services that

> ## SOCIOECONOMIC CONSEQUENCES OF CAPITALISM
> 1. Economic insecurity.
> 2. Labor union membership.
> 3. Advertising and consumerism.
> 4. Concentration of wealth and power.
> 5. Public and environmental irresponsibility.

are vital for human welfare (e.g., public health programs), and fosters the production of goods that are unsafe or harmful to people (e.g., Corvair cars).

Industrial capitalism has served the owners and managers of corporations extremely well, bringing them greater wealth and power than ever before possessed by any elite class in any society. It has served most professional, technical, and other white-collar workers quite well, creating well-paying jobs for them that do not exist in agrarian societies. It has served the bulk of blue-collar workers moderately well, providing the jobs they needed as they moved from rural to urban living, and also steadily raising their incomes so that they can live fairly comfortably. It has not, however, solved the problems of gross economic inequality, persistent class exploitation, or ever-present grinding poverty for many. Moreover, *capitalist economic systems have failed miserably and irresponsibly to provide citizens with many kinds of "public goods"* from clean air to quality education to fine arts. As expressed by John Kenneth Galbraith (1958), modern industrial corporate capitalism has succeeded in creating vast "private affluence" together with deplorable "public squalor."

SUMMARY

Under mercantilism, the economy serves as a tool of the political state to increase its wealth and power. The state directs the economy to serve those goals, not to meet the needs of the population. With traditional market capitalism, all economic enterprises are privately owned and operate within an unregulated free market, seeking to maximize their profits. Economic competition obeys the law of supply and demand, so that the invisible hand of market competition presumably ensures that the supply of available products remains in balance with the demand for them, and that prices are kept at reasonable levels. The idea of regulated capitalism arose as a response to imperfect competition in markets. To keep the economy functioning properly, government must impose a visible hand by formulating and enforcing monetary, fiscal, corporate, and distributive policies. Through such regulation, the economy presumably serves the needs of the entire society.

Welfarism asserts that the society as a whole has a responsibility to ensure that all its members receive at least minimal economic benefits. The emergence of this belief can be attributed to rational economic considerations and new cultural values. Socialism assumes that all societies rest on an economic foundation, especially the dominant mode of production in that society. Whoever owns and controls that mode of production will be extremely powerful. To eliminate that powerful elite class and its exploitive economic and political practices, socialism argues that the major means of economic production must be publicly owned.

In modern capitalist economies, the major business firms are privately owned corporations that operate on the profit motive but seek to minimize and control market competition. Their fundamental goal is always to make a profit, they are extremely wealthy, most corporate stock is owned by a small set of wealthy families and by other businesses and banks, their internal structure of authority is hierarchical in form, and most corporate policies are formulated by its board of directors.

The large business corporations within capitalist economies constitute an interwoven corporate system. They are interrelated through horizontal, vertical, and conglomerate corporate mergers, interlocking

directorates, and legal and illegal operating practices. In addition, the growth of multinational corporations is rapidly creating a single worldwide economic system. These corporations are immensely wealthy and are becoming major world economic and political powers. In addition to this industrial system of large corporations, capitalist economies also contain an entrepreneurial system of small businesses that are not very wealthy or powerful.

Corporations exert influence on government in many different ways in an effort to create conditions favorable to private business. Because government depends on the corporations to maintain a stable economy and a constant flow of revenues, government is continually concerned to keep the economy healthy and is therefore quite vulnerable to influences from the corporations. Corporations also contribute heavily to political campaigns, they supply many high-level executives for top government positions, and through lobbyists and advisory organizations, they provide a great deal of information to legislators and government agencies.

The process of industrialization has numerous socioeconomic consequences for all societies. The most direct of these is an immense increase in total wealth and personal income. A second consequence is a massive shift from agricultural to urban employment. Most types of urban occupations tend to expand with industrialization, with the largest increases occurring in the categories of professional and technical workers, managers and administrators, and clerical and sales workers. In addition, the hours in the work week have dropped significantly, and large numbers of women have entered the labor market. A final consequence of industrialization is that the average educational attainment of the population has risen steadily.

Capitalism, as a particular kind of economy, also has numerous consequences for individuals and societies. Because all employees, but especially blue-collar workers, have no claims to their jobs beyond their labor contract, they are quite vulnerable to economic changes. Unemployment and its resulting economic insecurity has been a constant threat or reality for many workers. To increase their bargaining power in the labor market, workers can organize themselves into labor unions. In the United States, unions operate mainly within the economic system and have never enrolled more than one-fourth of the labor force. In Western Europe, unions are generally closely linked with a political party, and much larger proportions of the labor force are unionized.

Capitalism depends heavily on advertising to expand markets and increase sales, which results in demand management of the economy. Advertising is a huge industry that seeks to create desires and needs, promote planned obsolescence, and influence the mass media. As a result, consumption becomes a major concern and activity of many people, and materialism becomes a dominant cultural value. Wealth and power are highly concentrated in a tiny proportion of the population in industrialized capitalist societies. This controlling stratum is immensely wealthy, owns large amounts of corporate stock, contains most members of corporate boards of directions, and holds most top executive positions within corporations.

Because capitalism is concerned with making profits for private firms, it tends to neglect both public services and environmental protection. Although individuals may act rationally in pursuit of their private gains, collectively those actions can lead to a "tragedy of the commons" with resource depletion, environmental pollution, inadequate public services, and dangerous products.

CHAPTER 13

MODERN POLITIES

How can modern political systems be described in terms of their
components, functions, and structures?

To what extent are all political systems oligarchical and repressive?

What is political democracy as viewed from classical, representative, party,
pluralist, and participatory perspectives?

In what ways does the government influence the economy in modern
capitalist industrial societies?

To what extent and in what ways do individuals participate in the political
system?

POLITICAL SYSTEMS

Although the economy is in many respects the dominant institution within modern industrial societies, the polity is of nearly equal importance. Through its political system, a society (or any other type of social organization) makes collective decisions and acts to attain collective goals. In modern societies, as we have already noted repeatedly, the economic and political systems are so highly interwoven that we often refer to them together as the "political economy." Nevertheless, sociologists frequently examine the polity as a separate institution, or system, with its own distinct characteristics and activities.

More specifically, *a polity is an interrelated network or system of beliefs* (e.g., concerning decision making, administration, obligations, and authority), *activities* (e.g, policy formation, program implementation, legal adjudication), *organizations* (e.g., legislatures, executive agencies, courts, political parties), *and relationships* (e.g., communication, legiti-macy, authority, enforcement) *that directs and regulates the collective functioning of a society or other organization.* In this chapter, the two terms "polity" and "political system" are used synonymously, as were "economy" and "economic system" in the previous chapter.

This first section discusses the nature of polities in terms of their various components, the kinds of functions commonly performed by governments, and the power structures of states and governments that are invariably dominated by small sets of elites.

Components

At the societal level, the principal components of political systems are states, governments, and political parties. Each of these components is described in the following paragraphs in terms of societal politics.

A state is the arrangement of political authority and other forms of political power within a society. The authority of the state rests on legitimacy granted to it as a result of cultural beliefs such as the "divine right of kings" or the right of citizens to form a government. As a consequence of this legitimacy, the state exercises ultimate sovereignty in a society. It can therefore make final authoritative decisions and exert power to enforce those decisions. This power system may be highly centralized in one person (King Louis XIV of France once insisted that "l'état, c'est moi" or "I am the state") or a small clique of military leaders. Conversely, it may be quite decentralized into many partially autonomous fiefdoms (as in a feudal society) or geographical regions (as in the semiautonomous cantons of Switzerland). The United States lies somewhere near the middle of this continuum, with the federal government exercising considerable centralized power while the various states retain jurisdiction over many other activities.

A government is the set of formal organizations that enact the power of the state and govern a society or one of its political subdivisions. Governments in Western societies are commonly divided into three main branches: a legislative branch (with either one or two houses) that makes the laws, an executive branch (with innumerable departments and agencies) that enacts those laws, and a judicial branch (with numerous courts) that enforces the laws. It should be added, however, that social scientists sometimes refer to additional branches of government, such as regulatory agencies or the military, which operate with considerable autonomy in some societies. Governments in many non-Western societies, in contrast, often merge the three main branches into one "all-purpose" organization, either formally (as in a military dictatorship) or informally (as when the ruling political party effectively controls all three branches, even though they are technically distinct). In addition to the national government, political systems also contain hundreds or thousands of local governments, including major geographical subdivisions (states in the United States, provinces in Canada, or departments in France), minor geographical units (counties, districts, town-

ships), city and town governments, and special-purpose units (such as school districts and water boards).

In the contemporary world, *the terms "nation" or "nation-state" usually refer to societies in which the state and its government are coterminous* (i.e., share common boundaries) *with the total society.* A nation is thus a modern society viewed from a political perspective. However, not all societies are nations, and not all nations are societies. Many citizens of East Germany and West Germany still think of themselves as belonging to a single society with a unique German culture, despite the fact that they have been divided into two separate nations since the end of World War II. Forty-five years later, they are moving to reunite that society. Conversely, many of the current nations in Africa contain two or more traditionally distinct tribal societies.

The polity of a modern nation also includes one or more political parties that functions within the political system. *A political party is a private association of persons with similar political ideologies and opinions that promotes candidates for public office and seeks to influence the government.* Although parties have no formal governmental status (they are not mentioned in the United States Constitution), they can become extremely powerful within a modern nation. A party sometimes dominates the formal government, as in the Soviet Union, in which the most powerful political position (until 1990) was First Secretary of the Communist Party, not the President. Political parties are not that powerful in Western societies, but they can be quite influential in nominating candidates for public office and shaping national political policies.

Other components of national political systems frequently include political interest associations (such as Common Cause and the American Civil Liberties Union in the United States); nonpolitical interest associations (such as the National Association of Manufacturers or labor unions) when they choose to enter the political arena; political policy advisory associations (such as the Heritage Foundation and the Brookings Institution), political action committees (PACs) that are formed to promote specific political causes; and news activities of the mass media. Because sociologists are generally most interested in relationships between the government and the total society, they often given considerable attention to these nongovernmental components of the national political system.

Functions

Social scientists frequently analyze political systems by examining the functions performed by governments. This kind of analysis seeks to identify the functions, or services, that governments perform for the larger society and its members. Those functions may be beneficial, neutral, or harmful, although primary attention is usually given to positive, or beneficial, outcomes. The most frequently mentioned functions performed by governments in modern societies are sketched in the following paragraphs (Easton, 1965).

External Protection. Since antiquity, political analysts have maintained that the first function of any national government is to *protect its society and citizens from external threats.* Most directly, this involves establishing a strong military organization and using military force when necessary to prevent invasion or conquest by another society. At times, moreover, this defensive function is interpreted to require and justify attacks on other nations when they are perceived as threats to the vital interests (usually territorial or economic) of the society. Consequently, throughout human history the function of national defense has frequently been transformed into military aggression. In addition to military actions, this external protection function also involves establishing and maintaining diplomatic relationships with other societies, negotiating with them over treaties and pacts, and participating in international organizations such as the United Nations. These nonmilitary interna-tional activities may be directed toward many different goals—such as creating commercial ties with other nations or preventing the spread of communicable diseases—but their ultimate justification is always protection of the interests and well-being of the society against external threats or disruptions, as well as maintaining the power of the state in relation to other states.

Internal Order. The second most important function of any government is usually said to be *preserving order and stability within its jurisdiction.* Again, the most direct expression of this function involves using coercion to prevent or control domestic riots, rebellions, or revolutions. On the individual level, it also involves use of the police power of the state to punish persons who commit crimes. To perform these functions, governments enact laws, maintain internal military forces (e.g., the National Guard in the United States), create police departments, and operate courts and detention facilities (e.g., prisons and rehabilitation centers). More indirectly, governments promote ideologies that explain the existing political order and legitimize its values and activities. Governments also reinforce social norms and rules ("Drive carefully" or "Don't litter"), and act as a mediator in resolving conflicts between various groups and organizations (such as labor-management disputes or interracial clashes). The ultimate justification for all such governmental activities is preservation of domestic order and social stability.

Economic Support. As we saw in the previous chapter, governments are always highly dependent on the economic system for financial resources, as well as to satisfy the material needs of the population and maintain economic stability. Consequently, a third function of all governments is to *support and enhance the economy.* To accomplish this objective, governments undertake such diverse activities as facilitating capital accumulation, providing tax incentives and benefits to industries, imposing tariffs and quotas on imported goods, establishing national

agencies, bureaucrats and technicians who operate those agencies, and communicators and propagandists who disseminate elite ideologies and values. (6) As societies and their political systems become increasingly large, the power of the elite class tends to be less visible because it is imbedded within established complex governmental organizations, but at the same time it becomes more pervasive and effective. (7) Elites may permit or even encourage limited social change within the society, but only to the extent that they see it as contributing to the goals they seek and not threatening their power. However, major transformation of the entire society—such as a shift from an agricultural to an industrial economy—are usually strongly resisted by established elites. Those fundamental societal transformations typically require the emergence of a new set of elites with a different power base who are able to replace or overthrow the old elite class.

In sum, elite theory argues that *to understand both social order and social change within any society, we must understand the power base, organizational structure, and power exertion of its dominant political and other elites.*

Causes of Elitism. Elite theorists generally agree on all of the preceding tenets of this perspective. There is considerable disagreement, however, on the underlying causes of elitism in society. Depending on the nature of their casual explanation, elite theorists may view the existence of elites as socially beneficial, regrettable but inescapable, or morally intolerable. The three principal formulators of elite theory—the Italian economist Vilfredo Pareto (1848–1923), his student, the political historian Gaetano Mosca (1858–1931), and the Italian-German sociologist Robert Michels (1876–1936)—each offered a different explanation of the existence of elites.

Pareto (1935) believed that elites are characterized by certain kinds of inherent abilities, such as organizing activities or manipulating people. Mosca (1939) agreed that

elites are often superior individuals in terms of ambition, drive, capacity for work, strength of will, and self-confidence. In addition, the eventual winners in the continual struggle for power and preeminence in society tend to come from privileged family backgrounds (which gives them a tremendous advantage over others), and usually represent the major economic, political, social, cultural, or other forces in their society.

Michels (1962) offered a much more extensive set of arguments to explain the existence of elites in all organizations. These causes of elite structures can be divided into three categories. (1) *Structurally,* all societies and other organizations are arranged into hierarchies of authority, so that those who occupy positions at the top of that structure are able to exercise legitimate authority throughout the entire organization. Even when ultimate authority is vested in the entire membership, organizational requirements for decision making and coordination result in that authority being delegated to and wielded by individuals located at the top of the structure. (2) *Operationally,* organizational leaders are able to control many kinds of organizational resources by virtue of their leadership roles and actions. These resources include experience in running the organization, established legitimacy, control of organizational finances and communications, the right to place people into organizational positions and reward or punish their actions, interpersonal relationships they create in the organization, and the aura of indispensability that develops around them as they lead the organization. (3) *Psychologically,* many ordinary members of organizations tend to be apathetic and indifferent toward organizational problems outside their immediate roles and are uninterested in assuming leadership tasks and responsibilities. They therefore welcome and desire leadership from above. As a result of all these observations, Michels formulated his "Iron Law of Oligarchy," which states that "Who says organization, says oligarchy" (p. 365).

POLITICAL OLIGARCHY

Oligarchy means rule by a few over the many. One of the first recorded uses of this term was by Aristotle over two thousand years ago, but it is equally applicable to contemporary political systems and other power structures. When applied to the political economies of modern societies, it often includes economic and other powerful elites as well as political leaders, although our focus here is primarily on government.

Oligarchic Democracy

The phrase "oligarchic democracy" may sound like a contradiction in terms, since democracy implies that political authority lies ultimately with all the citizens (however "citizen" is defined). In reality, nevertheless, *a considerable amount of oligarchy exists in the political systems of all democratic societies.* Behind the political procedures of campaigns, conventions, and elections, the real power of the state is typically concentrated in a very small set of political elites.

The reality of political oligarchy operating behind a facade of democracy is most evident in the Soviet Union. The constitution of the U.S.S.R. proclaims its political system to be a democracy and guarantees all adult citizens the right to vote. Elections are held periodically to elect representatives to its legislature, the Supreme Soviet, which meets when called to pass legislation and elect the national President. There are two limitations on the actual power of the Supreme Soviet, however. First, because (prior to 1990) there was only one political party—the Communist party of the U.S.S.R.—all candidates for the Supreme Soviet (prior to the 1989 election) have been uncontested and had to be party members or be approved by the party. Second, virtually all political decision-making has, until very recently, occurred within the inner ranks of the party, and the only function of the Supreme Soviet—prior to 1989—has been to ratify and legitimate those party decisions.

Other organizations and their leaders outside the party elite can sometimes influence national policies in the U.S.S.R. Industrial managers, scientists, engineers, economists, educators, and military leaders, for example, are periodically consulted on policy proposals, or may even bring uninvited pressure to bear on the party elites concerning specific issues. All of this does not negate the fundamental fact, however, that the political system of the U.S.S.R. has been extremely oligarchic in its structure and functioning.

Although political oligarchy clearly exists in the Soviet Union, we are repeatedly told that Western political systems are truly democratic. It is certainly true that competitive political parties exist in all Western societies, and that the formal government exercises political authority over the parties in all these countries. It is also true that for the past two hundred years there has been a continual struggle to establish meaningful democracy in Western societies by involving citizens in free elections and other forms of political decision making. Nevertheless, it is imperative that we not blind ourselves to the political realities of our own society. We must examine the power structures and governmental operations of Western nations to determine the extent to which they are in fact oligarchic in nature. Political scientists and sociologists have conducted considerable research on this question during the past several decades and have collected overwhelming evidence that extensive oligarchy does exist despite our democratic ideology and political practices. A sample of that research is summarized in this section. For simplicity, these examples are drawn only from the United States, but quite similar findings have been reported for all other Western nations.

Elitist Power Studies

By far the best known study of the national power structure of the United States is C. Wright Mills's *The Power Elite* (1956). Although published over thirty years ago, it is still the starting point for all sociological research on this topic. Mills began by arguing that the principal centers of power in modern societies are their major institutional networks and the large organizations that constitute those institutions. The dominant institutions in these societies are the economy, the polity, and the military. Mills examined each of those three institutions in considerable detail, demonstrating that over the past century each of them has become enormously large, extremely complex, and immensely powerful. Moreover, *in each realm the exercise of power has become highly centralized in a small set of top positions*—generally not more than 100 to 200. In the economy, these are the chief executives (the chairman of the board and the president) of the largest corporations and banks. In the polity, they are almost entirely within the executive branch of the federal government (the President and his staff, cabinet members, and heads of major agencies). In the military, they are the top-ranking generals and admirals (centering in the Joint Chiefs of Staff). Notice that it is the positions that carry power because of their command of these institutional realms; the men who occupy those positions (they were then and still are almost entirely men) exercise power only as long as they are in those positions.

Mills then argued that since World War II these three major institutions—and especially their top positions—have become increasingly interrelated and interwoven. Consequently, he maintained, *there are no longer three separate sets of institutional elites, but one integrated national power elite that rules the country.* "By the power elite, we refer to those political, economic, and military circles which as an intricate set of overlapping cliques share decisions having at least national consequences" (p. 18). He gave three reasons for this institutional and elite coalescence:

(1) Structural overlapping and functional interdependence, so that all three realms are highly interdependent and must coordinate their interrelated activities;

(2) International demands and pressures, stemming from our global interdependence and the Cold War, that force the three realms to act in unision in relationships with other countries; and

(3) Similarity among the people occupying the top positions in the three realms, which results from their common social backgrounds and values, their frequent interaction, and their periodic job shifts from one realm to another.

Mills did not suggest that there was any kind of hidden conspiracy among the power elite to dominate society, but rather that their responsibilities and activities require them to work together as a single entity. *Out of this cooperation at the highest levels of power come the major policy decisions that shape and influence the entire nation.*

Below the power elite, in Mills's model of society, lies a "middle level of power." It is composed of Congress, the judicial system, state and local governments, political parties, professional and business associations, labor unions, and many other kinds of organizations. When we read about issues being debated, political leaders opposing one another, and organizations conflicting over policies and programs, we are observing the activities of this middle level of power, not the power elite. The elites define the fundamental issues and determine the basic agenda of public politics, but they operate largely in private, behind the scenes, Mills insisted. Once they have established an underlying policy framework for society, they leave the process of thrashing out the operational details of those policies to middle-level organizations. Finally, at the bottom of this power structure is the mass of ordinary citizens who are, in Mills's analysis, virtually impotent in determining any important political or other decisions that affect the society. The structure of power in the United States, according to Mills, is diagramed in Figure 13-1.

FIGURE 13-1 Mill's model of the United States power structure

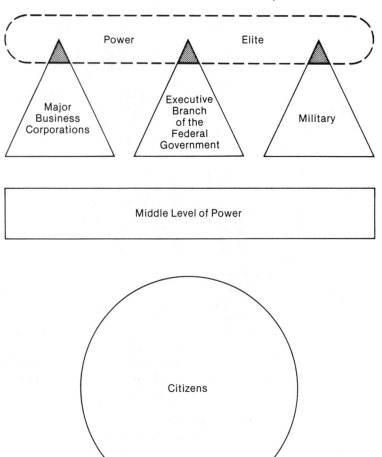

Subsequent researchers have elaborated or modified Mills's conclusions in various ways, but very few of them have disputed his basic thesis that power is highly centralized in contemporary United States society. For instance, three years after Mills's work, Floyd Hunter (1959) used a different methodological technique to identify what he called the "top leadership" of this country. Instead of looking at institutional structures and positions, he employed what is called the "reputational method." This procedure in- volves asking knowledgeable individuals, or "key informants," to name the people they believe exercise the most power in the soci- ety. Persons who are repeatedly named by many key informants are then presumed to be the top leaders, on the basis of their repu- tation as critical power wielders. In this man- ner, Hunter located 100 men who were con- sistently named as top national leaders. In agreement with Mills, most of these people held elite positions in the federal govern- ment, the major corporations, or the military. Hunter did not believe that they had coalesced into a single power elite to the extent claimed by Mills, but he did discover *a considerable amount of interlocking and cooperation among all the top leaders,* based primarily on their common concerns and interrelated roles.

Another variation on this theme is provided by G. William Domhoff in a series of studies beginning in 1967 and extending to the present (Domhoff, 1967, 1990). His research typically begins by identifying a set of persons who occupy top positions in the federal government and the major corporations. He then examines their social class standings in terms of family background, education, wealth, and listing in upper class social registers. He has consistently found that *almost all occupants of powerful positions also belong to an identifiable upper social class.* As a result, they tend to hold similar beliefs and values, share a common consciousness of purpose, and constitute a relatively closed and cohesive social unit, which Domhoff calls the "governing class."

The only feature of Mills's model of the United States power structure on which there is considerable disagreement among researchers is the extent to which powerful elites form a single ruling group. A number of social scientists (Keller, 1963; Bachrach, 1966; Dye and Zeigler, 1978) have argued that because of the increasing diversity and complexity of modern societies, no one set of elites is capable of making decisions and controlling activities across all institutional spheres. They agree with Mills that within each institutional arena there is considerable power concentration, resulting in a small set of powerful elites who largely dominate their sphere of activities. In other words, there are sets of economic elites, political elites, military elites, labor elites, communication elites, scientific elites, legal and judicial elites, educational elites, medical elites, cultural elites, sports elites, and so on. In disagreement with Mills, however, these writers argue that *the various sets of elites are relatively distinct and do not constitute a single*

unified power elite. Consequently, there is considerable conflict, bargaining, and power balancing among the various sets of elites. Suzanne Keller (1963) used the term "strategic elites" to indicate that each set of elites performs certain strategic functions within a defined sphere of activity. Other writers refer to them as "multiple elites" or "plural elites."

Finally, Gwen Moore (1979) discovered that within the network of national elites in the United States there is both diversification and concentration of power. Among almost 900 elites representing twelve major institutional sectors of society, she identified 31 relatively closed circles of interaction, each of which tended to focus on one particular issue area. Those specialized groups rarely contained more than 30 people, and there were relatively few overlapping membership or interaction linkages among any of them. In addition, however, she found one large "Central Circle" containing over 200 people who did not specialize in any particular issue area. Virtually all of the specialized circles of elites were linked with the Central Circle by numerous overlapping memberships and interaction linkages. Moore concluded that the major functions performed by the Central Circle of top elites were promoting communication among the small specialized groups of elites and resolving conflicts between them. In sum, *most national elites operate within small issue-specialized groups, but there is also an inner circle of power elites who coordinate the entire elite network.*

Governmental Repression

Social scientists who discuss the oligarchical nature of all modern governments are often highly critical of these power structures. Their basic argument is that as a result of governmental oligarchy, the state inevitably oppresses and represses the mass of ordinary citizens in order to maintain social and political order in society. Although these writers—such as C. Wright Mills—do not deny that modern governments perform many necessary and beneficial functions, they frequently ask the question: "Who benefits from these functions, and in what ways?" In general, their answer is that many governmental activities benefit primarily the dominant political and economic elites, the major corporations, and the more privileged classes in society.

The origin of this critical view of the state and government is often attributed to the French political philosopher Jean Jacques Rousseau (1712–89), whose writings provided much of the inspiration for the French Revolution and the American Declaration of Independence. French and American democracy are thus outgrowths of political analyses which stressed the extent to which governments repress their citizens. The writer who is most closely associated with this perspective, however, is Karl Marx, who was deeply influenced by Rousseau and other democratic theorists. One of his major concerns was how societies must be organized to ensure that democracy, rather than elitism, prevails throughout social life, so that all individuals are able to realize their full human potential, rather than being merely pawns in a societal chess game dominated by powerful rulers. Marx's historical analyses convinced him that whoever owns and controls the major means of economic production in a society will always exercise dominant power throughout that society. In all past and present societies, the dominant economic elites—the landed nobility in feudal societies and the industrial owners and managers in capitalist societies—have largely controlled the political system and used it to protect and promote their special interests and goals. This thinking led Marx to the conclusion that the only way of ensuring that state power and governmental organizations truly serve the interests of the entire society and all citizens is for the major means of economic production to be publicly owned and controlled. Economic and political power would then be shared by all. *Thus socialism, in its fullest development, is much more than just a type of economy; it is meant to be a way of organizing an entire society that promotes political democ-*

racy by empowering all citizens and eliminating government repression.

Contemporary social scientists who have been influenced by Marx tend to emphasize social conflict as a vital key to understanding modern societies and their political systems. They argue that relationships between the ruling class of economic and political elites (the bourgeoisie in capitalist societies) and the mass of ordinary workers (the proletariat in capitalist societies) have always been characterized by domination, exploitation, and potential or overt class conflict. To understand the primary social forces and tensions in past and present societies, therefore, they examine the dynamics of class and other forms of social conflict. In the future, they insist, if societies are to be radically transformed to eliminate domination and exploitation by elites, citizens must organize themselves so that they are capable of taking over the power now wielded by economic and political elites. Marx hoped that this process could be achieved through peaceful democratic means, and he looked to the United States—during Lincoln's presidency—to set an example for other societies. However, Marx's knowledge of the extent to which elites always resist change led him to believe that in most societies such change could only be achieved through overt or even violent class conflict.

Contemporary social activists who hold this perspective tend to stress the importance of social criticism. Critical examination and analysis of society is necessary to understand the ways in which economic and political elites control and repress citizens. Through socialization, education, and propaganda activities, these elites are extremely effective in persuading most people that the existing economic and political systems are effective and desirable and hence should be supported. Marx called this process the creation of "false consciousness," since it blinds people to the realities of elite control of society. The necessary first step in transforming any society, therefore, is to awaken citizens to these conditions by helping them achieve "true consciousness." Social criticism therefore lays the groundwork for social change toward a more equalitarian and humanistic society.

POLITICAL DEMOCRACY

Objecting to the pervasiveness of repressive oligarchical rule, many political philosophers and activists since the eighteenth century have proposed alternative versions of democracy as a means of distributing political power more equitably throughout society. Common to all these conceptions of democracy is the principle that *all citizens of a nation have the right to influence political decisions that affect them.* The term "right" implies that democracy is more than just a pragmatic blueprint for political systems; it is seen as a moral imperative that societies and individuals must struggle to attain. The concept of citizenship is critical for democracy, since it is distinctly different from the earlier status of subject. The prevailing definition of citizenship may be extremely restricted (such as adult, white, land-owning males—the prevailing definition when the U.S. Constitution was adopted in 1788), or quite inclusive (such as the current U.S. definition of citizens as all persons age 18 or older who are born in this country or have become naturalized citizens).

The various alternative forms of democracy can be divided into three sets. Traditional conceptions of democracy include classical and representative democratic theory. Pragmatic conceptions of democracy include elitist and party democratic theory. Reformist conceptions of democracy include pluralist and participatory democratic theory. These six forms of democracy are discussed in the following paragraphs and illustrated in Figure 13-2.

Traditional Conceptions of Democracy

Classical Democracy. As envisioned by Jean Jacques Rousseau, John Locke, and other early democratic theorists, government is a necessary but constraining social institution. As social life becomes increasingly complex, people find it necessary to enter into a social contract (meant as a metaphor, not an actual document) that binds them together as a political state and creates a government to operate that state. To govern effectively, however, governments must impose restrictions and restraints on individuals and organizations within society. Government is tolerable, therefore, only to the extent that it is controlled by the citizens rather than by elites.

Formulated as a reaction against the gross power inequalities of European feudal societies, with their extreme concentrations of power among small numbers of landholding nobles, classical democratic theory offered a radically different conception of how political power should be distributed and used. It rested on the assumption that all citizens are—or can be—essentially equal in both their concern with public issues and their competence to make decisions on those issues. Consequently, *the essential idea of classical democratic theory is that all citizens can and should participate equally in public decision making and exercise relatively equal amounts of influence in the political system.* "One man, one vote" became the rallying cry of this political theory in the eighteenth and nineteenth centuries. The prototype example of classical democracy in practice is a town meeting, at which all the citizens of a community discuss and then vote on whatever issues are confronting them.

Representative Democracy. Although town meetings maximize citizen involvement in political decision making, they are clearly impractical in large urban communities or total societies. The authors of the U.S. Constitution—especially James Madison and Alexander Hamilton—recognized this practical limitation of classical democracy, and they spent the decade of the 1780s searching for a workable and politically acceptable alternative form of democracy for the United States. In a series of writings that have become known as the Federalist Papers, they debated the merits of two other versions of

FIGURE 13-2   Alternative conceptions of political democracy

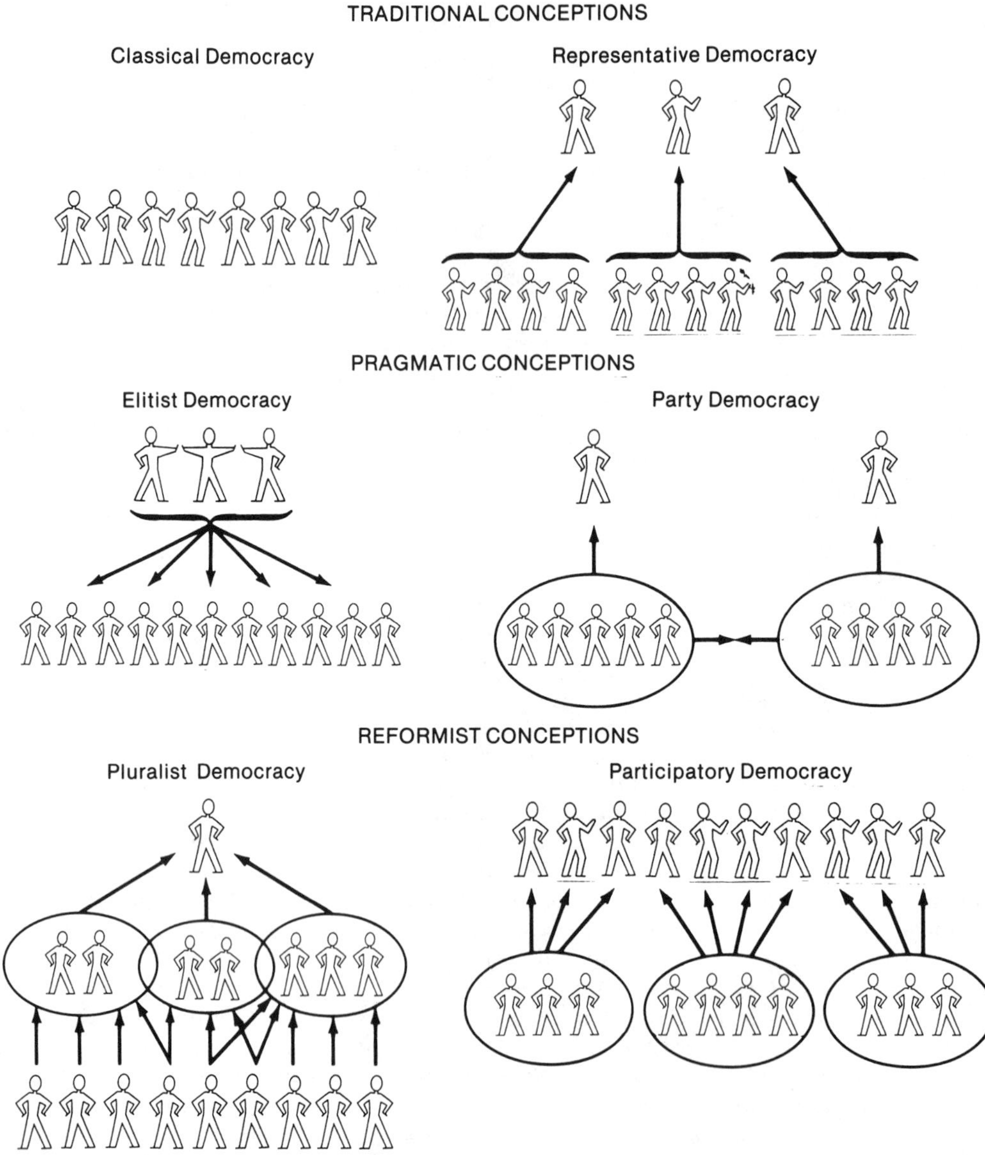

TRADITIONAL CONCEPTIONS

Classical Democracy

Representative Democracy

PRAGMATIC CONCEPTIONS

Elitist Democracy

Party Democracy

REFORMIST CONCEPTIONS

Pluralist Democracy

Participatory Democracy

democracy. In essence, Madison argued for a relatively decentralized theory of "pluralist democracy," while Hamilton argued for a more centralized theory of "representative democracy." Hamilton won this debate, in that his conception of representative democracy formed the basis of the Constitution. During the subsequent two hundred years,

however, Madison's theory of pluralism has come to play an increasingly pervasive role in American politics.

The basic idea of representative democracy is that citizens periodically elect political leaders who represent their interests and concerns in the legislative branch of government. Citizens do not vote on substantive policy issues but leave those decisions to their elected representatives. This conception of democracy therefore rejects the assumption that most citizens are competent to make decisions on political issues. Those decisions must be left to the judgment of elected political leaders who presumably are more knowledgeable about such issues than ordinary citizens. On the national level, the U.S. Constitution originally gave citizens the right to vote only for members of the House of Representatives. U.S. Senators were to be selected by the members of the various state legislatures, while the President was to be chosen by the Electoral College. The electors from each state could be chosen in various ways, but they were free to use their own personal judgment in selecting the President and Vice-President.

During the 200 years since the Constitution was adopted, our conception of representative democracy has expanded in several important ways to allow more citizen participation in elections. First, in response to mounting public pressure, the Constitution was amended to permit direct election of Senators. Second, the informal norm gradually developed that presidential electors should always be elected by the citizens and should be bound by the outcome of the popular presidential vote in their state. As a result, the Electoral College has now become a mere formality, except for the fact that the winning presidential candidate in each state takes all that state's electoral votes and the loser gets none of them, even if he loses the state by only a few votes. Third, as a consequence of the political reform movement that began in the 1920s, many states in this country now provide for popular referenda and initiatives to allow citizens to vote on substantive issues. In a referendum, the state legislature chooses not to make the final decision on a controversial issue, but rather places that issue on a statewide ballot for the citizens to decide. In an initiative, concerned citizens formulate a substantive petition, and if enough voters sign that petition it goes on a statewide ballot. However, there are still no provisions for referenda or initiatives at the national level in the United States or in most other democratic nations.

Pragmatic Conceptions of Democracy

Elitist Democracy. Many political theorists argue that the traditional Hamiltonian conception of representative democracy does not accurately describe the manner in which modern democratic political systems actually operate. This criticism was initiated by Max Weber, who pointed out that elections do not simply select political leaders who represent the citizens, but rather constitute a fundamental transfer of power from the people to government officials and their administrative staffs. Robert Michels's theory of oligarchic rule further emphasized that conclusion. Joseph Schumpeter (1943) added the observation that elections are in fact largely controlled by political elites who manipulate campaigns in a variety of ways to attract votes in a mass popularity contest. He characterized democracy as "that institutional arrangement for arriving at political decisions in which [elite] individuals acquire the power to decide by means of a competitive struggle for the people's vote" (p. 269).

More recently, many writers have taken account of the fact that political power in modern societies is highly concentrated in the major institutional spheres, each of which is dominated by a small set of very influential elites. Consequently, popular elections frequently have little effect on actual political policy formation and administration (Banfield, 1961; Dahl, 1961). As expressed by Emmette Redford (1969:44) in his analysis of "administrative states," "The attainment of the democratic ideal in the world of administration depends much less on majority votes than on the inclusiveness of the representation of interests in the interaction process among the decision makers."

The contemporary theory of elitist democracy holds that democracy exists in a society as long as there is competition for power and public office among the various sets of strategic elites, and the ruling elites take the interests of the public into consideration in their decision-making (Dahl and Lindblom, 1953; Bachrach, 1967). A further feature of this thesis is that democracy is protected and maintained by low levels of citizen participation (Berelson, et al., 1954:312–13). If too many people become involved in politics—especially persons with little knowledge of political issues—they generate conflicts that the system cannot handle. Hence citizen apathy and limited public involvement are seen as playing a useful role in maintaining the stability of the political system.

Party Democracy. In an effort to make elected representatives more responsive to the public and to restrict the power of political elites, all societies with democratic political systems have evolved political parties to mediate between citizens and the government. Although party democracy is not usually thought of as a political theory, in practice this form of political democracy has become the standard operating procedure in all modern nations.

The essence of party democracy is that political parties enact a crucial linking role between citizens and the government. They formulate and articulate policy positions on issues, represent the concerns of various segments of the population (such as classes or ethnic groups) and various interest organizations in the political arena, build coalitions among diverse sectors of the society that enable them to cooperate politically, select candidates to run in elections, define the basic political philosophies of candidates to the voters, raise funds and conduct campaigns, mobilize citizens to vote, build public support for candidates and the government, assign priorities to legislative proposals, and maintain discipline within the legislature so that bills can be passed.

To function in a democratic manner, a fully developed party system must meet several criteria.

(1) There must be two or more national parties that compete for popular support through party activities and election campaigns. Politi-

cal democracy is not possible with one-party systems.

(2) At least two of the parties must attract sufficient public support so that each of them periodically wins elections. One party must not dominate the political system.

(3) The parties must be private organizations not controlled by the government or too closely aligned with it.

(4) There must be freedom of speech and assembly throughout the society, so that the parties can communicate their ideologies and policies to all interested people.

(5) The party leaders must be relatively responsive to their supporters and committed to promoting the welfare of the entire society, not merely seeking political power to further their own interests.

Party systems that meet the preceding criteria can contain either two or several viable parties. In *two-party systems,* the major parties win virtually all major elections. Whatever small minority parties exist are merely protest groups, rather than serious contenders for public office. Within each electoral unit, whichever party receives a majority of the votes cast in an election wins that contest, so that the "winner takes all." In *multiparty systems* with three or more strong parties, either of two procedures may be followed in deciding elections. In some countries, the election is conducted in two stages, with all parties competing in the first round of voting, but only the two party candidates for each office with the most votes participating in the second round. In other countries, each party that receives some minimal proportion of the total vote (typically five percent) is awarded seats in the legislature in proportion to the number of votes it receives.

Two-party systems have the advantage of giving the winning party a clear majority in the legislature, which greatly facilitates enactment of its policies. In multiparty systems, it is fairly common for no party to win a majority of seats in the legislature, so that the largest party must form a coalition with one or more smaller parties if it is to carry out its policies. Those coalitions are often rather fragile and may dissolve over controversial issues. Two-party systems have the disadvantage, however, of precluding minority third parties from having any voice in the legislature. Another disadvantage of two-party systems is that both of the major parties usually express their policies in very general, inclusive, and noncontroversial terms so as to attract a majority of the voters. The result is that minority viewpoints are not expressed, and it may be difficult for the voters to distinguish between the two parties on many issues. Elections are therefore likely to be decided on the basis of the candidates' personalities, rather than their positions on relevant issues. In contrast, the various parties within a multiparty system with proportional representation are more likely to take distinctive stands on issues since they know that their position will be represented in the legislature even if they do not win a majority. Consequently, minority views are more likely to be advocated by politicians, and issues are often more critical than personalities in determining elections.

Reformist Conceptions of Democracy

Pluralist Democracy. The intellectual roots of traditional democratic theory lie in the eighteenth-century ideals of liberalism and rationality, both of which rejected the crumbling feudal social order with its emphasis on classes, guilds, churches, and communities. As a consequence, classical and representative democracy both stress the role of individual citizens in the political system and tend to distrust organizations, because they serve the special interests of their members and often conflict with the general welfare of the total society. The potential danger of this exclusive emphasis on individuals, however, is that people are likely to find themselves relatively powerless in the face of a strong national government and to be easily manipulated by political elites.

This potential danger of popular democracy was recognized by James Madison, who argued that citizens can exercise effective political power vis-a-vis the state only if they band together in various kinds of associations that represent their interests and enable them to speak and act collectively. The formation of political parties during the nineteenth century provided a partial solution to this political necessity. To gain public support and win elections, however, parties must attempt to appeal to as many different interests as possible, with the result that many specialized and minority interests are largely ignored. Consequently, Alexis de Tocqueville, in his classic 1840 analysis of *Democracy in America,* proposed an alternative version of democracy based on Madison's ideas. Tocqueville (1961:128–33) argued that the breakdown or absence of traditional hierarchies of feudal authority in modern societies leads to conditions of mass equality, which provide fertile ground for a "tyranny of the majority" that might destroy individual freedom in the name of popular democracy. To replace traditional aristocracies in contemporary societies, de Tocqueville called for the creation of multitudes of voluntary, special interest associations through which individuals could collectively exercise political power. This theory of democracy has subsequently become known as sociopolitical pluralism (Berry, 1970; Olsen, 1982b).

Pluralist democracy emphasizes the creation of a network of voluntary associations throughout society that mediate between citizens and the government. Sometimes called intermediate organizations because of their location between citizens and the government, each of these associations must possess its own power base and function independently of the government. They must be entirely private, composed of voluntary members who share common interests and concerns. Either separately or in cooperation with one another, interest associations must extend from the grass-roots level of individuals up to the national level, where they interact with the government. And if they are to affect political decision making, they must possess sufficient resources to enable them to exert influence on governmental bodies and leaders.

Some intermediate organizations—such as political action groups, lobbies, and citizens' associations—may participate frequently in the political system. However, most of them—including labor unions, business and professional associations, fraternal associations, ethnic organizations, and all kinds of special interest groups and clubs—are not basically political in nature and therefore enter the political arena only when their particular concerns are involved. Regardless of their concerns, nevertheless, all of these intermediate organizations must adhere to a common set of political norms and rules, so that conflicts can be resolved and collective decisions can be reached. Finally, within any particular area of activity, all of the involved organizations must be more-or-less equal in strength so that no one of them dominates the others.

The voluntary associations that pervade a pluralist polity are influence mediators between individuals and the government. Each organization brings together many people with similar concerns and interests, provides means through which their members can acquire information about relevant public issues, enables them to pool their resources to generate collective influence, and provides an established channel through which that influence can be exerted "upward" on political decisions and policies. To some extent, these associations also protect individuals from manipulation by elites through the mass media or state-controlled programs. At the same time, intermediate organizations serve government leaders by providing them with information about public needs and concerns, as well as an established route through which leaders can reach "downward" to large numbers of their constituents to deal effectively with their problems. In addition, government leaders are insulated from immediate dependence on mass public opinion and fear of overthrow by a mass movement or a revolution, which enables them to take necessary but unpopular actions (Kornhauser, 1959).

The mediation process performed by intermediate organizations in a pluralist political system thus bridges the influence gap between citizens and the government that is ignored by traditional forms of democracy. This process enables individuals to exercise far more influence on political decision making than would ever be possible through occasional mass voting in elections. Sociopolitical pluralism also limits the power of central government and political elites by "checking power with power," promotes negotiation and compromise in reaching collective decisions, and keeps the political process flexible and stable. Critics of sociopolitical pluralism have pointed out several limitations to this form of democracy, however. The most critical limitation is that many voluntary associations in modern societies are quite small and weak, with the result that they cannot exert any significant influence on the national government (Riesman et al., 1954), or they can easily be coopted by the government to support its policies (Olsen, 1982b).

Participatory Democracy. This second reformist version of democracy is essentially an attempt to make classical democracy theory applicable to modern societies. As pointed out by Carole Pateman (1970), the intellectual roots of participatory democracy lie in the classical writings of Jean Jacques Rousseau and John Stuart Mill. Participatory democracy retains two basic tenets of classical political liberalism: Individuals are the fundamental political actors in a democracy, and most people can act rationally if given adequate information about political issues (Ricci, 1971:10–11). At the same time, this conception of democracy rejects the third basic tenet of traditional liberalism, which holds that the personal and collective interests of individuals are adequately expressed through the electoral process. Popular election of government officials is only one way—and often not a very effective way—in which people can participate in and influence public affairs. *Participatory democracy expands political activities beyond voting to maximize both opportunities for and consequences of citizen involvement in all collective decision making.* As expressed by C. George Benello and Dimitrois Roussopoulos (1971:4–8):

"Participatory democracy seeks to reintroduce the concept of democracy from the ground up, which means introducing democratic processes into the major organizations of society, public and private. . . . In a participatory democracy, decision making is the process whereby people propose, discuss, decide, plan, and implement those decisions that affect their lives."

Five central features of participatory democracy are the following:

(1) All individuals must have full opportunity to participate as extensively as they wish in all collective decision making that affects them.

(2) Participation in collective decision making must not be limited to voting but should include a wide variety of activities requiring varying degrees of commitment and involvement.

(3) Responsibility for collective decision making is to be widely dispersed, so that it is not limited to officials and/or experts.

(4) Participation in collective decision making must not be limited to the political system, but should extend throughout all realms of social life.

(5) Participation in collective decision making within nonpolitical spheres of life will teach individuals political skills and norms and will motivate them to become involved in larger political issues.

Particularly crucial in this conception of participatory democracy is the insistence that full democratization of decision making within all local and private organizations is a necessary prerequisite for democracy in the political system. In Pateman's (1970:35) words: "For the operation of a democratic polity at the national level, the necessary qualities in individuals can only be developed through the democratization of authority structures in all political systems"—including the community, the workplace, and the family. In other words, as people become involved in collective decision making within those more immediate spheres of their life, they will acquire the skills and motivations necessary for effective participation in public affairs.

One way in which participatory democracy has been implemented in recent years has been through community-based citizen participation programs (Lind, 1975). In practice, citizen participation programs include many kinds of activities:

(1) Public meetings at which officials describe proposed plans or programs and ask for comments from the audience;

(2) Hearings sponsored by government agencies at which "intervenors" can respond to proposed policies or projects in a quasi-legal manner;

(3) Workshops in which citizens, planners, and public officials jointly discuss and develop action programs;

(4) Citizen advisory councils that meet regularly with public officials to formulate policies on community issues; and

(5) Citizen control boards that exercise final authority on various topics.

Such programs have been developed in countless communities throughout the United States in recent years, but thus far they have involved only small minorities of all citizens.

Despite the lofty ideals of participatory democracy, numerous questions can be raised concerning its practicability. Do most citizens really want to be involved in political decision making? Will knowledge and skills learned in local and private sectors of life actually carry over into national politics? How can citizens effectively exert influence on public officials, apart from voting? Is it realistic to think that most citizens can be involved in deciding major national and global issues? Will participatory democracy necessarily produce the best public decisions and policies?

Socioeconomic Base of Democracy

A critical problem faced by all proponents of political democracy is that this type of polity requires a particular set of economic and social conditions within a society if it is to be stable and effective. Unfortunately, those conditions have been rather rare throughout human history. *The principal features of this socioeconomic base of democracy are that citizens must enjoy considerable economic security and comfort, plus relative status equality.* In foraging societies, which often practiced collective decision making, those conditions were achieved by living in harmony with their natural environment, sharing their wealth relatively equally, and minimizing differences in social status. In ancient Greece, which is often described as the birthplace of political democracy, those necessary socioeconomic conditions were achieved by limiting the status of citizen to the small proportion of the population who were free, male, and affluent.

As societies slowly increased their wealth through settled agriculture, the expansion of commercial trade, and early industrialization, the surplus wealth being produced tended to become increasingly concentrated in the hands of a small class of economic elites. This enabled them to exercise more and more power, with the result that they came to dominate the political systems of their societies and actively resisted all attempts to redistribute political power more equitably. In short, *growing economic productivity and wealth tended to undermine the socioeconomic conditions necessary for political democracy, so that national political systems frequently became highly oligarchic in nature.*

That cumulative process of increasing wealth coupled with political oligarchy has only recently been reversed as modern societies have achieved relatively high levels of socioeconomic development (Bollen, 1983). In the United States, abundant natural resources, plentiful fertile land, and absence of a traditional rigid stratification system provided an adequate socioeconomic base for political democracy during the eighteenth and nineteenth centuries, prior to full-scale industrialization. Most other countries have not been that fortunate, however. In general, the socioeconomic base necessary for political democracy has not been attained in most societies until considerable industrialization and modern-

ization have been achieved. These societal developments tend to creat a fairly large middle class that enjoys considerable economic security and stability, as well as relative status respectability and equality (Rubinson and Quinland, 1977).

Numerous empirical studies (Lipset, 1959; Coulter, 1975; Olsen, 1982a) have demonstrated that political democracy is most likely to occur in societies that have attained all of the following conditions: full industrialization, high economic productivity and national wealth, an income distribution that gives most of the people an adequate income, an educated population (universal primary education and extensive secondary education), a sizable middle class composed of people in nonmanual occupations, extensive information flows (through newspapers and other mass media), and considerable normative cohesion (as evidenced by a common language and widely accepted norms of political tolerance). It is not surprising, therefore, that this type of political system has not yet been realized in most developing countries, and that even in industrialized societies, democracy is often threatened by authoritarian political movements.

GOVERNMENT INFLUENCES ON THE ECONOMY

The governments of all contemporary industrial societies continually attempt to influence, regulate, and direct their national economies. The pervasive role enacted by government in modern societies is nowhere more evident than in regard to the economy. The following discussion focuses on capitalist economies, but many of the practices discussed are also carried out in societies with socialist economies.

Throughout the nineteenth and early twentieth centuries, economic conditions in capitalist societies fluctuated widely and rapidly. Periods of economic growth and expansion were followed by disastrous business panics and depressions. This boom-and-bust cycle eventually resulted in a drastic economic breakdown in the 1930s—the Great Depression—that affected most industrial countries. In the United States, nearly a hundred thousand companies went bankrupt, economic production fell to half the level of the boom years of the 1920s, a quarter of the labor force was left unemployed, and millions of people suffered severe financial hardships.

As a direct consequence of that depression, the governments of the United States and all Western European nations began to regulate and direct their economic systems in the 1930s more extensively than ever before. Initially, most large corporations strongly resisted these changes, but over time they have generally come to realize that the visible hand of government can protect them from the uncertainties of the marketplace and hence stabilize their activities and increase their profits. Today, consequently, the principle of government regulation of the economy—although not all regulatory practices—is widely accepted and supported by the major corporations as an indispensable component of capitalist economies. As a result, *traditional market capitalism has been largely replaced by contemporary regulated capitalism in Western societies.* Most government influences on the economy can be classified into the five categories of governmental business regulation, governmental financial policies, government purchasing, foreign trade, and state enterprises.

Governmental Business Regulation

The process of regulation involves direct action by the government to influence the practices of corporations and to protect consumers in the marketplace. This can be accomplished in many different ways.

One way in which the U.S. government regulates business is through *independent regulatory commissions,* which are often called the "fourth branch of government." Beginning with the Interstate Commerce Commission in 1887, a set of regulatory agencies was created to oversee various sectors of the economy. These include the Food and Drug Administration, the Civil Aeronautics Board, the Federal Communications Commission, the Federal Trade Commission, and many others. In general, regulatory commissions establish operating standards and rules for the industries they supervise, which are enforced through the federal courts.

Over the years, many of the regulatory agencies have had considerable influence on business. The Food and Drug Administration, for instance, has been quite effective in ensuring that the foods and drugs offered to the American public satisfy stringent standards of purity and safety. Nevertheless, the influence of these agencies is severely limited by the fact that they usually depend heavily on the industries being regulated to provide them with personnel and relevant information. Realistically, the commissions can regulate their industries only to the extent that those corporations wish to be regulated. Consequently, the principal function of the regulatory agencies is to enable the major firms within an industry to act collectively, through the government, to regulate themselves.

Another form of government regulation is *antitrust laws.* Throughout the twentieth century, the U.S. government has passed numerous antitrust laws designed to regulate corporate mergers that would result in a single mammoth corporation controlling an entire industry. The Attorney General can bring suit to prevent or limit any corporate merger that would create a monopolistic restraint on trade. In practice, however, most of these antitrust laws have been rather ineffective. Companies that wanted to merge have generally been able to do so, regardless of the law, and only a tiny proportion of those mergers has been challenged in the courts by the government. Moreover, when a corporation has agreed to comply with a court order to divest itself of subsidiary divisions, it has usually been because the corporation had already decided that this action was in its own best financial interest. The breakup of the American Telephone and Telegraph Company in 1984 illustrates this point.

In addition to dealing directly with corporations, federal and state government agencies attempt to *protect individuals* from exploitation by business firms. Most of these efforts have focused on employees, who are at a tremendous disadvantage in relation to powerful corporations. One focus of these efforts has been to strengthen the labor union movement. Employees of private organizations now have the legal right to organize themselves into unions without being fired for their union activities, to bargain collectively with their employer to secure a union contract, and to go on strike to attain their goals. (Government employees may join unions, but they are generally prevented by law from striking and may be fired if they do.) Another focus of these protection efforts has been to specify minimum wages for all employees and to ensure that they enjoy safe working conditions. The most recent effort has been to assist women and minorities to obtain and retain jobs through affirmative action programs. Such programs specify that those individuals must be given equal preference for available jobs, that they cannot automatically be the first persons laid off in a cutback, and that the proportion of all employees in an organization who are women or minorities must be regularly monitored.

Governments have also begun to be concerned about *consumer protection* against unsafe and unsatisfactory products. Companies that sell unsafe items—from aspirins to automobiles—are now regularly pressured (through legal action or publicity) to recall and correct their products. Advertisers who make false claims for their goods may be forced to modify those advertisements or provide warning statements to the public, as in cigarette ads. It has also become easier for consumers to bring class action suits against corporations, in which a few people who have been harmed by a product sue the manufacturer for damages in the name of all consumers of that product.

Governmental Financial Policies

A second broad approach used by governments to influence their economic system is through monetary and fiscal policies. This is the principal strategy advocated by Keynesian economic theory, for it enables government to direct the entire economy in a relatively unobtrusive but effective manner. *Monetary policies* control the flow of money through the economy. In 1913, the U.S. government established the Federal Reserve System, governed by the Federal Reserve Board. It performs two major functions. First, the Board determines the rate at which the government prints money. In addition to replacing worn-out bills, the Treasury continually increases the total amount of currency in circulation to compensate for inflation and to allow for growth in economic transactions. A "tight-money" policy of slow increases in the money supply tends to minimize inflation but also limits economic growth. In contrast, an "easy-money" policy of a more rapid increase in the money supply tends to facilitate economic growth but also fuels inflation. Second, the Federal Reserve System regulates the flow of money through financial institutions. When the Reserve System sells Treasury notes or bonds, the buyers (usually banks or other financial institutions) pay for them in cash, which takes money out of private circulation—although it increases the national debt. Conversely, when the Reserve System buys back its obligations, it pays cash for them, which puts more money into circulation and decreases the national debt. By controlling the amount and flow of money circulating through the economy in these ways, the Federal Reserve System can strongly influence the activities of financial institutions, business firms, state and local governments, and individual consumers.

Fiscal policies influence economic activities by manipulating governmental income and expenditures. On the income side, governments may either raise or lower tax rates for individuals and/or corporations. If the economy is sluggish, the government may lower taxes in an attempt to promote greater consumption and hence stimulate economic activity and growth—but at a cost to its own revenues or its indebtedness. If the economy is expanding too rapidly, the government may raise taxes to reduce the amount of funds available to consumers and/or corporations. In addition, by altering specific tax rates, governments can affect particular segments of the economy. Lowering the tax rate on capital gains, for instance, is intended to encourage wealthy individuals to invest more heavily in corporations, while raising business taxes is intended to slow corporate growth.

On the expenditure side, governments continually make decisions concerning the allocation of their budgets. If a government wants to assist particular industries, it may give direct subsidies to some or all firms in that area. Perhaps the most prominent example of this practice in the United States is farm price supports, in which the federal government either buys surplus agricultural products that cannot be sold in the marketplace, or else pays farmers the difference between current market prices and higher "target prices" set by the Department of Agriculture. Governments also provide many kinds of indirect subsidies to businesses, such as tariff protection against foreign competition, constructing highways used by trucking companies and airports used by airlines, and cleaning up environmental pollution caused by toxic wastes from industries. A third kind of subsidy provided by governments is loan guarantees to financially troubled corporations, which enable banks to make large loans to them without fear of losing their money. The federal bailout of the Chrysler Corporation a few years ago illustrates this latter form of financial aid to business.

Meanwhile, if a government wants to boost employment, it may allocate funds to public works projects such as constructing dams or highways or public housing. This practice directly benefits the companies that receive the contracts for those projects and indirectly creates many new jobs. Alterna-

tively, a government may decide to increase various kinds of welfare payments in an effort to promote more consumer spending, which benefits wholesale and retail firms. All such decisions about the allocation of government funds are based on many political and social considerations in addition to influencing the economy, but these decisions always have countless direct and indirect effects on specific businesses, as well as the entire economy.

Government Purchasing

A third means by which governments exert immense influence on the economy is through their purchasing activities. In the United States, government units currently purchase over 20 percent of all goods and services produced, from pencils to space vehicles. Government decisions about what to purchase and how much to pay for those items can therefore have tremendous influence on the companies that supply them. In general, the largest corporations are the major suppliers of goods to the government, and hence are the main recipients of government expenditures.

Government contracts are highly lucrative to corporations for several reasons. They give the company a dependable customer for its products, so that once the contract is signed, the company no longer has to compete in the marketplace or spend money on advertising. These contracts are frequently very large, which enables a company to benefit from economies of scale in its operations. If research or development is needed to design or improve a product, the government will often pay those entire costs. If the costs of providing a product exceed its initial estimate in the contract, the government may absorb part or all of those cost overruns. Corporations are often able to charge many of their normal operating expenses, such as legal and consulting fees (and sometimes even executive entertainment), to government contracts. Finally, many government contracts are written on a cost-plus basis, which means that the government agrees in advance to pay the full cost of providing certain goods, no matter how high that may be, plus a guaranteed profit of perhaps eight or ten percent of the total contract.

The influence of government purchasing varies considerably among different industries, but government purchases are most extensive in the realm of defense contracts. The Department of Defense is the largest single consumer in the United States, spending over $100 billion a year for arms and many other items. More than 20,000 business firms sell products or services to the Defense Department, although 70 percent of all major contracts go to the 100 largest corporate contractors, and more than half of them are awarded to the 25 biggest firms. This linkage between the military and its suppliers is often called the "military-industrial complex," which reminds us of the extent to which many industrial firms are highly dependent financially on military contracts. Consequently, the major military suppliers—including General Dynamics, Lockheed, Boeing, and General Electric—constantly pressure Congress to spend ever-larger amounts on defense. The lobbyists in these efforts are often ex-military officers hired by defense contractors because of their "inside" contact with the Pentagon.

The existence of this military-industrial complex does not imply a conspiracy among industrialists, military leaders, and politicans, but it does indicate a tight convergence of interests among these interrelated parties, all of whom benefit from defense contracts.

Foreign Trade Promotion

A fourth manner in which government influences business interests is through promoting and regulating commercial trade with other countries. As world trade has expanded enormously since World War II, this aspect of the political economy has become increasingly important in capitalist societies. National governments in these societies continually enact many kinds of policies and programs to stimulate as well as to control foreign trade. Mar-

tin Marger (1981:176–77) summarizes that situation:

Just as the government's chief purpose at home is the maintenance of social and economic stability, the foundation of foreign policy is the preservation of a stable world environment in which the society's economic interest can be maximized. . . . Above all, the aims of foreign policymakers become: (1) protecting American business interests abroad and assuring an investment climate favorable to those interests; (2) stimulating the establishment of markets for American businesses; and (3) assuring the continued flow of raw materials from the underdeveloped nations to American industry. National security then becomes synonymous with corporate security.

To achieve those goals, governments take many different kinds of actions. They *negotiate trade agreements* with other governments, either bilaterally with individual countries or multilaterally with several others. These agreements commonly specify the kinds of goods that will be exported and/or imported, and sometimes goods that may not be traded. Such arrangements also frequently state how many items of particular goods will be exchanged and set minimum prices for those goods. The objective of all such trade agreements is to promote or protect domestic businesses.

Governments of nations that engage in extensive foreign trade, especially the United States, also attempt to *influence world financial conditions* so as to facilitate international sales. They are continually concerned about prevailing exchange rates between their currency and those of other countries. This may involve adjusting the value of their currency upward or downward in relation to other currencies. It may also involve buying or selling gold in an effort to keep their currency stable. These efforts are particularly crucial in regard to the U.S. dollar, since it has become the unofficial world currency in which well over half of all international sales are conducted. Governments are also concerned about their balance of trade with other nations. If a country sells much more abroad than it buys—as was the case with the

United States in the 1950s and 1960s—it may have to loan or give funds to other countries to enable them to keep purchasing its products. Conversely, if a country imports much more than it exports—as the United States has been doing recently—large amounts of its currency will accumulate in other countries rather than being returned through reciprocal trade. If either kind of trade imbalance continues for long, it can severely upset a nation's economy and create serious financial problems for many businesses.

Since a large proportion of the major multinational corporations have their headquarters in the United States, the federal government seeks to *assist the multinationals* in various ways. It enacts tax and other financial laws that enable those corporations to operate in the world market. It may represent their interests in international political and economic negotiations. It may overlook business practices abroad that are illegal in this country (such as paying pitifully low wages to workers or offering bribes to economic and political elites). And it may try to persuade foreign businesses or governments to invest capital in U.S. multinationals.

Finally, governments of industrial countries periodically attempt to *exert political or economic pressures* on other countries, especially developing societies. Sometimes these pressures are relatively indirect or subtle, such as praising the benefits of capitalism or the political leaders of countries who cooperate in trade agreements. Sometimes the pressures are more direct and overt, such as giving economic aid to foreign trade partners or setting limits on goods that are exchanged with them. And sometimes these pressures involve the use of military force, such as providing military aid to rebels seeking to overthrow an unfriendly government, or actually invading another country to protect our business interests there.

State Enterprises

The most direct way in which governments control businesses is by owning and operating them as

> ## GOVERNMENTAL INFLUENCE ON THE ECONOMY
> 1. Governmental business regulation.
> 2. Governmental financial policies.
> 3. Governmental purchasing.
> 4. Foreign trade promotion.
> 5. State enterprises.

state enterprises. Sometimes these enterprises make a profit and thus provide income to the government, but more frequently they operate at a loss and are kept functioning through government subsidies. In fact, the principal reason for the existence of state-owned enterprises in capitalist societies is that they are not able to earn a profit as private businesses. If the goods or services they provide are considered necessary for the public good, the government may operate them and cover their losses from the public treasury.

In the United States, government-owned enterprises include the postal service, many utility companies, most elementary and secondary schools and many universities, some hospitals and other medical care facilities, most local transit systems, and some railroads. In Western European countries, state enterprises are even more prevalent, including national railway and airline systems, radio and television networks, virtually all utilities, many insurance plans, and national health care systems. A number of those governments also partially or entirely own many industries, such as automobile manufacturers, iron and steel producers, and chemical firms. Consequently, several Western European economies are sometimes described as partially capitalist and partly socialist in nature.

POLITICAL PARTICIPATION

All forms of political democracy assume that citizens should participate in political activities. Widespread citizen involvement in politics does not ensure political democracy, as evidenced by the fact that the Soviet Union regularly claims that well over 90 percent of its citizens vote in all national elections. If citizens fail to participate actively in political affairs, however, they will certainly remain politically powerless, and democracy cannot succeed. In what ways and to what extent do Americans become involved in political affairs?

Political Participation Activities

Given the emphasis of traditional democratic theory on elections, it is not surprising that we commonly equate political participation with voting turnout. In reality, however, there are also many other ways of taking part in the political system. For illustrative purposes, we shall examine data for the United States, since most of the research on political participation has been conducted in this country (Milbrath, 1965; Verba and Nie, 1972; Olsen, 1982b).

At the most basic level of political involvement, about three-fourths of the public say that they pay at least some *attention to political news* and events. Exposure to political information has little effect on some people, but more than half of the citizens say that they have at least moderate *interest in political events,* and about two-fifths of them sometimes *discuss politics* with friends. In regard to voting, government statistics reveal that since 1930 the actual turnout in presidential elections has never exceeded 65 percent, and since 1976 it has consistently been below 55 percent (U.S. Bureau of the Census, 1987). In the 1988 presidential election, it was just 49 percent of all registered voters. In nonpresidential national elections for Congress the turnout rate has been below 40 percent since 1974. In local elections the rate of voting is rarely above 30 percent.

One way of becoming involved in politics beyond voting is to participate in *political activities within voluntary associations.* An interested individual can either join an organization that is specifically political in nature (such as the League of Women Voters or Common Cause), or take part in politically

oriented actions within nonpolitical special interest and community associations. About a third of the public say that they are active in at least one organization that is involved in some kind of local community problem. However, less than ten percent of the people in this country belong to any kind of political club or organization, and no more than another ten percent have ever personally taken part in political activities within nonpolitical organizations to which they belong.

Another way of becoming involved in the political system is to take part in *political party activities.* This may involve such simple acts as putting a political bumper sticker on one's car or contributing a small amount of money to a party, but it may also include attending party meetings or giving many hours of voluntary service to a party or candidate. Less than 15 percent of all citizens report that they have ever donated money to a party or candidate during an election campaign. About one-fifth of the public says that they have attended a political party meeting or rally during the past three years, while slightly more than that report that at some time in the past they have worked for a party or candidate in an election.

A more direct way of becoming politically active is to *contact public officials* or take part in *government functions* at the local, state, or national level. Most people's contacts with government officials are sporadic and transitory, as indicated by the fact that less than one-fifth of all citizens have ever contacted a state or national government leader about a political issue. A few individuals do become extensively involved in government through membership on public committees or boards, running for office, or actually holding public office, but less than five percent of the public report that they have ever done any of those things.

Quite clearly, these rates for all types of political participation in the United States are far below the expectations of democratic political theory. Data from other Western democracies indicate that voting turnout is generally higher in most of them than in the United States, but rates of organizational, party, and government participation in most other nations are generally even lower than in this country.

Political Participation Roles

In addition to examining these rates of participation in various kinds of specific political activities, we can also describe the kinds of political roles that people frequently enact. Table 13-1 lists six political participation roles identified in one study (Olsen, 1973), together with their definitions and the manner in which they were measured in that research. These roles can be thought of as strata in a hierarchy of political participation, since they are arranged in order of increasing activity and influence.

Political Leaders. By virtue of their elected or appointed positions in the governmental structure, Leaders normally exercise dominate power in the political system. There is considerable variation among them in the amount of authority and influence they exercise, however, depending on their positions and actions. They constituted about three percent of the population in the study reported here.

Political Activists. These active members of political parties, other political organizations, and politically involved voluntary associations operate outside the formal government, yet exercise a fair amount of influence on the political system through their organizational activities. Except for those involved in political parties, however, Activists typically enter the political arena only when issues impinge directly on their particular interests or concerns, so that their political involvement is relatively specialized. The Activist stratum included about 14 percent of the population in this study.

Political Communicators. As individuals, these people can have some impact on the political system through their communicative actions, but their influence is severely limited because their communications are not usually reinforced by other activities.

Hence the political effectiveness of Communicators depends largely on the willingness of Leaders and Activists to listen to their views and the receptiveness of Citizens to their messages. In this study, they accounted for about 13 percent of the adult population.

Political Citizens. Individually, Citizens have little impact on the political system, since their participation is largely limited to voting. Collectively, however, they constitute the foundation of a democratic political system. Nevertheless, many Citizens only marginally fulfill the requirements of the politically attentive public called for by democratic theory, and their voting choices are often affected more by their socioeconomic status, ethnicity, and childhood political socialization than by rational considerations of political issues. About 30 percent of the public enacted the Citizen role in this study.

Political Marginals. Their minimal contacts with the political system are almost entirely private actions, such as reading political news articles, so that they have virtually no impact on that system. Marginals are potentially available to give political support to candidates and parties if current issues touch directly on their personal lives, but such support is usually limited to occasionally voting. They numbered about 18 percent of the public in this study.

Political Isolates. As a result of being almost entirely cut off from the political system, Isolates take little or no part in political affairs. Their political ignorance and apathy normally result in either passive acquiescence toward, or withdrawal from, all political matters. They are outside the political system and tend to remain there. In this study, they constituted about 22 percent of the population.

Factors Related to Political Participation

Generalizing across all types of political activities and all political participation roles, we can draw several conclusions about the sociodemographic, socioeconomic, and

TABLE 13-1 Political Participation Roles, Conceptual Definitions, and Measurement

Stratum	Conceptual Definition	Operational Variables
Leaders	Persons who are directly involved in government.	At some time have either (a) served as a member of a public board, committee, or other body of some kind, or (b) been elected to public office.
Activists	Persons who engage in organized political action within private organizations.	At some time have either (a) done volunteer work or held office in a political party, or (b) participated directly in some kind of political activity conducted by a voluntary interest association (regardless of whether or not the organization's stated purposes are political in nature).
Communicators	Persons who receive and communicate political information, interests, beliefs or values.	At some time have both (a) received a political message by attending some kind of political meeting or speech, and (b) communicated a political message by writing to or otherwise contacting a public official, writing a letter to the editor of a newspaper, or displaying a political button, sticker, or other sign.
Citizens	Persons who perform the expected responsibilities of citizens, but take no other part in politics.	At the present time (a) have knowledge of the political system and recent political events, (b) hold opinions of some kind on several current political issues, (c) have a political party preference (including Independent), and (d) be currently registered to vote and have voted in at least half of all recent elections.
Marginals	Persons who have only minimal and transitory contacts with the political system.	Within the past few months have both (a) had some minimal exposure to political news via the mass media or reading partisan literature, and (b) felt some interest in a political issue or at least once discussed a political topic with another person.
Isolates	Persons who rarely or never participate in politics in any way.	A residual category containing all persons who do not qualify for any of the above strata.

Source: Olsen, Marvin E., "A Model of Political Participation Stratification," *Journal of Political and Military Sociology,* I (Fall, 1973), p. 188.

other characteristics of individuals that are related to—and presumably promote—involvement in the political system (Milbrath, 1965; Verba and Nie, 1972; Olsen, 1982b).

Gender. In the past, men have tended to be more active in politics than women, but in recent years those differences have virtually disappeared in the United States.

Age. Most forms of political involvement increase with age until retirement, after which they decline slowly.

Race and Ethnicity. Whites tend to score slightly higher than blacks on most political participation measures. However, when socioeconomic status is held constant by comparing blacks and whites at the same level, blacks often score equal to or slightly higher than whites. Members of several ethnic minorities (such as Hispanics) tend to be somewhat less active than nonethnic people, and those differences do not disappear when socioeconomic status is held constant.

Religion. Jews are the most politically active religious category. "Mainline Protestants" and Roman Catholics tend to be relatively active, while "Conservative and Fundamentalist Protestants" and persons with no religious preference are considerably less active politically.

Education. All forms of political participation increase with rising education. Amount of education is therefore a rather strong predictor of individual political activity.

Occupational Status. By itself, occupational status is almost as strong a predictor of political participation as is education. The higher the occupational status, the more politically active people tend to be. However, when other relevant factors—especially amount of education and involvement in voluntary associations—are held constant, occupational status has little independent effect on political participation.

Income. This indicator of socioeconomic status is less strongly related to political activity than either education or occupation. And when other relevant factors are held constant, that relationship often disappears entirely.

Parents' Political Activities. The more politically active one's parents were during one's adolescence, the more one is likely to participate in political affairs as an adult.

Voluntary Association Membership and Participation. The number of voluntary interest associations in which people are involved is the best predictor of political participation. Membership in such associations, regardless of level of involvement, is strongly related to political activity. This relationship holds at all levels of socioeconomic status. Frequent attendance at meetings and service on committees or in leadership positions in those associations further strengthen that relationship.

Community Residency. The longer people have lived in their community, the more likely they are to vote regularly, but this factor is not related to any other kind of political activity.

Community Involvement. People who participate in neighborhood and community activities are quite likely to participate in political affairs. This relationship remains moderately strong after socioeconomic status is held constant.

Mass Media Exposure. Although many forms of exposure to the mass media are not related to political participation, reading newspapers and watching news and other serious programs on television are strongly correlated with involvement in politics. This relationship also persists after socioeconomic status is held constant.

In general, these relationships between political participation and many different social characteristics suggest that *involvement in political affairs is strongly influenced by a person's location in the social structure.* Political participation is not just a consequence of an individual's personal attitudes or interest in politics, but is strongly affected by one's socioeconomic status, organizational memberships, and other social activities.

SUMMARY

The political system of a society includes all the beliefs, activities, organizations, and relationships that are concerned with collective decision making and regulation of collective activities. It includes the state, governmental organizations, political parties, political interest associations, and other organizations.

Governments typically perform many different kinds of functions for their societies. These involve protecting the society from external threats, preserving order and stability within the society, supporting and promoting the economy, distributing financial and other benefits, providing all kinds of public services, promoting societal cohesion, and planning for the future.

The political power of the state that enables governmental units to perform those functions tends to be highly concentrated in a small set of political elites in all societies. Elite theory argues that this concentration of political power is inevitable in all social organization. Political elites are usually well-organized; they strive to protect and preserve their power; they use whatever means they can to exercise that power; they may be divided into several levels; their power is pervasive if not always visible; and they tend to resist major social changes that might threaten or destroy their control of society. Elite theorists have offered numerous explanations for the existence and domination of elites, but the most comprehensive of those arguments incorporate a variety of structural, operational, and psychological factors that typically occur in all complex societies and other kinds of social organization.

Oligarchy, or rule by a few over the many, exists in all modern industrial societies. Although political oligarchy is most evident in the Soviet Union at the present time, it also occurs in all Western nations. In the United States, power is highly centralized within the three major institutional realms of the economy, the polity, and the military, as well as several other social institutions. There is some disagreement concerning the extent to which all of those sets of elites have become highly interwoven within a single power elite, but there does appear to be a central circle of top elites who act as overall coordinators of the political system.

All governments and political elites typically act in a variety of ways to control, protect, and perpetuate the existing political system. Marx made the elimination of this elite domination and repression the central focus of his writings. His solution to this problem was the creation of a socialist society characterized by democracy and equality in all realms of life.

To minimize the domination of political elites, democratic theory holds that all citizens have the right to influence political decisions that affect them. Political theorists have long searched for forms of democracy that are more relevant to modern societies than is classical democracy. The most widely practiced of these alternative forms is representative democracy, in which citizens elect leaders to make collective decisions for them. Many critics argue that contemporary democratic political systems are more accurately described as elitist democracy, because of the relative powerlessness of most ordinary citizens. To provide a link between citizens and political leaders, all modern nations have developed political parties. For party democracy to be effective, there must be at least two strong parties that compete for political power, they must be independent of the government, they must enjoy all civil liberties, and their leaders must be responsive and responsible. Both two-party and multiparty systems exist, and each has certain advantages and disadvantages.

In pluralist democracy, voluntary associations act as an intermediaries between the citizens and the government. These associations can perform many important functions, the most crucial of which is providing a channel through which citizens can act collectively to exert influence upward on the government. Such associations also protect citizens from manipulation by political elites, provide government leaders with a means of reaching downward to their constituents, and protect the government from mob rule. Participatory democracy seeks to maximize opportunities for citizen involvement in collective decision making throughout all realms of society, including the work place, the community, and the family. By taking part in all decision making that affects them, people can learn to become more active and effective political citizens.

Throughout history, as societies have become more wealthy, that wealth has tended to become increasingly concentrated in a small set of economic elites, which has led to oligarchy and autocratic government. Only with fully developed industrialization and socioeconomic development have some modern societies reversed that trend and fostered political democracy, as a result of increasing economic security, expanding education, growth of the middle class, extensive information flows, and other necessary conditions.

The pervasive role played by government in modern industrial societies is particularly evident in regard to its influences on the economic system, which have transformed traditional market capitalism into contemporary regulated capitalism. These influences include regulation of the economy by regulatory commissions; enactment and enforcement of antitrust laws; protection of workers and consumers; monetary policies to control the flow of money through the economy; fiscal policies that manipulate government income and expenditures; government contracts and other purchasing activities, especially with the military; policies and programs that stimulate and regulate foreign trade; and state ownership and operation of business enterprises.

Although political democracy assumes that citizens should be politically active, most forms of political involvement are limited to relatively small segments of the population. Voting turnout rates are quite low in the United States, and participation in other kinds of political activities through interest organizations, political parties, and government affairs typically involve a small minority of all citizens. Approximately two-fifths of the population enact the politically uninvolved roles of political Marginals or political Isolates. Another one-third of the public plays only the minimal role of political Citizens through voting. Only about one-fourth of the people are more involved in politics in the roles of political Communicators or political Activists. Very few people enact the role of political Leaders. Political participation is related to a variety of social factors, including age, race and ethnicity, religion, education, occupational status, income, parents' political activities, voluntary association membership and involvement, community residency, community involvement, and mass media exposure.

URBAN COMMUNITIES

Although cities have existed since antiquity, why has the urban revolution
  occurred so recently?

How have the patterns of land use in American cities changed during the
  twentieth century?

Does urban living have undesirable effects on the ways in which people
  interact with one another?

What kinds of economic and political problems are urban communities
  presently experiencing?

How are cities attempting to manage urban slums, urban housing, and
  comprehensive planning?

URBANIZATION

At the end of the twentieth century, it is
difficult to imagine a world without countless large cities. Urbanization is one of the
most pervasive trends in the modern world
but also one of the newest developments.
Although the first cities were established
more than 3,500 years ago, all early cities
were "islands in an overwhelmingly rural
sea" (Palen, 1987:3). Throughout history,
most of humanity has lived in rural areas or
small towns. In 1800, just three percent of
the world's population lived in towns of 5000
or more people. In 1985, in contrast, more
than 40 percent of all people were living in
communities of 20,000 or more, and by the
year 2000 that figure is expected to be over
50 percent. We are rapidly becoming an urbanized world.

Urban Concepts

As far as we know, human beings have
always lived in communities. As a form of
social organization, *a community consists of
a population of people who reside in a common
geographical area, corporate in many daily activities, and share a sense of communal belonging.* In foraging and early horticultural
societies, most of the members of a community were bound together by ties of kinship, but as communities became larger
and more complex, their unifying linkages were increasingly economic and political in nature. Geographical proximity,
functional interdependence, and cultural
identification nevertheless remain the distinctive features of all communities.

How large must a community be if it is to
be considered urban? Communities come in

all sizes, from a few families to many millions of people. Quite obviously, a village containing ten houses and a general store is vastly different—socially, economically, politically, and in every other respect—from Greater Tokyo (which is presently the largest metropolis in the world) with over 20 million people. However, there is no standard definition of what constitutes an urban community. The United States Census Bureau still classifies all communities with 2,500 or more people as urban, which reflects our predominantly rural past. More realistic is the United Nations definition of an *urban locality* as a community with 20,000 or more inhabitants, which is fairly widely accepted by urban demographers. The U.N. reserves the designation of *city* for communities with at least 100,000 residents.

The U.S. Census Bureau, meanwhile, uses several different terms to describe cities of 50,000 or more population. An *Urbanized Area* is a city (or two or more contiguous cities) of at least that size, plus the immediately surrounding densely settled land. A *Metropolitan Statistical Area* (MSA) consists of an Urbanized Area and the entire county in which it is located, and often also one or more neighboring counties that have close economic and social ties with the urban area. Other terms describe pairs or clusters of MSAs, although these urban complexes are often called simply *metropolises*.

In the contemporary world, the growth of urban communities is part of the broader social trend of urbanization. *Urbanization is a process of societal change in which an increasing proportion of the population resides in relatively large and dense communities that dominate the social, economic, and political organization and functioning of that society.* This process has both demographic and organizational components. Demographically, urbanization involves the concentration of a society's population into urban localities. This usually occurs as a result of two demographic changes: an increase in the number of cities in a society, and growth of the size of its cities. These two demographic changes generally occur together, although to varying degrees in different societies. Organizationally, urbanization is the expansion of urban social institutions (economic, political, and social) and urban ways of living (work, lifestyles, and values) within cities and throughout the society. Urbanization is thus a societal-wide process that involves much more than just population concentration. *Urbanization is one of the fundamental social transformations that are creating modern societies around the globe.*

The Urban Revolution

Although the process of urbanization began thousands of years ago and has slowly progressed through the ages, until quite recently it was a minor trend in societal development. As long as societies were essentially agrarian in nature, there was little reason for—or possibility of—extensive urban growth. *It was the industrial revolution and the transformation that it produced in the economies of Western nations that largely created the modern "urban revolution."* This linkage between industrialization and urbanization is demonstrated by two kinds of data.

Historically, the rate of growth in worldwide urbanization has risen sharply during the nineteenth and twentieth centuries (Davis, 1955; Chandler and Fox, 1974), as Western societies became increasingly industrialized. In 1800, at the beginning of the industrial revolution, no more than two percent of the world's population lived in cities of 20,000 or more, and there were fewer than 50 cities with populations of 100,000 or more. By 1900, the proportion of the world's population in cities of 20,000 or more had quadrupled, to nine percent, although this figure was still obviously quite low. By 1950, however, the world's urban population had risen to 21 percent, and 1985 it was over 40 percent (Population Reference Bureau, 1987). The recent growth of large metropolises has been even more striking. As late as 1900 there were only ten cities in the world with populations of one million or more, whereas in 1980 there were 235 such metropolises.

Alternatively, we can compute the statistical relationship between the degree of industrialization and the extent of urbanization in countries around the world at the present time. Several studies, using various definitions of industrialization and urbanization, have consistently found that correlation to be greater than .80, which is a very strong relationship. More graphically, of the 35 highly industrialized nations (in terms of the proportion of their Gross National Product originating in manufacturing and their total energy consumption), all but three (Albania, Portugal, and Yugoslavia) are also at least 50 percent urbanized. The proportion of the population living in urban communities (however these are defined by each country) in all 35 industrialized nations was given in Table 11-3. In 21 of them, the level of urbanization is 70 percent or higher, which is frequently used as an indicator of a high level of urbanization. The current average for all industrial nations is 72 percent urbanized, with the United States being slightly above that level (at 74 percent) and the Soviet Union being somewhat below it (at 65 percent) (Population Reference Bureau, 1987).

To explain this worldwide urban revolution more systematically, we must examine a number of interrelated factors that have made extensive urbanization possible and have propelled large numbers of people to migrate from rural areas and small towns to cities. These factors can be grouped under several broad headings (Hawley, 1964, 1971).

Agricultural Factors. Before large-scale urbanization can occur in a society, agricultural productivity must increase substantially so that there is enough surplus food for urban dwellers. This increased productivity, which results from improved farming technologies and practices, also reduces the need for agricultural workers and thus frees many of them for nonagricultural work. They become surplus labor in rual areas and are pushed into urban areas in search of jobs. More abundant and nutritious food in the cities also reduces the urban death rate (especially among infants) and allows natural population growth to occur there.

Industrial Factors. Factories and associated urban business enterprises require large numbers of workers. As these businesses are expanding during the early stages of industrialization, they attract displaced farm workers with offers of steady employment and wages. Other business activities that develop with industrialization—such as trade, commerce, service firms, and banks—also require many new workers. Urban job opportunities thus pull large numbers of people into cities in search of economic opportunities. The profits generated by these urban businesses also enable cities to obtain greater amounts of food and other resources from rural areas.

Transportation Factors. Cities cannot exist without a steady flow of resources into them from rural areas, as well as the commercial transport of manufactured goods. As long as the principal means of transportation were horse-drawn carts and sailing ships, they imposed severe limitations on urban growth. The development of railroads and steamships during the nineteenth century was therefore critical for the expansion of cities, as have been motor vehicles and airplanes during the twentieth century.

Health Factors. Medieval urban growth was severely retarded by the Plague that swept through Europe during the fourteenth century and killed at least one-third of the population of the continent. As late as the eighteenth century, large numbers of urban residents died each year from diseases caused by impure water, decayed food, and inadequate sanitation. Until cities learned to cope with these public health problems—which did not occur until the twentieth century in many societies—the urban death rate often equaled or even exceeded the combined urban birth and in-migration rates. As a result, cities were often hard-pressed to maintain their populations, let alone grow.

Political Factors. If cities are to flourish as viable communities, they must have governments that are capable of dealing with the many complex social problems that arise when a large number of people live in close proximity. Another requirement for urban growth, therefore, is the creation of viable and effective local governmental agencies. During the nineteenth century, the principal demands on urban governments were to create political and legal conditions that supported and facilitated the development of business enterprises. During the twentieth century, demands on these governments have expanded to include problems of housing, transportation, employment, health, education, recreation, and many other public issues.

Intangible Factors. A final set of factors influencing urban growth includes all of the intangible attractions of urban living. Some of the more prominent of these attractions are escape from traditional rural values, opportunities to experience new lifestyles, possibilities for obtaining formal education, availability of marriage partners, new recreational opportunities, and the general excitement of urban life. Such factors constitute a powerful pull on many people to leave rural areas and small villages and move into urban areas in search of a new way of life.

American Urbanization

The process of urbanization has been dramatically evident in the United States over the last 200 years. During the seventeenth century, a few port cities of moderate size—Boston, New York, Philadelphia, and Charleston—developed along the eastern seaboard, since the colonies were highly dependent on trade with England and Europe. At the time of the first national census in 1790, Philadelphia contained over 40,000 people, which probably made it the second-largest English-speaking city in the world, after London. Nevertheless, only five percent of the total population of the newly formed United States lived in urban settlements of 2,500 or more at that time. This was almost entirely a rural society.

Fifty years later, in 1840, the proportion of the population living in towns of 2,500 or more was still just eleven percent. The only city in the United States that grew dramatically during the first half of the nineteenth century was New York, which increased from about 60,000 people in 1800 to over one million in 1860. This expansion was due largely to the critical role of New York as the entry point for most immigrants and as the major port for trade with the Old World.

During the second half of the nineteenth century, the United States shifted rapidly from an agricultural to an industrial society. *Industrialization of the society was closely accompanied by a parallel growth of urban communities and cities.* In 1850, the total urban population (in towns of 2,500 or more) was only 15 percent, whereas by 1900 it had reached 40 percent. At the beginning of that period, there were just ten cities with more than 50,000 inhabitants in the United States, but at the end of the century there were 72 such cities. As an example, Chicago contained only about 4,000 people when it was incorporated in 1833, but by 1890 it had passed the million mark and by 1910 it contained over two million inhabitants.

The rush toward urbanization of the United States has continued unabated during the twentieth century. The proportion of the population living in urban communities of 2,500 or more population increased from 40 percent in 1900 to 74 percent in 1985. In addition, since the end of World War II, there has been a *steady movement of people out of central cities to surrounding suburbs and urban "fringe" areas* that are nevertheless still part of the overall metropolitan area. Consequently, urban growth in the United States is seen most clearly in the proportion of the population living within metropolitan areas (MSAs), consisting of a central city of 50,000 or more, the entire county in which it lies, and any surrounding counties that are economically dependent on that city. As previously mentioned, in 1900 there were 72 such metropolitan areas in the United States. As shown in Table 14-1, by 1950 there were 169 of these areas, which contained 63 percent of the total population. And in 1980 there were 281 metropolitan areas, containing 76 percent of the nation's population. The fact that 76 percent of all Americans live in metropolitan areas, but only 74 percent are classified as urbanized, is a result of the differing definitions of these two concepts. All metropolitan areas contain rural areas and small towns whose residents are not classified as urbanized but are included in the population of the metropolitan area. Conversely, residents of small cities between 2,500 and 50,000 population that are not located within metropolitan areas are classified as urbanized but not as living within metropolitan areas. In recent years, however, smaller cities—especially those outside metropolitan areas—have been growing rather rapidly. The proportion of the population living in cities with populations of 10,000 to 50,000 grew from 18 to 25 percent between 1960 and 1985.

As metropolitan areas in the United States have steadily sprawled outward, what were once independent smaller cities located outside metropolises have often been engulfed by metropolitan growth. Although these cities usually retain their political and cultural identity, functionally they become part of the total metropolitan area. Outlying farmlands and other previously open areas are also developed into housing tracts and shopping malls. As a result, in the more densely settled sections of the country, *metropolitan areas are rapidly growing together to form what are sometimes called megalopolises.* The largest of these, along the eastern seaboard, presently stretches from Boston to Washington, D.C. and is thus often called the "Bos-Wash" megalopolis. It is essentially a single long, urban complex containing over 45 million people. A second megalopolis extends along the south side of the Great Lakes from Pittsburgh to Milwaukee, and hence might be termed "Pit-Mil." The third—and most rapidly growing—megalopolis in this country is "San-San," stretching along the California coast from San Diego to San Francisco.

TABLE 14-1 Metropolitan and Suburban Growth in the United States, 1940–1980

Characteristic	1940	1950	1960	1970	1980
Number of Metropolitan Areas*	169	169	212	243	281
Total Metropolitan Population (in millions)	70	85	113	139	172
Total Metropolitan Population as Percentage of U.S. Population	53%	56%	63%	68%	76%
Total Metropolitan Land Area as Percentage of U.S. Territory	6%	6%	9%	11%	16%
Proportion of U.S. Population in Suburban Areas+	20%	24%	33%	37%	45%
Proportion of Metropolitan Population in Suburban Areas	37%	42%	52%	55%	60%

* Metropolitan areas in 1940; Standard Metropolitan Statistical Areas in 1950 through 1970; MSAs, PMSAs, and CMSAs in 1980.

+ Sections of metropolitan areas outside the central city.

Source: U.S. Bureau of the Census, *Statistical Abstract of the United States, 1987.* Washington, D.C.: U.S. Government Printing Office, Tables 1, 30, and 35.

Although the urban demographic growth that has dominated the United States during the twentieth century is quite striking, from a sociological perspective the process of urbanization involves much more than just expanding city populations. *Urbanization has become a total societal process, transforming the whole social structure of the United States and other industrial societies.* Large metropolitan areas not only contain the bulk of the population but also thoroughly dominate the entire society. Most of the major economic, political, and social activities throughout the society originate in, and are controlled by, metropolitan areas and their institutions. In addition, the mass media disseminate urban values, norms, and lifestyles across the land, infusing urban cultural ideas into even the smallest towns and rural areas. Urbanization is thus one of the most fundamental processes of societal change now occurring in all modern societies—and increasingly also in developing countries.

SPATIAL PATTERNS

The social organization of urban communities within contemporary industrial societies can be examined from several different perspectives. The perspective taken in this section focuses on the spatial patterns that characterize cities and metropolitan areas. This is often called an ecological perspective, since much of the sociological research dealing with these patterns has emphasized the manner in which people relate to the physical environment of the city. Consequently, many sociologists refer to this approach as "urban ecology." That term is somewhat misleading, however, since most of the research using this perspective has not attempted to deal with cities as total ecosystems. The concern has been limited largely to the ways in which urban communities are organized in space.

A second perspective that can be taken on urban social organization emphasizes urban social life, or "urbanism," which is discussed in the next section. A third perspective deals

with the political economies of cities, which is the topic of the following section. A fourth perspective, taken in the subsequent section, focuses on efforts to manage and improve urban communities.

Land Use Models

In the 1920s several sociologists at the University of Chicago became interested in the fact that the various activities constituting urban life are never randomly distributed throughout a city, but always form identifiable patterns of land use. Robert Park, Ernest Burgess, and their colleagues argued that these *urban spatial patterns are primarily a result of economic competition for land carried out in the marketplace, which results in differing land values.* Various activities are therefore located within a city according to their ability to pay prevailing market prices for land, so that similar kinds of activities tend to cluster together. These Chicago sociologists observed that the highest land values usually occur at the center of the city, as a result of the convergence of transportation lines that give that area the greatest access to all other parts of the city. Consequently, activities located near the city center are those that can afford to pay the highest prices for space. As a result of those prices, density of land use is usually greatest in the central business district. *Land values tend to decline at a fairly steady rate the further removed an area is from the city center, as does also density of land use,* primarily because of the economic and time costs of travel into the city center. As a city grows, therefore, activities that require cheaper and/or more land tend to move steadily further and further out from the city center.

Using Chicago as a prototype example, Burgess (Park and Burgess, 1925:47–62) developed an analytical model to display graphically the land-use patterns that typically result from this process. His ideal-type model was not intended to explain all patterns of urban land use, since the patterns that actually occur in any city are also influenced by many additional factors such as the natural topography, transportation routes, nonmarket land-use choices, and cultural values pertaining to historic landmarks or special activities. Nevertheless, the model does depict the most fundamental pattern of land use in most large American cities. Many European cities only partially fit the model, however, because of their much longer histories that predate modern transportation and construction techniques, while most cities in currently developing countries do not fit the model at all well.

Burgess's *concentric zone model* consists of a series of concentric circles extending outward from the city center, each of which tends to contain similar kinds of land uses. In theory, these should be more or less perfect circles, but in reality they are always quite irregular, with considerable overlapping of the zones represented by the circles.

Zone 1, the center business district, primarily contains office buildings, department stores, specialty shops, banks, major hotels, fancy restaurants, theaters, government agencies, and similar activities that can afford to pay extremely high prices for land and that use space very densely. At the outer edge of the central business district there is frequently a "red-light district" containing bars, massage parlors, strip joints, pawnbrokers, and other small businesses that are not very respectable, but for which there is considerable demand.

Immediately surrounding the central business district is Zone 2, which is called both the light manufacturing and wholesale district and the zone of transition. The businesses located in this area typically include small factories, auto and other repair shops, wholesale merchants, and warehouses, all of which require more space and lower rents than are available in the central business district. Also commonly found in this zone are cheap hotels and rooming houses, tenements, and large homes from the past that have been converted into many small apartments. Although the occupants of this housing cannot afford high rents, when large numbers of them are crowded into tiny living units, the total revenue obtained from

each building is sufficient to cover the high land costs. These slum areas house marginal individuals (rarely families) who are not very successful in life, and also newly arrived immigrants and other ethnic people (individuals and families) who cannot afford better housing. The term "zone of transition" refers to the fact that as the central business district expands outward, the existing buildings in Zone 2 are generally torn down to make way for new office complexes and retail stores. Consequently, the owners of the old buildings are often waiting to be bought out and do not want to invest the money necessary to keep their property in good repair. The buildings therefore become rundown and dilapidated, and the entire area tends to appear seedy and disreputable.

Zone 3 primarily contains working-class residences, which are a mixture of apartment buildings, duplexes, and small single-family houses crowded closely together, plus a few grocery stores and other retail businesses. Land in this zone is inexpensive enough to permit that kind of housing, but sufficiently expensive to require moderately high density. Most of the houses are of very standard design.

Still further out from the city center is Zone 4, which contains primarily middle-class residences. These tend to be moderate-size single-family homes on lots large enough to allow yards, plus better-quality apartment buildings. The houses are somewhat newer, larger, and display more architectural variation than in Zone 3. Except along major arterial streets, the land is usually zoned strictly for residential use, so that very few stores or businesses are located in this area.

Outside the city limits is Zone 5, consisting of residential suburbs inhabited by upper-middle-class and upper-class families. The houses are relatively new, much larger, located on spacious lots, and of many different architectural designs from modern single-story ranch style to traditional two-story colonial homes. The suburbs that existed in the 1920s when Burgess developed this model were almost exclusively residential in nature. Since then, however, these residential areas have become interspersed with shopping malls, industrial parks, and other enterprises that require large tracts of relatively inexpensive open land.

An alternative model of urban land use was proposed several years later by Homer Hoyte (1939), which has become known as the *sector model*. After studying growth patterns in 142 American cities during the twentieth century, he concluded that transportation routes extending outward from the city center—first railroads, and increasingly major thoroughfare streets—had been the principal avenues of development. He therefore argued that various land-use activities have tended to push outward along those transportation corridors in relatively homogeneous wedge-shaped sectors. Industries might follow one transportation route from the inner city clear to the suburbs, extending laterally on both sides of that route as they moved outward. Commercial establishments might follow another transportation route, ethnic settlements another route, low-income housing still another route, and so on. His model was also based on the thesis that market values determine land use, but the critical factor influencing those values in his view was access to transportation routes rather than distance from the city center.

Another alternative model was developed a few years later by Chauncy Harris and Edward Ulman (1945), which they called the *multiple-nuclei model*. They noted that different activities—such as manufacturing, warehousing, wholesaling, retailing, recreation, ethnic settlements, and exclusive residential areas—tend to cluster together around particular locations throughout the urban community. This occurs because similar activities need to be near one another for ease of access, and because once a particular kind of activity begins to dominate an area, it is no longer considered suitable (for economic and social reasons) for other activities. The result is a series of identifiable and relatively homogeneous areas scattered in no particular arrangement from the inner city to outlying suburbs. Nevertheless, this process of functional clustering is still a consequence of market forces that determine land values.

These three alternative models of urban land use are illustrated in Figure 14-1.

Anyone familiar with the complex, intermixed patterns of land use that exist in large cities today will realize that these models are grossly oversimplified, and that most cities display all three kinds of patterns, and possibly others as well. Concentric circles of different land uses, wedge-shaped sectors of similar activities, and scattered clusters of homogenous functions can all be identified, superimposed on top of one another. Consequently, *these land use models are most useful when applied in combination*.

In other societies, land use patterns are often quite different from American cities, so that long-established high-status residential neighborhoods may be located adjacent to a central plaza, while factories may have been constructed in outlying suburbs. Historical patterns of urban growth and cultural values concerning land use vary widely from one society to another and must always be taken into account. Nevertheless, *identifiable patterns of land use are a basic feature of urban communities in all societies*.

The Inner City

The most distinctive section of any metropolis is its *inner city,* or the areas located in and immediately around the central business district. In the Burgess concentric zone model, this is zones one and two. The principal activity in the inner city is business and commerce, although a considerable number of people also live there.

Since World War II, there has been a continual movement of many kinds of business firms from the inner city to outlying areas in all American and many European cities. Industries that were originally located between the central business district and residential areas have moved outward in search of large tracts of cheap land with low taxes on which to build new plants. This movement was greatly accelerated by the construction of the interstate highway system in the 1950s and 1960s,

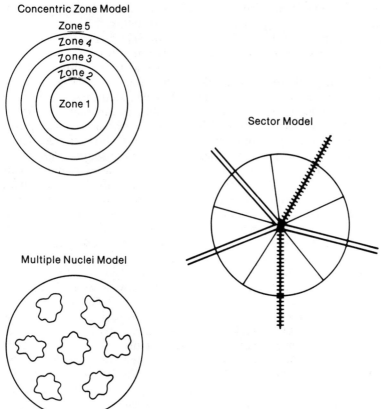

Concentric Zone Model

Zone 5
Zone 4
Zone 3
Zone 2
Zone 1

Sector Model

Multiple Nuclei Model

FIGURE 14-1
Alternative models
of urban land use

which bought up large amounts of land in the old industrial sections for highway construction and provided excellent transportation access to outlying areas. During the last thirty years, new manufacturing plants and industrial parks have therefore been constructed largely on the outskirts of cities. For the same reasons, wholesale firms have also tended to move from the inner city to outlying areas. Retail stores and service establishments, meanwhile, need to be located near residential areas. With the post-war growth of vast suburban residential housing, consequently, has come the development of suburban shopping malls that have drawn much of the retail trade away from the central business district.

This continuing movement of many kinds of businesses out of the inner city has been so extensive that during the 1960s and 1970s it appeared that many inner cities would become largely abandoned wastelands of decaying, unused buildings. Some urban planners even began to speculate that the inner city was a relic of the past, so that the metropolis of the future would resemble a donut with a hole in the middle that might best be converted to parklands. That speculation overlooked the fact, however, that there are still many kinds of activities that need to be located in the central business district for ease of access with one another and with the entire metropolitan area. These include corporate offices (even though their plants and warehouses are located on the outskirts of the city), financial institutions (banks, insurance companies, investment firms, etc.), government agencies (local governments and state and federal offices), major hotels and convention facilities, and cultural institutions (museums, libraries, concert halls, live theaters, etc.).

During the 1970s and 1980s, many large cities in the United States have been experiencing an urban renaissance in their central business district. Existing buildings in the inner city have been renovated, and new office towers and other kinds of buildings are being constructed at an unprecedented rate. This rejuvenation of the inner city has been due partially to private market forces spurred by economic growth. To a considerable extent, however, it is a result of intentional, planned efforts by business and civic leaders to reverse the trend of inner city decline and preserve the downtown area as the heart of the city. City governments have undertaken comprehensive planning efforts, established task forces of community leaders, provided land and financial incentives for new development, improved urban transportation systems, and taken many other steps to promote the rebirth of the inner city.

Suburbanization

This process, which has dominated American metropolises for the past half-century, refers to the *growth of suburbs that surround a central city and are politicially autonomous, but economically and socially linked with it.* Suburbs may be either incorporated towns or unincorporated areas governed by a township or county board. Despite their political autonomy, however, suburbs are socially and economically part of the total metropolitan area. The lifestyles, attitudes and values, and cultural orientations of suburban dwellers are decidedly urban rather than rural in nature.

Historically, the majority of people who have moved to the suburbs have come from the central city. From the perspective of the city, therefore, suburbanization represents a process of population dispersion and functional decentralization. For the metropolis as a whole, nevertheless, it represents expansion. People who have moved to suburbs from towns and rural areas outside metropolises, meanwhile, have contributed to urban and metropolitan growth.

Suburbanization in the United States began in the late nineteenth century, as upper-class families built summer homes outside the cities on railroad lines. Between roughly 1900 and 1920, suburban development was spurred primarily by the expansion of streetcar lines, which began to fill in the areas between railroad lines, with the result that the suburbs became increasingly upper-middle-class permanent residences. During the 1920s and 1930s the automobile became steadily more important in facilitating suburbanization, since it provided access to land not served by railroads or streetcars. As late as 1940, however, only 20 percent of the U.S. population lived in suburbs.

Massive suburban growth began immediately following World War II, and has never abated. Since 1950, almost all growth in metropolitan areas in the United States has occurred in the suburbs and outer urban fringes, not in the central cities. As was shown in Table 14-1, in 1950 only about one-fourth of the U.S. population lived in suburban areas. By 1970, however, more people resided in the suburban areas of metropolises than in their central cities (Kasarda and Redfearn, 1975). As also shown in Table 14-1, in 1980 approximately 60 percent of all metropolitan residents were located in the suburbs (defined by the U.S. Census as all areas within Metropolitan Statistical Areas outside their central city or cities), so that only 40 percent of metropolitan residents remained in central cities. Between 1970 and 1980, ten of the 30 largest central cities actually declined in population.

Prior to World War II, suburbs were composed almost entirely of residences, so that they became known as "bedroom communities." Most suburbanites still worked in the central city and had to commute into the city every day. Beginning in the 1950s and accelerating ever since then, however, businesses of all kinds have also joined the exodus to the suburbs, so that many people now work in the suburb where they live or in another suburb. Today, more than twice as many people commute from one suburb to another as commute from a suburb into the central city (*Time* Magazine, 1987:15). The most recent trend in this movement of jobs to the suburbs has been the construction of vast office complexes in outlying sections of metropolitan areas. In 1975, suburban office construction exceeded construction in central cities for the first time, and about 60 percent of all new offices are now being built in the suburbs. As recently as 1970, for example, Tysons Corner—an unincorporated part of Fairfax County in Virginia outside of Washington, D.C.—was little more than a crossroads with a gas station. Today it contains more office space than Baltimore.

As these suburban areas—which often encompass entire countries outside the central city—develop their own economic base of factories, shopping centers, and offices, they are no longer just bedroom communities. Although still part of the metropolitan region, they are increasingly becoming communities in their own right. Consequently, the term "suburb" is not very appropriate for many of them, and should probably be replaced with an alternative concept such as "satellite community." Nor is suburban living any longer a privilege of the affluent minority. Large numbers of middle- and working-class people now reside in suburban and satellite communities. On the whole, suburbanites are still above average in socioeconomic status, but people of all status levels can often be found in these communities. More distinctive than the class structure of these areas, however, is their racial composition, which is often 90 percent or more white. This situation is no longer due to legal segregation, but is rather a result of informal social pressures and the higher cost of housing in suburban neighborhoods. Nevertheless, considerable numbers of blacks have recently been moving out of central cities, so that about one-fifth of all black families now live in the suburbs.

Many interrelated factors have contributed to producing this massive suburbanization movement. Some of these factors are well-understood, despite their relatively intangible sociocultural nature. Most Americans have a strong desire to live in single-family houses rather than apartments. With the financial affluence that has characterized the American economy since World War II, large numbers of people have wanted and could afford newer, larger, and nicer homes, which were located primarily in the suburbs. They have sought to escape the congestion, noise, crime, and pollution of many inner-city neighborhoods. And they have valued the family-centered lifestyle and good schools that are generally available in suburban areas. In addition, considerable numbers of white families—although we don't know how many, since people rarely admit this—have moved to the suburbs to avoid an influx of blacks into their inner-city neighborhood or to keep their children out of racially integrated schools.

Other factors affecting suburbanization are more economically tangible, though often not so obvious. Most land available for new housing construction is located outside the central city, in what was once farms and pastures. Constructing new housing in the suburbs is therefore less expensive than refurbishing old housing in the inner city, especially when a contractor can put up a whole development at one time. Government loans from the Federal Housing Authority and the Veterans Administration are frequently easier to obtain for purchasing suburban houses than for houses in the city. And as more and more jobs have moved out of central cities, living in the suburbs eliminates expensive commuting to work.

SOCIAL LIFE

A second perspective for examining the social organization of urban communities is to focus on the ways in which urban residents live. This concern with urban living patterns and lifestyles, or *urbanism,* has been quite extensive in sociology.

Ideological Viewpoints

Two contrasting ideological viewpoints have pervaded much of the sociological research and writing on urbanism. The earlier, pessimistic view tended to idolize small town and rural life and to see urban living as the primary source of many contemporary social problems. The later, optimistic view, tends to exalt urban life as much more stimulating and sophisticated than found in small towns and rural areas.

The earlier viewpoint stems from the writings of the German sociologist Ferdinand Tönnies, who was concerned with the effects of industrialization and urbanization on social life. His major work, translated into English as *Community and Society* (1957), was first published in 1887. He argued that traditional societies tended to be characterized primarily by *Gemeinschaft,* or communal, relationships. Social interaction was informal and personal in nature, individuals had close ties with one another in their extended family and community, there was a strong sense of communal solidarity, and common cultural values and norms were widely shared and rigorously enforced through interpersonal influence. Modern societies, in contrast, tend to be characterized primarily by *Gesellschaft,* or associational, relationships. Social interaction is largely formal and impersonal in nature, individuals relate to one another mainly in functionally specialized roles at work and in other associations, people are more concerned about their personal interests than collective goals, and cultural values and norms are highly diverse and depend on formal sanctions for enforcement. Although this distinction between Gemeinschaft and Gesellschaft social relationships is clearly oversimplified, it has strongly influenced sociological theorizing about urban social life.

The Chicago urban sociologists placed great emphasis on this typology during the 1920s and 1930s. The classic statement of their thinking about urban living patterns was Louis Wirth's essay on "Urbanism as a Way of Life" (1938). Drawing heavily on Tönnies, as well as the earlier German sociologist Georg Simmel, Wirth stressed three features of cities that shape urban life: their *large size, population density,* and *social diversity.* Urban dwellers can know personally only a tiny fraction of all the people in their large community. Consequently, although they may interact with many other people in the course of their daily activities, those interactions are of necessity impersonal and superficial. The population density of urban communities leads people to deal with others as transitory role enactors, not as whole persons, and their actions are based on rational self-interest rather than communal trust and loyalty. Family and neighborhood ties are weakened or obliterated. The social diversity that occurs among urban dwellers contributes not only to impersonality and anonymity but also to segregation of people along class, ethnic, racial, religious, and other lines. Combined with extensive role specialization and economic division of labor, urban social diversity precludes any kind of cultural consensus. As a result, people became more tolerant of new or different ideas and lifestyles but lose all sense of collective cohesion.

In short, Wirth argued that *social life in the city becomes highly individualistic and Gesellschaft in nature, in contrast to the communal Gemeinschaft way of life found in rural areas and small towns.* Some people welcome and thrive in this kind of urban social environment. Many others, however—especially migrants from small towns and rural areas—experience great difficulty in coping with it. They feel isolated and alienated, encounter continual social tensions and conflict, and frequently fall into various kinds of deviance such as alcoholism, mental illness, drug abuse, delinquency, crime, and suicide. Implicit in this argument, obviously, is the belief that small town and rural life is more psychologically and sociologically beneficial for most people.

This theme of urban impersonality and anonymity pervaded sociological writings for several decades. Although Wirth's article was intended to be only an analysis of urban lifestyles, many sociologists interpreted it as a broad critique of the effects of societal modernization on the quality of social life. This theme was perhaps best expressed in a book by David Reisman, *The Lonely Crowd* (Reisman, et al., 1954). Portraying the members of modern societies as isolated and lonely individuals adrift in a vast crowd of strangers, the book became a best seller and influenced countless sociologists and popular writers.

A more recent view of urban life was developed by a number of sociologists during the 1960s (Gans, 1962; Greer, 1962; Wilensky, 1966). On the basis of in-depth studies of the ways in which city dwellers live, these researchers concluded that *urban social life is generally quite highly organized and stable.* Although urban living does involve more contacts with different kinds of people and more diversity of activities than commonly found in small towns and rural areas, urban people are generally not isolated or alienated or disorganized. They establish circles of friends and routines of daily activities, just as do small town and rural dwellers. They have a sense of shared community that centers on their family and neighborhood. And they are no more likely than other people to engage in deviant actions. If inner-city Chicago residents in the 1920s and 1930s were particularly prone to deviance, it was probably an outcome of their migration from rural to urban living, not an inevitable consequence of living in the city. In short, urban life displays considerable Gemeinschaft as well as Gesellschaft characteristics.

These later urban sociologists have been quite enthusiastic about the beneficial aspects of urban life. Urban dwellers can choose their friends on the basis of shared interests and values and don't have to restrict their friends to people who live near them. Urban school systems are generally far superior to rural schools, and the job market in the city provides a much wider array of employment opportunities. In the city, individuals enjoy more freedom to choose a lifestyle that suits them, rather than being forced to adapt to predetermined traditional patterns of living. And there is much greater cultural diversity and intellectual stimulation in the city, so that urban living encourages people to become cosmopolitan and sophisticated.

Numerous empirical studies have been conducted by sociologists to test these competing views of urban social life. The usual procedure has been to compare the number of personal friendships among urban residents with those among rural, small-town, and suburban dwellers. In one of those studies, for instance, Reiss (1959) found virtually no differences between urban, rural-nonfarm and rural-farm dwellers in their frequency of interaction with relatives, best friends, or other friends. He did discover, however, that urban residents were more likely than others to have frequent personal contacts with coworkers—which contradicted Wirth's prediction. This finding has been repeated in numerous subsequent studies, indicating that *urban settings, especially at work, generally provide as many or more opportunities for interaction with friends than do rural settings.*

Other studies have compared the frequency of interaction with neighbors, coworkers, friends, and relatives among residents of central cities versus suburbs. Quite consistently, they have found that this residential difference does not affect the amount of interaction that people have with relatives and coworkers, but that suburbanites do tend to have more interaction with neighbors and friends (Tomeh, 1964; Tallman and Morgner, 1970). Residential location within urban communities may therefore influence some friendship patterns, but this is probably largely a consequence of the fact that suburban residents are more likely to be married and have children, both of which factors tend to give people personal contacts with others.

These research findings clearly indicate that modern urban life has not eliminated personal friendships. Although it is true that we deal today with many people in a rather transitory and impersonal manner, *most members of modern societies do not appear to be socially isolated, but rather are enmeshed in fairly extensive webs of personal relationships with friends.* Instead of being lost in a "lonely crowd" of anonymous strangers, they tend to be linked with others in numerous ways.

The more optimistic view of urban social life is also supported by studies of recent trends in small towns and rural areas. Numerous developments in communications, transportation, education, employment, and other realms of social life have tended to make small town and rural living much more similar to urban living than was the case fifty years ago. Consequently, most sociologists today argue that *the size of the community in which people live is not usually a critical factor in shaping patterns of social life.* Much more important than place of residence are such factors as people's socioeconomic class, racial/ethnic status, age and sex, and occupational history—all of which vary widely among communities of all sizes.

Urban Neighborhoods

To a casual observer, the working- and middle-class residential sections of central cities may appear to be just block after block of nondescript small houses and older apartment buildings. Sociologists have discovered, however, that *urban neighborhoods are often highly organized small communities located within the urban environment.* In the United States, these neighborhoods are frequently based on ethnicity or race, as well as social class. Most large American cities contain several clearly identifiable ethnic neighborhoods. Depending on the history and location of the city, these people may be Poles, Italians, Puerto Ricans, Mexicans, Japanese, Chinese, or Scandinavians. The common ethnic culture of these neighborhoods often keeps them much more tightly knit and cohesive than other parts of the city.

Herbert Gans's (1962) study of the Italian West End neighborhood of Boston illustrates the characteristics that are common in many urban ethnic neighborhoods. He called these people "ethnic villagers" to indicate that, sociologically, they were living in a small village within the heart of Boston. They had a deep sense of neighborhood territoriality, could easily describe the boundaries of their neighborhood, and identified closely with this neighborhood. Much of their social life centered on strong social relationships with kin in the neighborhood, so that the extended family was the dominant social unit. Peer groups based on age and sex were also very important for youth and adults. People gave minimal attention to the external appearance of their house and yard, so that the area was often described by outsiders as a slum, but the residents placed great emphasis on keeping the interiors of their homes respectable and comfortable—which often meant filling them with as much furniture and knick-knacks as possible. The home was basically for family use only, however; most casual social interaction took place on front stoops or on the sidewalk. Because of the total orientation of these urban villagers to their ethnic neighborhood, they tended to be rather unaware of the larger city around them. As a consequence, they were quite unsophisticated about dealing with city government to secure public services and protect the interests of their neighborhood.

Ethnic villages persist because their residents choose to remain living in their neighborhoods. Even if their job relocates to a different part of the city or they become affluent enough to enable them to move to the suburbs, they tend to stay in the neighborhood because of its close social ties and cultural heritage. This is not usually the case with racially based neighborhoods, however. *Black neighborhoods—or black ghettos or black belts, as they are variously called—are much more likely to persist because of discrimination and segregation against blacks.* Although black neighborhoods may display many of the same characteristics as ethnic neighborhoods, they are heavily influenced by the external social forces of racial job discrimination and housing segregation. In some cities, these factors also apply to Orientals or other ethnic people, although rarely as extensively as to blacks.

Racial discrimination in employment in regard to hiring, job promotions, and wage levels keeps large numbers of black people relatively poor, so that they cannot afford to move out of the ghetto to higher-status neighborhoods. In 1985, the median annual income of all black households in the United States was about $15,000, compared to about $25,000 for all white households (U.S. Bureau of the Census, 1987:431). Although there is a sizable black middle class in the United States today, over one-third of all black households have incomes of less than $10,000, which places many of them below the federal poverty line.

Racial segregation in housing is no longer legal anywhere in the United States, but it is still widely prevalent—especially in large cities—because of racial attitudes and housing preferences of whites. In 1960, Karl and Alma Taeuber (1965) discovered that in the 207 largest American cities the average segregation index was 86 percent, which meant that this percentage of all nonwhites would have to move from their present housing if residential segregation were to be completely eliminated. This rate has declined somewhat in most cities since then, but is still over 75 percent in the majority of U.S. cities (Sorenson, et al., 1975). Basically, many white people do not want to live in neighborhoods that are predominantly black (Van Valey, et al., 1977).

Although most whites now say that they would not mind having some black families of their same socioeconomic level living in their neighborhood, they object when the proportion of blacks becomes too large. When a neighborhood begins to "tip" toward black residents—which is commonly between one-third to one-half black—many white families begin moving away as quickly as possible. When this occurs, they tend to be replaced by more blacks, until shortly the entire neighborhood is largely black and racial segregation is again perpetuated.

Social Participation

One of the major differences between the pessimistic and optimistic views of urban life concerns the extent to which individuals participate in informal social interaction with kin and friends and in more formal associations. Numerous sociological studies of these patterns of social participation have reached quite consistent conclusions (Reiss, 1959; Greer, 1969; Verba and Nie, 1972; Olsen, 1978; Suttles, 1978).

Interaction with family members is extremely important for most people, regardless of where they live or their social class. Frequency of kinship interaction varies considerably among individuals, but it is generally as extensive in urban and suburban settings as in small towns and rural areas. On the average, working-class people tend to interact somewhat more frequently with their relatives than do middle-class people, but this is probably more a consequence of social and geographic mobility than class. Individuals who have about the same level of education and the same kind of occupations as most of their relatives and who continue to reside in or near the community where they grew up generally find it easier to maintain close ties with their families. Kinship relationships are more difficult to sustain if a person is a college graduate when the rest of his or her relatives have only attended high school, if one enters a business or professional career when the rest of the family hold manual jobs, or if one moves far away from most other family members. Consequently, individuals who leave a farm or small town to go to college in the city and subsequently follow an urban-based career path may find themselves cut off socially and geographically from many of their kin. But this is a result of their mobility, not their place of residence.

Rural and small-town dwellers are more likely than urban residents to be acquainted with many of their immediate neighbors. In the past, limited transportation and communication forced rural and small-town people to find many of their friends among their neighbors. This is much less true today, however, as these people are able to broaden their circle of acquaintances. In the city and suburbs people are more likely to find their friends at work, in their place of worship, and in voluntary associations to which they belong. Urban residents may therefore not be very familiar with their neighbors—especially if they do not live in an ethnic or racially based neighborhood—but this does not mean that they are socially isolated. When urban dwellers do know their neighbors, this is often a result of friendships among their children, which brings the parents into contact with one another. But because families in the suburbs are more likely than those in the central city to have children living at home, interaction with neighbors tends to be more extensive in surburban areas.

Interaction with personal friends is very widespread regardless of where people live. Most individuals have a circle of close friends that may be limited to two or three others or may include eight or ten people. In addition, they are likely to have a much larger circle of acquaintances whom they know casually. Frequency of interacting with close friends varies widely, with about one-fourth of all people reporting that they do this several times a week, about one-fourth doing it approximately once a week, about one-fourth seeing their friends once or twice a month, and the remaining one-fourth doing this less often. In general, the higher one's socioeconomic status, the more personal friends one is likely to have, the more geographically dispersed those friends tend to be, and the more often one is likely to see one's friends. This tendency is not very pronounced, however, and many individual factors influence the extent and frequency of a person's relationships with friends. However, place of residence has no affect on these friendship patterns.

Voluntary association participation is often thought to be extremely prevalent in the United States, especially among urban residents, but that assumption is relatively invalid. Apart from a place of worship, approximately 40 percent of all Americans belong to no voluntary interest association, about 30 percent belong to only one such organization, and only about 30 percent belong to two or more of these associations. Rates of attendance or other forms of participation in voluntary associations are even lower. When asked how many associations they attend regularly, about 60 percent of all people say none, about 25 percent say one, and only about 15 percent report attending meetings of two or more associations fairly regularly. The most common kinds of voluntary associations to which people belong—again, other than a place of worship—are labor unions, educational organizations (usually a Parent-Teacher Association), fraternal associations (such as Rotary or Kiwanis clubs), and sports and recreational groups. Membership and participation in voluntary associations of all kinds—and also in places of worship—increases steadily with educational attainment, occupational status, and income level. It is also positively related to one's age and length of residence in the community, but it is not related at all to the size of the community. Suburban residents are somewhat more likely than those in the central city to become involved in these associations, but that is largely a result of their higher average socioeconomic statuses rather than their location. Finally, when socioeconomic status is held constant, blacks tend to participate in voluntary associations somewhat more frequently than do whites.

The principal point here is that *forms and rates of all types of social participation vary considerably among different kinds of individuals, but the size of one's community has very little effect on any of these activities.*

POLITICAL ECONOMY

An urban community is a highly complex form of social organization. As in all complex organizations, its economic and political systems constitute the core of its functioning.

Consequently, a third perspective for understanding urban communities is to examine their political economies.

Economic Base

A central concern in urban economics is the economic base of a community. *A city's economic base consists of those economic activities that provide its major sources of jobs, income, and wealth.* These basic economic activities exert widespread influence on the community's spatial patterns, buildings and other physical structures, population size and composition, government, and social structure.

Historically, the economic bases of most cities have fallen into one or more of six broad categories: *commerce*, including wholesale and retail trade, finance, and business management; *transportation*, including shipping ports, rail and road junctions, and storage facilities; *extraction*, such as mining, lumbering, and fishing; *government*, either local, regional (states, provences), or national; *manufacturing*, ranging from handicrafts through assembly plants to heavy industry; and *culture*, including higher education, church administration, and the arts. During their early stages of development, cities often concentrate their basic economic activities in one of those categories, but in later stages they frequently expand into several categories.

Economic base theory (Rasmussen, 1973; Richardson, 1977) argues that all aspects of a city's economic system are shaped by the nature of its base. The economic base is often divided into two sectors: the *export sector*, composed of those goods and services that are marketed or supplied outside the community, and the *local sector*, composed of all goods and services that are consumed within the community. Urban economists have traditionally assumed that the export sector was more critical for the economic well-being of the community, since it was seen as the primary source of financial capital for resource acquisition, economic investment, new employment, and community development. For example, one new job in the export sec-

tor can create two additional new support jobs in the local sector, and those three new jobs together can provide economic support for a total of six or more people. Consequently, the growth and economic well-being of the community has been thought to depend principally on expansion of the export sector of its economic base.

Paradoxically, however, as a city grows in size, the local sector of its economy tends to become increasingly dominant. Provided that the economy is viable, the demand for consumer goods and services often grows much more rapidly than the population size, as residents strive to improve their standard of living. As local businesses develop to meet those demands, the local sector becomes increasingly important. In addition, many business firms begin to produce goods and services for both the local and export markets, which tends to obliterate the distinction between those sectors. *Current thinking in urban economics therefore stresses that the export and local sectors are equally important.*

Two interrelated themes tend to dominate recent thinking about urban political economies. One of these is the many ways in which *the economies of all cities are closely linked with the national economy* through large corporations, financial institutions, and mass advertising and marketing. Neither the local nor the export sector of an urban economy can escape these pervasive external economic influences. Second, as urban economies are increasingly being regulated by governmental laws and agencies, it has become obvious that *these economies cannot be understood without also considering the political system* at all levels of government. Consequently, the concept of an interrelated urban political economy is rapidly replacing earlier ideas about the economy and the polity of a city as separate systems.

Labor Markets

An urban economy can be viewed as a highly complex labor market in which organizations are continually looking for employees and individuals are searching for jobs. How well these two sides of the urban labor market mesh together has multiple consequences for both the city's economy and its inhabitants.

The principal feature of an urban labor market, in contrast to a rural or small-town labor market, is extreme occupational specialization and diversity. Even a modest-sized city may provide thousands of different kinds of jobs, and in a large metropolis the labor market may encompass several hundred thousand job specialties. As a result, the process of matching workers with jobs is considerably more complicated than in nonurban areas. Two crucial aspects of this process of bringing workers together with jobs involve the kinds of workers available and the location of those people vis-a-vis existing job opportunities.

In regard to the kinds of workers available, some occupational capabilities tend to be oversupplied, while others are undersupplied in many cities. Very generally—recognizing that there are major differences among urban communities—there is often a surplus of unskilled manual laborers, semi-skilled factory workers and machine operators, sales clerks, clerical and other office workers, and small shopkeepers. Shortages, meanwhile, often occur for skilled craft trades, service workers, technicians of many kinds, administrative secretaries, high-status salespersons (insurance and securities), managers, and many kinds of semiprofessional (accountants and nurses) and professional (scientists and physicians) personnel. The fundamental problem here is that most of the available jobs either pay minimum wages (manual labor, many service occupations, fastfood workers, etc.) or require special training or skills (craftspersons, technicans, professionals, etc.). As a result, many of the people looking for work cannot afford to take the jobs available, or they are not qualified for them. Many cities today are therefore experiencing the twin problems of large numbers of low-skilled people unable to find work and large numbers of high-skilled jobs that cannot be filled.

In regard to the locations of workers, the major problem is that people seeking employment often live some distance from the available jobs for which they are qualified. In the past, the typical situation was that managers, administrators, professionals, and other higher-status persons tended to live in the suburbs, while their job opportunities were located mainly in the central city. This required them to make long and expensive commutes in and out of the city every workday. As businesses and offices have moved outward, that problem has tended to diminish, although many of these people still commute from one suburb to another. Today, it is primarily blue-collar and low-status white-collar workers who encounter a job location problem. Many of them still live in working-class areas of the central city, but the job opportunities available to them are increasingly found in the suburbs. Given their income levels, it is often difficult financially for these people to commute out from the city to the suburbs to find work. Consequently, industries and offices located in suburban areas are frequently hard-pressed to find enough blue-collar and clerical workers to meet their needs.

Power Structures

Within every urban community there is an elaborate structure of power relationships that centers in its political economy. Some of this power is formalized in the local political system, but much of it occurs in informal interpersonal interactions outside the government. These community power structures have been studied at great length since the 1950s by sociologists and political scientists.

Much of this research on community power has been concerned with the question of who determines basic policies on key community issues. There is general agreement that *in all communities most major decisions are made by a relatively small number of influential leaders.* There have been sharp disagreements, however, over such issues as "How can these elites be identified?", "How large is the set of elites in various commu-

FIGURE 14-2   Elitism and pluralism urban power perspectives

Elitism Perspective

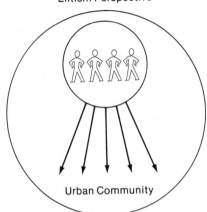

Urban Community

Pluralism Perspective

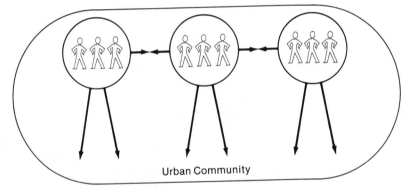

Urban Community

nities?", "What kinds of people are members of the power elite?", and "In what ways do elites exercise their power?" For many years, social scientists were sharply divided into two conflicting camps concerning these four questions. One of those camps was usually called the "elitism" perspective, while the other was known as the "pluralism" perspective. They are illustrated in Figure 14-2.

The *elitism perspective*, which was initially formulated by Floyd Hunter in his study of the power structure of Atlanta, Georgia, was often favored by sociologists (Hunter, 1953). These researchers generally agreed on the following matters:

(1) The best way of identifying powerful elites was by using the reputational method, in which community leaders are asked to name those individuals who are believed to exercise the most influence on major community issues. The persons identified in this manner are, in turn, asked the same question through several successive stages until consensus is reached on the circle of key elites.

(2) In most communities studied using this reputational method, the number of key elites was usually found to be quite small, often numbering no more than 30 to 50 people, most of whom knew one another personally, interacted very frequently, and were quite cohesive.

(3) With a few exceptions, these key elites tended to be executives of large business corporations and other major businessmen in the community, not government officials.

(4) In general, community elites exercised influence on policy issues through interpersonal interaction with one another, not through established political procedures.

In short, *the elitism perspective argued that key decisions on major community issues tend to be made informally in private by a small and highly interrelated set of private economic elites who agree on basic policies.*

The pluralism perspective, which was first developed by Robert Dahl in a study of the power structure of New Haven, Connecticut, was usually favored by political scientists (Dahl, 1961). These researchers held rather different views on the preceding four matters.

(1) The best way of identifying community leaders, they argued, was the decisional method, in which specific decisions that have been made in a community in recent years are examined in depth, and people who are knowledgeable about those decisions are asked who actually made them. The emphasis is thus on participation in decision making, rather than a reputation for being influential.

(2) Although the set of top leaders located in these studies was also usually no larger than about fifty, they were generally found to be organized into several subsets focusing on specific issues, so that there were very few general leaders who dealt with all issues. Because leaders tended to be issue-specific, community power structures were at least partially pluralist in nature.

(3) Most leaders were either local government officials or leaders of community organizations, not corporate executives or other businessmen. The political, rather than the economic, system tended to be dominant in the community.

(4) Each decision tended to be made by the subset of leaders concerned about it, and it was usually reached through relatively formal political procedures rather than informal interaction. Most issues involved considerable conflict, so that decisions were reached through compromise rather than consensus.

In short, *the pluralism perspective argued that policy decisions on major community issues tend to be made formally by specialized sets of public community leaders through negotiation and compromise.*

In recent years, we have come to realize that the findings of these two camps of researchers were much more similar than was first thought. There is a rather small set of elites or leaders within every community who generally formulate basic policies and make key decisions on major issues. In some cases these are business people, while in other cases they are public officials and/or leaders of community organizations. Sometimes they work together on numerous issues, while at other times they specialize on particular issues. A great deal of interpersonal interaction occurs among these elites or leaders, some of which is conducted in private and some of which occurs in public settings. On some issues there is general consensus on what should be done, while on the other issues there may be sharp differences of opinion that require negotiation and compromise. However, *very rarely do most community residents become involved in any community issues through public discussions, organizational activities, or voting.*

We have also come to realize that *cities vary considerably in their power structures.* After the power structures of more than a hundred communities had been examined, several social scientists (Aiken, 1970; Clark, 1968) looked at all of them to discover what features of cities are associated with relatively centralized versus decentralized power systems.

In general, they found that cities in the United States tend to have relatively diversified urban power structures if they display the characteristics listed below. Conversely, if they display the opposites of these characteristics, they tend to have relatively monolithic power structures.

(1) Had become a large metropolis prior to the twentieth century;

(2) Are located in the Northeast or North-central regions of the country;

(3) Have a population over one million;

(4) Contain a heterogeneous population in terms of race, ethnicity, and religion;

(5) Have a large proportion of their labor force working in manufacturing;

(6) Contain a large working class;

(7) Have strong labor unions;

(8) Contain many large, nonlocal business corporations;

(9) Have a diversified economy, with no single industry dominating the city;

(10) Contain many active voluntary associations;

(11) Experience numerous community conflicts;

(12) Have strong competitive political parties;

(13) Contain a Democratic voting majority;

(14) Have a dynamic mayor; and

(15) Have established an extensive local governmental structure.

Without going into the reasons underlying each of those relationships, it should be obvious that all of these factors tend to make a city more complex and diverse. *Social, economic, and political diversity tends, in turn, to give rise to a relatively decentralized power structure.* Conversely, in less complexly organized communities, it is easier for community elites to sustain a relatively centralized structure of power.

The comparative studies of urban power structures also analyzed the consequences of diversified versus monolithic power systems for community programs of various kinds. Again generalizing from studies of many communities, they concluded that the more dispersed the structure of power in a city, the more likely it was to have accomplished all of the following:

(1) Initiated extensive and adequate housing programs for low-income families;

(2) Conducted effective urban renewal programs;

(3) Developed numerous programs as part of the War on Poverty in the 1960s and 1970s; and

(4) Carried out comprehensive planning to improve the inner city.

URBAN MANAGEMENT

A fourth perspective from which to study urban communities is to examine ways in which community leaders—public and private—are attempting to manage and improve urban living conditions. Much of the early research done from this perspective focused on problems of individuals' adaptation to urban life, ranging from social isolation to deviant behavior. Since the 1950s, sociologists have been giving increasing attention to organizational problems of urban communities. Three types of urban management that are critically important in most large cities are explored in this section: slum removal, housing assistance, and comprehensive planning.

Slum Removal

As industries and wholesalers steadily moved out of the "zone of transition" surrounding the central business district, this area degenerated into slums of abandoned buildings and dilapidated tenements and rooming houses that became eyesores and the setting of a great deal of quasi-legal and illegal activities. The people living in these areas tend to be socially marginal individuals and ethnic minorities. To improve the buildings in these areas and thus eliminate slums, three different approaches have been tried in many cities.

The first approach, which was promoted primarily during the 1950s and 1960s, is *urban renewal*. Its objective is to replace inner-city slums and blighted areas with middle-class housing (usually apartment buildings) and retail stores. With federal money, the city buys, clears, and improves large areas surrounding the central business district. The land is then sold to private developers for about one-third the cost of acquiring and preparing it, with the understanding that they will construct new housing and other buildings in accord with the city's redevelopment plan. Since these are usually luxury apartments and office buildings, however, urban renewal programs have eliminated more than ten times as many housing units as they have constructed. Since the former residents of the slum housing that is torn down can rarely afford the new housing that is constructed, urban renewal projects often result in thousands of low-income individuals and families being displaced from their homes. And since large proportions of those former residents are usually blacks or other minorities, urban renewal has frequently been a synonym for "black removal." In short, *urban renewal is intended to upgrade inner-city areas, both physically and socially, not to provide housing for low-income urban dwellers.*

The second approach is *urban rehabilitation.* Many buildings in blighted areas—especially old factories and warehouses—are still structurally sound. Instead of tearing them down, the city (again using federal funds) provides grants and subsidies to developers who renovate those buildings into attractive commercial complexes containing specialty shops, restaurants, markets, and artists' studios, as well as middle- and upper-income apartments. Funds may also be given to individual residents to renovate their homes in these areas. However, the people who do this are usually relatively affluent families who buy inner-city housing expressly for this purpose, not the original residents of those buildings. Like urban renewal, *urban rehabilitation is intended to improve inner-city areas by changing them from slums into upper-middle-class neighborhoods.*

The third approach to urban redevelopment is called *urban gentrification.* It also preserves existing buildings by renovating them but focuses largely on residences rather than businesses. And instead of using federal funds and being directed by the city, gentrification is usually carried out entirely by private developers and residents. Since the developer who undertakes such a project can make a profit only if the market value of

---

FORMS OF URBAN SLUM REMOVAL

1. Urban renewal.
2. Urban rehabilitation.
3. Urban gentrification.

---

the renovated property rises sharply, it is crucial that an entire neighborhood be gentrified at the same time, since if even one or two old tenements remain, the neighborhood will not acquire a gentrified appearance and reputation. Because this process is done entirely with private funds, the resulting housing is normally extremely expensive. It typically attracts high-income business and professional people (usually without children) who enjoy urban living and want to reside near their place of work. *Many gentrified neighborhoods have become quite prestigious locations for affluent urbanites,* so that what was once a slum becomes a very high-status neighborhood. In Washington, D.C., for example, gentrified Georgetown is "the place" to live.

Although all three of these approaches to urban development have greatly improved the physical conditions of many inner-city areas, they have not solved the problems of urban deterioration, blight, and slums. Every large city attracts considerable numbers of individuals with little money and many serious personal problems. Their plight may be due to a variety of causes, including personal disabilities (mental illness, alcoholism, drug use), unemployment (lack of employable skills and unavailability of unskilled jobs), and racial and ethnic discrimination. Some of these individuals (few of them are family units) live literally on the streets, while many others exist in abandoned buildings, cheap hotels, flophouses, and run-down tenements. They cannot afford to live elsewhere, and they must live somewhere. Unless a city is willing to provide free or very inexpensive public housing for them, they will continue to congregate in the inner city, and the landlords who exploit them will continue to create urban slums.

Housing Assistance

In the United States, obtaining housing has traditionally been defined as a personal matter for each individual or household to deal with in the marketplace. Construction and financing of housing has therefore been largely the prerogative of private businesses, not the government. In many European countries, in contrast, housing has long been considered a public concern to be guided and assisted by governmental policies and programs. The U.S. government did not become involved in housing matters in any way until the depression of the 1930s, and not to any extent until after World War II. Even today the United States has no national housing policy. Federal and state concern with housing in this country can be divided into two broad categories: *home ownership assistance* and *low-income housing programs* (Palen, 1981; Bollens and Schmadt, 1982).

The United States government (as well as much of the public) has long assumed that *home ownership* is preferable to renting. To encourage bankers to invest in home mortgages during the depression, the federal government in 1934 created the Federal Housing Administration to insure home loans. Following World War II, the Veterans Administration began offering similar assistance to veterans to enable them to purchase homes. The FHA and VA do not loan money but rather insure home mortgages. This enables lower-income people who might not otherwise qualify for a mortgage to obtain one, usually with less downpayment and at a lower interest rate than with a conventional loan. These programs thus enable many more people to become home owners.

Both of these programs have frequently provided greater benefits to the purchasers of newly constructed houses than to those who bought existing houses. Since most new housing since World War II has been located in the suburbs, these programs have been a major factor promoting suburbanization. At the present time, approximately half of all home mortgages in the United States are insured by the FHA or the VA, so that the federal government is playing a very active role in promoting home ownership. In addition, the U.S. government allows home owners to deduct the interest payments on their home mortgage from their taxable income (renters cannot deduct any portion of their rent payments, however). The total amount of this indirect government subsidy, which strongly encourages people to buy rather than rent their home, is many times greater than all the funds allocated to low-income housing programs.

The first approach taken by the federal government to provide adequate housing for low-income families was to construct *public housing financed entirely with Federal funds*, which began in the late 1930s and reached its peak in the 1950s. Almost all of those projects consisted of a number of large, multiunit buildings located in inner-city neighborhoods and administered by the city government, with rents set somewhat below prevailing market rates. The rather naïve thinking behind this approach was that by putting poor people into better housing, many social problems—from delinquency to desertion—could be greatly reduced. In the words of John Palen (1981:278), this was to be "salvation by bricks and mortar" for the poor. At least one public housing project was constructed in every major city in the country (except San Diego), with a total of over a million rental units.

Initially, public housing was intended to be temporary quarters for low-income employed people who could not currently obtain adequate housing in the private market, but presumably would do so when their financial situation improved. Prospective tenants were carefully screened, rents were sufficient to cover operating costs, and the buildings were well-maintained. During the 1950s this situation changed considerably, however, as large numbers of people migrated to inner cities from rural areas, as the populations of these areas became increasingly black, as thousands of slum dwellers were displaced from their previous housing by urban renewal, and as many tenants became permanently unemployed because of the movement of jobs to the suburbs. By 1960, most public housing had become the residence of last resort for permanently unemployed people living on welfare, a large proportion of whom were black and many of whom were single-parent females with children.

Because of the extreme poverty conditions of most of these tenants, rents had to be lowered considerably, to the point where they no longer covered operating or maintenance costs. As a result, trash was not collected, routine building maintenance was not performed, damage was not repaired, and many projects became so run-down that no one would live in them. These physical conditions, combined with high rates of juvenile delinquency and other deviant behaviors that occurred in the projects because of the social and economic conditions of their residents, resulted in a widespread public reaction against public housing. In 1969, Congress finally authorized funds to cover operating costs and physical repairs in public housing, but at the same time it severely limited further construction of these projects. No public housing has been built since 1973, and it is doubtful if this form of low-income housing will be advocated again for some time to come.

In the 1960s, many legislators, city officials, and urban planners began to argue that instead of building public housing for the poor, the government should give direct *purchase subsidies* to these people so that they could become homeowners. Presumably, they would then have a financial stake in their home and a commitment to the neighborhood, so that their housing would not deteriorate into more slums. This movement culminated in the 1968 Housing and Redevelopment Act, which provided federal subsidies to low-income households for the purchase of homes with government-insured FHA and VA mortgages.

Unfortunately, in many cities this program encouraged widespread fraud and collusion by private developers. The typical pattern was for a developer to buy a large number of run-down inner-city houses at very low cost, make cosmetic improvements such as painting the outside and inside and installing cheap carpeting, and then get city inspectors to certify that the houses were worth a great deal more than their actual market value. The houses were then sold to low-income people at those inflated prices, with the Federal government contributing a large subsidy to reduce the interest rate to the purchaser, while the developer made a huge profit. When the new owners discovered the actual conditions of their homes, they often could not afford to make the necessary major repairs. Within a few years, consequently, many of them defaulted on their mortgages and abandoned their houses. The Department of Housing and Urban Development was left holding over 200,000 of these run-down inner-city houses and thus became the nation's largest slum landlord. Although strict administrative controls were eventually imposed by HUD to prevent this kind of fraud and the program is still in operation, the federal funds available for it have been severely reduced in recent years.

The Housing and Community Development Act of 1974 retained the idea of federal housing subsidies, but shifted the emphasis from purchasing to renting. Under this *rent assistance* program, HUD establishes a "fair rental value" for low-income apartments, certifies people as eligible for the program on the basis of their incomes, and stipulates that they should not pay more than 25 percent of their income for rent. The renter and the landlord sign a contract for that amount of rent, and the government gives the landlord the difference between the actual rent and the property's "fair rental value." In the late 1970s, nearly three-quarters of a million rental units were covered by this program, but it has also been considerably reduced in scope in recent years. The most serious disadvantage of this program is that it fails to provide for the extremely poor who cannot afford to spend even a quarter of their meager income on rent. Landlords, meanwhile, often make substantial profits from the program, since there are no requirements that the apartments be kept in adequate repair.

The latest trend in low-income housing assistance is *urban homesteading*. Since over 150,000 urban dwelling units are abandoned every year, most large cities contain hundreds or thousands of inner-city houses whose ownership has reverted to the city or the federal government. The city contracts with an interested resident to rehabilitate one of these houses to meet housing codes and to live there at least three years, after which the resident acquires full ownership of the building. Although this program appears extremely generous, it has several limitations. First, many abandoned houses are so deteriorated that they are beyond rehabilitation. Second, even if the building is still structurally sound, the cost of renovation is often very high, often running from $20,000 to $50,000. Few low-income people can afford these costs, even if they do all the labor themselves, and financial institutions have been very reluctant to loan this amount of money to low-income people on a house that initially has little market value. Third, since homesteading is done on a house-by-house basis, a rehabilitated house may still be surrounded by abandoned and burned-out buildings, so that the neighborhood remains quite unattractive and the market value of the house remains low. Fourth, homesteading does not apply to apartment buildings, which is where the majority of low-income people live. As a consequence of all these limitations, this program has been quite restricted in scope, with less than 40,000 houses having been homesteaded throughout the country.

URBAN HOUSING ASSISTANCE
PROGRAMS

1. Public housing.
2. Purchase subsidies.
3. Rent assistance.
4. Urban homesteading.

Overall, *the United States has a rather sad history of failing to provide adequate housing for low-income households.* Despite the various kinds of housing programs that have been implemented during the past fifty years, thus far no effective national low-income housing program has been adopted.

Comprehensive Planning

Since the days of ancient Rome, efforts have been made to plan cities in a rational manner. Many European cities that were developed during the medieval period—most notably, Paris—show evidence of geographical and architectural planning. In the twentieth century, urban planning has been widely practiced in a number of northern European nations. For a variety of historical and sociocultural reasons, countries such as Sweden and the Netherlands have been able to formulate and implement planning on a broad scale. In contrast, *planning has not fared well in the United States,* where most urban development has been done by private parties operating in the marketplace. The only American city that is based on any kind of overall plan is Washington, D.C., which was laid out by Pierre L'Enfant in 1791, although much of his master plan was later rejected.

Opponents of planning, particularly in the United States, argue that it tends to become a rigid bureaucratic process that rarely meets the actual needs of the city. It can become extremely expensive and time-consuming, they insist, and is generally quite inefficient. It may also lead to autocratic control of city development by a small set of elites who dominate the planning process. These opponents argue that although the market process of responding to what people want and are willing to pay for is never perfect, most of the time it is more responsible, especially in the long run, to what is actually occurring in a city. In addition, reliance on the market does not require the public funds that are necessary for planning and can be quite financially efficient.

Proponents of planning, on the other hand, argue that market processes are generally oriented to the interests of business and affluent residents and hence fail to serve the broad needs of the entire community. Market activities are always intended to make a profit for certain individuals. If a necessary activity will not be profitable—such as providing clean water or air, public parks, low-income housing, or crime prevention—it will not be undertaken by the private sector. Consequently, public planning is required if the common needs of all residents are to be satisfied. Moreover, if done well, planning need not be rigid, expensive, inefficient, or elitist. Proponents of urban planning are gradually gaining recognition and support in most American cities, so that this process is slowly beginning to prevail over traditional reliance on the marketplace for urban development.

In the twentieth century, urban planning—in the United States and in Europe—has become increasingly comprehensive in nature. Planning can be comprehensive in several different ways. First, *planning can encompass the entire metropolitan area* (and sometimes an entire region), rather than just the central city. Developing a metropolitan-wide plan obviously requires a great deal of coordination among all of the municipal governments in the area, as well as many other political units. This kind of metropolitan planning is presently being done in over 700 locations in the United States.

Second, *planning can be social as well as physical in nature.* It can expand beyond land use, building design, and other physical features of the city to include social organization. The profession of planning has historically been dominated by architects and engineers, who have generally given little attention to social aspects of urban living. For example, they have laid out streets on the basis of topography rather than actual patterns of travel and have designed high-rise apartment buildings without providing any common spaces in which the residents can interact informally. Planners are now beginning to realize, however, that slums are a result of complex social and economic forces as well as deteriorated housing, so that they

cannot be eliminated simply by tearing down old buildings and constructing new ones (Gans, 1968). They are also coming to realize, as another example of this trend, that suburban shopping malls are used as gathering places for friends to meet and interact as well as shop, so that many malls are now being designed to include places where people can sit and talk, garden restaurants, and play areas for children.

A third direction in which urban planning has sought to become more comprehensive has been *the development of master plans for cities or entire metropolitan areas.* Traditionally, plans have dealt only with particular features of a community, such as streets, parks, shopping areas or residences. Often they have been restricted to specific sections of the city that were targeted for redevelopment. A master plan, in contrast, attempts to address as many features of the entire urban area as possible. Early attempts to formulate master plans were frequently based on rather narrow, arbitrary, and biased assumptions of what constituted a desirable city (Meyerson and Benfield, 1955), and it is therefore probably fortunate that few of them were ever adopted or implemented. As planners have become more sophisticated, however, metropolitan master plans—such as the one that is currently guiding the modernization and growth of Stockholm—have become much more realistic and workable.

Fourth, *comprehensive planning can involve the creation of new towns.* A new town is totally designed and constructed according to a comprehensive plan and is usually not associated with any existing city. These new communities are intended to provide alternatives to urban living, since their size is usually limited to 30,000 to 50,000 inhabitants. And because they have their own economic base, schools, shopping facilities, and other facilities, they are intended to be largely self-contained. The idea of new towns was initially developed in England at the beginning of this century, where they were called "garden cities" because they were to be surrounded by "green belts" of publicly owned land. The early garden cities that were built outside London have long since become merely metropolitan suburbs, but since World War II numerous new towns have been established in England, the Netherlands, the Soviet Union, and throughout Scandinavia.

In the 1930s, the United States government designed, financed, constructed, and operated three demonstration new towns that were to provide low-cost housing for middle-income people. These communities (Greenbelt, Maryland; Green Hills, Ohio; and Greendale, Wisconsin) quickly became suburbs, however, and in 1949 they were sold to their residents. During the 1950s and 1960s, 64 new towns were begun by private developers in this country, most of which were completed and flourish today. Typical examples of these communities are Reston, Virginia, and Columbia, Maryland, both of which are now nicely laid out, comfortable, upper-middle-class suburbs of Washington, D.C. Columbia, for example, is arranged into many neighborhoods of about 900 residences, each with its own elementary school and neighborhood center, while four contiguous neighborhoods form a village with a central shopping area, middle school, and other public facilities. To promote further development of new towns, Congress in 1968 and 1970 passed legislation to provide financial and technical assistance to developers interested in this idea. About a dozen communities were planned and some were started, but in 1975 all federal funds were withdrawn and most of those towns have never been completed.

Fifth, *planning can become comprehensive as it involves citizens* as well as professional planners and government officials. Traditionally, citizen involvement in planning has been restricted to holding a public hearing at which the completed plan was presented and described, with no opportunity for input by citizens. This practice began to change in the 1960s, as a result of public concern about urban renewal, government housing projects, inner-city expressway construction, and community action programs. Citizens began to demand a voice in the development of plans and their final approval. Since then, extensive citizen participation programs have been carried out in many cities, and citizens have become highly involved in the planning process. These programs have faced two serious problems, however. Only a tiny proportion of the public ever participates, most of whom are relatively high-status community leaders and activitists. And even those people frequently lack the technical and financial knowledge necessary to make effective inputs to comprehensive plans.

The urban planning process is also changing in other ways at the present time. In the past, once a plan was adopted, it was commonly viewed as a fixed document that was to be implemented as fully and rationally as possible without change—at least for a considerable period of time. Today, *planning is coming to be viewed as an ongoing process,* so that plans become guidelines that are continually being reviewed and revised as conditions in the community change. As a result, *the planning process is becoming much more politicized* than it used to be. Originally, most planning offices or commissions were outside the established government bureaucracy, to depoliticize them and enable them to be more professional in nature. This rarely worked well, however, since there are always numerous political considerations that must be taken into account in planning. Consequently, planning agencies are now being brought back into the political process of local government. Because the resulting plans are grounded in political reality, they are much more likely to be accepted and actually implemented.

Finally, a few communities have begun to realize that they cannot continue to grow forever and do not want to become huge metropolises. They have therefore begun to experiment with *planning for nongrowth,* seeking to limit population in-migration and urban sprawl. Several legal battles have recently been waged over this issue, in which the courts have generally ruled that a community does have the legal right to restrict population growth. Urban nongrowth planning may likely become much more prevalent in the future, adding a whole new dimension to the planning process.

SUMMARY

A community consists of a population of people who reside in a common area, share many daily activities, and have a sense of communal belonging. Definitions of what constitutes an urban community are based on population size, but those criteria vary widely. As societies become urbanized, an increasing proportion of their population resides in relatively large and dense communities that dominate the social, economic and political organizations and functioning of the society. This fundamental process of societal transformation thus has demographic and organiziational components.

As a broad societal process, urbanization is a direct consequence of industrialization. Whereas in 1800 no more than two percent of the world's population lived in urban communities of any size, today that figure is over 40 percent. There is a strong relationship between the degree of industrialization and the extent of urbanization in all countries.

The contemporary worldwide urban revolution is a result of numerous interrelated factors: growing agricultural surpluses, expanding industry and other kinds of businesses, modern transportation systems, improved public health practices, viable and effective local governments, and the attraction and opportunities of urban living.

Urbanization has been quite extensive in the United States during the past 100 years. At first, this involved large-scale movements of people from rural areas and small towns into cities, but during the last half-century the dominant movement has been outward from central cities to suburbs and surrounding fringe areas. Although most central cities have not grown much for several decades, metropolitan areas and megalopolises are expanding at a rapid rate.

To explain urban spatial patterns, sociologists have developed three models of urban land use, all of which place considerable emphasis on land values. The concentric zone model focuses on the geographical distance between various land uses and the city center. The sector model focuses on the proximity of various land uses to major transportation corridors in the city. The multiple-nuclei model focuses on the clustering of similar land uses in various sections of the city.

Since World War II, there has been a continual movement of many kinds of business firms from the inner city to outlying areas in all American cities. Some kinds of businesses and other activities are remaining in the central business district, however, so that many cities are presently experiencing an urban renaissance.

Suburbanization has been the dominant urban demographic trend in American cities since World War II, so that since 1950 almost all growth in metropolitan areas has occurred in their suburban areas. Suburbs are increasingly developing their own economic bases, so that they are no longer simply bedroom communities for the central city. Massive suburbanization has been produced by economic forces concerning land and housing and sociocultural factors involving housing preferences and family-centered lifestyles.

Traditionally, many sociologists have tended to view urban living rather pessimistically, stressing the replacement of informal *Gemeinschaft* relationships by formal *Gesellschaft* relationships. Urban social life was described as impersonal, individualistic, isolated, and disorganized, and was thought to cause many kinds of social deviance. More recently, most sociologists have adopted a more optimistic view of urbanism as they have discovered that urban dwellers generally establish many kinds of interpersonal relationships and patterns of meaningful social organization. The size of the community, by itself, has very few effects on social life or individual behavior.

Many urban neighborhoods are highly organized small communities, especially those that center around a common ethnic heritage that creates strong social bonds. Black neighborhoods are also often quite organized, despite the fact that they are frequently a result of racial discrimination in employment and housing.

Numerous studies of social participation have discovered that interaction with family members is extremely important for most people, regardless of where they live; that while urban residents are frequently not well-acquainted with their neighbors, they make numerous friends at work and in organizations; and that interaction with personal friends is very widespread regardless of where people live. Membership and participation in voluntary associations is not too extensive, and is quite highly related to socioeconomic status.

A city's economic base consists of those economic activities that provide its major sources of jobs, income, and wealth. It usually rests on commerce, transportation, extraction, government, manufacturing, or cultural activities. Although the export sector of a city's economic base used to be considered more important than the local sector, as cities grow their local sectors become increasingly dominant.

Urban labor markets are characterized by extreme occupational specialization and diversity. Within the urban labor force, some occupational capabilities are frequently oversupplied, while others are undersupplied, which creates problems in matching workers with available jobs. In addition, workers often live some distance from the jobs for which they are qualified.

Within every urban community there is an elaborate structure of power relationships that centers in its political economy. The elitism and pluralism perspectives on urban power structures differ in their methodologies, descriptions of the composition of community leaders, and explanations of how those elites exercise power. There is

general agreement, nevertheless, that in all communities most major decisions are made by a relatively small number of influential leaders. In general, the greater the social, economic, and political diversity of a city, the more decentralized its power structure. And the greater the power decentralization, the more effective the power structure is likely to be in carrying out public programs.

Extensive urban redevelopment efforts in the areas immediately surrounding the central business district are occurring in many cities through urban renewal programs, urban rehabilitation efforts, and gentrification. Although these developments have greatly improved the physical conditions of those areas, they have not solved the problem of providing housing for lower-class people.

Governmental concern with housing in the United States has consisted largely of home ownership assistance and low-income housing programs. Home ownership assistance includes government-insured home mortgages and tax deductions for interest paid on mortgages. Low-income housing programs have included constructing public housing, giving direct purchases subsidies, providing rent assistance, and encouraging urban homesteading. None of those programs have been very effective.

Urban planning is practiced quite extensively in many European countries, but it has not been very popular in the United States until quite recently. Planning activities are becoming increasingly comprehensive in several different respects. They are encompassing entire metropolitan areas, incorporating social as well as physical concerns, stressing the formation of master plans, experimenting with creating new towns, and including citizen participation programs. Planning is also coming to be seen as a continual process, becoming more politicized, and starting to deal with community nongrowth.

15

BUREAUCRATIZED ORGANIZATIONS

What are the major features of the goal-oriented organizations that
   dominate modern societies?
What is the process of bureaucratization intended to accomplish, and how
   does it seek to achieve those ends?
How do the processes of goal attainment, environmental coping,
   organizational control, and organizational change occur in bureaucratic
   organizations?
What are some of the major operational problems that occur in
   bureaucratic organizations, and how might they be resolved?
In what ways do individuals respond to involvement in bureaucratic
   organizations, and what difficulties do they experience?

GOAL-ORIENTED ORGANIZATIONS

Modern industrial societies are pervaded by
organizations that are intended to attain specific goals. These goal-oriented organizations are usually referred to as formal organizations, associations, or bureaucracies. As
will be discussed in the following section,
however, the concept of bureaucracy has a
precise meaning in sociology that is narrower in scope than the other terms.

   This chapter is broadly concerned with all
organizations that are intended to attain specific goals, regardless of their nature. It
therefore overlaps somewhat with the chapters on industrial economies and modern
polities, since corporations and governments
are goal-oriented organizations. However,
the focus here is on single organizations
rather on economic or political systems. In
addition, this broad category of goal-
oriented organizations includes many other
kinds of social units besides business firms
and government agencies. Examples are

schools and colleges, churches, health-care
facilities, scientific laboratories, professional
organizations, special-interest associations of
all kinds, civic and charitable organizations,
labor unions, political parties, cultural organizations (libraries, museums, orchestras),
public service associations, military units,
and law-enforcement agencies.

Historical Development

   Relatively formal, goal-oriented organizations are certainly not a creation of the
twentieth century. In primitive forms, they
were probably developed soon after societies
began shifting from hunting and gathering
to agricultural economies, and they have existed in all subsequent types of societies. For
example, the Roman Catholic Church was
operating as a highly formal and complex
organization throughout Western Europe
by about the fifth century. Nevertheless, we
commonly consider goal-oriented organizations to be a distinctive feature of modern

industrial societies. There are two principal reasons for describing modern nations as "organizational societies" (Prethus, 1965). First, *goal-oriented organizations pervade all realms of social life to a much greater extent than ever before.* In preindustrial societies, such organizations were generally restricted to only a few spheres of activity—such as a central government, the military, or the church. Other parts of those earlier societies were usually organized in a much more informal manner. As a result, the daily lives of most people involved little contact with goal-oriented organizations. In marked contrast, such organizations exist throughout all areas of modern life. We encounter them first in school, then perhaps in the military, at work, within our community, in our religious activities, at all levels of government, and even in many of our recreational and other activities. Large goal-oriented organizations are thus a central feature of all modern societies.

The second reason for saying that we presently live in organizational societies is that *contemporary goal-oriented organizations tend to be much larger and more complex than ever before.* In earlier societies, most goal-oriented associations were not nearly as large or complex as contemporary corporations, governments, and many other kinds of organizations. Increased organizational size and complexity is partly a result of population growth, so that many more people are available today to participate in these kinds of organizations than in earlier societies. More important, however, are such factors as industrial manufacturing, which requires the coordinated efforts of hundreds or thousands of workers; electronic communications, which enable large organizations to transmit information rapidly to all their component parts; and administrative knowledge, which facilitates coordination and control throughout even the most complexly structured organization. Consequently, the goal-oriented organizations that we encounter in most spheres of our lives are often extremely large, formal, and complex.

Major Characteristics

The defining characteristic of all goal-oriented organizations is that they are intended to attain one or more *specific goals.* This goal orientation underlies their design, structure, and functioning. Any particular goal-oriented organization may have a single purpose or a whole set of objectives that it seeks to attain. These desired outcomes are the principal reason for its existence and guide many of its activities. Identifying the specific nature of an organization's goals—such as making money, serving the public, providing benefits to its members, or performing activities for clients—is therefore a crucial initial step in studying any goal-oriented association.

To achieve their goals, organizations utilize *relevant technologies* in their functioning. These may be machines in a factory, technical equipment in a hospital or laboratory, communication and control procedures in a government agency, or collaborative arrangements in a labor union or university. All these technologies—broadly defined to include physical and social instruments—are the principle means used by an organization to attain its desired ends. The organization is thus essentially a framework or context for employing whatever technologies are appropriate and available for achieving its goals. Consequently, the nature and requirements of those technologies will strongly influence the structure and functioning of the organization, and as its technologies change, so will the organization.

Some relatively simple technologies—such as handicraft skills—can be employed by one individual working alone or by a small group of people working together in an informal manner. Most forms of modern technology, however, require that large numbers of people—often hundreds or thousands—cooperate in an interrelated manner. To make this possible, the activities of all the members of a goal-oriented organization must be coordinated and controlled. One of the principle strategies used in modern organizations for promoting coordination and control is establishing *formal operating procedures* for all activities. Formalization of organizational functioning tends to ensure that all work is conducted in a standardized manner, that each person's activities mesh smoothly with those of others, that each unit of the organization knows what every other unit is doing, and that all their efforts flow together to produce the final desired outcome.

Organizational Structure

As previously emphasized, the starting point for investigating the patterns of social ordering within all goal-oriented organizations must be the objectives they are seeking to attain. An industrial organization that manufactures automobiles, for example, will have a very different internal structure from a government agency that administers housing and urban development programs, and both of those will be structured quite differently than a university or hospital that provides services to clients.

We have also noted that the technologies used by organizations to achieve their goals can have tremendous influences on the manner in which they are structured (Aldrich, 1972; Thompson, 1965). Within industrial manufacturing firms, for instance, different kinds of production technologies lead to quite distinctive organizational forms. Joan Woodward (1965) divided industrial firms into three categories depending on their major production technology:

(1) Unit production, in which each item is constructed separately by a work crew that performs many different operations on that item, as in building ships or houses.
(2) Mass production, in which the items move along an assembly line and each worker does the same operation on each item, as in manufacturing automobiles or refrigerators.
(3) Continuous production, in which the material being produced is continuously manipulated by highly automated processes, as in

petroleum refining and chemical manufacturing.

Woodward found that the structures of industrial firms in these three categories differed in numerous ways, ranging from the operations performed by individual workers to the arrangements of top management. As technologies change, therefore, so do organizational structures.

Several other factors can also affect the internal structure of goal-oriented organizations, including the availability of necessary natural and financial resources, political and economic pressures from other organizations, existing environmental conditions, cultural beliefs and values concerning how organizations should operate, and capabilities of organizational members (Aldrich, 1979; Argyris, 1972; Hall, 1982; Scott, 1981).

All these critical factors—by themselves and in interaction with one another—influence the patterns of social ordering that develop within goal-oriented organizations. Most of the research on this process, however, has focused on three interrelated dimensions of organizational structure: size, differentiation, and complexity.

Organizational size can be measured in terms of members, persons dealt with, tasks performed, amount of output, financial assets, or other criteria. In all cases, size is clearly affected by external demands for whatever the organization produces or does, by the current state of relevant technology, by the availability of natural and financial resources, by legal and governmental regulations, and by the ability of the organization's administrators to create and manage a large organization.

The larger an organization in terms of any criteria, the greater the task differentiation it tends to display (Blau, 1970 and 1971). Differentiation (or specialization) of tasks occurs at the level of individual duties and roles, among operating work groups and task forces, and between larger sections or departments of the organization. Each differentiated role, group, or section is assigned certain specialized tasks for which it is responsible, while at the same time it becomes highly dependent on other units in the organization for the functions it requires but does not perform. All parts of the organization are thus both specialized and interdependent. *In general, increasing differentiation tends to raise the operating efficiency of an organization,* since each individual and unit can concentrate all his/her or its efforts on a limited number of tasks and develop maximum competency in performing them. However, in every organization there is an upper limit of effective differentiation, beyond which greater task specialization creates severe management problems and therefore decreases organizational performance. After that critical point is reached, further increases in size do not normally produce more differentiation of tasks. Instead, organizations frequently divide into semi- or fully autonomous divisions, each of which operates as a relatively separate entity with its own pattern of task differentiation.

The greater the task differentiation within an organization, the more extensive its structural complexity, in the sense that it contains a vast number of positions, offices, sections, branches, departments, and divisions, all of which are arranged into numerous levels of authority. This kind of structural complexity is usually the most evident feature of any large goal-oriented organization. *Complexity occurs in two different dimensions in most organizations* (Hall, 1982:78–82).

(1) *Vertical complexity* refers to the number of hierarchically arranged levels of formal authority. It can vary from a "flat structure" with just two levels (one level of supervisors above all the rest of the members), to a "tall structure," with as many as ten or twelve levels from the bottom to the top of the hierarchy (each of which exercises a successively greater amount of authority).

(2) *Horizontal complexity* refers to the number of distinct positions and subunits at each level of the organization. Depending on the tasks, technologies, and personal capabilities in-

volved, the responsibilities assigned to each position and unit may be quite broadly defined, which produces relatively little horizontal complexity, or they may be very narrowly defined, which produces extensive complexity at each level.

These two dimensions of structural complexity tend to be related, in that the greater the horizontal complexity, the more levels of authority the organization is likely to contain, although this relationship varies widely among different kinds of organizations.

As the size, differentiation, and complexity of any organization increases, requirements for internal communication, coordination, and control multiply rapidly. As a result, the size of the administrative component of the organization—consisting of all supervisors, managers, administrators, and executives—tends to expand greatly, so that a progressively larger proportion of all personnel are engaged in such activities. This tendency has two serious consequences for an organization. First, it greatly increases opportunities for miscommunications, conflicts, and operational disruptions, as well as rapidly multiplying the flow of paperwork and administrative rules and regulations. Second, since none of these administrative personnel perform the basic work that contributes directly to the intended output of the organization—whether it is building cars or instructing students—the total operating costs of the organization rise, and its overall operational efficiency declines. For these reasons, organizations frequently tend to restrict the size of their administrative component as much as possible, which places limits on the degree of differentiation and complexity they can effectively maintain.

BASIC DIMENSIONS OF
ORGANIZATIONAL STRUCTURE

1. Size
2. Task differentiation.
3. Structural complexity.

Interpersonal Relationships

The arrangement of positions, offices, and other subunits within an organization—along vertical and horizontal dimensions—defines the official or formal structure of that organization that is depicted in its organizational chart. In practice, however, all organizations are composed of individuals who continually interact with one another. Many of those interactions are relatively routine in nature, conducted through established communication channels following prescribed rules and regulations. At the same time, *many interpersonal interactions are personal in nature, creating an unofficial informal social structure within the organization.* People chat with each other casually, come to like and trust some of their coworkers and dislike or distrust others, and create friendships that may extend outside the organization. To the extent that these informal relationships deal with private matters, they may have only minor effects on the total organization, although in a subtle manner the network of interpersonal feelings that develops among a set of coworkers can influence the manner in which they carry out their assigned duties.

Informal relationships among the members of an organization can also have direct and extremely important effects on its functioning. For example, when individuals develop personal relationships with others in different units or at other levels of the organization, they typically establish a communication grapevine that circumvents official communication channels. Depending on how that grapevine is used, it may either facilitate organizational operations (when individuals cut through official "red tape" to deal quickly and effectively with a pressing problem) or create problems for the organization (when individuals gain access to information they are not supposed to have or take actions without consulting their supervisors). Individuals may also collude with their trusted friends to bend or break standard operating rules and regulations and create their own personal procedures for dealing with certain situations or problems. Again, depending on how this practice is conducted and its effect on individuals' work performance, it may either help or harm the organization.

Perhaps the most critical outcome of such interpersonal relationships for organizations, however, is that they frequently give rise to *informal norms among groups of coworkers that strongly influence the manner in which they perform their assigned tasks.* Some of these informal norms may be relatively trivial, such as, "It's okay to be five or ten minutes late to work in the morning, as long as this doesn't happen every day," or "The office photocopier may be used to make copies of personal documents, provided you put money into the kitty for the annual office Christmas party." Frequently, however, the informal norms directly influence people's work much more effectively than any of the official norms or rules of the organization.

The classic study of this process was conducted between 1927 and 1932 by a team of industrial sociologists at the Hawthorne plant of the Western Electric Company, which manufactures telephone equipment. From lengthy observations of a crew of fourteen men who wired telephone switchboards, the researchers discovered that the work was almost entirely governed by a set of informal norms these workers had established over the years. Although each worker was paid at a piece rate according to the number of "banks" he wired each day, that financial incentive had little effect on anyone's actual output. Instead, the informal norms of the work group dictated that everyone should earn the same amount every day. The work group therefore established a quota for a normal day's work. Anyone who exceeded the informal quota was labeled a "rate buster" and was sanctioned by the other workers by hiding his tools so that he had to spend time hunting for them. At the same time, anyone who appeared to be not meeting the informal work quota was called a "chiseler" and was sanctioned through the practice of "binging," which involved one or more hard blows to the upper arm. The informal norms also recognized that some people were more experienced and skilled than others at various tasks, which was dealt with in two ways. First, people rotated jobs frequently, even though this was against company rules. Second, faster workers were expected to take time to help slower workers on particular tasks. The supervisor was fully aware of these informal norms and practices, but accepted them because they ensured that the workers produced the expected amount of work every day—which was what the company wanted—without any direct interference by him.

Numerous subsequent studies of interpersonal relationships and informal norms within many different kinds of organizations (Blau and Meyer, 1971) have repeatedly come to three fundamental conclusions.

(1) Interpersonal relationships and an "informal social structure" inevitably develop among the members of all organizations, regardless of the nature of the formal structure or any attempts to prohibit or limit such relationships.

(2) The informal norms and practices established by these networks of interpersonal relationships can be much stronger and more influential for individual members than most formal rules and regulations.

(3) Although the informal structure and its norms and practices may at times impede or obstruct particular organizational activities, wise managers can utilize these interpersonal relationships to augment the official rules and regulations and facilitate the operation of the organization.

BUREAUCRATIZATION

In traditional societies—in the past and at present—primary emphasis within most organizations is placed on observing established norms and practices and ensuring that traditional patterns of social ordering and cultural ideas are perpetuated. Effi-

ciency and effectiveness in accomplishing organizational goals are subordinate to maintaining the organization and benefiting its members. For example, problems have been commonly approached on the basis of, "How have we always dealt with this kind of situation?" rather than, "What is the best way of handling this problem?" In addition, the involved officials might ask, "How can we personally benefit from this situation?" rather than, "What approach to this situation would be best for the organization?" In addition, the individuals assigned to handle difficult situations would likely be selected on the basis of, "Whom can we trust?" or, "To whom do we owe a favor?" rather than, "Who is most qualified and competent to handle this kind of job?"

In modern societies, in contrast, we normally expect goal-oriented organizations to focus on the attainment of their intended objectives, to act as efficiently and effectively as possible in these endeavors, and to stress individual competence and impartiality rather than personal favoritism. This contemporary emphasis on organizational goal attainment is called bureaucratization.

The Bureaucratization Process

In formal terms, *bureaucratization is the process of rationalizing and controlling the activities of an organization to increase the efficiency and effectiveness of its goal attainment.* Because of the pervasiveness of bureaucracy in contemporary social life, this process is frequently included with industrialization, nationalization, and urbanization as one of the major trends shaping all modern societies.

Several aspects of bureaucratization require elaboration. First, it is an ongoing social process, not a particular kind of organization, although we often apply the term "bureaucracy" to goal-oriented organizations that clearly manifest this trend. Second, although the process of bureaucratization is observed most frequently within goal-oriented organizations, it can also occur in other kinds of organizations such as families or communities, to the extent that they seek to rationalize and control their col-lective activities. Third, "rationalization" of organizational activities means to select and carry out those activities as rationally and efficiently as possible to attain the organiza-tional goals being sought. Fourth, "control" of organizational activities means to coordi-nate and regulate those activities as exten-sively and effectively as possible to ensure that collective rather than personal goals are achieved. Fifth, rationalization and control of organizational activities are appropriate only with regard to the means employed by an organization to attain its goals. The selec-tion and nature of the ends being sought through collective action must be based on shared interests and values, not criteria of efficiency and effectiveness. Sixth, although the notion of bureaucracy is often equated in common speech with organizational rigidity, red tape, and inefficiency, the sociological concept of bureaucracy has exactly the opposite meaning. Although all kinds of operational problems do occur in goal-oriented organizations, they are frequently due to inadequate, misdirected, or exces-sive bureaucratization, not to the process itself.

Observers of the bureaucratization process in modern societies have identified several trends that have contributed to its development. Among the most important of these factors have been:

(1) Development of industrialization, with its de-mands for efficient production;

(2) Expansion of capitalism, with its emphasis on economic markets and profits;

(3) Creation of modern governments, with their requirements for effective public adminis-tration;

(4) Growth of urbanization, with its necessity for dealing with large-scale social problems of all kinds;

(5) Increase of organizational size and complex-ity, which compounds structural and opera-tional problems within organizations; and

(6) Spread of education, mass communications, science, and technology, all of which promote cultural secularization.

TRENDS CONTRIBUTING TO BUREAUCRATIZATION

1. Development of industrialization.
2. Expansion of capitalism.
3. Creation of modern governments.
4. Growing urbanization.
5. Increasing organizational size and com-plexity.
6. Spread of cultural secularization.

These basic trends that have produced mod-ern societies have placed increasing de-mands on all kinds of goal-oriented organi-zations to function as efficiently and effectively as possible in pursuing their in-tended goals.

The Weberian Model

One of Max Weber's major sociological concerns was to understand the process of bureaucratization that he saw occurring in governments, businesses, and other goal-oriented organizations within modern soci-eties. For this purpose, he devised the re-search methodology of constructing "ideal types." *An ideal type is a model of a social process or organization that identifies its most distinctive characteristics and exaggerates them to their maxi-mum possible condition.* It is not a description of an actual situation but rather an extreme characterization of that kind of situation that maximizes its dominant features. For in-stance, if the major characteristic of a uni-versity is the pursuit of knowledge, an ideal type model of a university would be totally devoted to research and teaching and would not conduct any public services, sports events, social activities, or other nonintellec-tual pursuits. Nor is such a model an ideal in any normative sense, so that it is not neces-sarily a goal to be pursued.

No real social process or organization ever approaches its ideal type, but that is not the point of this methodology. Its purpose, rather, is to provide a model with which to analyze existing situations. To do that, the researcher must also construct the polar op-

Offices

Position 1   Position 2

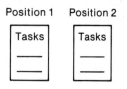

Competence

Careers

Impersonality

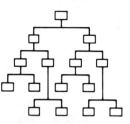

Procedures

Rules

Hierarchy

FIGURE 15-1
Characteristics
of the Weberian
bureaucratic model

posite of the initial ideal type, so that real situations can be located somewhere between those two extremes. For Weber, the polar opposite of an ideal-type bureaucracy is a traditional organization dominated by established customs and practices and operated on the basis of personal interests and concerns, rather than efficient and effective goal attainment.

Weber identified a number of features that he saw as indispensable for a modern bureaucracy based on the principles of rationalization and control for the efficient and effective attainment of organizational goals. These characteristics of his bureaucratic model can be grouped under the following six headings (Weber, 1947, Ch. 8; Lloyd, Mack, and Pease, 1979:209–14), which are illustrated in Figure 15-1.

Offices. All tasks to be performed within the organization are clearly defined, usually with considerable specialization, and assigned to specific positions or offices. Each person in the organization occupies a specific position or office, so that every individual's expected duties and responsibilities are precisely determined, as well as the relationship of that position to every other office in the organization. Each incumbent is expected to do exactly what is expected of that position; no more and no less. In addition, all offices exist independently of their incumbents, so that they are not dependent on any particular individual for their functioning and no one "owns" his or her office. As a result, the organizational structure remains intact regardless of the flow of personnel through various positions.

Competence. Individuals are selected for positions within the organization solely on the basis of their training, experience, and capabilities. This generally means that applicants must have completed a specified amount and kind of education or training, have acquired previous experience relevant to the position and/or pass a standardized proficiency examination. No person can claim a right to an office by virtue of family background or connections, personal friendships or obligations, or special privileges. In addition, position incumbents are periodically evaluated on the basis of their job performance, using objective criteria. All salary increments, promotions, and other rewards are determined solely by these measures of merit.

Careers. All the positions within an organization are arranged in sequences of increasing responsibility and authority, usually in terms of well-defined steps. Individuals who perform their assigned tasks in a satisfactory manner can therefore expect to follow an orderly career in the organization, advancing to increasingly more important and prestigious positions to the extent that they demonstrate competence for such promotions. In addition, all members are assured of job and financial security within the organization, as long as they perform in an adequate manner. This is accomplished through such procedures as granting tenure after a probationary period (which does not prevent an individual from being demoted or fired, but ensures that such actions must be based on rational reasons rather than personal consideration), a fixed salary, a retirement pension, and other fringe benefits.

Impersonality. The members of a bureaucratic organization are expected to relate to one another in terms of their official positions and roles, not on the basis of personal likes and dislikes or other emotional factors. Although individuals invariably develop personal feelings and relationships with others in the organization, all such considerations are to be put aside while one is carrying out assigned duties. This ensures that personal favoritism or conflicts will not disrupt the functioning of the organization. Interactions with clients, customers, or constituents are to be conducted in an impersonal and equitable manner, regardless of those people's personal characteristics.

Procedures. The procedures to be followed in all organizational activities are specified in written rules and regulations to which everyone is expected to adhere. In other words, "standard operating procedures" govern everything done within the organization, to ensure that all tasks are performed in the most efficient and effective manner. These rules and regulations can be relatively flexible, allowing for adaptations to specific cases as new situations develop. All such alterations must, however, be justified on rational, not personal, grounds. In addition, written records or files are kept on all activities to ensure that established precedents are perpetuated through time and to provide a basis for evaluating individual and organizational performance with accurate information.

Hierarchy. The organization is structured in a hierarchy of authority, and every position is precisely located within that hierarchy. Each level of authority in this structure is responsible for all levels below it and is responsible to its next higher level. Normally, the higher the level, the fewer offices and units it contains, so that the overall structure resembles a pyramid of authority. A hierarchical structure defines the explicit location of all responsibilities, so that no incumbent can either dodge or overstep his or her assigned authority. It also enables those at the top of the hierarchy to control all activities throughout the entire organization. In addition, a hierarchical structure establishes official lines of communication, so that all orders, reports, and other messages follow a chain of command and everyone who needs to know about a particular situation is kept informed.

All these characteristics of the Weberian bureaucratic model are in sharp contrast to traditional forms of organization in which individuals define their own duties and responsibilities according to personal interests, offices may be sold to the highest bidder or given to friends or relatives, incumbents are selected and evaluated on the basis of personal characteristics or other irrelevant criteria, organizational members are never sure of their future in the organization, people deal with one another in terms of individual likes or dislikes, each situation is handled in a unique manner depending on the people or conditions involved, and lines of authority and communication are constantly shifting.

Advantages of Bureaucracy

For Weber, the principal advantages of bureaucratic organizations over their traditional alternatives were their efficiency and effectiveness in attaining collective goals. In addition, three other advantages of bureaucratic organizations are that they tend to be more equitable, accountable, and stable than traditional organizations.

Efficiency is attained by minimizing the costs required to achieve desired goals. Many kinds of costs are involved in operating complex organizations, including finances, politics, personnel, resources, social and environmental impacts, and time. Direct financial costs are usually the easiest to calculate, so that businesses often concentrate on them and ignore many other indirect, hidden, or external costs. Politicians, meanwhile, are particularly sensitive to the political costs (public support, votes, political alliances, and legitimacy) of governmental actions. Sociologists and psychologists tend to emphasize human costs, such as requirements for qualified personnel, emotional and interpersonal demands on individuals, and problems created by organizations for the communities and societies in which they are located. More recently, environmentalists have made us acutely aware of the extent to which organizations can deplete scarce natural resources, consume large amounts of energy, and pollute the environment. And in today's world, time is a vital concern for most organizational activities. All features of the bureaucratic model are intended to minimize these organizational costs by ensuring that activities are conducted in as rational a manner as possible. However, the model tends to focus primarily on financial and temporal costs and does not deal extensively with many kinds of human, political, or environmental costs.

Effectiveness is determined by the extent to which an organization achieves its desired goals. In other words, does the organization accomplish what it is intended to do? To maximize effectiveness, the bureaucratic model emphasizes organizational control over the actions of individual members and subunits. In particular, specified task definitions, standardized rules and regulations, and a hierarchy of official authority are designed to ensure that all persons and units within the organization perform their assigned tasks and do not deviate from those expectations. Those control procedures are enforced through a variety of social sanctions. Those sanctions may be either rewards or punishments and can range from informal praise or criticism to more formal actions such as raises, promotions, reprisals, and firing. The effectiveness of all these control procedures if often limited, however, by the web of informal interpersonal relationships that exists within all organizations.

Equity is treatment of individuals that is fair and just, with no discrimination against any categories of people. Several features of the bureaucratic model are designed to accomplish that objective, for both organizational members and outside clients, customers, or constituents. Its emphasis on competence as the only criterion for selecting and evaluating members ensures that everyone will be treated and judged on the basis of what they do, not who they are in terms of their social class, family background, race, ethnicity, gender, age, or other such characteristics. In other words, bureaucracies should recognize only achieved status, not any form of ascribed status. Impersonality is meant to ensure that individuals will relate to one another on the basis of their organizational roles, regardless of personal feelings, and that all persons enacting a particular role will be treated in a similar manner. The exis-

tence of career paths within the organization, meanwhile, gives all members financial
and personal security.

*Accountability occurs when responsibility for
every activity and decision is assigned to a specific
position or office.* All such responsibilities are
clearly defined and precisely located within
the organizational structure, so that everyone knows exactly what everyone else is to do
and not to do. With full accountability, individuals cannot dodge taking actions for
which they are responsible, or "pass the
buck" when problems occur. If something
needs to be done, the people involved know
who is supposed to handle the situation and
are assured that it will be dealt with by the
appropriate office. If an individual over-
steps his or her assigned responsibilities or
authority, that person can be sanctioned for
those actions without taking reprisals against
innocent parties. If the organization as a
whole engages in socially unacceptable or illegal activities—such as polluting the environment or bribing government officials—
those individuals at the top of the hierarchy
who have overall responsibility for the entire
organization can be held accountable for its
actions.

*Stability is the capability of an organization to
cope with external stresses and internal strains and
to preserve its existence and cohesion.* Because of
their functional rationality and control procedures, bureaucratic organizations are
adept at weathering many kinds of storms,
external and internal, resolving conflicts,
and protecting their functional capabilities.
They are not likely to be seriously disrupted
by deviant actions of members, conflicts
among subunits, or pressures from other organizations. In modern, highly demanding
societies, the ability of an organization to
maintain stability can be quite beneficial for
its members and the larger society.

All these advantages of the bureaucratic
model can turn into serious problems and
liabilities if they are abused or carried to excessive extremes—as we shall see in a later
section—but if handled wisely, they make
bureaucracies indispensable in the modern
world. In Weber's (1947:337) words, "Bureaucratic administration is, other things being equal, always, from a formal, technical
point of view, the most rational type. For the
needs of mass administration today, it is indispensable."

Misdirected Bureaucratization

Most of the operational and personal
problems that occur in large, formal, complex, goal-oriented organizations occur because of either inadequate or excessive bureaucratization. Two critical dangers are
inherent in the process of bureaucratization,
however, and can have serious consequences
for society if the bureaucratic emphases on
rationality and control are misdirected.
Weber was acutely aware of both of these
dangers and he was intensely concerned that
if bureaucratization were applied to realms
where it was not appropriate, humanity
would find itself imprisoned within an "iron
cage" from which there would be no escape.
Numerous subsequent studies of complex
organizations and bureaucratization (e.g.,
Abrahamson, 1977; Blau and Scott, 1971;
Mannheim, 1940; Slater, 1970) have clearly
demonstrated that these two dangers are indeed outcomes of misdirected bureaucratization and can be disastrous for modern
societies.

*The first potential misdirection of bureaucra-
tization would be to apply rationality and control
to the attainment of all goals in personal and social
life.* Within goal-oriented organizations
there are clear benefits from emphasizing
rationality and control, as long as those procedures are used judiciously and wisely.
When these criteria of rationality and control are applied to other realms of social
life outside goal-oriented organizations,

ADVANTAGES OF BUREAUCRACY

1. Efficiency.
2. Effectiveness.
3. Equity.
4. Accountability.
5. Stability.

however, serious problems may arise. Within families, for example, exclusive emphasis on rationality and control can destroy intimacy, create a very harmful atmosphere for children, and rob family life of all joy and love. Personal recreational pursuits, meanwhile, are deliberately intended to be enjoyable and relaxing, not goal-oriented in any specific sense. Although organized sports may be quite bureaucratized, a fishing trip that was conducted according to someone's rule book would not likely be very pleasant. In religious activities, the emphasis is on individual spirituality, worship, and self-realization, not rational goal-attainment, even though the church or synagogue as a formal organization may attempt to function in a rational manner.

The second potential misdirection of bureaucratization would be to apply rationality and control to the selection of desired ends in social life. Weber carefully distinguished between "instrumental rationality," which pertains to the means of social action, and "value rationality," which pertains to the ends being sought through these means. When used appropriately, bureaucratization can greatly facilitate instrumental rationality. Beliefs, values, and goals in social life are inherently nonrational, however, and must be chosen on other grounds. Value rationality, Weber warned, may appear "scientific" and desirable, but it could destroy meaningful social life. We may place high value on political democracy and individual freedom, for instance, but those are valuative choices that cannot be subjected to rationalization. If political, religious, or other leaders proclaim ultimate goals for their society and justify their selection on the grounds of efficiency and effectiveness, open discussion and debate concerning those goals will be foreclosed; they will no longer be valuative choices.

BUREAUCRATIC PROCESSES

Many dynamic processes are continually occurring in all goal-oriented organizations.

Four of the most important of these processes are sketched in this section: goal attainment, environmental coping, organizational control, and organizational change.

Goal Attainment

For organizations that are designed to accomplish specific purposes—especially organizations that are highly bureaucratized—the process of goal attainment is extremely crucial. However, determining how well any organization is actually achieving its goals can be quite difficult for the organization itself and for social scientists.

One reason for this difficulty is that *most organizations have several different goals*. There are usually one or more *official goals* that are "the general purposes of the organization as put forth in the charter, annual reports, public statements by key executives, and other authoritative pronouncements." In addition, there are typically several *operative goals* that are "the ends sought through the actual operating policies of the organizations" (Perrow, 1961:855). Although some of the operative goals may reflect the official goals, other operative goals may be of a totally different nature. For example, while the official goal of a civic association may be to "promote the welfare of the community," its operational goals may include such purposes as enhancing the business interests of its members or preserving the established power structure of the community. Whereas official goals are easily identifiable from public statements, at least in broad terms, operative goals can only be determined by examining the actual policies, decisions, and activities pursued by the organization. Moreover, there are often two different kinds of operative goals within an organization: *external goals,* which pertain to desired conditions or changes in the larger social environment (such as attracting new businesses to the community), and *internal goals,* which pertain to the functioning of the organization itself (such as keeping the organization financially solvent). Finally, many of the subunits within a complex organization may have their own operative goals (such as expanding their particular activities) that have only partial or no relevance to the total organization.

A second reason for the difficulty in determining how well organizations are achieving their goals is that *the criteria used to evaluate the extent of goal attainment are often quite imprecise* (Blau and Scott, 1971:130–31). To continue the preceding example of a civic association, how might one measure an improvement in the welfare of a community? One possible procedure would be to focus on a few specific operative goals, such as constructing a new city park or attracting new businesses to the community, and ignore the broader official goals. Another procedure would be to measure the activities performed rather than the actual goals attained, such as preparing a booklet describing the desirable features of the community. Still another procedure would be to note the size of the budget or other resources expended on organizational goal attainment. All these measurements have obvious limitations, especially when either the official or operative goals of an organization are stated in rather broad and abstract terms. Consequently, it is always desirable for organizations to translate their general goals into more specific and measurable objectives.

A third reason why goal attainment is difficult to determine is that *organizations frequently alter their goals through time.* They may fully achieve their initial goal and then decide to adopt a new goal rather than disband. This occurred when the National Foundation for Infantile Paralysis (which conducts the March of Dimes) achieved its goal of eradicating polio among children as a result of the development of the Salk and Sabine vaccines and adopted the new goal of promoting research on birth defects (Sills, 1957). More commonly, organizations gradually shift their operative goals as conditions change, without ever proclaiming new official goals. Our illustrative civic association, for instance, might over time focus an increasing amount of its efforts on supporting the election of a new city council.

Regardless of the goals being sought by an organization, to the extent that it is bureaucratized it will attempt to function in as rational a manner as possible. To act in a totally rational manner, however, an organization must acquire complete information about all factors in its environment that affect it, all its internal activities, and the efficiency and effectiveness of its goal-directed efforts. In reality, of course, no organization ever begins to possess such complete information, so that considerable uncertainty pervades all organizational activities (Thompson, 1967). Consequently, *the ability of all organizations to operate rationally in pursuit of their goals is always severely limited by uncertainty.* There are several possible ways of responding to this situation. One common procedure is simply to "muddle through," acting in whatever ways appear feasible and appropriate at the time, without giving much attention to operational rationally. Another procedure is to establish "norms of rationality," which stress the importance of acting rationally as far as possible, but also to develop operating procedures for dealing with situations when all the necessary information is not available (Thompson, 1967). Still another procedure is to adopt a "satisficing" rather than a "maximizing" strategy for decision making (Simon, 1957). With this strategy, the organization searches for solutions to problems that adequately satisfy its requirements, given its limited information, rather than seeking maximum rational solutions. All these procedures are less than perfect from the perspective of bureaucratic rationality, but they do enable organizations to pursue desired goals in spite of severe constraints on the amount and kinds of information available.

Environmental Coping

The most basic internal operative goal of most organizations is to survive and function in its social and natural environments. *Organizations must therefore constantly deal with or adapt to environmental conditions and pressures.* Environmental coping is crucial if an organization is to obtain necessary resources from the environment (such as new members, financial support, relevant information, or natural resources) and return its products to the environment (such as educated persons, manufactured goods, new information, or social services). Sociologists frequently speak of these transactions between an organization and its environment as system "inputs" and "outputs," indicating that they are normal functions of all "open systems" that interact with their environments.

Satisfactory input and output flows are vital for attaining most organizational goals. If necessary resources cannot be obtained and finished products disposed of, an organization often accomplishes only very little. Imagine a university, for example, that is prevented from obtaining any new students or outside funding for even two or three years and whose graduates are not wanted by employers. The university might struggle along for a time, but it would undoubtedly have to close before long. Some sociologists even argue that the functional effectiveness of an organization should be measured in terms of its ability to deal with its environment, rather than the attainment of its stated goals (Aldrich, 1979).

Because of the operational importance of inputs and outputs for goal-oriented organizations, *the positions and subunits in an organization that control environmental flows enact a critical role.* The organization depends heavily on these "gatekeepers" to perform their roles in an adequate manner. As a result of that dependence, gatekeepers can exercise a great deal of power over organizational activities. By closing the organization's gates to its environment—or even threatening to do so—they can severely disrupt the functioning of the organization. (To a lesser extent, opening the input and output gates too wide may also disrupt the organization). In a business, for example, the subunits that procure needed raw materials and sell finished products are often capable of dictating major corporate policies if they choose to exercise that influence. As a result, top organizational administrators are often particularly concerned to maintain control over gatekeeping activities.

At the same time, the environments with which organizations must deal are rarely passive. Environmental conditions are continually changing, and other organizations or individuals—such as competitors or government officials—may frequently exert pressures on the organization. Consequently, the social and natural environments are major sources of operational uncertainty for most bureaucratic organizations as they attempt to function in a rational manner. *To minimize or eliminate external uncertainties, organizations frequently seek to influence or control their relevant environments as much as possible* (Thompson, 1967). For instance, a manufacturing firm may negotiate long-term contracts with its major suppliers and its principal wholesalers, or it may even seek to acquire them through vertical mergers. This is also the main reason why large corporations make such extensive efforts to develop close ties with government regulatory and other agencies.

James Thompson and William McEwen (1958) have described four strategies that organizations commonly use in their interactions with their environments, all of which are designed to minimize external uncertainty.

(1) *Competition* involves ordered procedures for dealing with other organizations concerning inputs and outputs. Businesses compete with one another for sales, government agencies for financial allocations, and universities for students.

(2) *Bargaining* involves direct negotiations with other relevant parties concerning inputs and outputs. Businesses bargain with their suppliers, government agencies bargain among themselves, and universities bargain with funding sources.

(3) *Cooptation* involves bringing leaders of other important organizations into the policy-making structure of the organization in order to gain their cooperation and support. Bankers are given positions on the board of directors of manufacturing corporations, government agencies place influential com-

---

**STRATEGIES FOR COPING WITH
SOCIAL ENVIRONMENTS**

1. Competition.
2. Bargaining.
3. Cooptation.
4. Coalition.

---

munity leaders on their advisory committees (Selznick, 1966), and universities appoint important businesspersons as trustees.

(4) *Coalition* involves establishing close working relationships or mergers between an organization and relevant portions of its environment. Businesses establish horizontal mergers with other competing firms, national governments create permanent alliances with other nations, and universities join in academic associations to promote their common interests. All these strategies help to ensure that an organization will be able to survive and function in a changing and uncertain environment.

Organizational Control

To cope with their environments and attain their goals, all organizations must exercise some degree of control over their members and their internal and external activities. As goal-oriented organizations grow in size and complexity, and as they become bureaucratized to function more efficiently and effectively, control processes become increasingly critical. *Organizational control is the utilization of social power by organi-*zational administrators to ensure that the organization operates as intended.

Organizational control activities may be directed toward many different objectives. They may be used to protect organizational boundaries against external pressures, prevent undesired or disruptive actions by members, encourage members to perform their assigned roles in a satisfactory manner, ensure that organizational survival and operational requirements are adequately met, coordinate relationships among various parts of the organization, provide for collective planning and decision making, maintain established patterns of social ordering within the organization, perpetuate cultural values and norms, contribute to overall organizational goal attainment, or promote organizational change.

Weber's bureaucratic model attempts to maximize organizational control in two different ways: through a hierarchy of official authority and through formalization of operating procedures. These two approaches to exercising organizational control can be viewed as part of a broader scheme that includes three distinct control strategies: command, standardization, and internalization. As depicted in Figure 15-2 and discussed in the following paragraphs, each of those strategies can be accomplished through two different means, and each of those means tends to have a particular effect on organizational activities.

A command strategy for exercising organization control depends on issuing action directives.

FIGURE 15-2 Organizational control strategies, means, and effects

Officials exercising this type of control tell others what to do and demand compliance. Command control can be exerted through *coercion* involving the use of force, which produces *obedience* among organizational members but not voluntary cooperation. In contrast, the bureaucratic model relies entirely on legitimate *authority*, which is accepted by the members of the organization and therefore results in voluntary *compliance*. This authority is arranged in a hierarchical structure in which the flow of directives and control is entirely downward from the apex to the base, so that the organization has a unitary power structure. Weber argued, moreover, that to be accepted as legitimate, bureaucratic authority must be rational-legal in nature, as opposed to either traditional or charismatic authority.

Rational-legal authority has two dimensions: rational authority derived from technical expertise in performing a role or set of actions, and legal authority derived from occupancy of an organizational office. With rational/expert authority, a person is granted the legitimate right to exercise power within a specific set of activities because of his or her personal competence as acquired through training and/or experience. With legal/official authority, a person is granted the legitimate right to exercise power within a specified domain because of his or her organizational position. Weber assumed that in a highly bureaucratized organization these two dimensions of rational and legal authority would be identical, since officeholders would be selected strictly on the basis of their competence and merit. In reality, however, the two dimensions frequently do not coincide. There can be either "knowledge without office," as in the case of a staff specialist who advises but never commands, and "office without knowledge," as in the case of a president who knows very little about what is actually occurring within the organization.

A standardization strategy for exercising organizational control depends on establishing operating procedures. Officials exercising this type of control decide how tasks should be performed and expect those procedures to be followed. Standardization control can be exerted through *routinization,* in which all tasks are precisely specified, so that they are always conducted in the same manner, but this tends to minimize performance by organizational members. In contrast, the bureaucratic model relies primarily on *formalization,* or creating detailed rules and procedures to cover all situations, which results in overall *regulation* of organizational activities, but at the cost of flexibility to respond quickly to new or unique situations.

In practice, most complex organizations utilize both forms of standardization in varying degrees. However, in recent years there has been a movement away from extreme task specialization. In many organizations, workers are being organized into task forces, each of which is assigned a broad sphere of responsibilities or problems to handle (Bennis, 1970). The procedures and rules governing each task force are stated in fairly broad terms, so that its members have considerable latitude in deciding how to apply those guidelines to specific situations.

An internalization strategy for exercising organizational control depends on obtaining capable personnel. Officials exercising this type of control appoint or train organizational members to carry out organizational tasks and expect satisfactory performance. One way of doing this is to recruit and *select* individuals who already have desired qualifications such as formal education, relevant technical training, particular personality characteristics, or a certain social class background. However, this approach tends to be rather *exclusive,* eliminating many individuals who might be capable of becoming effective organizational members. Another approach is to appoint members on the basis of their potential and *train* them—through either formal instruction or on-the-job training—to become *competent* organizational members.

Neither form of internalization control is explicitly included within Weber's bureaucratic model, but both are compatible with its emphases on rationalization and control. Moreover, this control strategy is often more effective than either command or standardization, since it does not depend on administrators continually issuing and enforcing directives or establishing and monitoring rules. The selection approach has typically been more common, because it does not require the organization to conduct any training activities. Professional organizations such as hospitals and schools rely primarily on obtaining personnel who have already undergone extensive professional training and presumably are fully prepared to perform their jobs. However, large corporations and other organizations that have the resources to conduct their own training programs or to hire others to do this for them frequently give new (and newly promoted) members several weeks or months of specialized training. For example, a military officer normally receives more than three years of full-time training during his or her career, and some businesses are now sending promising executives to graduate school for up to four years.

Underlying these three control strategies is the more fundamental question of the extent to which power and control within an organization are centralized or decentralized. *In Weber's bureaucratic model, all power is centralized at the top of an authority hierarchy, which he believed was necessary for effective control and coordination of organizational activities.* Michels's "iron law of oligarchy," based on the bureaucratic model, provided further theoretical and empirical support for the inevitability of power centralization. As a result, many organizational theorists and administrators assume uncritically that all bureaucratized organizations must have a hierarchy of centralized authority. This assumption is more or less justified under some conditions—such as moderate organizational size and complexity, simple and routine tasks, uncomplicated and unchanging technologies, relatively untrained personnel, and stable environmental conditions.

As we have learned more about organizational dynamics, however, we have come to realize that *power centralization often detracts from efficient and effective organizational functioning.* Under many kinds of conditions, a more decentralized structure is preferable (Hage and Aiken, 1967; Hall, 1982). Those conditions include large size and extreme complexity, nonroutine goals and tasks, rapidly developing new technologies, highly trained personnel, changing environmental conditions, and ideological commitment to democratic decision making. Under these kinds of conditions, a centralized hierarchy of authority tends to be too rigid and cumbersome and does not give organizational members enough autonomy and flexibility to deal adequately with the expectations and responsibilities placed upon them. Some organizations, faced with demands for greater power decentralization, have tried to sidestep this issue by pacifying or manipulating their members. Pacification involves giving members more benefits, such as higher wages or more privileges, but not changing the structure of authority. Manipulation involves making members believe they have more authority—as in "human relations management" (Coch and French, 1958)—while final control is actually retained in the hands of management.

With true power decentralization, authority and decision making are moved down the hierarchy to the units that are actually performing goal-oriented tasks, so that they have full responsibility and control over those activities. The organizational structure then becomes rather "flat," with a minimum number of authority levels. Experiments with this kind of decentralized structure have demonstrated that it can increase worker productively while simultaneously greatly improving member satisfaction with and loyalty to the organization (Morse and Reimer, 1956; Blumberg, 1969; Abrahamson, 1977). Decentralization is particularly effective when organizational members are highly professionalized, so that they control their own activities on the basis of internalized professional norms. Professionals often strongly resent adminstrators trying to tell them how to perform their professional roles (Litwak, 1961).

Overall organizational planning, coordination, and other administrative functions are still necessary in a decentralized organization, but these can be carried out by specialized administrative units that are not given responsibility for overall organizational decision making. In other words, administrators do not have to be decision makers. Functional administration can remain centralized in the hands of professional administrators—as is in done in many hospitals, for instance—while decision making and control can be carried out by all organizational units within their assigned spheres of responsibility. This allows all units and members to participate in making decisions that affect their particular activities and to exercise control over their own actions.

Organizational Change

All organizations are at least periodically faced with the option or necessity of changing their operating procedures and/or structure to deal with new conditions or problems. Change is particularly crucial for bureaucratized organizations, with their demands for efficient and effective goal attainment. Paradoxically, however, purposeful change is an extremely difficult process for many organizations, especially bureaucracies. Quite often they tend to become locked into existing modes of operation and structural arrangements, so that change is viewed as a disruptive threat to established and time-tested practices. A fundamental problem for many goal-oriented organizations, therefore, is how to promote and incorporate desired changes while also maintaining organizational viability and cohesion.

One approach to understanding organizational change is to examine characteristics of proposed innovations that affect their eventual adoption or rejection. A lengthy list of such characteristics has been compiled (Zaltman, Duncan, and Holbeck, 1973:33–45), the most important of which are the following.

(1) Source: innovations originating within an organization are more likely to be adopted than those originating outside it.

(2) Basis: innovations based on scientific research are more likely to be adopted than those based on speculation.

(3) Cost: the less costly an innovation is for an organization, the more likely it is to be adopted.

(4) Risk: the less risk posed by an innovation for an organization, the more likely it is to be adopted.

(5) Complexity: the less complex an innovation, the more likely it is to be adopted.

(6) Compatibility: the more compatible an innovation is with existing organizational practices, the more likely it is to be adopted.

(7) Modifiability: the easier it will be to modify an innovation in the future, the more likely it will be adopted.

(8) Reversibility: the easier it will be to eliminate an innovation that later becomes undesirable, the more likely it will be adopted.

(9) Benefits: the greater the perceived advantages or benefits of an innovation for an organization, the more likely it is to be adopted.

(10) Ramifications: the fewer the ramifications of an innovation for other parts of an organization, the more likely it is to be adopted.

A second approach to understanding organizational change is to determine which organizational features facilitate or impede the change process. Jerald Hage and Michael Aiken (1970:30–53) found that both of the organizational control strategies emphasized by the bureaucratic model—hierarchy of authority and formalization of procedures and rules—tend to reduce the adoption of innovations, as does centralization of power. Conversely, change is more likely to occur in organizations that have little hierarchy, low formalization, and relative decentralization of power. Change is also associated with the number of professional roles in an organization, suggesting that the internalization strategy for organizational control is more compatible with adoption of innovation than are the other two control strategies. These researchers also found that two aspects of the goal-attainment process within organizations apparently affect the rate of organizational change. Adoption of innovations is more likely to occur if an organization stresses effectiveness more than efficiency in achieving its goals and if it emphasizes quality, rather than quantity, of output.

A third approach to this question of organizational change is to explore the ways in which organizational members affect the change process. For instance, change is more likely to occur when the members of an organization participate in the decision to adopt an innovation (Zaltman, Duncan, and Holbeck, 1973:33–45) and when they are highly satisfied with the change (Hage and Aiken, 1970:53–60). Even more important than the attitudes and actions of the rank-and-file members, however, is the manner in which the leaders of an organization view change. Studies focusing on the political economy of organizations (Zald, 1970; Corwin, 1973) have discovered that the nature of their economic and political systems affect the change process in many ways. Power conflicts frequently occur among leaders within those two realms of organizations, and the outcomes of these struggles influence whether change occurs and what kinds of innovations are adopted. In general, organizations change if and when their leaders or dominant elites promote change, and they are unlikely to change if these persons are opposed to it.

Finally, a fourth approach to understanding organizational change is to analyze the stages through which this process occurs. Hage and Aiken (1970:94–106) have divided the process of change into four stages, each of which is characterized by distinctive kinds of problems for organizations. In the *evaluation stage,* organizational decision makers determine that the organization is not attaining its goals as efficiently or effectively as possible or that it should adopt one or more new goals. The major problems encountered at this initial stage involve fundamental conflicts over what the organization should be doing. In the *initiation stage,* a decision is made to adopt a particular innovation and plans are made for its implementation. The problems at this stage are mostly concerned with obtaining the funding, personnel, and other resources needed to adopt the innovation. In the *implementation stage,* the change is actually put into practice. Most of the problems that develop at this time center around conflicts among members and subunits, as the power structure of the organization shifts to take account of the innovation. In the final *routinization stage,* decision makers determine whether to reject or retain the innovation, and, in the latter case, how to integrate it into the normal operations of the organization. Most of the problems that occur as innovations are routinized result from disruptions of previously existing operating procedures.

BUREAUCRATIC PROBLEMS

People who work or otherwise participate in bureaucratic organizations often complain bitterly about all the frustrating, ridiculous, and impossible problems with which they must constantly deal, and everyone has their own favorite horror story about "when I worked at. . . ." or "when I was in the military. . . ." Complex bureaucratic organizations are indeed beset with all kinds of operational problems, which sociologists have studied at great length. Two general statements can be made about all such organizational problems.

(1) They are frequently generated by the structure and functioning of goal-oriented organizations, not by the personality characteristics of the individuals involved. These problems tend to occur regardless of who the participants happen to be.

(2) They generally result from placing excessive or distorted emphasis on the rationality and control aspects of the bureaucratic model, so that those operational means for goal attainment become ends in themselves. This tendency is particularly common in regard to hierarchies of authority and formalized operating procedures.

The following paragraphs describe eight operational problems that frequently occur in bureaucratic organizations.

Rule Ritualization

One of the most frequently expressed complaints about bureaucracies is that they function strictly by the rule book in a rigid and inflexible manner. All situations falling within a defined category are treated in the same standardized manner, regardless of their unique features, and organizational members refuse to bend the rules to accommodate situational variations. Over time, this tendency to adhere blindly to existing rules and procedures can create what the social critic Thorstein Veblen called "trained incapacity" and sociologist Robert Merton described as a "bureaucratic personality." Such organizational members become incapable of using any initiative or creativity. They also create much of the red tape of purposeless procedures and countless forms and records that are perpetuated without ever being questioned. Slavish conformity to rules and obsessive concern with procedures and forms can cause many serious difficulties for organizations, their members, and the people with whom they deal. This is especially true when conditions change rapidly and new situations arise that are not covered by established rules and procedures. The roots of this problem often lie in the manner in which the rules are formulated and enforced. If operating rules and regulations are specified in minute detail, and if individuals are rewarded for following them blindly and punished for deviating from them in any manner, rule ritualization is especially likely to develop. *The solution to this problem lies in formulating rules and regulations as broad guidelines, encouraging organizational members to use their own initiative in applying them to specific situations, and continually searching for new and more appropriate operating procedures.*

Job Incompetence

Ideally, all positions in a bureaucracy are filled on the basis of competence and merit, and each person's job performance is periodically evaluated. Yet we often find people in positions for which they are partially or completely incompetent. Sometimes this results from failing to adhere to the bureaucratic principles concerning merit selection and job performance. At other times it is an outcome of rule ritualization, so that position incumbents know only how to follow the rule book and cannot deal with novel situations. It may also be due to what Lawrence Peter and Raymond Hull (1969) called the "Peter Principle": "In any hierarchy every employee tends to rise to his level of incompetence." Individuals who perform their jobs competently tend to be promoted, which continues until they reach a position that is beyond their abilities, and there they remain. In time, states "Peter's Corollary," "every post tends to be occupied by an employee who is incompetent to carry out its duties." *The solution to the "Peter problem" requires that individuals who are incompetent in their present position be moved back down the hierarchy to a job they can perform adequately,* but such demotions are usually very strongly resisted.

Impersonal Treatment

Customers, patients, constituents, and other outside clients of bureaucratic organizations are often distressed to discover that they are treated by the organization in a standardized, impersonal manner that seems to ignore their individual needs and concerns. To some extent, such impersonality is inherent in any situation in which large numbers of people are being handled. Sheer numbers make it impossible to treat each individual in a unique manner. Categorization of clients as nonrepeat customers or undergraduate majors or single parents becomes necessary if the organization is to cope with the needs of many people. Impersonal treatment may also be a result of rule ritualization among organizational members, so that they are unwilling to make any individual exceptions to established procedures. Nevertheless, people often fail to realize that the impersonal treatment they are receiving tends to insure that everyone is dealt with in a relatively equitable manner. The bank official who tells his brother that, "I can't approve this loan to you, even if you are my brother and desperately need the money, because your credit rating is not strong enough," may appear to his brother as totally insensitive and impersonal. However, the bank official has acted in a fair and impartial manner and has avoided personal favoritism that would violate the objective of operating the bank in a rational and equitable manner. *Solutions to this problem may include flexibility in applying procedures to individual cases and consideration in explaining the reasons why rules must be followed.*

Internal Conflicts

No matter how bureaucratized or centralized organizations may be, they are never single, monolithic entities. The myriad subunits comprising an organization will often have objectives and interests of their own, some of which may likely conflict with the goals and objectives of other units and the total organization. For example, one government agency may be conducting programs to conserve energy, while another agency offers tax incentives for increased oil production. Such interunit conflicts can be highly confusing and frustrating for organizational members and outside clients. Other sources of conflict within organizations may be discrepancies between the formal and informal social structures; divided loyalties between professional or occupational norms and actual job requirements; and organizational objectives that violate the norms of the larger society. In short, social conflict is inevitable within complex, goal-oriented organizations. In itself, however, conflict is not the real problem. Operational problems arise, rather, from the way in which conflicts are handled and resolved. *Consequently, the solution to this problem lies in developing effective and wise procedures for managing organizational conflict.*

Split Authority

In the bureaucratic model, "authority of office" and "authority of expertness" are supposed to be combined within every position (Blau and Scott, 1971:71–76). In reality, however, these two bases of legitimate authority are often split among different people. Persons in line positions—from top executives down through administrators, managers, and supervisors—have authority by virtue of their office, but they frequently have relatively little direct knowledge of the tasks performed within the units for which they are responsible. This is especially likely to occur when technologies and procedures are changing rapidly, so that whatever knowledge and expertise these officials may have acquired before they assumed their present positions have become largely obsolete. Meanwhile, persons in staff positions—technical experts, researchers, public relations specialists, accountants, and many others—have authority based on their personal capabilities, but they can only advise rather than make decisions and policies. This situation of split authority is becoming widespread in most complex organizations and can create endless conflicts and problems between line and staff personnel (Dalton, 1961). It is also a frequent source of confusion for subordinates and outside clients, especially when they receive conflicting directives or information from line and staff officials. Since the bureaucratic ideal of combined official and expert authority is clearly impractical in many modern organizations, there is no obvious solution to this problem. *Much of the resulting conflict and confusion can be avoided, however, by closer cooperation between line and staff persons and a willingness by each to respect the responsibilities and authority of others.*

Communication Distortion

Hierarchical structures give rise to numerous communication problems, despite the fact that they specify precise communication channels. As directives and other messages flow down the hierarchy, they are often reinterpreted and elaborated at each successive level, so that what reaches individuals at the bottom of the structure bears little resemblance to what was originally issued at the top. For example, a simple directive from top management to observe all safety precautions may become for shop workers an elaborate set of procedures covering all kinds of situations, some of which directly interfere with their ability to perform assigned tasks. At the same time, the flow of information up the hierarchy is also often distorted. Since people at each level may be reluctant to pass on negative or undesirable information to their superiors, many operating problems or deficiencies never reach top administrators. Their decisions and policies are then based on incomplete or inaccurate information about what is occurring in the organization. Lateral communications across separate branches of the hierarchy, meanwhile, tend to be officially discouraged, since they prevent higher officials from being fully informed about what their subordinates are doing. In many situations, however, a direct memo or phone call from one office to another across the hierarchy is much more efficient than sending a memo up one branch of the hierarchy and down another branch, since it avoids all intervening distortion. Again, there are no simple solutions to these communication problems, but *much communication distortion can be avoided by providing for more direct and unfiltered communications among all organizational units and positions.*

Goal Displacement

The principle goals of bureaucratic organizations generally pertain to the outside world. Their intent is to affect clients, customers, other organizations, or the society in some manner. Nevertheless, a considerable portion of any organization's resources and efforts must be expended on internal maintenance activities rather than external goal attainment if the organization is to survive

and remain viable. There is always a tendency, therefore, for an organization to lose sight of its external goals and give primary or exclusive attention to internal organizational maintenance goals. This process of goal displacement (Merton, 1968:256–57) is particularly likely to occur in organizations with rather complex structures that require considerable coordination and regulation. As emphasized by Parkinson's (1957) Law, which states that in any bureaucracy, "Work expands to fill the time available for its completion," there is a reciprocal relationship between work flow and organizational maintenance activities. As the amount of work being handled increases, organizations tend to add more personnel and create more complex structural arrangements. This, in turn, requires an ever-expanding number of administrative and supervisory persons who do not contribute directly to external goal attainment but merely keep the organization operating. To carry out their tasks, they institute more and more forms, reports, and other paper work, so that all organizational members are forced to take an increasing amount of time away from goal-oriented activities to deal with administrative paper work. As that trend progresses, even more personnel are needed to achieve the original goals, and so the process of goal displacement through growth continues endlessly. *The solution to this problem lies in learning how to administer and coordinate complex organizations with minimal personnel, activities, and paper work,* but that is a truly demanding challenge.

Change Resistance

Despite the fundamental importance of change for goal-oriented organizations if they are to keep abreast of developing technologies and other shifting conditions, bureaucratized organizations often strongly oppose internal changes. Bureaucracies frequently prefer to continue their established practices indefinitely, no matter how inefficient or out-of-date they may have become, and they resist most attempts to introduce innovations. They appear to be committed to perpetuating current conditions and practices forever. Explanations for this tendency—which is completely antithetical to the bureaucratic model's emphasis on efficiency and effectiveness—can be found in all of the previously mentioned problems. In particular, rule ritualization, job incompetence, and goal displacement contribute directly to organizational resistance to change. In addition, aversion to change is built into the promotion systems of many organizations. Individuals advance up the hierarchy if they do their job as directed and don't create any problems for the organization. By the time they reach top administrative and executive positions, therefore, they have had years of experience in faithfully following established rules and procedures. Any tendencies these individuals may have toward expressing initiative or creativity is likely to have been snuffed out. Paradoxically, however, top positions need individuals who are farsighted, innovative, and creative and who can promote planning and change. *One solution to this problem is to recruit top policy makers from outside the organization, in hopes that they will not have acquired a trained incapacity for innovative thinking. Another solution is to create a different kind of reward system within the organization, so that individuals are promoted when they demonstrate creativity rather than conformity.*

INDIVIDUALS IN ORGANIZATIONS

Our focus thus far in this chapter has been largely on organizations themselves. All large goal-oriented organizations contain numerous people, of course, most of whom perform their assigned tasks with little concern for the organization as a whole. Much of the social scientific research on organizations has dealt with ordinary rank-and-file members, the ways in which they participate in bureaucratic organizations, and the difficulties they encounter. This final section dis-

cusses four aspects of individual involvement in goal-oriented organizations that have been extensively studied. These are only a few of the many kinds of situations and difficulties that individuals experience in complex organizations, but they are all quite common and critical for many organizational members.

Compliance

Why do most individuals most of the time comply with the rules and directives of the organizations in which they work or otherwise participate? Amatai Etzioni (1961) has developed a typology of three bases for individual compliance, depending on the principal form of power exercised by an organization over its members.

Some organizations rely primarily on *coercive power* to control their members by punishing individuals who do not comply. Prisons, mental institutions, and basic military training units are common examples of this kind of organization. *Individuals subject to coercive control obey organizational rules and directives to avoid undesirable sanctions of various kinds.* Obvious difficulties with this approach are that the organization must continually watch all individual actions, it must devote considerable effort to imposing sanctions, and it obtains only minimal compliance. Individuals typically do as little as they can get away with and constantly attempt to beat the system in devious ways.

Other organizations rely primarily on *remunerative power* to control their members by giving financial or other rewards to individuals who comply. Common examples of this type of organization are businesses, government agencies, and schools. *Individuals subject to remunerative control abide by organizational rules and dictates to obtain desired benefits.* Two frequent difficulties with this approach are that it creates inequality among members, since some people receive more rewards than others, and that frequently distributed benefits often come to be viewed as rights rather than rewards. Remunerative

BASES FOR INDIVIDUAL COMPLIANCE

1. Coercive power.
2. Remunerative power.
3. Normative power.

control usually produces greater compliance than coercive control, but most individuals tend to do only what they are rewarded for and no more.

Still other organizations rely primarily on *normative power* to control their members by socializing them to accept organizational goals and norms as their own. Common examples of such organizations are families, churches and synogogues, and voluntary associations. *Individuals subject to normative control follow organizational rules and dictates because they identify with the organization and accept or internalize its norms.* This approach can be highly effective in eliciting maximum member participation, so that individuals often do even more than is asked of them. It does have the limitation, nevertheless, of diminishing individual autonomy and encouraging overconformity.

In reality, most organizations employ all three types of power to varying degrees under differing circumstances and with different categories of members. Consequently, many difficulties can arise for individuals as they shift their compliance from one basis to another.

Supervision

In what manner should supervisors treat their subordinates so as to elicit adequate task performance and member satisfaction with the organization? This issue has been one of the most widely discussed aspects of organizational management.

One supervisory style, developed at the beginning of this century, was known as *scientific management* (Taylor, 1911). Its intention was to rationalize supervision by discovering the "scientifically most efficient procedure for performing every task." For example, the precise motions and time re-

quired to carry out each task were to be measured precisely and taught to all workers. Similarly, research was to determine exactly how much pay was required to ensure that each job was done adequately. This kind of supervision was undoubtedly an advance over traditional forms of authoritarian and idiosyncratic order giving, but it completely ignored all human aspects of work and organizational participation.

In the 1930s and 1940s, partly as an outgrowth of the Hawthorne studies of interpersonal relationships among workers, *human relations management* became very popular (Likert, 1961). By practicing good human relations in the work place, supervisors would presumably increase output and promote greater job satisfaction among workers. Supervisors were to communicate fully and openly with their subordinates, be supportive of them in terms of their work and personal lives, encourage informal relationships among them, and listen to what they had to say. Numerous evaluations of this style of supervision have found that it definitely enhances worker satisfaction and reduces interpersonal tensions and conflicts, but it is questionable whether it significantly improves job output (Filley and House, 1969:399–400).

More recently, *interest has shifted from supervisory styles to direct worker participation in decision making, which alters the role of the supervisor from a director or controller to a coordinator or facilitator.*

Human relations management included the idea that managers and supervisors should discuss operating procedures, problems, and changes with workers, and a number of experiments along those lines were conducted in the 1950s (Blumberg, 1969: Chs. 5 and 6). Although most of those experiments with *worker discussions* demonstrated improved satisfaction and morale, they had two serious limitations:

(1) They all contained an element of worker manipulation by management; and
(2) They rarely produced major increases in job productivity (Coch and French, 1958).

Some of the experiments that grew out of the human relations tradition went a step further by reorganizing the work place to allow workers to participate in making actual decisions about some features of their work. This practice of *limited worker decision making* is particularly effective in reducing worker absenteeism and turnover, which lowers labor costs and hence increases organizational efficiency (Morse and Reimer, 1956). It is still questionable, however, whether this practice substantially improves worker productivity. Moreover, because of the limited scope of the decisions that workers are normally allowed to make and the fact that the new arrangements are still incorporated within a hierarchy of managerial authority, they cannot be described as true worker participation in management.

The most far-reaching attempts to reduce hierarchy and directly involve workers in administrative decision making for the entire organization have been conducted in Yugoslavia, beginning in the 1950s and continuing through today. The constitution of that country stipulates that all large industrial and business firms must have a worker's council. This group of about twenty elected employees has extensive authority and responsibilities. It adopts the bylaws of the enterprise; develops long-range plans for the organization; handles employee hiring, grievances, complaints, and dismissals; sets pay rates; distributes the financial proceeds of the firm; and selects the director of the company. A management board, consisting of the officers of the council, oversees the daily functioning of the organization. Workers' councils give employees an opportunity to participate in the actual management of their organizations, and involvement in these groups appears to be extensive and enthusiastic (Institute of Social Science, 1962). However, over time there has been a marked tendency for managers to perpetuate themselves in office and to coopt these councils so that they become oriented primarily toward managerial, rather than worker, concerns (Blumberg, 1969: Ch. 9).

Alienation

As organizations become increasingly large and complex, with narrowly specialized job and tasks, the roles of most individual members may become rather meaningless. This is particularly likely to occur in manufacturing plants in which each worker performs only one small, repetitive operation on an assembly line, although it can also occur among secretaries and other white-collar workers. This condition of *worker alienation* was one of Marx's major concerns (Fromm, 1963). He argued that workers in modern industries were becoming alienated from the products of their labor and ultimately from themselves. The process of bureaucratization, with its emphasis on routinization and formalization of operating rules and procedures, further contributes to worker alienation (Mills, 1956). *In addition to the meaningless nature of much work in modern organizations, most employees have very little control over their own activities.* They become simply minute, interchangeable parts in a vast organizational machine.

Two frequently proposed solutions to this situation have been to give workers more leisure time or company-sponsored leisure activities and to automate the most dull and repetitive jobs (Blumberg, 1969:48–64). Increased leisure time and opportunities obviously do not eliminate worker alienation but possibly makes it more bearable. Automation does eliminate some of the most unrewarding and meaningless tasks, although even highly skilled technicians often discover that monitoring automated processes is not very satisfying work.

A more meaningful solution to worker alienation is *job enlargement* (Blumberg, 1969:66–69). With this approach, the scope of tasks and responsibilities assigned to individuals is expanded, so that each person performs a complete activity that produces a meaningful product or outcome. Although job enlargement requires that workers be broadly trained and creative, it offers them more challenges and an opportunity to identify with a completed task. As an example of this approach, the Volvo automobile factory in Sweden has eliminated all assembly lines and organized its workers into task groups. Each group is responsible for all aspects of assembling a major section of a car, from ordering parts to testing the final product. This experiment has given workers a great deal of satisfaction with their jobs, and it has also increased worker productivity and greatly reduced the rate of assembly errors that plague automobiles coming off assembly lines.

Individuality

Bureaucratic organizations not only alienate individuals, but they also shape their personalities and self-identities. Some years ago, William Whyte, Jr. (1956) wrote a caustic account of the "organization man" that became a best seller. His central thesis was that people who work in large organizations come to belong to the organization so that it is an essential part of their identity. As a consequence, they become committed conformists to all company policies, on the job and in their personal lives. Michael Maccoby (1976) later identified three other prominent types of "organization persons": the "craftsman" who is primarily concerned about producing a quality product; the "jungle fighter" who seeks to exercise as much power as possible in the organization; and the "gamesman" who thrives on competition and strives to win all the "games" that go on within the organization.

The principal point of both those studies was that organizations shape individuals. One of the most thorough analyses of this process was conducted by Rosabeth Moss Kanter (1977). She found that the characteristics of organizations that have the most influence on individuals are opportunities, power, and numbers. Job *opportunities* are limited by the pyramidal structure of most organizations, so that although everyone is continually encouraged to advance, only a small number of individuals can ever achieve high positions. Sooner or later, most people find that they are locked into dead-end jobs or have advanced as far as they will ever go in the organization. This discovery can be a severe blow to one's self-esteem and work motivation. The ability to exercise *power* in an organization is always sharply limited by people's positions in the hierarchy, narrowly prescribed job definitions, occupancy of staff, rather than line, positions, and other persons who exercise power through their positions or their numbers. Individuals react in many different ways to these limitations on their power, ranging from passivity to belligerence. Two common examples of the difficulties that arise in such situations are the middle-level manager who constantly attempts to wield power beyond her designated authority, and the relatively powerless foreman who compensates by insisting on rigid conformity to all organizational rules. The importance of *numbers* depends on whether one is in the majority (white males) or a minority (women, blacks, and others). Individuals in the majority not only tend to feel more comfortable in the organization, but they also have better prospects for raises and advancement. Individuals in minority categories often become frustrated by their more limited possibilities for recognition and by the tendency of majority members to treat them as tokens or representatives of their categories rather than as individuals.

In short, *the kind of person one becomes, and even one's most basic self-identity, are often strongly influenced by the structural and cultural characteristics of the bureaucratic organizations in which one participates.*

SUMMARY

Modern societies are pervaded by organizations that are oriented toward the attainment of specific goals. To achieve their intended goals, organizations utilize relevant technologies and establish formal operating procedures. The major structural dimensions of all goal-oriented organizations are their size, differentiation, and complexity (vertical and horizontal). In addition to their formal structure, all such organizations also contain an informal structure of interpersonal relationships that can have considerable influence on their functioning.

Most goal-oriented organizations in modern societies are relatively bureaucratized. Bureaucratization is the process of rationalizing and controlling the activities of an organization to increase the efficiency and effectiveness of its goal attainment. Bureaucratization is interrelated with several other fundamental trends in modern societies, including industrialization, capitalism, nationalization, urbanization, organizational growth, and cultural secularization.

Weber's ideal-type model of a fully bureaucratized organization sought to maximize rationality and control processes. This is accomplished by defining offices and duties precisely, stressing personal competence, providing stable careers, operating impersonally, establishing standard operating procedures and rules, and arranging all formal authority into a hierarchy.

The principal advantages of bureaucratic organization over more traditional forms of organization are its efficiency and effectiveness in attaining desired goals, its equitable treatment of all persons, its accountability for all activities and decisions, and its stability in the face of stresses and strains. The bureaucratization process is misdirected, however, if it is applied to all realms of human life, or if it is used to determine social values and goals.

Four fundamental processes that occur within all bureaucratic organizations are goal attainment, environmental coping, organizational control, and organizational change. Determining how successfully an organization is in achieving its goals can be quite difficult because most organizations have several goals, both official and operative, because the criteria for such evaluations are often imprecise, and because organizations frequently alter their goals through time. In addition, uncertainty severely limits goal attainment.

The process of coping with environmental conditions and pressures is vital if an organization is to obtain necessary resources and dispose of its products. The gatekeeper subunits that control those inputs and outputs can therefore exercise considerable power within an organization. Because the social and natural environments are major sources of uncertainty for most organizations, they frequently seek to influence those environments through competition, bargaining, cooptation, and coalitions.

To exercise control over their members and activities, bureaucratic organizations utilize various combinations of command, standardization, and internalization strategies. The Weberian model particularly emphasizes the use of formal authority (rational and legal) and formalization of operating procedures. In addition, many contemporary organizations attempt to select and/or train members who are competent and committed to the goals of that organization. In the Weberian model, all power is centralized at the top of an authority hierarchy to ensure effective control and coordination, but a more decentralized power structure is often more compatible with the goals and activities of contemporary organizations.

Organizational change can be investigated by examining the numerous characteristics of proposed innovations that affect their eventual adoption or rejection, by determining which features of organizations facilitate or impede the change process, by exploring the ways in which organizational members affect change, and by analyzing the stages through which organizational change occurs.

Most bureaucratic organizations encounter numerous operational problems that typically result from placing excessive or distorted emphasis on rationality and control, so that those means to goal attainment become ends in themselves. These problems include rule ritualization, in which procedural rules are applied minutely and inflexibly; job incompetence, in which individuals are promoted above their level of ability; impersonal treatment, in which organizational clients are handled in a standardized manner; internal conflict, which can arise from a variety of sources; split authority, when authority of office and authority of expertness do not coincide; communication distortion, which occurs as information travels up and down the hierarchy; goal displacement, in which an organization loses sight of its external goals and places all emphasis on internal goals; and change resistance, which is an outcome of all the previous problems as well as organizational promotion procedures.

Individual members of bureaucratic organizations frequently experience many kinds of personal difficulties as they enact their organizational roles and confront numerous operational issues. These difficulties involve pressures for compliance with organizational directives based on coercion, remuneration, and normative appeals; styles of supervision employed in the organization; alienation resulting from lack of control over one's activities; and organizational influences on one's personality, self-esteem, and self-identity.

CHAPTER 16

SOCIOECONOMIC STRATIFICATION

How do power inequality and distribution processes create socioeconomic
stratification?

How are status inequality and social classes distributed in modern industrial
societies?

In what ways do socioeconomic status and class positions affect various
aspects of one's life?

What social forces and processes tend to maintain existing patterns of
socioeconomic stratification?

How can socioeconomic stratification systems be changed and inequality
reduced?

EXPLANATIONS OF STRATIFICATION

The pervasiveness of socioeconomic inequality throughout social life has already
been discussed at several points in this book.
In Chapter 6, stratification was described as
the process through which social benefits
are unequally distributed and those patterns
of organized inequality are perpetuated
through time. Also mentioned there were
the three basic components of inequality—
power, privilege, and prestige—the numerous dimensions of stratification, and the central concept of social class. The examination
of agrarian societies in Chapter 8 showed
how socioeconomic inequality steadily increases with growing agricultural productivity. Chapter 12, dealing with industrial economies, demonstrated that capitalism can
create extreme concentrations of power and
wealth within an upper stratum of society.
Chapter 13, on modern states, dealt with the
unequal distribution of political power and
participation in industrial societies.

This chapter continues our exploration of
socioeconomic stratification in modern industrial societies. The initial section discusses factors that produce socioeconomic
inequality. Subsequent sections deal with
patterns of status and class stratification in
contemporary societies, consequences of
stratification for individuals, the processes
and forces that maintain existing patterns
of stratification, and ways of altering those
systems and reducing socioeconomic inequality.

Power Inequality

Underlying most socioeconomic stratification in all societies is an unequal distribution among individuals and organizations of
the ability to exercise power in social life
(Weber, 1958; Lenski, 1966). *Power inequality
is the root cause of most social stratification.* To
exercise power over others, social actors
must control and utilize valuable resources.
The most fundamental of these are natural

375

resources such as land, water, agricultural products, ores such as iron, precious minerals such as gold, and fuels such as coal and oil. As the technology available in a society develops, people are able to exploit the natural environment with increasing efficiency and to acquire greater amounts of various resources such as food, energy, and minerals. As that occurs, some segments of the population inevitably gain control of disproportionate shares of the additional resources and thus become more powerful than other members of the society.

On that ecological base, all societies past the hunting and gathering stage create patterns of social organization to protect, perpetuate, and promote social inequality. Individuals and organizations that control valuable resources utilize them to exercise power over others, establish organizational structures and hierarchies of authority within which to enact that power and increase their resources, establish rules and norms to ensure that others comply with their dictates, distribute rewards to those who comply and punish those who do not, and create beliefs and ideologies to explain and justify their superior power. Consequently, socioeconomic stratification becomes a complex sociocultural as well as an ecological process, so that patterns of social ordering and cultural ideas further expand and solidify socioeconomic inequality within the society.

Although power inequality underlies all socioeconomic inequality, the ability to exercise power is generally viewed as only a means of acquiring other desired benefits in social life. In most situations, power is sought not as an end in itself, but because it can be used to generate all kinds of desired social privileges such as wealth, material possessions, financial security, access to roles and organizations, education, leisure and recreation, or enjoyment of the arts. Power can also be transformed—either directly, or indirectly via the privileges it provides—into social prestige, esteem, and honor. Hence, *most powerful actors constantly seek to employ their power in ways that will enhance their privileges*

and prestige relative to others, which expands social inequality even further. As a result, those who have power, privilege, and/or prestige frequently acquire even more, while those who do not, often have few opportunities to improve their conditions in life.

Along with power exertion, social conflict is also inherent in most socioeconomic stratification. As actors employ power to acquire privileges and prestige, they frequently come into conflict with other powerful actors seeking the same goals. These struggles among competing elites and would-be-elites have pervaded human history. In addition, disadvantaged members of a society may also create conflict by demanding a larger share of the available benefits, sometimes resorting to such strategies as strikes, riots, or rebellions. However, these challenges to existing systems of inequality are much less common than conflicts among powerful elites seeking to control the system. Throughout history, most disadvantaged people have been so thoroughly controlled, exploited, and socialized to accept their lot in life that they have rarely even considered rebelling. And when they have occasionally attempted to alter the stratification system to gain more benefits for themselves, they have generally been swiftly punished or eliminated.

Numerous social theorists have developed differing explanations of how power exertion creates socioeconomic stratification. These are not alternative theories of stratification, but rather complementary perspectives on power inequality. They all concur on the basic thesis that power exertion underlies all socioeconomic inequality.

Marx's Perspective. Karl Marx focused on the economic production dimension of stratification (Marx, 1956). The primary concern of any society, he maintained, is to obtain economic sustenance from the natural and social environments in order to survive. The prevailing "mode of production" in a society shapes the manner and effectiveness with which this is accomplished. For example, in agrarian societies the dominant mode of production is settled agriculture, while in industrial societies it is manufacturing. The major mode of production in a society has two components:

(1) The "forces of production," consisting of the scientific knowledge, technological applications, and machinery that are used in that productive process; and

(2) The "relations of production," or social arrangements, that determine who owns and controls the dominant productive process.

Although the forces of production shape the overall structure of a society, the relations of production determine its prevailing patterns of socioeconomic stratification.

In Marxian theory, *social classes are defined by their relationship to the major means of economic production in a society.* Hence the class that owns or controls the production process exercises vast power and constitutes the dominant elites. In fully industrialized societies, this is the small proportion of the population who own controlling blocks of stock in the major corporations, plus the top executives of those companies (who are often also major stockholders). Marx called this business elite class the "bourgeoise." The principal subordinate class in industrial societies is the "proletariat," composed of all workers—blue-collar and white-collar—who sell their services to the bourgeoise in the labor market. Other subordinate classes in these societies are the middle class of independent professionals and small businesspersons, the classes of farmers and artisans who are essentially holdovers from the old agrarian way of life, and the "lumpenproletariate" (literally, the "ragamuffin proletariat") of unemployed or otherwise dispossessed people. All these subordinate classes are relatively powerless in relation to the dominant class of industrialists who exercise pervasive power throughout all parts of the society.

Weber's Perspective. Max Weber agreed with Marx that the exercise of power shapes all forms of stratification. Since he was primarily interested in how inequality affects individuals, however, he focused on the economic consumption dimension rather than the production dimension of stratification (Weber, 1958). In capitalist societies, most goods and services are obtained by people through market transactions. Consequently, Weber argued that the principal determinant of social class for individuals is their ability to exercise power in the consumption market. Such power is most often based on wealth, but it can also be derived from control of organizations, the ability to provide necessary services, or such intangible resources as fame or beauty. Whatever its sources, the amount of power that people exercise in the marketplace and their ability to use it to obtain necessary goods and services will largely determine their life chances, standards of living, and lifestyles. *Social classes are therefore composed of sets of people who exercise similar amounts of power in the consumption marketplace and consequently exhibit similar lifestyles.*

Dahrendorf's Perspective. The contemporary German sociologist Ralf Dahrendorf also holds a power perspective on stratification, but he insists that the principal shapers of social inequality in modern societies are large goal-oriented organizations (Dahrendorf, 1959). The central feature of all such organizations is a formal hierarchy of authority. The top position holders in corporations, governments, universities, and all other complex organizations set policies, make decisions, and exercise authority over all other parts and members of those organizations. These organizational elites therefore comprise the controlling class within each organization, and collectively they constitute the dominant class in society. All the other members of an organization who do not hold positions of formal authority constitute a subordinate class. Although an individual may occupy an elite position in one organization but not in another, most people belong to the subordinate class within all organizations to which they belong. In short *social classes in modern societies are determined* *primarily by the exercise or nonexercise of formal authority in large organizations.*

Sumner's Perspective. The early twentieth-century American sociologist William Graham Sumner is typical of many past and contemporary social theorists who argue that culture plays a crucial role in shaping patterns of socioeconomic stratification. He began with the assumption that the first requirement of all societies is to survive in their natural and social environments. As people develop effective ways of meeting their needs and perpetuate those actions through time, established social practices become expressed symbolically as folkways that are viewed as the proper or right ways of carrying out collective social activities. Those people who are most skillful in meeting their needs and achieving their goals form a powerful and wealthy dominant class within a society. That controlling class is able to formulate the folkways followed by all other members of the society, to reward those individuals who abide by the existing norms, and to punish those who do not. In other words, *the dominant class uses its power to shape the culture of a society, which defines the statuses of all other classes.* The working class is taught to accept its place in society below more privileged classes, the members of racial and ethnic minorities are culturally defined as inferior, and women are socialized to enact roles that are subordinate to men.

Benefit Inequality

The various power perspectives point to the basic cause of socioeconomic stratification, but by themselves they do not fully explain how privileges and prestige become distributed unequally among the members of a society. When sociologists examine the effects of socioeconomic stratification on social life, they are typically concerned with more immediate manifestations of status, such as income and wealth, occupational prestige, educational attainment, housing location and quality, material possessions,

social esteem, intellectual sophistication, and overall lifestyles. To understand how people acquire or do not acquire such status benefits, we must ascertain how social power is transformed into privileges and prestige.

In some cases, this transformation is quite obvious. When statuses are acquired through ascription, the son of a king becomes the next king, and the child of a peasant remains a peasant. In a modern society, the son of a wealthy corporate executive is sent to the best schools, may be given a relatively high position in his father's business upon graduation, quickly moves up the corporate hierarchy, and eventually inherits the family's wealth. As more and more roles in contemporary societies are opened to competitive achievement, however, this process becomes very complex. Individuals must demonstrate their personal capabilities and perform their assigned roles in a competent or superior manner. Consequently, the distribution of privileges and prestige in modern societies is increasingly being determined by the skills one possesses, the positions one achieves, and the manner in which one enacts social roles. Nevertheless, this process is still highly influenced by the actions of powerful elites.

At the present time, sociology contains two quite different approaches to explaining how benefits are distributed among the members of a society. *One approach focuses on the actions of elites*—corporate owners, government officials, wealthy families, organizational authorities, and culturally defined dominant classes—in influencing the distribution of privileges and prestige throughout the society. This approach emphasizes such processes as social control, decision making, exploitation, oppression, and legitimization. Social scientists who emphasize this perspective are often labeled as "elitists" if they defend the actions of societal elites as necessary and/or desirable, or as "radicals" if they criticize or condemn those actions as unjustified or immoral.

The other approach views the distribution of benefits as a natural process that is inherent in organized social life and is not controlled by dominant elites. This approach emphasizes such processes as status competition, individual effort and capabilities, incentives and rewards for adequate role performances, and the fulfillment of necessary functions for society. Social scientists who emphasize this perspective are commonly labeled as "functionalists" if they argue that these practices are necessary for the functioning of society, or as "conservatives" if they believe that such activities justify social inequality.

The two alternative approaches to benefit inequality are evident to varying degrees in the complementary perspectives proposed by several writers. They all concur on the basic thesis that benefit inequality results from an interplay between social structural conditions and the power and role resources of individuals.

Marx's Perspective. *Karl Marx held that the distribution of benefits is determined by the dominant class through its control of all major organizations in the society.* The process occurs primarily through work, in the payment of wages for labor. In a capitalist economy, Marx believed, business owners pay their workers (blue-collar and white-collar) less than the true value of their work and hence inevitably exploit them. This is not because the bourgeoise are evil persons, but because (according to the prevailing economic theory of Marx's time) this is necessary to make a profit and remain in business. In other words, Marx saw exploitation of the labor force as an inherent feature of profit-oriented capitalist production. Workers could join together in unions and collectively demand higher wages—which Marx urged them do—but this could diminish profits and eventually lead to the failure of many firms. The distributive process is further influenced by government, which is closely allied with the bourgeoise and acts to ensure that business owners retain a large proportion of their profits for investment in economic growth. In addition, families and schools teach workers to perform their as-

signed roles in the stratification system, while religion and secular ideologies convince members of the subordinate classes to accept that system and grant it legitimacy.

Weber's Perspective. *Some aspects of Max Weber's thinking favored the elite control approach, while other aspects leaned toward the natural process approach.* To the extent that consumptive power in the marketplace is derived from wealth or occupancy of high organizational positions, elites heavily influence the distribution of benefits to all other individuals and hence their life chances. Weber held a broader perspective than did Marx, however, pointing out that a person may acquire wealth or high position from many sources other than ownership of the means of economic production. These include inheriting wealth, acquiring political office, and being fortunate in one's financial transactions. Consumptive power in the marketplace may also be derived from particular skills or knowledge a person possesses, which enables some nonelites to do well in the marketplace and improve their life chances through their own efforts. Weber also identified two other dimensions of stratification in addition to socioeconomic class, both of which operate to a considerable degree through natural processes. One of these dimensions is social prestige or honor, which he termed "status." Prestige status is accorded to individuals by others on the basis of their standing in the community. To some extent, this is determined by one's possessions and lifestyle, which are shaped by the marketplace. In addition, prestige can also be acquired as a result of one's family background, education, role performances, personal accomplishments, and contributions to the community. The other dimension of stratification is political party standing, which is a result of one's political activities and involvement. An individual's party standing is partially determined by party elites, but it is also partially a result of one's own efforts and contributions within the political system.

Davis and Moore's Perspective. The American sociologists Kingsley Davis and Wilbert Moore (1945) formulated the functional perspective on stratification, which holds that *unequal distribution of privileges and prestige is a natural process necessary for the functioning of society.* They began with the assumption that all societies must satisfy numerous functional requirements if they are to survive and attain goals. Various roles in a society contribute differentially to the fulfillment of those functional requirements, and the roles that contribute the most are of the greatest functional importance. If the society is to operate adequately, those crucial roles must be enacted by qualified persons in a satisfactory manner. In general, however, such roles require more training, abilities, and effort than do other social roles. Consequently, the supply of people who can and will enact these critical roles is normally rather limited. All societies are therefore faced with the functional problems of inducing qualified persons to fulfill functionally important roles and encouraging them to enact those roles to the best of their abilities. Societies resolve these problems by awarding differing amounts of privileges and prestige to roles and actors according to their functional importance for the society. The more important and demanding the role, the greater the benefits given to its incumbents to ensure that the best available people choose that role and enact it as well as possible. In the words of Davis and Moore, "Social inequality is thus an unconsciously evolved device by which societies ensure that the more important positions are conscientiously filled by the most qualified persons."

Simpson's Perspective. Richard Simpson (1956) sought to describe how the functionalist process of stratification actually occurs in contemporary societies. In so doing, he created a perspective on benefit inequality that blends insights from Marx and Weber with those of Davis and Moore. In reality, there is never consensus in any society as to which roles are functionally critical for society as a whole. However, powerful organizations and individuals within a society frequently determine that particular roles are important for their own interests and goal attainment. These powerful actors—not society as a whole—therefore attempt to ensure that roles which they believe are important are enacted by qualified people in a satisfactory manner. This results in a "role market" in which privileges and prestige are accorded to roles as a consequence of (1) the demand for those roles by powerful actors, and (2) the supply of people qualified and willing to enact them. Several factors influence the demand for certain roles. Those factors include prevailing cultural views, existing technologies, and public opinion concerning the roles. Similarly, several factors influence the supply of persons available to enact those roles. These include the talents and training required by the roles, family and interpersonal influences on educational attainment and role selection, social restrictions on who may acquire these roles, the openness of the society to geographical and status mobility, and the uniqueness of the role demands and responsibilities. In short, *unequal privileges and prestige in social life result from a continual bargaining and exchange process in the "role market" between "buyers" and "sellers" of roles that powerful actors believe are important.*

PATTERNS OF SOCIOECONOMIC STRATIFICATION

The fact that most members of industrial societies enjoy a much higher material standard of living than exists among all but the elite members of agrarian societies does not negate the fact that socioeconomic power, privileges, and prestige are still distributed very unequally in the United States and all other modern nations. Two different patterns of socioeconomic stratification that occur in all of these societies are examined in this section: distributions of people on various status dimensions and clusters of people who form identifiable social classes.

Status Distributions

One way of describing patterns of socio-economic stratification is to determine how people are distributed along such dimensions as power, wealth, income, occupation, and education. Countless empirical studies, using several different methodologies, have investigated all of these stratification dimensions and have consistently discovered wide variations among individuals on all of them. Their major findings clearly demonstrate the great extent of socioeconomic status inequality that exists within industrial societies. The data used in the following paragraphs to illustrate these patterns are taken from the United States, but studies in many other modern nations have revealed quite similar patterns.

Power. We have already examined the manner in which the structure of power in modern societies is extremely concentrated in multinational corporations and the national government, and to a lesser extent in the military, special-interest associations, labor unions, and other large organizations. What does this structural power concentration mean for the socioeconomic statuses of individuals?

Most of the research that has been conducted on this topic has focused on the distribution of social power in specific communities (Aiken and Mott, 1970; Troustine and Christensen, 1982) or in complex organizations (Bachrach and Lawley, 1980; Zald, 1970). Quite predictably, these studies have discovered that a very small set of people formulate most of the major policies and make most of the crucial decisions within all communities and organizations. In formally structured organizations with an established hierarchy of authority, these are usually the persons who occupy top organizational positions, while in communities they are more likely to be an informally organized network of leading business executives and government officials. Below this level of top elites there are frequently several successively lower levels of semielites, directors and managers, and activists, all of whom exercise some amount of power within specified areas of activity. The actions of people at these lower levels of power are almost invariably shaped and constrained, however, by the policies and decisions of the top organizational or community elites. Moreover, all the members of these lower power levels constitute only a minority of the total membership of the organization or community.

The vast majority of people have almost no influence on the functioning of the organizations or the community or the society to which they belong. Occasionally, they may band together in a protest movement or strike and force the elites to make some concessions to them. Very rarely, however, do such actions alter basic policies or practices. In short, *the distribution of social power appears to be highly skewed toward the top in all large social systems, so that most individuals are relatively powerless in most spheres of their lives.*

Wealth. We have already seen that wealth is extremely highly concentrated in the United States, with the top one-half percent of families owning about 20 percent of all private assets. The distribution of wealth across the entire population—depicted in Figure 16-1—demonstrates this concentration even more clearly. (These figures from 1973 are the latest available, but there is no evidence that the distribution of wealth has changed significantly since then.) The bottom fifth of all households own essentially no wealth (the precise figure is 0.2 percent of all private assets), and many of these people owe more than they own. The second fifth possesses merely two percent of all wealth; the third fifth just six percent; and the fourth fifth only about 16 percent. In contrast, the top fifth of all households owns over three-fourths of all privately held assets, primarily corporate stocks, bonds, and real estate. In short, *some people possess a great deal of wealth, but most people have very little.* Their entire worldly wealth often consists only of whatever equity they have in a house (usually heavily mortgaged), a small savings account, a car or two (often with a lien), their household furnishings, and their clothes

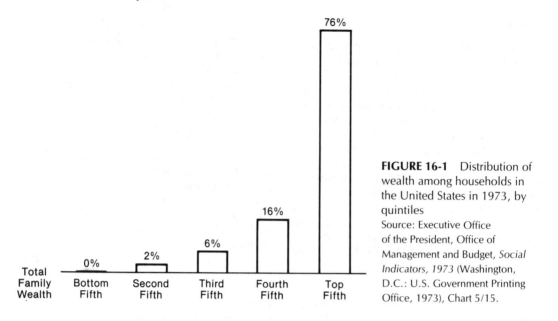

FIGURE 16-1 Distribution of wealth among households in the United States in 1973, by quintiles
Source: Executive Office of the President, Office of Management and Budget, *Social Indicators, 1973* (Washington, D.C.: U.S. Government Printing Office, 1973), Chart 5/15.

and other personal possessions. They own virtually no assets to invest in any kind of money-making ventures.

Income. The money income received by families is not quite as concentrated at the top as is total wealth, but it is far from being equally distributed. In 1986, the median income of all families in the United States was about $29,500, but those incomes ranged from nothing to millions of dollars.

As shown in Figure 16-2, the bottom fifth of all households in this country had a me-dian income of about $13,000 in 1985, which meant that they received only five percent of all money income. The second fifth had a median income of approximately $23,000, which gave them 11 percent of all income. The median income of the third fifth was about $33,000, so that they received 17 per-cent of all income. The fourth fifth, with a median income of about $46,000, received 24 percent of all income. And the top fifth, which had a median income of approxi-mately $78,000, received 43 percent of all income.

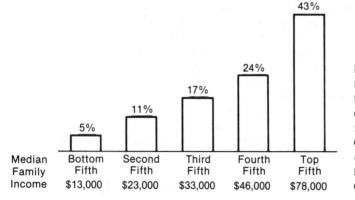

FIGURE 16-2 Distribution of money income among families in the United States in 1985, by quintiles
Source: U.S. Department of Commerce, *Statistical Abstract of the United States, 1987.* (Washington, D.C.: U.S. Government Printing Office), Table 733.

TABLE 16-1 Distribution of Money Income Among Families in the United States, 1930–1985, by Quintiles

Income Fifths	Percent of All Income						
	1930	*1940*	*1950*	*1960*	*1970*	*1980*	*1985*
Lowest fifth	⎰ 13%	5%	5%	5%	5%	5%	5%
Second fifth	⎱	12%	12%	12%	12%	12%	11%
Third fifth	14%	17%	17%	18%	18%	18%	17%
Fourth fifth	19%	23%	24%	24%	24%	24%	24%
Top fifth	54%	43%	43%	41%	41%	41%	43%
Top five percent	30%	18%	17%	16%	16%	16%	17%

Source: U.S. Department of Commerce, *Statistical Abstract of the United States, 1987* (Washington, D.C.: U.S. Government Printing Office), Table 733.

This pattern of income inequality among quintiles of families in the United States has not changed significantly since 1940. As seen in Table 16-1, there was a major reduction in income inequality between 1930 and 1940, caused by the Great Depression of the 1930s and the social welfare programs introduced during that decade. In 1930, the top fifth of all families received 54 percent of all income, and the top five percent received 30 percent. In 1940, in contrast, those figures had declined to 43 and 18 percent, respectively. Since 1940, however, the proportion of all money income going to each quintile of families has not varied by more than two percent, and there were no changes at all between 1960 and 1980. Since 1980, however, there has been a slight trend toward greater income inequality, with the top quintile increasing its proportion of all income from 41 to 43 percent, and the top five percent increasing from 16 to 17 percent.

An alternative way of viewing the distribution of money income among families is to calculate the proportion of all families falling within various income categories. In 1985, five percent of all American families were extremely poor, with total annual incomes of less than $5,000. Another eight percent were rather poor, with incomes between $5,000 and $10,000, so that 13 percent of all families lived on less than $10,000. The income bracket of $10,000 to $20,000, which might be described as semi-poor, contained another 21 percent of all families. At the high end of the income distribution, 19

percent of American families had incomes between $35,000 and $50,000, which might be described as a comfortable level of living. Another 18 percent received more than $50,000, which enabled them to live affluently. At the very top, more than two million people had incomes of a million dollars or more. In short, *a considerable number of American families have very low or quite modest incomes, while a good number of families enjoy comfortable or affluent incomes, and a fair number are rich.*

Occupations. The status of various occupations is most frequently measured by asking large samples of people to assign prestige scores to different jobs. As seen in Table 16-2, on a scale of 0 to 100, Supreme Court justices have the highest occupational prestige, followed closely by physicians. As might be expected, street sweepers and shoeshiners have the lowest prestige. Three things about these occupational prestige scores are quite remarkable (Hodge, et al., 1964; Trieman, 1977).

(1) People at all occupational levels generally agree on the prestige accorded to each job. Physicians and street sweepers both agree that the former are at the top of the scale and the latter are at the bottom.

(2) These scores have not changed significantly since they were first obtained in 1927, and the 1963 rankings given in Table 16-2 still generally hold today.

(3) The prestige rankings of most jobs are very similar in all industrial countries.

TABLE 16-2 Occupational Prestige Ratings in the United States in 1947 and 1963

Occupation	1947 Score	1963 Score	Occupation	1947 Score	1963 Score
U.S. Supreme Court justice	96	94	Newspaper columnist	74	73
Physician	93	93	Policeman	67	72
Nuclear physicist	86	92	Reporter on a daily newspaper	71	71
Scientist	89	92	Radio announcer	75	70
Government scientist	88	91	Bookkeeper	68	70
State governor	93	91	Tenant farmer—one who owns livestock and machinery and manages the farm	68	69
Cabinet member in the federal government	92	90			
College professor	89	90	Insurance agent	68	69
U.S. representative in Congress	89	90	Carpenter	65	68
Chemist	86	89	Manager of a small store in a city	69	67
Lawyer	86	89	A local official of a labor union	62	67
Diplomat in U.S. Foreign Service	92	89	Mail carrier	66	66
Dentist	86	88	Railroad conductor	67	66
Architect	86	88	Traveling salesman for a wholesale concern	68	66
County judge	87	88	Plumber	63	65
Psychologist	85	87	Automobile repairman	63	64
Minister	87	87	Playground director	67	63
Member of the board of directors of a large corporation	86	87	Barber	59	63
			Machine operator in a factory	60	63
Mayor of a large city	90	87	Owner-operator of a lunch stand	62	63
Priest	86	86	Corporal in the regular army	60	62
Head of a department in state government	87	86	Garage mechanic	62	62
Civil engineer	84	86	Truck driver	54	59

Occupation			Occupation		
Airline pilot	83	86	Fisherman who owns his own boat	58	58
Banker	88	85	Clerk in a store	58	56
Biologist	81	85	Milk route man	54	56
Sociologist	82	83	Streetcar motorman	58	56
Instructor in public schools	79	82	Lumberjack	53	55
Captain in the regular army	80	82	Restaurant cook	54	55
Accountant for a large business	81	81	Singer in a nightclub	52	54
Public school teacher	78	80	Filling station attendant	52	51
Owner of a factory that employs about 100 people	82	80	Dockworker	47	50
Building contractor	79	78	Railroad section hand	48	50
Artist who paints pictures that are exhibited in galleries	83	78	Night watchman	47	50
Musician in a symphony orchestra	81	78	Coal miner	49	50
Author of novels	80	78	Restaurant waiter	48	49
Economist	79	77	Taxi driver	49	49
Official of an international labor union	75	76	Farmhand	50	48
Railroad engineer	76	76	Janitor	44	48
Electrician	73	76	Bartender	44	48
County agricultural agent	77	75	Clothes presser in a laundry	46	45
Owner-operator of a printing shop	74	75	Soda fountain clerk	45	44
Trained machinist	73	73	Sharecropper—one who owns no livestock or equipment and does not manage farm	40	42
Farm owner and operator	76	74	Garbage collector	35	39
Undertaker	72	74	Street sweeper	34	36
Welfare worker for a city government	73	74	Shoeshiner	33	34
			Average	70	71

Source: Robert W. Hodge, Paul M. Stegel, and Peter H. Rossi, "Occupational Prestige in the United States: 1925–1963," *American Journal of Sociology 70* (November 1964), 290–92.

From these findings we can conclude that *occupations differ greatly in the amount of status or prestige associated with them, and these occupational rankings are quite stable.*

For ease of reporting and interpretation, the many thousands of different occupations found in modern societies are often combined into several broad categories. The distribution of employed persons in the United States in 1985 among those categories is given in Figure 16-3, with occupational prestige increasing from left to right across the categories.

Workers in extractive industries—farming, fishing, and forestry—today constitute only three percent of the total labor force, while unskilled laborers in all other industries are another four percent of all employed persons. Most blue-collar workers fall into one of three categories—semiskilled machine operators, service workers, and skilled craftspersons—each of which constitutes 12 or 13 percent of the labor force. Altogether, these five categories of blue-collar workers account for 44 percent of the employed labor force at the present time. Clerical workers are the largest category in today's labor force, with 16 percent of all employees, while sales workers are 12 percent of the labor force. Traditionally, the 28 percent of all employed people in these two categories have been considered white-collar

workers, but most of them are more similar to blue-collar workers in the nature of their jobs, their occupational prestige, and their incomes. The final three categories are clearly white-collar workers, with a total of 27 percent of the labor force. The category of technicians is quite small, with just three percent of all workers. Executives, administrators, and managers account for 11 percent of the labor force, while professionals of all kinds are 13 percent of all employed persons.

Education. Two generations ago, most people left school after the eighth grade, only a small number completed high school, and just a tiny minority graduated from college. That picture has changed markedly during this century as more and more people have gone on to high school and college, so that the median educational level of all persons age 25 or older is now 12.7 years. Nevertheless, *there is still considerable inequality in amount of education attained*—as depicted in Figure 16-4. In 1985, among persons age 25 or older, about 14 percent had not gone beyond grammar school. Another 12 percent had not completed high school. By far the most common level of educational attainment was high school graduation, accounting for 38 percent of the adult population. Approximately 16 percent of all adults

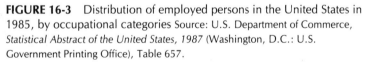

FIGURE 16-3 Distribution of employed persons in the United States in 1985, by occupational categories Source: U.S. Department of Commerce, *Statistical Abstract of the United States, 1987* (Washington, D.C.: U.S. Government Printing Office), Table 657.

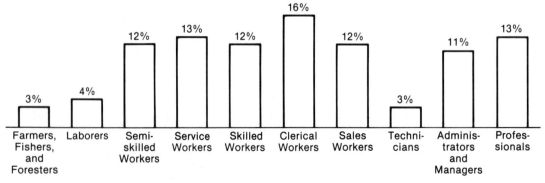

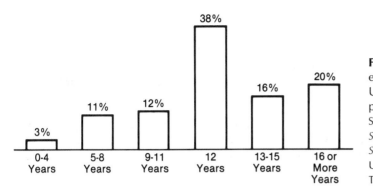

FIGURE 16-4 Distribution of educational attainment in the United States in 1985 among persons 25 years or older
Source: U.S. Department of Commerce, *Statistical Abstract of the United States, 1987* (Washington, D.C.: U.S. Government Printing Office), Table 198.

had completed one to three years of college, while 20 percent were college graduates. If current levels of college enrollment continue in the future, the sizes of the latter two categories should continue to expand, while the bottom two categories will decline even further.

Relationships Among Dimensions. Since status on any one stratification dimension can often by transformed into status on other dimensions, *all of the preceding indicators of socioeconomic status are fairly highly related to one another.* As an example, let us examine the consequences of educational attainment and occupational prestige for household income—as shown in Table 16-3. The top panel of the table indicates that median family income increases steadily and rather

sharply with each level of education, from $10,000 for families with 8 years or less of schooling to $32,300 for those containing a college graduate in 1985. The bottom panel demonstrates a similar pattern among broad occupational categories, ranging from $15,400 for farm workers to $32,100, for all white-collar workers in 1981. Unquestionably, educational attainment and occupational status pay off in higher income.

Social Class

A second way of describing patterns of socioeconomic stratification is to identify the social classes existing in a society. Whereas status dimensions are relatively continuous graduations from low to high, *social classes are*

TABLE 16-3 Median Income by Educational Level and Occupational Status in the United States in 1981–1985

Educational Level	Median Family Income in 1985
0–8 Years	$10,800
9–11 Years	$12,800
12 Years	$17,800
13–15 Years	$20,800
16 or More Years	$32,300

Occupational Status	Median Household Income in 1981
Farm Workers	$15,400
Service Workers	$17,400
Blue-Collar Workers	$24,600
White-Collar Workers	$32,100

Source: U.S. Department of Commerce, *Statistical Abstract of the United States.* (Washington, D.C.: U.S. Government Printing Office), 1984, Table 757; 1987, Table 735.

identifiable sets of people who have relatively similar amounts of power, privilege, and prestige. Classes are more than just population categories. They are organizational units within society, displaying some amount of social ordering and a shared class culture. To identify and describe the various classes comprising any society, therefore, we must locate the boundaries that distinguish them from one another and then investigate the patterns of social relationships and cultural ideas that characterize each class (Landecker, 1981).

In recent years, numerous sociologists have described the socioeconomic class structure of the United States as containing five major classes (Beeghley, 1978; Roosides, 1976; Vanneman, 1977). These are socioeconomic classes, so we must remember that the complete stratification system of this society also contains political, racial/ethnic, gender, intellectual, and other sets of classes. Although this set of five socioeconomic classes pertains most directly to the United States, relatively similar structures of classes are becoming increasingly evident in most other highly industrialized nations. The boundaries separating the five classes are fairly identifiable and pervasive throughout the United States, although they are certainly not as clear or as rigid as the class or caste boundaries that exist in many agrarian societies. In modern societies, many people move upward or downward from one class to another during their lifetime, thus experiencing class mobility. Moreover, because Americans like to think of their society as "a land of equals," we are often not as aware of class distinctions as are most Europeans with their long history of sharp class divisions. In addition, within each social class there are numerous status gradations among its members, which further complicates the overall picture. Because of all these factors, class differences in the United States are more blurred and subtle than in many other societies, but they are nevertheless extremely important in social life.

There are no standard names for the five classes in contemporary American society, so for convenience we shall refer to them as the elite, influential, middle, working, and dispossessed classes.

Elite Class. As we saw in Chapter 12, *the elite or upper class in American society is immensely powerful and wealthy.* Many of its members derive their power from their positions as top executives and directors of major corporations, while others are high government officials, military leaders, heads of national organizations, or members of wealthy and famous families such as the Rockefellers, Kennedys, Fords, and Vanderbilts. Their great wealth generally comes from ownership of large blocks of corporate stocks and state and municipal bonds, and much of it is inherited from previous generations. Most of these people enjoy six-figure incomes, and salaries of half a million or more are not at all uncommon. Money alone will not pay membership in the elite class, however, since a truck driver who wins ten million dollars in a state lottery will never gain entry. To be a member of the elite class, one must also hold a powerful position in the economic, political, or other major sphere of society—or marry someone who does, or be descended from someone who has.

Less tangible criteria for membership in the elite class often include white Anglo-Saxon ethnicity, at least a bachelor's degree from a prestigious university or college, evidence of "proper" etiquette and personal values, membership in exclusive clubs, personal relationships with other elites, and listing in a Social Register of high-status people. Individuals who have recently acquired power and wealth but have not yet transformed these resources into social prestige and other indicators of high status are frequently excluded from the elite class until they demonstrate that they have adopted the proper values and norms. Some sociologists place those people in a separate "semielite" or "lower-upper" class as long as they are excluded from full membership in the elite or upper class.

The elite class in the United States probably comprises no more than one percent of the total population, although if semielites are included that figure might increase to two or three percent. Those relatively few people in the elite class nevertheless occupy most high economic and political positions, own over half of all corporate stock, control at least one-fourth to one-third of all wealth in the country, and generally have personal assets of at least a half million dollars. *In short, elites are located at the apex of the socioeconomic class structure and dominate many spheres of activity throughout society.*

Influential Class. Although they are not extremely powerful or wealthy, members of the influential or upper-middle class enact critical social roles and are generally financially affluent. *The distinguishing feature of the influential class is the exercise of significant social influence within organizations, professions, or other realms of society.* Many of these people occupy executive or administrative/director positions in businesses, government agencies, special-interest associations, labor unions, universities, medical centers, the mass media, and other organizations. Others are prominent in such professions as science, law, religion, medicine, literature, and the arts. Still others are leaders of community and other local groups, and some are well-known entertainment and sports figures. In short, by virtue of their roles, knowledge, and skills, these people are able to exert influence on what other people think and do.

There are no established criteria for membership in the influential class beyond wielding influence, so that one can gain entry into it by climbing an organizational hierarchy, developing a professional skill, being elected or appointed to a public office, or enacting an occupational or other role in a manner that becomes critical for others. Many commentators on postindustrial societies, however, point to the rapidly growing importance of expert knowledge as the primary resource for exerting social influence in modern societies (Bell, 1973). Since possession of such knowledge is usually certified by a higher degree or license of some kind, entry into the influential class is in-

creasingly dependent on possession of requisite credentials such as a certificate of educational or professional attainment.

Economically, members of the influential class typically own only small amounts of personal wealth and perhaps a few stocks or bonds. Nevertheless, their incomes—which commonly range from about $50,000 to $200,000 in current dollars—usually enable them to live quite comfortably or even affluently. In terms of education, an undergraduate degree is almost mandatory for most positions in this class, and graduate and professional degrees are quite common today. These people typically own single-family homes in attractive neighborhoods, participate in a wide variety of community and other organizations, travel widely, and expect their children to attend college.

At present, the influential class probably constitutes roughly 15 percent of the total United States population, but as we move steadily toward a postindustrial society it will undoubtedly expand. These people are in no sense elites, but *influentials shape the actions of most organizations and other social activities and hence influence the lives of many other people.*

Middle Class. The distinctions between the influential class and the middle class are subtle, but nevertheless crucial. Influentials, as the name implies, are proactive. That is, they shape the course of activities to at least some extent within some sphere of social life. Members of the middle class, in contrast, are basically reactive in their major social roles, following the lead or directives of others. In their personal lives—such as their family, friendship groups, neighborhood, work group, or church or synagogue—they may likely influence other individuals, but they do not normally shape courses of events within broader organizational, community, or occupational settings. Nevertheless, within those latter realms they are able—because of their intellectual and/or interpersonal skills and abilities—to enact roles that are considered functionally important. In addition, those roles are often entrusted with some degree of responsibility. In short, *members of the middle class enact occupational and other roles that are valued by organizations or the society and that require particular kinds of knowledge or social skills.*

In their jobs, members of the middle class occupy a wide variety of white-collar positions as semiprofessionals (e.g., school teachers, nurses), technicans, office managers, lower-level public officials, sales representatives, and small business and farm owners. (Owners of small businesses and farms used to be considered part of the influential or upper-middle class, but in today's economy of large corporations their ability to exercise significant influence within the economic system is severely limited.) Clerical workers and retail sales clerks have traditionally also been included in the middle class, but recent evidence indicates that the social and economic conditions of most of these people are today closer to the working class (Vanneman, 1977), so that many sociologists now place them there. As a consequence of the functional roles they perform, middle-class people receive above-average salaries, ranging from around $25,000 to $50,000, although some families enjoy higher total incomes when both spouses are employed.

There is considerable overlap in amounts of income, standards of living, and lifestyles between the influential and middle classes, although on the average the middle class does not live as affluently as the influential class. Their houses are typically somewhat less expensive and are located in less prestigious neighborhoods, they do not usually own as many luxury possessions, and their total wealth is significantly smaller than that of the influentials. A generation ago, most members of the middle class were high school graduates with perhaps some postsecondary vocational or technical training, but today most of them have some college education and an increasing number of them are college graduates.

In the contemporary United States, the middle class is generally estimated to comprise about 30 or 35 percent of the popula-tion. It has grown steadily in size since World War II in this and all other industrial societies, since as *complex technology and bureaucratic organizations have become increasingly prevalent in modern societies, the roles performed by middle-class persons are indispensable in keeping the society functioning effectively.* However, much of this recent growth in the size of the middle class has been due to a tremendous expansion in all kinds of clerical and other paper-handling occupational roles. In the future, as more and more of this work is routinized and computerized, the middle class may cease growing.

Working Class. Whereas middle class people react to existing social conditions by fulfilling important roles, members of the working class are subject to those conditions and hence must struggle to find a place for themselves and earn an adequate living. In other words, *the working class consists of ordinary people who do all the routine jobs—typically involving manual skills or simple white-collar tasks—in industrial societies.* Traditionally, the working class has included all blue-collar workers—skilled craftspersons, semiskilled machine operators, and regularly employed laborers—as well as all service and farm workers. And, as previously noted, many clerical and retail sales workers also fall into this class today, despite the fact that their jobs are technically white-collar in nature. Virtually all of these people have completed at least some secondary education, high school graduation is the most common level of educational attainment, and many of them also have additional technical or vocational training.

Workers in modern societies typically enjoy a modest material standard of living, with incomes ranging from approximately $15,000 to $30,000—and more if both spouses work. This amount of income provides adequate housing in an apartment or small house, plus a few luxuries, but little or no personal wealth. Moreover, the real income of most working-class people, after taking account of inflation, has not increased significantly in the past twenty years. More significant than any differences in income between the middle and working classes, however, is the status of workers in the occupational marketplace. Whereas members of the middle class commonly have higher education or skills that give them a fair amount of employment flexibility and enable them to pursue a career, most members of the working class simply hold a job that typically requires only a few weeks or months of training, so that they are much more dependent on whatever jobs are available in their location at the present time.

Symbolic of the differing relationships of these two classes to the occupational marketplace is the fact that middle-class employees typically receive a fixed salary (or fees or commissions) and traditionally have not been laid off during economic slowdowns, whereas most workers are paid on an hourly basis only for the time they actually spend on the job and are always subject to layoffs. The resulting differences in economic security and occupational status between the middle and working classes are presently being obliterated, nevertheless, as much office and factory work is automated, many skilled craftspersons gain fairly comfortable incomes through union bargaining, and most workers acquire high school educations. Moreover, the economic slow-down of the 1980s resulted in many white-collar employees being laid off or experiencing a declining real income (taking account of inflation), so that their standard of living is today often no better than that of the majority of working-class people.

Nevertheless, many studies have reported that the traditional distinction between the middle and working classes is still quite real in terms of occupational status and mobility, economic security, residential patterns, material possessions, recreational patterns, and social and political attitudes (Beeghley, 1978; DeFronzo, 1973). Depending on whether or not clerical and retail sales workers are included as workers, this class comprises about 35 to 45 percent of the population, and its size has been relatively stable for some time.

In short, *members of the working class perform necessary jobs and have enough income to live modestly, but their occupational roles typically carry no special status, they are essentially interchangeable parts of the occupational structure, and their economic condition is always somewhat precarious.*

Dispossessed Class. We have characterized the elite class as wielding immense socioeconomic power, the influential class as shaping particular spheres of social activity, the middle class as enacting valued roles, and the working class as performing necessary jobs in society. In contrast, members of the dispossessed or lower class are largely victims of the industrial system and have little control over the course of their lives. For one reason or another, these people cannot function adequately within society and consequently live largely at its mercy as marginals or outcasts. *The distinctive characteristic of the dispossessed class is that it cannot participate effectively in the occupational marketplace and hence is not regularly employed.* Some of these people are unemployable because of physical or mental handicaps; a considerable number of them cannot find regular jobs because today's economy has less and less need for unskilled manual laborers; some work irregularly but are frequently unemployed for long periods of time; quite a few are divorced women with preschool children living on very low-paying jobs or welfare; some are migrant farm laborers who drift with the crops; some work the streets as prostitutes or petty thieves; some are retired people living on small fixed pensions; and a few have rejected involvement in the normal occupational world for ideological or personal reasons.

Economically, most of the dispossessed exist below or just barely above the federal poverty line, depending on their eligibility for various public benefits. Their poverty is a result, not the cause, of their location at the bottom of the socioeconomic class structure,

---

SOCIAL CLASSES IN AMERICAN SOCIETY

1. Elite class.
2. Influential class.
3. Middle class.
4. Working class.
5. Dispossessed class.

---

however. Many of them are also very poorly educated, and this handicap severely limits their ability to find regular employment and move into the working class. In addition, many members of the dispossessed class suffer from racial and/or gender discrimination, which further restricts their employability. And in numerical terms, the largest number of people in this class are minor children of dispossessed adults, who are frequently single parents.

Considering the great prosperity of American society at the present time, relative to all other industrial nations, it is often a shock to realize that from ten to 15 percent of the population falls into this class. Whatever the reason for their relegation to the ranks of the dispossessed, however, *all members of this class share the common fate of being socioeconomically powerless and hence are locked into the bottom of the class structure.*

Poverty

Poverty is a condition of extremely low income, so that poor people constitute an income category, not a social class. Consequently, being poor does not automatically place one in the dispossessed class. College students, recently divorced women, and retired people living on a small pension may fall into the poverty category and still retain many other characteristics that place them in the working or middle class. However, since virtually all members of the dispossessed class are quite poor, poverty is closely associated with membership in that class.

Although there has always been poverty in the United States and all other industrial nations, Michael Harrington's landmark 1963 book, *The Other America: Poverty in the*

U.S., made many Americans dramatically aware of the fact that postwar affluence in this country had by no means eliminated the problem of abject poverty among a considerable portion of the population. It also made clear that poverty involves much more than just lack of money, but also malnutrition, disease and poor health, low self-esteem, lack of hope for the future, and sometimes premature death. As a result of the public outcry created by this book, poverty became a major social and political issue in the United States that led directly to President Lyndon Johnson's War on Poverty and subsequent governmental efforts to eliminate poverty as much as possible.

In 1967, the federal government established an official "poverty line," and since then has regularly published data on the number and kinds of people living below that line in this country. The government's poverty line was initially set by determining the minimum amount of money needed for food to keep people alive under short-term emergency conditions, calculating that amount for a year, and then tripling that figure. It was never intended to represent even a minimally adequate income on a permanent basis. Nevertheless, the official poverty line has since become enshrined in all kinds of government statistics and reports. It takes account of the number of persons in a household, and it is periodically adjusted for inflation. Consequently, while the original 1967 poverty line was about $3,000 for an urban family of four, by 1985 that figure had reached approximately $11,000. For smaller families, it was about $5,500 per one person, $7,000 for two people, and $8,500 for three people.

Because the official poverty line is a totally inadequate amount of income to sustain a family indefinitely, the federal government also regularly provides data based on two other indicators of low income. One of these is the lower level living standard established by the U.S. Department of Labor, which is intended to represent the minimal amount of income necessary to sustain life on a permanent basis. In 1985, it was about $15,000

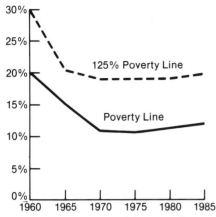

FIGURE 16-5   Proportion of the United States population below the federal poverty line and 125 percent of the poverty line, 1960-1985 Source: U.S. Department of Commerce, *Statistical Abstract of the United States, 1987* (Washington, D.C.: U.S. Government Printing Office), Table 749.

for a family of four. The other indicator is the arbitrary figure of 125% of the poverty line, which was approximately $13,750 for a family of four in 1985.

In 1960, when Harrington gathered statistics for his book, 40 million Americans, or 22 percent of the population, had incomes below what later was established as the official poverty line. As shown in Figure 16-5, by 1970 that number had dropped sharply to 13 percent, as a result of increasing affluence and the War on Poverty. In 1973, it reached a low of 11 percent, but since then it has risen slightly. In 1985, 33 million persons, or 14 percent of the population, were still living below the official poverty line. The corresponding figures for people below 125 percent of the poverty line are somewhat higher, since they include many people who exist just above the poverty line, but they have displayed the same pattern since 1960.

What kinds of people live below the official poverty line? Table 16-4 provides several answers to this question. The data in this table are all expressed in terms of families rather than individuals in the United States.

More than two-thirds of all families below the poverty line are white, while slightly more than one-fourth are black, and one-sixth are Hispanic. However, racial and ethnic minorities are quite disproportionately represented among the poor. Among all black families, 31 percent are officially poor, while among Hispanics that figure is 29 percent. In contrast, only 11 percent of all white families are classified as poor.

Male-headed families constitute about half of the poor, but only nine percent of all such families fall into this category. Female-headed families account for the other half of the poor, but 34 percent of all these families without a man present are below the poverty line. Among female-headed families with children under age 18, 54 percent are poor.

In terms of age, families headed by a person under 25 constitute only about one-eighth of the poor, but 30 percent of all such families are below the federal poverty line. Young families are more likely than any other age category to be poor. Although there is a widespread belief that many retired families are struggling with poverty, this is not true. These families account for only one-tenth of the poor, and only seven percent of them fall into this category.

Lack of education is markedly related to poverty. Although families in which the head of the household has less than an eighth-grade education constitute only about one-sixth of the poor, 26 percent of all those poorly educated families fall below the poverty line. Families in which the head has completed eight years of education fare somewhat better, since they are less than one-tenth of the poor, and only 16 percent of such families are poor. Completing some high school but not graduating actually hurts people, since those families are one-fifth of the poor, and 19 percent of them are in poverty.

Not surprisingly, families in which the head of the household is unemployed are very likely to be poor. These families constitute nearly half of the poor, and 25 percent of them fall into this category. Families in which the head is employed part of the time fare somewhat, but not greatly, better. They account for nearly one-third of the poor,

TABLE 16-4   Characteristics of United States Families Below the Federal Poverty Line, 1985

Characteristic	Percent of All Families Below the Poverty Line	Percent of Families in that Category Below the Poverty Line
Race/Ethnicity		
White	69	11
Black	27	31
Hispanic	16	29
Sex of Household Head		
Male	51	9
Female	49	34
Age of Household Head		
24 or younger	13	30
65 or older	10	7
Education of Household Head		
Less than 8 years	15	26
8 years	8	16
1–3 years of high school	20	19
High school graduate	30	8
More education	13	3
Employment Status of Household Head		
Employed full-time	21	4
Employed part-time	30	21
Unemployed	49	25

Source: U.S. Department of Commerce, *Statistical Abstract of the United States, 1987* (Washington, D.C.: U.S. Government Printing Office), Tables 745, 746, 749, 750.

and 21 percent of these families are below the poverty line.

In sum, poverty is especially prevalent among families that are black or Hispanic, or who are headed by an unmarried woman, a person under age 25, a person with less than a high school education, or a person who is not employed full-time. Nevertheless, no more than one-third of the families with any one of those high-risk characteristics were below the federal poverty line in 1985. Therefore, having any one of these characteristics does not automatically doom a family to poverty. When a family has several of these characteristics, however, its likelihood of being poor increases sharply.

CONSEQUENCES OF STRATIFICATION

Patterns of status and class stratification within a society have numerous consequences for many other realms of social life.

As emphasized by Weber (1958), people's ability to exercise power in the consumption marketplace largely determines their life chances and lifestyles. All the consequences mentioned in this section have been substantiated by a number of sociological studies, so that we can have considerable confidence in their validity within the United States and most other industrial nations. The precise nature and magnitude of these relationships vary through time and across different settings and societies, however. Some of them vary continuously along status gradations, while others display sharp differences among social classes. Some of them are most closely related to particular stratification dimensions, such as education or income, while others are more broadly associated with people's overall socioeconomic status or class. Nevertheless, all these factors are associated with one's position in the socioeconomic structure of society and are frequently described as outcomes or consequences of stratification.

All the factors mentioned here are usually viewed as either desirable or undesirable for individuals. The most noteworthy feature of all these relationships—beyond their scope and diversity—is that *all of the undesirable consequences are associated with lower status or class positions, while all of the desirable consequences are associated with higher positions in the stratification system.* In other words, in all these areas of social life, the higher a person's class or status position, the greater the benefits or advantages he or she generally experiences. Conversely, people who occupy lower positions in the stratification system are generally disadvantaged in many aspects of their lives.

A number of other neutral consequences of stratification that cannot be described as desirable or undesirable have also been identified by sociologists. For example, these include differences in the manner in which children are socialized, the churches or synagogues that people attend, their political party preferences, how they spend their leisure time, and their aesthetic interests and preferences. In this section, however, we focus only on status and class differences that are valued as desirable or undesirable, to emphasize the wide range of advantages or disadvantages that result from one's position in the socioeconomic stratification system in modern societies. These relationships are discussed in the following paragraphs and summarized in Table 16-5.

Health

The lower one's socioeconomic status or class, the higher the rate of infant mortality, the greater the incidence of most serious illnesses, the less adequate one's diet, and the shorter one's life expectancy at birth. The higher one's status or class, the better one's general health is likely to be, the more adequate the medical care one receives, and the longer one is likely to live. Mental health is also related to socioeconomic stratification,

with most forms of mental illness being considerably more common among people with lower status or class positions.

Marriage and Family

People with higher status or class positions tend to be older and more mature at time of first marriage, are more likely to report that they are happy in their marriage, are more satisfied with their sex lives, and are less likely to have their marriage end in desertion or divorce. The lower a women's status or class, the more likely she is to become pregnant outside of marriage, especially as a teenager, and the more children she is likely to bear even though she may have difficulty supporting them. (For example, women with no more than a grade school education have an average of 3.5 live births, compared to 2.2 for college-educated women.) And the higher the status or class position of a couple, the more likely they are to make major decisions jointly and to operate the household in an egalitarian manner rather than the wife being submissive to the husband.

Education

We have already seen that amount of education attained is directly related to the socioeconomic position of one's parents and oneself. In addition, adequacy of school facilities improves steadily with rising status or class. And children from higher-status or class homes are much more likely to attend college, regardless of their intellectual abilities.

Housing

One does not have to be a sociologist to know that people with higher status or class standing generally live in larger, more expensive, and better-quality housing. In addition, different neighborhoods within a community clearly reflect the socioeconomic positions of their occupants in terms of

TABLE 16-5   Typical Disadvantages and Advantages of Socioeconomic Status

People With Lower Statuses Are More Likely To. . . .	*People With Higher Statuses Are More Likely To. . . .*
Die in infancy	Survive infancy
Eat a poor diet	Eat a good diet
Experience many serious diseases	Experience few serious diseases
Experience mental illness	Avoid mental illness
Receive poor medical care	Receive good medical care
Have overall poor health	Have overall good health
Die before average life expectancy	Live past average life expectancy
Marry at a young age	Delay marriage past the average age
Say that their marriage is unhappy	Say that their marriage is happy
Become pregnant outside of marriage	Avoid pregnancy outside of marriage
Have three or four or more children	Have none, one, or two children
Have family decisions made by the man	Have family decisions made jointly
Receive a poor public education	Receive a good public education
Drop out of high school	Complete high school
Value work over education	Believe education is vital
Receive poor grades in school	Receive acceptable grades in school
Not attend college	Attend college
Live in a smaller, poor-quality house	Live in a larger, good-quality house
Have poor-quality home furnishings	Have good-quality home furnishings
Live in a high density area	Live in a low density area
Live in a low-prestige neighborhood	Live in a high-prestige neighborhood
Have only a few close friends	Have many close friends
Not participate in community activities	Participate in community activities
Not belong to voluntary associations	Belong to voluntary associations
Attend church irregularly	Attend church regularly
Ignore news reports	Pay attention to news reports
Not travel frequently or far from home	Travel fairly frequently and far
Be dissatisfied with one's job	Be satisfied with one's job
Be uninformed about public issues	Be informed about public issues
Avoid discussing political affairs	Frequently discuss political affairs
Not vote regularly	Vote regularly
Not be active in a political party	Be active in a political party
Never hold any public positions	Hold public positions
Not support civil liberties	Support civil liberties
Be strongly nationalistic	Hold an international perspective
Commit violent crimes	Commit white-collar crimes
Be arrested and convicted of crimes	Escape arrest and conviction for crimes
Be victims of crimes	Avoid being victims of crimes
Suffer from alcohol and drug abuse	Avoid alcohol and drug abuse
Express unhappiness with life	Express happiness with life
Hold a short time perspective	Hold a long time perspective
Feel that others control one's life	Feel in control of one's life
Reject social nonconformity	Accept social nonconformity
Be intolerant of complexity in life	Be tolerant of complexity in life
Live for the present	Live for the future

housing quality, size of lots, upkeep, and prestige.

Social Participation

Many different indicators of the extent and nature of one's participation in social life are strongly related to socioeconomic status or class. The higher one's position in the socioeconomic system, the more extensively an individual is likely to participate with others in numerous kinds of activities. These include the number of one's close friends and frequency of interaction with them, involvement in community activities and voluntary interest associations, frequency of church or synagogue attendance, diversity and richness of recreational activities, amount of travel, and exposure to news and other information via the mass media. Nor should it be surprising to find that the higher the status of one's job, the more satisfied one is likely to be with it.

Politics

Individuals with higher-status or class positions are more aware of public issues and more interested in political affairs, discuss politics more frequently, and vote more regularly. They are also much more likely to be active in party activities, to belong to other political organizations, and to hold public positions, such as serving on a school board. In terms of political attitudes, socioeconomic status or class is strongly related to support of civil liberties such as free speech for all persons, protection of civil rights for minorities, advocacy of public interest concerns such as environmental protection, and holding favorable views toward other countries and international organizations such as the United Nations.

In short, a person's socioeconomic status or class affects most other aspects of his or her life, from the most personal to the most public kinds of attitudes and actions. Whenever these differences are generally valued as desirable or undesirable, the lower one's status or class position, the more likely one is to experience the consequences of stratification as disadvantages, while the higher one's status or class, the more likely one is to experience them as advantages.

MAINTAINING STRATIFICATION SYSTEMS

Socioeconomic stratification systems are remarkably stable through time. In preindustrial societies, most people remain at the same status or class level as their parents, generation after generation. In advanced industrial societies, as more and more social positions and roles can be achieved through one's own efforts and accomplishments, status inheritance becomes less prevalent, and the stratification system is more open and fluid. Nevertheless, *status and class inheritance is still the most common condition in modern societies.* The reason for this is that many powerful forces in all societies—industrial as well as agrarian—operate to maintain existing patterns of socioeconomic inequality and to "keep people in their place"—wherever that may be in the stratification system. In this section, we examine several important mechanisms through which existing socioeconomic stratification patterns are maintained and perpetuated.

Differential Opportunities

Some kinds of status benefits are passed on directly from one generation to the next, such as wealth, a family business, the family estate, or political power. This process occurs primarily within the elite and influential classes, however. *For most people, the inheritance process is indirect, operating through differential opportunities for educational and occupational attainment.* As we have already seen, the higher the status or class position of a family, the more likely its children are to attend good schools and receive superior instruction, the more education they will likely receive regardless of their mental abilities or academic interests, and the more prestigious the college or university they will probably attend.

In addition to the job opportunities provided by these educational advantages, children from higher status or class families receive many other advantages in securing desirable jobs. Some of these are quite subtle, as when parents teach their children communication and interaction skills, instill in them the value of deferring immediate gratification for long-term goals, and introduce them to prospective employers. Other advantages are more obvious, as when a parent brings his or her children into the family business, loans or gives a child money to start a business or make a downpayment on a house, or pressures a friend to give their son or daughter a job.

Socialization and Ideology

Perhaps the most remarkable feature of socioeconomic stratification systems most of the time is that the majority of people—members of subordinate classes as well as those of dominant classes—accept the existing system as natural, proper, and legitimate. Consequently, they rarely question or challenge patterns of structural inequality but simply accept them as "the way things are." How does this come about? The apparent answer is that *parents, teachers, the media, and other socialization agents teach children at all status and class levels a "culture of inequality" that justifies and supports socioeconomic inequality* (Lewis, 1978). At lower status or class levels, children are socialized into a belief system that stresses apathy and cynicism, distrust of existing social institutions, and a sense of personal powerlessness to alter their life conditions. At middle-status or class levels, children are taught that if they work hard and conform to established norms, they will succeed in life and attain a comfortable standard of living. And at upper-status or class levels, children are socialized to believe that they are inherently superior to most other people and are

entitled to the opportunities and benefits that the stratification system bestows upon them.

In addition, *every society contains a dominant ideology—or set of beliefs and values—that justifies and legitimates the prevailing patterns of inequality.* This ideology is formulated and perpetuated by the higher classes to explain and justify their privileged positions in society, and in most situations is widely accepted by other people. In feudal societies, the dominant ideology typically emphasized the preordained and fixed nature of social inequality, while in modern industrial societies the prevailing ideology commonly asserts that everyone can get ahead if they try hard enough. For example, a survey of the American public found that between 80 and 90 percent of people at all status and class levels agreed with the belief that "there is plenty of opportunity" in this society (Rytina, et al., 1970). As a result, people at the bottom of the stratification structure tend to blame themselves—or "bad luck"—rather than the stratification system for their powerlessness and poverty, while those toward the top of the structure believe that they have personally earned and are entitled to the benefits they enjoy. Karl Marx referred to this acceptance of the existing system among disadvantaged people as "false consciousness," and insisted that only when they acquire "true consciousness" of the extent to which they are manipulated and exploited by dominant classes will they ever question or challenge established patterns of socioeconomic inequality.

Social Control

The processes of differential educational and occupational opportunities and socialization into an established ideology of inequality are often sufficient to perpetuate a system of stratification almost indefinitely. If those processes should prove to be insufficient, however, the dominant classes can always resort to a variety of social control techniques.

Resource Monopolization. This technique of social control is quite straightfoward. In an agrarian society, the elites generally own most of the land, so that the vast bulk of peasants have no chance of becoming land-owners. In industrial societies, corporate owners and executives control the majority of jobs and hence can reserve most high-status positions for members of their own class and keep the rest of the population dependent on them for employment.

Economic Exploitation. This control technique carries monopolization one step further by taking resources from disadvantaged people. In medieval agrarian societies, peasants were typically compelled to turn over as much as half of their crops to the nobility and the established church as land rents, taxes, or tithes. In industrial societies, many employees—both blue-collar and white-collar workers—are often paid the minimal wages necessary in the prevailing job market to secure their labor. If a person refuses to work for those wages, he or she will normally not be hired, since the employer can generally find someone else who will accept them. Marx condemned this practice as exploitation of the proletariat and urged workers to organize themselves into unions and bargain for higher wages. Since then, unions have been effective in raising wages in many crafts and industries, but most employers still pay only the lowest wages they can convince unions to accept, while many blue-collar and white-collar workers are not unionized and hence are at the mercy of whatever wages their employers are willing to pay. And although the United States government specifies a minimum hourly wage, it is not high enough to bring a family of four above the federal poverty line.

Tax laws also facilitate economic exploitation. Some taxes, such as sales taxes on purchases, are regressive in nature, extracting a larger proportion of earnings from low-income people than from higher-income people. Although income taxes are supposed to be progressive, the numerous deductions and loopholes that are available primarily to higher-income households greatly limit the actual amount of taxes they pay. In fact, many quite wealthy individuals manage—quite legally—to pay few or no taxes at all. Perhaps the most flagrant example of this was the late billionaire John Paul Getty, who in the 1960s had a daily income of over $300,000 and yet paid only a few thousand dollars a year in income taxes because of oil depletion, sheltered income, business loss, and other tax loopholes clearly designed to benefit the very rich.

Coercion. If all other methods of social control prove ineffective in maintaining the existing structure of socioeconomic inequality, powerful classes can always employ direct coercion. Whenever possible, this is done through established governmental and legal systems by passing and enforcing laws to protect one's privileges and control groups who challenge them. An interesting historical example of such control in feudal times was a law outlawing the crossbow, because it enabled common foot soldiers to attack armored knights. In modern societies, business leaders have often succeeded in obtaining laws that prohibited the formation of unions, kept wages as low as possible, discriminated against minorities, closed many jobs to women, and in other ways ensured that there would be an adequate supply of cheap wage labor. Today we witness numerous political struggles between elites and concerned citizens over such issues as false advertising, dumping toxic wastes into the environment, and affirmative hiring practices. Because elites control immense financial and political resources, they are usually quite successful in using the governmental and legal systems to their advantage.

Even in contemporary industrial societies, however, elites often resort to illegal actions. They may hire strike-breakers to disrupt a legal strike, stuff ballot boxes, bribe legislators, market a product they know is dangerous, blacklist certain individuals from securing employment, violate environmental protection laws, or hide profits by claiming nonexistent business losses. In recent years, such actions—when detected—have increasingly resulted in convictions and fines or imprisonment. Even when this does happen, however, the punishments rarely have serious consequences for more than a few individuals, leaving the offending corporation or government agency largely intact and as powerful as ever.

ALTERING STRATIFICATION SYSTEMS

In all modern societies, many—if not most—people hope to improve their socioeconomic position. Basically, there are two ways of doing this. One way is through personal mobility, in which individuals and families raise their occupational or income status through time and may eventually move into a higher social class. The other way is through structural change, in which the distribution process is altered so that more benefits flow to disadvantaged categories of people or social classes. In general, most people find it easier to focus their efforts on improving their own position through mobility rather than by attempting to bring about the kind of major structural change advocated by social reformers. Nevertheless, social movements in several advanced industrial societies during the last fifty years have sought to create more equitable patterns of stratification. This section examines both approaches to reducing socioeconomic inequality, as well as poverty programs that have been implemented in the United States.

Social Mobility

Folk tales about individuals—such as Andrew Carnegie or John Rockefeller, Sr.—who are born into poverty but rise to become millionaires, abound in all modern societies. Although we realize that these are extremely rare cases, most people hope that they can improve their lot in life through their own efforts (called generational or intragenerational mobility) or at least ensure that their children do better than they have done (called generational or intergenerational mobility). How realistic are such hopes?

Amount of Mobility. As long as mobility aspirations have remained relatively modest, large numbers of people in modern societies have been able to achieve their goals. Several studies of occupational mobility in the United States have found that from one-third to one-half of all people have achieved an occupational status at least one level above that of their fathers (Blau and Duncan, 1967; Hauser, *et al.,* 1975; McClendon, 1977). A considerable proportion of this intergenerational upward mobility has been caused by shifts in the occupational structure of the society, which sociologists call "structural mobility" to distinguish it from "exchange mobility," resulting from efforts by individuals to improve their personal socioeconomic status. Approximately similar rates of observed mobility have been discovered in many other industrial countries (Grusky and Hauser, 1984; Slomczynski and Krauze, 1987).

Nevertheless, *most status/class improvements are quite limited.* The son of a factory worker may succeed in becoming a skilled mechanic, and the daughter of a clerk may rise to a low-level managerial position. Neither of them, however, has much chance of becoming a corporate executive or a U.S. Senator. For example, Lipset and Bendix (1959) discovered that more than two-thirds of the business executives they examined had come from the upper class, while only about ten percent had risen from the working class. Moreover, if less than one-half of the population is upwardly mobile, this means that the bulk of the population in industrial societies either remains at the same status/class level throughout their lifetime (although they will probably increase their income as they grow older), or they may experience the shock of downward mobility (which happens to roughly one-fifth of the population in the United States).

Causes of Mobility. Although the rates of upward mobility that have occurred during the twentieth century within industrial societies have been relatively modest, they are still much higher than typically exist in agrarian societies, where such mobility is limited to an extremely small proportion of the population. What factors have accounted for the notable rises in overall education, occupational, and income levels in modern societies? The basic answer to this question lies in the impacts of industrialization on societies.

Economic development alters the entire socioeconomic structure of society, not as a result of intentional social reform movements, but as a consequence of economic growth. Industrial economies require a more skilled labor force than do agrarian societies, so that greater educational opportunities must be made available to more individuals. Unskilled and semiskilled jobs decline in availability, so that large numbers of people are forced by the shifting occupational structure to move upward into skilled manual or white-collar clerical and sales jobs. As the economy produces immense amounts of wealth, many people receive higher incomes and improve their standard of living, even if they remain at the same occupational level. The essential point is that this *structurally forced upward mobility is not due to ambitious indivduals working hard to raise their socioeconomic status or class positions, but rather to broad developments in the economy that push them upward in order to obtain jobs, regardless of their personal motivations or efforts*—and sometimes in spite of their lack of mobility aspirations or abilities. These structural economic changes may also push some people downward into lower status or class positions despite their personal desires.

Two additional structural forces that also facilitate upward mobility in modern societies are differential birth rates and immigration. Since higher-status couples typically have fewer children than do lower-status people, this creates openings toward the top of the socioeconomic ladder and provides opportunities for some lower-status people to move upward. And because a large proportion of the immigrants to the United States have been relatively unskilled laborers and farm workers who were willing to work for low wages, their presence in the labor pool has tended to push nonimmigrants into higher-status jobs. As a result of these and other consequences of industrialization, much of the upward social mobility that occurs in modern societies is caused by broad social forces, not individual efforts.

Determinants of Mobility. Structural changes in the stratification system make possible upward mobility, but they do not determine which individuals are able to take advantage of those opportunities. The search for factors that influence the occupational and other statuses attained by individuals—which is called *status attainment*—has been one of the most frequently studied topics in American sociology during the last twenty years (cf. Blau and Duncan, 1967; Hauser and Featherman, 1978; Hout, 1984; Sewell, Hauser, and Wolf, 1980). At first, all of these status attainment studies were limited to white males, but later they were extended to include females and blacks. In general, these later studies demonstrated that the status attainment process is roughly similar for all people, although some specific factors affect women and blacks that are not important for white males. Seven major sets of conclusions have emerged from those studies.

First, the *status/class level of one's family of origin* heavily influences the occupational and income levels that a person is likely to achieve during his or her lifetime. The educational and occupational statuses of one's father are both quite important, but so is the educational attainment of one's mother, and the occupational status of one's mother is critical for women. Rather interestingly, the total amount of wealth possessed by one's parents is more important than their income level.

Second, the *amount of education* one receives is the single most influential factor affecting the occupational level that one attains later in life. However, education is more important for women than for men and more important for whites than for blacks.

Third, the *status level of one's first full-time job* (which is obviously affected by one's family background and the amount of one's education) has considerable impact on the occupational level that one eventually acquires. This factor is much more important for men than for women, however.

Fourth, *blacks are severely disadvantaged* in the status attainment process, compared to whites. This is particularly evident in regard to education, since educational attainment does not give blacks anywhere near the advantages it does whites. Most white minority persons (e.g., nationality ethnics and Jews) fare about as well as the white majority in the status attainment process, although this is less true of Hispanics.

Fifth, some *personality characteristics* appear to influence one's status attainment. Of particular importance is the time perspective one applies to his or her life. Individuals who are able to formulate long-range plans for their life and put aside immediate benefits for more distant goals are more likely to achieve higher status later in life. Such personality characteristics are largely a consequence of the kind of socialization one receives, however, and the higher the status /class position of the parents, the more likely they are to instill those characteristics in their children.

Sixth, for *women, the status or class of the man they marry* is still quite important in determining their subsequent socioeconomic position. The status attained by men is essentially unaffected by whom they marry, however. Employed women who do not have children tend to follow a status attainment process that is relatively similar to that of men, while employed women with children experience more limitations in their status attainment.

Seventh, *situational opportunities* during one's life still have a lot to do with the status level that a person eventually achieves. These include being in the right place and time when a job opportunity opens up, having personal connections with people who know of job possibilities, being sponsored by

---

DETERMINANTS OF SOCIAL MOBILITY

1. Family of origin.
2. Amount of education.
3. First job.
4. Race.
5. Personality characteristics.
6. Spouse (for women).
7. Situational opportunities.

---

an older high-status person who opens doors for one, and just plain good luck. Most of these situational opportunities are more dependent on receiving help from others than on one's own aspirations or capabilities, however.

In short, just as the underlying causes of upward mobility are primarily social rather than individual in nature, *the factors that influence the status/class positions a person attains during one's lifetime are also primarily social, not personal.* This generalization does not deny that ambition and hard work are important for getting ahead in life and achieving a desired status or class position. It does emphasize, however, that it is vitally important to "choose one's parents carefully," since their status/class level and the socialization opportunities they give to their children will generally be critical in one's later status attainment.

Poverty Programs

The purpose of poverty programs—initiated in the United States by President Lyndon Johnson's call for an "unconditional war on poverty" in 1967—was to assist extremely poor individuals and families to escape from that condition. They were essentially public assistance programs designed to enable those at the bottom of the stratification system to be upwardly mobile. They thus relied almost entirely on a mobility rather than a structural change strategy for improving the socioeconomic conditions of the poor. One structural change program—a guaranteed minimum monthly income—

was proposed and tested, but it was never implemented. At the present time, moreover, most of the more far-reaching programs that were initiated in the 1970s have been severely cut back or eliminated, so that the remaining poverty programs in this country—such as food stamps—are no more than public welfare and do not alter the structure of inequality. The following paragraphs answer some questions that are frequently asked about poverty programs.

Are Poverty Programs Necessary? A majority of the American public is extremely skeptical about the necessity of poverty programs. A national poll by the *New York Times* and CBS News in 1978 found that 54 percent of the population believed that "most people who receive welfare could get along without it if they tried." How valid is that belief? First, consider that over one-third of all people under age 65 who fall below the federal poverty line receive no public assistance of any kind, often because they are too proud to "go on welfare." Many of these people are employed full-time or part-time, but they cannot earn enough to escape poverty. Among those who do receive some kind of assistance, approximately 88 percent are parents with preschool children, children of all ages who are in school, disabled persons, elderly people, or persons employed full-time. Of the 12 percent who might be employed, over four-fifths are women, most of whom remain at home to care for small children. Less than two percent of all persons on welfare are able-bodied unemployed males, and most of them lack any kind of employable skill (Department of Health, Education, and Welfare, 1972; Mears, 1977).

Many other common assumptions about welfare recipients are equally invalid.

(1) Although a disproportionate number of blacks are poor, over two-thirds of all welfare recipients are white.
(2) Welfare families do not have large numbers of illegitimate children; most have no more than two or three children, and more than two-thirds of these are legitimate.

(3) Most people do not remain on welfare year after year; more than half of all recipients receive benefits for less than 21 months.
(4) Very few of these people prefer "handouts" to jobs; almost all of those who are able to work take jobs whenever possible.

What Was the War on Poverty? Despite widespread invalid beliefs about poverty and welfare, the American public became quite concerned about poverty during the 1960s and 1970s. We discovered that in this "land of plenty" over one-fifth of the population lived in poverty at a level inadequate to sustain life on a permanent basis. Numerous programs of various kinds—both expansions of existing programs such as Social Security and entirely new programs such as Headstart—were enacted by Congress in a concerted effort to eliminate poverty. These programs included:

(1) Medicaid, which provides low-cost medical care to the poor;
(2) Headstart, which provides preschool enrichment centers for children from low-income families to prepare them for public schools;
(3) Aid to Families with Dependent Children (AFDC), which provides financial assistance to poor parents (largely women) with small children;
(4) Food Stamps, which low-income people can purchase at a fraction of their face value and use to buy food;
(5) The Comprehensive Employment Training Act (CETA), which provided free vocational training in classrooms and on-the-job;
(6) The Community Assistance Program (CAP), which provided federal funds to communities to establish centers to conduct a variety of local programs (ranging from child care to legal assistance) for the poor; and
(7) Several different housing programs intended to help low-income families improve their housing conditions.

What Is the Present Status of These Poverty Programs? During the 1980s many of these poverty programs were eliminated, and the remaining ones suffered severe budget reductions. Consequently, the United States is no longer waging any kind of direct war on poverty. The Reagan administration, as part of its supply side economic policy, chose instead to promote economic development through tax reductions and other governmental actions designed to stimulate production, on the grounds that this would eventually provide jobs for poor people. In other words, that administration relied on the more traditional approach of promoting upward individual mobility through economic growth. Meanwhile, the number of people in this country living below the poverty line has been rising since 1980.

Structural Change

The social mobility approach to reducing socioeconomic inequality makes no effort to alter the processes by which desired benefits are distributed throughout a society. It seeks merely to facilitate the upward movement of capable people within the existing system, without changing the structure of that system. Or, in times of economic prosperity and growth, the resulting societal changes improve the standards of living of many people upward without affecting their relative positions in the stratification system. In contrast, the structural change approach attempts to alter basic distribution processes and patterns of socioeconomic stratification. Two contrasting ways in which this can be attempted are illustrated by Sweden and the Soviet Union.

Sweden. Sweden has a democratic parliamentary political system and a largely capitalist economy. Working within those parameters, the Social Democratic Party—which has controlled the government since the 1930s (except for a few years in the 1970s)—has introduced numerous structural changes aimed at significantly reducing socioeconomic inequality (Fleisher, 1967; Thomasson, 1970).

To limit the accumulation of great wealth and power, Sweden has a steeply progressive income tax with rates as high as 75 or 80 percent for high-income persons, very high

inheritance and wealth taxes that make it impossible for individuals and families to inherit or accumulate any great amount of wealth, and various regulations that prevent business executives from exercising dominant power in the government. To assist the middle and working classes, Sweden provides free education and technical training for all persons at all levels; ensures that labor unions (to which most employed persons belong) can bargain effectively with employers for adequate wages; and has established procedures through which employees can buy stock in the company where they work and can influence corporate policies and practices. For people at all income levels—but especially low-income families—Sweden has created one of the world's most extensive and generous systems of public services, including free medical care, child and family allowances, day care facilities for children, and unemployment and retirement benefits. *As a consequence of these innovations introduced by a democratic socialist political party, there is neither great wealth nor severe poverty in Sweden today.* There is still considerable status and class stratification, but it is much less extensive than in the United States.

Soviet Union. The U.S.S.R. has taken a quite different route to reducing stratification through structural change (Hough, 1977; Parkin, 1971). The Soviet Union has a fully socialist—not a communist—economy, in which all major industries and other businesses are owned and controlled by the state. Therefore, if social classes are defined solely in terms of the people's relationship to the means of economic production, this society contains no classes. However, if classes are defined more broadly in terms of possession of power, wealth, and other privileges, the Soviet Union is a highly stratified society.

Because the political system is still at the stage which Lenin called the "dictatorship of the proletariat," it is quite authoritarian and highly centralized in nature. As a result, the dominant class is composed of members of the Communist Party who hold high government positions, administer state industries and other businesses, or are well-educated professional and technical experts. The members of this bureaucratic elite of approximately one million persons wield immense power, receive incomes many times higher than ordinary people, and enjoy numerous advantages such as better housing, better medical care, access to higher education, the right to shop at special stores, and the use of state-owned vacation facilities. Moreover, the rest of the population is stratified in terms of education, occupation, and income to at least the same extent as in most other industrial societies.

The Soviet stratification system differs in two important ways from capitalist societies, however. At the top of the class structure, there is no leisure class that lives off accumulated wealth, and people cannot inherit large amounts of money. Party elites enjoy many special privileges, however. At the bottom on the class structure, a fairly extensive system of public benefits—including free medical care, free education, and pensions programs—ensures that most people have at least a minimally adequate standard of living. Therefore, *although the Soviet Union has a long way to go before it will have eliminated socioeconomic stratification, it has introduced a number of structural changes that have reduced some of the extremes of status and class inequality.*

SUMMARY

Power inequality is the root cause of most socioeconomic stratification. Unequal distributions of social power rest on ecological conditions but become embodied in complex sociocultural processes. Individuals and organizations employ power to enhance their social privileges and prestige, thus creating stratification systems and also generating considerable social conflict. Alternative but complementary explanations of power inequality in modern societies include control of the major means of economic production, resource advantages and disadvantages in consumption marketplaces, exercises of au-

thority in organizations, and creation of cultural beliefs about inequality.

The transformation of social power into unequal privileges and prestige occurs as these benefits are distributed throughout the members of a society. That process can be explained in terms of the fairly deliberate actions of elites in shaping the distribution process, or by viewing the distribution of socioeconomic benefits as a natural process in organized social life. Marx's theory of a dominant social class that owns the major means of economic production illustrates the first approach, while the second approach is illustrated by Davis and Moore's argument that differential rewards are necessary to ensure that socially important roles are adequately enacted. Weber's writings on stratification incorporate aspects of both approaches, emphasizing individuals' life chances in the marketplace and community evaluations of people's social standing. Simpson integrated these two approaches by pointing out that the distribution of socioeconomic benefits occurs within a "role market" that is largely shaped by powerful elites.

One way of describing patterns of socioeconomic stratification in modern societies is to determine how various kinds of social benefits are distributed throughout the population. Power, wealth, income, occupations, and education are all very unequally distributed in industrial societies, with vast distances between their top and bottom positions. All of these stratification dimensions are interrelated to a considerable extent.

Another way of describing patterns of stratification is to identify and describe the social classes existing in a society. Five classes frequently identified in the contemporary United States are the elite class, the influential class, the middle class, the working class, and the dispossessed class. Each of these classes is distinguished by several factors that constitute a class boundary, and each class displays numerous distinctive characteristics in its occupational levels, educational attainment, income and wealth, housing, lifestyles, attitudes and values, and many other features.

Poverty, or extremely low income, is defined by the federal poverty line, although this level of income is not considered adequate to sustain an individual or family on a permanent basis. The proportion of the American population below this line was 22 percent in 1960, dropped to 11 percent in 1973, and has since risen to 14 percent. People in "high risk" categories are particularly likely to be poor, especially when they fall into several of these categories: being a racial or ethnic minority, living in a female-headed household, being under age 25, having less than a high school education, and not being employed full-time.

A person's status or class position in the socioeconomic stratification system affects most other aspects of his or her life. In general, the higher one's status or class position, the more desirable these consequences, while the lower one's status or class position, the less desirable they are. Numerous consequences of socioeconomic status and class have been discovered in the realms of health and life expectancy, marriage and family living, housing conditions, social and community participation, political affairs, social deviance, and broad attitudes and values.

Strong social forces operate in all societies to maintain the existing stratification system. One of these is the differential opportunities that are afforded to members of various statuses and classes, through direct inheritance and indirect educational and occupational advantages. Another is socialization and ideology, which justify and legitimate the existing stratification system and teach individuals at all status/class levels to accept their lot in life and not attempt to alter existing patterns of inequality. A third set of social forces falls under the heading of social control, which includes such techniques as resource monopolization, economic exploitation, and coercion.

At the same time, within all societies many people attempt to improve their status/class positions. One way of doing this is to strive for individual upward mobility. In reality, however, those individuals who are upwardly mobile generally achieve only modest gains in the status/class standings. Status inheritance from one generation to the next is the most common condition, and a considerable number of people experience downward mobility. Although a great amount of upward mobility has occurred in industrial societies during the last hundred years, much of this structurally forced mobility has resulted from economic growth that has pushed people upward regardless of their personal abilities. Many social factors influence which individuals are upwardly mobile, including one's status/class origin, amount of education, level of first job, race and ethnicity, learned personality characteristics, marriage partners, and situational opportunities.

The poverty programs initiated in the United States during the 1960s and 1970s attempted to reduce the worst aspects of poverty. Despite widespread public beliefs that the poor are to blame for their own misfortunes, a variety of public programs were enacted. Most of these programs sought to assist individuals in becoming upwardly mobile, not to change the distribution of socioeconomic benefits. In the 1980s, all those programs were either abolished or severely reduced.

Another way of reducing socioeconomic inequality is to initiate broad structural changes within a society. Sweden has moved further in this direction than any other nation, adopting many policies and programs that have effectively eliminated great wealth and severe poverty. The Soviet Union has also attempted to reduce socioeconomic inequality through governmental action, but it has created a politically based dominant class instead of a class of economic elites.

SOCIOCULTURAL INEQUALITY

What social factors determine race and ethnicity in contemporary societies?
How have minority groups been treated throughout history?
How effectively have African-Americans used individual mobility and
  collective action to improve their status?
How are Native Americans, Hispanic-Americans, and Asian-Americans
  faring in the United States today?
What is socially structured sexism, and what are some of its consequences
  for women?

RACE AND ETHNICITY

Socioeconomic stratification is the most pervasive form of inequality in all modern societies, but it is certainly not the only way in which people are treated unequally. This chapter examines several other forms of sociocultural inequality that pervade modern societies and produce social divisiveness, oppression, and conflict. This first section deals with the meaning of race and ethnicity in social life, while the second section examines various ways in which minority groups have been treated in various societies. The remaining sections discuss African-Americans, three other racial and ethnic minorities, and gender inequality.

In explaining socioeconomic stratification, considerable emphasis is placed on power inequality as the basic cause of status and class systems. Power differences are also extremely important in the various kinds of sociocultural inequality examined in this chapter, since in all cases the subordinate

people exercise considerably less power in social life than do those who oppress them. The disadvantaged power positions of these subordinate people is always a critical handicap in their efforts to improve their social status. At the same time, *these other forms of stratification all have a distinct cultural component in addition to patterns of structural inequality.* They are created and maintained by cultural belief systems that define various categories of people—blacks, ethnic populations, or women—as inferior human beings. These cultural beliefs are expressed by individuals as attitudes of prejudice, ethnocentrism, disdain, and even hatred. Consequently, a complete analysis of racism, sexism, and other kinds of sociocultural inequality must include historical, cultural, and social-psychological factors as well as structural patterns of inequality. With our emphasis in this book on societal dynamics, however, we shall focus primarily on the broad social and economic conditions of these minorities in modern societies.

Race and Racism

In biology, the species is the smallest category that is of any scientific importance, since it identifies which organisms can and cannot interbreed. A race is a minor subcategory of a species, composed of organisms that display some common physical characteristics, such as a particular strain of wheat or breed of cattle. Among humans—all of whom are members of a single species—the most common racial categories are Negroid, Caucasoid, and Mongoloid. Three features of these racial categories are extremely important for understanding sociocultural inequality.

First, *the physical differences typically associated with these three racial categories—skin color, hair texture, facial features, etc.—are of relatively recent origin* in the panorama of human history. They probably have not existed for more than 50,000 years and have clearly resulted from adaptations to environmental conditions that have been perpetuated through in-breeding. A dark skin, for instance, protects people in the tropics from the strong rays of the sun, whereas a light skin enables people in northern latitudes to absorb more of the limited sunlight. Similarly, more profuse body hair helps people in cold climates retain body heat, while less body hair helps people in warm climates keep cool through evaporation.

Second, *as populations have migrated and interbred, their physical features have become highly intermingled.* There are today no "pure" human races—if there ever were any. The people of India have dark skins but Caucasoid facial features. The Ainu of Japan have Mongoloid facial features but light skin. The San of Africa have dark skins but Mongoloid facial features. And millions of people—most noticeably in Hawaii and Indonesia—display combinations of physical characteristics associated with all three races.

Third, *there is no convincing evidence that members of any particular racial category share any common intellectual or personality characteristics.* Intelligence, artistic ability, athletic skill, mechanical aptitudes, personal ambi-

tion, and all other such qualities of individuals are widely distributed throughout all racial categories. Because of geographic isolation and social barriers, a population of people with similar physical characteristics may likely develop a common culture or subculture that is quite distinctive from other cultures, but these cultural differences have no basis in biology. The extent to which culture is often confused with biology is evident in regard to Jewish people. Although Jews are frequently called a "race," they are, in fact, a religiously based subculture that has no relationship to biology. There are Jews around the world with all kinds of skin color, hair types, and facial features. Indeed, the only way the Nazis could distinguish Jews from Aryans (another nonracial category) was by forcing them to wear a yellow Star of David—a religious symbol—on their clothing at all times.

If race is so unimportant in biological and psychological terms, why does it provide a basis for severe sociocultural inequality? There are two principal reasons for this, which are highly interrelated. The first reason stems from cultural differences among societies or other populations. If the members of one culture define another culture as inferior—applying such labels as uncivilized, barbarian, primitive, savage, subhuman, etc.—then those labels are likely to become associated with whatever physical characteristics are prevalent among the despised population. For instance, because Native American Indians possessed less complex material technology than the European colonists, the belief arose that all "redskins" (who are actually descendents of Mongoloid migrants from Asia) were "primitive" people.

The second reason for the sociocultural importance of race rests on power differences between societies or other populations. If one population is able to enslave or otherwise dominate another population—as in the case of whites dominating blacks for 300 years in the United States—then whatever physical characteristics are prevalent among the subordinate people are likely to be used as a basis for identifying them and "keeping them in their place."

In short, among humans *race is primarily a sociocultural categorization, based on a few minor physical characteristics, which differentiates sets of people in terms of culture and/or power and thus provides a basis for structured inequality.* It doesn't really matter what those physical characteristics are, as long as they can be associated with people who have a different culture of lack social power. The dominant population defines the subordinate population as inferior and subordinate, associates that lower-status position with some physical characteristics that are evident among members of the subordinate population, and uses those physical features as a basis for legitimizing its discriminatory and oppressive actions. *The creation of patterns of sociocultural inequality based on physical differences among sets of people is called racism.*

Ethnicity

Like race, ethnicity is also a social categorization that divides populations of people and is frequently used as a basis for discriminatory actions and structured social inequality. However, *the primary basis of ethnicity lies in cultural differences among people,* rather than biological characteristics. These cultural differences may be derived from people's national origins, language, religion, traditions, historical background, or other factors. Not all cultural differences give rise to ethnic categories, however. Ethnicity rests on three features of one's cultural heritage.

First, *a cultural background must be fairly easily identifiable.* Immigrants from Poland who live in a Polish neighborhood, continue to speak Polish, and maintain traditional Polish lifestyles and customs are clearly identifiable as ethnic people. In contrast, a woman whose grandparents came from Sweden 60 years ago and who is fully assimilated into the dominant American culture would not likely be considered an ethnic. She might be proud of her Scandinavian ancestry and even belong to a Scandinavian-American association, but her cultural heritage would not be visible or influential enough to place her in an ethnic category.

Second, *a cultural background must be defined as ethnic by the society in which it exists.* A person of Italian descent might be considered an ethnic in the United States, but obviously would not be so labeled in Italy. Japanese-Americans are an ethnic minority in California, but not in Hawaii. All Jews are placed in a single ethnic category in the United States, but in Israel they are classified into three categories—Sabras (native-born Israelis), Sephardim (Jews of Spanish or Portugese descent), and Ashkenazim (Jews of European or American background)—of which only the latter two are defined as ethnic groups. In short, the dominant culture determines what subcultures are considered ethnics.

Third, *a cultural background must be defined as inferior by the dominant culture if it is to be considered ethnic.* If a subculture is considered to be merely different and not inferior in any way—such as Christian Science, which rejects modern medicine—it is not likely to be labeled as ethnic. The Amish subculture, in contrast, is labeled as ethnic because its nineteenth-century rural lifestyle is considered by the dominant culture to be totally out of date. These definitions of cultural inferiority change through time and hence are never static. At the turn of the century, Irish people were widely despised in the United States, but in 1960 we elected an Irish-American as President.

Ethnicity often overlaps with race, as in the case of Japanese-Americans who are frequently viewed as both an ethnic and a racial category. A third-generation American of Japanese ancestry named Bill Jones who is a lawyer and lives in an affluent suburb would not likely qualify as an ethnic, even though he might have some Mongoloid facial features that put him in that racial category. Similarly, all African-Americans are sometimes referred to as ethnics as well as members of a racial category, since it is assumed that they share a distinctive black subculture. However, an African-American college-educated business executive who has lived all his life in the "white upper-middle class" might have no more ties with the black sub-culture than his white colleagues, although racially he would still be classified as a Negro.

There is no word such as "ethnicism" with a meaning similar to "racism," but there are certainly similar patterns of discrimination and social inequality toward ethnic populations. Ethnic inequality is not as prevalent or evident in the United States today as it has been in the past, but it still exists, and it is rampant in many other societies. For example, ethnic hostility and conflict are presently tearing apart Northern Ireland and Lebanon. Together with racism, *ethnicity provides a pervasive basis for sociocultural inequality in contemporary social life.*

MINORITY GROUPS

The term "minority group" is widely used in sociology as a general concept that includes subordinate racial categories and ethnic populations, as well as women, the aged, the handicapped, and other kinds of people who are in some way discriminated against by other members of their society. It is a rather misleading term, however. Not all minority groups are necessarily numerical minorities. Females outnumber males in most societies, and in South Africa blacks comprise over three-fourths of the entire population. These are not groups in the sociological meaning of a small set of people who interact frequently and personally. The term "subordinate population" would therefore be much more precise. Nevertheless, the term "minority group" is widely used in everyday language as well as in sociological writings.

Characteristics of Minority Groups

Robertson (1981) has identified five characteristics of all minority groups, which together considerably clarify the meaning of this concept.

(1) *The members of a minority group are disadvantaged in relation to the rest of the population of that society.* In addition to being less powerful, they are commonly viewed as socially inferior and often suffer discrimination, persecution, oppression, and exploitation.

(2) *The members of a minority group are socially visible in some way.* This visibility may be based on skin color, surname, gender, age, language, or other features of the individual. Whatever the identifying characteristic, it is believed to be socially important and is used to distinguish those individuals from others.

(3) *The members of a minority group typically feel a sense of common affinity with one another.* This "consciousness of kind" or common identity is a direct result of being treated as a distinct category and of being discriminated against by others.

(4) *The members of most minority groups are placed into that category by others.* Consequently, no matter how successful a person is in his or her life, it is usually quite difficult—if not impossible—to escape one's minority status. This is not always true of ethnic people who may cherish and perpetuate their religion or cultural heritage, but most minority group members do not voluntarily choose this status.

(5) *The members of a minority group generally find most of their friends and their spouse within their group.* This results from social pressures and personal choice. Other people are frequently reluctant to have close personal relationships with minorities, and the sense of common identity among the members of a minority group leads them to seek friends among themselves. This tendency of minority people to relate to one another further separates them from other members of the society.

Prejudice versus Inequality

Oppression of minority people results from a combination of several factors: individual attitudes of prejudice, individual discriminatory actions, cultural beliefs and ideologies, and social patterns of subjugation, exploitation, and segregation. All these factors are highly interrelated and tend to reinforce each other. To understand why minority groups are oppressed, however, we need to unravel these interwoven factors and determine which ones are the fundamental causes of the process.

The most common way of explaining minority group oppression is to take a social-psychological approach that gives causal priority to prejudicial attitudes held by individuals. Prejudice is a negative prejudgment about a category of people that is based on false assumptions about them (Seeman, 1981:379). These attitudes are often based on *stereotypes*—or cultural images—that depict all members of a minority group as "lazy" or "conniving" or "irresponsible" or otherwise undesirable. Such stereotypes usually have little or no basis in reality. Indeed, prejudiced individuals often hold negative attitudes toward all kinds of people about whom they know nothing. For example, Hartley (1946) found that nearly three-fourths of all persons who were prejudiced against blacks and Jews also expressed such attitudes toward "Wallonians," "Pireneans," and "Danireans"—all of whom are fictitious categories of people. Most prejudice is clearly a mental attitude that people learn at an early age—as in the song from the musical "South Pacific," which states that to be prejudied "you've got to be carefully taught, by six or seven or eight."

Prejudice is particularly likely to occur when people need a scapegoat to blame for their personal difficulties. The clearest example of this occurred during the 1920s and 1930s in Germany, which experienced massive unemployment and runaway inflation as a result of the financial retributions imposed by the allies after World War I. Many German people were severely hurt by these financial conditions that they did not understand, and blamed them on "Jewish financiers." The resulting scapegoating of all Jewish people paved the way for the Nazis' attack on Jews and the extermination of over six million of them.

This social-psychological perspective argues that *prejudiced people express their attitudes by discriminating against members of a minority group,* treating them as social inferiors and denying them opportunities for jobs, housing, personal freedom, or even life. As these discriminatory practices become widespread, the culture and social structure of the entire society become locked into beliefs and patterns of social inequality toward the minority group. The outcome is societal racism.

The major limitation of this social-psychological explanation is that it ignores the effects of the social environment on people's actions. Regardless of their personal attitudes, people tend to act in accord with the cultural norms and social practices of the situations in which they find themselves. No matter how prejudiced individuals may be toward blacks, for instance, when they are in a social situation in which blacks are treated the same as whites they will generally not discriminate against them. Conversely, no matter how unprejudiced individuals may believe themselves to be, if they are placed in a situation in which discrimination is expected, they will generally conform to the prevailing practices and support social inequality. In short, the existing sociocultural organization heavily influences individual behavior.

An alternative social-organizational explanation of minority group oppression gives causal priority to patterns of structured inequality existing in a society. Under various circumstances, a society may become organized to treat one or more minority groups unequally. For example, when colonists from Europe came to North America, they wanted the land for themselves. Over the following 300 years, their more advanced material technology and their increasing numbers enabled them to subjugate completely the native population. Colonists in the South also quickly realized that huge profits could be made from growing cotton and tobacco and shipping these crops back to Europe, where there were strong markets for both products. However, cotton and tobacco plantations required large numbers of laborers to till the fields and harvest the crops. Because the Native American Indians refused to perform this work, southern plantation owners began importing blacks from Africa as laborers. To maintain absolute control over these laborers, they were treated as subhuman slaves. Regardless of the personal attitudes of white southerners toward blacks—which in fact, could be quite personal and even intimate—the whites became economically dependent on their black slaves and hence were locked into the social practice of slavery to preserve their economy, patterns of social organization, and way of life.

Following the Civil War, much of the plantation system in the South was destroyed, and slave labor became less of an economic asset on the smaller farms that replaced the plantations. The Emancipation Proclamation issued by President Lincoln legally ended slavery, but it was the changing economic system of the South that actually freed the slaves, along with northern soldiers and subsequent legal controls initiated by the federal government. For some time after the war, Southern blacks benefited from a variety of short-range accomplishments of Reconstruction (van den Berghe, 1978). In 1885, a Boston newspaper assigned a black reporter to travel throughout the South and report on racial conditions there. He wrote that, "I found traveling more pleasant than in some parts of New England. I think the whites of the South are really less afraid to have contact with colored people than the whites of the North."

In the 1880s and 1890s, however, the economic and political systems of the South again began to shift, as industry entered the South and a new generation of southern political leaders struggled to regain political control of their region. One way of doing this was to establish legal patterns of segregation against blacks, to ensure once again that they would provide a docile and powerless labor force. The first Jim Crow, or segregation, laws were passed in the South in 1895, and by 1905 the entire region was legally segregated. Those patterns of structured inequality persisted until the 1950s and 1960s, when actions by the federal government brought an end to legal segregation and discrimination against blacks in the South.

The social-organizational pespective on minority group relations stresses the fundamental importance of prevailing social, economic, and political conditions, which create broad patterns of structured social inequality. Those sociocultural patterns pressure individuals to act in discriminatory ways toward the members of minority groups. As a consequence of those actions, people then develop prejudical attitudes and beliefs toward minority persons. In short, organized societal racism is a cause of discrimination and prejudice, rather than an outcome of those conditions.

The social-psychological and social-organizational explanations of minority-group relations are both useful, since personal prejudices and structural inequality tend to reinforce one another. However, each perspective leads to a distinctive course of action as we attempt to improve intergroup relations.

Treatment of Minority Groups

The dominant members of a society may treat minority groups in several different ways. These policies and patterns of intergroup relations may be formally proclaimed by the government, or they may evolve informally through social practices. A society may hold quite different policies toward various minority groups, and these policies frequently change through time with shifting societal conditions. Six alternative policies of intergroup relations identified by George Simpson and Milton Yinger (1972) are described (with minor modifications) in the following paragraphs and illustrated in Figure 17-1.

Assimilation is the policy of encouraging or forcing a minority group to give up its separate identity and join the dominant majority. With ethnic minorities, this policy may be promoted by teaching all children English in school, ridiculing foreign traditions and ways of life, or forcing Jews to accept Christianity. With racial minorities, assimilation occurs through intermarrying, as in the case of Brazil where interracial marriages are widely accepted. Some minorities may voluntarily and actively seek assimilation, but many resist it as best they can because they value their own cultural heritage. In the

FIGURE 17-1   Alternative policies for treatment of minority groups

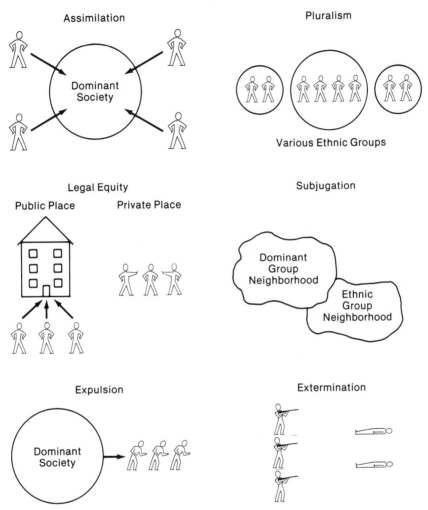

early decades of this century, the United States was often described as "the great melting pot" in which all minority groups (except blacks) would eventually be assimilated into a homogeneous society. We now realize, however, that this vision was both naïve and ethnocentric.

Pluralism, or coexistence, is the policy of encouraging the retention of ethnic and racial differences while treating all categories of people equally. Minorities may become assimilated to the extent they desire, but ethnic and racial differences are respected and valued. In

addition, no forms of minority group discrimination are tolerated in the society. This is obviously a high ideal that can be extremely difficult to achieve in practice, but it is possible. Switzerland is composed of German, French, and Italian ethnic populations, each of which speeaks its own language and maintains its own cultural traditions and lifestyles. Yet all three populations, plus smaller ethnic groups, live together harmoniously on equal terms in a well-integrated society. To the extent that the United States now has an "official" policy concerning intergroup relations, it is pluralistic coexistence, but we are still far from achieving full equality among all minorities.

Legal equity, or constrained discrimination, is the dual policy of establishing legal constraints againt formal discrimination by organizations toward minority groups, while accepting informal discrimination in interpersonal relations with minority individuals. This stance acknowledges that some persons will inevitably treat others in an unequal manner in their interpersonal relations, housing preferences, friendship networks, religious practices, and other daily activities. The society as a whole, acting through its govenmental agencies, is incapable of preventing or controlling most such actions. Government can, however, act to constrain more visible forms of discrimination such as legal segregation of housing and schools, organizational practices of not hiring or promoting members of particular minority groups, or refusal to provide public services to people because of their race, ethnicity, or gender. In addition to protecting minority groups in these ways, government can enact laws designed to rectify past discrimination, such as Affirmative Action programs, which require organizations (businesses, public agencies, colleges, etc.) to actively seek out minority persons as employees, members, or students. Although the official policy of the United States may be pluralism, its operating policy at the present time is much closer to legal equity toward most minority groups.

Subjugation is the policy of intentionally organizing a society to promote and maintain the social inequality of one or more minority groups. In the eighteenth and nineteenth centuries, European colonists around the globe assumed that they were superior to the native peoples of their colonies and that they were therefore entitled to subjugate and oppress them. Slavery completely subjugated African-Americans by denying them all legal, political, economic, and social rights, and many of those practices were maintained through segregation until the middle of the twentieth century. The clearest current example of this practice is found in South Africa, where the official policy of apartheid is intended to ensure that the small white minority that controls the society can totally dominate the large black majority. Subjugation of religious minorities, meanwhile, can be obarved in many contemporary societies, especially in the Middle East. A policy of minority group subjugation may be enforced in many ways, including physical violence, denial of political and legal rights, segregation in housing and public facilities, legal (or *de jure*) discrimination, established social patterns (or de facto) of discrimination, economic exploitation, and ideologies that proclaim the superiority of the dominant people. This policy, in its many diverse forms, has been the most common form of intergroup relations throughout human history.

Expulsion, or population transfer, is the policy of physically removing the members of a minority group from participating in the society. Minority persons may be forced to leave the country, often forfeiting all their possessions, as happened to hundreds of thousands of Jews in Europe in the 1930s. They may be permanently relocated on reservations and be prohibited from living elsewhere, as in the case of most Native American Indians in the United States during the nineteenth and early twentieth centuries, and with blacks in South Africa today. Or they may be forced into temporary relocation centers, as were more than 100,000 Japanese-Americans in 1942. Sometimes population transfer appears to be voluntary, as when the black leader Marcus Garvey led several thousand African-Americans back to Africa to create the new nation of Liberia, or when the Black Panthers demanded in the 1960s that blacks be given several states in which to create their own separate society. Such movements are generally a direct result of severe repression of the minority group, however. Various forms of expulsion have been almost as common as minority subjugation in many societies past and present.

Extermination, or genocide, is the policy of de-

liberately killing all or most of the members of a minority group. This practice has also been fairly frequent throughout history, when invading armies ruthlessly killed the conquered men and enslaved the women. In the United States, from the seventeenth through the nineteenth centuries, the pioneers assumed this task themselves, eliminating approximately two-thirds of all Native American Indians as they pushed continually westward. We should not have to be reminded, moreover, that humanity has not abandoned the practice of genocide. The Nazis' "final solution" to the "Jewish problem" was to exterminate over six million Jews in concentration camps during the 1930s and 1940s. More recently, in Burundi in 1972 the dominant Tutsi tribe massacred an estimated hundred thousand members of the subordinate Hutu tribe.

These alternative policies of minority group relations are often applied in various combinations within a society. Different policies are applied to various minority groups with varying degrees of success. Moreover, all such policies are constantly changing through time, so that minority group relations are always highly fluid and variable. Nevertheless, the essential point is that *patterns of sociocultural inequality toward minority groups are not just a matter of how individuals treat one another; they are an integral component of the manner in which a society is organized and the policies it adopts toward minority groups.*

AFRICAN-AMERICANS

African-Americans are the largest minority in the United States. In 1986, there were almost 30 million in this country, or about 12 percent of the total population. They are also the minority group that has suffered by far the worst forms of discrimination and oppression (except for Native American Indians). When we speak of racism in the United States—both interpersonal and structure—we are generally referring to the past and present conditions of black people.

Slavery

Between 1619 and 1863 (when slavery was legally abolished) approximately 400,000 black Africans were shipped to this country in chains and sold as slaves in the South. As we have seen, *Africans were brought here for economic reasons, to provide cheap labor for cotton and tobacco plantations and for other forms of agriculture,* since the colonies did not have an indigenous class of peasants to perform this work. They were stripped of their past cultural heritage, forced to learn English and adapt to American ways of living, prevented from forming stable family units, denied all legal and political rights, and considered to be merely property—like animals—rather than human beings.

From our twentieth-century perspectives, slavery is a despicable practice that violates all our beliefs about human rights. To understand it, however, we must view it in its historical context. First, slavery was not invented in the United States. Many societies throughout history—including the "enlightened" ancient Greeks—have held slaves. Second, despite popular images of Simon Legrees beating their slaves mercilessly, most slaves in the U.S. South were treated no worse than were peasants and laborers in many European countries at that time. Although they were often forced to work 12- to 14-hour days in the fields during the busy seasons, this was considered normal for farm laborers. Most slave owners fed their slaves reasonably well, treated their physical ailments, provided them with some kind of housing, gave them some time off from work for rest and relaxation, and allowed them to hold religious services. Slaves were valuable property, representing large capital investments (usually several hundred dollars apiece, which today would be the equivalent of several thousand dollars), as well as an essential labor force. Economically, therefore, slave owners could not afford to abuse their slaves too badly.

Third, some black slaves in the South acquired positions of moderate responsibility as farm overseers or managers, household domestics, mechanics, and craftsmen. (At the time of the Civil War, for example, almost all mechanics in the South were black.) Fourth, over time, many blacks were voluntarily freed by their owners, saved their wages and bought their own freedom, or escaped to the North. By the beginning of the Civil War, there were more free African-Americans than slaves in the United States. These developments suggest that *the conditions of African-Americans in the United States at that time were not too different from the way in which many other oppressed minorities have been treated in the past* (van den Burghe, 1978). Nevertheless, that fact does not justify human slavery under any conditions, since slaves are denied all human rights.

After the Civil War, although the former slaves were legally free to do what they wanted, most of those who had been working on Southern plantations remained on the land as hired agricultural laborers (at subsistence wages) or as sharecroppers. Their economic condition was therefore no better—and often worse—than it had been during slavery. Those African-Americans who had acquired other skills were able to begin participating more fully in the economic life of the nation, but they were generally at the bottom of the socioeconomic stratification system.

Racial Segregation

Meanwhile, a new form of racial inequality replaced slavery. *African-Americans throughout much of the United States were increasingly subjected to racial segregation* under which they were prohibited (legally and/or socially) from using white facilities such as schools, churches, housing, hotels and restaurants, trains, hospitals, or even public lavatories and drinking fountains, and from holding many kinds of desirable jobs. Whereas slavery was based on the economic system of plantation agriculture in the South, segregation rested directly on the sociocultural categorization of Negroes as infe-

rior human beings. In other words, black slaves were oppressed because of their role in the Southern economic system, but under segregation all African-Americans were oppressed simply because they were Negroes, regardless of their economic roles. Legal segregation of technically free blacks began not in the South, but in the border and southern-midwest states during the early part of the nineteenth century, as a strategy for preventing free blacks from competing effectively with whites for land, better-paying jobs, and social status (Woodward, 1974).

During the Reconstruction Period in the South following the Civil War, northern political influences (and sometimes military force) prevented the establishment of legal segregation in that region. After Reconstruction ended about 1890, however, all the southern states rapidly enacted extensive segregation laws. As industry and other forms of nonagricultural business developed in the South, the new economic and political elites had two main reasons for instituting racial segregation. Economically, segregation ensured that there would continue to be a large labor force of disadvantaged workers to perform unskilled labor in factories and other businesses at minimal wages. Politically, segregation was a way of securing the electoral support of the white working class, who were thus assured that blacks could not compete with them for more desirable jobs, housing, and other benefits.

By 1910, complete racial segregation prevailed not only throughout the former Confederacy, but also quite extensively in the border states and some south-central states. African-Americans were legally forbidden to hold most higher-status jobs, to live in white neighborhoods, to patronize white hotels and restaurants, to attend white schools, to be treated in white hospitals, or to worship in white churches. Or, if they were allowed to enter these places, they had to do so through separate entrances and remain in areas designated for blacks. In the South, blacks even needed a pass to travel and were often told to "get out of town before dusk." Segregation was strictly enforced by the police and also by extralegal vigilantes and organizations such as the Ku Klux Klan. The federal armed services were also segregated, so that as late as World War II most African-Americans served in all-black units commanded by white officers.

Segregation was not legally mandated outside the South, but it was nevertheless widely practiced throughout the country during the first half of this century. Informal segregation enforced through organizational practices and interpersonal relations can be as discriminatory as legal segregation. Although white employers were often anxious to hire blacks as laborers at minimal wages—especially after the 1920s when large-scale immigration was halted—in all other aspects of their lives African-Americans were expected to keep to themselves and not impinge upon "white society."

Most African-Americans were forced—by economic necessity, social pressures, and legal restrictions such as neighborhood convenants that forbid whites to sell or rent to blacks—to live in the most undesirable sections of communities. As a result, black ghettos developed in all northern cities, where black people were crowded into run-down tenements and other housing that had been abandoned by whites as they moved outward to better neighborhoods and suburbs. As a consequence of this residential segregation, churches, schools, and other organizations in the ghettos became predominantly or entirely black. A further consequence was that most interpersonal interaction, especially outside the work place, was sharply divided along racial lines. Whites therefore had little personal contact with African-Americans, which increased their prejudical and stereotypical attitudes. *Until the middle of the twentieth century, the United States was truly a racially divided and oppressive society.* And in many extralegal ways, it remains so today.

African-Americans reacted to this racial discrimination and segregation in the same two ways that have characterized most oppressed people: through individual mobility, in an effort to improve their personal statuses in society, and through collective action to eliminate racism.

Individual Mobility

Before they can improve their positions in society, many disadvantaged people find it necessary to be geographically mobile. *Throughout this century, large numbers of blacks living in the rural South have migrated to urban communities and to the North.* In 1910, almost 90 percent of all African-Americans lived in the South, primarily in rural areas. By 1980, three-fourths of them lived in metropolitan areas, and over half of them were located outside the South. This massive migration was prompted by the same kinds of factors that have created rural-to-urban population movements in all developing countries: "push" forces of overpopulation and agricultural depression in rural areas, combined with the "pull" forces of new job opportunities in urban industries and other organizations. In addition, of course, blacks who moved to the North prior to the 1950s were seeking to escape at least the legal segregation that prevailed throughout the South. The peak of this migration occurred during the 1940s, when war industries in the North were desperate for workers, but it continued during the economic boom years of the 1950s.

The primary goal of most African-Americans pursuing this route of individual mobility, nevertheless, has been to improve their personal socioeconomic statuses. How successful have they been in this endeavor? By all criteria, many blacks have greatly improved their socioeconomic condition during the last fifty years—but so have many whites. The critical consideration, therefore, is how well blacks are doing in comparison with whites at the present time. Table 17-1 compares whites and blacks in the United States in 1985 on a number of different socioeconomic status indicators. Overall, these figures show that *African-Americans are pres-*

TABLE 17-1 Comparisons of African-Americans and Whites on Socioeconomic Status Indicators in the United States, 1985

Status Indicators	African-Americans	Whites
Median years of school completed (persons age 25 or older)	12.3	12.7
Completed secondary school (persons age 25 or older)	60%	76%
Completed college (persons age 25 or older)	11%	20%
Enrolled in college (persons age 17–24)	27%	35%
Unemployed	15%	6%
Skilled workers (among employed persons)	8%	12%
Technical, clerical, or sales workers (among employed persons)	23%	30%
Professional or managerial workers (among employed persons)	12%	24%
Persons below the federal poverty line	31%	11%
Median family income	$16,800	$29,200
Family income of $25,000 or more	33%	58%
Family income of $50,000 or more	7%	20%

Source: U.S. Bureau of the Census, *Statistical Abstract of the United States*, 1987. (Washington, D.C.: U.S. Government Printing Office), Tables 197, 198, 213, 662, 731, and 746.

ently least disadvantaged in regard to education, moderately disadvantaged in occupational status, and still greatly disadvantaged by income.

Education. There is relatively little difference between the races in median number of years of school completed, with whites having 12.7 years and blacks 12.3. There is still a racial gap in completing high school, however, since 76 percent of all whites but only 60 percent of blacks have attained this level. Many more blacks than whites drop out of school before earning their high school diploma. In addition, almost twice as many whites (20 percent) as blacks (11 percent) have graduated from college. This latter gap is slowly being closed, however, since nearly as many black high school graduates

(27 percent) were enrolled in college in 1985 as were whites (35 percent).

Occupation. The most glaring difference between blacks and whites in regard to work is seen in the unemployment rate. In 1985, that rate was two and one-half times as high among blacks (15 percent) as among whites (6 percent). Among employed persons, blacks are less likely than whites to hold all kinds of more desirable jobs. This difference is not too great among skilled craftspersons, who are eight percent of employed blacks and 12 percent of employed whites. The racial difference is somewhat greater among technical, clerical, and sales workers, who account for 23 percent of employed blacks and 30 percent of employed whites. This difference is most evident among professional and managerial persons, since twice as many whites (24 percent of employed persons) as blacks (12 percent of employed persons) hold such jobs.

Income. Black socioeconomic inequality is most evident in this realm. Whereas only 11 percent of all whites live below the official poverty line, that figure is 31 percent among blacks. Median family income was about $29,000 for whites in 1985, but only about $17,000 for blacks. Nearly twice as many white families (58 percent) as black families (33 percent) had household incomes of $25,000 or more. And at the level of $50,000 or more, the racial difference is much greater, with 20 percent of white families but only 7 percent of black families earning that amount of income.

It is quite clear from these statistics that the majority of African-Americans experience two interrelated forms of inequality. In addition to all the subtle—if no longer legal—kinds of racial discrimination that still prevail in this society, they are also disadvantaged on all dimensions of socioeconomic status. Current statistics do indicate that a minority of African-Americans— between one-fifth and one-third, depending on the indicators used—are presently living moderately comfortably as members of the middle or influential class. They have at least some college education, and are increasingly graduating from college. They hold white-collar jobs and are rapidly moving into technical and professional fields. They enjoy at least a median-level income. The large majority of African-Americans, however, are still poorly educated, work in blue collar jobs, and survive on low- to poverty-level incomes. It appears, in other words, that *the African-American population is today becoming rather sharply divided into two distinct socioeconomic classes: a minority black middle class that is moderately successful in the socioeconomic marketplace, and the majority of blacks who are more or less locked into the working and dispossessed classes* (Wilson, 1987). In short, the strategy

of individual mobility has worked for some African-Americans during the last thirty years, but not very well for the large majority of them.

Collective Action

Many African-Americans in the South and the North have viewed individual mobility as an inadequate route to improving their status in society. In addition to the fact that the majority of black people have not been able to climb very far up the socioeconomic ladder, this approach does not deal effectively with organized racism. In an effort to eliminate racial segregation and discrimination in society, large numbers of blacks have turned to collective social and political action.

The civil rights movement is often said to have begun in 1954 with the historic Supreme Court case of *Brown* v. *Board of Education* of Topeka, Kansas, in which the Court ruled that segregated schools were inherently unequal regardless of the quality of black schools. It ordered nationwide elimination of all legally segregated school systems "with all deliberate speed." For several years after that, however, relatively little progress was made in ending *de jure* school segregation in the South, while de facto school segregation in the North—created by segregated housing patterns—was not affected by the Court decision.

A more appropriate birth date for the civil rights movement might well be December 1, 1955. On that day, Rosa Parks, a black women in Montgomery, Alabama, refused to obey the order of a public bus driver to give up her seat to a white man and move to the section at the rear of the bus where blacks were supposed to sit. She was then forcibly removed from the bus. In response, the black community of Montgomery—led by Dr. Martin Luther King, Jr.—began a mass boycott of the buses, which lasted many months until the bus company finally gave in and eliminated segregated seating. Sparked by this success, King and other black leaders—joined by a considerable number of white activists—began organizing civil rights protest activities throughout the South and in many northern cities.

King and his followers adopted the strategies of civil disobedience and nonviolent resistance that had been developed by the Indian leader Mahatma Ghandi in the late 1940s as a means of gaining India's independence from Great Britain. (Ghandi had, in turn, taken this idea from the nineteenth-century New England writer Henry David Thoreau.) The basic idea of these protest strategies is to deliberately, but nonviolently, disobey laws that are seen as immoral and then passively accept the consequences. Their twin goals are to disrupt the normal course of events and thereby create problems for officials, and to challenge the moral validity of unjust laws and thereby attract public attention and support for one's cause. Nonviolent resistance is a crucial component of this strategy, in order to demonstrate the moral justice of the cause and to avoid provoking—as far as possible—the use of violence by public officials.

During the late 1950s and the 1960s, the civil rights movement gave rise to hundreds of nonviolent boycotts, sit-ins, pickets, voter registration drives, mass marches, and demonstrations against racial segregation and discrimination. Although the participants in these activities were frequently jeered by white onlookers, arrested and beaten by police, jailed by courts, and occasionally murdered, the movement persisted and steadily gained public sympathy and support. Gradually, most southern segregation laws and public discriminatory practices in all states were abolished, and many states passed voting rights and anti-discrimination laws. The high point of the movement came in 1965, when King led the historic March on Washington and delivered his "I have a dream" speech from the steps of the Lincoln Memorial. A few months later, Congress passed a national voting rights act, although continued action by civil rights groups and federal officials and courts was required to enforce it throughout the South.

The movement suffered a severe loss when King was assassinated in 1967, but other black leaders stepped into the void and continued his efforts. However, because change was often painfully slow and widespread racial discrimination and inequality continued to exist, the civil rights movement took on two new dimensions in the late 1960s and early 1970s. Frustration and resentment among many African-Americans resulted in *serious racial riots* in the black ghettoes of Detroit, Los Angeles, Washington, and many other non-southern cities. Quite a few lives were lost and a great deal of property was destroyed in those riots, without producing many immediate improvements in interracial relations. The other new dimension of this movement was the *emergence of black militancy* and the creation of organizations such as the Black Panthers that rejected the strategy of nonviolence and vowed to use all means necessary to improve the conditions of black Americans. Adopting the philosophy of "Black Power" proclaimed by Stokely Carmichael (Carmichael and Hamilton, 1967), these militants rejected the goal of racial integration that had been held by the earlier and more moderate black leaders. Instead, many of these militant leaders and organizations sought to establish a separate black society within the United States. Their use of violent tactics quickly brought them into direct clashes with police and public officials, and many of these black leaders were arrested and sentenced to long prison terms. By the end of the 1970s, black militancy had virtually ended.

Overall, *the civil rights movement was quite successful in abolishing most forms of legal segregation and discrimination in the United States.* It also gave African-Americans renewed hope for the eventual elimination of organized racism. The movement was not very successful, however, in dealing with more subtle forms of racial discrimination in housing, employment, private organizations, and interpersonal relations that are not based on legal statutes. These forms of racism still prevail throughout most parts the country today.

A less recognized, but extremely promising, outcome of the civil rights movement was a marked reduction in racial prejudice among whites. Desegregation led to much greater interpersonal contact between blacks and whites, and as a result of these contacts many whites have discarded their earlier prejudicial attitudes toward blacks. For instance, in 1963, 52 percent of all whites reported that they would be concerned if a black family moved in next door, but by 1978 that figure had declined to 28 percent (Louis Harris and Associates, 1978). Similar reductions occurred in the attitudes of whites concerning many other interracial situations, ranging from a black sitting next to them on a bus to a friend or relative marrying a black person. This declining reduction in prejudicial attitudes toward African-Americans suggests that *although the civil rights movement is now rather dormant, interpersonal relationships between blacks and whites in this society should continue to improve gradually in the future.* As new generations of white Americans grow up in a society that no longer tolerates at least overt segregation and discrimination, they will have more personal contacts with African-Americans, which should further reduce the prevalence of prejudical attitudes.

The civil rights movement of the 1960s and 1970s clearly illustrates the difference between an educational strategy for improving race relations and a social action strategy. The educational strategy is based on the social-psychological explanation of minority group oppression, which begins prejudiced attitudes among individuals. It attempts to change these attitudes through informational, persuasive, educational, and other kinds of programs that are intended to demonstrate to individuals the fallacies, inhumaneness, and harmfulness of racial prejudice. *The underlying assumption of this educational strategy is that if prejudice can be reduced or eliminated, people will stop discriminating against minorities, and over time racism will gradually disappear.* Although this strategy is occasionally effective with some individuals, it has two serious limitations.

First, deep-seated attitudes formed early in childhood and reinforced throughout one's life are extremely resistant to change through any kind of cognitive messages. Second, even if this reeducational process is successful in altering individuals' attitudes, as long as those people remain in a social environment that condones or encourages discrimination and racism, they will very likely continue to act in discriminatory ways toward minority people.

The social action strategy, in contrast, is based on the social-organizational explanation of racism. It is aimed at changing broad sociocultural conditions in a society, not individuals. *This action strategy holds that if structural and cultural racism can be prevented, most individuals will cease acting in discriminatory ways regardless of their personal attitudes.* Moreover, as they experience equal status and rewarding interaction with minority people, these encounters will lead them to reevaluate and reject their prejudices. Very briefly, this strategy of intentional social change involves five interrelated stages.

(1) People who are seeking change form social-action organizations, acquire resources, and gain public support.

(2) Those organizations take direct actions—as done in the civil rights movement—that challenge racist laws and practices and bring pressures to bear on discriminating organizations and bigoted officials.

(3) If those pressures are successful in disrupting normal activities and creating difficulties for powerful actors and key functionaries, those people will be forced to negotiate with the protesting organizations and make concessions to them in the form of new laws, regulations, policies, and procedures.

(4) As the legal system and various organizations change in this manner, segregation and discrimination will be gradually eliminated, and increasing numbers of people will have more direct contacts with minorities.

(5) Through time, this will reduce racial prejudice, as is now occurring as a consequence of the civil rights movement.

OTHER RACIAL AND ETHNIC MINORITIES

In addition to African-Americans, the United States today contains many other racial and ethnic minorities. In this section, we briefly examine three of these minority groups that have been the victims of severe discrimination and prejudice: Native Americans, Hispanics, and Asian-Americans.

Native Americans

Although there is no accurate count of the number of people living in what is now the United States in the early 1600s when the first European settlers arrived, estimates range as high as several million (Dobyns, 1966). They were the descendants of people who migrated here from Asia at least 12–15,000 years ago—and perhaps considerably earlier than that—when there was a land bridge across what is now the Bering Strait. Native American "Indians" (so named by Columbus when he thought he had landed in India) are thus both a racial and ethnic minority.

Because of the hunting and gathering economies and the low levels of technology prevailing among most Native American tribes, Europeans did not consider them to be legitimate owners of the land. Instead, they were viewed as "savages" to be subdued or eliminated as rapidly as possible to make way for the colonists. Many Native Americans were quite friendly and helpful to the early settlers, and the Pilgrims in New England could not have survived the first years there without the food and other assistance provided by the natives. *As more and more colonists arrived and began taking over increasing amounts of land, however, the Indians began to realize that they were literally being invaded.*

They responded as any invaded people would—by resisting in whatever ways they could. They refused to give up the land that had been theirs for thousands of years without fighting for it. They also refused to be enslaved, which led to the importing of black slaves from Africa. These Native Americans were proud people with strong bonds of tribal organization and loyalty that enabled them to act collectively—as Africans brought here as individuals in chains could not—to resist the white invaders. From their perspective, they were struggling heroically against superior military technology to protect their homeland. The white colonists, however, were intent on either pushing the natives further and further west out of their way, or else killing them. The practice of scalping, for instance, was not initiated by Native Americans, but by the colonists. In the 1750s, the Massachusetts House of Representatives offered a 50-pound reward (a large sum of money in those days) for every adult male Native American scalp brought in and 20 pounds for every female scalp.

Profound cultural differences between the European colonists and the Native Americans further intensified animosity and hatred toward Indians. For example, many Native American tribes held a concept of personal property that might be described as "ownership in use." In their view, all goods were ultimately the collective property of the tribe, and an individual "owned" an item only when he or she was using it. When a Native American saw a colonist's axe or gun lying unused, from his cultural perspective it was perfectly legitimate to take it and use it. Europeans, however, viewed this action as theft, which led to the belief that no Indians could be trusted.

Even more critical in the prolonged struggle between colonists and natives for control of the land was their fundamental cultural difference concerning land ownership. Native Americans viewed the land as part of the given natural environment, of which they were an integral part, and to think of owning it was as absurd to them as the idea of owning air. The land was simply there, to be used as needed by all living creatures, but never to be owned. The European settlers, of course, held a totally different view of the land. Coming from societies in which all land had been owned for centuries—by individuals, estates, or the state—and in which land ownership was basic to the economy, they were extremely eager to acquire their own parcels of land in the New World. Since the natives did not originally claim ownership of the land, the colonists simply moved in, staked out their claims, demanded exclusive rights to "their" land, and sold plots of it to each other. As the Native Americans came to understand what was happening and were pushed out of more and more of the land they had traditionally inhabited, they became incensed. From their perspective, the white settlers had no right to claim ownership of the land or deny use of it to native tribes. They therefore frequently went to war against the settlers in an effort to retain their traditional territories.

The federal government negotiated nearly 400 treaties with Native American tribes in an effort to settle these conflicts over the land, but most of those agreements were really "articles of surrender" by the Indians. They were forced, by the superior military power of the federal government, to give up their traditional homelands and move further and further west. Although most tribes accepted these treaties in good faith and attempted to abide by them, the government repeatedly broke the treaties whenever pressures mounted from pioneers moving westward to "get rid of the Indians." Thousands of Cherokees, for instance, were forced to walk a thousand miles in midwinter from their homeland in the Southeast to Oklahoma. Over four thousand of them died on that "Trail of Tears." "White man's diseases" also took a heavy toll among the natives, who had no natural immunity to many infectious diseases imported from Europe. By the middle of the nineteenth century, no more than about 250,000 Native Americans remained alive.

In 1871, the federal government adopted the policy of making all Native Americans "wards of the state" on the assumption that they were not competent to take care of themselves. This status was used to legitimate rounding up most of the remaining Native Americans and placing them on reservations. These were largely lands in the West that were so desolate and infertile that no white settlers wanted them. Until well into the twentieth century, the Na-

tive Americans were expected to survive on those barren reservations without any governmental assistance—or to die. Not until 1924 were Native Americans granted citizenship in the United States.

Today, slightly less than 1.5 million people in this county are classified as Native Americans, divided into several hundred tribes. However, over six million Americans have some Native American ancestry (U.S. Bureau of the Census, 1984:39 and 42). About 30 percent of the 1.5 million Native Americans have left their reservations and are more or less assimilated into the dominant culture of this society, while the other 70 percent still live on 267 reservations.

Many of the Native Americans who left the reservations have been moderately successful in raising their socioeconomic statuses. For example, in 1980 over half of all Native American adults had at least a high school education (about the same as blacks), and about 16 percent were college graduates (almost as high as the rate for whites). Their median family income in 1980 was over $16,000 (compared to $12,000 for blacks in that year). These average figures nevertheless mask the grinding poverty that exists on many reservations. For instance, in 1980, one-fourth of all Native Americans had only an elementary school education, 27 percent of them lived below the poverty line (compared to 21 percent of all blacks), and over half of them had annual family incomes below $15,000 (U.S. Bureau of the Census, 1984:39). *Consequently, Native Americans still constitute one of the most impoverished minority groups in the United States.*

In recent years, Native Americans have attempted to follow the example of African-Americans in organizing collective action movements to improve their conditions. They have adopted the slogan of "Red Power," created the American Indian Movement (AIM) to speak and act on their behalf, and have filed hundreds of lawsuits in states from New England to the Southwest to regain their traditional lands. Although courts have typically been unwilling to grant them those lands, in a number of cases state governments have been ordered to pay them large cash settlements as compensation. Beyond those legal disputes, *Native Americans are today demanding respect for their traditional cultures and an opportunity to become self-supporting and self-determining participants in American society.*

Hispanic-Americans

This term is loosely applied to all people with Spanish surnames or ancestry living in the United States. They number about 17 million, or roughly seven percent of the total population, and hence are the second largest racial-ethnic minority in this country. Almost 11 million of these 17 million Hispanics are Mexican-Americans, or Chicanos, and there are probably another three to five million Mexicans living illegally in this country who are not counted by the Census. Other Hispanics include about two million Puerto Ricans, almost one million Cubans, and roughly three million persons from other Central and South American countries.

Hispanics are basically an ethnic minority, distinguished by their Latin-American cultural heritage and the fact that most are bilingual, speaking Spanish and English. Since Mexico and many other Latin American societies are racial and cultural blends of the indigenous Indian population and Spanish colonists, however, a considerable portion of the Hispanics in the United States are a racial minority as well as a mixture of three cultures.

Mexican-Americans. In 1835, the white settlers in Texas rebelled against Mexico and temporarily created an independent nation. In 1845, Texas was granted statehood in the United States, even though Mexico still claimed it. The resulting Mexican-American war between 1846 and 1848 ended with a treaty in which Mexico relinquished its claim to Texas and ceded large parts of the Southwest to the United States. As a consequence of that treaty, hundreds of thousands of Mexicans living in those areas automatically—and involuntarily—became residents of the United States.

Since the beginning of the twentieth century, many million Mexicans have emigrated to this country. Like most large migrations, this movement of Mexicans has been a result of both "push" and "pull" social forces. An early push factor was civil unrest in Mexico, but the principal one—especially in recent years—has been the grinding poverty of many Mexican people caused by poor land, low wages, and extremely high unemployment. The corresponding pull factor from the United States has been opportunities for better-paying jobs. *For a long time, the United States actively encouraged this immigration, since Mexicans were viewed as a source of extremely cheap labor.* They were recruited and imported in large numbers during the early decades of this century to build railroads and work as farm laborers. They were guaranteed good working conditions and adequate wages, but those guarantees were systematically ignored. During World War II, they were again actively recruited to fill labor shortages and to replace Japanese-Americans who had been interred. Large-scale importation of Mexican workers continued until the 1960s.

The United States has been equally active, however, in attempting to shut off the flow of Mexican workers whenever they have not been needed. During the depression of the 1930s, the Mexican-American border was largely sealed, and more than a half-million Mexican workers (many of whom were United States citizens born in this country or naturalized) were deported to Mexico. And for the last twenty years, the federal government has been attempting to limit severely the flow of Mexican immigrants. The border patrol catches several hundred thousand illegal migrants every year and returns them to Mexico, but many of them just turn around and try again and again until they are successful. Some of them work in this country for a while and then voluntarily return home, but many remain here more or less permanently as illegal aliens—or more recently as legal residents. They are able to remain because many employers—

especially in the Southwest—are anxious to hire them for menial work from crop picking to dishwashing. They are commonly paid very low wages that are frequently below the country's legal minimum wage, but are nevertheless far above prevailing wages for laborers in Mexico (Acuna, 1980).

Mexican-Americans are the most poorly educated minority group in the United States. Nearly 40 percent of them have only eight years or less of schooling, and slightly less than half have a high school education (U.S. Bureau of the Census, 1987:121). One reason for this condition is that while Spanish is spoken in many of these homes, until quite recently most schools attended by their children were conducted entirely in English. In addition to having to learn a foreign language, the children often felt caught between two cultures and alienated from school. In the last few years, however, many schools in heavily Mexican areas—primarily in California, Arizona, New Mexico, and Texas—have begun offering bilingual classes in the primary grades in an effort to make these children feel comfortable in school and to ease the process of assimilation into Anglo culture. Another reason for the limited school attendance of many Mexican-American children is that they are frequently put to work at an early age to help the family survive economically.

A large proportion of this minority group is also extremely poor. In 1985, 29 percent of them fell below the poverty line, and 40 percent had annual incomes below $15,000, so that their median family income at that time was only about $19,000 (U.S. Bureau of the Census, 1987:438).

Like most other minority groups, however, *Mexican-Americans have recently begun demanding better wages and living conditions.* Much of this effort has centered in labor unions of agricultural workers, led by militant union organizers such as Cesar Chavez. In addition to seeking greater benefits for Mexican workers, this movement is attempting to instill in them a sense of pride in their culture and awareness of the political influence they can wield in local and state politics through collective action (Hermendez, et al., 1976).

Puerto Ricans. The island of Puerto Rico was taken by the United States from Spain in 1898 at the end of the Spanish-American War, and the people of this territory were made citizens of the United States in 1917. In 1952, they voted to adopt the status of an associated free state. As U.S. citizens, they are legally entitled to emigrate to the mainland without limitation. Because of the great poverty and lack of economic opportunities in Puerto Rico, a great many of them have chosen this option.

Of the approximately two million Puerto Ricans on the mainland at the present time, *nearly three-fourths live in ghetto areas of New York City.* On the whole, these immigrants have not fared well on the mainland. They are as poorly educated as Chicanos, with about 40 percent having only an elementary school education and only another 40 percent being high school graduates. They are not farm laborers like the majority of Chicanos, but rather tend to work in very low-paying urban jobs that no one else wants. As a consequence, 43 percent of them were living below the poverty line in 1982, 60 percent of them had annual family incomes below $15,000, and their median income was just over $11,000, although it has improved slightly in the last few years. *Puerto Ricans are today the poorest minority group in the United States* (U.S. Bureau of the Census, 1984:41). As many of these people return home each year as migrate to the mainland. This keeps their population size relatively stable, but it also means that a majority of the Puerto Ricans in this country at any given time are recent immigrants who are not well-assimilated into the dominant culture.

Asian-Americans

The U.S. Census in 1982 classified approximately 3.75 million Americans as being of Asian or Pacific Islands descent. The largest group was Chinese-Americans, numbering about 800,000. The number of Filipino-Americans was almost as large, at about 775,000, while Japanese-Americans ranked third, with about 700,000. There were also about 350,000 Koreans, approximately 260,000 Vietnamese, and roughly 800,000 people from other parts of Asia and the Pacific Islands (U.S. Bureau of the Census, 1984:36 and 39).

Despite the severe discrimination experienced by many Asian-Americans as racial and ethnic minorities, on the whole they have been remarkably successful in adapting to this society and climbing the ladder of socioeconomic success. As a result of the great emphasis placed on higher education by most Asian cultures, these people have become much better educated than the general American population. Fully one-third of all Asian-Americans are college graduates, compared to only 20 percent of white Americans. Although 13 percent live below the poverty line, large numbers have obtained relatively high-status and well-paying jobs. Consequently, the median family income among all Asian-Americans in 1982 was over $27,000, compared to about $21,000 for whites at that time, while nine percent of them had annual incomes over $50,000 a year (U.S. Bureau of the Census, 1984:39).

Among all Asian-Americans, Chinese and Japanese immigrants to the United States have experienced the most severe racial and ethnic discrimination.

Chinese-Americans. Large-scale immigration of Chinese workers—mostly single male laborers—began in 1850 and continued until 1882. Over 300,000 of them were brought to California as contract laborers to build railroads and work in mines. In many ways, their lot was not much better than had been endured by African slaves, except that after they had worked long enough to pay for their passage, they were free to return home if they wished and could afford it.

The Chinese immigrants were vehemently resented by American workers, who feared that they would be displaced from their jobs by "coolies" who worked for very low wages.

Much was written at that time about the "yellow peril," and there were frequent anti-Chinese riots, lynchings, and even wholesale massacres of Chinese laborers. The police acted quickly to arrest and imprison Chinese immigrants on any pretense, at which time they cut off the men's queues (a long single braid of hair) that were an important symbol of adulthood and citizenship in Chinese culture.

In 1882, Congress passed the Chinese Exclusion Act, which suspended the immigration of Chinese laborers for ten years and decreed that all persons born in China were permanently ineligible for U.S. citizenship. That law was later extended indefinitely and remained in effect until it was repealed in 1943. At that time, a quota of 100 Chinese immigrants per year was established, which was not increased until 1968.

After the railroads were constructed and white miners succeeded in organizing unions that excluded Chinese from mining, large numbers of these people moved into urban areas where they created Chinatowns to preserve their culture and way of life. At first they frequently worked as menial laborers in small sweatshop factories or as domestic servants. As soon as they were able to accumulate some savings, however, many Chinese-Americans energetically began forming their own businesses, such as importing firms, retail stores, restaurants, and laundries.

While adopting American business practices, these people nevertheless strived to perpetuate traditional Chinese social and cultural patterns. Their Chinatown communities were highly self-contained, organized around clan loyalties, and largely governed by secret societies (or *tongs*) which settled disputes, provided social welfare services, and protected Chinese merchants from interference by white officials and competitors. Residents of these urban Chinatowns also continued to speak Mandarin or other Chinese dialects, to marry almost exclusively among themselves, and to preserve traditional Chinese customs and traditions. The result has been that—even today—many Chinese-Americans are relatively insulated from the dominant American culture and are only partially assimilated into United States society (Lyman, 1974).

Japanese-Americans. Japanese people began migrating to the United States in large numbers during the 1880s, after Chinese immigration had been cut off. They came as families rather than as single males, settled largely on the West Coast (primarily in California), and commonly took up farming. *They quickly became objects of the anti-Oriental prejudice that had arisen toward the Chinese,* which culminated in California's Alien Land Law that forbid them from owning any land. By forming protective agricultural associations that provided credit to rent land and regulated prices for farm products, however, Japanese farmers were able to undercut their competition and control a considerable portion of California's farm production (Daniels, 1974). In 1922, in an attempt to limit the growing political power of Japanese-Americans, the Supreme Court ruled that persons born in Japan could not become citizens of the United States.

This was not the last atrocity imposed upon Japanese-Americans, however. In 1942, three months after Pearl Harbor, President Roosevelt issued an executive order that authorized the military to move all persons of Japanese ancestry living on the West Coast (whether citizens or aliens) into internment camps located inland. They were given one month to dispose of all their possessions, with the result that most of them lost considerable amounts of money. *Without any due process of law, approximately 110,000 Japanese-Americans were confined against their will for the duration of the war.* Although they were not physically abused, starved, or killed, they were nevertheless treated as prisoners of war within concentration camps surrounded by barbed wire fences and gun turrets.

The justification for this total abridgment of civil rights was that Japanese-Americans might possibly commit subversive acts. The racist nature of this governmental policy is indicated by the fact that no such action was taken against the several million German-Americans or Italian-Americans in this country, even though there were a number of cases of espionage and sabotage by German immigrants sympathetic to their homeland. No Japanese-Americans living in Hawaii or other parts of the country (who were not interred) were convicted of any acts of subversion throughout the war. And the Army division composed entirely of Japanese-American troops (many of whom were released from the internment camps to join the Army) that fought in Europe was the most highly decorated unit of the Armed Forces during World War II.

The internment of Japanese-Americans did have one unintended benefit for them after the war. It dispersed the high concentration of these people on the West Coast throughout much of the rest of the country, which in the long run facilitated their assimilation into mainstream American society. *Since the war, most Japanese-Americans have fared quite well, and they are now by far the most successful racial-ethnic minority in this country.* Traditional Japanese values stressing education, initiative, hard work rationality, loyalty to the family, and concern for the welfare of the community have enabled them to become extremely upwardly mobile. In comparison with the total population, Japanese-Americans are more likely to finish high school, graduate from college, hold white-collar jobs, pursue professional careers, and earn above-average incomes. Nevertheless, they still experience discrimination, frequently find their friends and spouses among their own people, and hence, like Chinese-Americans, remain a less than fully assimilated minority group (Wilson and Hosokawa, 1980).

GENDER INEQUALITY

In all societies there has been an established division of labor between men and women. In addition to the biological function of procreation, each sex has been assigned and held responsible for certain kinds of social roles. As we have seen, this role distinction is most obvious in foraging societies, in which hunting is almost universally a male activity, while gathering edible plants is largely done by women (and children). In agrarian societies, preparing the soil and planting the crops are primarily the responsibilities of men, although women frequently assist in these tasks. Tending and harvesting the crops are generally defined as women's work, however, while herding and tending cattle is normally done by the men and boys. Food preservation and preparation is almost always done by women in all societies, while conducting religious and other collective ceremonies is generally reserved for men (Murdock, 1935).

As the economy of a society shifts from agriculture to industry, many of these traditional gender roles are no longer relevant. Gender-based role distinctions do not disappear, however. They are simply redefined to fit the new conditions. Males are everywhere considered to be the principle income earners, while women are still held responsible for most tasks associated with child rearing, food preparation, and household maintenance. In other words, although the many diverse roles performed by men in preindustrial societies are largely collapsed into one dominant role of breadwinner in industrial societies, women continue to enact as many—or even more—demanding roles in modern societies as they did in the past.

Socially Structured Sexism

Although the traditional roles of men and women are quite different in most preindustrial societies, neither set of roles is necessarily less important or less valued than the other. Again, this is most evident in foraging societies, in which a majority of the food consumed is provided by the women through plant gathering, and most goods used by families are made by the women. In agrarian societies, meanwhile, no farming family or community could function for long without the diverse economic tasks performed by women, including tending vegetable gardens, caring for chickens and other small animals, preserving and preparing food, making clothes, and keeping the household running smoothly. *In preindustrial societies, therefore, gender-based division of work is normally viewed as inevitable and imperative.* Moreover, women are not necessarily treated as the "weaker sex." Quite the opposite. They are expected to work as long and hard as men, as well as rear the children, care for the sick and elderly, and assume other responsibilities.

There is one major realm of activity, however, in which women have almost always been kept subordinate to men. Regardless of the nature of economic roles in a society, men have almost universally dominated collective decision making. This has occurred within the family, in the community, and in the broader sphere of politics and government (Friedel, 1975). The related activity of making war has also been exclusively a male prerogative. In short, in most societies throughout history men have wielded greater social power than women, despite the vital economic and household roles performed by women.

In medieval Europe, a new conception of women and their social roles developed within the upper classes. Enough surplus wealth was being produced by the peasants to enable a very small proportion of the population (often no more than one or two percent) to be freed from productive labor (provided they could extract the surplus from the peasants). The men within this elite nobility class could still find plenty of activities to keep themselves occupied: managing their estates, operating the government, making war, and running the Church. The women of the nobility class had little to do, however, since all necessary economic and household work was performed by others. Consequently, the belief arose that upper-class women were frail and delicate and were not capable of doing anything more strenuous than supervising the servants, sewing, bearing children, and providing emotional support to their husbands. This belief—and the roles it imposed upon women—persisted for several hundred years in Europe and reached its peak in the nineteenth-century Victorian era. The only major change that occurred during those centuries was that as new social classes acquired surplus wealth—first merchants and later industrialists and businessmen—this conception of women was gradually expanded to encompass an ever-larger proportion of the female population. Women were expected to be mothers, wives, and objects of adoration—but not competent adults or contributors to the economy.

Remnants of that belief still persist today in Western societies, as seen in the practices of men opening doors and giving up seats for women. This view of women and their proper social roles is also still widespread in the much more fundamental realm of work. *Until quite recently, a woman's place was socially defined as in the home, rearing children and doing housework.* Women were not expected to be gainfully employed—at least after marriage—or to pursue other vocational roles outside the home. Although this role definition was not strenuously applied to working-class women—for whom employment was often an economic necessity—it was strictly imposed on most middle- and upper-class women.

When this restrictive economic role for women is combined with exclusion from collective decision making, the result is socially structured sexism. *Sexism is the belief that women are innately inferior to men in social and intellectual capabilities, together with established role definitions and practices that severely limit the activities in which women are permitted to participate and the roles they may enact.* Since the concept of gender refers to social conceptions of appropriate roles, behavior, and personality characteristics for men and women, the term "gender inequality" more precisely describes conditions in which females are socially defined and treated as subordinate to males. However, because this inequality is commonly believed to be rooted in biological differences between the sexes, the term "sexual inequality"—or sexism—has become more popular.

In contemporary industrial societies, socially structured sexism is most evident in the two realms of family roles and socioeconomic status. (Gender differences in family roles will be discussed in Chapter 18 which deals with the family.) Our focus in this chapter is on the socioeconomic status of women. Illustrative data are drawn from the current status of women in the United States, but the general conditions described occur in virtually all industrial societies. Because this book focuses on macrosociological dynamics, we do not deal with the social-psychological side of gender inequality, including personality and emotional differences between males and females, the socialization practices that largely produce those differences, or their consequences for personal interaction and relationships between men and women.

Education of Women

Traditionally, women have received much less formal education than men. By the middle of this century, however, women in the United States were completing more education than men, as seen in the top panel of Table 17-2, which gives the median number of years of school completed by women and men age 25 or older from 1960 through 1985, divided by race. In 1960, white women had attained a median of 11.2 years of school, while the corresponding figure for white men was only 10.7 years. At that time, blacks were still much more poorly educated than whites, but black women were completing more school (8.6 years) than were black men (7.7 years).

Between 1960 and 1985, men eliminated the gender difference in median amount of education completed. Although the figure for white women increased to 12.6 years, the corresponding figure for men rose to 12.7 years. Meanwhile, black women and men

TABLE 17-2 Educational Attainment of Women and Men Age 25 and Older, by Race, in the United States, 1960–1965

Category	Median Number of Years of School Completed			
	1960	*1970*	*1980*	*1985*
White women	11.2	12.1	12.6	12.6
White men	10.7	12.1	12.5	12.7
Black women	8.6	10.1	12.0	12.3
Black men	7.7	9.4	12.0	12.3
	Percent of College Graduates			
	1960	*1970*	*1980*	*1985*
White women	8.1	8.4	13.3	16.3
White men	10.3	14.4	21.3	24.0
Black women	3.3	4.6	8.3	11.0
Black men	2.8	4.2	8.4	11.2

Source: U.S. Bureau of the Census, *Statistical Abstract of the United States*, 1987 (Washington, D.C.: U.S. Government Printing Office), Table 197.

made gigantic strides in educational attainment during this period, so that by 1985 their median years of school almost equaled that of white people, at 12.3 years.

Much more striking, nevertheless, was the unprecedented trend of completing college that occurred during this same time period, which is reported in the bottom panel of Table 17-2. The proportion of white women who were college graduates doubled between 1960 and 1985, from 8.1 percent to 16.3 percent. White men were completing college at an even greater rate, however, so that the proportion who were college graduates increased from 10.3 percent in 1960 to 24.0 percent in 1985. A similar trend occurred among blacks, but to an even greater extent. The proportion of black women college graduates rose from 3.3 percent to 11.0 percent during this period, but the rate of college graduation among black men increased from 2.8 percent to 11.2 percent.

Overall, the general trend in educational attainment in recent years is quite clear: the American population is becoming much more educated. At the present time, however, *men are completing more education than women*, especially among whites. Even more critical is the trend for *many more men than women to complete college*, which is steadily becoming the primary credential necessary for entry into higher-status and better-paying managerial and professional occupations.

Employment of Women

Women have always worked—usually very hard and for long hours every day. Indeed, it is probably safe to say that in most societies women have always worked at least as much—if not more—than men. Nevertheless, most of women's work has traditionally been carried out in the home or in a home-related work place, such as a family farm, workshop, or store. In the nineteenth century, as industrialization expanded rapidly, many factories began employing large numbers of single working-class women to tend machines because they could be hired at considerably lower wages than men. Some middle-class women, meanwhile, began finding employment as school teachers or nurses. Nevertheless, *employed women were normally expected to leave the labor market as soon as they married and never to return.*

This pattern did not change significantly until the 1940s. During the war, when many factories were operating almost around the clock to produce military goods, and a considerable proportion of the male labor force was in the armed services, large numbers of women were employed. When the war ended, however, women were expected to relinquish their jobs to the returning veterans and go back to being homemakers. Many—though not all—of them did that, so that as late as 1960 only 38 percent of all women in the United States were employed outside the home (U.S. Bureau of the Census, 1984:407 and 414).

Since 1960, however, more and more women have sought employment outside the home, as seen in the first panel of Table 17-3, which pertains to all persons age 16 and older. For many women, seeking paid employment has been an economic necessity, either because they were single heads of households (often with dependent children), because their husband's income was not keeping up with inflation, or because they needed the extra income to purchase a house. For other women, employment is a critical step in breaking away from traditional homemaker roles. The proportion of all women who were gainfully employed rose to 43 percent in 1970, to 52 percent in 1980, and it was 55 percent in 1985. These figures were essentially the same among married women. Especially noteworthy, however, was the rapid growth in employment among women with children at home. Among married women with school-age children between six and 17, the proportion who were employed rose from 39 percent in 1960 to 68 percent in 1985. Married women with preschool children under 6 have been even more likely to go to work in recent years, so that their employment rate has risen from 19 percent in 1960 to 53 percent in 1985. Women are dramatically challenging the belief that they cannot be both mothers and wage earners.

In contrast, the employment rate among men has slowly been declining, from 83 percent in 1960 to 76 percent in 1985. This trend has been caused primarily by the gradual aging of the population, so that an increasing number of men are living into their retirement years.

As women have entered the labor force, what kinds of jobs have they taken? A review of several broad occupational categories in the second panel of Table 17-3 shows some sharp differences between men and women. Virtually as many women (24 percent) as men (25 percent) held professional, administrative, and managerial positions in 1985. The category of technical and sales jobs was also nearly balanced between women (15 percent) and men (14 percent). The largest difference between the sexes occurred in clerical jobs, which were held by 29 percent of all employed women but only six percent of all men. In addition, there were almost twice as many women (19 percent) as men (10 percent) in service jobs. In sharp contrast, almost all skilled craft jobs were held by men (20 percent of the male labor force), whereas only a tiny minority of women (two percent) held such jobs. A similar, although less drastic, difference existed in the category of semiskilled and unskilled workers, with 20 percent of all employed men but only nine percent of all employed women doing this kind of work.

More revealing about the kinds of jobs held by women, however, are the proportions of women versus men in various specific occupations, a few of which are listed in the third panel of Table 17-3. Within each occupational category, women tend to be highly concentrated in a few kinds of jobs and severely underrepresented in many other kinds of jobs. *The occupations in which women are concentrated usually have one or both of two characteristics:*

(1) *They are traditionally defined as "women's work,"* such as nursing or teaching school; *or*

(2) *They are quite low-paying relative to other jobs in that category,* such as private household services compared to protective services (e.g., police officers).

In the professional and administrative category, for instance, women dominate the

TABLE 17-3 Employment Status of Women and Men in the United States, Age 16 and Older

Category of Persons	Percent Employed Part- and Full-Time, 1960–1985			
	1960	*1970*	*1980*	*1985*
All men	83	80	77	76
All women	38	43	52	55
All married women	31	41	50	55
Married women with no children under age 17	35	42	46	48
Married women with children age 6–17	39	49	62	68
Married women with children under age 6	19	30	45	53

Occupational Categories	Percent of Employed Women and Men in Each Category in 1985	
	Women	*Men*
Professional and administrative	24	25
Technical and sales	15	14
Clerical	29	6
Service	19	10
Skilled crafts	2	20
Semiskilled and unskilled	9	20
Other	2	11

Selected Occupations	*Percent of Women in 1985*
Professional and administrative	
Registered nurses	95
Librarians	87
Elementary and secondary teachers	73
Social workers	67
Social scientists	43
Administrators and managers	29
Lawyers and judges	18
Physicians	17
Engineers	7
Technical and sales	
Health technicians	83
Retail sales	83
Real estate sales	52
Science technicians	33
Insurance sales	28
Securities and financial sales	25
Engineering technicians	18
Clerical	
Secretaries	98
Information clerks and receptionists	98

TABLE 17-3 *Continued*

Selected Occupations	Percent of Women in 1985
Bank tellers	93
Bookkeepers, accounting, and auditing clerks	92
Computer operators	66
Administrative supervisors	53
Materials clerks	40
Services	
Private household	96
Health services	90
Personal services	81
Food services	64
Building services	40
Protective services	13
Crafts	
Electricians	8
Construction crafts	2
Auto mechanics	1
Semi- and Unskilled Work	
Machine operators	40
Laborers	17
Transport operators	8

Source: U.S. Bureau of the Census, *Statistical Abstract of the United States,* 1987 (Washington, D.C.: U.S. Government Printing Office), Tables 639, 657.

fields of nursing, library science, elementary and secondary school teaching, and social work. In sharp contrast, women are distinct minorities among administrators and managers, lawyers and judges, physicians, and engineers. Moreover, even within the fields dominated by women, men tend to hold the higher-status and better-paying positions. Although most public school teachers are women, most school administrators are men. Among administrators and managers, women tend to hold fairly low-level positions, while top executives are almost universally men.

Similar patterns can be seen within all other occupational categories. Health technicians are largely women, since this is relatively low-paying women's work, while engineering technicians are almost all men, since this is relatively high-paying men's work. Most retail sales clerks are women, while most securities and financial salespersons

are men. Secretaries are almost entirely women, but materials clerks (traditionally defined as men's work) are still predominantly men. Most personal service jobs are done by women, but the majority of building services jobs are still held by men. In short, *there is a great deal of status inequality between men and women within all occupational categories and all specific occupations.* This gender difference is very slowly being eliminated at the present time, but most women still have a long way to go before their jobs will be equal to those of most men.

Income of Women

Gender inequality is even more striking when the income of employed women is compared to that of employed men in the United States, as seen in the top panel of Table 17-4. Among full-time employed persons in 1970, the median annual income of

TABLE 17-4 Income Status of Women and Men in the United States, 1970–1987

Category of Persons or Families	Median Income			
	1970	*1980*	*1985*	*1987*
Persons employed full-time				
Women	$5,400	$11,600	$15,400	$16,000
Men	$9,200	$19,200	$23,500	$23,100
Proportion of women to men	59.2%	60.5%	65.5%	69.4%
Families by composition				
Female-headed, no man present	$5,000	$10,400	$13,700	*
Male-headed, wife not employed	$9,300	$19,000	$24,600	*
Proportion of male to female	54.2%	54.9%	55.7%	
Percent of employed persons earning $25,000 or more				
Women	*	*	7%	*
Men	*	*	30%	*

Category of Families or Persons	Poverty Income 1985			
	Poverty Line		125% of Poverty Line	
	Number (millions)	*Percent*	*Number (millions)*	*Percent*
Families, by composition				
Female-headed, no man present	16.4	33.5	20.1	41.4
Persons in all families	33.1	14.0	44.2	18.7
Children under age 18 in female-headed families	6.7	53.6	7.6	60.7

* Data not available.

Source: U.S. Bureau of the Census, *Statistical Abstract of the United States,* 1987 (Washington, D.C.: U.S. Government Printing Office), Tables 737, 742, 743, 746.

women was about $5,400, compared to about $9,200 for men. On the average, therefore, women then earned only 59 cents for each dollar earned by men. By 1980, the dollar amounts had risen greatly (due largely, but not entirely, to inflation), but the proportional difference between women and men was still almost the same, at 60 cents to the dollar. During the 1980s, however, this gender gap in income began to close, as women's earnings rose proportionally faster than men's. *In 1987, full-time employed women had a median income of about $16,000, compared to about $23,000 for men, so that women were earning about 70 cents for each dollar earned by men.* Nevertheless, *women are still greatly disadvantaged in income relative to men.*

When the incomes of families are compared, the gender difference is even greater. In 1970, female-headed households earned only 54.2 percent as much as male-headed households in which the wife was not employed. In 1985, that difference had decreased only slightly, to 55.7 percent. Finally, in 1985 only seven percent of all employed women earned $25,000 or more a year, whereas 30 percent of all employed men earned that much.

Part of this gender income difference can be attributed to the fact that, on the whole, women are not as well-educated as men in this society, as previously noted. As of 1985, more women (42 percent) than men (35 percent) had ended their formal education with high school, while more men (24 percent) than women (16 percent) had completed college (U.S. Bureau of the Census, 1987:121). Part of the difference is also explained by the fact that women are more likely than men to move in and out of the labor force, so that they frequently do not acquire as much seniority and work experience as men. Together, these structural factors account for roughly half the income difference between employed women and men (Beeghley, 1978:286–290). Conversely, *half of the gender-income discrepancy appears to be a result of discrimination against women based solely on their sex.* Even when we compare the income

of males and females in the same kinds of jobs, women are often paid considerably less than men for doing exactly the same work.

As a result of the lower-status jobs and lower incomes of so many women, large numbers of them today suffer severe financial deprivation. It is bad enough when a married woman can only earn about two-thirds as much as her husband. Much more serious is the plight of women who are the sole income-producers for themselves or their families. Approximately 30 percent of all households in the United States today are headed by women who either have never married, are separated or divorced, are widowed, or whose husbands are unemployed (U.S. Bureau of the Census, 1987:45). Over two-thirds of these female-headed households contain one or more children under age 18.

As a consequence of this situation, *poverty is rapidly becoming extremely widespread among women and their dependent children* who must survive on "female-level" incomes. As seen in the bottom panel of Table 17-4, of the approximately 33 million Americans existing below the federal poverty line in 1985, nearly half lived in female-headed households. Expressed differently, one-third of all female-headed households in this country are below the poverty line. If we consider the higher criteria of 125 percent of the poverty line which is still a very marginal income level, over 40 percent of all female-headed households fall below it. Even worse is the fact that over half (54 percent) of all children under age 18 living in female-headed households exist below the poverty line, and 60 percent are below 125 percent of that line. Thus the children of women who must support themselves are especially likely to be the victims of gender income inequality. Many sociologists have recently begun referring to this situation as the growing "feminization of poverty," although it might more properly be called the "feminization and childrenization of poverty." The United States, meanwhile, is the only fully industrialized nation in the world that does not have some kind of public program of children's allowances for all persons under age 18.

Women's Liberation Movement

A social movement calling for the liberation of women has been growing steadily in the United States and many other societies around the world since the mid-1960s. Unlike the women's suffrage movement of the late nineteenth and early twentieth centuries, which had the specific goal of gaining the vote for women, the contemporary women's liberation movement has several broad objectives. First, it seeks to eradicate the traditional belief that women's roles must be limited to homemaking, childbearing and rearing, and providing emotional nurturing. Second, it aims to open all social roles to women on the basis of individual capabilities, so that no one is denied opportunities for personal achievement on the basis of her sex. Third, it is dedicated to eliminating all forms of gender inequality in education, work, income, politics, community affairs, and other realms of social life. Fourth, it aspires to help women acquire the skills and self-confidence necessary to take full advantage of new social roles and opportunities as they develop.

Public support for women's liberation has been growing steadily in the United States for the past twenty years. Since 1970, the national Roper Poll has repeatedly asked the question, "Do you favor or oppose efforts to strengthen and change women's status?" When this question was first posed, only 42 percent of the public responded favorably. Each successive poll discovered increased support for the movement, however, so that by 1980 a majority of 64 percent of the population said they favored this objective. Interestingly, men have consistently supported the goals of the movement to almost the same extent as women, and in 1980 the two sexes were equal in their rate of favorable responses to the Roper question. Explicit opposition to this statement was expressed by only 24 percent of women and 23 percent of men in 1980. The strongest opposition to the movement occurs among older people who hold more traditional beliefs and are perhaps fearful of the social changes that women's liberation is creating.

Although the women's liberation movement began in the United States, it has since spread around the globe. Nor is it limited to industrial societies. The United Nations proclaimed the years 1975 to 1985 as the Decade of Women, which culminated in a worldwide conference of women in Nairobi, Kenya, in 1985. Thousands of women from many developing, as well as industrial, societies gathered at that conference. They represented both national governments and hundreds of nongovernmental organizations, such as the American-based National Organization for Women (NOW). These delegates celebrated the achievements of the decade and renewed their dedication to promoting women's rights and opportunities in all societies in the years ahead.

Many diverse strategies are being utilized by the women's liberation movement to achieve its goals.

Public information and education programs attempt to make people aware of gender inequality and to support the objectives of the movement. One seemingly minor but very critical aspect of this struggle is the elimination of sexist language. It is no longer acceptable, for instance, to use such words as "he" or "chairman" in a generic sense to refer to women as well as men, since this traditional practice ignores women and implies that they are not worth mentioning.

Political campaigns push for the enactment of laws that forbid discrimination on the basis of sex and open new opportunities for women. In the United States, there has been a concerted effort over many years to adopt an Equal Rights Amendment to the federal Constitution that would guarantee equal rights for all women. Although the ERA has thus far failed to gain ratification by enough state legislatures to become part of the Constitution, its supporters have no intention of abandoning their efforts.

A policy of *Affirmative Action* has been adopted in the United States by the federal government for itself and all public and private organizations receiving federal funds. This policy has also been adopted by many state and local governments and numerous nongovernmental organizations. Under this policy, an organization seeking to hire new employees must deliberately search for qualified women and minority persons and—provided they are fully qualified—give them first priority for those positions as long as they are underrepresented in that organization. Although numerical quotas for women and minorities are illegal, the principle of taking affirmative hiring actions to redress years of past discrimination is becoming quite widespread.

Other policies and programs are also being proposed and gradually adopted by numerous public and private organizations. These include provision of maternity leaves (or parental leaves that may also be taken by fathers) before and/or after the birth of a child; establishment of daycare centers by communities and employers; and creation of special educational and vocational training programs for women, especially those who are reentering the labor force for the first time or after a long absence.

The newest strategy for promoting greater general equality is the idea of *comparable worth pay*. This proposal goes beyond "equal pay for equal work," by insisting on "equal pay for comparable work." In many realms of work, jobs that are heavily dominated by women—such as those of secretaries, teachers, and nurses—receive much lower pay than male-dominated jobs that require much less preparation and entail considerably less responsibility. Comparable worth programs attempt to determine the qualifications, duties, and contributions of all jobs and then assign equal pay to jobs with the same comparable worth, regardless of who occupies them. School teachers, for example, would no longer be paid less than street repair workers, but would receive the same salaries as other equivalent semiprofes-

sionals. Implementing a comparable worth program on a large scale is clearly a huge and difficult undertaking. Nevertheless, in 1984 the Supreme Court of the state of Washington ordered the state government to institute such a program for all its employees, which is presently being done.

These many accomplishments achieved by the women's liberation movement during the last two decades in the United States and many other countries have unquestionably helped to improve the roles and status of women. Nevertheless, there is still widespread structured sexism and gender inequality in all societies, as we saw with regard to employment. Because sexism and gender inequality are so deeply ingrained in the social ordering and cultures of all societies, they are not likely to disappear rapidly. This is a fundamental process of social change that affects all aspects of social life, and such change generally occurs quite slowly. Still, *it is quite evident that equality for women is a goal whose time has come and will continue to be vigorously pursued.*

SUMMARY

Sociocultural inequality is created by belief systems that define various categories of people as inferior, which leads to structured differences in power and status. Race, as a basis of inequality, rests on a few minor physical characteristics but is primarily a sociocultural categorization that defines some races as inferior to others. Racism is the creation of structured patterns of inequality on the basis of those racial definitions. Since ethnicity lacks those minor physical differences as a basis for social differentiation, it is entirely a sociocultural phenomenon in which a population of people who share an identifiable subculture are defined as inferior by the dominant culture.

The concept of minority groups includes all categories of people who are culturally defined as inferior or subordinate on the basis of their race, gender, ethnicity, age, physical handicaps, or other characteristics. The social-psychological explanation of minority group discrimination and oppression emphasizes prejudical attitudes within individuals, which lead them to scapegoat others and discriminate against them. The social-organizational explanation, in contrast, begins with patterns of structured inequality within a society, which in turn cause people to discriminate against minorities and feel prejudice toward them.

Six broad patterns of intergroup relations in regard to minority groups in modern societies are assimilation, in which minority groups are forced to give up their separate identities; pluralism, in which minority groups are encouraged to retain their differences and are treated the same as the majority; legal equity, in which legal constraints are established against discrimination toward entire categories of minorities, while informal discrimination is practiced against minority individuals; subjugation, in which a society is intentionally organized to promote the inequality of minority groups; expulsion, in which minority groups are physically removed from participation in the society; and extermination, in which the members of minority groups are deliberately killed.

African-Americans are the largest minority in the United States today. Their ancestors were brought to this country as slaves to provide cheap labor for southern plantations. Following the Civil War, the southern and border states established legally based racial segregation in all realms of social life, while the northern states developed extensive informal segregation centering on residential patterns.

African-Americans have attempted to improve their status in society in two ways. Acting individually, they have sought to move up the socioeconomic ladder through physical and social mobility. In this effort, they have been moderately successful in regard to education, somewhat successful in regard to occupational achievement, and rather unsuccessful in regard to income. Black people are increasingly becoming divided into a

small, but moderately successful, black middle class and a large, disadvantaged working/dispossessed class. Acting collectively, blacks initiated the civil rights movement to oppose structured racism. Using the strategies of civil disobedience and nonviolent resistance, this social movement was quite successful in eliminating all *de jure* segregation, but considerably less successful in combatting de facto segregation and discrimination.

Throughout the colonial period in the United States, Native Americans were treated brutally, and often killed, by the white settlers. In the 1870s, the remaining Native Americans were placed on federal reservations, where the majority of them still live. Although some Native Americans who have moved off the reservations are becoming moderately well assimilated, on the whole these people are one of the most impoverished minority groups in the country.

Hispanic-Americans from Latin America and the Caribbean include Mexican-Americans, Puerto Ricans, Cubans, and people from many other countries. Mexicans have been encouraged to come into this country whenever cheap labor has been needed, but they have been blocked from emigrating when they were not needed. They are the least educated minority group, and many of them are quite poor. As American citizens, Puerto Ricans can legally emigrate to this country, and nearly three-fourths of those immigrants live in New York City. They are the poorest minority group in the country today.

Asian-Americans from China, Japan, the Philippines, Southeast Asia, and the Pacific Islands have a different history from other minority groups. The early Asian immigrants came to this country as laborers and experienced severe discrimination and oppression. They were frequently forbidden from becoming citizens or owning land. During World War II, all Japanese-Americans living on the West Coast were placed in internment camps. Since the war, however, many Asian-Americans have been remarkably successful in acquiring education, high-status jobs, and comfortable incomes.

Gender inequality and socially structured sexism rest on the traditional division of labor between men and women that occurs in all societies. In preindustrial societies, most women usually contribute to economic production in many vital ways. But in industrial societies they have commonly been relegated to the role of mothers and homemakers and denied opportunities for employment. In almost all societies, moreover, women exercise less social power than men. Sexism is the belief that women are inherently inferior to men, together with the practice of keeping them in subordinate social roles.

At mid-century, women were, on the average, slightly better educated than men, but in the last ten years this difference has been reversed. A smaller proportion of women than men are now graduating from college. Beginning with World War II, an increasing number of women—including those with children—have been entering the labor market. Although over half of all women are now employed, most of them work in relatively low-status and low-paying "women's jobs." On the average, employed women earn only about 70 percent as much as men, with the result that large numbers of self-supporting women and their children live in poverty. The women's liberation movement has sought to eliminate gender inequality and improve the status of women through Affirmative Action and several other programs.

18

FAMILIES

What is a family, and what social functions are performed by families in all
societies?

In what ways are families changing as a consequence of industrialization
and urbanization?

Why are so many marriages failing today?

How are family roles being modified in contemporary societies?

What new trends in marriage and family living are emerging today?

FAMILY ORGANIZATION

Friends come and go, but the family remains
forever. We all have some kind of family,
and although as adults we can choose which
family members we interact with and in what
manner, we can never completely escape our
family bonds. Because of that, and also because the family performs many functions
that are vital for individuals and society, the
family is often said to be the most fundamental type of social relationship and social institution. Nevertheless, the family as a form of
social organization has changed drastically
during the last two hundred years as a result
of industrialization, urbanization, and other
changes that have been occurring in modern
societies.

Kinship

Families rest on ties of kinship among individuals. *Kinship ties may be based on common
ancestry, marriage, birth, or adoption.* Your kin

thus include all the people to whom you are
related in some manner. But to whom are
you related? *Kinship is a culturally defined social linkage, not necessarily a social relationship.*
In the United States, for example, you are
related to your uncle even if you have never
met him or have any contact with him. Social
relationships of varying degrees of closeness
or intimacy frequently develop among kin,
and these relationships can be greatly
strengthened—or sometimes strained—by
their kinship basis. Nevertheless, social relationships must be created and maintained
through social interaction, whereas kinship
ties exist by cultural definition.

If we could trace our ancestry back a hundred generations and fill in our family tree
up to the present, each of us would probably
share common ancestry with several million
other living persons. Yet we do not consider
all those people to be our kin, since our culture defines kinship much more narrowly.
Kinship in the United States is normally re-

stricted to our grandparents, their children (our parents and aunts and uncles), those persons' children (our siblings and cousins), and the offspring of those people (our own children and grandchildren, and our cousins' children and grandchildren). Even with this restriction, however, most people undoubtedly have dozens of living relatives, which is usually far more than we usually can—or want—to keep track of. Consequently, we frequently distinguish between our immediate relatives—our grandparents, parents, uncles and aunts, first cousins, children, and grandchildren—and our other distant relatives, whom we may generally ignore.

Other societies handle this problem of superfluous relatives in different ways. For example, some cultures define only persons on the mother's side of the family as kin— her parents, siblings, and their children— and exclude all persons on the father's side from the kinship network. Even a child's biological father may be culturally defined as nonkin, with one of the mother's brothers assuming the role of social father to the child.

However they are culturally defined, *kinship ties are continually being created through marriage and birth, so that most kin networks continue indefinitely.* Only rarely does an entire line of immediate relatives end as a result of no marriages or children. As new kinship linkages are created through marriage or birth, they are always recognized by the culture and acknowledged by other kin. The children of nonmarriage unions pose a problem of kinship definition, however. Will they be accepted as part of the kinship networks of both partners, or will they be rejected by one or both sets of relatives? In the past, this problem has typically been resolved by labeling such children as "illegitimate" and either rejecting them or only partially accepting them into the kinship network of one (usually the mother) or both parents. Another common solution to this problem is to place strong social pressures on the parents to marry—provided they are

both unmarried—in order to legitimize their children. The distinction between "legitimate" and "illegitimate" children is no longer legally recognized in the United States and many other societies, however, and children of nonmarriage unions are increasingly being accepted by kinship networks.

The extensiveness of divorce and remarriage in modern societies is presently creating havoc in defining kinship ties. Are the divorced parents still part of each other's kin networks? For instance, should a divorced women still consider her ex-husband's parents and siblings as her relatives, and vice versa? Legally, divorce severs all those previous kinship ties, but in practice it is becoming quite common for people to maintain these ties despite the divorce. The view that, "I divorced him, but not his whole family" is often expressed today. The situation is even more complicated for the children of divorced parents. The parents' separation does not legally or culturally sever their kinship links with either side of the family, but maintaining close relationships with relatives on both sides can become quite difficult for these children. When one or both of the parents remarry, the situation becomes even more confusing for their children. They now have three or four sets of relatives, and keeping track of all of them can become almost overwhelming.

The crucial point about kinship ties, regardless of how they are culturally or personally defined, is that they are qualitatively different from friendships. One may like or dislike, love or hate, feel close to or distant from, and interact with or ignore one's relatives—but they still remain one's kin. Moreover, in all societies, *kinship ties carry some amount of social obligation to one's kin.* This may be as minimal as sending a birthday card, or as involved as providing financial assistance or a home for a relative who is experiencing personal difficulties. Consequently, kinship everywhere constitutes a culturally defined interpersonal linkage that generally provides considerable social stability and continuity for individuals and society as a whole.

Family Units

The family constitutes the core of all kinship networks, and each of us has a conception of who constitutes our family. At first glance, it would seem that no social arrangement is more clearly understood than the family. As sociologists and anthropologists have studied families through history and in all types of societies, however, they have discovered almost endless varieties of family forms. Although some of these forms have existed only in preindustrial societies of the past and are not important in the modern world, they show us that society can define almost any kind of social group as a "family." Modern societies, meanwhile, continue to display a wide variety of family forms.

In broad terms, *a family is two or more people who are linked by some kind of kinship tie, who live together at least part of the time, who share economic resources, and who function as a cooperative social unit in numerous ways.* Let us examine each of these features of the family in more detail.

Kinship Bonds. The most fundamental and pervasive kinship linkage within families is marriage, and all human societies have recognized this type of social relationship. Indeed, a marriage bond is normally thought to be sufficient to define a family, so that all married couples are, by definition, families. Yet some married couples in contemporary societies maintain separate households and live apart much of the time. In addition, almost three million couples in the United States presently live together and function as a family even though they are not married.

Although *monogamy*—marriage between one man and one woman—is by far the most common form of marriage throughout the contemporary world, this has not always been the case. *Polygamy*—marriage involving three or more people—has been fairly common throughout preindustrial societies. Most commonly this has been *polygyny*—in which one man has two or more cowives—usually as a way of demonstrating his wealth and status in society. Since there are generally about as many men as women in most

societies, this practice is necessarily limited to a small minority of high-status men. Nevertheless, a large majority of all preindustrial societies have viewed polygyny as the most desirable form of marriage (Murdock, 1949). It was often associated with the practice of women bringing large dowries to their marriage, so that if a man could afford to support two or more wives and their children he might acquire considerable land and other wealth through multiple marriages. Polygyny was practiced by the Mormons in the United States until late in the nineteenth century, is still permitted in many Middle Eastern societies, and is fairly widespread in Africa today (Welch and Glick, 1981).

In contrast, *polyandry*—in which one women has two or more cohusbands—has always been relatively rare, occurring only in societies that practiced female infanticide and consequently had a surplus of adult males. *Communal* or *group marriage*—in which several people view themselves as a single marital unit—has never (as far as we know) been a widely established practice in any society. Occasionally, however, it has been attempted in utopian communities such as the Oneida community in upstate New York during the nineteenth century and in counterculture communes during the 1960s. Finally, modern societies are gradually accepting the practice of *homosexual marriage*—usually two women but sometimes two men—living together as a family unit and sometimes rearing children.

Families may also be based on kinship bonds other than marriage or a committed sexual relationship. Roughly twenty percent of all families in the United States at the present time consist of a single parent (usually a woman, but sometimes a man) and her or his children. These single-parent families are usually the result of divorce or death of a spouse, although some unmarried women are now choosing to have or adopt children without marrying, and a few men are also doing this. Another kind of nonmarital kinship bond within families is an elderly parent living with his or her adult child. Generally this adult child is married, so that if that couple has children, the family contains three generations. It is not uncommon, however, for the adult child to be single (either never married or divorced or widowed), with or without children.

Social scientists frequently use the concept of *nuclear family* to refer to the standard family form of a married couple and their preadult children living as a unit by themselves, although it also includes single-parent families. The concept of *extended family* refers to all families that contain other relatives, such as elderly parents or siblings. The argument is often made that while extended families—usually three-generation families—have been fairly common in preindustrial societies, the nuclear family now prevails in all modern societies. It is true that in agrarian societies elderly parents frequently live with their adult children, primarily because they are no longer physically capable of farming on their own and have nowhere else to go. Given a typical lifespan of no more than about fifty years in such societies, however, that arrangement is not likely to last too many years. In industrial societies, meanwhile, even if elderly parents maintain separate residences, it is not uncommon for them to live close to at least one of their adult children and to interact with them quite frequently. This also occurs among siblings. Consequently, *although most households in modern societies contain only a nuclear family, extended family ties are still quite important for most people today.*

Common Residence. The family is usually thought of as a social unit that lives together in a common residence, at least part of the time. Historically, however, this has not always been the case. In preindustrial societies, it has been quite common for a married couple to live with either the husband's parents or other relatives (called *patrilocal residence*) or the wife's relatives (*matrilocal residence*). Nor is this practice unknown in modern societies, especially when housing is scarce or expensive. Because housing is currently in very short supply in most cities within the Soviet Union, for example, these practices are fairly common during the first years of marriage. In addition, in most contemporary societies it is often economically advantageous for single adult children—either never married or after a divorce—to reside with their parents for a period of time.

Another pattern that is becoming increasingly prevalent among professional and managerial couples is *commuter marriage,* in which they work and live in separate communities and cohabitate only on weekends and holidays. Still another practice that has recently been emerging is for an unmarried couple (either heterosexual or homosexual) to maintain separate residences (often apartments in the same building or close together) but to function much of the time as a family unit. In short, *although families in contemporary societies are normally expected to live together in their own home, this has not always been the case and is not always practiced today.*

Economic Sharing. Perhaps the most pragmatic way of identifying family units is to ask, "What groups of people regularly share their economic resources?" *Families in all societies, however they are defined or constituted, commonly pool their financial resources and operate as a single economic unit.* In preindustrial societies, this often involves productive resources, since the family unit works together to farm its land and produce the goods and services it needs. Although there may be considerable task specialization among family members, they share the fruits of their labor and distribute those benefits in terms of individual needs rather than the kind or amount of work performed.

In industrial societies, individual family members are likely to work separately—either in a paid job or in the home—but pooling and sharing of resources still occurs in terms of economic consumption. To a considerable extent, this economic sharing is a necessary consequence of living in a single residence in which all the family members use common facilities. In addition, however, there is also a normative belief that all family members share a common responsibility for the welfare of the family group and each of its members. In this sense, the family operates in terms of the communistic principle of "from each according to his/her abilities to each according to his/her needs." In formulating this principle, Marx looked to the family as an example of the manner in which communities and societies should ideally function.

Many contemporary families depart somewhat from this ideal of complete sharing, however. For example, each family member may receive a specified amount of the total family funds—a personal allowance—to spend as he or she desires, although most of the family's economic resources are still pooled. Much more important in most families is the question of who decides how those collective funds will be used. Is this done unilaterally by the head of the household—usually the eldest male—or is it done through some kind of shared decision making? Since control of the family's purse strings provides a fundamental basis for exercising power within the family, the manner in which these decisions are handled is a crucial determinant of how the family functions as an economic unit.

Social Cooperation. Collective cooperation extends far beyond economics in most families. It ranges from mundane matters, such as performing housekeeping tasks, to crises, such as serious illnesses. It also extends outside the home to community and public affairs, from routine social activities to political action. *If a family is to operate effectively as a cohesive social unit, its members must cooperate in a responsible manner.* Family members are expected—by one another and by society as a whole—to support each other and to present a united front to the outside world. If one family member has a hard day at work or school, the other members are expected to be understanding and supportive. If a friend knocks at the door during a family argument, the argument will usually be quickly put aside during the visit so as not to involve the outsider. If one family member has community responsibilities, such as

serving on a school board, the rest of the family is expected to accommodate those activities internally and support them publicly. Family cooperation never encompasses the entire lives of all the members, since each of them usually pursues numerous individual activities, but it can normally be expected whenever necessary.

A critical aspect of family cooperation is its authority structure and modes of decision making. Traditionally, many families in preindustrial and modern societies have operated as a *patriarchy,* in which the husband or other dominant male exercises all final authority and makes all major family decisions. The opposite extreme—which is less common but occurs in many families—is a *matriarchy,* in which this role is performed by the wife or other dominant female.

In most contemporary families, however, authority and decision making are shared somewhat more equally by both spouses and sometimes with older children. Few families are totally egalitarian, since even with shared decision making it is quite common for one person to prevail in the majority of decisions. But the traditional pattern of total patriarchy is rapidly disappearing, especially when both spouses are well-educated. Relative egalitarianism has become the norm within most families in modern societies, although the translation of this norm into everyday practice can entail numerous difficulties. Does it mean that the husband makes some decisions while the wife makes others, which has been the typical practice in the past? Or do both spouses participate in all family decision making? If this latter practice prevails, how do they reach decisions in situations in which they strongly disagree? These family power dynamics are critical for family cooperation and stability,

---

CHARACTERISTICS OF ALL FAMILIES

1. Kinship bonds.
2. Common residence.
3. Economic sharing.
4. Social cooperation.

but they can cause endless conflicts and disruption.

Universal Family Functions

In all societies at every level of economic development, family units perform a number of social functions for their members and the larger society. The anthropologist George Murdock (1949) compiled a list of these activities, which he called universal functions of the family, and documented their existence in a wide variety of different societies. Although there have been countless societies throughout human history in which the family was not responsible for every one of these activities, most of them are so widespread that we can think of them as the principle functions of the family as a social institution. The importance assigned to each of these family functions varies widely among societies, of course, as well as among specific families within any society. Families also differ greatly in the effectiveness with which they carry out the various functions. In broad terms, nevertheless, *these universal family functions are as crucial in modern industrial societies as they are in preindustrial agrarian societies.* The following paragraphs describe the most important universal family functions.

Regulating Sexual Activity. Sexual interaction is obviously not confined to married couples, and in some societies—including the United States—there may be considerable sexual activity outside of marriage as well as within it. Nevertheless, the marital relationship is everywhere viewed as the morally desirable setting for sexual intercourse. This moral norm therefore constitutes the accepted standard against which all other sexual activity is judged and sanctioned. At the same time, the cultures of all known societies have included some form of incest taboo that specifies which family members may not be sexually intimate. Most commonly, incest is culturally defined as a sexual relation between father and daughter, mother and son, or siblings, although some

societies have occasionally permitted one or more of these relationships. In other societies, the incest taboo extends to first or second cousins, or even to all the members of one's clan. The most likely explanation of the universality of this taboo is that these forms of sexual intimacy can be severely disruptive of family cohesion and stability.

Replacing Societal Members. Although a society may allow or even encourage a considerable amount of sexual activity outside of marriage, procreation is always expected to occur within the family. When it does not, most societies have traditionally stigmatized the offspring as "illegitimate." In modern societies this moral norm is gradually losing strength as increasing numbers of single women (and some men) insist on keeping and rearing their children without marrying. This practice is still labeled as deviant by a large portion of the population, however, which indicates that the traditional norm continues to be widely accepted. The cultural insistence that reproduction occur within marriage is unquestionably beneficial for children, since the family provides a socially stable and emotionally secure environment for them, which is especially vital during the early years of childhood. From the perspective of the larger society, meanwhile, these norms insure that the population will continually be replaced in an orderly manner.

Rearing and Socializing Children. A stable family unit undoubtedly provides the most psychologically and emotionally desirable setting for rearing children. Although other relatives and friends—as well as agencies such as nurseries and child care centers—frequently participate in the process of rearing children, primary responsibility for this activity almost always rests on the parents and immediate family. The task of socializing children, or teaching them the culture of their society and one or more of its subcultures, also falls heavily on the family. In modern societies, it is assisted by numerous other socialization agents, including the extended kin network, schools, churches and synagogues, youth organizations, peer groups, and the mass media. Nevertheless, societies everywhere rely on the immediate family as the primary socialization agent.

Satisfying Physical Needs. Young children are almost totally dependent on their family to provide for their basic physical needs such as food, clothing, and shelter, as well as many other material comforts and luxuries. This dependence does not end with childhood, however. As previously noted, the family is a fundamental economic unit in which material and economic resources are shared to provide for the needs of all its members. Moreover, many families contain one or more adults who are largely or entirely dependent on it, either temporarily or permanently, for their economic survival. These may include individuals with physical or mental illnesses or handicaps, pregnant women, full-time students, unemployed persons, and the elderly. All modern societies have various kinds of public programs that provide financial and other forms of support for such people under various conditions, but these programs are generally viewed as supplements to family care.

Providing Emotional Intimacy. In addition to our physical needs, all humans have strong needs for acceptance, caring, companionship, support, and love. To satisfy these emotional and psychological needs, we need close personal relationships with others. Our friends, coworkers, and relatives often meet some of these needs, but those relationships generally lack the interpersonal intimacy that is necessary for full satisfaction of all our personal needs. The immediate family can provide that closeness and intimacy, and consequently it is normally the primary source of our emotional nurturance and psychological fulfillment. This dependence on the family is greatest during early childhood and diminishes somewhat as the individual matures and broadens his or her circle of friends who can provide companionship and support. Nevertheless, the depth of interpersonal intimacy that can oc-

cur in the family is rarely duplicated within friendship groups.

Exercising Social Control. Whereas the previous function primarily benefits individuals, this one serves the larger community and society. If all persons fully internalized all the norms of their culture and abided by those norms in all social situations, they would be entirely self-controlling and require little or no external social control. In reality, of course, that never happens. A great deal of our individual behavior is guided and directed by social expectations and pressures from those around us. These external social controls are generally most effective when they are exercised by persons with whom we have close personal ties, since we normally place great importance on maintaining their respect and acceptance. The family unit is therefore usually capable of exercising strong and pervasive control over the actions of its members. A disapproving word from parents or a spouse can often have much greater influence on a person's actions than anything that might be done by anyone else.

Performing Social Placement. This family function is important to the extent that people acquire social roles, positions, relationships, and statuses through ascription rather than achievement. If a society operated exclusively on the principle of personal achievement, people's family origins and current family situation would have no effect on the roles and statuses they achieved. Although modern societies are moving increasingly in that direction, a great deal of social life is still influenced by ascription. Family background is one of the most important determinants of one's educational opportunities and attainments, political and religious beliefs, opportunities in the marriage market, and particularly the occupational roles and statuses one achieves later in life. One's current family situation, meanwhile, likely influences with whom one interacts and who one's friends are, one's social standing in the community, economic condi-

> ### UNIVERSAL FUNCTIONS OF THE FAMILY
>
> 1. Regulating sexual activity.
> 2. Replacing societal members.
> 3. Rearing and socializing children.
> 4. Satisfying physical needs.
> 5. Providing emotional intimacy.
> 6. Exercising social control.
> 7. Performing social placement.

tion, and many of the things one does outside of work or school. In the past, the social statuses of women and children have been almost entirely determined by their family, especially their father and/or husband. Although that practice is slowly diminishing, the social placement function of the family is still more critical for women than for men.

THE FAMILY IN TRANSITION

In preindustrial societies, the household is normally the principal economic production unit of society, primarily in the areas of agriculture, handicraft manufacturing, and shopkeeping. The term "household" is most appropriate in this context, since in addition to the immediate family, it often includes other relatives, hired laborers, apprentices, boarders, or servants. The household is therefore a fundamental part of the economic system, providing goods or services for the community and society and simultaneously satisfying its own economic needs. All other functions of the family are usually subordinate to this economic production activity, and all members of the household participated in it according to their assigned roles. The work place—farm, pastures, shop, or store—is normally located in or close to the household residence, so that economic production and other household roles are highly intermingled. In addition, the household unit often performs many other functions for its members, such as educating the children, caring for the sick and

elderly, providing recreation, settling conflicts, and conducting religious services.

Changing Family Functions

The advent of industrialization and urbanization in a society drastically changes many functions of households and families. Most critically, virtually all economic production activities move out of the household into factories, offices, stores, and other large organizations. Although farming may continue to be largely a family-based activity, the proportion of the population engaged in agriculture declines sharply. As a result of this economic shift, several fundamental alterations occur in the family. It loses its primary basis of economic power as a producer of goods and services and becomes merely a consumer of them. The individual wage earner, rather than the household, becomes the source of family income. Work is physically separated from the home. To the extent that outside employment is restricted to men, women lose their role as contributors to the household economy and become merely homemakers and child rearers. And the family loses one of its most vital sources of internal cohesion and stability. In short, *in modern societies the household/family changes from being the fundamental economic production unit to occupying a peripheral position outside the industrial economy.*

In addition, the family is also beset with numerous other challenges to its previously dominant role in society. As elaborated by William Goode (1963), these challenges come from all of the following sources.

(1) Other specialized organizations and institutions have taken over many of the noneconomic functions once performed by the family. These include schools, churches and synagogues, medical facilities, social service agencies, commercial recreation, and the courts.

(2) In urban settings, families often lose their sense of being part of a tightly knit community. Although people still interact with many

of their neighbors, those relationships often become rather sporadic.

(3) To obtain or retain a job, the nuclear family is often forced to move periodically, which severs established social ties with neighbors, friends, and even relatives. A mobile nuclear family may experience considerable social isolation for some period of time, so that its members depend on one another to satisfy most of their emotional and personal needs.

(4) As occupational attainment and other forms of personal achievement and success in life are increasingly determined by the roles that people enact outside the family, individuals spend decreasing amounts of time in family activities and give less attention to family relationships and responsibilities.

(5) Children become an economic liability rather than the asset they were on the farm or in the family shop or store, and rearing children becomes extremely expensive. The responsibilities of child rearing also detract from the time and energy that parents have for outside employment or community activities.

Given the movement of economic production activities out of households, the loss of many noneconomic family functions, and the numerous other challenges to the family in modern societies, some observers have wondered whether the family is becoming an obsolete social unit. These pessimistic predictions overlook the fact that all of the universal family functions are still crucially important today. In fact, it can be argued that since most families no longer have to perform so many different kinds of functions, they can now concentrate on their basic functions of providing emotional intimacy and support to their members, rearing and socializing children, meeting the physical needs of members, and controlling their actions. *Although the family does not appear to be disappearing in modern societies, its functions and structure are rapidly changing in response to the fundamental trends of industrialization and urbanization.*

Family Composition

Thus far we have been focusing on changing family functions, but let us now briefly examine the corresponding alterations that have recently been occurring in the composition of households and families.

We often think of households in preindustrial societies as consisting of large extended families with numerous relatives, in contrast to contemporary small nuclear families. The argument is then made that one of the most fundamental changes resulting from industrialization and urbanization is a widespread shift from extended to nuclear families. This view is overly simplistic, however, since it is doubtful if the majority of families in any society have ever contained three generations with all their offspring, plus other assorted relatives. Although it is true that households in preindustrial societies sometimes contain as many as ten or twelve people, many of those individuals are not family members. It is also true that the extended family is a very important social unit in some contemporary societies—such as China—but the entire extended family does not often live together in a single household. In the United States, the first national census in 1790 found the average household size to be only 5.8 persons, most of whom were undoubtedly children of the married couple in the household.

More realistically, *the major change that has occurred in the extended family with industrialization and urbanization is a decline in frequency of interaction among all its members.* In preindustrial societies, it is quite common to find several households of kin all living in close proximity to each other, or at least in the same village. Consequently, there is often a great deal of interaction among extended family members on almost a daily basis. In modern societies, in contrast, adult offspring often move far away from their parents and siblings, so that opportunities for interaction with kin are considerably diminished. Although many people still interact fairly often with their relatives, these relationships typically play a considerably less prominent role in their daily lives than in agrarian societies.

To illustrate the changes that are occurring at the present time in the composition of American families, let us examine some recent data (Hacker, 1983; U.S. Bureau of the Census, 1987:42). During the decade from 1970 to 1980, the total population of this country increased by 11 percent, but the number of households grew by 27 percent. The rate of household formation was thus much greater than the rate of population growth. From 1980 to 1985, the population increased by 5.0 percent, while the number of households increased by 7.4 percent.

One major cause of this growth in the number of households has been a steady increase in the proportion of people living alone, especially young single and elderly widowed persons. Approximately seven million more people were living by themselves in 1985 than in 1970, so that single-person households rose from 17 to 24 percent of the total. Because the U.S. Census does not classify a household as a family unless it contains two or more persons related by marriage or birth, however, those single-person households are excluded. Consequently, the proportion of family households declined from 81 to 73 percent of all households between 1970 and 1985. Another cause of this drop in the number of families has been the expanding practice of unmarried couples living together. This type of nonfamily household increased by over 70 percent during those 15 years.

The average size of American households declined from 3.14 to 2.69 persons between 1970 and 1985, so that *households are significantly smaller today than they were in 1970*. The expansion of single-person households has contributed greatly to this decline in household size. Another important cause of this trend has been a rapid growth in the number of female-headed families with children but without a man present, which rose from 21 to 31 percent of the total between 1980 and 1985. This situation is largely a result of divorce, since it is customary for the mother to retain custody of the children after a divorce. The number of male-headed households with children but without a woman present remained fairly constant at about two percent.

As a consequence of so many people living alone, cohabiting, or rearing children without a spouse, the proportion of all households containing a married couple declined from 71 percent in 1970 to 58 percent in 1985.

Very clearly, the composition of households and families in the United States—and in most other industrial societies—is currently changing quite rapidly and drastically. This does not indicate that the family is disappearing in modern societies, however. Rather, *households are altering their compositions in response to new residence patterns, divorce rates, and living arrangements.*

Marriage

The large majority of all families are formed through marriage. In the United States today approximately 95 percent of all people marry at least once, one of the highest marriage rates in any society. Why do almost all people in this country marry? The common-sense answer is that they "fall in love." Throughout most human history, however, this would have been considered a frivolous, if not a silly, answer.

In preindustrial societies, marriage is a serious "business" arrangement for the families and the individuals involved. For families, it is a permanent alliance that often involves considerable amounts of land, cattle, or other forms of family wealth. Consequently, the common practice in these societies has been for the parents to arrange the marriages of their children—often at an early age—to achieve the greatest possible economic advantage for the family unit. It was unimportant whether the two individuals loved or even liked each other. Sometimes they did not even know each other prior to marriage, especially when the marriage was arranged or even performed when they were young children. For most individuals in preindustrial societies, meanwhile, marriage is virtually an economic necessity. Men cannot handle a farm or shop without a woman to assist them and provide a home for them. Most women are totally dependent on having a husband to provide for them economically. And when contraception is almost unknown, men and women need each other to rear the children that are the inevitable result of a sexual relationship.

The notion of "romantic love" arose during the twelfth and thirteenth centuries among the nobility in medieval Europe, who had excess time on their hands and were seeking diversions from boredom. It had nothing to do with marriage, but was rather an idealistic emotional state that might or might not lead to sexual consumation between lovers outside of marriage. Over time, this ideal was gradually adopted by the rising middle class, but it was still not considered an appropriate or sufficient basis for marriage. Spouses might eventually come to love each other, but this was not a necessary component of a successful marriage. Much more important was the couple's ability to work together to create a viable economic unit and a stable home for their children. Not until the industrial revolution provided expanding educational and occupational opportunities for young people did romantic love come to be viewed as a sufficient basis for marriage.

Perhaps all that was true in the past, but don't most people today marry because they are in love with one another? Romantic love is undeniably a major theme in contemporary cultures, endlessly glorified by the mass media and desired by most people. In fact, Goode (1959) has argued that romantic love is functionally indispensable for young people today, since it enables them to loosen their emotional bonds with their parents, lures them into marriage, and gives them the emotional support they need to create a new family of their own. Nevertheless, many people marry for numerous reasons other than love. They may be lonely, need economic support, be pregnant, be seeking companionship, or simply feel that getting married is the expected and "normal" thing to do.

Regardless of their motivations for marrying, *most people tend to marry someone who is fairly similar to themselves in several critical ways,* which is called *homogamy.* These similarities are evident in several respects.

(1) Most married couples are approximately the same age or only a few years apart in age. Modern societies frequently contain a cultural norm that the man should be slightly older than the woman, although in practice this age difference has been steadily declining and is now only about two years.

(2) For a variety of social and cultural reasons, most people marry within their own racial category. Although interracial marriages have become somewhat more common in recent years, only 1.4 percent of all marriages in the United States are interracial, with 0.4 percent of those being black-white couples and most of the remaining 1.0 percent being white-Oriental couples (U.S. Bureau of the Census, 1985:38).

(3) For fairly obvious reasons, couples tend to have about the same amount of education. When a difference in education does exist, the man tends to be somewhat better educated than the woman, although the reverse pattern is not uncommon. Because of the tendency for some men to marry downward on the educational scale, however, well-educated women often have a more difficult time finding a spouse than do well-educated men.

(4) Most people also tend to marry within their own social class, although the rather vague class boundaries that exist within modern societies make this tendency less obvious. Many factors contribute to this pattern, including people finding marriage partners through their work, the differences in interests and lifestyles that accompany social class position, and the fairly marked value differences that occur among people of different classes.

The process of creating a marriage bond involves several stages that are rather well-defined in contemporary cultures. The first stage in this process occurs when young people begin to break away from their parental ties by going off to college, getting a job and supporting themselves, and/or moving out of the family home and living on their own. This leads to the second stage (begun in high school but later intensified) of meeting new people and making friends of the opposite sex. The third stage of dating (which also generally begins in high school but becomes much more intensive after that) is a direct outgrowth of meeting new and interesting people. Contemporary dating practices, unrestricted by parental preferences or chaperoning, give young people wide opportunities to experiment with relating to persons of the opposite sex on a variety of bases: friendship and companionship, affection and love, and/or intimacy and sexuality. The fourth stage in this process, living together, has only become prevalent during about the last twenty years and is still not undertaken by the majority of young people or accepted by their parents. For those who do cohabit, however—either on a part-time or full-time basis—this arrangement enables them to discover whether or not their relationship can withstand the demands of rent payments, different eating preferences, housekeeping chores, and all the other details of daily living.

If the relationship continues and deepens, with or without cohabitation, the next stage is engagement. In the past, betrothal was typically considered a very serious moral or even legal commitment. The young man was expected to ask the woman's father for permission to marry his daughter, and he might be sued for breach of contract if he later broke the engagement. (Interestingly, women often had more freedom than men to break an engagement, although they rarely did this.) Today, engagement is treated as a private agreement between the couple that either one can terminate, although it is still commonly announced to friends and family with a symbolic ring. The final stage of getting married is normally a public action that is celebrated by the families and their relatives and friends through a ritualistic ceremony (either religious or civil) and sanctioned by the state as a legal status. Public confirmation of a marriage can be viewed as simply a holdover from the time when it was primarily a liaison between two families, but it also serves to impress upon the couple the fact that the larger commu-

---

STAGES IN CREATING A MARRIAGE

1. Loosening parental ties.
2. Meeting new people.
3. Dating.
4. Living together.
5. Becoming engaged.
6. Getting married.

---

nity views their union as a serious commitment and has an interest in its continuation—especially after the birth of children.

Marital Rates and Statuses

More people are marrying today than at any time in the recent past. Whereas in 1960 there were 8.5 marriages per 1,000 population, in 1985 there were 10.6 marriages (U.S. Bureau of the Census, 1987:80). However, people are waiting a bit longer today to begin married life. In 1960, the median age at first marriage was 22.8 years for men and 20.3 years for women. In 1983, those ages were 24.4 for men and 22.3 for women. Despite the popularity of marriage, during this 23-year period there was also *a sharp rise in the divorce rate.* Calculated as the number of divorces per 1,000 married couples, the divorce rate rose from 7.1 to 21.3. (It was 22.0 in 1980 but has dropped slightly since then.)

The reason why the marriage rate is increasing despite the rising number of divorces is that about three-fourths of all divorced people remarry, usually within a few years. Men are somewhat more likely than women to remarry, however. More than 80 percent of all divorced men remarry, regardless of their age, but only about two-thirds of all divorced women marry again. For women, age is a crucial factor in remarriage. Although over 75 percent of all women who divorce before age 30 remarry, this rate declines to about 50 percent of those divorced in their thirties, and after age 40 only about one-fourth of all divorced women remarry.

TABLE 18-1 Marital Status of the United States Population and of Males and Females Age 18 and Older, in 1960 and 1985

Marital Status	Percentage of Population		Percentage of Males		Percentage of Females	
	1960	*1985*	*1960*	*1985*	*1960*	*1985*
Single	22.0	21.5	25.3	25.2	19.0	18.2
Married	67.3	63.0	69.1	65.7	65.6	60.4
Divorced	2.3	7.6	1.1	6.5	2.6	8.7
Widowed	8.4	7.9	3.7	2.6	12.8	12.6

Source: U.S. Bureau of the Census, *Statistical Abstract of the United States, 1987* (Washington, D.C.: U.S. Government Printing Office), Table 44.

Table 18-1 shows the marital statuses of the United States population and of men and women separately in 1960 and 1985. The proportion of the population that was single remained about the same throughout the period, but there were more single males than females at both points in time. The proportion of the population that was married dropped slightly between 1960 and 1985, with the rate being somewhat higher for men than for women. The proportion of people who were divorced rose sharply among both men and women. The proportion of widowed people declined slightly, with most of that change occurring among men.

There appear to be two paradoxes in the figures cited in Table 18-1. First, if the marriage rate is higher today than in 1960, why are fewer people married now? This paradox is explained by the fact that there were three times as many divorced people in 1985 than in 1960. In other words, somewhat more people are marrying today, but a great many more people are divorcing. Second, if there are more single men than women, why are there also more married men than women? This paradox is explained by the fact that many more women than men remain either divorced or widowed. The greater number of divorced women occurs because they tend to wait longer after divorce before remarrying than do men, and a greater proportion of them never remarry. The greater number of widowed women—

five times the number of widowed men—occurs primarily because females live an average of about six years longer than males.

MARITAL BREAKDOWN

As in any social relationship, over time a marriage can become dull and uninteresting, full of conflict, or even emotionally and psychologically destructive for its participants. Because of the psychological, social, parental, economic, and legal responsibilities associated with marriage, however, unhappy marriages are much less likely than other relationships to be dissolved when they are no longer viable. We have no exact knowledge of the proportion of current marriages that are truly satisfactory for their members. When people are asked in surveys to evaluate their marriage and family life, more than 90 percent usually give a positive response. The current divorce rate, as well as popular literature on married life, however, suggests that the actual rate of marital satisfaction is much lower.

Separation and Divorce

One solution to an unhappy marriage that is taken by many couples is to separate, or cease acting as if they were married. Sometimes one of the spouses—usually the man—moves out of the family home and establishes a separate residence. Much more common, especially when there are children at home, is to remain in the same residence but live largely separate lives with minimal interaction, no emotional involvement, and often no sexual activity with each other. The marriage is thus retained in name only. This situation of social, emotional, and physical separation within the household is probably much more extensive than we typically realize.

Divorce—or marital dissolvement, as it is now often called—is merely the final stage of marital breakdown, often occurring after years of dissatisfaction with a marriage. As we have seen, that rate has been steadily rising during recent years. More than one out of every three marriages now ends in divorce, compared to one in four in 1960 and much lower rates prior to that. Moreover, there is some truth in the old adage about the "seven-year itch" in marriage, since the median length of marriages that are dissolved has remained about seven years throughout the last thirty years. In general, the longer a marriage lasts the less likely it is to end in divorce, although again this tells us nothing about the level of happiness existing in long-term marriages that are not legally terminated.

To understand the reasons for marital breakdown, we must ask two separate questions. First, what are the major causes of unhappiness in marriage? Second, what factors affect the divorce rate? Although these two questions are clearly linked, they have somewhat distinct answers.

Causes of Marital Unhappiness

Several causes of marital unhappiness (or conversely, marital happiness) are fairly obvious. One of the most basic is *marriage at a young age,* especially under 20. The younger a person is, the less likely he or she is to make a wise choice of a spouse. Many young people are still too immature to be able to select someone with whom they can live happily for the rest of their lives (Lee, 1977). They are still changing and growing rapidly and do not yet have enough experience relating

closely to others to know what kind of person would be best for them. Conversely, the older people are when they marry, the more likely they are to have a happy marriage.

Regardless of the age at which they marry, couples with one or more *critical dissimilarities in their social backgrounds* are less likely to remain happy together over the years. Sharp differences in social-class background are especially disasterous for marital satisfaction, but interpersonal difficulties may also arise if the spouses differ in race, ethnicity, or religion, or if there is a wide disparity in their ages. Whatever the nature of these differences, they almost inevitably create additional problems for a couple beyond the usual demands of maintaining a viable marital relationship.

Differences that develop between the spouses after marriage can also drive them apart emotionally and socially. A common example is a husband who goes on to obtain a college or graduate degree and develops a career as a high-level manager or professional, while his high school-educated wife remains a homemaker. Eventually, he is likely to discover that one of his female colleagues at work is much more interesting and challenging than his wife. The reverse pattern has not been very common in the past but could become so as many women go on to obtain higher education and establish a career outside the home.

The myth of romantic love continuing forever is frequently blamed for much marital dissatisfaction. Since this kind of emotional fervor rarely lasts very long after marriage, individuals who believe that it is a necessary component of a successful marriage are certain to become disillusioned rather rapidly. All the routine demands of daily living, the conflicts that inevitably occur in any close relationship, and the process of becoming thoroughly familiar with all the personality characteristics of one's spouse can quickly destroy the emotional bliss of romanticism. Couples who are able to transform their initial romantic feelings into a deeper form of love can create a much more stable emotional basis for their relationship. If they are unable to do that, their marriage will likely become devoid of any emotional involvement.

Another cause of marital unhappiness that is often discussed is *sexual incompatibility or unfaithfulness.* If a couple experiences serious problems in their sexual life, for whatever reasons, this can obviously create tension and conflict that may eventually pervade their entire relationship. However, many sexual problems are probably a result rather than a direct cause of marital dissatisfaction, although over time sexual difficulties can contribute to their unhappiness. Whether or not sexual infidelity creates problems for a marriage depends largely on the attitudes of both spouses toward such activity. Since about two-fifths of all married people have at least one extra-marital affair, this does not necessarily destroy a marriage; but if it becomes a regular practice it will certainly create stress for one or both partners.

Other causes of marital unhappiness are less obvious. For example, although children are supposed to strengthen marital ties, couples with *children in the home* are on the average less happy than couples without children. Children make great demands on parents, often necessitate major changes in their life plans and activities, and may become an emotional barrier between the parents (Miller, 1976). Despite the emotional trauma that is often thought to occur when the children all leave home and the parents are left with an "empty next," many couples report that this is one of the best periods in their marriage, since they can begin relating to each other again.

As families have given up many of their earlier economic and other functions and are now concerned largely with providing companionship and emotional support, it might be expected that the interpersonal bonds between spouses would be strengthened. They are no longer primarily a work team but rather an emotional partnership. The difficulty with this expectation is that it often becomes overly demanding for the spouses. Many people come to *depend almost entirely on their spouse to meet all their psychological and emotional needs.* This often places more demands and burdens on one's spouse than she or he can possibly fulfill. When these expectations are not satisfied within the marriage, the partners may blame each other for not giving enough to their relationship.

Another popular misconception is that employment of the wife tends to disrupt the marriage relationship and create tensions that produce dissatisfaction. There is no evidence that working wives have less happy marriages than homemakers, and there is some indication that such marriages may be stronger because the wife feels more personally fulfilled (Locksley, 1980). There may be problems in the marriage, however, *if the husband strongly objects to his wife's working*, or if he expects his wife to perform all of the traditional homemaking tasks in addition to her job, without any assistance from him.

Finally, despite the common belief that money cannot buy marital happiness, *couples with relatively low incomes often experience conflicts over family finances* that can interfere with their relationship (Glick and Norton, 1977). Conversely, couples with comfortable incomes tend to report greater satisfaction with their marriage. An especially traumatic experience for some couples is loss of work by the husband. In addition to the economic hardships this imposes on the family, one or both of the spouses may define the husband as a failure because he cannot support his family. This can be devastating for their marriage.

CAUSES OF MARITAL UNHAPPINESS

1. Young age at marriage.
2. Dissimilarities in social backgrounds.
3. Different stages of personal development.
4. End of romantic love.
5. Sexual incompatibility or unfaithfulness.
6. Children in the home.
7. Extensive dependency.
8. Low income.

Causes of Divorce

All the preceding causes of marital unhappiness can contribute to an eventual divorce. Whether or not an unhappily married couple finally dissolves their marriage also depends on several other factors, however. The steadily rising divorce rate in modern societies may not be due to any greater amount of marital dissatisfaction today, but rather to the fact that there are many fewer obstacles to divorce than in the past.

For example, *a divorce is no longer legally difficult to obtain.* Whereas it used to be treated in the courts as an adversarial contest in which one spouse had to prove the other guilty of adultery, mental cruelty, or some other serious transgression, divorce is increasingly being treated as a nonadversarial problem in which neither spouse is solely at fault. In many U.S. states, a marriage can now be dissolved simply because the spouses wish to end it, without any further justification. In addition, courts now routinely award child support to the parent who retains custody of the children or permit joint custody of the children, so that neither parent is left with the entire burden of providing for the children.

Another factor influencing the decision of many people to leave their marriage is *the increasing availability of employment for women.* As long as women are economically dependent on their husbands and have no way of supporting themselves, they are not very likely to divorce no matter how unhappy they may feel. If they know that they can support themselves financially, however, that economic barrier to divorce is removed. Consequently, although employment of wives does not necessarily produce marital dissatisfaction, it does contribute to the current divorce rate.

Public opinion concerning divorce and divorced people has also shifted markedly in recent decades. In the past, divorce was commonly viewed as a personal and moral failure, and divorced people—especially women—were often stigmatized as social outcasts and shunned by their former

> **CAUSES OF DIVORCE**
> 1. All factors contributing to marital unhappiness.
> 2. Legal ease of divorce.
> 3. Employment opportunities for women.
> 4. Public acceptance of divorce.
> 5. Longer life span.
> 6. Properous economic conditions.

friends. Today, in contrast, divorce is accepted by most people as simply the end of an unsuccessful marriage, without any moral stigma. Most divorced people now find it much easier to put their lives back together, make new friends and begin dating again, and eventually remarry.

The steadily increasing *length of the average life span* is probably also influencing the divorce rate. When many people died in their 40s or 50s, death, rather than divorce, ended many marriages. With people now typically living into their seventies, middle-aged persons in unhappy marriages are more likely to feel that they can't bear the thought of spending another 20 or 30 years with a spouse they detest, and so seek a divorce.

Finally, the *general economic conditions prevailing in a society* can affect the divorce rate. In bad economic times, such as the depression of the 1930s, couples are more likely to stay together. The pressing demands of financial survival apparently tend to override their personal difficulties. With greater economic prosperity, such as has generally prevailed during the last thirty years, they tend to feel less commitment to keeping the family together and more capable of handling the financial stresses of divorce.

Divorce Trauma

Regardless of the causes of marital dissatisfaction or the factors that facilitate marital dissolution, *divorce is an extremely traumatic experience for many people.* They are losing a relationship to which they may have given many years of their life, their entire life pattern is being disrupted, they frequently have to leave or sell their family home, their economic standard of living often declines sharply, they have to begin coping again with the demands and loneliness of single living, and they are very likely to feel considerable guilt and loss of self-esteem over the divorce. Moreover, if they have children—which is the case in about two-thirds of all divorces—they may no longer be able to live with their children, they worry about the psychological effects of the divorce on the children, and they have to arrange such matters as child custody and visiting rights.

Many divorced people report that this experience was one of the most stressful and upsetting experiences in their lives, emotionally, psychologically, and socially. It is quite common for recently divorced people to suffer numerous kinds of mental or emotional problems, often to the point where they seek professional mental health services. The typical emotional recovery period from a divorce, especially after a lengthy marriage, is at least two to three years, and it can take much longer than that. Consequently, although ending a bad marriage may be the wise course of action in the long run, in the short run divorce can be emotionally devastating for all the family members.

SHIFTING FAMILY ROLES

Romantic fairy tales often end with the line, "And so they were married and lived happily ever after." In reality, of course, the marriage ceremony is only the beginning of the process of creating a marital relationship and a family that can continue throughout one's life. Within that setting the participants must learn to enact a wide variety of new and different roles if the marriage and family are to be viable and enduring. Several of these family roles—all of which are currently being modified—are sketched in this section.

Gender Roles

What should a woman and a man do as marriage partners? Traditional cultures are very clear about the expected division of labor within the family. The role of the husband is to provide income for the family, handle the family finances, and do maintenance work on the family dwelling (to which modern societies have added maintenance of the family car). The role of the wife is to perform all homemaking tasks (cooking, cleaning, doing the laundry, sewing, etc.), rear the children, care for family members when they are ill or have other problems, and be a companion to her husband. In addition, women in traditional societies often assist with running the family farm or business, carrying out such tasks as tending a vegetable garden, milking the cows, cleaning the shop, or waiting on customers. As long as both spouses accept these traditional gender roles and carry them out satisfactorily, the family is able to function as a viable social unit, and the spouses are likely to feel fairly satisfied with their marriage.

Many of these traditional gender role expectations have tended to persist in modern societies. Despite such social changes as separation of employment from the household, shifts in the occupational structure, rising educational levels of men and women, declining length of the work week, employment of women outside the home, and a falling birth rate, many men (and many women) still believe that the wife should be responsible for all homemaking, child rearing, and other traditional "wifely" tasks. Even when the wife is employed full-time, the average husband is not likely to do much more in the home than if she is not employed (Pleck, et al., 1980). As a consequence, married women often find themselves holding down two full-time jobs: at work during the day and at home in the evening. A typical married man can accomplish all his employment and household responsibilities in an average of 62 hours per week, but an employed woman who also handles all the homemaking and child rearing duties traditionally assigned to a wife and mother performs an average of over 80 hours of labor a week (Vanek, 1980). Needless to say, severe marital dissatisfaction and conflict can result from this situation.

Expectations concerning family gender roles are slowly changing in modern societies, however, especially among middle-class and upper-middle class people. Some men are beginning to assume at least partial responsibility for various household tasks such as cleaning, shopping, or cooking. They are also becoming more involved in helping to care for their children. Women, meanwhile, are contributing significantly to the income of over half of all families, learning to perform home maintenance jobs, handling family finances, and even doing car repairs. *Men's and women's roles in the family are gradually becoming more blended, so that traditional gender distinctions are slowly disappearing.* Nevertheless, it will undoubtedly be a long time before all traditional gender role expectations totally disappear, since the majority of married couples still believe in them to a considerable extent.

Authority Roles

It would be reasonable to assume that in traditional families each spouse would exercise authority and make decisions within his or her assigned sphere of responsibility. Authority and decision making within the family would then be relatively equally divided between the husband and wife. This is not typically the case, however. Instead, the traditional male role includes being head of the household, which gives him the legitimate right to exercise all authority and to make all major decisions for the family. He alone decides what job he will hold, whether or not his wife will work outside the home, how the family income will be spent, where they will live, how the children will be reared and disciplined, what household tasks each family member will perform, and even many of the details of housekeeping. He may decide to delegate some of these decisions—especially those concerning the home and the children—to his wife, but that is his decision to make. His wife and the children are expected to do as they are told and to defer to him on all important decisions. Commonly, the wife does not even know how much money her husband earns or how most of it is spent. She is simply given a monthly allowance—just like the children—with which to operate the household, and she is expected to keep her expenses within that amount.

This traditional pattern of male dominance can be contrasted with a totally egalitarian family. In this ideal case, both spouses share fully and equally in the exercise of all authority within the family. Neither one dominates the other, and they make all decisions jointly. In reality, of course, no family is totally egalitarian. Although both spouses may participate in making major decisions about employment, finances, housing, and child rearing, one of them will usually exert more influence than the other on any specific decision. In addition, each spouse will usually have his or her particular areas of specialization or expertise, to which the other spouse will defer on most occasions. "George really has a way with the flower garden, so he takes care of it, while I handle the monthly bills because I like to work with numbers." The crucial feature of a relatively egalitarian family is not that both spouses make all decisions jointly and equally. It is, rather, that both participate extensively in the exercise of authority, they decide together how family decisions will be made and who will do this on various topics, and each one can choose at any time to become more or less involved in any area of decision making. Moreover, these choices are made on the basis of individual preferences and mutual agreements, not cultural definitions of traditional family roles.

As a broad trend, *families in modern societies are shifting gradually from patriarchal to somewhat more egalitarian patterns of authority and decision making.* Although research findings differ considerably on the extent of this trend, a large majority of all families in the United States at the present time appear to have moved somewhat away from total patriarchy. Most families are still far from being fully egalitarian, however, and the lower the socioeconomic status of a family the less egalitarian it is likely to be (Blood and Wolfe, 1965). Women still tend to defer to their husbands on major family decisions—although they may silently resent their husbands' exercise of authority and their own acquiescence to it. In the future, the trend toward greater equality in the family will likely continue or intensify as women become better educated, seek employment and develop careers outside the home, and liberate themselves (and their husbands) from traditional beliefs about family authority and decision-making roles.

Sexual Roles

Human sexual roles have both physical and psychological dimensions. Physical sexual activity is defined in all societies as an appropriate and expected form of interaction among spouses. A marriage is usually not considered to be complete until it is consummated through sexual intercourse. Regardless of what the cultural norms hold to be proper and improper sexual behavior outside of marriage, spouses are expected to be sexually intimate.

In marriages based on traditional role expectations, however, the spouses do not enjoy equal sexual rights. In such relationships, the husband believes that he has the right to satisfy his sexual demands with his wife whenever he wishes, regardless of her desires. She is expected to participate in sexual activities whenever he wants them (except, perhaps, during her menstrual period or in the final stages of pregnancy) and at least appear to enjoy them. She is not granted this same right, however and she must subordinate her sexual desires to his wishes. In this realm—as in all other aspects of traditional marital relationships—the male exercises power and the female is submissive.

In modern societies, *sexual relationships within marriage are gradually becoming more egalitarian.* Women are coming to feel that their own sexual desires are legitimate and that they have a right to satisfy them. They are also gaining the courage to say "no" to their husbands and not feel guilty. At the same time, men are beginning to be more understanding and considerate of their wives' sexuality. Nevertheless, it is doubtful if most marriages are today fully egalitarian in the realm of sex. Men still tend to dominate sexual activity in most marriages, at least subtly, and to hold their wives responsible if there are sexual difficulties in their relationship (Gagnon, 1977). In this area, role expectations and actions change very slowly.

There is one realm of sexual activity, however, in which women in the United States have apparently achieved equality with men. In the past, the "double standard" held that extramarital sexual affairs were condoned for men but vehemently prohibited for women. Today, extramarital sexual relationships are almost as common among women as among men, with about two-fifths of both sexes reporting that they have had at least one affair outside their marriage (Thompson, 1983).

The psychological dimension of sexuality is much more complex. Traditional role expectations clearly define the meanings of masculinity and feminity. Traditionally, if a man is to be considered masculine, he must be self-confident, assertive, independent, competent, and strong, and he must not express his feelings through any display of emotionality. If a woman is to be feminine, she must be self-denying, submissive, dependent, inadequate, and weak, but she may display her feelings in overt emotionality. Although few men or women have probably ever fully achieved these "ideals," they have traditionally exerted strong influence on individuals' feelings and actions.

In modern societies, *many men and women are rejecting traditional conceptions of masculinity and feminity.* Men are slowly learning that they can sometimes be passive or dependent or emotional and still be accepted as males in their own and others' eyes. Women are learning that they can be assertive, independent, and competent without sacrificing their feminity. In other words, men and women are coming to realize that they can be more complete human beings and need not always conform to traditional definitions of masculinity and feminity. As with sexual behavior, this blending of masculine and feminine roles is occurring very slowly, but apparently steadily, especially among people of higher socioeconomic status. Nevertheless, considerable confusion presently exists among men and women about what it means to be masculine or feminine, and whether these concepts are even relevant in the modern world.

Parental Roles

Parenthood has always been an expected—and usually highly desired—part of marriage and family life. Traditionally, married women who could not or would not have children were looked upon with scorn, as being less than a complete woman. Although a small, but increasing, proportion of women are today choosing to remain childless—usually to pursue a career—the vast majority of couples still want children. Childbearing and rearing have decidedly not gone out of vogue, although many women are delaying their families until after they have completed their education and begun a career.

From a purely rational perspective, we might wonder why anyone wants to have children. Children are extremely demanding in terms of time, attention, effort, emotions, stress, and conflict. The birth of a couple's first child typically requires vastly more readjustments in their lifestyle and activities than did their marriage. These demands do not lessen when the children start school or become teenagers—they just change in nature. In addition, rearing children in modern societies can be extremely expensive—at least $100,000 per child, and much more if they go to college. Clearly, couples do not have children for rational

reasons. They want and have offspring because bearing and rearing children is one of life's deepest and most emotionally satisfying experiences, regardless of how difficult that process may be or how much it costs. Having children is sometimes said to be life's biggest gamble, but—fortunately for the human race—most people do it because they want the experience, without any thought of costs or demands.

Nevertheless, couples are now becoming more rational about the number of children they bear, thanks largely to modern contraception. A hundred years ago, married women in the United States had an average of more than five living children. By the 1930s, this figure had dropped to about three children, but during the post-World War II Baby Boom it rose again to almost 3.5 children. Since 1960—when the Pill first came on the market—the number of children per family has declined steadily, and it is currently about 2.1. *Most young women today say that they want—and expect—to have just two children,* while about ten percent want only one child and another ten percent want no children. This trend is one of several factors that are contributing to the continually declining size of households.

It is becoming increasingly common today for *fathers and mothers to believe that the responsibilities and tasks of child rearing should be shared equally.* This is particularly true in regard to teaching children values, developing their mental abilities, and meeting their emotional needs. In practice, however, the daily demands of caring for children still fall more heavily on mothers than fathers, regardless of the childrens' ages or whether or not the mother is employed. Providing economic support for the children is the only responsibility that is typically seen as primarily the father's (Gilbert, et al., 1981).

In the contemporary United States, over 60 percent of all mothers with children at home are employed, either part-time or full-time. Many critics have claimed that having a working mother is emotionally harmful for children, especially during their early years. There is no research evidence to support this contention, however. Children of employed mothers do not appear to have any more emotional or behavioral problems than do children whose mothers are not employed (Clarke-Stewart, 1977). The only exception to this generalization occurs when the father is unemployed or very poorly paid, so that the family experiences psychological and financial stresses. *The crucial factor in child rearing is the quality of the relationships between the parents and with their children*—not the amount of time either parent spends with the children. Consequently, a woman who wants a career but is intensely frustrated because she spends all her time at home caring for children may be a less adequate mother than a working woman who is satisfied with her life and is able to give warmth and emotional nurturing to her children when she is with them.

Divorce obviously creates major disruptions in parental roles. The parent with whom the children live must be both mother and father to them most of the time, so that the demands of parenting are doubled. Since this is usually the mother, and since her income level is often drastically reduced after the divorce, she is also likely to experience serious financial stresses that make the double parenting role even more difficult. The other parent (usually the father) loses daily contact with the children and can no longer play an active parenting role. Despite weekend or other periodic visits with the children, he is likely to feel that his relationship with them has become severely weakened and tenuous.

Parenting problems also continue if the parent with whom the children live remarries. This is especially likely if his or her new spouse also has children from a former marriage, so that they create a "blended family." Parenting can be difficult enough with one's own children. When one also has to act as a stepparent to additional children, the demands can become overwhelming. The most frequent source of conflict among remarried couples with children is child rearing practices with stepchildren (Duberman, 1975). In addition, the couple must also cope with the parenting wishes and demands of one or two ex-spouses. Moreover, if the new couple have children of their own, the situation becomes even more complicated. In short, *divorce with children and subsequent remarriage and stepparenting often make the parental role one of life's most demanding experiences.*

One additional aspect of parenting roles has aroused great concern in recent years. In the United States today, over a million parents (or sets of parents) either seriously neglect their children or assault them physically or sexually. About one-fifth—or 200,000—of these child victims die each year from the abuse they receive from their parent or parents (National Institute of Mental Health, 1974:6). Child neglect and assault are more common among families with relatively low socioeconomic status, but they occur at all status levels. Numerous factors undoubtedly contribute to this problem, including poverty, unemployment, parental conflicts, and alcohol and drug abuse. Moreover, many parents who abuse their children were themselves victims of abuse as children, so that they learned this pattern of behavior early in life. Whatever the causes, it is clear that parents who abuse their children are acting out their own personal or interpersonal problems upon their children, who become helpless victims of their parents' immaturity, lack of self-control, or mental illness.

Child Roles

Traditional family patterns also contained well-defined role expectations for children. They were to be totally subservient to their parents, especially their father, and do exactly what they were told as long as they lived in their parents' home. They were typically given a set of tasks to perform on a regular basis—totally different for boys and girls—and were punished if they failed to carry out those responsibilities. They had no say in the assignment of these tasks or in any other family decisions. Their play activities and interaction with friends were also strictly controlled by the parents. In adolescence, boys might be given some freedom to work for another farmer in the community or to become an apprentice to a local craftsman—or possibly to continue in school—as well as to interact with friends without supervision. Whatever money they earned, however, belonged to their father as long as he was supporting them. Adolescent girls, meanwhile, were strictly controlled by their parents and allowed very little personal freedom. Their education often ended with elementary school, since girls were thought to have no need of "book learning," and after that they were usually kept busy helping with housework and caring for younger siblings. The parents decided if and when a daughter might begin seeing a young man of whom they approved, and those meetings were commonly chaperoned. When a young woman was ready to marry, her father had to give his consent, from which comes the tradition of the father "giving away" his daughter to a husband who assumes the role of providing for and supervising her.

Vestiges of those traditional childhood roles still prevail in some families in contemporary societies, in that female children are frequently more protected and controlled than male children. On the whole, however, *children's family roles have been changing even more drastically than those of adults.* In most families today—although more frequently in higher-status homes—*the emphasis has shifted from controlling children to nurturing, supporting, and encouraging them to develop their own autonomous lives.* They are encouraged to remain in school and do as well as they can there, to make friends of their own and to particpate in peer-group activities, to take part in family discussions and decision making, to earn their own money through such jobs as delivering newspapers or babysitting, and to accept responsibility for directing their own lives. In adolescence, moreover, boys and girls are today given almost complete freedom to date whomever they wish and eventually to decide for themselves whom they will marry. Although most parents atempt to provide standards and guidelines for their children in these various activities, the emphasis is on the children

learning to exercise internal self-control over their own actions rather than the parents exercising external control over them.

At the same time, however, *young people are now remaining financially dependent on their parents to a later age than ever before.* A century ago, most youths were providing for themselves and/or were married by age 18. Today, most youths remain in school until that age and hence are almost entirely dependent on their parents financially. After that, over 40 percent of all young people in the United States go on to college and continue their financial dependency for another one to four years (although they may provide part of their own support), and another large proportion of people in this age range continues to live at home and are at least partially supported by their parents. Consequently, although children and youths are being given considerable independence in many realms of life at relatively early ages, in the crucial sphere of financial support most of them are remaining dependent on their parents until they are into their 20s. This condition creates a potential for considerable stress and conflict between parents and children.

Many forms of deviant behavior are becoming increasingly prevalent among youths in modern societies, including juvenile delinquency, vandalism, alcohol and drug abuse, and teenage pregnancy. Critics of contemporary family life and parenting practices frequently blame these problems on parental permissiveness and call for a return to stricter controls by parents over their children. In contrast, professionals working in the areas of child development and family life generally contend that these problems result primarily from failure by parents to give their children adequate socialization, emotional support, and guidance. Other social scientists, meanwhile, point to conditions in the larger community that contribute to problems among youth, such as inadequate recreational and other programs for young people, insufficient opportunities for part-time jobs, poor housing and neighborhood conditions, schools that neither interest nor challenge youths, and lack of neighborhood and community social cohesion.

All these parental and community factors undoubtedly contribute to the currently soaring rates of problems among young people, although we do not know precisely how important each factor may be. Moreover, there is the additional consideration that young people are today growing up in a world that is radically different from that of any previous generation. Technological and social changes are occurring more rapidly and extensively than ever before, the possibility of nuclear devastation cannot be ignored, and the ecological future of our entire industrial civilization and its affluent standard of living can no longer be taken for granted. Under these conditions, it is perhaps not surprising that the process of becoming a psychologically mature and socially responsible adult is an extremely demanding challenge for many young people today.

EMERGING FAMILY TRENDS

Family forms, structures, functions, and roles are undergoing extensive modification in contemporary industrial/urban societies. As a consequence of all these changes, several new trends in marriage and family living have emerged in recent years.

Remaining Single

Adults may be single at three different times during their lives: before they marry for the first time, after a divorce or death of one's spouse in midlife, and in old age after the death of the spouse. All three types of single living have been increasing dramatically in recent years. The number of young singles has risen because many people are entering their first marriage at somewhat older ages today; the number of middle-aged singles has increased sharply because of the divorce rate; and the number of older singles (primarily women) has expanded somewhat because of their increased longevity relative to men. As a result of all three of these trends, many observers have predicted that living alone will become a very common lifestyle in the future.

That prediction is open to considerable doubt, however. As we have already seen, the marriage rate has also been rising steadily since 1960. Over 95 percent of all people in the United States marry at least once, and although nearly 40 percent of all marriages now end in divorce, about 75 percent of all divorced people eventually remarry. Of those who do remarry, nearly half go through a second divorce, but a large proportion of them remarry again. In short, relatively few people choose to remain single throughout their entire lifetime. (Even gay and lesbian people who reject heterosexual marriage often form long-term paired relationships.) *Single living is becoming increasingly common at all stages of life but only for relatively short periods of time,* and it does not appear to be replacing marriage.

Single-parent families are a variation on single living that has also become much more common recently. The two causes of this trend are the rising divorce rate (since about two-thirds of all divorces involve children) and the current desire of many unwed mothers to keep their children (about nine-tenths of them do this today, compared to only about one-third in 1960). As mentioned previously, single parents often experience severe financial and psychological difficulties. Fortunately, this is usually only a temporary condition, since a large majority of single parents eventually marry or remarry (Glick, 1979).

Cohabitation

This trend of couples living together without marriage has already been discussed as a new development of the last twenty years, although it still accounts for only slightly less than three percent of all households. Cohabitation is particularly common among college students who want a stable bonded relationship but are not yet in a position to marry. About one-fourth of all undergraduates have done this at least temporarily, and a large majority of them say they would be willing to do so if they found a suitable partner. The other category of people who are increasingly trying cohabitation are recently divorced persons who want companionship but are not yet ready to recommit themselves to marriage.

Although living together is likely to become even more common in the future, it is rarely a permanent substitute for marriage. Most couples who cohabit for a period of time either break up or go on to marry within a few years. This practice provides companionship and emotional and sexual intimacy during periods when marriage is not feasible, as well as a useful form of trial marriage for couples who have not yet decided to marry. It does not, however, provide the depth and security of interpersonal commitment that comes with marriage. In addition, it can also carry legal liabilities, since courts in several states have recently ruled that if the arrangement ends, one partner can sue the other for all shared property and even for financial support (or "palimony"). In short, most cohabiting couples are eventually likely to break up or marry rather than maintain a permanent living-together arrangement.

Serial Monogamy

Looking at current rates of marriages, divorces, second marriages, second divorces, third marriages, and so on, many observers of contemporary family life have concluded that we are today practicing serial monogamy. In other words, marriages are monogamous, but many people have more than one marriage and some people have a whole series of them. Most people are committed to marriage, but not necessarily "till death do us part." Instead, they remain in their current marriage only as long as it is satisfying to them, at which point they leave that partner and look for another one. The argument commonly given to justify this practice is that because individuals and social conditions are changing so rapidly in modern societies, and because people are living longer, it is naïve to expect two people to remain fully compati-

ble with each other over a span of fifty or sixty years of adult life. A couple in their mid-forties are not the same people who married in their mid-twenties, nor are the social conditions with which they must cope still the same. Twenty years later, when they are in their sixties, they and society will have changed even further. So, when a marriage no longer works adequately, the best thing to do is end it and start a new one.

There is a fair amount of validity in this description of modern marriage as serial monogamy, and we can probably expect it to continue or expand in the future. At the same time, we should not lose sight of the fact that at least sixty percent of all people remain married to the same spouse throughout their entire life, and that over half of those who divorce and remarry continue that second marriage for the rest of their life. In short, we should not overly exaggerate the extent of serial monogamy in modern societies.

Open Marriage

In the 1970s, many couples became quite enthusiastic about the possibility of "opening" their marriage to new kinds of personal and interpersonal experiences. As described by O'Neil and O'Neil (1972:74) in their widely read book on this topic, a "closed" marriage is characterized by ownership of one's mate, denial of one's self-identity, playing the "couples game" in all activities, rigid expectations for marital roles, absolute sexual fidelity, and total exclusivity of the spouses from all other emotional relationships. In contrast, an ideal "open marriage" would be marked by minimal dependence of the spouses upon one another, a commitment to individual freedom and personal growth, flexible expectations for marital roles, mutual trust between spouses, and expansion of their marriage through various kinds of relationships with others. As countless couples attempted to open their marriages in these directions, they typically sought to redefine their marital and parental roles, engage in more activities such as work or community organizations or recreation as separate individuals, develop close friend-ships with people of the opposite sex, and sometimes engage in extramarital sexual re-lationships.

From a broad perspective, the marital changes advocated by proponents of open marriage are merely a recognition and legiti-mization of the trends in marriage and fam-ily living that are already widespread in con-temporary societies. In other words, *the basic concept of open marriage merely expresses the fun-damental shift from traditional to more egalitar-ian marriage and family life*. From a narrower perspective, meanwhile, the idea of open marriage encourages men and women to es-tablish cross-sex friendships, love, and sex-ual liaisons outside of their marriage. In practice, such relationships often create se-vere stresses for marriages, and not infre-quently lead to divorce. Open marriage is no longer so widely discussed today, partly be-cause its broader implications for more egal-itarian marriages are now fairly widely ac-cepted, and partly because its narrower focus on personal relationships outside of marriage were too difficult for many people to handle. The extent to which people will seek to make their marriages more open in either the broad or narrow sense remains to be seen.

Group Marriage

In the nineteenth century, several uto-pian communities were established in the United States in which—at least theoret-ically—all the men were married to all the women and there were no pair bondings. All the adults were also considered to be parents of all children in the community. There were no sociological studies of any of those com-munities, so that we do not know how their members really related to one another, but it is highly doubtful if everyone felt equally close to everyone else. A century later, in the 1960s, quite a number of communes were created as part of the counterculture move-ment of that time, many of which rejected the idea of monogamous marriage. We do have detailed accounts of several of them,

---

> **EMERGING FAMILY TRENDS**
> 1. Remaining single.
> 2. Cohabitation.
> 3. Serial monogamy.
> 4. Open marriage.
> 5. Group marriage.

---

describing the attempts of these young peo-ple to relate to one another in new ways. For a variety of reasons, almost all of those com-munes failed after a few months or at most a few years, often as a result of interpersonal conflicts.

A group marriage does not have to be part of a larger communal living arrange-ment, however. In contemporary terms, *a group marriage consists of three or more adults who consider themselves to be a single marital unit*. During the 1960s and 1970s, several hun-dred group marriages were established that were known to sociologists, and the total number may have been much larger. Most of them consisted of three to six people. Ideally, a group marriage provides its partic-ipants with much richer, more diverse, and more satisfying emotional and sexual rela-tionships than are possible in a monogamous two-person marriage (Constantine and Constantine, 1974). In practice, virtually all known group marriages have failed rather quickly. Although emotional and sexual jeal-ously and conflicts contributed to many of those failures, the most critical problems in most cases arose from interpersonal conflicts concerning personality and value differ-ences, disputes over finances or housework, or controversies over child rearing practices. At the present time, consequently, there is no indication that group marriage will even-tually replace monogamy.

SUMMARY

Kinship ties are culturally defined linkages based on common ancestry, marriage, birth, or adoption. Cultures severely restrict the categories of people who are defined as kin, and in practice people frequently distinguish between immediate kin and more distant kin. New kinship ties are continually being created through marriages and births, but the extensive changes that are presently occurring in marriage and family practices often create considerable confusion concerning kinship lines. Nevertheless, kinship ties are qualitatively different from friendships, since they always imply some amount of social responsibility to one's kin.

Although family forms have differed widely throughout history, in broad terms families are characterized by four features. First, family members are linked by kinship bonds, the most important of which is marriage. Monogamous marriage involving two people of the opposite sex is by far the most common form, but many societies have allowed some men to have more than one wife. Single-parent families are becoming increasingly common. In modern societies, the nuclear family is often said to have replaced the traditional extended family, although extended kinship ties are still vitally important for many people. Second, the family is a social unit that lives together in a common residence, at least part of the time, but many variations on this pattern can be observed today. Third, the family is an economic unit that shares its financial resources among its members according to their needs. Fourth, the members of a family cooperate in a variety of ways to maintain it as a viable unit, but these patterns of cooperation are highly influenced by the family's authority structure and modes of decision making.

In all societies, families perform a number of universal functions for their members and the larger society. These include regulating sexual activity, replacing societal members, rearing and socializing children, satisfying physical needs, providing emotional intimacy, exercising social control, and performing social placement.

In preindustrial societies, the household is normally the principal economic production unit of society. In modern societies, this function has largely moved out of the household, so that most families are now only consumption units. Contemporary families have also lost many other traditional functions to specialized organizations in the community, they often no longer feel part of a closely knit community, they may be highly mobile geographically, their members spend much of their time in activities outside the family, and children have become an economic liability. However, the family is not disappearing in modern societies; it is merely changing its functions and structure in response to the fundamental trends of industrialization and urbanization.

At the present time, the rate of household formation in the United States is much greater than the rate of population growth, primarily because of the growing number of single-family households and cohabiting couples. Meanwhile, the average size of the American household has declined significantly.

In preindustrial societies, marriage is a serious business arrangement for the families and the individuals involved, and love is not a serious consideration in these arrangements. Only recently has romantic love been considered the appropriate basis for marriage, and many couples still marry for other reasons. Most people tend to marry someone who is fairly similar in terms of age, race, education, social class and other characteristics. The process of creating a marriage bond typically involves the stages of breaking away from the parental home, meeting new people, dating, living together, engagement, and a public marriage ceremony.

Most people in contemporary societies apparently want to be married, and the marriage rate has been rising recently. However, people are now remaining single a bit longer before marrying for the first time. The divorce rate has risen very sharply in recent years, but a large proportion of all divorced people remarry—especially if they are a man or a childless woman. Women are much more likely than men to experience widowhood for several years at the end of their lives.

Marital relationships break down for many reasons, including unwise marital choices by young people, dissimilarities in social backgrounds, differences that develop between the spouses over time, loss of feelings of romantic love, sexual incompatibility or unfaithfulness, demands of child rearing, excessive emotional dependency, and husbands' objections to their wives working. Whether a dissatisfied couple continues to live together or seeks a divorce depends on several other factors, such as legal requirements for divorce, availability of employment for women, public opinion regarding divorce, increasing lifespans, and economic conditions in the society. In most cases, divorce is an extremely traumatic emotional experience.

The roles that people play within the family have shifted markedly in recent years. Although many traditional expectations concerning proper gender roles for men and women still persist, these roles are slowly becoming blended in large numbers of families. Traditional patriarchal roles based on male dominance are gradually giving way to somewhat more egalitarian patterns of authority and decision making, although few families are fully egalitarian. Male dominance in marital sexual roles is also declining, and traditional concepts of masculinity and feminity are slowly being discarded by many men and women.

Most couples want and do have children, despite the demands of parental roles, but the number of children they have is declining and fathers are starting to share more in child rearing. Employment of mothers is not harmful for children, but unemployment of the father can be. Divorce creates major disruptions in parental roles, especially if one or both parents remarry. Child neglect and abuse are rather widespread in contemporary societies. Children's family roles have been changing quite drastically in modern societies, shifting from parental obedience to personal development and autonomy. However, young people are now remaining financially dependent on their parents to a later age than ever before. Many forms of deviant behavior are becoming increasingly prevalent among youth in modern societies, probably as a result of numerous changes occurring in family life and the larger society.

Single living is becoming increasingly common at all stages of life, although this is only a temporary state for most people. A considerable number of young and recently divorced people are cohabiting, but within a few years most of these couples either break up or marry. Serial monogamy is fairly widespread today, but the majority of people still marry only once, and few marry more than twice. In a broad sense, the idea of open marriage is a recognition of the shift that has been occurring from traditional to more egalitarian marriage patterns. Group marriages have been tried by some people in recent years, but virtually all of these arrangements have failed very quickly.

CHAPTER
19
SOCIOCULTURAL INSTITUTIONS

Why are education and schools so critical in modern societies, and what factors presently limit their effectiveness?

In what ways does education perpetuate socioeconomic and racial/ethnic inequality in modern societies?

What is religion, and what functions do religion and religious organizations perform in contemporary societies?

What trends are currently occurring in religious participation in the United States?

How do legal systems serve modern societies, and who benefits from them?

EDUCATION AND SCHOOLS

The term "sociocultural institutions" refers to those major subsystems of society that are primarily oriented toward the shared culture of that society. Their basic concerns are to preserve, perpetuate, expand, and/or change the societal culture or subcultures within it. Three critical sociocultural institutions in modern societies are education, religion, and the law, which are the concerns of this chapter.

Education can be informal and interpersonal, such as when a father teaches his young child to catch a ball. It can also be quite formal and organized, as in a university lecture. Needless to say, there are countless gradations between these extremes, but *when sociologists examine education as a social institution, they are primarily concerned with the transmission of knowledge, skills, beliefs, and values in organized classes within schools.* In modern societies, formal education is the principal sociocultural institution for pre-

serving and perpetuating the cultural heritage, as well as much of their social structure. Education is also an important agent of socialization—together with the family—for teaching individuals how to function as members of society. Only during the last two hundred years has formal education performed these functions, however.

Historical Background

In agrarian societies of the past, most education was conducted in a rather informal manner. Children of farm families learned most of the practical skills they needed for farming and housekeeping from their parents, while religious organizations attempted to instill basic beliefs and values in young people. If a boy wanted to become a skilled artisan, he was apprenticed to a carpenter or blacksmith or baker and learned his trade by working beside his master. Even basic reading and writing were considered unnecessary luxuries that most people did not need, and all further education was reserved for the sons of the nobility, to be acquired from private tutors or clergy. With few exceptions, schools as separate institutions did not exist in such societies.

One consequence of the growth of commercial trade in the seventeenth and eighteenth centuries, however, was the creation of a considerable number of schools throughout Western Europe. Most of these schools were intended not for sons of elites but for those of merchants and businessmen. To succeed in business, merchants had to be literate, know how to keep records, and be familiar with law and politics. Although many of these schools were private, *by the middle of the seventeenth century, England had begun to establish free public schools,* which provided the model for public education in the United States.

Early settlers in the New World—who were generally better educated than the average Europeans of that time—carried with them a deep faith in the benefits of education. As early as 1647, the Massachusetts Bay Colony passed a law requiring every town to establish a school system and compelling all children to attend school. The primary purpose of this schooling was not to teach practical knowledge and skills, but to preserve the cultural heritage the settlers brought with them and to teach the moral virtues that were thought necessary to preserve civilization in the wilderness.

During the eighteenth and nineteenth centuries, public schooling gradually expanded throughout the United States. Although it was generally limited to elementary education and was rarely compulsory, it was strongly supported by local communities, by the developing labor movement, and by immigrant families as a vital way of improving their lot in life. Even on the expanding frontier, pioneer families were eager to build a schoolhouse—if only a one-room log cabin—and bring in a teacher. Members of the growing urban merchant and industrial classes were also anxious that their children be educated, although they frequently sent their sons to private or church-sponsored schools.

By 1850, every state that was then in the Union had provided for free, tax-supported elementary schools. The major impetus for expanding public education came after the Civil War, however, as the nation began to industrialize rapidly and demand a more educated citizenry. By 1900, there were several thousand public high schools (compared to almost none in 1850), as well as normal schools for training teachers, land-grant colleges to teach agriculture and mechanics to the sons of farmers, adult education programs to assist immigrants in becoming assimilated to their new homeland, liberal arts college for aspiring professionals, and universities offering graduate programs. Since then, the educational system in this country has continued to grow at a phenomenal rate.

The expansion of formal education in the United States during the last hundred years is best illustrated by the proportion of persons 25 years or older who were high school graduates. In 1870, just two percent of the adult population had completed that much education, and in 1900 high school graduates were still merely six percent of the population. As late as 1950, that rate had only risen to 34 percent, but in 1985 it was 76 percent (U.S. Bureau of the Census, 1987:121). In that year, over 58 million people in this country—approximately 24 percent of the total population—were enrolled in some kind of school, and the country was spending over $240 billion a year on education. In terms of the total number of people involved—students, teachers, administrators, and other staff—education is now the largest organized activity in the United States.

The development of formal educational systems has been an integral part of the general process of societal modernization. As industrialization, nationalization, urbanization, and bureaucratization have transformed social life in contemporary societies, demands for education have steadily increased. Industrial workers have to know how to operate and repair complex machinery. Citizens in democratic nations are expected to be familiar with numerous public issues and to vote wisely for public officials. Urban residents are called upon to deal competently with all kinds of collective problems. And office workers must be capable of handling written directives, records, and data sets. *The growth and development of formal schooling in modern societies can therefore be seen as a direct response to demands from the larger society for a more educated population.*

United States Schools

In three major ways, elementary and secondary schools in the contemporary United States are very similar to those in most other modern societies. In three other important ways, however, education in this country differs significantly from almost all other countries (except Canada). The following paragraphs deal first with the three similarities, and then with the three differences.

Similarity: Secularization. One of the basic purposes of formal education is to transmit cultural values to new generations. Traditionally, those values have always included the basic religious beliefs prevailing in a society. However, *during the twentieth century there has been a steady trend within most industrial societies to secularize public education.* The public schools provide an education that is oriented toward the humanities and the sciences (natural and social), not toward religious beliefs and values. This trend still arouses considerable controversy in the United States and other countries, as seen in the current struggle over school prayers. Nevertheless, the content of contemporary public education is today almost entirely secular in nature.

Similarity: Bureaucratization. Schools and school systems in all modern societies are highly formal and relatively complex organizations. *A bureaucratic organizational structure is as prevalent in education as in most other parts of social life.* Authority is hierarchi-

cal, with students at the bottom; standardized procedures and rules cover most situations, both within and outside the classroom; and there is built-in resistance to organization change. Consequently, some of the most important lessons that children must learn if they are to be successful in school include obeying their teachers, complying with established rules and regulations, following a standardized time schedule, and not challenging the existing system. A growing number of educators, however, question the effects of these lessons on the development of students' capabilities for original, innovative, and creative thinking.

Similarity: Professionalization. Not long ago, teaching was looked upon as an occupation for unmarried women who did not have children of their own to raise, and a few years of secondary school were considered adequate preparation for teaching. During this century, however, *teaching has become increasingly professionalized in all industrial societies.* This trend is most evident in the steadily rising educational requirements for teachers, so that new teachers in all school systems throughout the United States must now have at least a B.A. degree and have completed a teacher-training program. Quite recently, a national panel of professional educators proposed that in the future all teachers should have a Master's Degree. Other important aspects of the professionalization of teaching have been greater emphasis on improving the process and techniques of teaching; expanding the curriculum far beyond the basic "three R" skills of reading, writing, and arithmetic; and creating many specialized educational roles such as student counseling, teaching the handicapped, and training in vocational skills.

Difference: Mass Education. Since its founding, the United States has been strongly committed to providing free public education for everyone. At first, this commonly meant no more than three or four years of basic literacy training, and as recently as the end of the nineteenth century an eighth-grade education was considered quite adequate for most people. Moreover, the country was slow to put its commitment to public education into practice, so that free public schools were not available to everyone until the 1870s. Two fundamental transformations have occurred in the U.S. secondary schools during the twentieth century, however (Trow, 1961). At the turn of the century, high schools were intended almost entirely for the children of relatively high-status, affluent families. Gradually, secondary education was redefined as a right and then as a requirement for all adolescents, as it became evident that a high school education was necessary for a person to participate adequately in this society. The second transformation occurred after World War II, when secondary education was again redefined for nearly half of all students as preparation for college, rather than being the termination of one's formal education.

Other industrial societies have been gradually adopting the American ideal of mass education as a right of all citizens, but in most cases at a considerably slower pace than has occurred in this country. The equivalent of nine or ten years of U.S. schooling is still considered adequate in most European and other developed societies, while secondary education (which commonly extends through the equivalent of at least one year of college in the United States) is is viewed primarily as preparation for university-bound students.

Difference: Community Control. In most other industrial countries, the public schools are organized on a national basis under a Ministry of Education, with administrative control, curriculum design, and financial support coming largely or entirely from the national government. In contrast, *all school systems in the United States are locally controlled, politically autonomous units*. Each school system is governed by an elected school board that operates independently from all other political bodies. The federal and state governments provide on the average about half the funding for local school systems, establish operating standards and guidelines for them, and impose some requirements (such as minimal graduation criteria or racial integration) upon them. But ultimately the local community—acting through its elected school board—controls its own public elementary and secondary schools.

This practice of community control over the schools results in benefits and problems for education. The benefits derive largely from the fact that citizens can exercise direct influence on the administration, curriculum, educational quality, and other activities of the schools that their children attend. The problems arise from the fact that schools differ widely in quality among communities, and even between neighborhoods within the same community. A principal factor underlying these differences is that there are gross disparities among states and communities in the amount of expenditures per student for education. In 1986, the average for the United States was almost $3,500 per student for primary and secondary education. However, 13 states spent less than $3,000 per student, while 14 states spent more than $4,000 per pupil (U.S. Bureau of the Census, 1987:130). Differences among school districts are even greater, varying from less than $500 to more than $15,000 per student.

Difference: Pragmatism. *Americans have long held a pragmatic view of education, believing that it should have immediate relevance to people's lives.* During the 40 years from 1880 to 1920, when massive waves of immigrants were coming to this country, one of the primary requirements of the public schools was to Americanize the children of these new residents. This was followed by an emphasis on vocational education for working-class children, so that schools began offering courses in such skills as auto repair, woodworking, sewing, and typing. More recently, Americans have expected their schools to deal with such social problems as poverty, racial discrimination, and drug abuse.

The belief that education alone—apart from any other changes in society—can

> ## CHARACTERISTICS OF UNITED STATES SCHOOLS
>
> 1. Secularized curriculum.
> 2. Bureaucratized organizations.
> 3. Professionalization of teaching.
> 4. Mass education.
> 5. Community control of schools.
> 6. Pragmatic goals.

solve all kinds of social ills is distintively American. Most other industrial countries continue to hold a more academic view of education, although in many of these societies the schools are becoming increasingly pragmatic as vocational training and sociopolitical concerns enter the curriculum.

Functions of Schools

As a sociocultural institution in modern societies, schools at all levels perform a variety of functions for students and the larger society. Many of these functions are manifest, or intended and recognized, while others are latent, or not fully intended and/or recognized. The following paragraphs sketch the most important of these functions of schools.

Manifest Function: Promoting Personal Development. The fundamental purpose of schooling is to educate students in many different ways. They are taught basic reading, computational, analytical, and other academic skills. They are expected to absorb massive amounts of information about numerous substantive areas, from biology to history to sociology. More subtle—but perhaps more crucial—are the effects of education in *shaping personalities, teaching social skills, creating broader and more sophisticated perspectives on life, and developing intellectual abilities of critical and innovative thought.* In general, the more education one acquires, the more likely one is to think analytically about issues, understand diverse points of view, and be able to make informed judgments and decisions.

Manifest Function: Transmitting the Cultural Heritage. To participate effectively in one's community and society, a person must be familiar with its cultural heritage, belief systems, basic values, prevailing norms, and current rules and customs. This process of transmitting the dominant culture and specific subcultures from one generation to the next occurs in many settings—through one's family, informal interaction with friends, one's church or synogogue, other organizations to which one belongs, and the mass media—as well as in school. Indeed, apart from some history and literature courses, schools do not explicitly describe any of the subjects in their curriculum as "cultural transmission." In a broad sense, however, *everything the schools teach is part of the cultural heritage of that society, and much instruction reflects prevailing cultural beliefs, values, and norms.* This is quite obvious in a civics course that emphasizes the virtues of democracy and the evils of dictatorships. But even in a supposedly objective math class, students are taught not to cheat and to persevere on a problem until it is solved. As observed by Durkheim (1961) at the turn of the century, schools in modern societies have largely replaced religion as transmitters of moral values and thus play a crucial role in maintaining the normative cohesion of society.

Manifest Function: Preparing for Employment. In a broad sense, much of what one learns in school—from the primary grades through college and graduate school—is intended to prepare one for adult employment. *In addition to academic skills and abilities, schools teach numerous employment-oriented lessons.* These include how to compete or cooperate with others, how to carry out an assigned task, how to follow rules and regulations, and how to observe a time schedule. Beyond the primary grades, the schools also provide job training in all kinds of manual trades, technical skills, managerial and administrative activities, and the professions. Moreover, as students progress through school they are continually tested for various aptitudes, channeled toward some academic and vocational areas and away from others, encouraged to continue their education or to leave school and seek employment, and taught to view themselves as potential manual workers or white-collar employees or professionals. Finally, as students complete various academic or vocational programs, the schools certify them as prepared for particular kinds of employment. In today's "credential society," such certification—whether it be a high school diploma, a certificate of technical training, a bachelor's degree, or a Ph.D.—is increasingly a necessity for employment. Employers specify minimal educational requirements for most jobs, and they often hire candidates with the most education. The state also requires licensing based on education and/or vocational training for many kinds of jobs from cutting hair to practicing law.

Manifest Function: Facilitating Social Mobility. As we saw in Chapter 16, *formal education is by far the most effective route for achieving upward social mobility.* The more education one completes, the more likely one is to attain a high-status job and a comfortable income later in life. Without a secondary education it is extremely difficult in today's society to obtain any but the most menial kinds of jobs at low wages. The more desirable and prestigious jobs that provide comfortable incomes generally require at least some training or education beyond high school, if not a bachelor's or even a graduate degree. Consequently, ambitious young people are remaining in school for longer and longer periods. This emphasis on credentialism can have two harmful consequences for the process of education, however. First, it often leads students to place more value on getting a degree than obtaining a meaningful education. Second, it is steadily producing an oversupply of persons with college and graduate degrees, far above what can often be absorbed by the labor market.

Manifest Function: Encouraging Innovation and Change. Although the principal concern of all education is to preserve and perpetuate knowledge, we also look to the schools to *create new knowledge and solve all kinds of technical and social problems.* At the individual level, this is accomplished by giving students the information and intellectual training needed to understand current issues and make decisions in an informed manner. Particularly crucial in this endeavor is teaching students to be skeptical of received wisdom from the past or from established authorities, and helping them to develop the ability to think analytically and creatively about conditions and problems. At the organizational level, this innovative function is performed primarily in the major research universities. Faculty members in all disciplines—from art to zoology—are expected to conduct research or other scholarly work and to publish the results, as well as to teach. A great deal of research is also carried out in other settings—government agencies, industrial labs, and independent research institutes—but most basic research and scholarly work is still done in universities. Moreover, universities are increasingly being called upon today to address applied technical and social problems.

Latent Function: Teaching Social Control. Although schools may proclaim that they are teaching students to be independent and creative thinkers, the real message they frequently convey is, "If you want to get ahead in school and life, follow the rules and don't try to rock the boat." Schools are formal organizations with all kinds of established rules and regulations, and after a few years of primary school most students learn that they are rewarded if they are on time, have done their homework, don't talk with one another in class, turn in assignments when due, and accept whatever the teacher says without question. Failure to observe these established guidelines frequently results in some kind of punishment, from a scolding to a failing grade. All organizations must have some rules and regulations to control the actions of their members if they are to operate effectively. Hence the real problem does not lie in the existence or enforcement of these standards for action. *The fundamental problem, rather, lies in the fact that in most schools at all levels the students have no voice in establishing the guidelines that they are expected to observe* (Ewens, 1984). In political terms, they are treated as powerless subjects rather than as enfranchised citizens within their school.

Latent Function: Providing Custodial Care. Although we don't like to think of schools as "baby sitters," this function is quite evident today. *With two-thirds of all mothers of school-age children employed, having their children cared for during the day is vitally important.* The principal problem here, in regard to younger children, is that they usually come home in the afternoon two or three hours before their parents. In this situation, "latchkey" children are frequently left unsupervised—except perhaps by older siblings—which sometimes results in serious behavioral difficulties. In the Scandinavian countries, all communities provide an after-school care center where children can go until their parents finish work, but such facilities are rare in the United States. With older adolescents and young adults, this custodial function of the schools serves to keep them out of the labor market. If so many young people between 16 and 22 were not in school, many of them would be flooding the labor market and greatly increasing the unemployment rate.

Latent Function: Teaching Competitiveness. Organized social life basically involves cooperating with others to achieve common goals. Almost all schools in modern societies operate on the principal of competition rather than cooperation, however. *At a very early age, students are taught to compete with one another* for the teacher's attention, good grades, positions in the starting lineups of athletic teams, peer popularity, academic honors, and other rewards. Very rarely are they given collective projects—either in the classroom or in extracurricular activities—in

which they must work together in a cooperative manner to attain a collective goal. In the classroom, competition for good grades is often so fierce—especially in college—that many students deliberately look for "soft courses" and easy instructors, regardless of whether or not they will learn much in those classes. Considering the pervasiveness of competitive training throughout people's school careers, it is not surprising that societies such as the United States place overriding emphasis on competition and individual achievement on the job and in many other realms of social life.

Latent Function: Creating Youth Subcultures. In preindustrial societies, by the time most children reach adolescence they are being assimilated into the adult society and learning adult roles. For boys, this involves learning a trade or other occupation, while for girls this means learning to run the household and care for younger siblings. In modern societies, however, we do not expect young people to begin assuming adult roles until they are in their late teens or early twenties. Instead, throughout adolescence they are isolated in schools with their age peers where they have little contact with adults other than teachers and are not expected to perform any adult roles. As a consequence, *students tend to create their own youth subcultures with distinctive values, norms, and role expectations.* Youth subcultures are not necessarily detrimental—unless they stress deviant activities of one kind or another—

FUNCTIONS PERFORMED BY SCHOOLS

1. Promoting personal development.
2. Transmitting the cultural heritage.
3. Preparing people for employment.
4. Facilitating social mobility.
5. Encouraging innovation and change.
6. Teaching social control.
7. Providing custodial care.
8. Teaching competitiveness.
9. Creating youth subcultures.

but they do little to prepare young people for adult life.

Quality of Public Education

During the 1980s, large numbers of educators and citizens expressed concern about the quality of education in American public schools. Average scores of high school seniors on the Scholastic Aptitude Test declined steadily throughout the 1970s, and although these scores stabilized during the 1980s they are still significantly lower than during the 1950s and 1960s. Moreover, the average scores of American students are lower than those in many other industrial nations. This latter difference is probably caused by the fact that a much larger proportion of all youth in this country take the SAT than in any other country. Nevertheless, many critics of American schools point to both of these facts about SAT scores to support their argument that the quality of education in this society is inadequate. Along these same lines, a Gallup Poll recently found that over three-fifths of all Americans believe that elementary and high school students are not working hard enough in school and on homework (Gallup Report, 1983). Still other critics argue that the public schools are failing to teach students to think analytically and critically, to challenge existing social and economic conditions, to be capable of coping with a rapidly changing world, or to envision ways of improving society in the future.

To investigate these charges, a National Commission on Excellence in Education was established by the federal government. Its report, issued in 1983 with the title, "A Nation at Risk: The Imperative for Educational Reform" (Gardner, 1983), was extremely critical of the quality of public education in this country. For instance, it estimated that 13 percent of all 17-year-olds are functionally illiterate, so that they cannot read a daily newspaper or do simple arithmetic, and this rate may be as high as 40 percent among minority youths. In comparison with students in 21 other nations on 19 standardized achievement tests, American youths had the worst average scores on seven tests and did not rank higher than third on any of them. Overall, *the Commission concluded that a "tide of mediocrity" pervades U.S. schools,* which it blamed on "weakness of purpose, confusion of vision, underuse of talent, and lack of leadership" (Gardner, 1983:13). This is indeed a serious indictment of the quality of education in the United States.

What should be done about this problem? Most of the recommendations offered by the Commission were fairly traditional in nature. These include longer school days, stricter educational standards and requirements, more attention to basic subjects such as English, mathematics, and science, and increased homework. It also recommended more adequate and extensive teacher training programs in colleges and universities, better funding for public schools, especially those whose students are predominantly from minority groups, and reconceptualizing education as a lifelong process for all persons rather than just for children and youths.

Another direction of educational reform that has long been advocated by many professional educators is to alter the teaching/learning process carried out in schools. Instead of attempting to "teach" students an established curriculum, school should be a "learning experience" for students in which they are encouraged to explore and expand their own curiosities and interests. In such schools, students would work much more on their own and in small groups rather than just listening to classroom instruction. This might involve exploring topics of relevance to them, carrying out projects, conducting experiments, preparing reports, and utilizing the community outside the classroom as a "learning laboratory." This approach to learning would clearly require a much lower teacher-student ratio than the traditional practice of having one teacher handle a class of 25 to 35 students. It would also require greater financial and other resources for the schools, development of new pedagogical techniques and materials, and a quite different understanding of the entire educational process.

These mounting criticisms of the public schools and demands for educational reform do not necessarily indicate that the quality of public education has deteriorated drastically in recent years. More likely, they are a consequence of six converging trends in United States schools and society:

(1) The low level of funding that has always existed and continues today;

(2) Our commitment to mass education of all youths through at least secondary school;

(3) Lack of knowledge about the learning process and how to educate students;

(4) The poor quality of most teacher training programs in the past;

(5) Recent rapid expansions in the total amount of information existing in many fields; and

(6) The demands of a rapidly changing society for a continually better-educated population.

As a result of these trends, *the rather mediocre quality of public education that we have accepted in the past is no longer adequate for the present or the future.* As expressed some years ago by Peter Drucker (1972), "Today's school does no poorer a job than it did yesterday; the school has simply done a terribly poor job all along. But what we tolerated in the past we no longer can tolerate. . . . The school has suddenly assumed such importance for the individual, for the community, for the economy, and for society that we cannot suffer the traditional, time-honored incompetence of the educational system."

EDUCATION AND INEQUALITY

Despite its many benefits for individuals and society, education also contributes directly to maintaining and perpetuating established patterns of socioeconomic, racial, and gender inequality. Although this process is no longer intended, as it often was in the past, it is nevertheless quite pervasive in modern societies.

Education and Socioeconomic Status

The relationships between education and socioeconomic status can be viewed as a vicious circle that continues across generations. The higher the status of one's parents, the greater the amount and quality of education a child is likely to receive. Subsequently, the amount and quality of one's education will heavily influence the status/class position one attains as an adult. This, in turn, will enable one to secure more and better education for one's children, and so the cycle continues. The following discussion focuses on the initial step in that cycle, examining factors that foster educational attainment by children of higher-status parents and hinder such attainment by children from lower-status families.

Four sets of factors enable parents with above-average socioeconomic status or class positions to ensure that their children receive an extensive and beneficial education, regardless of the children's intellectual abilities, interests, or motivations (Jencks, et al., 1972).

Economic Factors. We have already seen that per pupil expenditures on education differ widely among school systems and between schools within a given system. *The higher the average income level of the residents of a school district, the more funds that system is likely to have for physical facilities, teachers' salaries, and educational materials.* School systems in affluent communities and suburbs often spend two or three times as much per pupil as inner-city systems. These differences stem largely from the fact that at least half of all funds for education come from local residential property taxes based on the market value of those properties. In addition, college-educated people are more likely than others to vote for higher property tax rates to support good schools, so that communities with well-educated populations generally have the best schools. Within a particular school system, moreover, school administrators often allocate more funds to schools in "better" neighborhoods because of parental demands to provide good schools for their children.

At the family level, parents with higher educations can more easily afford to send their children to good private schools if they are dissatisfied with the quality of the public schools. Low-income parents, on the other hand, often find it necessary to urge their older children to drop out of school and go to work to help support the family or to become financially self-supporting. Needless to say, parents with higher incomes can afford to send their children to college, whereas low-income parents frequently cannot. And the higher the family income, the better the quality of the college their children will likely attend.

Home Environment Factors. The higher the educational level of the parents, the more education they will generally expect their children to obtain and the more encouragement and support they will give to their children's school efforts and activities. Well-educated parents expect their children to stay in school—generally through college—and to perform to the best of their abilities. They are more likely to stress the importance of education to their children, to assist them with homework, to praise good grades, and in general to encourage learning and intellectual achievement. Conversely, poorly educated parents may give their children little encouragement and support to do well in school, make disparaging remarks about education as a waste of time, and stress the importance of getting a job and earning a living rather than pursuing higher education.

Better-educated parents also encourage intellectual attainment in many subtle ways that are absent in the homes of poorly educated parents. Children from more privileged families are likely to be exposed to books and intellectual discussions from an early age, given educational toys, encouraged to watch educational programs on television, taken to museums, and exposed to cultural activities such as concerts or lectures. Finally, higher-status parents are more likely to teach their children to defer immediate gratification of desires in order to attain long-range goals. All these family experiences are likely to be reinforced, moreover, by the children's friends, who will generally be of the same socioeconomic status or class. If all one's friends believe that doing well in school and going to college are important, these social pressures will reinforce the home environment and further encourage the child to take education seriously.

Classroom Instruction Factors. Almost all school teachers in the United States today have a college education and speak standard American English. Children from middle- or higher-status homes normally have no trouble understanding this language. *Children from lower-status homes, however, are often unfamiliar with many of the words used by their teachers.* Those from Hispanic families where Spanish is spoken in the home, and those from lower-status black families that speak Black English, are particularly disadvantaged by their linguistic background. Most of the textbooks used in all schools are also written in standard English. In addition, the living conditions and other situations portrayed in elementary school texts are typically middle class in nature, so that children from disadvantaged homes often have great difficulty relating to the content of these books.

In high school, many of the subjects included in the curriculum may have little relevance to the lives of lower-status students. When their families are struggling to find a job or secure adequate housing or keep enough food on the table, it is difficult for them to see any point in studying European history or solid geometry. As a result of all these conditions, disadvantaged children often feel alienated from school and frequently come to define themselves as poor students who really don't belong there.

Performance Expectation Factors. Teachers frequently expect children from higher-status or class backgrounds to do well in school, regardless of their intellectual abilities. They tend to aim their teaching primarily at these students, to give them more personal attention, and to challenge them intellectually. Conversely, teachers often hold lower expectations for children from disadvantaged backgrounds, again regardless of their individual abilities.

These differing expectations are further intensified by the common practice in high schools of placing students into various "tracks"—college preparatory, general education, vocational training, clerical training, or remedial instruction. The justification for this procedure is quite rational, since it enables courses and instruction to be tailored to individual abilities and interests. The students within each track can be given the kind of education that best suits them, and teachers are not hampered by trying to deal in one classroom with students of widely varying academic abilities and goals. In practice, however, tracking frequently harms many students who are placed in the less prestigious vocational, clerical, and remedial tracks. Students are often assigned to these tracks on the basis of their social class background, rather than their intellectual abilities and educational goals. Teachers generally hold higher expectations for students in the college prep and general tracks than for those in the other tracks, with the result that the latter students receive inferior instruction. Once a student becomes "locked into" one of these lower tracks, it can be very difficult to escape from it and prepare oneself for college or technical training.

The expectations that teachers and the school structure create are also commonly adopted by student subcultures. College prep students often look down on vocationally oriented students, for example, and express those views. *Over time, this labeling by teachers, the school, and peers becomes a "self-fulfilling prophecy" for students.* They develop a self-image that reflects what others think and expect of them, which then guides their actions so that they fulfill those expectations. Students from higher-status homes come to view themselves as deserving of respect and recognition in school and in the larger society. Those from lower-status homes, meanwhile, "learn their place" in the school and the societal stratification system and become content to remain there rather than strive for advancement.

Racial Segregation in Schools

Racial and ethnic segregation has been widespread in American schools in the past and is still extensive today. The common definition of a "segregated school" is one in which more than half the students are members of minority groups. In 1980, 65 percent of all minority children attended segregated schools, according to that definition (U.S. Bureau of the Census, 1984:149). In the South, racially segregated schools used to be required by law, although those laws were rescinded in the 1970s. Most racial and ethnic segregation in schools is now a result of underlying segregation in housing patterns. This section deals solely with racial segregation, since it has been the focus of most public attention in recent years, although numerous patterns of ethnic segregation also occur in many communities.

Desegregation Efforts. In 1954, the U.S. Supreme Court ruled in *Brown v. Board of Education* that segregated schools are inherently unequal in terms of their consequences for the intellectual and social development of minority children. Although the Court ordered that segregation be eliminated from public schools "with all due speed," for many years compliance was very slow and sporadic, in the South and in the rest of the country. During that period, however, the civil rights movement gained considerable strength and public attention. As a direct result of this movement, Congress passed the *1964 Civil Rights Act, which authorized the federal government to withhold educational funds from communities that intentionally maintained segregated schools.* Armed with this leverage, the U.S. Department of Justice began putting pressures on all southern states to eliminate their laws requiring racially segregated schools.

The Civil Rights Act had relatively little effect on nonlegal school segregation outside the South, however, since it resulted from segregated housing rather than legal mandates. As a consequence, by the early 1970s school systems in the South were more racially integrated than those in much of the rest of the country. The first court case involving housing-based segregation outside the South did not reach the Supreme Court until 1973. In that case, involving the Denver school system, the Court ruled that the federal government must demonstrate an intention by school officials to impose segregation before federal funds could be withheld. Subsequent court cases challenged that decision, however, so that by the late 1970s it was only necessary to demonstrate that the schools were, in fact, segregated and that school authorities were failing to eliminate that condition. As a result, school systems in many non-Southern communities were ordered by the federal courts to establish desegregation programs.

The Coleman Report. The Civil Rights Act of 1964 also required the U.S. Civil Rights Commission to conduct a thorough study of the effects of racial segregation and integration on children's school achievement. This nationwide study, conducted by a group of social scientists headed by sociologist James Coleman, examined the records of several thousand students in segregated and integrated schools. Its report (Coleman, et al., 1966), published two years later and popularly known as "The Coleman Report," quickly became the focus of an intense national policy debate that lasted for many years. Since then, more than thirty additional studies on this topic have been conducted by sociologists and other social scientists. All these studies have arrived at remarkably similar conclusions, with only minor variations. The main findings from the Coleman and subsequent studies were the following:

(1) On all standardized tests of academic achievement (verbal, mathematical, and other abilities), the average scores of African-American children were significantly lower than those of white children. These differences were much greater for blacks in segregated schools than for those in integrated schools and tended to widen each year as children progressed through those schools.

(2) The school environment—physical facilities, curriculum, teacher qualifications, instructional methods, etc.—had relatively few effects on racial differences in academic achievement. Consequently, improving the quality of all-black schools without altering their racial composition did very little to help these children overcome their academic handicaps.

(3) The most important factor determining how well all children performed in school was their home environment, including the educational level of their parents and the intellectual atmosphere in the home. The second most important factor was the extent to which a child's classmates are academically oriented and motivated to do well in school. Both these findings were similar to—and closely related to—the effects of socioeconomic status and class on school performance.

(4) Holding constant the effects of home environment, African-American students in integrated schools scored significantly higher than those in segregated schools, indicating that the racial composition of the school was important. In addition, the greater the number of years that black children spent in integrated schools, the more their scores improved and the smaller the gap between them and white children.

(5) School integration did not benefit blacks if classes remained relatively segregated, with whites in academic classes and blacks in vocational training programs. It is crucial that classrooms be integrated, so that black students share the same learning experiences as white children.

(6) On the average, test scores of white children in integrated schools did not differ from those of children in predominately white schools. In other words, while racial integration of schools clearly helped African-American children, it had no negative effects on the academic achievements of white children in those schools.

The policy implications of these findings for school systems were quite clear. *Since the* schools can do little to alter the home environment of students, if they wish to improve the academic performance of African-American children, they must be racially integrated. How could that be achieved, when most neighborhoods are heavily segregated? The conclusion reached by the Coleman Report was that the established policy of requiring children to attend the school in their immediate neighborhood had to be changed. The Coleman study examined several voluntary approaches to achieving racially integrated schools, but it concluded that none of those alternatives was likely to be effective in reducing large-scale school segregation. It therefore recommended mandatory busing of students among schools throughout a community. This recommendation was subsequently imposed by courts on numerous school systems.

School Busing. Over time, mandatory busing was discovered to have three serious limitations, however. First, many parents (black and white) favor neighborhood schools and object strongly to having their children ride a bus across town every day to another school. Second, in many large cities the population is so heavily black—95 percent in Washington D.C. and 80 percent in Detroit, for example—that no amount of busing can achieve school integration within the city. And since the predominantly white suburbs have separate school systems, inner-city children cannot legally be bused to the suburbs. Third, because many white parents object to busing and/or racial integration of schools, when courts have imposed mandatory busing on urban public school systems large numbers of white families have moved to the suburbs or sent their children to private all-white schools. In numerous cities, this process of "white flight" has resulted in the schools becoming more segregated than before busing was initiated.

Because of these problems with mandatory busing, Coleman later withdrew his original recommendation and suggested that more attention should be given to integrating neighborhoods. Meanwhile, *many*

communities—with the approval of the courts—have been searching for other ways of promoting school integration. Some of these approaches are merely disguised ways of forcing busing, such as closing schools in black neighborhoods so that black children have to be bused, or restricting each school to only two or three grades so that all children must eventually be bused. Alternative approaches attempt to encourage voluntary busing. One method is to adopt an open enrollment policy in which parents can send their children to whatever public school in the city they choose. Another method is to create high-quality programs in "magnet schools" (such as science in one school and art in another) that will attract interested students from throughout the city. Other suggested approaches are much broader in scope. For instance, several large cities are presently considering the policy of busing on a metropolitan-wide basis, involving all the suburbs. This would solve the problems of white flight and all-black central city schools, but it is being strongly resisted by many suburban families.

Ultimately, *elimination of segregated schools will depend on eliminating patterns of racial segregation in housing, so that neighborhoods become more integrated—within the inner city and in the suburbs.* That process will take a long time to achieve and will undoubtedly lead to bitter social and legal conflicts. But at least there is now widespread recognition among educators and many parents that segregated schools are inherently harmful to minority children.

RELIGION AND RELIGIOUS ORGANIZATIONS

Human life is beset with fundamental questions to which we have no definitive answers. What is the origin of the universe? What is the nature of existence? What is the ultimate purpose of human life? What basic values should we hold, and what kinds of ethical principles should we follow? Why is there evil in the world? Is there some kind of existence after death? In short, all people yearn to find meaning and purpose in life, individually and collectively. To bridge the gap between our unanswered questions and our need for meaning in life, we create belief systems. For the most part, beliefs and belief systems are based not on information or knowledge, but on intuitive feelings and convictions that we accept on faith. Nevertheless, we tend to hold our beliefs very deeply and resist changing them. Organized belief systems shared by large numbers of people often become established religions. The human need to create and share belief systems is so fundamental and pervasive that all known societies have contained one or more religions.

Sociologists study religion as a sociocultural institution, but they do not attempt to ascertain the truth of any religious belief systems. Sociology cannot answer such questions as, "Does God exist?". But it can, for instance, investigate relationships that occur between the social structure of a society and its religious beliefs. In agricultural societies, religion tends to focus on environmental conditions and fertility; strongly patriarchal societies tend to have strictly masculine gods; and societies ruled by autocratic elites tend to have highly authoritarian religions. Sociologists also investigate such topics as the functions performed by religion for societies and individuals, the linkage between religion and socioeconomic class, the ways in which religious organizations are structured and function, and the distribution of religious beliefs and practices within a society. In short, *sociologists treat religious belief systems and the religious organizations based on these beliefs as critical components of all societies.*

Nature of Religion

Although most individuals hold personal religious beliefs, religion as a sociocultural institution is part of the shared culture of a society. Not all cultural belief systems constitute religions, however. As pointed out by Émile Durkheim, *the most common element in all religious belief systems is a sense of the sacred.*

Sacred beliefs are viewed as holy or spiritual because they transcend normal human experience and hence inspire feelings of reverence, awe, and piety. Nonsacred beliefs, in contrast, are described as secular and do not inspire such feelings. Magical beliefs commonly contain both sacred and secular elements.

Two additional components of all religious belief systems are symbols and rituals. A religious symbol is anything that represents or is embodied with a sense of the sacred. It may be a physical object such as a Holy Grail or holy stone, a place such as Mecca or a temple, or an abstract design such as a cross or a six-pointed Star of David. A religious ritual is any activity or practice that expresses one's sacred beliefs. It may be as simple as saying a prayer or wearing a veil, or as complex as a worship service or a funeral ceremony. In sum, *religion is a system of shared cultural beliefs that are viewed as sacred and are expressed through symbols and rituals.*

Because religion is part of the culture of one's society, the particular sacred belief system held by an individual is usually determined by the social and historical conditions in which that person lives. *Most people acquire their religion as a child through socialization from their parents and other members of their community.* If you had lived in ancient Greece, you would probably have believed that Zeus was the father of all the gods; if you had been a member of the nobility in medieval Europe you would undoubtedly have been a Catholic; if you grew up in contemporary Saudi Arabia you are almost certainly a follower of Islam; and if you are from a Jewish family in the United States today you likely identify yourself as part of the Jewish community. We are not total slaves to our religious socialization, however. Many individuals modify their religious beliefs somewhat during their lifetime. Some persons intentionally change their religion and undergo a resocialization process into the new faith. And quite a few people in contemporary societies reject formal religion altogether and become agnostic, atheistic, or totally indifferent toward religion.

Religious Beliefs

The wide range of religious belief systems that exist throughout human societies can be loosely categorized into six broad types, although there are countless variations within each category.

Supernaturalism is the belief that some kind of supernatural force or power pervades and influences all existence. This power does not take any specific forms such as spirits or gods and is not directly concerned with human beings. Nevertheless, this belief system holds that it is important for humans to respect and be in touch with the supernatural power. Such beliefs are often associated with very simple societies, such as the concept of *mana* held by the Melanesan islanders of the South Pacific. More sophisticated versions of supernaturalism are also fairly common in modern societies, as expressed in the "Star Wars" injunction, "May the Force be with you," and in the belief that there is some kind of ultimate power guiding the universe.

Animism is the belief that numerous animate spirits are active in the world, in human life and in natural phenomena. These spirits are not worshiped as gods, but rather are personified as humanlike but nonphysical beings with motives and intentions that may be either good or evil. Since they are more powerful than humans, however, they must be placated and influenced as much as possible through religious or magical rituals. Animistic beliefs have been quite common among foraging and simple horticultural societies around the world, but they also occur in modern societies in such forms as black magic and worship of the occult.

Ancestralism is the belief that an all-powerful sacred "presence" exists throughout nature and in all people. This presence is addressed by worshiping nature and the wisdom of one's ancestors. This type of religion thus combines features of supernaturalism and animism, but it does not include any concept of gods or a supreme God. It also incorporates codes of ethical principles to guide human life, and thus blends into ethicalism, as discussed shortly. The principal ancestral religion in the contemporary world is Shinto, "the way of the *kami,*" which is the national religion of Japan, although many Japanese are also Buddhists, Confucianists, Taoists, or Christians.

Polytheism is the belief that there are a number of gods who rule the world and must be acknowledged. Although these gods are often depicted with human characteristics, they are infinitely more powerful than human beings or animistic spirits. One of the gods is generally viewed as the "father of the others, and there may also be a "mother" god. The other gods—who may be depicted as their "children"—have specialized realms of concern such as crops, weather, war, love, or music. All the gods are presumed to play an active role in directing human affairs, but they are not necessarily seen as all-powerful. Because polytheism is most likely to occur in agrarian socities, it has been a very common type of religion throughout human history.

Monotheism is the belief that there is a single supreme diety who is all-knowing and all-powerful. This supreme being is believed to be responsible for and to control all existence, and it is the sole object of all religious worship. It does not play as active a role in human affairs as the various polytheistic gods, but it is concerned about human beings and can be addressed by priests or by individual believers. A monotheistic God is believed to communicate its laws or commandments to humans through one or more prophets, who thus become the founders of religions. There are three monotheistic religions in the modern world—Christianity, Islam, and Judaism—and they are the dominant religions at this time.

Ethicalism is the belief that there are sacred principles that should guide all human activities. These principles, as we come to understand them, provide ethical and moral guidelines for human life. This type of religion does not include any concept of diety or gods. Instead, it urges its believers to open themselves—through meditation and other rituals—to achieving understanding of, and living in harmony with, the sacred principles. There may be several stages of open-

TYPES OF RELIGIOUS BELIEF SYSTEMS
1. Supernaturalism.
2. Animism.
3. Ancestralism.
4. Polytheism.
5. Monotheism.
6. Ethicalism.

ness or awareness, but ultimately one seeks to be "at one with the universe." Ethicalism is usually associated with the Eastern religions of Buddhism, Confucianism, and Taoism, but it also exists in the West in the form of humanism, Ethical Culturalism, and other religious belief systems.

In terms of number of adherents, Christianity is the most widespread religion in the world today, with approximately one billion believers. Since there are three principle branches of Christianity, however, it is important to divide the total number of Christians into Roman Catholics, who number about 600 million; Protestants, with about 350 million; and Eastern Orthodox Christians, who are approximately 75 million. Christians are located primarily in Europe and North and South America, although Christianity has spread to all parts of the globe. The second largest religion today is Islam, whose adherents are often referred to as Moslems. Its nearly 600 million believers are concentrated largely in the Middle East, as well as in Africa, Indonesia, and the Soviet Union.

Hinduism, which exists primarily in India, claims about 500 million members. Buddhism also originated in India, but it has spread throughout Asia and is thought to have about 250 million adherents. Confucianism and Taoism both came from China, but they are also widely accepted in Japan and elsewhere in Asia. Membership figures for these religions are put at about 150 million and 30 million, respectively, although several hundred million Chinese are at least nominally believers in some combination of Confucianism, Taoism, and Buddhism.

Shintoism has about 60 million members, largely in Japan, although many Japanese also accept other Eastern religions or Christianity. Judaism, finally, has about 15 million members worldwide, a considerable portion of whom reside in Israel.

Religious Organizations

All the major world religions are more than shared belief systems with associated symbols and rituals. They are also social organizations with many of the same characteristics as other associations of people who share a common concern. The sense of sacredness that pervades religious beliefs, symbols, and rituals may also extend to some features of religious organizations, such as the reverence that is accorded to Buddhist monks or the Roman Catholic belief that the Pope can speak on religious matters as the direct spiritual descendant of Jesus. On the whole, however, *religious organizations are generally viewed as humanly created bodies whose purpose is to express and preserve a religion through a variety of activities* ranging from worship services to social and political action. Sociologists therefore study these organizations in the same manner that they examine schools or businesses or governments.

Types of Religious Organizations. Numerous sociologists have attempted to identify the fundamental characteristics of religious organizations and to classify them into basic categories. This effort was begun by Ernst Troeltsch (1931), a colleague of Weber's in Germany, and has been continued by such contemporary sociologists as J. Milton Yinger (1970) and Ronald Johnstone (1975). Their work has focused largely on Christianity, however, and cannot be applied to other world religions without modifications.

Christian religious organizations can be placed along a broad continuum, the end points of which may be described as "established" versus "nonestablished" churches. This continuum displays a number of interrelated characteristics that tend to vary together from one end to the other. The most important of these tendencies are as follows:

(1) *Social structure.* More established churches tend to have a rather formal structure, with a hierarchy of authority embedded in several levels of church positions and a well-defined set of organizational rules and procedures. More nonestablished churchs tend to have a much more loose and informal structure.

(2) *Clergy.* As a consequence of their formal structure, more established churches usually have professionally trained full-time clergy and other personnel, whereas more nonestablished churches may have only volunteer part-time leaders.

(3) *Worship services.* The more established churches generally hold fairly formal and restrained worship services, with relatively little participation by the members. The services of more nonestablished churches tend to be much more informal and spontaneous, with considerable activity and expression of emotions by the participants.

(4) *Number and involvement of members.* Established churches typically have large numbers of members, but their level of personal involvement in the church may be fairly minimal except for attendance at formal services and other rituals such as weddings and funerals. Nonestablished churches are usually much smaller, but their members tend to be highly involved and often view the church as the center of their life.

(5) *Social status.* The closer a church is to the established end of this continuum, the more privileged its members tend to be in terms of socioeconomic class, racial and ethnic status, and other social rankings. Consequently, these churches are generally rather prestigious, wealthy, and powerful. In contrast, the closer a church is to the nonestablished end of the continuum, the lower its members and the church as a whole tend to be in terms of status and power.

(6) *Relationship to society.* The more established a church is, the more it tends to reflect and support the values and social arrangements prevailing in the larger society. It will therefore have numerous links with many other social institutions. More nonestablished churches, on the other hand, frequently reject many or most features of the society, sometimes denouncing them as "evil." They therefore tend to be relatively isolated from other social institutions (except the family). The relationship of a church to the larger society is often the most crucial factor determining most of its activities as a social organization.

This continuum of established to nonestablished churches is frequently divided into four broad types of religious organizations, although the boundaries between these categories are not very sharp.

An ecclesia is a religious organization that is closely allied with the prevailing political and economic systems in the society, and to which most or all members of the society belong at least nominally. It thus falls at the extreme "establishment" end of the preceding continuum. As the "official" church of its society, an ecclesia typically receives funds from the government, exercises considerable influence on public policies and laws, shapes the prevailing culture, and affects the lives of most people in that society. Individuals who reject the established state church and desire to form an alternative religious organization or practice a different religion may be tolerated, or they may be banished or executed. The Roman Catholic Church was an ecclesia for many centuries in Europe until the Protestant Reformation challenged its dominance. Today, the Catholic Church in Italy and Spain, the Anglican Church in England, and the Lutheran Church in Sweden are often placed in this category, although none of these bodies exercises the sweeping power of an exclusive ecclesia. Perhaps the clearest examples of ecclesia in the contemporary world are Islam in Saudi Arabia and Iran and Judaism in Israel.

A denomination is a relatively well-established religious organization with a large number of members, but it is only one of many kinds of such organizations in the society. It is not supported by the state and does not exercise the social and cultural dominance of an ecclesia. A denomination usually accepts the existing social order and culture, although it may be critical of particular social, economic, or political policies and conditions. It thus falls toward the more established end of the preceding continuum of religious organizations, with a formal structure and a professional clergy. In the United States, the Catholic Church is today considered to be a denomination, as are the major Protestant bodies such as the Episcopalian, Presbyterian, Methodist, Lutheran, and Baptist Churches. Judaism can also be considered a denomination within the United States today, but not in other countries such as Israel.

A sect is a considerably less established religious organization with fewer members and a more informal structure. Most sects are created as offshoots from denominations by people who feel that the more established churches have either lost touch with "pure" religion or are too accepting of existing social conditions. Within Christianity, sects generally stress fundamentalism, or a literal intepretation of everything in the Bible, together with intense emotional involvement and "moral purity" of their members. Sects also commonly proclaim a rather dogmatic belief that they are the only true religion. They tend to reject many or most existing social, economic, and political conditions, emphasizing otherwordliness and salvation through faith rather than attempting to change society. They generally appeal primarily to lower-status or other disadvantaged people and hence lack the social respectability and power of the mainline denominations. Many sects are fairly short-lived, but some evolve gradually into more established denominations. Methodism, for instance, began as a sect that broke away from the Anglican Church in England, and this process is occurring today with Jehovah's Witnesses and the Assembly of God. Contemporary sects also include a wide variety of Pentecostal, Evangelical, and other religious organizations ranging from the Old Order Amish to the Hare Krishna and the Unification Church (the "Moonies").

A cult is a very loosely organized and nonestablished small set of believers who subscribe to *some kind of esoteric idea.* It usually has relatively few adherents and little or nor formal structure. Whereas sects are attempting to "purify" more established religion and churches, cults have no roots in any existing religious organizations or traditions. Most of them are formed by an individual who claims to have received a divine revelation and who has great charismatic appeal to his or her followers. Cultists tend to be intensely devoted to their particular beliefs and leader, feeling that they are creating a wholly new religion or are preparing themselves for a cataclysm such as the imminent end of the world. Most cults are very transitory in nature, although sometimes they become transformed through time into more established churches. The Church of the Latter Day Saints (the Mormans) is an example of a religious body that began as a cult, developed into a sect, and is today a well-established denomination. More contemporary cults have been the People's Temple founded by Jim Jones, who led his followers to Guyana and then in 1978 persuaded over 900 of them to commit mass suicide, and the Rajnesh who took over the town of Antelope, Oregon until their guru was expelled from the United States for violation of immigration laws.

Among all modern societies, the United States is by far the most highly organized in terms of church membership and participation. In addition to the approximately 200 generally recognized denominations in this country, there are at least 400 sects and 500 identifiable cult movements (Stark and Bainbridge, 1981). In contrast, other developed countries typically contain only ten to 15 major churches and a handful of sects and cults. In Canada, for example, three-fourths of the population are affiliated with the Catholic Church, the

---

TYPES OF RELIGIOUS ORGANIZATIONS

1. Ecclesia.
2. Denomination.
3. Sect.
4. Cult.

Anglican Church, or the United Church of Canada. The distribution of preferences among the largest denominations in the United States is as follows:

Roman Catholic = 28 percent; Baptist = 19 percent; Methodist = 10 percent; Lutheran = 6 percent; Presbyterian = 4 percent; Episcopalian = 2 percent; other Protestant churches = 18 percent (none of which contains more than one percent of the population); Jewish = 2 percent; other religions = 4 percent; and no religious preference = 7 percent

(Gallup Report,1982).

Approximately two-thirds of all adults in this country report that they are a member of a church or synagogue, and 40 percent say that they attend religious services weekly (Gallup, 1982). That rate of attendance is higher than in any other modern country. As shown in Table 19-1, attendance varies by

religion, with Catholics having the highest rate, although there is considerable variation among the various Protestant denominations and sects; by gender, with women attending more frequently than men; by age, with attendance rising as people become older; and by region, with the Midwest being highest. There is relatively little variation in attendance by education, however.

People in this country also tend to feel that religion is very important to them. Approximately 55 percent of all adults in the United States make this claim, whereas no more than 40 percent do so in any other modern country. As also seen in Table 19-1, this feeling also varies by religion, being highest among Protestants (but with members of sects generally feeling much more strongly about religion than members of denominations); by gender, being much higher among women; by age, showing a steady increase as people grow older; and by region; being highest in the South. The im-

TABLE 19-1   Religious Participation and Importance in the United States, 1980

	Percent of Adults	
	Attend Religious Services Weekly	*Say that Religion is Very Important*
Nationwide	40	55
By Religion		
Catholic	53	56
Protestant	39	61
Jewish	25	31
By Gender		
Women	44	62
Men	36	48
By Age		
Below 30	31	43
30–49	40	55
50 and older	47	65
By Education		
Grade school	43	69
High school	39	55
College	40	50
By Region		
East	40	49
Midwest	45	54
South	42	66
West	29	51

Source: The Gallup Report, 1982.

portance of religion for people tends to decline with rising education.

Functions of Religion and Churches

Since religious beliefs and practices have existed in all human societies, sociologists have long been interested in the the functions that religion performs for societies and individuals. These functions do not explain the initial origins of religion—which are lost in prehistory—but they help to explain why religious beliefs are preserved through time and why people are continually creating and perpetuating religious organizations. Émile Durkheim (1915) and Max Weber (1970) made substantial contributions to these inquiries, which have been pursued by many later investigators. The most important beneficial functions of religious beliefs and organizations—some of which are relatively manifest and some of which are largely latent—are sketched in the following paragraphs.

Manifest Function: Giving Meaning to Life. Weber saw religion as performing many of the same kinds of social functions as did Durkheim, but he stressed its cognitive, rather than its moral elements. All people have a deep need to find some meaning and purpose in life, individually and collectively. Such meanings can be derived from many sources, including cultural heritages and traditions, political ideologies, scientific knowledge, and interpersonal relationships. None of these secular sources are fully adequate, however, in providing an overall worldview that can integrate all aspects of human existence into a meaningful whole. *This function of providing a coherent worldview that makes life truly meaningful is best performed by religion,* Weber suggested, because of its encompassing and sacred nature. The framework of ultimate meaning derived from religion often pervades many other realms of social life. It gives legitimacy to the political order, stability to the economic order, and sanctity to the family.

Manifest Function: Celebrating Life Passages. Major transition points in people's lives—especially birth, marriage, and death—are commonly occasions for public ceremonies. *All churches and synagogues have established rituals for such life passages,* and many people turn to their church or synagogue at these times even if they do not otherwise participate in religious activities.

Manifest Function: Creating Community. The concept of community, used in this context, refers to a set of people who share common beliefs and ways of living, interact with one another in personal ways, and identify themselves as a collective body. In modern societies—especially the United States—*religion and religious organizations provide one of the most important bases for creating a sense of community* in an otherwise highly urbanized, bureaucratized, and impersonal society. In a broad sense, suggested Will Herberg (1960), this process occurs within each of the basic religious traditions—Protestantism, Catholicism, and Judaism—in American society. Jews are particularly likely to think of themselves as members of a Jewish community even if they do not attend religious services regularly. Within all three traditions, people have tended to form friendships with—and especially to marry—other members of their religious community (Lenski, 1961). On a smaller scale, some of the primary reasons why many individuals attend church are to find people with whom they feel congenial, to make friends, and to take part in informal social activities.

Manifest Function: Providing Social Services. Before the days of public welfare programs and agencies, churches were usually the primary providers of assistance to the poor, the homeless, the abused, and other needy people. Today, such assistance is typically provided by social service agencies, but *many private agencies are operated by, affiliated with, or supported by churches.* Moreover, since persons with problems—ranging from spouse abuse to eviction from their housing—frequently go first to their church for help, churches often act as intermediaries in referring these individuals to appropriate social service agencies. Many religious leaders also do psychological counseling with individuals on a wide variety of topics—such as marital problems, deviant children, severe illness, and death—although they generally refer more serious cases to professional counselors and agencies.

Manifest or Latent Function: Stimulating Social Change. Religious beliefs and organizations are often described as performing a conserving function in social life, preserving and perpetuating values, norms, and traditions. At the same time, however, *religion may constitute a dynamic force for extensive social change.* Sometimes religious proclamations are used merely to legitimate other intentions, as when members of the nobility in late medieval Europe adopted Protestantism as means of freeing themselves from the political and economic control of the Roman Catholic Church. At other times, religious ideas may unintentionally foster social change, as suggested by Weber's thesis that the Protestant Ethic accidently encouraged enterpreneural economic activities and thus paved the way for industrialization. At still other times, religious organizations strive actively to create social change, as seen in the movements for civil rights, prevention of war, economic justice, and women's rights in the United States in recent decades.

Latent Function: Expressing Awareness of Society. Society, argued Durkheim, exists as a reality that is external to individuals and influences many of their actions. However, the concept of society is difficult for many people to grasp, and its influences on them often seem to be quite amorphous and impersonal. Consequently, although people are generally aware of the existence of society and its affects, they frequently have great difficulty understanding and coping with it. Moreover, because society as a whole is so much more powerful than any individual, it inspires a sense of awe and reverence in many people. Durkheim therefore suggested that *religious beliefs, symbols, rituals, and other practices provide a means whereby people can express their awareness of and feelings toward their collective life.* Although it is an oversimplification to say that Durkheim described religion as "the worship of society," he did believe that religion provides a vehicle through which people can collectively express and acknowledge their dependence on one another and their society.

Latent Function: Maintaining Social Cohesion. The essence of society (or more generally, all social organization) for Durkheim is a set of "collective representations," or widely shared beliefs, values, and norms. General acceptance of these cultural ideas among most members of a society is the basis of what sociologists now describe as normative cohesion. Many of these fundamental ideas—such as democracy or freedom—may be essentially secular in nature. However, *to the extent that shared beliefs, values, and norms are infused with a sense of the sacred, they become much more binding on individuals and groups in the society.* Durkheim referred to collective representations that are infused with sacredness as the "collective conscience" of a society, and argued that they are fundamental for maintaining cohesion in all societies, primitive and modern.

Manifest Function: Promoting Social Control. Collective social life requires that individuals frequently put aside their personal interests and goals and cooperate by adhering to social norms and rules. Although people may abide by these social standards for purely expedient reasons, *norms become much more forceful when they are viewed as moral imperatives derived from religion.* People then accept the norms of society as the right or moral ways of acting and comply with them voluntarily from a sense of "oughtness." When that occurs, external control through sanctions imposed by others is unnecessary. Consequently, Durkheim argued that commitment to religious beliefs and ethical codes is in effect a commitment to social order and

FUNCTIONS PERFORMED BY RELIGIOUS ORGANIZATIONS

1. Giving meaning to live.
2. Celebrating life passages.
3. Creating community.
4. Providing social services.
5. Stimulating social change.
6. Expressing awareness of society.
7. Maintaining social cohesion.
8. Promoting social control.

collective cooperation. Participation in religious activities continually reaffirms and strengthens that commitment.

Religion and Elite Dominance

Although religious beliefs and organizations clearly perform many beneficial functions for individuals and society, religion also has a dark side that is not often recognized or acknowledged. In many—if not most—societies, *the major religion is largely controlled by the dominant political and economic class and used by it as a vehicle for exercising power throughout the society.* Elites use religion to justify the established economic and political orders, to legitimate their privileged positions, to discourage attempts at changing the stratification system, and to persuade disadvantaged classes and individuals to accept their lot in life without protest. Religious doctrines often stress the beliefs that submissiveness is a requirement for salvation, that "servants should obey their masters," and that "the meek shall inherit the earth."

Karl Marx (1864) explicitly pointed out this dark side of religion, arguing that religious doctrines and organizations are a major factor in preserving class inequality and exploitation and preventing oppressed classes from challenging the rule of elites. In his early 1848 writings, he denounced established religion in a phrase that has since been widely repeated, "Religion is the sign of the oppressed creature, the sentiment of a heartless world, and the soul of soulness con-

ditions. It is the opiate of the people." Paradoxically, however, Marx's vision of a future "classless society" in which there would be no more class domination and exploitation and in which all people would be treated equally was derived directly from the ethical teachings of Judaism and Christianity. Essentially, therefore, Marx was criticizing not the ideas of religion, but its institutionalized practice by religious organizations.

There is abundant historical evidence to support Marx's contention that religion frequently supports elite domination of society. For example, the pharaohs of ancient Egypt were regarded as divine incarnations of the gods, so that it was unthinkable even to question their proclamations and heresy to challenge their rule. The Hindu religion in India teaches that persons who fail to perform the social obligations of their caste or who attempt to attain a higher caste position will be reborn in their next life into a lower caste or even as an animal. This belief, which has prevailed for many hundreds of years, effectively controls the actions of lower-caste people and limits upward social mobility. In late medieval Europe, kings usually claimed that they ruled by "divine right" and that no one could challenge their autocratic regimes. The Roman Catholic Church of that time supported these royal claims as a means of assuring the protection and support of the state for its own power and wealth, so that new kings were typically crowned or annointed by church officials. And for centuries the Biblical story that Eve was created from Adam's rib and later tempted him to eat the apple of "original sin" has been used to justify the domination of men over women, on the grounds that women are physically and morally inferior beings.

Western colonialism made extensive use of religion to justify and support dominance and exploitation. Over a period of three hundred years the dominant Western nations—Portugal, Spain, England, France, Germany, and later the United States—seized vast territories and millions of people around the world as colonies. The basic purpose of these invasions and subjugations of weaker societies was clearly economic. The colonial powers wanted gold, land, natural resources, slaves, workers, or crops. At the same time, colonial exploits also enhanced their political and military power around the world. Colonialism was explained and justified not on any of those grounds, however, but by the religious claim that the colonists were bringing Christianity to the heathens and thus saving their souls. The churches—Protestant and Catholic—were active participants in the colonization process, creating elaborate doctrines describing the "white man's burden" to "enlighten the savages" by bringing them Christianity and European "civilization." Missionaries were sent out to colonies around the world to establish churches and schools and convert the "heathens." Although individual missionaries were undoubtedly well-intentioned, their efforts had drastic unintended effects. In addition to legitimizing the colonial enterprise, they commonly destroyed the traditional sociocultural patterns of the native people and left them disorganized, confused, and vulnerable to foreign domination. Moreover, in the process of converting the natives to Christianity, they taught them to be submissive to their colonial masters and to perform whatever labor was demanded of them by the European colonists. The legacy of that practice of religiously sanctioned colonial domination and exploitation still pervades much of Africa, Asia, South America, and the South Pacific today.

In the United States, organized religion was one of the principal supporters and legitimizers of slavery in the nineteenth century. Although a few small religious bodies vigorously condemned slavery from the outset, all of the major churches initially endorsed it. In fact, they frequently taught that human slavery was in accord with the will of God, and slaveholders in the South used religion to teach their slaves submission and obedience with the promise of attaining salvation after death. At the time of the Civil War, several of the major denominations—including the Baptists, Methodists, and Presbyterians—split into opposing camps over the issue of

the war and slavery, and most of these organizational divisions still remain. After the war, when racial segregation and discrimination replaced slavery, these practices were generally condoned by southern churches and ignored by northern ones. Not until the civil rights movement of the 1960s did the major northern churches become active in promoting racial integration and equality, while the white southern churches were mostly quite passive on this issue. Many church leaders and members from the North were active participants in civil rights marches and demonstrations, but in the South only the black churches were involved in the movement. And despite all the civil rights activities conducted by the churches in the 1960s and 1970s, most churches throughout the United States today remain highly racially segregated. It is sometimes asserted that the clearest examples of racial segregation in the United States today are found in churches on Sunday mornings.

Finally, it should also be noted that *throughout history, religion has been used to justify and legitimate wars of all kinds.* The medieval Crusades, whose underlying purpose was to open trade routes from Europe to Asia, were depicted as "holy crusades" to convert or destroy Muslims. The Hundred Years War in Europe, in which the old landed nobility struggled with the emerging national kings for political dominance, was widely described as a conflict between Protestants and Catholics. During World War II, American soldiers sang "Praise the Lord and pass the ammunition." Today, religious beliefs and proclamations are being used to legitimate numerous armed conflicts over more fundamental economic and political issues in Lebanon, Northern Ireland, Iran, and other areas of the world.

RELIGION AND MODERN LIFE

In all preindustrial societies—from simple hunting and gathering tribes to elaborate agrarian empires—religion has pervaded most areas of life. Religious beliefs and practices have been integral parts of family life, work and business, politics and government, law, education, art, science, and many other activities. In contrast, *a fundamental trend within the process of societal modernization has been expanding secularization of social life.* Religion has been deemphasized or excluded from numerous kinds of activities in modern societies. Perhaps the clearest example of this process has been in the realm of science and technology, where norms of rational inquiry have almost entirely replaced acceptance of religious dogma (although the recent emphasis on creationism as an alternative to biological evolution is a countertrend). In the economic realm, meanwhile, pragmatic cost-effective criteria have largely replaced all concerns with "serving God's will."

Religion and Politics

The U.S. Constitution makes a clear distinction between church and state, so that government in this country is generally more secularized than in most other modern nations. Nevertheless, our religious heritage is still expressed in many subtle ways in political activities, which Robert Bellah (1975) has called our "civil religion." The Pledge of Allegiance declares that we are one nation "under God," and our coins all carry the phrase, "In God we trust." The President is inaugurated while placing one hand on the Bible, and most religious leaders pay at least lip service to religion. Many political events frequently include a religious invocation, carefully worded to be nonsectarian. When John F. Kennedy was elected as the first Catholic President, this event was hailed as evidence of growing religious tolerance in the United States, yet in his inaugural address Kennedy did not hesitate to ask for God's blessing and help with his administration. In short, *the American political system is still far from being completely secularized.* Moreover, at the present time we are witnessing renewed efforts by a number of religious movements to reinsert explicit religious beliefs and concerns into partisan politics.

Declining Religious Involvement

Considerable sociological research has investigated the growing secularization of social life in the United States and other industrial nations. For instance, numerous surveys during the last thirty years have asked Americans about their church activities and religious beliefs. *The results of these surveys have shown a consistent but not overwhelming decline in religious involvement.* From approximately 1950 to 1980, the following trends occurred in this society.

(1) The proportion of adults who belonged to a church or synagogue dropped somewhat, from 76 to 69 percent.

(2) The proportion who attended religious services most weeks went down slightly, from 46 to 40 percent.

(3) A larger decline occurred among those who said that religion was very important in their life, from 75 to 55 percent.

(4) The largest change occurred among people who said that the Bible is the actual word of God, to be taken literally word for word, which went from 65 to only 37 percent (Gallup Report, 1982).

Similar surveys in several other modern nations have shown considerably sharper declines in religious involvement—with the exception of Canada, where the trends are roughly the same as in the United States. The continuing relative viability of American and Canadian churches may be due, suggests Peter Berger (1969), to the fact that in most other countries the churches generally perform only traditional religious services. In contrast, many North American churches have taken on a variety of other functions—from social events to personal counseling—that have kept them more relevant to many people's daily lives.

Among Christians, the most notable decline in religious involvement in the United States has occurred with Catholics. Weekly attendance at Mass dropped from 72 percent to 53 percent between 1954 and 1981. Because Judaism does not place as much emphasis as Christianity on formal worship services, attendance at Jewish services has traditionally been rather low. Nevertheless, attendance rates among Jews have also dropped considerably in recent years, so that less than 20 percent of all Jews go to a synagogue even once a month.

At first appearance, therefore, there does seem to have been a considerable decline in religious involvement in the United States in recent years. The preceding data do not present the entire picture, however.

Growth of Religious Fundamentalism

Although mainline churches have been experiencing some decline in participation over the past forty years, that trend has been countered by a steady growth of religious fundamentalism. Consequently, some sociologists argue that the United States is not becoming any less religiously involved, but is merely continuing its historical process of constantly diversifyng its forms of religious expression (Stark and Bainbridge, 1985). The fundamentalist movement is not new, having begun early in the twentieth century as an effort to "purify" the established churches and return religion to its "fundamentals." It was essentially a reaction to the increasing liberalism and modernism of the mainline churches as they strove to take account of contemporary physical and social science, ethical humanism, theological scholarship, and changing societal conditions. However, *since the 1960s, religious fundamentalism has been expanding rapidly in this country.*

Fundamentalism is most prevalent within Protestantism, where there are both fundamentalist denominations (such as the Southern Baptist Convention and the Seventh-Day Adventists) and sects (countless variations of Evangelical, Pentecostal, and Holiness organizations). Many mainline Protestant churches are also experiencing fundamentalist movements among some of their members. In addition, the movement toward fundamentalistism is now occurring within the Catholic Church (where it is known as "charismatic renewal of faith") and

among some Jews (who often call themselves "Jews for Jesus").

Although there are many varieties of religious fundamentalism, fundamentalists generally share two features in common:

(1) *A traditional conservative theology* that focuses on the Bible as the direct "word of God" and insists that everything in it must be accepted as literal truth; and

(2) *A strong emphasis on personal salvation* through a total commitment of faith, which is described as being "born again."

Many (although not all) fundamentalist churches believe in evangelicalism, or "spreading the word" through all possible means and continually attempting to recruit new members. Some of them also believe in pentecostalism, or the infusion of the Holy Spirit into religious rituals and personal actions, which may be expressed through "speaking in tongues," physical gesticulating, and faith healing.

Most religious fundamentalists are highly critical of many current social and political trends. They tend to oppose abortion, Women's Liberation, Gay Liberation, population control, and similar movements; they favor saying prayers in public schools and teaching such beliefs as creationism; and they are frequently strong anticommunists who distrust all actions of the Soviet Union and want the United States to expand its military forces continually. Syndicated television evangelists such as Jerry Falwell and Oral Roberts, who preach fervently on these social and political topics, as well as traditional religious themes, attract over 25 million viewers on a regular basis and raise more than $50 million a year through solicitations (Bollier, 1982). In addition, fundamentalists have recently become quite active politically, through such organizations as the Moral Majority. The goal of these efforts is to bring religion back into government and the schools. They oppose liberal candidates for public office and sometimes run their own candidates, exert pressures on public officials, seek to gain control of school boards, initiate court suits, and sponsor political rallies. With enormous financial resources and television exposure at its disposal, this Christian Right political movement has had considerable success in recent years in achieving some of its goals.

Emergence of Religious Cultism

Hundreds of new religious sects and cults have been created in the United States throughout its history, and some of these—including the Mormons and the Christian Scientists—have since become well-established denominations. During the last thirty years, however, a number of new religious cults have attracted thousands of followers. These cults generally center on a highly charismatic leader who claims to have some kind of new religious message, and who attracts throngs of followers. Unlike more traditional fundamentalism, which seeks to return Christianity to what are thought to be its "original doctrines," *these new cultists believe that they have a novel vision of spirituality that transcends traditional religion.* Two of these cults are briefly described as follows.

The Children of God is an outgrowth of the "Jesus Freak" movement of the hippie counterculture of the 1960s. It preserves the counterculture rejection of materialism and its emphasis on psychodelic drugs, blending them with an entirely personal and experiential approach to religion through personal salvation. The leader of this movement is Moses David, who claims to be a prophet inspired by God and who periodically issues new scriptures to the Children of God, telling them how to survive in an alien and hostile world. Members of the cult surrender all of their worldly goods to it, perform no employed work, and spend their time in contemplation or on the streets seeking new converts.

The Hare Krishna movement, which is part of a Hindu sect called the International Society for Krishna Consciousness, was brought to the United States from India in the 1960s. Its guru, or teacher, is not believed to be a god but is viewed as a living representative of the diety. The goal of the Krishna movement is to achieve Krishna consciousness, or oneness with the eternal. In its original Indian form, this could be attained only through many years of study, contemplation, and meditation. The American version has been streamlined, however, to allow attainment of Krishna consciousness simply by joining the movement, rejecting all worldly concerns (materialist, egoistic, and sexual), dressing appropriately (in saffron robes), and performing rituals (chanting, dancing, and begging). Members must commit themselves totally to the movement, associate only with each other and disassociate themselves even from their immediate families, and live in special Krishna houses.

Understanding Religious Trends

There are no simple explanations of the current trends toward religious fundamentalism and cultism. Several observations about these movements provides some understanding of them, however.

First, *they have been especially pronounced since the 1960s.* That decade and the ensuing years have been periods of very rapid and extensive social change. During such times, many people experience feelings of uncertainty, instability, confusion, and even loss of personal identity. Inevitably, many of them will turn to religion to find meaning and purpose in life. By providing definite—although oversimplified—answers to these basic questions, fundamentalism and cultism appeal strongly to peoples' need for certainty in life.

Second, *they provide a religious community for people.* As societies such as the United States become increasingly urbanized and bureaucratized, many people experience impersonality, lack of close personal relationships, loss of community, and social isolation. Most relegous sects and cults are tightly organized, involve their members extensively or exclusively with one another, and thus provide a social haven where individuals can obtain a sense of acceptance and belonging.

Third, *these new religious movements are attracting different kinds of people than in the past.* Whereas fundamentalist sects used to draw their members primarily from the most disadvantaged people in society, today they are making strong inroads into the working and middle classes. And the new cults are drawing their adherents largely from among young, middle-class, relatively well-educated people. The established churches are clearly failing to provide something—often described as a sense of spirituality and emotional involvement—that many people at all levels of society feel is extremely important in their lives.

Fourth, *the fundamentalist and cultist movements can be viewed sociologically as a response to the expanding secularization of modern societies.* Religion is vitally critical for large numbers of people, many of whom are deeply distressed by the overall withdrawal of organized religion from many areas of social life, or by specific "moral" issues such as abortion or homosexuality or school prayers. By participating in the new religious movements, they shed their sense of personal powerlessness and feel that they are contributing to maintaining morality and religion as a dynamic force in society.

LAW AND SOCIETY

All societies contain rules to direct and regulate collective activities. In foraging and horticultural societies, the rules are unwritten and are enforced through interpersonal sanctions. Although they are thus totally informal in nature, they may be quite extensive and demand strict compliance. As writing developed in agrarian societies, operating rules were increasingly specified in a formal manner and enforced by the government. Social rules thus become legal statutes. Depending on their level of structural development, such societies may also contain police systems and courts for administering the laws and prisons for handling persons who break the law. These nascent legal systems are commonly an integral part of the governmental administration, however, and do not exist as a separate social institution. The king, the land-owning nobility, and other political elites commonly proclaim and enforce laws as they please, while ordinary people are completely at their mercy without any means of legal protection or redress.

Modern Legal Systems

The heart of a modern legal system consists of laws that have been formulated and adopted through a specified process by a governmental body that is authorized to perform this function. That authorization may be derived from a constitution, tradition, or a higher government unit. *Formal statutes* may be created by any level of government on any specific topic, provided that the originating body is authorized to deal with that topic and provided that it follows established procedures in creating the laws.

In addition to formal statutes, modern legal systems typically contain three other kinds of laws. *Administrative laws* are detailed regulations issued by government agencies that are charged with enacting public policies. The legislature or other policy-making body lays out broad guidelines in an area and then leaves it to the appropriate administrative agency to write the specific regulations required to carry out that policy. These administrative regulations carry the weight of law and are enforceable through the courts. *Case laws* are legal precedents that have been established over time through the resolution of previous legal cases dealing with a common topic. Although the precedent that has emerged from those cases may not be stated explicitly, it may be cited by lawyers and judges in deciding a current case. *Common laws* are well-established social traditions and customs that are unwritten but are strongly supported by most people in a society. If no other type of law applies to a particular case, legal officials may cite common law as a basis for resolving that situation.

In most modern societies, the legal system is a separate branch of government that functions with some autonomy from the legislative and administrative branches. The legal system normally contains several components. Police agencies (local, state, and federal) enforce the existing laws and apprehend those who violate them. The courts (again at all levels of government) determine when laws have been violated and by whom, and decide upon punishments for offenders. The prisons and other correctional agencies punish offenders in various ways and may also attempt to rehabilitate them into law-abiding citizens.

Another vital component of modern legal systems is the profession of law. Professionally trained lawyers and judges prosecute and defend those charged with crimes, debate the pros and cons of civil suits, administer trials, decide legal cases (in the absence of a jury), set sentences for offenders, and perform many other roles crucial for the legal system. A hundred years ago, law was not very professionalized. Like Abraham Lincoln, an aspiring lawyer could simply read law books until he felt ready to begin practicing. Today, lawyers must be certified by the state as professionally competent, on the basis of their educational preparation and written examinations, and the field is rather strictly regulated by its professional associations.

Legal systems in most contemporary industrial societies are relatively decentralized structurally. Each level of government has its own laws and legal agencies. These separate local, state or regional, and national legal systems exercise considerable autonomy in dealing with cases that fall within their jurisdictions. For example, if a person violates a community building code, that case is handled by the local authorities, not by the state or federal legal systems. A case of murder, meanwhile, will be handled by the state legal system and cannot be appealed to the federal courts (except on other grounds), since there are no federal laws against murder. A case of espionage against the United States government, however, must go directly into the federal courts.

Most modern legal systems specify the legal rights of citizens and procedures for protecting those rights. The purpose of these "Bills of Rights" is to set explicit limits on the ability of governments to make and enforce laws on particular topics, and to ensure that individuals charged with violating the law receive a fair hearing at which they can adequately defend themselves. In legal systems based on the British model, the most basic of these citizens' rights is the presumption that one is innocent until proven guilty beyond a reasonable doubt. In contrast, Germanic-based legal systems presume that a person charged with a crime is guilty until one can prove oneself innocent.

Functions of the Law

Manifest Functions. The major functions of the legal system are fully intended and recognized. The most basic of these manifest functions is to *handle criminal cases* by identifying, apprehending, judging, and punishing individuals and organizations who violate criminal laws. A criminal law is a legal statute that requires or prohibits specified actions that are considered necessary or harmful to society as a whole. A criminal law case therefore always involves an action by the state (at some level) against the alleged offender, and any resulting punishment is carried out by a government agency.

A second manifest function of the legal system is to *settle civil disputes* between two or more private parties, either individuals or organizations. In these civil suits, the state is not a party to the dispute, even though it may involve an alleged violation of a legal statute or administrative regulation. The role of the legal system in these cases is to ensure a fair hearing for the contesting parties, determine who is at fault in that situation, and impose an appropriate settlement of the dispute.

A third manifest function of the legal system is to *provide legal protection* of several kinds. It protects the public against potentially dangerous individuals by incarcerating them in prisons or mental hospitals, and against organizations (such as businesses or government agencies) that are acting in ways that might harm citizens or the society. It also protects persons accused of a crime by preventing the alleged victim from attempting some kind of violent revenge or a vigilante group of aroused citizens from attempting to take the law into their own hands by lynching or otherwise punishing the accused in a extralegal manner.

Modern legal systems are increasingly assuming an additional function that is not formally intended but which is becoming widely recognized and accepted, and is therefore in the process of shifting from a latent to a manifest function. As the courts interpret the Constitution, legal statutes, and administrative regulations in innovative ways to fit contemporary situations, their decisions often have the effect of *creating new laws.* The most famous example of this process was the 1954 decision by the U.S. Supreme Court that racially segregated schools are inherently unequal and discriminatory. That court decision led to the eventual elimination of legally based racial segregation in this country. More recently, the courts have taken proactive stands on several other controversial issues such as abortion, school prayers, and women's rights.

Latent Functions. Legal systems perform several latent functions that are not formally intended and not generally recognized by the public, although the legal profession and social scientists are often aware of them. Perhaps the most important of these is *managing and mediating social conflicts.* This function goes beyond settling specific criminal or civil cases, since it involves defusing or resolving fundamental social conflicts that might otherwise seriously disrupt society. Although the legal system formally deals only with specific cases, the legal settlement of one or several key cases within a broad sphere of fundamental social conflict will often reduce or resolve the entire underlying controversy.

FUNCTIONS PERFORMED BY THE LEGAL SYSTEM

1. Handling criminal cases.
2. Settling civil disputes.
3. Providing legal protection.
4. Creating new laws.
5. Managing and mediating social conflicts.
6. Reaffirming cultural values and norms.
7. Transforming the exercise of power.

A second important latent function of the legal system is *reaffirming existing cultural values and norms,* thus contributing to the normative cohesion of society. As individuals and organizations are convicted of, and punished for, violating laws that reflect basic cultural values and norms, the relevance of these values and norms for the society as a whole is reaffirmed.

Finally, modern legal systems perform a critical role in *transforming the exercise of power* within contemporary societies. Through a gradual but continual process, the "rule of might" is being transformed into the "rule of right." In other words, the direct exertion of physical and economic force by elites over the rest of society is increasingly being mediated through the legal system. This legalization of social power is intended to—but certainly does not always—provide nonelites with some amount of legal protection against outright coercion and enables them to challenge the actions of elites.

Beneficiaries of the Law

Legal systems in modern societies are intended to benefit society as a whole, protecting it from illegal activities, and also to benefit individuals and organizations who have been or might be harmed by others. The gradual transformation of coercive force into legal procedures is a clear example of this process. However, this intention is far from being fully achieved in any society.

Throughout history, and still to a large extent today, *legal systems have benefited primarily the more powerful and higher-status components of societies.* These include members of privileged social classes, corporations and other business organizations, government agencies, and established churches and other sociocultural institutions. Conversely, legal systems have often discriminated against weaker and lower-status components such as the poor, minorities, groups that expose new or unpopular ideas and practices, and even the broad middle class. In the past, as well as in many developing societies today, this bias of the legal system is quite evident. Kings, members of the nobility, economic elites, government agencies, ecclesiastic churchs, and other powerful persons and organizations have often openly controlled and manipulated the legal system for their own advantage. In contemporary industrial societies, this process is generally less flagrant and more subtle, as corporations and other dominant organizations attempt to influence the legal system through indirect influences rather than direct pressures, but the bias still operates continually.

One interesting illustration of this subtle use of the law by powerful organizations is "intimidation lawsuits" (Canan and Pring, 1986). In recent years, numerous public-interest groups have increasingly challenged practices by businesses and governments, which they claim are harmful to the environment or other public concerns. In retaliation, the challenged organizations have begun filing lawsuits against the public-interest groups and their members, charging them with everything from defamation of character to infringement of constitutional rights. Although the lawsuits ask for financial compensation for the alleged damages to the business or government agency, their primary purpose is legally to intimidate citizen groups from trying to interfere with the activities of those organizations.

As societies continue to increase in technological and sociocultural complexity, their legal systems will undoubtedly become even more influential and critical for organized social life. At the same time, the historical tendency for legal systems to benefit primarily the more powerful and higher-status components of a society is still quite evident, although it is less blatant and more subtle today. Justice is supposed to be blind and to treat all members of society equally, but that ideal is still far from reality.

SUMMARY

The development of formal educational systems has been an integral part of the overall process of societal modernization. Free public education was begun in England and the United States in the seventeenth century and has been gradually expanding since then. For most of that time, however, most people have received only a primary education, and widespread secondary education did not become common until after World War II.

Public schools in the United States are similar to those in most other modern societies in three ways: the educational process is quite secularized, schools are organized as bureaucracies, and teaching is becoming increasingly professionalized. In three other ways, American schools are rather different from those in almost all other countries: free public education is provided for everyone through secondary school, school systems are controlled by locally elected school boards, and the public holds a very pragmatic view of education.

The major manifest functions performed by schools include promoting the personal development of students, transmitting the cultural heritage of the society, preparing persons for employment, facilitating upward social mobility, and encouraging innovation and change in society. Among the numerous latent functions performed by schools are teaching students to conform to cultural norms and rules, providing custodial care for children and youth, and teaching the norms and skills of competitiveness.

Four sets of factors enable parents with above-average socioeconomic status/class positions to maximize the amount and quality of education received by their children. Higher-income communities and neighborhoods provide more funds for their schools. Better-educated parents stimulate and encourage their children to do well in school. Much school instruction is oriented toward middle- and upper-status children. Teachers' expectations, school tracking systems, and student subcultures combine to create a labeling process that becomes a self-fulfilling prophecy for many students.

Considerable concern about the general quality of education in American public schools has been expressed in recent years, and a National Commission concluded that a "tide of mediocrity" pervades the schools. Several interrelated social trends have contributed to this condition, and professional educators are today exploring numerous possible ways of improving the quality of public education.

The 1954 Supreme Court desegregation ruling, followed by the 1964 Civil Rights Act, have eliminated legally based racial segregation in American schools, but there is still a great deal of segregation derived from housing patterns. The Coleman Report and many other studies of racial segregation in the public schools have all concluded that black students in integrated schools consistently score higher on standardized achievement tests than do those in segregated schools, holding constant the effects of the students' home environments. And the more years that black children spend in integrated schools, the higher their test scores. The Coleman Report initially recommended mandatory busing as a means of integrating urban school systems, but several serious problems have arisen with that strategy. Emphasis is currently being placed on voluntary busing schemes.

The common element in all religions is a set of beliefs that are viewed as sacred and are expressed through symbols and rituals. These sacred beliefs are acquired through childhood socialization, so that the religion held by an individual is largely a result of the social setting in which one is reared. Six broad types of religion are supernaturalism, animism, ancestralism, polytheism, monotheism, and ethicalism, although each of these categories contains many different specific religions. The major world religions today (in order of number of followers) are Christianity, Islam, Hinduism, Buddhism, Confucianism, Taoism, Shintoism, and Judaism.

Christian religious organizations can be placed along a continuum from established to nonestablished churches. The major characteristics of this continuum include formalness of church structure, professionalization of the clergy, nature of religious services, number and involvement of members, social status of the church and its members, and the relationship of the church to the larger society. This continuum of religious organizations is often divided into the four broad categories of ecclesias, denominations, sects, and cults. Among all modern societies, the United States is the most highly organized in terms of church membership and participation, and a majority of Americans say that religion is very important to them personally.

The most important manifest functions of religion include promoting social control, giving meaning to life, intentionally stimulating social change, creating a sense of community, providing social services, and celebrating life passages. Some vital latent functions of religion are expressing awareness of society, maintaining social cohesion, and encouraging social change.

The "dark side" of religion is that in most societies the major religion is largely controlled by the dominant class and used by it as a vehicle for exercising power over all parts of society. This process has occurred throughout human history, but was particularly evident during the era of European colonialism and during the period of slavery in the United States. Religion has also repeatedly been used to legitimate war.

A fundamental component of the process of societal modernization has been the expanding secularization of many areas of social life, although this process is far from complete in any contemporary society. In the United States, involvement in religious activities and concern for religion has declined steadily during the last forty years, which is often taken as an indication of increasing secularization. During this same period, two religious trends have been steadily expanding in the United States. Religious fundamentalism emphasizes traditional conservative theology, personal salvation, and rejection of many current social and political trends. Religious cultism involves religious movements that believe they have a novel vision of spirituality that transcends traditional religion. These recent developments provide a sense of religious community for many people, are increasingly attracting middle-class people, and can be viewed as a response to the growing secularization of modern societies.

Modern legal systems are much more formal and complicated than those in preindustrial societies, and they are crucial for the operation of industrial societies. The laws comprising these systems consist of legal statutes, administrative regulations, case laws, and common laws. Modern legal systems include police units, courts, correctional agencies, and the legal profession, all of which are relatively decentralized. They also normally include provisions to protect the rights of citizens.

The major manifest functions of legal systems in modern societies are to handle criminal cases, settle civil disputes, and provide legal protections. The courts are also increasingly creating new laws through their interpretations of constitutions and existing statutes. Among the latent functions performed by these systems are managing and mediating social conflicts, reaffirming existing cultural values and norms, and transforming the exercise of social power.

Throughout history, legal systems have generally benefited primarily the more powerful and higher-status components of society, and that bias continues today in all modern societies. However, it now tends to be more indirect and subtle than in the past.

CHAPTER

20

SOCIAL DISRUPTION

Why are some actions considered deviant, while others are not?

What are the major social causes of crime?

How do social movements develop through time, and what action strategies are used by movement organizations?

What kinds of social conditions tend to produce sociopolitical revolutions?

How is war affected by basic ecological conditions and the level of societal development?

SOCIAL DEVIANCE

Imagine a society in which everyone always did precisely what they were supposed to do according to prevailing role expectations, organizational rules, and cultural norms, so that no one's actions were ever "out of line." It would certainly be a very well-ordered, predictable, and stable society with relatively little conflict and few serious social problems or disruptions. It would also undoubtedly be a rather dull, uninteresting, and unchallenging society in which to live. And it would be a society that was largely incapable of adjusting to changing technological, environmental, social, and other conditions.

Fortunately, that kind of society has never existed in the past and is quite unlikely ever to exist in the future. Numerous writers have depicted various utopian societies in which social disruptions were minimized, and a few of those visions have been translated into experimental communities (Erasmus, 1977). However, most of those experiments have been rather short-lived, and all of them have fallen far short of the utopian ideal.

In reality, all societies constantly experience countless forms of deviance and social disruption. Moreover, many social scientists argue that modern industrialized/urbanized/bureaucratized societies display more extensive and more varied activities of this sort than most premodern societies. In this section we examine the general nature of social deviance. The following sections deal with four kinds of social disruption: crime, social movements, revolutions, and war.

Meaning of Social Deviance

If we define deviance broadly enough, all of us are frequently deviant in one way or another. We deviate from the role expectations that our role partners hold for us, fail to practice proper etiquette, say and do impolite or inconsiderate things, don't observe all of the customs of our culture, hold unconventional ideas, or sometimes act in ways that others consider "weird." In short, we are each a unique individual as well as a member of society, and at many times our personal actions are not precisely what other people or society as a whole think we should do. Such nonconforming actions can be fascinating to examine and frequently tell us a great deal about the ways in which individuals relate—or fail to relate—to their social world. For the most part, however, they do not constitute social deviance as sociologists usually define this concept.

In contrast to such idiosyncratic or non-conforming behavior, social deviance involves more critical actions that have serious consequences for shared social life. *Social deviance consists of actions that violate significant cultural norms and are negatively valued by a considerable number of people.* Such activities are viewed as a threat to established patterns of social ordering and cultural values, and the society (through its authorized agents) seeks to prevent them as far as possible and punishes people who commit them.

Social deviance is a process with five distinct steps.

(1) A cultural norm, operating rule, or law is established within a culture or subculture, which people are expected to observe.

(2) One or more persons act or interact in a way that appears to violate that cultural standard.

(3) Other people observe the deviant action and report it to community, organizational, or societal authorities.

(4) Some persons—such as a government official, a judge, a jury, a governing board, organizational administrators, or the public as a whole—determine that the observed action violates an important cultural standard and is socially undesirable or unacceptable.

(5) Either that evaluator or some other designated agent of society sanctions the violator(s) in some manner to inflict punishment and to deter such activities in the future.

This process conception of social deviance points to two fundamental generalizations. First, *no actions are inherently deviant; deviance is always socially defined.* In other words, social deviance is always relative to the conditions in which it occurs. An action that is defined as deviant by one culture or subculture, for instance, may not be considered deviant in another society. Premarital sex is absolutely prohibited in Islamic societies, widely accepted in Western societies, and frequently expected in the youth subculture of the United States. Social deviance is also relative to time and place. To continue the example of premarital sex, two or three generations ago it was severely condemned in the United States, but times have changed. Even today, however, having sex on a public beach would be treated as an offense. Finally, social deviance is relative to the person or persons who commit the activity. Premarital sex is still less acceptable to many middle-class parents than to working-class parents, and it is less accceptable for women than for men of all classes.

The second generalization follows from the first one. *No individuals are inherently deviant; they become labeled as deviants only as their actions are observed, judged, and sanctioned by others.* The person who claims to have talked with God and carries out the instructions he or she says were received in that communication might be labeled and treated as a heretic, a saint, a cultist, a mass murderer, the founder of a religion, or a psychotic. In practice, we often label individuals who act in deviant ways as criminals, perverts, or other kinds of evil persons. In doing this, however, we are judging the total individual on the basis of one or a few actions and are forgetting that most of his or her other actions may be quite conforming or "normal," as well as the fact that other people in other circumstances might judge that individual to be a hero or a pioneer.

Despite the totally relative nature of all social deviance, such activities frequently create serious problems for societies, with the result that great efforts are made to prevent, detect, and punish many kinds of unwanted deviance. Some deviant actions are seen as harmful to the persons committing them, as in "victimless crimes" such as marijuana smoking or gambling. Most serious deviant actions involve one or more victims, however, so that the negative judgment of these actions imposed by society is intended to protect the innocent persons. From a broader perspective, social deviance can also have numerous serious consequences for the community or society as a whole. It tends to undermine public acceptance of established norms and compliance with them, it weakens normative cohesion, it disrupts existing operating procedures, and it requires the expenditure of enormous financial and personnel resources for police, judicial, and incarceration services.

At the same time, however, some instances of social deviance can have beneficial consequences for society. As pointed out by Durkheim, it reaffirms cultural norms and reinforces the desirability of social ordering for society. It may also bring out hidden problems or defects in existing conditions, such as poverty or racial discrimination. Deviance may also serve as a safety valve to reduce social tension, such as political demonstrations or prostitution. And it may promote desirable social change, as when many people ignore obsolete tax laws or traditional feminine roles.

Categories of Social Deviance

There is no standard typology of different forms of social deviance. The ten categories discussed in the following paragraphs and illustrated in Figure 20-1 only indicate the wide range of activities that are commonly viewed as socially deviant in contemporary industrial societies. *These broad categories of social deviance are generally recognized in all modern societies, but the specific actions that are defined as falling within each category vary considerably across the cultures and subcultures of those societies.* Consequently, the actions mentioned for each category are merely illustrative. In addition, the typology does not differentiate between forms of social deviance that are legal or illegal—except for crime—since that distinction depends totally on the laws of particular political units. Some of the actions within each category may be illegal in

some settings, and thus constitute crimes, but they may be entirely legal in other settings.

Crime. Technically, a crime is any intentionally committed action that violates the legal code of the political jurisdiction within which it occurs. However, many such actions are never brought to the attention of the police, and of those that are, many never result in a criminal conviction. Moreover, an action that is treated as a crime in one jurisdiction—such as gambling—may be completely legal in a neighboring jurisdiction. In practice, criminologists tend to focus primarily on the most serious crimes that are generally illegal in all jurisdictions. These include crimes against people, such as murder, robbery, aggravated assault, and forcible rape; and crimes against property, such a burglary, larceny-theft, motor vehicle theft, and arson.

Mental Illness. In the past, mental illness was often considered a crime, but today it is usually defined as a form of sickness to be treated medically rather than legally. This historical legacy still influences our thinking about mental illness, however. Persons with serious mental illness are generally considered to be deviant from established norms of acceptable behavior. In contrast, persons with physical illnesses—no matter how serious—are not usually labeled as deviant, but merely sick. Psychologists frequently divide mental illness into the two broad categories of neuroses (such as anxiety or obsessions), which create problems for individuals but do not totally dominate their personalities; and psychoses (such as schizophrenia and acute depression), which can completely incapacitate a person. Individuals with severe psychoses are particularly likely to be defined as deviant.

Sexual Deviance. As illustrated by the example of premarital sexual relations, what is and is not considered deviant sexual activity varies widely across cultures and through time. Incest (however it is defined) is considered deviant everywhere, as is bestiality,

Crime

Robbery

Sexual Deviance

Homosexuality

Communicative Deviance

Slander

Political Deviance

Protests

Lifestyle Deviance

Begging

Mental Illness

Depression

Personal Deviance

Drug Use

Administrative Deviance

Ignoring Rules

Religious Deviance

Satanic Worship

Collective Actions

Riots

FIGURE 20-1   Ten categories of social deviance

but premarital and extramarital sex are becoming widely accepted and practiced. Undoubtedly the most controversial sexual practice at the present time is homosexuality, as increasing numbers of people "come out of the closet" and openly admit their homosexual preferences. Also highly controversial is the issue of abortion. The fact that homosexuality and abortion arouse strong emotions on both sides of these topics indicates that the norms concerning them are currently in flux, and many people no longer consider them deviant.

Personal Deviance. This broad category includes a variety of actions that an individual performs on himself or herself. These may involve a male wearing female clothing (a woman wearing male clothing is not considered deviant in Western societies) or wearing no clothing at all. Personal deviance may involve body mutilation, such as voluntary scarification or extensive tattooing (but not piercing one's earlobes). These actions involve food, such as cannibalism. Personal deviance can involve excessive consumption of alcohol when it leads to public drunkenness, and use of many kinds of drugs, from marijuana to crack or heroin. Although in most such cases the only "victim" is the person performing the action, these kinds of activities are often defined as deviant because they are viewed by others as morally offensive.

Communicative Deviance. The most common form of communicative deviance is lying to deceive others, although there are many shades of partial lies—such as a polite "white lie" or telling only part of the truth—that are often exempted from the label of deviance. In contrast, perjury—lying under oath—is considered a serious crime. Other forms of communicative deviance include fraud, when a situation is intentionally misrepresented; cheating on an examination; slander, or intentionally making false and harmful statements about another person; and libel, or making such accusations in writing.

Administrative Deviance. This extremely broad category includes all kinds of actions that violate some kind of administrative rule and are viewed as wrong but not morally offensive or evil. Common examples include being late to work, disregarding organizational operating regulations, violating minor traffic ordinances, gambling, drinking alcohol when under the legal age, and hundreds of other minor infractions of established social rules. The sanctions imposed for most of these actions are usually fairly mild, but the fact that they are sanctioned indicates that they are viewed as socially deviant.

Political Deviance. In autocratic societies, many kinds of political activities are often defined by the government as deviant, and these actions may be severely punished. For instance, people may not be permitted to criticize government officials or form opposition parties. Democratic societies usually permit their citizens to engage in a much wider range of political activities, but they also establish boundaries of acceptable political action. In the United States, for example, one may not advocate violent overthrow of the government, let alone attempt it— even though the country gained its independence in this manner. Other forms of political action, such as mass demonstrations or boycotts, are tolerated but are viewed by the majority of citizens as illegitimate. Another category of political deviance is participating in extremist organizations such as the Ku Klux Klan or the American Nazi Party. Finally, "Iranascam" demonstrated that high public officials may also be sanctioned for violating established political norms.

Religious Deviance. To be religiously deviant in the contemporary United States, one must belong to an esoteric religious cult, such as one that worships Satan. Virtually all other forms of religious belief and practice are accepted as legitimate, and their adherents are not defined as deviant. This has not been true in most societies throughout history, however, including many non-Western societies today. The most common situation has been to tolerate only one established religion, often supported by the state, and to define all other religious beliefs and practices as deviant. In some societies these deviant groups have been grudgingly tolerated, but in many cases their members have been severely persecuted or even executed. In addition, it has been—and still is—common for established churches to impose sanctions on their own members who question orthodox beliefs or practices. In the Middle Ages, heretics were burned at the stake; today they may be excommunicated.

Lifestyle Deviance. In all societies, some individuals either voluntarily reject or are involuntarily rejected from customary living patterns, and they consequently live in a very different manner from the majority of people. Examples of involuntary lifestyle deviance are people who spend their lives in prisons or mental hospitals. Deviant lifestyles such as those of street people, beggars, migrant laborers, and prostitutes are in one sense chosen voluntarily, but in a broader sense they are often forced upon individuals by social conditions, such as poverty and discrimination. Other deviant lifestyles are entirely voluntary, such as that of recluses (either religious or secular), hippies, paramilitary survivalists, and people who participate in group marriages.

Collective Actions. When large numbers of people congregate in one place and participate in some kind of collective action, the outcome may become socially deviant. If established social norms prevail—as in an audience watching a performance—the situation is not defined as deviant. However, a process of emotional contagion can occur among crowds of people, leading to panics, mobs, riots, and rebellions. In addition to the high level of emotionality in such situations, there is usually a shared sense of frustration, outrage, or fear that triggers collective actions that ignore established norms and often involve violence. Under such conditions, people participate in activities they would never consider doing by themselves, such as looting stores, setting cars on fire, or lynching minority persons.

Deviance in Modern Society

Critics of contemporary societies frequently argue that social deviance is now much more extensive than in the past. They often portray preindustrial rural societies as relatively harmonious and tranquil, in contrast to modern nations that are rife with conflict, social disorder, cultural confusion, and widespread deviance. Whether or not there is any validity to this accusation is impossible to determine for several reasons. First, statistics on rates of most types of deviance are woefully incomplete and inaccurate even in contemporary societies, and they are virtually nonexistent for preindustrial societies past or present. Second, cultural definitions of what constitutes deviance differ so greatly among societies and through time that such comparisons are virtually mean-ingless. Third, because modern societies tend to be more tolerant of many forms of deviance than are traditional societies, actions that were once carefully concealed—such as religious nonconformity or homosexuality—are today much more openly acknowledged.

Without attempting to resolve this debate, we can, however, identify a number of conditions in modern societies that certainly contribute to or even encourage social deviance. The following list of these conditions is undoubtedly incomplete, but it suggests that considerable social deviance of all kinds is to be expected as an integral aspect of modern social life.

(1) Modern societies have extremely *complex patterns of social ordering*, with extensive role specialization, countless diverse kinds of organizations, and complicated sets of operating procedures.

(2) Much *role acquisition* is based on personal competition and achievement, rather than traditional status ascription.

(3) The *cultural diversity* existing within modern societies creates considerable ambiguity of values, norms, and rules, as well as accommodating a wide variety of subcultures.

(4) Extensive *population heterogeneity* contributes to social and cultural diversity and leads to a wide variety of differing lifestyles.

(5) The relative *impersonality* of much contemporary life in large organizations and urban communities limits the effectiveness of direct interpersonal social control.

(6) Many forms of *social inequality*, including economic, political, racial, and gender status rankings all influence rates of social deviance.

(7) The relative *economic affluence* of a considerable proportion of the population gives many people the resources with which to engage in activities that are not available to people with meager economic means.

(8) High levels of *education* increase many people's awareness of alternative courses of action and ways of living.

(9) *Political democracy* directly contributes to greater diversity in political activities, and it

indirectly contributes to widespread variation in such realms as religion.

(10) Perhaps the most important of all these conditions in modern societies is the rapid and extensive rate of *social change,* which constantly undermines established sociocultural patterns and opens many areas of social life to innovation and experimentation, some of which will invariably be defined as deviant.

As social scientists have become increasingly aware of all these social conditions and trends that can influence or produce social deviance in modern societies, they have often challenged the traditional assumption underlying all conceptions of deviance. *Traditionally, most forms of deviance have been viewed as voluntary and intentional actions.* This "personal voluntarism" perspective is considered crucial if individuals are to be held responsible and accountable for their actions, if some actions are to be judged as socially deviant, and if the persons who take them are to be punished by society.

This assumption is open to question, however, if social conditions rather than personal choices are the main causes of many deviant actions. In such circumstances, can individuals always be held personally accountable or responsible for those actions? Instead, should not many deviant actions be viewed as a result of sociocultural conditions and forces over which most individuals have little or no control? From that perspective, *people who commit actions that are defined as deviant ought to be treated as casualties of inequality, discrimination, oppression, cultural conflicts, social change, or other sociocultural factors.* They should then be helped or treated, not punished. If we take this sociocultural determinism perspective seriously, however, are we then led to accept or at least excuse most deviant actions, no matter how seriously they violate established values and norms? This issue of voluntarism versus determinism in regard to social deviance has no clear resolution and is being vigorously debated today by social scientists, public officials, and many concerned citizens. Most instances of social deviance probably result from a combination of sociocultural pressures and individual choices, but the mixture of these two kinds of causes may be unique to each case.

CRIME

Although crime is only one of many categories of social deviance, it receives by far the greatest attention from government officials, the media, and the public. Opinion polls in the United States and several other countries have repeatedly found that crime is considered to be a very serious social problem in modern societies. And the costs of crime to society are enormous. In addition to the human and financial costs directly caused by crime, society must support police forces, legal systems, and penal institutions to cope with criminal activity.

Concept of Crime

A crime is any action that (1) violates the legal code of the political jurisdiction in which it occurs, through commission or omission; (2) is done intentionally or in reckless disregard of the law; and (3) is considered to harm society as a whole rather than just another individual. The first criterion is extremely inclusive as well as relative to a particular time and place. Legally, jaywalking and overtime parking are crimes, as are robbery or murder. The second criterion must always be proved. Many actions that would normally be crimes are not criminal when committed entirely unintentionally (unless there is reckless disregard of the law, as in manslaughter resulting from an automobile accident caused by speeding), by a young child, by a mentally deficient person, or by an insane person (which is a legal status, not a medical diagnosis). The third criterion distinguishes criminal cases from civil suits. Assault is a crime, even though only one person may be hurt, since it is considered harmful to society as a whole, and the indictment is made in the name of the "People of the state of _____," not the victim. In contrast, a suit for slander is a civil case, since it is not viewed as harmful to society, and the person convicted of it is not labeled a criminal.

Categories of Crime

Criminal actions are commonly categorized in several different ways, depending on the age of the offender, the severity of the action, the nature of the action, the setting in which it occurs, and the type of offender.

Age of the Offender. Criminal actions committed by persons who are considered old enough to know what they are doing (typically about age 11 or 12, but sometimes younger), but not mature enough to understand the full consequences of their actions (usually under age 18, but sometimes as young as 15 or 16) are commonly termed *juvenile delinquency.* These violations are often the same ones committed by adults, such as theft or disorderly conduct, but there are also "children's crimes" such as truancy, running away, curfew violation, and incorrigibility. A juvenile delinquent is usually treated by the legal system differently than is an adult. His or her case may be handled in an informal closed hearing, rather than a formal public trial. A convicted juvenile is likely to receive a reprimand, a suspended sentence, or an assignment to perform several hours of community service rather than a fine or prison sentence. When the case is considered serious enough to warrant confinement—usually only after repeated offenses—juveniles are frequently set to a detention home rather than to jail.

Severity of the Action. Violations of the law that do relatively little harm are classified as *misdemeanors,* while more serious crimes are called *felonies.* Examples of common misdemeanors are minor traffic violations, loitering, public drunkenness, a petty theft (usually under $50). Such cases are usually handled in a less formal manner than are felonies, as when one pleads guilty to speeding and pays a small fine without going to court, or through a judicial hearing rather than a formal trial.

Nature of the Action. Felonies committed by adults are commonly divided into three broad categories, depending on the nature of the act committed. *Crimes against persons* involve threatened or actual violence toward the victim, and are usually considered the most serious kind of criminal action. They include murder and manslaughter, assault (threatening or attacking another person), forcible rape (regardless of whether or not the victim actively resists), and robbery (regardless of whether or not the victim is physically harmed). *Crimes against property* comprise approximately 90 percent of all serious offenses in the United States. They include larceny-theft (stealing money or goods belonging to someone else), motor vehicle theft (classified separately because of its frequency), burglary (entering private property such as a home or business to steal), and arson (intentionally starting a fire). One form of larceny-theft that is extremely common in modern societies is embezzlement, ranging from the secretary who takes home company office supplies to the vice-president who manipulates company sales records and pockets thousands of dollars. *Crimes against morality* are often called "victimless crimes," because the only person who might possibly be harmed is the individual who commits them (Schur, 1965). Nevertheless, they are treated as crimes because powerful groups or the public as a whole consider them to be morally offensive, no matter how many people engage in them. These crimes include gambling, prostitution, drug use, and many other activities.

Setting of the Action. A popular image of crime is a robber who mugs a man in a deserted alley or a rapist who attacks a woman in a park. These and other kinds of street crimes are quite common, but *public places* are only one of many settings in which crimes occur. *Private residences* are another common setting for much crime. In addition to burglary by an outsider, tax evasion is committed in the home, as are many "crimes of passion," such as unpremeditated murder of a family member in a fit of anger. A third setting in which much crime occurs is the *work place*. These are mostly crimes against property, ranging from simple theft to elaborate embezzlement, from forgery to fraud, from false advertising to price fixing, and from padded expense accounts to stock manipulation. A fourth setting that has attracted much public attention in recent years is the *political system*. When such actions are committed by persons outside the government—such as occupying a government building, hijacking an airplane for political purposes, engaging in political terrorism, or kidnapping or assassinating a public official—they usually occur in public places, but are often defined as political in nature. When the actions are committed by people within the government—such as conspiracy, falsification of records, bribery, repression of dissent, illegal detention, or torture and murder of prisoners—they are even more clearly part of the political system.

Type of Offender. The vast bulk of petty crimes are committed by *amateur criminals* who only once or occasionally engage in such actions and for whom crime is not a way of life. These include shoplifters and tax evaders, as well as people who take home hotel towels. They also include most "victimless crimes," although these people may engage in a particular illegal activity fairly regularly. In addition, a large proportion of all assaults, rapes, and murders are committed by individuals who have never before engaged in any criminal activity.

In contrast, *professional criminals* are persons who make most or all of their living through crime, and for them it is a well-defined way of life. They include professional bank robbers, safecrackers, confidence gamesmen, and currency counterfeiters.

Many crimes are committed by *criminal organizations,* or businesses that regularly engage in illegal activities but otherwise operate as do all other businesses. Activities that are particularly favored by organized crime, because of their high profits, are transporting drugs (marijuana, cocaine, heroin, etc.),

illegal gambling (bookmaking and numbers rackets), loan sharking (loaning money at illegally high rates), and prostitution rings.

Corporations and other *legal organizations* may commit criminal actions in the course of their normal operations. When the corporation as a whole engages in such activities —such as tax evasion, price fixing, false advertising, copyright infringement, political bribery, bid rigging, or overcharging on contracts—it is often referred to as *corporate crime*. When the action is committed by an individual executive, administrator, or other "person of respectability and high status in the course of his occupation," it is usually called *white-collar crime* (Sutherland, 1961). These activities include embezzlement, stock manipulation, fee-splitting, expense account falsification, and computerized theft. The distinction between corporate and white-collar crime is often blurred, however, since the decision to commit a corporate crime must be made by a number of top executives, while the individual white-collar criminal takes advantage of the corporate or other organizational setting in which he or she works to commit those actions.

Rates of Crime

All modern societies make extensive efforts to record rates of various types of crimes. In the United States, the Federal Bureau of Investigation collects data each year from approximately 8,000 local police jurisdictions and compiles them into its annual report titled "Crime in the United States: Uniform Crime Reports." However, *all official crime statistics are known to be grossly incomplete*, for two principal reasons. First, many crimes are never reported to the police. This is particularly true of "victimless crimes," such as using drugs or visiting prostitutes, because the persons who take these actions often view the pertinent law as illegitimate and are not about to turn themselves into the police. Many white-collar crimes are also never reported after they are discovered because the corporation involved wants to avoid bad publicity, and so it merely fires the offending employee. We do know, however, that the total cost of the major kinds of white-collar crimes—embezzlement, forgery, tax evasion, and fraud—is at least three times as great as all other crimes against property (President's Commission on Law Enforcement and the Administration of Justice, 1967). Second, many local police departments do not inform the FBI of all the crimes known to them, often because they do not keep accurate records. Underreporting of crime rates is also done for political reasons, as when a police commissioner or sheriff is running for reelection and wants to present a favorable public image of his administration.

More accurate, but unofficial, statistics on rates of criminal activity are periodically obtained from victim surveys that ask respondents how frequently they have been victimized by a crime. For instance, a survey by the Law Enforcement Assistance Administration (*New York Times*, 1974) covering 200,000 people in eight major cities found that these respondents reported about twice as much crime as shown by official statistics. More specifically, although the official rates for murder and auto theft appear to be relatively accurate, the actual rate of robberies is about fifty percent higher than the official rate, the rates for larceny-theft and aggra-

vated assault are about twice the numbers reported, there are three times as many burglaries as shown in official figures, and there are at least four times as many rapes as are reported.

Despite these serious reporting limitations, the known crime rates in the United States are quite disturbing to public officials and citizens. Table 20-1 gives the official rates for eight major types of crime in the United States in 1960 and 1980 and shows the percentage increase in each rate during that period. In twenty years the rates of murder doubled, aggravated assault and burglary more than doubled, larceny-theft and burglary more than tripled, and known forcible rapes and robbery both quadrupled. Particularly disturbing is the fact that these rates of violent crimes in the United States are much higher than in most other industrial societies. For example, there are more homocides each year in Detroit than in all of Great Britain (FBI, 1975:11).

One explanation of these rising crime rates is undoubtedly better reporting in recent years, as citizens and organizations have become more concerned about crime and as police reporting procedures have improved. Another explanation of rising crime rates is the growing proportion of the population between the ages of 16 and 25, who account

TABLE 20-1 Official National Crime Rates in the United States in 1960 and 1980

Type of Crime	Rate Per 100,000 Population		Percent Increase
	1960	*1980*	
Murder	5	10	100
Aggravated assault	110	291	165
Forcible rape	9	36	300
Robbery	60	244	307
Larceny-theft	1,028	3,156	207
Burglary	506	1,688	234
Suspected arson	—*	64	—*

* No data available.

Source: U.S. Bureau of the Census, Statistical Abstract of the United States, 1975, 1981, and 1984. Washington, D.C.: U.S. Government Printing Office.

for over half of all arrests. A third explanation is the expanding traffic in narcotics, which is a major source of income for organized crime and which leads many users to commit crimes to obtain money to pay for drugs. Nevertheless, we do not presently understand many of the complex factors that are contributing to the recent increases in all types of reported crimes.

We can, however, discard the traditional idea that most crimes are committed by particular types of people, such as lower-class persons or minorities. It is true that the FBI's "Uniform Crime Reports" indicates that some categories of individuals are much more likely than others to be arrested. These include males, persons under age 25, nonwhites, urban dwellers, and persons with low socioeconomic statuses. However, those figures reflect only crimes known to the police for which an arrest was made. In addition to gross underreporting of white-collar and victimless crimes, there is a strong bias within police departments to arrest the previously named kinds of individuals much more frequently than women, older people, nonminorities, and higher-status persons.

An alternative source of data on criminal activity is the self-report studies that ask respondents to mention (completely anonymously) the crimes they have committed. These studies show that *almost everyone has committed some kind of legal offense,* and most people report more than one such action (Doleschal and Klapmuts, 1973; Tittle, et al., 1978). At one time or another, we all engage in criminal activity, but only a small proportion of those actions are reported to the police. An even smaller proportion of them lead to arrests, only some of those cases are prosecuted, and just a tiny fraction of all crimes result in a formal conviction and punishment. Moreover, at each stage in this process, cases involving higher-status and nonminority persons are more likely to be dismissed. Conversely, *cases involving persons with disadvantaged socioeconomic or minority statuses are much more likely to be acted upon by the authorities.* Justice is never blind to people's statuses in society.

Social Causes of Crime

When we read a newspaper account of someone who robs banks for a living, embezzles a million dollars from their employer, or randomly kills twenty people, we may likely wonder, "What went wrong with his socialization?" or "What conditions led her to do that?". To understand why a particular individual commits a criminal action, or why he or she commits one particular kind of crime rather than another, we must examine that individual's biological and psychological characteristics and the circumstances of their personal lives. In particular, judges and penal authorities must obtain such information about each individual criminal if they are to impose an appropriate punishment and handle the person in a just and beneficial manner.

When sociologists study crime, however, they seek answers to very different questions. They are concerned with the sociocultural conditions that produce crime as a social activity, as well as various kinds of criminal actions. A number of sociological theories have been proposed to explain the occurrence of crime, and many empirical studies have been conducted on this topic. The current sociological explanations for the occurrence of crime in modern societies can be grouped into five categories, each of which is briefly described in the following paragraphs. These are not competing theories, in the sense that only one of them will eventually be found to be true. Rather, they offer complementary explanations of the social causes of crime, and all of them are undoubtedly valid to one degree or another. They merely focus on different aspects of the criminal process, so that some are more relevant than others in particular situations, but they must all be considered if we are to understand why modern societies produce crime.

Social Control Theory. The central argument of this theory of criminal activity is that *the process of social control of individuals' actions is inadequate in particular situations.* This perspective does not argue that normal social controls fail completely with criminals, since most of those people's actions conform to existing social norms. What it does argue is that under some conditions the process of social control breaks down. This may occur within the individual, as a result of a norm not being adequately internalized or being rejected. It may also occur in interpersonal interaction, as a result of role expectations not being clearly conveyed or informal sanctions not proving effective (Reckless, 1961). In either case, the individual acts entirely on the basis of his or her personal motives, without regard to social expectations or responsibilities. Depending on the nature of those motives, the person's actions may be quie "normal," they may be deviant in some manner, or they may violate the law and be considered criminal. To explain why some individuals repeatedly commit criminal actions, Travis Hirschi (1971) focused on people's bonds to society. When that bond is severely weakened or broken, criminal actions are particularly likely to occur. This bond has four elements, all of which are important in the process of social control: attachments to other individuals; commitment to social roles and activities; involvement in social relationships and organizations; and belief in established values and norms.

Opportunity Availability Theory. Durkheim (1964) coined the term "anomie" to describe a situation in which societal norms have broken down or become inadequate to guide much social activity, with the result that in many situations people find themselves in a condition of "normlessness." Although this concept of anomie pertains to ineffective social control, Robert Merton (1968, Chs. 6 and 7) used it in a different manner. He focused on situations in which the established norms and institutionalized patterns of a society are not adequate to enable some people to achieve its valued cultural goals, such as occupational achievement or financial success. In such situations, individuals may seek new, nonnormative ways of attaining those goals. Some of these innovative actions—such as stealing a car

that one cannot afford to buy, or manipulating a company's stocks to increase its profits—will likely be defined as criminal. In short, *restricted or unavailable opportunities to follow normatively accepted means to attain culturally valued goals will lead some people to take innovative actions that violate the law.* (Merton also identified several other possible ways of coping with such situations, including ritualistic adherence to existing inadequate norms, retreat into non-goal-oriented activities such as drinking or drug abuse, and rebellion against prevailing cultural goals. These alternative coping strategies may lead to other forms of deviance, but are less relevant to crime.) Several sociologists (Cohen, 1955; Cloward and Ohlin, 1960) have demonstrated that limited opportunities for achieving middle-class success goals such as employment and money are especially relevant for explaining lower-class delinquent gangs.

Cultural Transmission Theory. Criminal actions, like all other social activities, are learned from the cultures and subcultures in which we live. If our culture tells us that falsifying our income-tax return is acceptable (because "Everyone does it"), or we belong to a subculture that glorifies violence (as a way of demonstrating one's manhood), we are very likely to adopt and enact those norms, regardless of the fact that they violate the law. In particular, through "differential association" with deviant and criminal subcultures, individuals learn the techniques of crime and accept norms that justify criminal activities (Sutherland, 1939). This theory has often been applied to juvenile gangs (Cloward and Ohlin, 1960), but it is equally applicable to professional criminals (who often learn the "tricks of the trade" from other inmates in prison) and to white-collar corporate criminals (when the corporate culture stresses maximizing profits in any way possible) (Akers, 1977). In short, *criminal activity is learned through socialization into deviant subcultures.*

Symbolic Labeling Theory. As discussed earlier, deviance is a process that involves not only an action that violates the existing norms or laws, but also detection, judgment, and sanctions by others toward the offender. This perspective is particularly relevant to crime. Although almost everyone commits a criminal action at one time or another, most people are never socially defined as criminals. This is because their actions are never detected, are judged to be trivial or excusable, or are not punished. To take account of this process, sociologists use the concept of "labeling" to explain how some individuals become viewed by society as criminals (Becker, 1963; Lemert, 1967). Individuals who are labeled and treated by others—especially law-enforcement officials—as a "delinquent" or a "professional thief" or a "gangster" are much more likely to continue engaging in such actions in the future than are persons who are not so labeled. (This process of labeling also occurs with "nuts," "sluts," "queers," "terrorists," and many other kinds of deviants.) In other words, *through symbolic labeling, society reinforces criminal activity and influences people to enact further criminal roles in the future.* Other symbolic rituals that contribute to this process include "degradation ceremonies," in which the offender is forced to admit the immorality of his or her action and the power of legal authorities (Garfinkel, 1956), and "stigmatizing" a person as a socially unfit or undesirable individual (Goffman, 1963). Numerous studies have demonstrated, however, that labeling and other symbolic rituals are applied quite selectively by authorities, so that middle-class "respectable" people are much less likely to be treated in this manner than are lower-class "disreputable" persons (Chamblis, 1973; Piliavin and Briar, 1964).

Power Manipulation Theory. Powerful economic, political, and other elites can often shape the legal system of their society to legitimate and protect actions that are important to them, while ensuring that other actions which harm their interests are defined as criminal. As expressed by Richard Quinney (1974:8), "Law is the tool of the ruling class." The political leader who starts

---

THEORIES OF CRIME CAUSATION

1. Social control theory.
2. Opportunity availability theory.
3. Cultural transmission theory.
4. Symbolic labeling theory.
5. Power manipulation theory.

---

a war or the corporate executive who approves dumping toxic wastes into the environment are not likely to be treated as criminals, while the lobbyist who tries to bribe a politician or the office worker who falsifies company records are more likely to be prosecuted as criminals (Liazos, 1972). The point stressed by this perspective is that *law and crime are rarely a black-and-white matter of right and wrong but are often defined and administered by powerful interests in society for their own benefit.* Consequently, criminality always reflects the power structure and dominant interests of society. Very frequently, elites use the legal system to prevent social changes that they oppose, such as the formation of labor unions during the early decades of the twentieth century or the antiwar movement of the 1960s and 1970s. When elites want to promote social change, however, they can use the legal system for that purpose, as in Affirmative Action laws.

Although there are many important theoretical differences among these various explanations of crime, they all share one common assumption. Criminal activity is an integral part of society, and it can only be understood by taking account of a variety of relevant social conditions and processes. To explain and control crime, therefore, we must examine society, not just individual criminals.

SOCIAL MOVEMENTS

Crime and social movements disrupt established patterns of social and cultural ordering. Some of the tactics used by social movement organizations may violate the law, and elites sometimes succeed in having movement organizations declared illegal. Despite these similarities, crime and social movements are quite different social activities. The most fundamental of these differences is that people generally commit crimes to benefit themselves in some way, whereas people usually participate in social movements to change society. Such changes, if realized, may benefit some participants directly, but many people support or join social movements without any thought of personal gain. Their concern, rather, is to contribute to changing society in a manner that they believe is desirable and/or necessary.

Nature of Social Movements

A social movement is a loosely organized effort by a relatively large number of people to change their society in some critical way. Although the nature of the desired change is unique to each social movement, all of them share several common characteristics.

(1) They are *goal-oriented,* in that they seek to promote intentional social change. The objectives of some movements are fairly specific, such as eliminating discrimination against homosexuals, while other movements espouse quite vague goals, such as the desire of the counterculture movement of the 1960s and 1970s to create a new lifestyle.

(2) They focus around an *ideology,* or shared belief system that describes how society should be changed and improved. This ideology not only defines the goals of the movement, but it also provides a rationale for the importance of these goals. It is the primary focus of whatever overall cohesion the movement generates.

(3) They attract relatively *large numbers* of people, often in the thousands or even millions. However, there are many degrees of participation in social movements, including casual sympathizers, committed supporters, active participants, and highly involved leaders. Even though a woman might deny being an active "women's libber," for instance, she might nevertheless support the goal of equal rights for women or contribute money to a women's organization.

(4) They are often organized into a number of action-oriented *movement associations.* Although all of the organizations within a social movement usually share a common ideology and may sometimes collaborate in joint activities, they frequently operate independently of each other and may at times conflict over objectives to be sought or strategies to be pursued.

(5) Movement organizations usually have several fairly prominent *leaders* who act as spokespersons for the movement to the public. Most of these leaders are deeply involved with their organizations, but sometimes they are independent writers or public lecturers. One of the principal activities performed by these leaders is legitimizing the movement to the public.

Social movements typically originate within a particular society, since their concern is to change that society in some way. The civil rights movement in the United States, for example, is largely confined to this country. With contemporary electronic communications, however, a movement that begins in one society may spread to other societies that contain similar conditions or problems. Although the student/youth movement of the 1960s began in the United States, it rather quickly spread to most other Western industrial societies. Other social movements that have developed in this country during the past few decades, but have spread in varying degrees to other societies, include the women's movement, the peace movement, the gay rights movement, the abortion movement, and the environmental movement.

It is important to *distinguish between a general social movement and its specific movement organizations.* The movement as a whole will usually be focused around a common ideology, such as the concern of the environmental movement to protect and preserve natural resources, environmental quality, and wildlife. Members of the public who sympathize with the movement or support its goals will likely identify with the movement as a whole, while critics and opponents of the movement will frequently criticize or condemn it as a whole. People who are more actively involved in the movement, however, will frequently belong to only one or a few movement organizations. Active participation in one organization often leaves little time or energy to become equally involved in other movement organizations. In addition, these involved members typically feel that their particular organization is dedicated to the most desirable objectives within the movement or is pursuing the most effective action strategies. Because movement participants tend to differ in these assessments, it is not uncommon to find a number of separate action organizations within a single movement, each of which has its own particular objectives and strategies. For instance, within the broad environmental movement there is the Sierra Club, Friends of the Earth, the Natural Resources Defense Council, the Audubon Society, the Wildlife Society, Environmental Action, the Environmental Defense Fund, and many other environmentally oriented associations.

Types of Social Movements

Considering the almost unlimited variety of goals that might be sought by social movements, it is difficult to classify them into neatly defined categories. One simple typology is fairly commonly utilized, however.

Reform movements seek to improve some specific aspect of society. At the same time, they accept the basic social/political/economic structure of the society. The social movements previously mentioned are all essentially reform movements, as were earlier movements to abolish slavery, establish labor unions, and promote prohibition.

Revolutionary movements attempt to create an entirely new kind of social, political, and/or economic system and thus a totally new society. Revolutions frequently involve a direct attack on the existing political system, as in the French Revolution of 1798, the Russian Revolution of 1917, and the more recent revolutions in Cuba, Iran, and many other countries. This is not always the case, however, as exemplified by the Social Democratic political parties

in Western European nations that are attempting to replace capitalism with socialism through democratic actions within the existing political systems. Revolutions will be discussed more extensively in the next section of this chapter.

Reactionary movements desire to "turn back the clock" and recreate conditions they believe existed at some time in the past. In the United States, the Moral Majority, the Ku Klux Klan, and the anti-abortion movement are current examples. Such movements usually begin with fairly specific objectives, but sometimes expand to advocate a broader revolution, as occurred when the Nazis gained control of the government in Germany in 1933.

Utopian movements seek to "move the clock forward" to some imagined and desired ideal future conditions. Although they rarely engage in direct political action, their advocates may attempt to create a community based on their utopian ideas. A number of such experimental communities, such as New Harmony, Indiana, were established in the United States during the nineteenth century, but none of them survived for long. More recent examples of utopian social movements include the communal movement of the 1960s (which also created many short-lived communities), and the current voluntary simplicity movement (which has resulted in a few experimental communities).

Expressive movements attempt to change society by modifying the psychological and emotional states of their members. They believe that change must originate within the individual, and that if enough people experience such change, this will eventually alter society. Many such movements are religious in nature, such as the "Moonies" and the "Jesus

---

TYPES OF SOCIAL MOVEMENTS

1. Reform movements.
2. Revolutionary movements.
3. Reactionary movements.
4. Utopian movements.
5. Expressive movements.

people." In the 1970s, however, an entirely secular expressive movement arose, under the general heading of humanistic psychology, which was expressed in such activities as Transcendental Meditation, est (Erhard Seminar Training), Transactional Analysis, and encounter groups.

Development of Social Movements

The process through which social movements develop has been studied by many sociologists in recent years. By combining the findings of a number of researchers (Gamson, 1975; McCarthy and Zald, 1977; Oberschall, 1973; Smelser, 1962), we can identify eight stages through which social movements often progress as they develop. In reality, these stages are not clearly distinguished, they frequently overlap, and they do not necessarily occur in the sequence given here. Nevertheless, these eight features do occur in most social movements, particularly reform movements.

Strains. Some kind of serious strain exists in the social ordering and/or culture of a society. These strains frequently center on inequalities among social classes or other parts of the society, discrimination or exploitation toward disadvantaged segments of the society such as racial or ethnic minorities, severe economic problems such as widespread unemployment, or a crisis in the political system, such as loss of legitimacy by the government. At least some members of the society become aware of this strain, define it as a social problem, and come to feel that existing conditions are unacceptable or intolerable.

Beliefs. As these perceptions and feelings develop and become increasingly widespread, some individuals articulate and discuss them as a situation that can and should be changed. Secularized cultures, in which social change is seen as possible and desirable, are therefore much more hospitable to social movements than are traditional or relatively sacred cultures. In addition, these social critics formulate a plausible explanation

of the causes of the undesirable situation and suggest the changes that are necessary to rectify it. In other words, they create a coherent ideology that will become the focus of the social movement.

Support. As the problem, its causes, and its potential solution are discussed and debated by the spokespersons for the movement and their opponents, public opinion coalesces on the issue. Growing numbers of citizens become aware of the situation, sympathize with the ideology and goals of the developing movement, and begin to support it. At this stage, most of these people will not be active participants in the movement, but they will provide an expanding base of support for it. Conversely, if most of the public ignores the emerging issue or feels that it is unimportant, the movement is likely to remain merely a topic of discussion among intellectuals and social critics.

Mobilization. This is perhaps the most crucial stage in the development of a social movement. If it is to become more than merely an issue for public discussion, the movement must mobilize resources that can be committed to creating organizations and promoting social change. The most vital resources that must be mobilized are people willing to become actively involved in the movement with their time and efforts, plus financial contributions from them and/or other movement sympathizers. To mobilize such resources, the spokespersons for the developing movement not only proclaim its ideology as widely as possible, but they also attempt to dramatize the seriousness and unacceptability of the underlying problem and the necessity for social change to resolve that problem. This process can be greatly expedited if some incident occurs that attracts media attention and shocks and angers public opinion, such as the Kent State University killings did for the student movement and the Three-Mile Island accident did for the anti-nuclear movement.

Organization. Thus far, the movement is still likely to be rather amorphous and unorganized. Before concerted efforts can be made to promote social change, one or more action-oriented organizations must be established, often with relatively complex structures. As mentioned previously, a number of separate organizations are likely to emerge, each with its own particular objectives and preferred strategies of action. This diffuse network of separate organizations can be quite beneficial for the movement, for two reasons.

(1) Supporters can locate and join the particular association with which they feel most comfortable, which maximizes opportunities for participation.
(2) There is no single entity that opponents of the movement can attack and seek to destroy.

However, these various movement organizations must all share a common ideology (at least in broad terms), communicate among themselves, and be willing to cooperate rather than quarrel over objectives and strategies. To establish and operate these movement organizations, the original spokespersons for the movement who formulated its ideology and generated public support must often be replaced by new leaders who are more skilled in organizational dynamics.

Action. Movement organizations are created to take action to promote social change. They develop objectives to pursue, strategies for achieving those objectives, and specific tactical actions to enact their strategies. To achieve success they must then carry out their strategies and tactics and accomplish at least some of their objectives. This stage of the process is discussed in greater detail in the following section.

Reaction. Social movements and movement organizations are rarely, if ever, unopposed. Since they are attempting to change society in some critical way, there will almost inevitably be strong opposition to their efforts. Moreover, their opponents are likely to be powerful elites within the established economic, political, legal, and other systems of the society. Those opponents may be protecting their own interests, or they may sincerely believe that the movement is harmful to society. In either case, they are usually in a position to mobilize extensive resources—organizations, funds, people, and public opinion—to counter the movement. Most social movements therefore face an uphill struggle against overwhelmingly superior resources. An alternative strategy sometimes used by established organizations—especially the major political parties—is to coopt the movement by adopting some or all of its ideology and persuading leaders of movement organizations to "join the system" and work for change within it rather than from the outside.

Resolution. Several alternative outcomes may eventually develop from a social movement. It may be successful in attaining some or all of its goals, thus initiating significant social change. It may be completely suppressed or defeated by the opposition, or else be coopted by it. It may slowly fade away as people lose interest in it, regardless of whether or not it has achieved any of its goals. Or it may become an established and relatively permanent part of the society, continuing to work for desired social changes and gradually realizing at least partial success. This last possibility is often described as "institutionalization" of the movement, since it becomes accepted by the public and elites as a legitimate activity, and the various movement organizations become increasingly formalized and self-sustaining. If this happens, a third set of leaders will likely emerge who are skilled in fund raising, pub-

---

STAGES OF SOCIAL MOVEMENTS

1. Social strains.
2. Shared beliefs.
3. Widespread support.
4. Public mobilization.
5. Movement organizations.
6. Direct actions.
7. Official reactions.
8. Eventual resolution.

lic relations, and organizational management, replacing the previous leaders who founded the movement organizations and guided their initial activities.

Action Strategies

Most social movements are acting from a position of weakness in relation to established authorities and elites. If they are to succeed in changing society in the way they desire, they must carefully choose their broad strategies of action and specific tactics for enacting those strategies. Four basic types of strategies—each of which has numerous tactical variations—are most commonly utilized by social movements (Williams, 1977).

Persuasion. Many movements will initially attempt to use information and *rational arguments* to persuade the public, elites, and authorities of the seriousness of the problem with which they are concerned and the need for social change. Such arguments generally have little impact, however. Much more effective are *emotional appeals*, especially ones that portray innocent victims being seriously exploited, economically or physically harmed, or even killed as a result of the present situation. Again, an event such as Kent State or Three-Mile Island that attracts extensive media coverage can be extremely useful to a social movement in presenting its emotional appeal. These appeals are usually aimed at the general public to gain large numbers of sympathizers and supporters. Public opinion polls are often used to measure the strength of this public support. Movement leaders can then approach elites and officials with the assertion that "a large majority of the public is behind us in this matter." If elites and authorities become convinced that this is true, they are much more likely to negotiate with the movement leaders and make concessions to them.

Pressures. Social movements cannot offer jobs or other financial incentives to their supporters or to elites and officials, as is frequently done by leaders of established orga-

nizations such as corporations and governments. If they have sufficient public support, however, they can threaten to have their supporters *withhold actions* that elites or authorities believe are necessary. With business firms, this typically involves organizing a boycott of their products or services. With elected officials, this usually involves threatening to vote for their opponents in the next election. There is always a certain amount of bluffing with this strategy, since movement leaders never know how many of their sympathizers and supporters will participate in a boycott or vote for opposing candidates. Nor can they command those people to take such actions. However, if movement leaders can present a convincing threat, elites and officials will often respond even if they are doubtful about the validity of the threat. Maintaining the goodwill and support of the public is extremely important to most established leaders, so that they are frequently unwilling to "call the bluff" of the movement leaders, in case they might lose the contest. Another kind of pressure that has been extensively employed in recent years is threatening to, or actually filing, a *lawsuit* against elites or officials. This tactic has been particularly effective in the civil rights movement, since the courts have generally ruled in favor of civil rights organizations. The consumer movement also uses class action suits, which are filed in the interest of all consumers of a particular product without specifically naming all those individuals. Finally, some social movements organize *initiatives* for public voting.

Protests. Leaders of social movements often organize various kinds of *mass activities* such as mass meetings, marches, sit-ins, walk-outs, picketing, and demonstrations. One purpose of such events is to gain publicity, especially when the mass media cover them, and thus attract more sympathizers and supporters. This strategy can be quite effective (Gamson, 1974) even if a majority of the public views such actions as illegitimate (Olsen and Hovey, 1974). A second purpose of these mass activities is to disrupt normal social life and bring strong pressures to bear on elites and officials in an effort to force them to initiate changes. With this strategy, however, there is always the possibility that elites and officials will instead attempt to prevent or constrain the demonstration by obtaining a court injunction, calling out the police or National Guard, or having the participants arrested. Organizers of mass activities therefore always take a calculated risk that the established system will tolerate and respond to them rather than oppose or attack them. Another variation of this strategy is *civil disobedience,* in which protesters deliberately violate an existing law, passively accept arrest, and tolerate whatever official sanctions are imposed on them. The idea of civil disobedience was formulated by Henry David Thoreau in the nineteenth century and was very effectively used by Mahatma Ghandi in his campaign to gain political independence for India from Great Britain, as well as by the more recent civil rights and anti-nuclear movements in the United States. This approach depends on authorities treating the protesters in a relatively humane manner, however. If the protesters are imprisoned indefinitely or executed—as occurred when civil disobedience was attempted against the Nazi treatment of Jews—their efforts may be totally ineffective.

Violence. Threatened or actual *physical violence* is always a possibility with social movements, either as an intentional strategy or as an unintended outcome of demonstrations that get out of hand. Riots, bombings, hijackings, kidnappings, assassinations, terrorism, and other violent events occur quite frequently in developed and developing countries around the world. Individuals and organizations that engage in such activities are almost always condemned by the public as "extremists" and severely punished by authorities if apprehended. Although this strategy therefore appears to be suicidal for a social movement, it is sometimes adopted as a last-ditch effort by movement organizations that have been unsuccessful in using

other strategies. If peasants, workers, or minorities come to feel that all other strategies are hopeless and that they have "nothing to lose but their chains," they may resort to violence to gain public attention, even if the result is repression of the movement by authorities. At the same time, the opposite side of this issue of violence must not be overlooked. In many demonstrations and other events that are intended to be nonviolent, violence is initially and most extensively utilized not by the protesters, but by police and other public officials. *Official violence* has been quite common in early efforts by unions to organize workers, the civil rights movement, the antiwar movement, and early stages of revolutions.

REVOLUTIONS

Sociopolitical revolutions have often been major turning points in the development of societies. Historians, consequently, have devoted considerable attention to describing these critical events. Only recently, however, have sociologists begun to study them in depth. Whereas historians are usually concerned with describing the details of specific revolutions, sociologists use these historical events as case studies. Their concern is to formulate generalizations that can be applied to all sociopolitical revolutions.

Meaning of Sociopolitical Revolution

The term "revolution" is used in several ways in the social sciences. Sometimes it refers to a gradual, but fundamental, transformation of the basic organization of society, such as the agrarian revolution, the urban revolution, or the industrial revolution. At other times, it is applied to widespread changes in particular areas of social life, such as the "sexual revolution" or the "communications revolution." In this section, however, we are specifically concerned with sociopolitical revolutions that involve the political system of a society. Although such revolutions often begin as reform movements, they frequently escalate in scope and intensity until they become a total revolution.

As previously mentioned, a revolutionary sociopolitical movement attempts to change the social, economic, and/or political systems and thus create a new kind of society. A full-scale revolutionary movement usually seeks to alter the power structure of the society and consequently its social class structure; it frequently wants to make major alterations in the control and operation of the economic system; it almost always insists that the existing government must be replaced; and it often desires to modify the state, or basic structure of political authority within the society. The process of promoting such extensive societal change invariably provokes severe social conflict. Powerful sectors of the society—economic elites, government leaders, the dominant class, the legal system, the military, and the established church—will usually oppose the revolutionary movement. When conflict becomes that widespread and acute, violence is extremely likely to erupt. In short *a sociopolitical revolution attempts to make fundamental and radical changes in the organization of society and the state, often through extensive social conflict and possibly through violence.*

Causes of Sociopolitical Revolutions

As with all social disruptions, there is no single or simple cause of sociopolitical revolutions. We can, however, identify a variety of societal conditions that may contribute to the outbreak of an attempted revolution. Theorists emphasize these various conditions to differing degrees, but all of them have been important in the major sociopolitical revolutions that have occurred during the past two hundred years. Five types of conditions that contribute to the creation of sociopolitical revolutions are described in the following paragraphs and illustrated in Figure 20-2.

Severe Social and Cultural Tensions. It usually takes more than a few problems in a society to spawn a revolution. Prerevolu-

FIGURE 20-2   Factors contributing to sociopolitical revolutions

Severe Social and Cultural Tensions

Widening Gap between Expectations and Reality

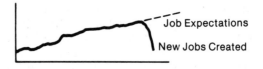

Ineffectiveness or Breakdown of the State

Development of a Revolutionary Movement

Creation of an Alternative Authority Structure

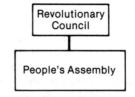

tionary societies often exhibit a wide range of serious social and cultural problems that affect large numbers of people, create severe tensions throughout the society, and come to be viewed as intolerable. As emphasized by Marx and Engels (1948), these tensions might center caround class exploitation and inequality, or they might focus on a fundamental crisis in the cultural values of a society (Johnson, 1964). If these problems and tensions remain unresolved and continue to escalate for a long period of time—and especially if established elites refuse to recognize or deal with them—the society becomes increasingly ripe for a revolution. Alternatively, elites may make halfhearted, but unsuccessful, efforts to deal with these situations, or they may actively oppose all initial attempts at social reform. In any case, more and more people gradually come to believe that revolution is the only viable course of action.

A Widening Gap Between People's Expectations and Reality. Paradoxically, sociopolitical revolutions tend to occur not when problems and tensions are at their worst, but as conditions are improving. When problems and tensions are extremely severe, any effort by elites to deal with them will appear desirable, and most people will tend to go along with these efforts rather than attempt to change their society radically. As conditions slowly improve, however, people's expectations for the future will often begin to soar until they far exceed actual conditions. This situation may be the result of elaborate but unrealistic promises by political leaders, or it may be caused by a sudden cessation or even reversal of the trend toward better conditions. In either case, the gap between public expectations and sociopolitical reality widens rapidly, producing extreme frustration and despair among large numbers of people. At this point a revolution is especially likely to erupt. "The actual state of socioeconomic development is less significant than the expectation that past progress, now blocked, can and must continue in the future" (Davies, 1962:9). Such a condition is usually described by sociologists as *relative deprivation*. The actual level of deprivation that people are experiencing is not as important as their perception and belief that they are

much worse off than they might and should be. Actual conditions at the present time may be compared to either public expectations for the future (which might be termed "temporal deprivation"), or to another society that appears to be making much faster progress in dealing with similar problems (which might be termed "comparative deprivation"). In either case, many people experience a sense of intolerable deprivation between what is and what might be.

Operational Ineffectiveness or Breakdown of the Existing State. As stressed by Theda Skocpol (1979), societies in which the state is functioning effectively and remains strong rarely experience revolutions. There are two principal reasons for this. First, if the state and its government appear to be operating relatively effectively, most people will tend to support it in hope that it will eventually resolve the problems and tensions besetting the society, no matter how severe they may be. Second, if the state and its government appear to be relatively strong economically and politically, dissident groups of citizens will tend to believe that they have little hope of successfully overthrowing it, and if they do attempt to initiate a revolution they will likely be quickly suppressed. Revolutions—especially successful ones—therefore usually occur in societies in which the state is weak and ineffective. Although a breakdown of state effectiveness and power can result from several causes, it is especially likely when the national government is experiencing severe pressures and stresses from other countries within the world system. Those international stresses most commonly result from either economic competition or war. Both of those conditions force the government to devote most of its resources and efforts to external affairs and to ignore domestic conditions and problems. The state is particularly susceptible to breakdown if it loses this economic competition or war, so that its citizens feel deprived at home and defeated abroad.

Development of a Revolutionary Movement with Strong Leadership. As long as the citizens of a society remain unorganized in regard to their problems, a sociopolitical revolution is not likely to develop, no matter how deprived they may feel. Initiating and conducting a revolution requires organization among its supporters and the emergence of capable leadership (Britain, 1952). Intellectuals must become dissatisfied with existing conditions and formulate a radical alternative and an ideology to justify it. Politically oriented movement organizations must be created and attract large numbers of sympathizers and supporters. There must be overall leadership of the entire movement, either by one dominant movement organization or through a coalition of several of them. And a revolutionary party must be formed with the explicit goal of overthrowing the present government and capturing the state.

Creation of an Alternative Authority Structure That Claims Political Legitimacy and Sovereignty. Although sociopolitical revolutions often begin through relatively spontaneous uprisings and demonstrations by peasants, workers, students, or other dissident sets of people within the society (Skocpol, 1979), their ultimate success depends on the creation of "multiple sovereignties" (Tilly, 1975). That is, an alternative body or "counterstate" is created that claims a legitimate right to form a government and to which large numbers of people give allegiance. This alternative body will be in direct conflict with the existing state, so that the society becomes polarized between the two competing authority structures. Successful completion of the revolution will depend on the ability of the counterstate to gain the allegiance of large numbers of supporters, to overthrow the existing government, and to create a new and viable state in its place. Otherwise, the existing state and its government will remain in power, and the revolution will be crushed.

Revolutionary Outcomes

Conducting a successful revolution in the face of powerful opposition by an estab-

lished government and economic and other elites is an extremely difficult and risky endeavor. Revolutionary leaders are quite likely to lose their movement and their heads. Consequently, it is not surprising that most nascent sociopolitical movements are suppressed or defeated. Conversely, it is quite surprising that there have been a number of successful sociopolitical revolutions during the past two hundred years. The United States and France carried out revolutions in the eighteenth century, and the twentieth century has witnessed successful revolutions in Russia, China, Cuba, East Germany, and several other nations.

Overthrow of the existing government is not the end of a major sociopolitical revolution, however. *The most critical period in a revolution comes after the existing government is overthrown, as the revolutionary party and its new state attempt to implement extensive social, economic, and political changes throughout society.* Altering the major patterns of social ordering and culture of a society can be much more demanding and difficult than toppling a weak government.

Once the state has been seized by a revolutionary movement, the initial outcome is likely to be the formation of a new government by the more *moderate leaders* of the movement. Although they typically desire extensive social change, they are usually committed to preserving much of the old society and are willing to work for gradual change of the economy, the class structure, and other features of their society. If they can govern effectively, begin to deal with underlying problems and tensions, and slowly improve conditions throughout the society, these moderate leaders may retain political power for some time and guide society through a gradual social and cultural transformation.

Quite frequently, however, the moderate leaders do not move fast or extensively enough to satisfy the more *radical leaders* of the revolutionary party. Those radicals often want to change the entire society immediately, and they are unwilling to follow the gradual route of the moderates. If the radicals are strong enough, after a few months or years they are likely to push out the moderates (often imprisoning or executing them to prevent further challenges from them) and establish another new government that they control. Moreover, radicals often want a strong authoritarian state that can immediately instigate social change without dealing with opposition and are willing to use coercion to achieve those goals. If they control the government, therefore, it is likely to become an authoritarian dictatorship that tolerates no opposing parties, and the society is likely to experience much more coercion than existed under the old regime and much more violence than occurred when that regime was overthrown.

Under these conditions, radical social change may be imposed upon the society, but with no pretense of democracy and with great human suffering. If the radicals are successful in controlling the military, they may remain in power for some period of time. If the *military leaders* retain some autonomy and become increasingly dissatisfied with the radical political leaders, however, they may stage a "coup d'etat" and substitute a military dictatorship for the radical revolutionary government. After that, depending on the values and goals of the military leaders, a more moderate civilian government may eventually again be established, or the military may continue to rule for as long as it can retain power.

WAR

Foraging societies rarely engaged in organized warfare. They did not normally have the excess population or material resources necessary to carry out such activities on a large-scale or sustained basis. Most disputes between these societies—over such issues as hunting territory or an unfulfilled marriage agreement—were settled through negotiation and an exchange of goods and/or promises. When they did resort to violent conflict, it was usually more of a symbolic ritual than organized war.

With the development of horticulture, however, the nature of war began changing dramatically. Particularly with advanced horticulture, societies frequently possessed sufficient population and material resources to organize and equip armies (and later navies) and to engage in extensive warfare. For at least the past seven thousand years, organized war has been an integral part of human history. The first known military empires were established in Mesopotamia and the Nile Valley about five thousand years ago, and ever since then war has been one of the principal means of resolving conflicts within and between societies, as well as for acquiring additional land, wealth, and population. As we saw in Chapter 9, war has played a central role in the emergence of most modern nations during the last several hundred years. And no one living in the twentieth century needs to be reminded of the prevalence of warfare in contemporary international relations.

Nature of War

War is organized violent conflict between sociopolitical units for the purpose of defeating or destroying the enemy. Three aspects of this definition require elaboration. First, *war is a highly organized form of social conflict.* In addition to complex organizational structures within the military forces of each side, the conduct of warfare itself tends to follow ordered patterns. Strategies of attack and defense are carefully planned, and both sides often observe unwritten "rules of combat," although these rules have changed greatly through time. In the American Revolutionary War, for example, the proper way to fight was to line up one's solders in several ranks across an open field, so that the British considered the Americans to be cowards for shooting from behind trees and rocks. And even in this age of mass warfare, we still observe rules concerning treatment of prisoners of war and armistice negotiations.

Second, *the sociopolitical units that fight each other in a war may be either parts of a single society or separate societies.* Internal wars between parts of a society—such as regions, ethnic populations, or subcultures—are usually called *civil wars*. *Revolutionary wars* involve a large proportion of the population of a society seeking to overthrow its government, whether controlled by domestic elites or by a foreign nation. (In the latter case, the term *colonial war* may also be applied.) Internal civil, revolutionary, and colonial wars share at least two common features.

(1) They frequently grow out of a revolutionary social movement within the society.
(2) There are frequently strong value differences between the antagonists, so that both of them believe they are fighting for a fundamental cause.

As a result, these internal wars are often highly ideological in nature.

External wars between two or more societies have traditionally been more pragmatic in nature, centering on efforts by at least one side to expand its sphere of military and political control and to acquire additional land, material resources, or population. These are usually called *international wars,* although in the twentieth century we have used the term *world war* when both sides consisted of coalitions of several nations. This century has witnessed at least three important changes in the nature of external wars.

(1) Like internal wars, external wars have tended to become highly ideological, focusing on antagonistic belief systems such as democracy, nazism, and communism.
(2) Also like internal wars, external wars have increasingly involved civilians as well as military forces.
(3) The distinction between internal and external wars has frequently become rather cloudy. For example, the North Vietnamese insisted they were fighting a civil war to reunite their country, while the United States defined that war as part of the global conflict between the West and the Soviet Union.

Third, *the goal of war is to defeat or destroy the enemy.* This broad objective differentiates war from social movements and from other conflicts that typically seek more limited and specific outcomes. That distinction has also become increasingly blurred in the twentieth century, however. Sociopolitical movements—especially within colonial societies—have frequently escalated into revolutionary wars aimed at defeating externally imposed governments. Other nations, meanwhile, sometimes view sociopolitical movements as domestic conflicts and sometimes as manifestations of global political struggles.

War and Modern Societies

The occurrence of war is directly linked to the three basic ecological factors of technology, resources, and population, as well as the economic surpluses that are generated when those ecological factors are combined into national socioeconomic development. First, technological innovations in the instruments of warfare have repeatedly given short-term advantages to their inventors and have led to long-term changes in the nature of war. Critical military inventions have included the stirrup (which made it possible to fight on horseback rather than just on foot), the longbow (which enabled soldiers to fight at a distance rather than just hand-to-hand), the musket (which is much more deadly than bows and arrows or swords), the exploding shell (which made the cannon a truly deadly weapon), steel-plated ships (which revolutionized naval warfare), tanks (which revolutionized land warfare), and airplanes (which added a whole new dimension to war) (Rybczynski, 1983: Ch.7). Most recently, the development of nuclear weapons has threatened to change warfare from military combat into mass destruction of human civilization.

Second, war consumes all kinds of natural resources in a destructive, rather than a constructive manner. To wage war, a nation must have access to such resources as surplus food to feed military personnel, iron and other minerals with which to manufacture weapons, petroleum with which to operate military machinery, and now uranium with which to produce nuclear weapons. Those resources are largely consumed in the process of waging war, without contributing to the overall development of society. In addition, war often destroys cities as well as valuable farmland, forests, and other natural resources.

Third, if a society is to engage in warfare, it must have surplus population that can be freed from normal occupations for military service and that is expendable. Consequently, the larger the population of a society, the greater its potential for engaging in war, providing it is able to organize its population into military forces.

Finally, modern warfare is extremely expensive economically. Therefore, the higher the level of socioeconomic development in a nation and the greater its surplus wealth, the more capable it is of waging war. Surplus wealth for war can be derived from a highly productive agricultural economy, but much greater surplus wealth becomes available to societies as they achieve self-sustaining industrialization (Rostow, 1969).

As an outgrowth of the development of modern nations during the past few hundred years, there has been a rather steady increase in the incidence of wars throughout the world. As shown in Figure 20-3, during the sixteenth century (the count actually begins in 1480) there were 63 wars, and a similar number (64 wars) during the seventeenth century. The eighteenth century—which is often called the "Age of Reason" in the West—saw many fewer wars (38) than might have been expected. During the nineteenth century, when nations began to industrialize, the number of wars rose drastically, to 89. And the twentieth century (through 1980) has already experienced 118 wars. Warfare is clearly a major component—and likely a direct consequence—of social modernization.

To prepare for or conduct a war, a nation must divert a large proportion of its available goods and services from domestic activities into the military. In addition to creating serious shortages in consumer requirements, this diversion can seriously impede the social, economic, and political development of a society. It is true that a full-scale war effort can bring a society out of an economic slump, as occurred in the United States with World War II. In the long run, however, there is considerable evidence that military preparations and expenditures do not stimulate societal development to anywhere near the extent that typically occurs with nonmilitary production (Gold and Quinn, 1981).

War can also affect the social organization of a society in various ways. On one hand, if the war is seen as "defending the homeland" or "defeating a tyrant who threatens the world," it can unite the population of a society and strengthen its normative and functional cohesion. On the other hand, many

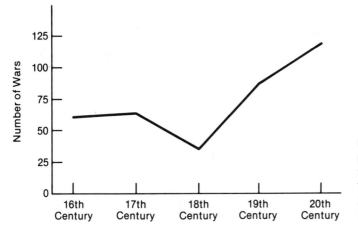

FIGURE 20-3 Number of wars per century, 1480-1977

Source: Based on data given in Jonathan Turner, *Sociology: The Science of Human Organization* (Chicago: Nelson-Hall, 1985), p. 425.

wars sharply divide a society—as occurred in the United States over the Viet Nam War— and lead to severe internal conflicts and loss of societal cohesion. War is also often used as an excuse for increased discrimination against minorities, as this country did with Japanese-Americans in World War II, or increased inequality among social classes, as when working-class youths are sent to war and middle-class youths receive deferments to remain in college.

Beyond these consequences of "normal war" looms the terrifying possibility of global nuclear warfare that could end human civilization. If a nuclear war itself did not have that result, detonation of large numbers of nuclear weapons would likely produce a prolonged "nuclear winter." Dust and ashes in the atmosphere would block out so much sunlight that plants could not grow and hence animals and humans could not survive for long. Since the end of World War II, we have avoided global warfare through the possibility of "MAD"—or "mutually assured destruction." Since there would be no victors in a global nuclear war, the superpowers have been held in check by the realization that if they started such a war, they would be as completely destroyed as their opponent. Obviously, however, this "balance of terror" is an extremely tenuous basis on which to ensure world peace. In the late 1980s, as a result of arms limitations negotiations between the United States and the Soviet Union, the world began slowly to move away from its MAD policy.

Meanwhile, there will undoubtedly continue to be a steady stream of more limited and conventional wars around the world for a long time to come. Underlying most of our recent wars and probably most future conventional wars among nations are the conditions of gross inequality that exist between developed and developing societies, coupled with the struggles of developing societies everywhere to raise their standards of living and to compete economically and politically in a world system that severely discriminates against them.

SUMMARY

Social deviance consists of activities that violate significant cultural norms and are negatively valued by a considerable number of people. Deviance is always socially defined by a particular culture or subculture in reference to a specific set of circumstances. No actions are inherently deviant. Nor are any individuals inherently deviant, since they become labeled as deviants only as their actions are observed, judged, and sanctioned by others. However it is defined, social deviance usually creates many serious problems for societies, as well as some positive effects.

Ten broad categories of social deviance are crime, mental illness, sexual deviance, personal deviance, communicative deviance, administrative deviance, political deviance, religious deviance, lifestyle deviance, and collective actions. Each of these categories includes numerous kinds of specific deviant activities.

Several conditions within modern societies contribute to the occurrence of social deviance. These include complex social ordering, role acquisition based on achievement, wide cultural diversity, population heterogeneity, impersonality of much social life, many forms of social inequality, widespread economic affluence, high levels of education, political democracy, and extensive and rapid social change. These factors suggest that much deviance is socially caused, which raises the question of the extent to which individuals should be held personally accountable or responsible for those actions.

A crime is any action that violates the legal code of the political jurisdiction in which it occurs, is done intentionally or in reckless disregard of the law, and is thought to harm society as a whole. Criminal actions are commonly categorized in several ways, according to the age of the offender; the severity of the action committed; whether the action is against other persons, property, or public morality; the setting in which the action occurs; and the type of offender. The latter factor distinguishes among amateur crime, professional crime, organized crime, corporate crime, and white-collar crime.

All official crime statistics are grossly incomplete. However, crime rates are known to be quite high in modern societies, particularly the United States, and have risen rapidly in recent years. Some categories of individuals—particularly those with disadvantaged socioeconomic or minority statuses—are much more likely to be arrested, prosecuted, and punished for crimes than are other categories of people. Nevertheless, almost everyone commits some legal offenses during his or her lifetime.

A number of sociological theories have been proposed to explain the occurrence of crime, all of which are undoubtedly relevant to some extent in various circumstances. These theories point to inadequate social controls; restricted or unavailable opportunities to follow normatively accepted means for attaining culturally desirable goals; socialization into deviant subcultures; symbolic labeling of individuals as criminals; and manipulation of laws and the legal system by powerful elites.

A social movement is a loosely organized effort by a relatively large number of people to change their society in some critical way. Social movements are goal-oriented; they focus around a shared ideology; they attract large numbers of people; they often give rise to several movement organizations; and they usually have a number of prominent leaders. Movement organizations and their leaders are the principal actors in social movements, but they often have many additional participants, supporters, and sympathizers.

Social movements can be classified into five broad types: reform movements that seek to change some specific aspect of society; revolutionary movements that desire to create an entirely new kind of society; reactionary movements that want to recreate some past conditions; utopian movements that desire to create some imagined ideal conditions; and expressive movements that seek to modify the psychological and emotional states of their members.

Social movements typically progress through eight identifiable stages, although these stages often overlap or are thoroughly intermingled. These involve serious social strains; shared beliefs about the causes and potential solutions of those social problems; growing support by large numbers of people; mobilization of those supporters and sympathizers; creation of several movement organizations; actions by those organizations and their leaders; reactions to the movement by other parts of the society; and some kind of eventual resolution.

Movement organizations utilize a variety of action strategies to attain their goals. These include: logical persuasion and emotional appeals; pressures such as withholding desired actions, filing lawsuits, or organizing referenda; protest actions such as mass activities of various kinds and civil disobedience; and threatened or actual physical violence.

A sociopolitical revolution attempts to make fundamental and radical changes in the organization of society and the state and involves extensive social conflict and probably violence. Several sets of social conditions can lead to the outbreak of a sociopolitical revolution. These include severe social and cultural tensions; a widening gap between people's expectations and social reality, which produces a perception of relative deprivation; operational ineffectiveness or breakdown of the existing state; development of a revolutionary political party or other politically oriented organizations with strong leadership; and the creation of an alternative authority structure that claims political legitimacy and sovereignty.

Several outcomes typically result from a successful sociopolitical revolution, in addition to overthrowing the state and its government. A new government must be organized, and efforts must be initiated to produce extensive social change. At first, these activities are often spearheaded by the more moderate leaders of the revolution, but frequently they are pushed aside by more radical leaders who desire drastic and rapid change. Those radical leaders often establish a strong authoritarian state that rules by decree and that tolerates no opposition to its sweeping changes. Those efforts, in turn, are sometimes toppled by a military coup d'etat, which may or may not return the society to civilian control.

For the last seven thousand years, organized warfare has been an integral aspect of human history, and war has played a central role in the emergence of most modern nations. War is organized violent conflict between sociopolitical units for the purpose of defeating or destroying the enemy. It is a highly organized form of social conflict. It may occur within a society as a civil, revolutionary, or colonial war, or it may occur between societies as an international or world war. Most wars seek total victory over the enemy rather than more limited objectives.

The occurrence of war is directly linked to the three basic ecological factors of technology, resources, and population, as well as the economic surpluses that are generated when those ecological factors are combined into national socioeconomic development. Technological innovations in the instruments of warfare have repeatedly altered the nature and outcomes of wars. War consumes all kinds of natural resources in a destructive manner. War requires excess population that is not needed for other activities. And because war can be extremely expensive, the greater the economic surplus in a society, the greater its potential for engaging in war. The frequency of wars around the world has risen dramatically during the nineteenth and twentieth centuries.

Wars generally have many harmful consequences for societies, although they may also benefit a society in some ways. With the advent of nuclear weapons, the entire nature of warfare has changed. It no longer involves just military forces, but entire civilian populations. Global nuclear war has thus far been avoided through the possibility of mutually assured destruction. If such a war should occur, it might likely eliminate all human civilization—as well as most other forms of life—as a result of a prolonged nuclear winter.

EMERGING ECOLOGICAL CRISES

What is a societal crisis?
What is presently happening to the earth's supplies of minerals and fuels, and why are we having an energy shortage?
In what ways are industrial societies destroying the natural environment?
How overpopulated is the world today, and why is this crisis most acute in the industrial nations?
How serious is food scarcity around the world today, and what will happen in the future as world population continues to grow?

SOCIETAL CRISES

A crisis is much more serious than a mere problem that requires attention. The word, *crisis,* comes from a Greek word that means a critical dividing or turning point. As a problematic situation becomes increasingly severe, it may reach a decisive point at which it must be resolved if it is not to destroy the system in which it occurs. A medical crisis is the point in an illness when the patient either begins to recover or dies. A societal crisis can be thought of in the same way, as a time when a society or other organization either manages to deal successfully with a serious problem or starts to decline or disintegrate.

Although numerous societal crises, or critical turning points, have occurred throughout human history, many observers of the contemporary world have become convinced that *we are presently facing a more complex set of interrelated, fundamental crises than ever encountered before.* All these crises are emerging rapidly at the present time.

Consequently, during the final decade of the twentieth century and the first several decades of the twenty-first century—roughly the life span of most present college students—we will have to find ways of coping with them if human civilization as we know it is to survive. Some of these crises involve the world's ecosystem, in conjunction with population growth. Other crises are occurring in the economic and political systems of modern nations. Still others pertain to organizational structures and patterns of socioeconomic inequality.

All these emerging societal crises are highly interwoven, so that they cannot be resolved separately but must be dealt with in combination as an interrelated system. This chapter deals with several crises that are presently developing in the world's ecosystem. Chapter 22 focuses on a number of crises in the social and economic organization of contemporary industrialized societies. In combination, these two sets of crises will undoubtedly influence human social life for the next several hundred years. And the manner in which they are handled may largely determine the nature of postindustrial societies.

Since the ecosystem in which humans presently exist has become worldwide in scope, the emerging ecological crises are not restricted to highly industrialized societies but affect the entire human race. Nevertheless, their potential effects could be much more destructive for highly developed nations than for less developed ones. Many of these ecological crises involve quite technical and complicated physical and biological factors that are beyond the scope of sociology. Since our concern here is with the consequences of these crises for human societies, their technical aspects are only briefly sketched to indicate their scope and seriousness. Readers who want to learn more about the details of these ecological crises can explore them in a number of excellent books, including Lester Brown's *Building a Sustainable Society* (1981) *and State of the World* (1989), Donella Meadows et al.'s *The Limits to Growth* (1972), William Ophuls's *Ecology and the Politics of Scarcity* (1977), and the Council on Environmental Quality's *The Global 2000 Report to the President* (1980).

Four critical ecological crises are examined in this chapter: natural resource depletion, which includes mineral exhaustion and energy shortages; environmental destruction, which pertains to air, water, and land; overpopulation, viewed in conjunction with the earth's carrying capacity; and food scarcities resulting from distributional problems and rapid population growth. All these crises are closely linked with our current modes and levels of industrial production, and are being intensified by the explosive rate at which populations are growing throughout the world.

NATURAL RESOURCE DEPLETION

Industrial production in modern societies demands a constant flow of mineral and fuel resources that are extracted from the earth's crust. The earth's deposits of all these resources are finite, however. When they are exhausted, they will be gone forever. Unless adequate substitutes can be found for all these minerals and fuels, industrial production of many material goods and modern transportation systems must end. Without industry and transportation, contemporary societies will be drastically altered.

Mineral Exhaustion

Throughout most human history, the supplies of all mineral resources have been so vast in relation to their rates of extraction and consumption that they have been viewed as virtually inexhaustible. *Only during the last 20 to 30 years have we become fully aware of the rapidly diminishing supplies of most minerals and the fact that they will not last much longer.*

This situation would be alarming enough if we were consuming these minerals at constant rates, but that is not the case. Throughout the twentieth century, consumption rates of all these natural resources have been steadily rising as a result of continually increasing industrial production. Constantly, we are exhausting the supplies of all minerals at faster and faster rates. In other words, their consumption is increasing and their supplies are decreasing at exponential rates, so that with each passing year the situation becomes considerably more serious than it was even the preceding year. No exponential growth rate can continue forever, since sooner or later such a curve would be skyrocketing straight upward and the world ecosystem would collapse. Even in the short run, however, a deceptively slow exponential growth rate can have disasterous consequences. For instance, a mild growth rate of three percent per year in the consumption of a finite resource will mean that in just 23 years we will be using twice as much of it per year as we are presently. At that rate, no finite resource can last very long.

The top section of Table 21-1 lists 15 minerals that are important for contemporary industrial production processes. The figures in this table were compiled about

TABLE 21-1 Expected Reserves of Important Minerals and Fuels, as of 1970

Mineral or Fuel	All Known Reserves				Possible Reserves	
	Duration with Constant 1970 Use Rate	Expected Annual Growth Rate of Use	Duration with Exponential Use Rate	Approximate Year of Exhaustion	Duration with Exponential Use Rate	Approximate Year of Exhaustion
Aluminum	110 years	6.4%	33 years	2001	49 years	2019
Chromium	730 years	2.6%	115 years	2085	137 years	2107
Cobalt	190 years	1.5%	90 years	2060	132 years	2102
Copper	52 years	4.6%	27 years	1997	46 years	2016
Iron	840 years	1.8%	154 years	2124	*	*
Lead	38 years	2.0%	28 years	1998	119 years	2089
Manganese	710 years	2.9%	106 years	2076	123 years	2093
Mercury	25 years	2.6%	19 years	1989	44 years	2014
Molybdenum	390 years	4.5%	65 years	2025	92 years	2062
Nickel	130 years	3.4%	50 years	2020	75 years	2045
Platinum	100 years	3.8%	41 years	2011	49 years	2019
Silver	18 years	2.7%	15 years	1985	23 years	1993
Tin	88 years	1.1%	62 years	2032	92 years	2062
Tungsten	39 years	2.5%	27 years	1997	*	*
Zinc	280 years	2.9%	76 years	2046	115 years	2085
Coal	3,100 years	4.1%	118 years	2088	132 years	2102
Natural gas	30 years	4.7%	19 years	1989	58 years	2022
Petroleum	38 years	3.9%	23 years	1993	43 years	2013

* Not available.

Source: Adapted from Dennis L. Meadows, et al., *The Dynamics of Growth in a Finite World* (Cambridge: Wright-Allen), 1974, Table 5–1.

1970, but since no major new deposits of any of these minerals have been discovered since then, the figures are still essentially valid. However, since 20 years of additional consumption—at continually increasing rates—must be taken into account, the current situation is considerably more serious than it was in 1970. The first four columns in the table pertain to all known supplies of these minerals. The first column gives the number of years that each mineral would last if consumption had continued at a constant 1970 rate, rather than steadily increasing. The second column gives the annual percentage rate at which the use of each mineral was increasing in 1970. The third column then gives the number of years (from 1970) that the supply of each one was expected to last with that growth rate, and the fourth column gives the approximate year when all known reserves of each mineral were expected (in 1970) to be exhausted. Moreover, it must be kept in mind that as the supply of a mineral becomes increasingly limited, its price usually begins to rise sharply. Even though there may still be unused deposits of all these minerals, therefore, in the near future they are likely to become so expensive that their use will be severely limited.

Five of these minerals—copper, lead, mercury, silver, and tungsten—are already in severely short supply. The fact that we have not yet entirely run out of mercury and silver, as was predicted in 1970, indicates that in the intervening 20 years we have begun to curtail their use and to substitute other materials for them. Copper wire, for example, is rapidly being replaced by optic fibers made of silicon, the principal ingredient of which is ordinary sand. Nevertheless, known deposits of all five of these minerals are today quite limited and will not last many more years. The expected life spans of all the other minerals are not much longer. Even iron ore, on which we depend for the steel used in countless industrial products, will be largely depleted early in the twenty-second century. However, the critical point here is not to predict precisely when each mineral is likely to be exhausted, but to understand that *supplies of most minerals will be gone within about a hundred years.*

Some optimists argue that the situation is not as bleak as these figures portray, insisting that with more geological exploration we will undoubtedly discover additional reserves of all these minerals. Consequently, the figures in the last two columns of the table are based on the most optimistic speculations that have been offered concerning possible future discoveries. The fifth column gives the number of years that those speculative reserves might be expected to last after 1970, and the last column gives the approximate year (counting from 1970) in which each mineral would be exhausted if those optimistic speculations should prove valid. Even if we should discover large additional reserves of all these minerals, given the exponential rates at which they are presently being consumed, most of them will still be exhausted before the end of the twenty-first century. Again, exponential rates of consumption of finite resources cannot go on indefinitely.

Other optimists argue that as these minerals become depleted, we will undoubtedly intensify our technological efforts to develop substitutes for them. The substitution of optic fibers for copper wire and fiber glass for steel in many current products are cited as examples of this solution. Beyond the fact that many of these expectations assume the development of technologies that do not presently exist, there is an additional serious flaw in this reasoning. Most of the substitute technologies that we presently have—and presumably most of the additional technologies that might be discovered—require the use of large amounts of energy. With unlimited energy supplies, it is conceivable that we could discover how to produce vast amounts of new or artificial minerals. Unfortunately, this kind of technological utopianism ignores the equally serious crisis of energy shortages.

Energy Shortages

The industrial revolution in all modern societies has depended on the consumption of vast amounts of fossil fuels that have provided the energy needed to operate machines, factories, transportation systems, offices, stores, and homes. These fuels—primarily coal, oil, and natural gas—have been available in what appeared to be abundant supplies for the relatively small costs of extracting them from the earth, refining or otherwise preparing them for use, and transporting them to where they were needed. Not until the 1973–74 oil embargo by the Organization of Petroleum Exporting Countries (OPEC) was much serious attention given to the fact that these fuels are also finite resources. Even then, many policy makers and most of the public saw the problem in political and economic, rather than ecological terms. The prevailing view was that OPEC countries had the oil that western nations needed but were restricting sales in order to keep the price high. Consequently, the industrial countries decided that we had to begin exploiting new petroleum reserves in Alaska, the North Sea, and other areas not controlled by OPEC. Nevertheless, that initial oil crisis did alert scientists and engineers to begin examining the extreme dependence of all industrial nations on fossil fuels.

In 1979, five major studies of the world's energy situation were published almost simultaneously: *Energy Future,* a report of the Energy Project at the Harvard Business School; *Energy in America's Future,* a report of Resources for the Future; *Energy: The Next Twenty Years,* a report to the Ford Foundation; *The Good News About Energy,* by the Council on Environmental Quality; and *Energy in Transition: 1985–2010,* a report by the Committee on Nuclear and Alternative Energy Systems of the National Academy of Sciences. These reports all came to essentially the same conclusion. *The world's known reserves of fossil fuels are rapidly being depleted and will become prohibitively expensive or essentially exhausted during the twenty-first century.* Consequently, unless industrial societies drastically reduce their consumption of these fuels, it will be impossible to sustain current levels of industrial production for more than 50 to 75 years.

The bottom section of Table 21-1 gives the basic data underlying this prediction. Coal is the most abundant of these fuels. If the rate of coal consumption continues to increase, however, all known resources will last for just over one hundred years. If the consumption of oil and natural gas had continued to increase at the rate of seven percent per year as occurred during the 1960s, world supplies of both these fuels might have been depleted before the end of this century. Fortunately, those consumption rates have decreased considerably since 1970, so that world supplies will last a few decades longer.

The last two columns of the table give the possible durations of these fuels if vast new reserves should be discovered. In that case, coal supplies would last at least into the twenty-second century, but oil and natural gas would still be essentially exhausted before the middle of the twenty-first century. Some additional reserves of both fuels have been discovered since 1970, so that the more optimistic projections may be more accurate than the 1970 ones. Nevertheless, those discoveries—as well as all future possible discoveries of further reserves—only postpone the inevitable depletion of oil and gas by a few years. As with minerals, the crucial point is not precisely when they will be gone, but the fact that *the world is presently running on finite and very limited supplies of fossil fuels, and when they are gone there will be no more available.*

The five 1979 reports, as well as numerous studies done since then, have extensively explored three alternative energy sources that might ease or solve the impending energy crisis. The first alternative is nuclear energy, which has two forms. All existing nuclear power plants utilize nuclear fission, in which atoms of uranium or plutonium are split apart to release huge amounts of heat that is used to boil water or another liquid, and the resulting steam drives an electric generator. There are approximately 100 of these fission plants in the United States (although many of them are not presently operating), and several hundred more in other industrial countries.

The numerous problems associated with nuclear fission power plants have become painfully evident in recent years. These include the cost of constructing such plants, which has risen from about a half-billion dollars to over five billion dollars apiece in the last twenty years; malfunctioning of the plants, such as occurred at Chernobyl when the containment structure ruptured and radioactive water vapor was spread over much of Europe; and permanent storage of dangerous radioactive wastes, which we still do not know how to accomplish. In addition, the nuclear fuels used in fission reactors are finite resources that will also be exhausted within a few decades at the present rate of use. Finally, nuclear energy produces only electricity and cannot be used to power motor vehicles or planes. As a result of all these factors—as well as widespread public concern and fear regarding the safety of nuclear reactors—no new fission plants have been started in the United States since 1980, and many other countries are also slowing or stopping their construction.

The other form of nuclear energy is fusion, in which atoms of heavy hydrogen are fused together. Nuclear fusion has the two advantages of using a nearly inexhaustible fuel and producing much more energy than fission. The limitations of this form of nuclear energy are presently overwhelming, however. The technology is still in the experimental stage, and we do not presently know how to construct commercial fusion plants; the cost of a single particle accelerator to create nuclear fusion is measured in tens of billions of dollars; and we currently have very little understanding of the potential safety problems that may be associated with nuclear fusion.

For all of these and other reasons, all of the 1979 studies concluded that *nuclear energy cannot—at least in the foreseeable future—provide a permanent solution to the energy shortages we will soon be experiencing.* That conclusion has been echoed by numerous subsequent studies. Although there are still many staunch advocates of nuclear energy, a number of them now concede that

nuclear fission is at best only a short-term answer to the energy crisis, and that we must find other permanent solutions.

The second energy alternative that has received widespread scientific and public attention since the mid-1970s is conservation. At first, energy conservation was viewed primarily as an immediate means of reducing the demand for energy and thus reducing the consumption of fossil fuels (Sawhill, 1979). Conservation can be accomplished in many different ways. These include changing the manner in which people use energy, from turning down the furnace thermostat to driving more slowly; constructing more energy-efficient new buildings and retrofitting existing buildings to reduce their heat loss; designing energy-efficient appliances and machinery for homes and factories; altering industrial production processes to require less energy; developing new agricultural procedures; and producing more fuel-efficient motor vehicles and planes.

During the 1970s and early 1980s, extensive programs to promote energy conservation were initiated by many governments, utilities, businesses and industries, and environmental organizations (Ester, et al., 1984). In the United States, this effort was spurred by the realization that the nation was consuming almost twice as much energy per person as any other industrial country (except Canada). Despite numerous difficulties in designing, implementing, and funding these convention programs, they were remarkably successful. Instead of continuing to grow, energy use in the United States leveled off in 1979 and has remained at a relatively constant per capita rate since then. Whereas we first thought that conservation would just slow the energy growth rate, we now realize that *a serious nationwide conservation effort could eventually reduce our total energy consumption by one-third to one-half of the 1980 level.* As a result, many energy planners now view conservation as a source of energy rather than simply as a way of reducing demand. Despite these successes with energy conservation and its future potential, however, most conservation programs were sharply reduced or totally eliminated during the 1980s because the U.S. federal government adopted the policy of stimulating increased energy production rather than supporting conservation programs.

Although energy conservation programs will undoubtedly again be supported in the future as fossil fuels become increasingly expensive and scarce, *conservation by itself cannot permanently solve the energy crisis.* That will require the development of entirely different energy sources that do not depend on finite fossil fuels and that avoid the severe problems of nuclear energy.

The third alternative to fossil fuels, which thus far we have only begun to explore, is solar energy. Technically, fossil fuels are a form of solar energy, since they come from the remains of plants and animals that once drew on the sun's energy. In practice, however, solar energy refers to energy that presently or quite recently reached the earth through solar radiation. Solar energy is therefore an infinite resource—as long as the sun keeps burning—that cannot be exhausted. Quite clearly, *the ultimate solution to the energy crisis lies in converting solar radiation into useful forms of energy* (Brown, 1981; Hayes, 1977; Lyons, 1978).

The critical problem with solar energy is learning how to utilize it for human purposes. All humanity presently uses less than one percent of the sun's energy that reaches the earth, primarily because it is so widely dispersed. To be useful to us, energy must be concentrated so that it can be stored, transported, and used for specific purposes. Nature's primary way of concentrating solar energy is through photosynthesis in plants. These plants are, in turn, eaten by animals and people so that the energy becomes stored in their bodies and can be used to do work. Humans also release the energy stored in plants by burning wood and using plants for many other purposes. Solar energy is also stored—but not concentrated—in the earth and in bodies of water, and then slowly released back to the atmosphere. All life on earth depends on a continual inflow of solar energy that is concentrated and stored

through these natural processes. Nevertheless, beyond growing plants, raising animals, burning wood and fossil fuels, and otherwise utilizing these natural processes, humanity has thus far not been very successful in harnessing solar radiation to meet our energy needs.

There is one important exception to that generalization. Running water is often classified as solar energy, even though it is responding to gravity rather than solar radiation, since it is an infinite natural resource. For hundreds of years, people have been using running water to turn wheels for grinding and other purposes, and in the twentieth century we have constructed dams on many major rivers to generate electricity. Hydroelectric power is very inexpensive and nonpolluting, but unfortunately there are only a limited number of rivers that can be dammed. In the United States and many other countries, virtually all the sites feasible for large dams have already been utilized, so that we cannot expect any significant increase in hydroelectric power in the future.

Another partial exception to that generalization is wind, which is a direct result of solar radiation. People have, of course, been using wind for several thousand years to propel ships and turn windmills. Fossil fuels almost entirely displaced those uses of wind power, however. In recent years, some experimental efforts have been made to construct wind turbines to generate electricity, but their usefulness is obviously limited to windy areas and windy days.

Most current efforts to develop solar energy fall into two broad categories. The first category of solar technologies involves *direct absorption of radiation to heat buildings and/or water.* These techniques can be either passive or active in nature. Passive solar technologies are ways of designing and constructing buildings to maximize their absorption of solar radiation. They vary from simple procedures such as having large south-facing windows, to more complex techniques such as tromb walls made of cement blocks or other similar materials to absorb and hold the sun's heat. Insulation and other energy-conserving construction techniques can also be considered aspects of passive solar energy. Active solar technologies add some kind of moving material to facilitate heat absorption and concentration. Most commonly, this material is air, water, or another liquid that passes through a solar collector on the roof and then into the building where it is either used immediately or else stored in a tank, a rock bed, trays of special salts, or other devices.

The second category of solar technologies involves the *transformation of radiation into electricity*. Again, this can be done in two different ways, either indirectly or directly capturing solar energy. With an indirect procedure, solar radiation is collected by mirrors and/or lenses and focused on containers of water, which boils to produce steam that drives a generator. This is normally done with a large, centralized system much like other generating plants. With a direct procedure, photovoltaic cells turn sunlight into electricity. This kind of system can be as small and decentralized as desired. Thus far it has been used with space vehicles and satellites, houses and office buildings, and most recently in experimental solar-powered cars and planes. Currently, these cells are still fairly costly to manufacture, so that solar-generated electricity is at least twice as expensive as power generated by burning fossil fuels. Sometime in the near future, however, as prices of fossil fuels rise and the costs of making photovoltaic cells decline with mass production, this new solar technology will probably provide affordable electricity in unlimited amounts.

ENVIRONMENTAL DESTRUCTION

Pollution of the natural environment—air, water, and land—by the waste products of industrial production and consumption is the ecological crisis that has attracted by far the greatest amount of media attention and public concern. Paradoxically, however, the most serious consequences of pollution may not be felt nearly as soon as those from mineral exhaustion or energy shortages. This does not mean that the consequences of pollution may not become extremely severe, but only that it will likely take time for their full effects to be experienced. The primary reason for the widespread media and public attention to environmental pollution is that some instances of it are quite visible and dramatic, especially in contrast to dwindling supplies of minerals and fuels hidden in the ground. When pollutants in the air above a community become so thick that people start coughing and have other respiratory problems, when poisonous gases escape from a chemical factory and kill several thousand people, or when a river is so polluted that all life in it dies and the water is unfit for drinking or any other use, people take notice and demand that something be done immediately.

Most pollution of the air, water, and land is a direct consequence of our industrial way of life in modern societies. Many factories produce large amounts of dangerous chemical wastes as by-products of their industrial processes, most of which are buried in the ground or dumped into rivers and lakes. Coal- and oil-burning electrical generating plants continually spew hundreds of tons of noxious fumes and ash particles into the air. All machines that burn petroleum, from furnaces to automobiles, put out enormous amounts of carbon dioxide and other polluting gases. And the massive use of fertilizers and pesticides by modern agriculture leaves huge amounts of nitrates and harmful chemicals in the soil, air, and water. Although human activities have been discharging pollutants into the environment since people first discovered how to make fires, until the twentieth century the forms and amounts of those pollutants remained well within the ability of the earth's ecosystem to absorb them with little or no permanent damage to the natural environment. That ecological balance has been seriously upset during this century, however, as modern industry and its products have expanded enormously and spread around the globe. The current rates of many forms of pollution are already far in excess of the earth's ability to absorb these wastes, so that the excesses are steadily accumulating in the environment. Moreover, many pollution rates are increasingly exponentially every year. *Unless we discover how—and are willing to pay the costs—to reverse and eventually eliminate these pollution trends, the earth's environment could become totally unfit for human life within a few centuries.*

Air Pollution

Pollution of the atmosphere occurs whenever hydrocarbons are burned, and as a result of many chemical processes. For example, the smoke from electrical generating and large heating plants that burn coal with a high sulfur content contains large amounts of sulfur molecules. When they reach the upper atmosphere and are pushed around the globe by stratospheric winds, these molecules often become the cores of raindrops and snowflakes which, when falling back to earth as *acid rain and snow,* may be deposited hundreds or thousands of miles from their originating source. When this acidic water is absorbed by plants, it frequently kills them. Vast tracts of forests, aquatic life in hundreds of lakes, and thousands of acres of grasslands are presently being destroyed throughout the northern hemisphere by acid precipitation. For example, many lakes in the Adirondack Mountains are now so acidic that they sustain little or no life.

Burning of fossil fuels in plants, furnaces, and motor vehicles also releases huge amounts of carbon dioxide into the atmosphere. As this gas accumulates in layers in the troposphere, it reflects heat from the earth back downward and thus prevents it from escaping into space. This process is called the *greenhouse effect,* since it traps heat in the same way that a glass greenhouse does. As a consequence, many scientists now believe that the earth's atmosphere is slowly but steadily beginning to heat up. The rate of increase in atmosphere carbon dioxide almost exactly matches the growth of the world's population during the past 25 years. By the year 2050, this greenhouse effect is expected to raise the average temperature on earth as much as 9°F. This is five to ten times the rate of global warming that occurred at the end of the last Ice Age.

Such warming will have profound effects on human life. Within the next century, the fertile mid-latitude farmlands (including all farmland in the United States) that presently feed most of the world's population could become desert wastelands, devoid of enough water to grow any crops. The climate would become much hotter, so that life in many cities would become almost unbearable. In addition, as the atmosphere heats up, the polar icecaps will begin to melt, raising the levels of all the oceans by several feet. Most coastal land and cities would then be flooded and lost to human use. Countless species of wild plants and animals would become extinct. World weather patterns, tropical storms, and ocean currents would also be altered by a global warming trend. Increasingly, scientists are no longer asking whether these changes will occur, but what effects will they have on the world.

Another kind of air pollution is caused by the release of chlorofluorcarbons (CFCs) into the atmosphere. These chemicals are used as coolants in refrigerators and air conditioners and are an important ingredient in aerosols and plastic foams. They appear to be slowly destroying the *ozone layer* in the stratosphere that shields the earth from the sun's dangerous radiation. This has recently become most evident over Antarctica, where a large hole has been discovered in the ozone layer. As humans are exposed to increased amounts of solar radiation, they are likely to develop skin cancers (which have risen sharply in recent years and have become one of the most rapidly increasing causes of death), cataracts than can produce blindness, and lowered resistance to many kinds of infection. Although at the present time the ozone layer is estimated to be diminishing only about two percent per century, that is sufficient to cause an additional 20,000 cases of life-threatening skin cancer per year in the United States alone. The long-term effects of increased solar radiation on the global ecosystem are not well-understood, but they will certainly not be beneficial.

Water Pollution and Depletion

Pollution of ground water has been increasing very rapidly in recent years for a variety of reasons. In the past (and until today in many developing countries), most cities dumped all their raw sewage into the nearest river. City sewer systems in all developed nations now include treatment plants that reduce the sewage into harmless organic materials. However, *sewage dumping* still occurs quite frequently, as a result of treatment plants breaking down or becoming overloaded. At those times, cities simply empty their sewer systems into the most convenient body of water. Another extensive cause of water pollution is *fertilizer runoff* from farms. Nitrates and other chemicals that are not absorbed by the earth or plants, a common result of heavy applications of fertilizers, are washed away by rain and flow into creeks and rivers and may eventually make their way into urban water systems.

In recent years, we have become increasingly aware of the extent to which industrial plants discharge chemical wastes into rivers and streams. Sometimes these toxic *chemical discharges* are accidental, as in the spill that killed all life in the Rhine River in Germany in 1986. More frequently, however, they are deliberate acts by factories that need to get rid of industrial wastes—often highly toxic materials such as acids or mercury—but don't want to pay the costs of safe disposal procedures. Toxic dumping is usually illegal, but factories may get away with it for years before their actions are detected.

Fresh water will soon become one of our most precious natural resources, since people, crops, and animals all depend on it for life. Worldwide demand for water is expected to double during the next 20 years. Over two-thirds of all water used by humans goes into agricultural irrigation, and most of that water is not immediately available for any other uses.

By 2000, virtually every country in the world is expected to be experiencing serious water shortages. The problem will be most severe in the developing nations of Africa, South Asia, Latin America, and the Middle East, where fresh water has already become scarce in many areas. Within ten to 20 years many of those countries will be consuming their full available water supply, so that they will be unable to expand their water resources any further, despite constantly rising demands for water by growing populations and irrigated agriculture (Council on Environmental Quality, 1980:26).

In many industrial nations, meanwhile, major aquifers of underground water are rapidly being drained much faster than the water is replenished through natural processes. For example, the huge Ogallala aquifer beneath the southwestern plains from Nebraska to Texas has made possible irrigated farming throughout this six-state area. However, that deep aquifer is essentially nonrechargeable and will be largely depleted by 2000. At that time, irrigation will no longer be possible throughout the southwestern United States (Brown, 1981:26).

Land Pollution and Depletion

Pollution of the land is also frequently caused by toxic industrial wastes that are buried and forgotten until they begin leaking into the soil and causing illness and death, as in the infamous Love Canal incident in New York State. There are thousands of *industrial dumps* throughout the United States and in all other industrial societies, most of which could potentially become serious health problems. Also contributing to land pollution is the use of *dangerous chemicals,* such as dioxine in the construction of roads and other physical facilities, and many pesticides and herbicides. Every acre of land that is *paved over* to make a new highway or shopping mall parking lot is totally polluted in terms of sustaining life. Finally, every year we are generating tons of *radioactive wastes* that are being buried in the ground. Wherever that occurs, the land may become so radioactive that it cannot be used for any other purpose for hundreds or thousands of years.

Erosion of fertile topsoil from agricultural lands is presently occurring at alarming rates in many parts of the world, as farmers attempt to squeeze more and more food production from their land. Traditional farming practices, in which each plot of land was allowed to remain fallow every three or four years or was planted with a legume such as clover to restore the soil, generally resulted in only two or three tons of topsoil loss per acre each year. Since new topsoil is continually being formed by natural processes at rates of two to five tons per acre per year, those practices did not deplete the soil. In recent years, however, mounting demands for more food, plus the availability of cheap nitrogen fertilizers, has led farmers to abandon these traditional practices and plant all their land in cash crops every year. The result has been topsoil erosion at rates up to twenty tons per acre every year (Brown, 1981:18). As the topsoil is lost to wind and water erosion, subsoils become part of the tillage layer. This reduces the soil's organic components, nutrient content, water-retention capacity, and aeration, leaving it less fertile each succeeding year. Rising food demands have also pushed farmers to till additional plots of land with little water and steep slopes, which are extremely susceptible to rapid soil erosion.

Farmlands that require irrigation are losing productivity through waterlogging and salinization in many parts of the world. These natural processes occur whenever surface water from rivers is used to irrigate land that has inadequate underground drainage. Adding water to this land gradually raises the water table, and when it comes within a few feet of the surface it begins to impede the growth of deep-rooted plants. As the water table rises even further, water starts evaporating through the soil. This concentrates salt and other minerals near the surface, which harm plants. It has been estimated that one-fifth of

the world's total irrigated farmland is either waterlogged or salinized and that the productivity of these lands has fallen by at least 20 percent (Brown, 1981:25).

Large amounts of croplands are being lost to nonagricultural uses such as village expansion, urban development, energy production, and highway construction. In many industrial countries, urban development has steadily been taking over as much as one percent of the prime farmland every year. Highway construction and parking lots also devour cropland. In developing countries, village expansion and rapid urban growth are extending further and further into surrounding farmlands, thereby reducing these countries' ability to produce food for their exploding populations. Finally, energy production projects, such as hydroelectric dams that flood rich valleys and coal strip mining that digs up vast areas, also decrease the supply of agricultural land.

Deforestation is occurring very rapidly in many parts of the Third World, where large proportions of the people still rely on wood for most of their fuel and building needs. In many of these countries people are cutting down trees at much faster rates than they grow. Consequently, it has been estimated that the number of acres that are forested and the total amount of growing woodstock will decline by 40 percent between 1980 and 2000 in the developing countries. If that happens, those 80 percent of the world's population will then have only about 45 percent of the world's forests. The per capital volume of growing woodstock in these nations, which is now 57 cubic meters of biomass, will be reduced to 21 cubic meters. In the industrial nations, in contrast, the current volume of logging is not greatly above the natural growth rate. They presently have 142 cubic meters of growing woodstock per capita, which is predicted to decline to 114 cubic meters by 2000 (Council on Environmental Quality, 1980:23). Even that slower rate of logging will eventually destroy most remaining old forests, however.

All of the world's major deserts are spreading

relentlessly outward, covering thousands of acres of land with sand every year. The Sahara Desert has received the most attention, since it is spreading fairly rapidly across Northern Africa. However, this process is also occurring in the Middle East, Western Asia, India, and Brazil (Brown 1981:22). Although some of the causes of spreading desertification are natural, the process is greatly intensified by human abuse of the land through overgrazing, deforestation, and overcultivation.

Grasslands for livestock are being seriously depleted through overgrazing. Although roughly twice as much of the earth's land is used for grazing as for farming, most of these grasslands are too dry or too steep for any other use. Historically, the number of grazing animals (beef and dairy cattle, water buffalo, sheep, and goats) has increased in direct proportion to growth of the human population. That expansion can no longer continue, however, since almost all available grasslands are now being used, and in many parts of the world the number of grazing animals is two or three times what the land can permanently support. At the same time, world demand for livestock products is doubling every generation, as a result of population growth and desires for more consumption of meat. There is no way in which that rising demand can be satisfied without overgrazing grasslands to the point at which they will no longer sustain any vegetation (Brown 1981:47).

OVERPOPULATION

As discussed in Chapter 11, the world's population has been growing extremely rapidly during the twentieth century. It did not reach one billion until roughly 1825. In 1925 it was still only about two billion. By 1960 it had risen to three billion. By 1975 it was up to four billion. And in 1987 it reached five billion. The world growth rate in 1987 was 1.7 percent per year, which may seem low, but which would result in a doubling of the world's population to ten billion in just another forty years. In short, *the total number of human beings on this planet has grown six-fold in just over 150 years, and the rate of this population growth has been increasing exponentially.* We are clearly in the midst of a population explosion.

The world's population growth rate did slow down somewhat between 1975 and 1987, dropping from 1.9 to 1.7 percent per year. That decline was most evident in the industrial nations, where the rate was cut almost in half, from 0.9 percent to 0.5 percent. In contrast, the rate in all the less developed countries of the world declined only slightly, from 2.4 percent to 2.1 percent.

World Population Projections

Population projections into the future are always risky, since many possible factors can effect birth and death rates. The exact figures produced by these projections must therefore always be taken as only rough approximations of what may actually occur in the future. The basic trend, however, is absolutely clear and nearly unavoidable. Unless some catastrophic event such as a global nuclear war or epidemic or mass starvation should occur, the world's population will continue to expand rapidly for some time to come. World population growth cannot continue indefinitely, of course, since sooner or later a continually increasing population would exceed the food supply, exhaust all natural resources, and eventually fill the land so densely that there would be "standing room only." Extensive population growth will almost certainly continue for the next several generations, nevertheless, since this process has a built-in momentum that is extremely difficult to slow or reverse.

The present world population growth rate is high enough to create massive overpopulation during the coming century, as illustrated in Figure 21-1. If this growth rate continues, in 2000 the total world population will be at least 6.2 billion, in 2020 it will reach 8 billion, in 2050 it could be 10 billion, and by 2075 it may be as high as 12 to 16 billion (U.S. Bureau of the Census, 1987:814). Because less developed

FIGURE 21-1 World population growth and overpopulation Source: U.S. Bureau of the Census, *Statistical Abstract of the United States, 1987* (Washington, D.C.: U.S. Government Printing Office), Table 1435.

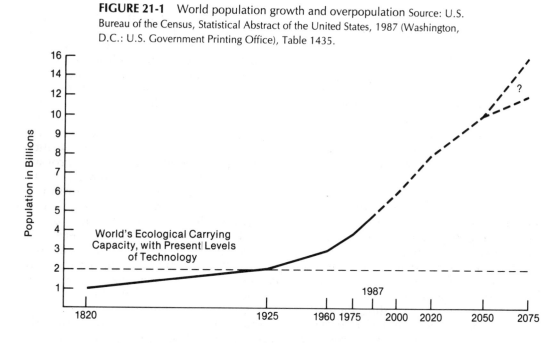

nations have a much higher growth rate than do more developed ones, at least 90 percent of that population increase is expected to occur in those societies. They presently contain about 76 percent of the world's people, but that figure is predicted to be 79 percent by 2000, 83 percent by 2020, and as high as 87 percent by 2075.

Overpopulation

How many people are required to create an overpopulation crisis, in the world as a whole and in various parts of it? With five billion people, is the world presently overpopulated? Or will that point be reached in 2000 or 2020? The exact date when world overpopulation occurs is essentially irrelevant, since it is quite clear that this crisis has occurred or will soon occur. More importantly, the concept of overpopulation is entirely relevant to several other considerations. If overpopulation is defined as the point at which there is not enough food available to keep everyone alive, that time will not come for at least several decades, and some people think it could be put off

indefinitely if we discover how to manufacture sufficient quantities of synthetic food with biogenetic engineering. In contrast, if overpopulation is defined as more people than can be provided with a minimal adequate standard of living (e.g., at least 2,500 calories of food per day and an annual family income equivalent to at least $15,000) then the world probably already contains two or three times too many people. All such criteria for defining overpopulation are obviously rather arbitrary, depending on the standard of living that is considered necessary and/or desirable.

A somewhat more objective criteria for defining overpopulation is provided by the concepts of ecological balance and carrying capacity. A population of any species is in balance with the carrying capacity of its ecosystem as long as the rate at which it consumes natural resources remains at or below the earth's ability to replenish them. *When the resource consumption rate exceeds the replenishment level on a continuing basis, the ecosystem is out of balance because population is overshooting the earth's ecological carrying capacity.* As we saw in Chapter 5, a society may exist in a condition of resource overshoot for some period of time by using a variety of techniques, such as drawing down supplies of finite resources. Overshoot cannot continue indefinitely, however, for sooner or later the environment "bites back" and the population declines sharply through starvation, disease, or other calamities. This natural ecological process is as inescapable for humans as it is for any other species.

Technically, the human race was exceeding the ecological carrying capacity of the earth the first time a bit of copper or iron ore was dug out of ground, since those metals could not be replaced. More realistically, though, the critical point came at the time when the consumption of metals and fossil fuels became so great that we could foresee the exhaustion of all known deposits. And in terms of renewable resources such as food and water, we began exceeding the earth's carrying capacity when our agricultural production and water extraction practices began to have permanent harmful effects on the natural environment. Any estimate of the earth's total carrying capacity for human life, and hence the point at which we first began exceeding that capacity, is at best an informed guess. Our best estimate, however is that *the human race began to overshoot the carrying capacity of the earth's ecosystem early in the twentieth century* (Catton, 1980). Almost certainly that point was reached by about 1925, when the total world population reached two billion. In other words, *two billion people may be the maximum number that the earth's ecosystem can sustain on a permanent basis with an adequate standard of living*—at least given present levels of technology. From this perspective, there are already at least three billion too many people in the world, and the situation is becoming worse each year.

Developing Nations

The initial reaction of most people to the realization that the world is almost certainly already overpopulated and that this crisis is continuing to worsen is to point to the less developed nations around the globe. With approximately 3.8 billion people, or over three-fourths of the world's total population, isn't it those societies that are overpopulated? Since all the industrial nations, in contrast, contain only about 1.2 billion people, or less than one-fourth of the total, they don't seem to be too overpopulated. Even more serious is the fact that the less developed nations, which have a current growth rate of 2.1 percent and a population doubling time of only 33 years, are growing much faster then the industrial nations. The latter societies presently have a growth rate of only 0.5 percent and a doubling time of 150 years. Therefore most further population expansion will occur in less developed societies, not in industrial societies. In short, the population explosion and its resulting crisis of overpopulation appear to be occurring largely in the Third World.

From the straightforward perspective of population size, those observations are obviously correct. The populations of most developing countries are increasing at alarming rates every year. *Many developing countries are already seriously overpopulated in terms of the fundamental criterion of having enough food to keep everyone alive.* They desperately need to follow the example of China, which has reduced its rate of growth from 1.9 to 1.3 since 1970 by implementing a nationwide population control program. Otherwise, the populations of most of those societies will soon far exceed all their natural resources, with resulting mass starvation, disease, and death.

Industrial Nations

From a broader ecological perspective, however, laying the blame for the entire overpopulation crisis on the doorsteps of developing societies severely distorts reality. At the present time, all of the industrial nations together constitute only about one-fourth of the world's population but are consuming between one-half to three-fourths of all kinds of vital resources. In other words, the members of these societies are using two to three times their "fair shares" of all natural resources. Therefore, *if overpopulation is de-*

fined in terms of exceeding the carrying capacity of the ecosystem, it is the industrial societies that are creating most of the overpopulation problem. It is these 1.2 billion residents of highly developed societies who are rapidly pushing the earth toward ecological collapse, not the 3.8 billion people in the rest of the world.

When this ecological perspective is applied to future population projections, we can calculate that each one percent growth in the total population of all industrial nations will probably increase overall consumption of natural resources by at least 2.5 percent. Since their total population is predicted to grow from 1.2 to 1.33 billion by 2020, or about 11 percent, their consumption of natural resources could increase by another 30 percent above their already high current levels. In 2020, therefore, the more developed nations could be consuming as much as four-fifths of all natural resources. In contrast, each one percent growth in the total population of all less developed nations will increase overall consumption of natural resources by less than 0.5 percent. Consequently, although their total population is predicted to grow from 3.8 to 6.7 billion by 2020, or about 76 percent, their consumption of natural resources might not increase by more than about 35 percent above their current low levels. In reality, since they are much less powerful economically and politically than the industrial nations, their proportion of the earth's natural resources might likely decline even further. In short, if present resource consumption trends continue, the rich nations will continue to become even richer as they extract the last remaining reserves of many natural resources from the earth. Meanwhile, the vast numbers of people in less developed nations will not seriously disrupt the earth's ecosystem because they will be dying from mass starvation and disease.

FOOD SCARCITY

Food is the most basic natural resource for human life, yet it poses the most difficult problems of assessment and prediction. To a large extent, this difficulty stems from the fact that it involves two distinct, yet interrelated, problems.

Uneven Distribution

The first of these problems concerns *the present uneven distribution of food among societies and among individuals within every society.* Daily food consumption varies widely among societies, roughly corresponding to their level of economic development. Many people in less developed nations barely manage to eat the 2,000 calories per day that are required for survival, while in more developed countries most people eat at least 3000 calories per day. Moreover, food is distributed very unequally within every society. Even in highly developed nations such as the United States, low-income people are malnourished in terms of total calories and the composition of their diet. This problem of unequal food distribution among nations and individuals is largely economic and political in nature; and although it can be extremely serious for the people suffering from malnutrition, it is not a fundamental ecological crisis.

Inadequate Production

The second problem concerns *the total amount of food produced per capita, both now and in the future.* Overall, are we now producing enough food to feed the world's population? Will future food production keep pace with growing populations? In regard to the current situation, the apparent answer is slightly, but not severely, negative. That is, if all presently available food were equally distributed among the world's more than five billion people, everyone would be less than adequately nourished, but no one would be starving to death. (Ophuls, 1977:50). Moreover, in the past few years, world food production has begun to fall behind population growth. In regard to food production in the future, the answer is much less clear.

Some optimists believe that the earth

could potentially feed at least fifteen billion people, although that hope rests on several dubious assumptions, such as:

(1) Essentially even distribution of food consumption among all people;
(2) Everyone eating no more than about 2,500 calories per day, with little or no red meat;
(3) Massive use of fertilizers (which are produced from our dwindling supplies of petroleum) and pesticides (which are often highly polluting);
(4) New biogenetic technologies that would greatly increase crop yields; and
(5) New techniques for farming lands that are presently too dry, cold, or otherwise too infertile to yield crops.

Somewhat more realistic predictions promise to feed perhaps eight billion people by 2000, although those hopes also rest on extensive use of fertilizers, pesticides and irrigation—all of which have serious environmental impacts. Moreover, it is expected that these developments, if they were possible, would likely double the real cost of most food products by 2000 (Council on Environmental Quality, 1980:16–17). An even more realistic prediction suggests that in 2000 world food production will be sufficient to feed no more than six billion people, again at considerably higher food prices.

The Future

Consideration of rising food prices—caused primarily by the increasing cost of petroleum, various chemicals, and irrigation water—takes us back to the issue of food distribution. Since many people in less developed societies are unable to pay higher prices for food, the distribution of food products around the globe will likely become even more unequal in the future than it is today. The World Bank has estimated that by 2000 at least 1.3 billion people in less developed countries could be suffering from serious malnutrition (Council on Environmental Quality, 1981:17). Consequently,

simply increasing food production at any cost—economic and environmental—will not solve the world's food problem. *If a catastrophic food crisis is to be avoided, the interwoven issues of production and distribution of food must be solved.*

The world is not currently teetering on the brink of mass starvation, although considerable numbers of people in less developed nations and many low-income people in more developed nations are not presently receiving adequate nutrition. In the near future, this situation will undoubtedly become somewhat worse in terms of the amount of food per capita that is available and how it is distributed. *Looking further into the twenty-first century, the world food crisis will unquestionably become extremely serious as populations continue to grow.*

SUMMARY

The ecological crises that are presently emerging are all worldwide in scope and becoming increasingly serious. They are primarily the consequences of industrial production, consumption, and rapid population growth, all of which are highly interrelated.

The earth's deposits of all the mineral resources that are vital for industrial production are finite, and most of these deposits are presently being depleted at rapid rates. Most of them are expected to be totally exhausted or prohibitively expensive before the end of the twenty-first century, even if all potentially possible reserves should be discovered.

The fossil fuels of coal, oil, and natural gas that have made possible the industrial revolution in modern societies are also finite and are presently being consumed very rapidly. All known and potential reserves of oil and natural gas will be exhausted or prohibitively expensive before the end of the twenty-first century. Nuclear fission as an alternative source of energy is beset with numerous serious problems, and it does not appear to offer a viable substitute for fossil fuels. Nuclear fusion is still in the experimental stage of development, and there are serious doubts that it will ever be suitable for most energy needs.

Widespread adoption of energy conservation practices could reduce current energy consumption demands by as much as fifty percent. This strategy could therefore postpone the impending energy crisis for several decades, but by itself cannot provide a permanent solution to this problem. That ultimate solution appears to lie in various forms of solar energy, provided that technologies can be developed to concentrate it and make it readily available for all energy needs. The most promising of these new technologies involve direct absorption of solar heat and transformation of solar radiation into electricity.

Most environmental pollution of the air, water, and land is a direct consequence of our industrial way of life. Serious air pollution problems include acid rain and snow, the greenhouse effect of atmospheric warming, and destruction of the ozone layer. Water pollution problems result primarily from discharges of toxic chemicals, dumping of municipal sewage, and fertilizer runoff. Most land pollution is produced by industrial dump sites, use of dangerous chemicals, and paving over large tracts of land.

As populations grow, the land and water available to meet expanding human needs has become seriously depleted. Fertile topsoil is rapidly eroding from agricultural lands as they are used more intensely. Irrigated farmland is losing productivity through waterlogging and salinization.

Croplands are being lost to nonagricultural uses. Deforestation is occurring extensively in the Third World. The major deserts are all spreading outward. Grasslands are being depleted through overgrazing. And by 2000 vitually every country is expected to be experiencing a shortage of fresh water.

Overpopulation has resulted from the fact that the world's population has grown from two to five billion people in this century, and it is expected to increase to as much as 12 billion during the next century. Most of that future population growth will occur in less developed countries. Overpopulation is always relative to some criteria, such as the earth's ecological carrying capacity. In terms of number of people in relation to available food supplies, most overpopulation is occurring in less developed countries. From a broader ecological perspective, this problem lies primarily in the industrial nations, since they are presently responsible for most mineral exhaustion, energy shortages, and environmental pollution.

Most current problems of food scarcity are being caused by the unequal distribution of food products among nations and individuals. At the present time, the world's total food production is minimally sufficient to feed all people, if it were evenly distributed. Various new agricultural techniques may expand food production considerably in the near future, but that expansion cannot continue indefinitely. By the end of the twenty-first century, the world's supplies of food could very likely become inadequate to feed all the people then living.

CHAPTER 22

EMERGING SOCIAL AND
ECONOMIC CRISES

Why is the likelihood of continual industrial growth being questioned?
What fundamental crises are besetting contemporary governments?
What critical crises are presently undermining urban communities?
Why are bureaucratic organizations becoming unmanageable?
Is socioeconomic inequality inevitable among individuals and societies?

ECONOMIC CRISIS

Even if the numerous ecological crises discussed in the previous chapter can somehow be surmounted in the future, modern societies are also beginning to experience a multitude of economic and social crises that pose a fundamental threat to their continued viability, or even their existence. Let us begin with economics.

A wide variety of existing and possible future economic crises could be discussed here, ranging from poverty in the midst of plenty to prospects for a worldwide depression. For brevity, however, this section focuses on the most fundamental and potentially most severe of these crises: *the possible cessation of industrial-based economic growth.* If this possibility becomes reality, it will affect all aspects of modern economies.

The Coming Crisis

Ever since societal economic systems began to evolve beyond the hunting and gathering stage, all societies have sought to increase their economic productivity and wealth. Economic growth and higher standards of living have been universally valued goals, despite repeated periods of temporary economic stagnation or decline. Moreover, *economic growth has traditionally been viewed as a potentially endless and infinite process.* Even if the economy of a particular society was not growing or was expanding only slightly, people have almost always assumed that with more and better land or technology they could improve their economic productivity and wealth.

The industrial revolution that transformed Western societies during the past two hundred years has immensely stimulated and expanded our vision of unlimited economic growth and ever-increasing societal wealth. This expectation is quite understandable, considering the tremendous expansion in economic productivity and wealth that has occurred in fully industrialized societies during the twentieth century. Two extremely destructive world wars and a devastating worldwide depression have failed to stem the tide of economic growth more than temporarily. And since the 1950s, the United States, Western Europe, the Soviet Union, Japan, and some developing nations have experienced unprecedented economic expansion. As a consequence, visions of continued unlimited economic growth thoroughly pervade contemporary industrial societies. We assume that a constantly increasing Gross National Product is possible and desirable and become gravely concerned whenever it fails to meet our growth expectations.

During the last twenty years, however, we have slowly begun to realize that this expectation of unlimited growth is very likely a myth derived from the economic expansion of the past two centuries. Increasing numbers of economists and other social scientists (e.g., Heilbroner, 1976; Henderson, 1978; Meadows, 1972; Olson and Landsburg, 1973) have recently argued that the kind of economic growth we have experienced with industrialization cannot continue indefinitely. *There is a strong possibility that economic growth based on ever-increasing industrial production will cease within the next hundred years.* If that occurs, it would not necessarily mean that all economic development would end or that national economies would stagnate or collapse. It would mean, however, that the economies of the presently industrialized societies would have to undergo massive transformations from an industrial base to other kinds of economic activities.

Most of these analyses of current and projected economic trends agree that future national economies must have at least two fundamental characteristics if they are to remain viable. First, they must be based on resources and processes that are unlimited rather than finite. Information processing and human services are often mentioned as possible economic bases for the future. Second, they must remain in balance with ecological conditions so that they do not inflict any further damages on the world's ecosystem. In short, *future economies must be able to operate on a sustainable basis* (Daly, 1977). Such sustainable economies should be capable of gradually improving the standards of living of all people around the globe.

Limits to Industrial Growth

Three broad arguments are frequently made to explain why unrestrained industrial-based economic growth cannot continue indefinitely. These arguments pertain to ecological conditions, capital availability, and cultural values.

Ecological Limits. Prior to the industrial revolution, the economies of all societies normally remained within the earth's ecological carrying capacity. As a society industrializes, however, its economy develops the capacity to exceed that carrying capacity. As long as only a relatively few societies were living beyond their ecological means, they survived by using their wealth and power to appropriate the natural resources they needed from other lands and by drawing down reserves of finite resources. As industrialization began spreading around the globe, however, the economies of an increasing number of societies exceeded the earth's carrying capacity, and the situation became steadily more critical for the world as a whole. As previously mentioned, *early in the twentieth century humanity was probably already exceeding the earth's total ecological carrying capacity,* and the situation has obviously now become much more serious (Catton, 1980).

We did not become fully aware of the global nature of this problem until the early 1970s, when a group of European businessmen formed an organization called the Club of Rome, which sponsored a research project to investigate world ecological and economic trends. The resulting report, titled *The Limits to Growth* (Meadows, et al., 1972), gave us a totally new perspective on economic growth. The team of researchers who conducted this study compiled massive amounts of data on a number of critical world conditions and trends pertaining to natural resources, population size, environmental pollution, food availability, and industrial output. They combined these five variables into a complex computer model of the world ecosystem that took account of all the ways in which those factors affect one another. They then used this World Model to project future trends in all five variables to the year 2100. *This model predicted that the entire world system would probably collapse before the year 2050.* Their "standard run" of the model, which predicts collapse of the entire world system by 2100, is shown in Figure 22-1. The clear conclusion to be drawn from this analysis is that we cannot expect to continue indefinitely exceeding the earth's ecological carrying capacity.

To discover how this catastrophe might be avoided, the researchers successively altered each of the five variables in the model and observed the resulting effects on future trends. For example, they first made the hypothetical assumption that unlimited natural resources would become available. In a second run, they assumed that the world population stopped growing. In subsequent runs, they assumed that environmental pollution would cease and that abundant food would be available for all people. With each of these modifications, the estimated date at which the world system broke down was delayed a few decades, but none of them prevented its occurrence. *The only way in which this worldwide ecological and economic catastrophe could be avoided permanently was to assume that industrial growth ceased.* Under that condition, the world model became stable and sustainable indefinitely. Many subsequent studies have

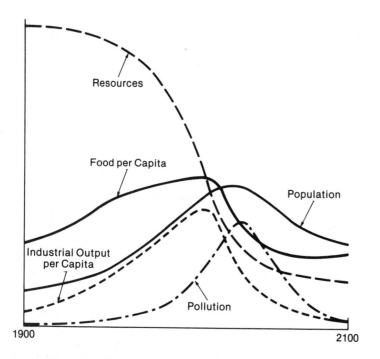

FIGURE 22-1 Standard run of the world model

Source: *The Limits To Growth: A Report from the Club of Rome's Project on the Predicament of Mankind*, by Donella H. Meadows, Dennis L. Meadows, Jørgen Randers, William W. Behrens, III. A Potomac Associates book published by Universe Books, N.Y., 1972. Original graphics by Potomac Associates. Redrawn by Wadsworth Publishing Company for inclusion in *Environment, Energy, and Society* by Craig R. Humphrey and Frederick R. Buttel. Copyright 1982. Reprinted by permission of both publishers.

The "standard" world model run assumes no major change in the physical, economic, or social relationships that have historically governed the development of the world system. All variables plotted here follow historical values from 1900 to 1970. Food, industrial output, and population grow exponentially until the rapidly diminishing resource base forces a slowdown in industrial growth. Because of natural delays in the system, both population and pollution continue to increase for some time after the peak of industrialization. Population growth is finally halted by a rise in the death rate due to decreased food and medical services.

questioned various features of the Club of Rome study, but none of them have negated its basic conclusion that world ecological stability depends ultimately on ending economic growth based on industrial expansion.

Financial Limits. Economic growth is not an automatic or spontaneous process. To increase economic productivity and wealth, at least four critical factors are necessary: technological knowledge, natural resources, investment capital, and the organizational ability to bring the other three factors together and create a viable economy. Presumably there is no limit to continual advances in science and technology, and we hope that our organizational capabilities will also continue to develop. Let us assume for the moment that somehow we solve the ecological problem of finite natural resources (as well as the related problems of overpopulation and environmental pollution). We are then left with the question of *how to continue expanding the capital available for investment in new productive facilities and techniques.*

In the past, surplus capital for investment in expanding economic ventures has come primarily from four sources:

(1) Discovering and cultivating additonal arable land;

(2) Taking natural resources and wealth from other societies;

(3) Keeping the total consumption level of a society lower than its economic output, which has invariably meant that large portions of the population were forced to endure relatively low standards of living; and

(4) Exploiting previously unused natural resources, especially fossil fuels.

All four of these sources of surplus capital have been crucial for industrialization during the past two hundred years. But what about the future?

The amount of arable land around the globe is obviously finite, and most of it is now being cultivated. In fact, soil erosion and expanding deserts in many parts of the world are currently reducing the total amount of arable land. In the past few decades, societies have been able to increase agricultural productivity considerably through widespread applications of fertilizers, herbicides, and pesticides. However, fertilizers are largely derived from petroleum, which is a finite resource, and we are now discovering that many chemical herbicides and pesticides cause serious harm to the natural environment and to human beings. Agricultural productivity has also been increased recently through biotechnical discoveries such as new hybrid seeds—generally called the "green revolution"—but many experts now believe that there are also definite limits to that line of development. Consequently, we cannot depend on steadily increasing agricultural productivity to provide most of the surplus capital necessary for unlimited economic growth.

Nor can the industrial nations any longer continue to expropriate resources and wealth from less developed countries. The era of colonialization is over, and developing societies no longer tolerate such exploitation.

Hypothetically, the standard of living of most of the world's population might be kept at or near the subsistence level, so that the resulting economic surplus could be used for capital investments—provided that continual population growth did not consume that surplus as fast as it was produced. Realistically, however, that situation is highly unlikely. People in the industrialized societies would not likely tolerate drastic reductions in their standards of living and would undoubtedly overthrow any government that attempted to take such actions. Moreover, most people in developing countries are fully aware that higher standards of living are possible. As a result of this "revolution of rising expectations," they are determined to achieve a better life for themselves or their descendants. If the global economic system breaks down as a result of an ecological catastrophe or a nuclear war, the people remaining may all be reduced to living at the subsistence level. Barring that possibility—which would leave no surplus capital at all—

we cannot expect to finance continued economic growth by permanently depriving masses of people of an adequate standard of living.

The fourth major source of investment capital—drawing down the earth's supply of petroleum and other finite natural resources—has been especially crucial for the latter stages of industrialization in the West. We have withdrawn billions of dollars worth of resources from our "earth bank account" and used the resulting capital to finance industrial development. Without doubt, however, this source of capital is limited and will not be available for more than another century.

The grim conclusion is that there may not be enough surplus capital available from any source to sustain high levels of industrial growth for many more decades (Forrester, 1977). By placing strict limits on population growth, resource depletion, and consumption levels, all of humanity could conceivably continue to live relatively comfortably on an indefinite basis. But the financial limits to unending industrial-based economic growth appear to be as severe as the ecological limits.

Cultural Limits. Whereas the ecological and financial limits on industrial growth are factual in nature, the cultural limits are intangible—but no less critical. Various writers have expressed this problem in different ways, but its central theme is that *the pursuit of unlimited economic growth is a hollow cultural goal that will ultimately prove to be inadequate for human life* (Bennett, 1976). In the words of Robert Heilbroner (1976:113), there is "a hollowness at the center of business civilization—a hollowness from which the pursuit of material goods diverts our attention for a time, but that in the end insistently asserts itself."

This hollowness has two facets, Heilbroner suggests. The first is "the tendency of a business civilization to substitute impersonal pecuniary values for personal nonpecuniary ones" (p. 113). Material possessions, no matter how abundant, are no substitute

for more meaningful values and activities such as close personal relationships or individual self-fulfillment. The second facet of this cultural hollowness is "the disregard of business for the value of work. A business civilization regards work as a means to an end, not as an end to itself. The end is profit, income, consumption, economic growth, or whatever; but the act of labor itself is regarded as nothing more than an unfortunate necessity to which we must submit to obtain this end" (p. 114). Marx warned us of the alienating effects of labor in industrial economies over a century ago, and it continues to be a major concern of many writers today. Meaningful and satisfying work is crucial to human existence, but when work becomes merely paid labor that is performed to earn money to purchase material possessions, it loses much of its intrinsic value.

The cultural argument for limits to industrial growth does not suggest that all material possessions or all income-producing work are undesirable and lead to cultural alienation and hollowness. Obviously, we require food, clothing, and other material goods, and in a market economy we must earn money to obtain those necessities. This argument does assert, however, that *the pursuit of perpetual economic growth destroys much of what is most meaningful and satisfying in human life.*

Future Prospects

If these various limits to endless industrial-based economic growth have any validity, what are our prospects for the future? Quite conceivably, they might include sharply reduced material standards of living in presently industrialized societies, as well as the prospect that much of the rest of the world will never be able to improve their economic conditions. Those prospects are ethically intolerable to many people, and politically unacceptable to many others, but they are fully within the realm of possibility. If we wish to avoid the outcomes, it appears mandatory that *all societies must develop econo-*

mies that are oriented toward permanent economic sustainability rather than unlimited industrial growth.

POLITICAL CRISES

Modern political systems are beset not by one major crisis, but by a wide array of diverse crises. They penetrate to the cores of contemporary states and threaten the ability of governments to function with any effectiveness. Four of these political crises are very briefly examined in this section, each of which involve a basic contradiction within modern political systems.

State Illegitimacy

In all Western societies, the fundamental legitimacy of the state rests on two ideologies: liberalism and democracy. As originally formulated in the seventeenth and eighteenth centuries, liberalism was the political ideology of market capitalism. Its basic tenet was that all persons should be free to exploit economic opportunities in capital, commodity, retail, labor, and other markets with minimal interference by the government. During the nineteenth and twentieth centuries, as governments became more involved in economic affairs, liberalism adopted two additional ideas, both of which are fully compatible with contemporary capitalism. First, governments should facilitate the accumulation and investment of capital to promote economic growth, which usually involves a variety of fiscal and monetary policies. Second, governments may regulate markets to improve their functioning and thereby benefit businesses, which is often accomplished through tariffs and trade policies.

In current usage, however, the meaning of liberalism has shifted considerably. It now usually refers to such ideas as civil liberties or welfarism—which are not contradictory to the original concept of liberalism, but which compound its meaning. Today, the term conservatism—which was originally a defense of feudalism and other traditional social conditions—is closer to the original idea of liberalism, although many contemporary writers prefer "neoconservatism." Its basic tenet is that governmental involvement in economic matters should be minimized as much as possible.

The essential meaning of democracy, as developed by Rousseau and other eighteenth-century political theorists, is that all citizens should have an opportunity to participate in political processes and decision making. In the nineteenth century, Marx and other writers added the idea that democratic political systems should strive to create conditions of socioeconomic, as well as political, equality among all citizens. Although contemporary theories of party and elitist democracy have modified the original concept of classical democracy, this ideology still emphasizes the idea that government should rest on the consent of its citizens.

The central thesis of Alan Wolfe's book, *The Limits of Legitimacy: Political Contradictions of Contemporary Capitalism* (1977) is that *the ideologies of liberalism (used in its original meaning) and democracy are fundamentally incompatible.* Liberalism emphasizes free market competition, which tends to produce extensive socioeconomic and political inequality, while democracy emphasizes the empowerment of all citizens through political participation, so as to promote greater political and socioeconomic equality. In other words, although both ideologies stress personal freedom, liberalism emphasizes the freedom to be unequal, while democracy emphasizes the freedom to be equal.

Despite this basic contradiction, all contemporary Western political systems derive their legitimacy from both ideologies and hence rest on the precarious ideology of "liberal democracy." Over the past two hundred years, Western polities have devised a series of uneasy and unstable accommodations between liberalism and democracy, which Wolf analyzes in considerable depth. None of those accommodations have proven effective for long, however. As a result, *the basic contradiction between liberalism and democracy is becoming increasingly apparent and pervasive at the present time and consequently is undermining the legitimacy of all Western political systems.*

Wolfe argues that this crisis in political legitimacy is causing stagnation of state functioning, political alienation, increasing state oppression of citizens, and a willingness among many government leaders to adopt manipulative or authoritarian solutions to the functional problems of modern societies. He offers no easy solution to the legitimacy crisis but warns that if it is not soon resolved, we will undoubtedly witness the collapse of many Western states and the loss of the personal freedom that both liberalism and democracy cherish.

Fiscal Insolvency

This second political crisis is closely related to the first one, but it has its own distinct character. As described by James O'Connor in *The Fiscal Crisis of the State* (1973), *contemporary governments are finding it increasingly impossible to meet all their financial commitments and responsibilities, because they are being pushed in two incompatible financial directions.*

All modern governments are committed—because of their liberal ideologies and capitalist economies or because of their state socialist ideologies and economies—to facilitating the continued accumulation and investment of capital to support economic growth. In recent decades, this task has become steadily more difficult for most governments, for numerous reasons. These include the end of colonialism, the immense demands by multinational corporations for additional capital, the finite nature and consequent rising prices of oil and other natural resources, trade imbalances among nations within the world economy, and many other factors.

At the same time, all Western governments have also accepted the responsibility—because of their democratic ideology and public demands for improved standards of living—of serving the public welfare and

assisting disadvantaged citizens. This responsibility is also becoming increasingly expensive for most governments. People everywhere are demanding more and more public services such as health care, high education, and transportation facilities, and the costs of all these services have skyrocketed. Citizens also generally expect their government to ensure them continually rising incomes and higher standards of living. The ideology of welfarism, meanwhile, insists that government has a responsibility to sponsor programs to assist the poor, the unemployed, the disabled, the elderly, and many other categories of disadvantaged people. Regardless of whether such welfare programs are based on humanitarian concerns or are merely a political strategy to attract votes and keep the people from demanding more fundamental economic changes, they are extremely expensive.

The contradiction in this case is that *to satisfy these competing sets of financial demands for capital accumulation and public services, governments must constantly raise taxes.* For a variety of reasons, however, they usually find this to be a difficult or impossible task. If a government attempts to raise business taxes, large corporations exert tremendous influence on legislators to block that action or else find legal (and sometimes illegal) ways of avoiding paying taxes. If a government tries to raise individual income or other taxes, many citizens complain loudly, vote against these officials in the next election, or organize initiatives and political movements to reduce taxes.

Faced with these limitations on increased tax revenues, governments often search for alternative courses of action. They may cut back their efforts to promote capital accumulation and economic growth. They may severely reduce public services and programs. They may borrow heavily from other countries or international agencies and steadily increase their foreign debt. Or they may borrow money from their own citizens and increase the national debt, thereby fueling inflation. However, *none of these alternatives will permanently resolve the basic contra-*

diction between the competing financial demands on modern governments and politically acceptable limits of taxation. In addition, when a government spends hundreds of billions of dollars on military forces, the fiscal crisis of the state becomes even more severe. If modern governments are to remain financially solvent, some permanent solution must be found to this fiscal crisis—although the nature of that solution is not presently evident.

Elite Dominance

As we saw in Chapter 13 on contemporary political systems, elitism and oligarchy exist everywhere. All modern states and governments display these characteristics, despite their ideological commitments to political democracy. We also noted that many recent studies have discovered that even in the United States and other Western democracies, a relatively small set of political and economic elites tends to dominate the political system. Although proponents of the theory of pluralist democracy argue that numerous voluntary associations exercise considerable political influence within modern societies, we find that in reality they are merely describing a system of pluralistic, rather than monolithic elites.

Ralph Miliband, a British political theorist, has argued forcefully in *The State in Capitalist Society* (1969) that *all modern states are profoundly oligarchical and elitist.* Moreover, on the basis of our present knowledge of the linkages between the economic and political systems in these societies, he maintains that economic elites thoroughly dominate national political leaders on most crucial issues. Contemporary corporations—within societies and throughout the world economy—have become so powerful that governments cannot control them. Governmental leaders—even of socialist governments such as France in the 1980s—are forced to support and promote corporate interests, since their legitimacy and their revenues are derived from corporate production. If they were to advocate basic changes in the economy, they would quickly

be pressured or voted out of office. Consequently, the best they can do is attempt to regulate the economy and provide public services and welfare benefits to citizens in an effort to keep them committed to the existing economic system of corporate capitalism.

Although Miliband's analysis is limited to capitalist societies, his charge of elite dominance of the political system is equally applicable to the Soviet Union. The major difference in those nations is simply that party leaders rather than economic elites constitute the ruling political class. Nevertheless, those dominant party leaders are thoroughly dedicated to supporting and promoting their economic system.

The fundamental contradiction in this situation within all industrial nations—as well as many developing countries—is that *public policies resulting from elite control of the political system often fails to serve the broader needs of the entire society.* Many public goods—including education, health care, science, the arts, urban planning, public transportation, assistance to the disadvantaged, and environmental protection—do not generate financial profits or contribute directly to economic growth. As a result, they tend to receive minimal support from governments and corporations. The only times when many of these public services receive anything approaching adequate financial support from the ruling class are when they are linked to the interests of corporations or perceived threats to national security. Much of the time, the organizations and systems that provide public goods for their society are forced to operate with minimal financial and other support from the dominant elites.

Another dimension of this crisis is that *economic and political elites frequently have little concern with socioeconomic, racial, gender, and other forms of social inequality.* Despite their democratic rhetoric, they often ignore the democratic goal of eliminating inequality in society. Because they occupy positions at the top of the stratification system, elites tend to assume that existing structures of inequality are relatively immutable or even morally justified. In recent decades, some political parties and leaders have taken limited steps to deal with the worst forms of inequality—such as racial discrimination against blacks in the United States—but those problems are far from being eliminated. Poverty, racism, and sexism are still highly evident in all modern societies.

The essence of this crisis, in short, is that *political elitism—whether dominated by economic or party elites—is not capable of adequately serving public needs or eliminating social inequality.*

Citizen Apathy

Classical democratic theory is dedicated to the proposition that all citizens have the right to participate in political decision making. Carole Pateman's review of the writings of early democratic theorists in *Participation and Democratic Theory* (1970) makes this abundantly clear. If individuals are to learn how to participate effectively in political affairs, they must acquire and practice those skills in their home, their workplace, and their community. Consequently, the contemporary theory of participatory democracy insists that people must have opportunities to take part in all forms of collective decision making.

The contradiction confronting all efforts to promote greater political involvement is that *large numbers of citizens do not exercise their participatory right even when it is available to them.* As we have seen, more than one-third of the citizens in the United States and other Western democracies have little or nothing to do with the political system, while another one-third limit their political participation to the single act of voting. No more than one-third of the public makes any effort to be active in politics beyond voting—and for most of those people such activities are quite limited and sporadic. This widespread public apathy toward political affairs is one of the main reasons why small numbers of economic and other elites are able to exert so much influence on government. In the long run, *low levels of citizen participation in politics*

CURRENT CRISES OF THE STATE

1. State illegitimacy.
2. Fiscal insolvency.
3. Elite dominance.
4. Citizen apathy.

---

can undermine or even destroy political democracy.

Many factors undoubtedly cause people to be politically inactive, including the complexity of modern government and political issues, lack of experience in political affairs, the feeling that one is powerless to influence the political system, and preoccupation with one's personal affairs and problems. Nevertheless, if political democracy is to be sustained, we must find ways of encouraging all citizens to take an active role in public affairs. As stressed by Pateman, one way of moving toward this goal would be to create many more opportunities for people to participate in decision making at home, in school, at work, within voluntary associations, in religious organizations, and in local community affairs. *By building participatory decision making into all realms of social life, we would also be strengthening political democracy.*

URBAN CRISES

Large cities in contemporary societies are also beset today with numerous major crises that, taken together, often make them almost unmanageable. In addition to the urban management problems that were discussed in Chapter 14, two conditions that exist in virtually all large cities are frequently mentioned as devastating urban crises: financial peril and governmental fragmentation.

Financial Peril

This crisis is similar to the fiscal crisis of the state discussed in the previous section, but in this case it pertains to city governments. These governments are increasingly encountering severe difficulties in obtaining the funds necessary to provide all the municipal services that their residents demand. And some cities—including New York and Cleveland—have teetered on the edge of bankruptcy. In most cities, this financial crisis is caused by the dual factors of rising demands for public services and declining tax revenues.

Governments of central cities within metropolitan areas are presently being called upon to provide more public services than ever before (Bollens and Schmadt, 1982:203–04). Some of this demand is for expansion of services that cities have long provided, such as police and fire protection, health care, welfare programs, and sanitation systems. As middle- and upper-middle class people have moved to the suburbs, the populations of the central cities have become increasingly composed of working- and lower-class people who are the principal users of most of those traditional municipal services. In addition, affluent suburban dwellers and residents of gentrified inner-city neighborhoods expect the city to continue providing high-quality hospitals, schools, cultural facilities, and recreation opportunities for them. At the same time, some of this increased demand has been for new kinds of services—often required by federal regulations—such as environmental protection, low-income housing projects, legal aid for the poor, and consumer protection programs.

Although demands for municipal services have been soaring, *the amount of tax revenues available to central cities has been steadily declining in recent years* (Bollens and Schmadt, 1982:205–14). In general, city governments obtain funds from three kinds of sources, each of which has traditionally supplied about one-third of their total revenues: property taxes on real estate and other tangible property, revenue sharing and grants from federal and state governments, and nonproperty taxes and fees (e.g., local sales taxes, local income taxes, business operating

taxes, and user fees). Several things have been happening to these municipal revenue sources.

First, as central cities have lost residents and businesses to suburban areas, their *property tax base* has steadily been diminished. This has been particularly serious, because businesses and affluent households typically pay much more money in property taxes than the value of the municipal services they receive. In effect, they have been subsidizing the costs of public services for less affluent city residents. A large proportion of the people who now remain in the central city pay less in property taxes than they receive in public services. And when city governments attempt to raise property tax rates on the businesses and more affluent households that remain in the city, this often drives even more of them to the suburbs.

Second, *federal and state government funds* allocated to cities are frequently computed on a per capital basis. As central cities lose population to the suburbs, therefore, those state and federal funds decrease. Even more serious has been the policy of the national administration during the 1980s that the federal government should minimize the funds it gives to cities for public housing, education, police protection, and many other kinds of municipal services. Many federal programs that used to provide large amounts of money to city governments for those kinds of services have been severely cut back or totally eliminated.

Third, revenues from *local sales taxes*—which are levied by over 4,000 city governments—depend on the level of consumer spending. As more affluent people move to the suburbs and as suburban shopping malls attract large numbers of shoppers from the central city as well as the suburbs, the volume of retail expenditures within the city diminishes sharply. In turn, this decreases the amount of funds the city receives from its sales tax.

Fourth, *local income taxes* draw revenues primarily from higher-income households and large businesses. As those people and firms move to the suburbs, this source of municipal revenues also declines.

Fifth, *user fees* can only be imposed on some kinds of services, such as public transportation, recreational facilities, health services, and cultural activities. If the city raises any of those fees, however, fewer people tend to use them, diminishing the total amount of revenues received. This is most apparent with buses and other forms of public transportation, which often find it impossible to charge high enough fees to cover their operating costs.

In a sometimes desperate effort to balance their budgets, *city governments have recently been experimenting with a variety of new fiscal procedures.* In one way or another, most of these procedures attempt to obtain tax revenues from suburban areas for services provided by the central city. They include:

(1) Creating special metropolitan-wide political districts to provide particular services such as mass transportation or hospitals.

(2) Metropolitan-wide sales or income taxes, of which a specified portion goes to the central city.

(3) Metropolitan property tax sharing, in which a proportion of all property taxes levied on new buildings constructed in the suburbs is returned to the central city.

Needless to say, all such financial innovations have been strongly opposed by large numbers of suburban residents and businesses, so that thus far they have not been very widely implemented.

There is no obvious solution to the current urban financial crisis, but clearly it must be resolved if central city governments are to remain financially solvent.

Governmental Fragmentation

One of the most serious crises confronting almost all metropolital areas in the United States—and to some degree in many other industrial societies—is governmental fragmentation. *The typical metropolitan area in the United States has not one government but an average of 95 separate governmental units.* And the large metropolises with over a million population have an average of nearly 300 local governments within the boundaries of their Metropolitan Statistical Area (MSA) (Bollens and Schmadt, 1982:89).

There are several different kinds of local governmental units, most of which occur in profusion in virtually every metropolitan area. First, there are numerous *municipal governments.* In addition to the central city, there will likely be anywhere from a handful to several dozen politically autonomous cities, towns, or villages. They may be suburbs of the central city, satellite cities with their own economic bases, or outlying towns within the metropolitan area. Second, there are likely to be a large number of autonomous *special districts* and *public authorities* that provide particular services such as water, sewage, public transportation, fire protection, or an airport for the central city or the entire metropolitan area. Each of these districts has its own governing body, administrative structure, tax base, and operating rules, so that each functions as a separate governmental unit. Third, *school districts* are also autonomous in most metropolitan areas, again with their own boards, administrators, and taxes.

Fourth, twenty of the states in this country are divided into *townships* (called towns in New England), which provide local municipal services to unincorporated territories. A large metropolitan area may contain quite a number of these units, covering all the territory within the MSA that is not incorporated as a municipality. Fifth, most metropolitan areas encompass several *county governments* (except in Connecticut and Rhode Island, where the towns function as counties, in Louisiana where they are called parishes, and in Alaska, boroughs). Finally, metropolitan areas are affected by large numbers of *state and federal agencies,* which are independent of all local governments, and sometimes by the *governments of adjacent states* when the MSA crosses state boundaries.

There are several interrelated reasons for this proliferation of local governmental units. Suburbanization is a major factor, as new suburbs are created and incorporated as independent municipalities, rather than as part of the central city. In many cases, the metropolitan area has expanded outward to encompass communities that were originally separate from the central city. As demands for new municipal services arise, it is often easier to create autonomous special districts to provide them, rather than making them part of the municipal government. School districts have traditionally insisted on being politically distinct from municipal governments in an effort to keep political interests out of the schools. And as state and federal governments impose new regulatory provisions on cities, additional administrative structures are frequently established to carry out those roles.

Regardless of the underlying reasons, *governmental fragmentation has extremely serious consequences for all metropolitan areas.* These include overlapping political jurisdictions, duplication of public services, uncertainty concerning responsibility for various services, incapacity for overall governmental planning, inability to coordinate or regulate metropolitan-wide services, conflicting administrative rules and procedures, and general political confusion and inefficiency. In short, in most metropolitan areas the governmental system is very ineffectively organized and, as a result, often experiences many serious problems in performing its functions.

The solution to this problem that is most often suggested is to establish some form of *metropolitan government for the entire area.* Many variations on this approach are potentially possible. When the MSA includes only one county, all governmental functions might be given to the county government and all smaller governmental units abolished (as in Honolulu). When several counties are involved, a single metropolitan-wide government might be created, with the county governments subordinate to it (which is the case in New York and Toronto, although both those metropolises still have numerous autonomous outlying suburbs). Another approach might be to turn all metropolitan-wide services over to the county government, while the central city and all other municipalities retain their autonomy and continue to provide local services to their residents (as in Indianapolis and Miami).

Despite these numerous possibilities, at the present time only 12 metropolitan areas in the United States and four in Canada have any form of metropolitan government. Some kind of governmental consolidation has been proposed in about 30 other metropolitan areas in this country during the last 40 years, but all those proposals have been defeated in public referenda. All these efforts—whether successful or unsuccessful—have been bitterly opposed in campaigns, elections, and court suits by all kinds of individuals and organizations who believed that governmental consolidation would harm their particular interests. For example, suburban residents and businesses have generally been strongly opposed to consolidation, because they felt it would increase their taxes while depriving them of control over local governmental services.

In those few metropolitan areas that have initiated some form of governmental consolidation, the new system has generally worked quite well. Governmental costs have decreased, public services have been improved and expanded, effective coordination has been implemented, and comprehensive planning has been undertaken. Given the extreme political difficulties involved in obtaining public approval of governmental consolidation proposals in most metropolitan areas, however, this does not appear to be a viable solution to governmental fragmentation in the near future.

Consequently, *many metropolitan areas in this country have adopted various kinds of less formal and less integrated procedures for coping with governmental fragmentation.* The most common of these procedures is to establish a metropolitan *Council of Governments (COG),* which now exists in about 600 communities in the United States. A COG is not a governmental unit but simply a voluntary council composed of representatives from all governmental units in the area. It typically meets once a month to discuss common problems, consider comprehensive plans proposed by its professional staff, and coordinate common activities. A COG has no legislative, financial, or enforcement powers and hence depends entirely on voluntary participation and compliance. For that reason, COGs are usually quite weak bodies, although in a few cases (e.g., San Francisco and Minneapolis-St. Paul), they do exercise considerable influence over metropolitan-wide affairs.

A second procedure is *interlocal agreements* between two or more municipalities. The usual pattern is for small suburbs to contract with the central city for a specified period of time to provide one or more services for them that they are not capable of performing themselves. These frequently include such services as police and fire protection, but sometimes they cover a wide range of municipal activities. Los Angeles County presently offers a full package of fifty municipal services to all interested incorporated and unincorporated communities within the county.

A third, less common, procedure is known as *functional transfers*. As with interlocal agreements, suburban or other local governments turn over responsibility for specific public services to the central city government, the county government, or occasionally a Council of Governments. In this case, however, the transfer of functions is permanent, rather than a temporary contract.

Although these various attempts to deal with metropolitan fragmentation have helped to resolve specific problems, none of them have eliminated the underlying crisis. *Governmental fragmentation is an extremely serious crisis in virtually all metropolitan areas today that severely limits the provision of adequate public services to the residents of the entire area.*

BUREAUCRATIC CRISES

Max Weber's bureaucratic model for goal-oriented organizations was intended to facilitate effective and efficient organizational functioning. In practice, however, as such organizations become increasingly bureaucratized, they generally experience all kinds of operational problems and often fail to attain their desired goals. In an effort to cope with those conditions, organizations commonly add more levels and units to their structures and more rules and regulations to their procedures, until they reach the point of being totally unmanageable (Meyer, Stevenson, and Webster, 1985). *The fundamental crisis prevading most large bureaucratized organizations in all modern societies—as well as many developing countries—is how to manage these organizations in an efficient and effective manner so that they can attain their goals.* This management crisis stems primarily from two basic features of the bureaucratic model: hierarchy of authority and commitment to routinization.

Hierarchy of Authority

As we have previously seen, the traditional bureaucratic model assumes that the most effective way of maintaining control over all organizational activities is to create a hierarchy of authority in which all directives flow downward. The legitimate right to make policy decisions for the organization is vested in a few positions at the apex of the hierarchy (such as a board of directors) and is then delegated downward to successively lower levels of its structure. Incumbents of positions located near or at the bottom of the hierarchy are expected to carry out their assigned tasks in a dutiful and adequate manner, without deviating from or modifying their work directives. Two arguments are often given to justify a hierarchy of authority.

(1) Persons occupying top positions are the best-qualified and most competent individuals in the organization and hence will usually make the wisest decisions for the organization as a whole.

(2) Persons occupying low-level positions are not competent or qualified to make important organizational decisions and must be continu-

ally supervised from above to ensure that they perform their assigned tasks adequately.

The first argument is often negated, however, by the fact that *many of the operational problems that beset bureaucratized organizations are a direct consequence of centralized decision making by bureaucratic elites.* Top officeholders frequently make decisions that are uninformed, unwise, or not in the best interests of the organization. This may occur because much of the information needed to deal with critical issues is never communicated up the hierarchy, so that their decisions are based largely on misconceptions or ignorance of actual conditions in the organization. It may occur because the organization is so large and complex that no one, no matter how well-informed, can fully understand all its components and activities. It may occur because individuals in high positions are not competent to perform their roles, having achieved those positions on the basis of seniority or organizational loyalty, rather than ability. Or, finally, organizational elites may place advancement of their personal careers or other interests ahead of the needs of the organization.

Whatever the reason, abundant research evidence demonstrates that whenever decision-making authority is highly centralized in one or a few positions at the top of a power hierarchy, organizational functioning tends to suffer (Abrahamsson, 1977). On one hand, many of the decisions handed down from the top are not appropriate or adequate to deal with the conditions and problems being encountered throughout the organization. On the other hand, individuals occupying positions at lower levels of the hierarchy—where the actual work of the organization is performed—are often prevented from carrying out their tasks in an efficient or effective manner because they have no authority to make decisions concerning their own work.

The argument that most rank-and-file organization members are not competent to make organizational decisions and require continual supervision can be countered in two ways. First, although many of these individuals may appear apathetic or even irresponsible, this is often a learned response to powerlessness. If one is never given opportunities to make decisions and is continually subjected to directives from above, the best way of surviving in the organization is often to do just as one is told and never "make waves." However, a number of experiments have shown that when workers are given the authority to make decisions about their own work, they generally act responsibly (Morse and Reimer, 1956; Burns, et al., 1979). Second, if we take democracy seriously, all individuals have the moral right to participate in making decisions that directly affect them (Abrahamsson, 1977). The theory of participatory democracy insists that if people are to be actively involved in societal political affairs, they must have opportunities at work and in other organizations to learn how to participate in collective decision making. Democracy in society begins at home and in the work place.

Commitment to Routinization

The purpose of bureaucratization is to maximize rationality and control within organizations. This control process is achieved partly by establishing a hierarchy of authority and partly by creating formal operating procedures, such as standardized rules and regulations, written records and files, and other techniques. Formalization of operating procedures can contribute immensely to rationalizing organizational activities, as along as those activities are routine and repetitive. Highly bureaucratized organizations can often operate quite rationally in determining the most efficient and effective means of carrying out a particular task and standardizing that procedure to ensure that it is repeatedly performed in the same manner. In short, *bureaucratized organizations tend to be committed to operating as routinely as possible.*

As long as an organization encounters no serious external changes or pressures from its natural or social environments and experiences no disruptive internal conflicts or disruptions, a commitment to routinization can serve it quite well. In the modern world, however, such relatively static conditions rarely occur. In reality, most organizations must cope with a continual stream of external stresses and internal strains. New technologies are developed, other organizations attempt to influence or control them, critical resources become scarce or expensive, their outputs are no longer desired or valued by society, key individuals leave and replacements must be recruited, units and individual members conflict with one another for any number of reasons, communication channels within the organization break down, exchange obligations are not fulfilled, individuals or units fail to perform their tasks adequately, and so on.

In all such stressful situations, rigid commitment to routinization can create serious problems or even disaster for an organization. *To deal with nonroutine and often unpredictable situations, an organization must be able to respond with flexibility and creativity.* Standardized operating procedures, codified in written rules and regulations, do not usually promote flexibility and creativity. On the contrary, they tend to encourage rigid adherence to "doing things by the book" and thus stifle initiative and creativity. The result is that the organization is frequently incapable of coping with many of the stresses and strains impinging upon it. The very techniques that were intended to promote operational rationality become impediments to efficient and effective functioning, and the organization becomes progressively less capable of achieving its goals.

It is possible to build into an organization various procedures to promote planning, flexibility, creativity, and intentional change (Hage and Aiken, 1970). To the extent that such dynamic practices are adopted by an organization, it may largely avoid the management crisis that plagues so many bureaucracies. However, this approach to management demands that *an organization move beyond the traditional bureaucratic model and devise new procedures for promoting rationality and*

control. The "catch 22" here is that the process of creating procedures to encourage intentional organizational change is itself a fundamental change that most organizations are programmed to resist. Until bureaucratized organizations discover a way of escaping this dilemma, they are likely to experience an ever-deepening management crisis.

INEQUALITY CRISES

There is nothing new in the fact that individuals and societies are grossly unequal in the power they exercise, the privileges they enjoy, and the prestige they acquire. Socioeconomic inequality is as old as human civilization and is certainly not a novel condition or crisis in the contemporary world. However, the process of industrialization, especially in its early stages, considerably magnifies the status differences between social classes and among societies. Inequality is therefore a fundamental characteristic of modern social life, which many people believe is morally indefensible.

An optimistic argument is often made that full-scale industrialization, with its resulting fantastic increases in total societal wealth and power, is at last providing a means of eliminating socioeconomic inequality (Lenski, 1966). Mature industrial societies offer their citizens unprecedented opportunities for educational attainment, better jobs, higher incomes, a more comfortable standard of living, and greater social prestige. According to this argument, it is only a matter of time—and continual economic growth—until most members of these societies will enjoy at least the benefits of a middle-class lifestyle. Why, therefore, should we expect any kind of fundamental crisis of inequality in the future?

Growth Versus Redistribution

In one sense, this optimistic argument is correct. A great deal—though by no means all—of the wealth and other benefits provided by full-scale industrialization is gradually diffused throughout much of the population in these societies. Education levels rise from one generation to the next, which can be considered a definite advance. Increasing numbers of workers escape from backbreaking menial labor on farms and in factories, attaining at least semiskilled jobs, if not skilled or technical employment, white-collar jobs, managerial positions, or professional careers. For many people, such occupational advancement—either during their own lives or through generations—is unquestionably an improvement in job satisfaction and social status. Although many blue-collar and white-collar employees still feel that their jobs provide considerably less personal fulfillment than they would like, they have no desire to return to the days in which most workers toiled 50 or 60 hours a week at unskilled jobs to keep bread on the table.

The strongest case for the optimistic argument, however, lies in the constantly rising personal and family incomes produced by industrialization, plus the vastly improved standards of living enjoyed by large portions of the population as a result of those higher incomes. There is no doubt that most members of industrial societies are better off economically today than ever before. If we ignore the fact that grinding poverty still remains a stark reality for at least one-sixth of the United States population, are we not at least slowly eliminating the worst forms of socioeconomic inequality?

In another sense, unfortunately, *the optimistic argument is misleading and invalid. It is misleading because it confuses improved levels of living with equality.* Inequality is always a relative manner. No matter how well-off one may be economically or in any other sense, if many other people are much better off, inequality still exists. Although material and other levels of living have improved greatly for many people in fully industrialized societies during the past fifty years, income distributions have remained highly skewed. As we saw in Chapter 16, the distribution of personal incomes in the United States has not changed significantly for over two generations. In 1940, the fifth of the population

with the lowest incomes received only five percent of all money income, while the fifth with the largest incomes received over 40 percent of all money income. That unequal income distribution remains the same today. Although figures for the distribution of total wealth are less complete, we know that it is much more unevenly distributed, with one percent of all Americans owning over 25 percent of all personal wealth in this country (Turner and Starnes, 1976:19).

Mature industrialization and explosive economic growth have done nothing to reduce income and wealth inequality in this country for over fifty years. Many people have considerably higher incomes (even allowing for inflation) and live much more comfortably than their parents and grandparents, but there is still as much economic inequality as ever. *We have relied on constant economic growth to avoid the necessity of redistributing income and wealth and thus reducing economic inequality.* And the poor are still with us.

Inequality in a Sustainable Economy

The optimistic argument is invalid because it rests on the assumption that extensive economic growth will continue indefinitely. As long as the economy continues to expand, proponents of this perspective may insist that what really counts for most people is their actual level of living, not their relative status in an abstract income distribution. As long as they are living quite comfortably and can look forward to even more income in the future, why should they care if other people are making five or even ten times as much money as they are? They have no basis for serious complaints, according to this argument, since all of their reasonable needs are being satisfied quite adequately.

As we have seen, however, the basic assumption of unlimited industrial-based economic growth appears highly unwarranted. Even if we put aside the possibility of global nuclear war, there are inescapable ecological and financial limits to economic growth through perpetual industrial development.

If we move toward a sustainable economy, it will no longer be possible to continue constantly raising most people's material standards of living through constantly expanding production. What will this mean for socioeconomic inequality?

Most societies have experienced times when their economies were not growing, such as the worldwide depression of the 1930s. It is very common during such periods for many people who had previously been located around the middle of the income and wealth distributions to move downward. As a result, the lower levels of those distributions increase in size, and relative socioeconomic inequality increases. Economic downturns since World War II have deviated from that pattern somewhat, however, since all industrial societies have implemented welfare programs that redistribute a portion of the total national wealth to people located toward the bottom of the income distribution. In some societies, including the United States, these programs have been rather limited in scope and have had only minimal effects on the overall income and wealth distribution. In other societies—especially in Scandinavia—these programs are much more extensive and have considerably reduced socioeconomic inequality. The essential point is that *when economic growth cannot be relied upon to raise the standards of living of most people more or less continually, socioeconomic inequality is likely to increase unless the society adopts programs to redistribute income and wealth.* Economic inequality could be considerably reduced in a society with a sustainable economy, but this would have to occur through redistribution of income and wealth, not through constant economic growth.

Class Bifurcation

Is socioeconomic inequality likely to increase in Western industrial societies in the future? Paul Blumberg's book, *Inequality in an Age of Decline* (1980), indicated that this is already occurring in the United States. Although this society pays lip service to the idea of a welfare state, in practice it has been rather resistant to public programs that would significantly redistribute income and wealth. Consequently, the real incomes (adjusted for inflation) of the majority of people in this country have not improved significantly during the last twenty years.

Blumberg described the structure of socioeconomic inequality that appears to be developing in the United States as economic growth continues to slow down. A minority of the population—perhaps as large as one-fourth—will probably be able to continue improving its standard of living. These are people who hold relatively privileged socioeconomic statuses and who have the advanced education and the occupational skills (professionals, managers, computer and other technicians, entertainers, etc.) required to continue riding the crest of the economy as it moves away from industrial manufacturing. The middle half of the population will not be so fortunate, however. This large middle and working class is composed of people who have a high school education and perhaps a year or two of technical training or college, are employed as white-collar clerical and salesworkers or blue-collar skilled and semiskilled workers, and receive middle-level incomes but have very little accumulated wealth. During the next two or three decades, Blumberg argued, they will find it increasingly difficult to find steady employment at a pay rate adequate to sustain a comfortable standard of living. They will therefore very likely go deeper and deeper into debt as they struggle to maintain their past standard of living or else will experience a declining level of living. In either case, *the gap between the minority of privileged "haves" and the large majority of increasingly disadvantaged "have-nots" could become a virtually unbridgeable gulf.* The bottom one-fourth of the population, meanwhile, will have few opportunities to escape economic deprivation, severe poverty, or dependence on public welfare.

If Blumberg's predictions become reality, they would create a politically explosive situation. Many members of the sinking middle and working class are likely to become highly resentful and angry, turn their frustration and wrath on vulnerable scapegoats, such as racial and ethnic minorities, and support politicians who promise simple and quick solutions to their problems. Eventually, if the situation continues to worsen, the society could become ripe for either the emergence of an authoritarian political demigod or a political revolution.

In sum, *the crisis of socioeconomic inequality in advanced industrial societies is how to implement extensive programs of income and wealth redistribution so as to prevent increasing inequality and political unrest as economic growth slows down.*

International Bifurcation

Thus far we have been focusing on individual socioeconomic inequality within industrial societies. *Much the same pattern could well occur on a global scale, with increasing international inequality and a steadily widening gulf between the highly industrialized and the developing societies.* The 35 advanced industrial nations will probably continue to enjoy relatively comfortable levels of living (at least by a privileged minority of their citizens) for some time to come. And those societies that manage to make a successful transition from an industrial-based growth economy to some kind of postindustrial sustainable economy should be able to maintain their superiority in the world economy indefinitely. Future prospects for most of the over 120 developing nations in the world could become increasingly bleak and hopeless, however. As we have already seen, it may prove impossible for many of them ever to industrialize fully and attain current Western standards of living. If their development is permanently blocked, the world will likely become even more divided than it is today into a small set of relatively privileged nations and a much larger set of grossly disadvantaged nations with no realistic hopes of further socioeconomic development.

That kind of rigid international stratification would provide no basis for political stability in the world. Many of the disadvantaged societies—especially those that have begun the process of industrialization and presently have high expectations for future development—could easily become politically desperate and radicalized. Leaders of those societies might well come to believe that their only hope lay in taking the wealth they desire from the privileged societies through forceful means. Incidents of international terrorism, military threats, blackmail, or armed conflict could likely escalate rapidly. And since a number of developing countries now possess nuclear weapons, the threat of nuclear war between "have" and "have-not" nations might become an increasingly likely final outcome.

There is an obvious way of avoiding this explosive international situation. As on the individual level, *global socioeconomic inequality could be reduced or even eliminated by redistributing wealth among societies.* International programs could be established through which the privileged nations freely shared their technology and capital with all the developing countries around the globe. For the industrial or postindustrial nations, this would necessitate lowering their economic outputs and levels of living somewhat, so as to enable all people to live with at least moderate comfort and some hope for future betterment. This would not be international altruism but *a realistic understanding that socioeconomic inequality inevitably breeds political conflict, combined with public acceptance of the fact that all humanity is linked together in a single world ecological/economic system.*

SUMMARY

Humanity's centuries-old vision of continual and potentially endless economic growth, which was greatly magnified by the industrial revolution, is no longer viable. We now realize that industrial-based economic growth is inherently limited, so that unrestrained economic development cannot continue forever.

Three broad arguments lead to this conclusion. (1) The ecological limits of the earth's total carrying capacity will very likely produce a complete collapse of the world economic/ecological system within a hundred years, unless industrial growth ceases. That collapse will be a combined outcome of population growth, resource depletion, environmental deterioration, and food shortages, in combination with the attempt to promote ever-expanding industrial growth. (2) The sources of surplus investment capital that financed the industrial revolution are rapidly being eliminated as all arable land is brought into cultivation, exploitation of less developed societies is no longer tolerated, masses of people around the world are demanding better levels of living, and fossil fuels and other finite natural resources become exhausted. (3) The pursuit of unlimited economic growth is a hollow cultural goal that will ultimately prove inadequate for human life. It substitutes pecuniary values for human based values and disregards the intrinsic importance of meaningful and satisfying work in human life.

The legitimacy crisis in modern states is a result of an inherent contradiction between the ideologies of traditional liberalism, with its emphasis on market capitalism, and political democracy, which emphasizes equality of political participation and socioeconomic conditions. This ideological contradiction has not been resolved despite two hundred years of effort and is today undermining the legitimacy of all Western political systems.

The fiscal crisis is occurring because modern governments are constantly being pressured to perform the dual financial functions of promoting capital accumulation and providing all kinds of public services. At the same time, governments are facing severe limitations on their ability to increase tax revenues without arousing strong public hostility.

The elitism crisis results from the fact that all modern states are profoundly oligarchical and elitist, dominated either by powerful corporations or by leaders of dominant political parties. Elite control of the political system often fails to serve the broader needs of society and also tends to ignore social inequality.

The participation crisis facing all democratic nations arises because large numbers of citizens choose not to exercise their right to take part in political affairs even when it is available to them.

In recent years, many cities have been experiencing severe financial crises. Governments of central cities are being called upon to provide more public services than ever before, while at the same time the amount of tax revenues available to them has been steadily declining. Municipal governments have begun experimenting with a variety of new fiscal procedures to deal with this financial crisis, but no solution has yet been found.

Another major crisis in all metropolitan areas is governmental fragmentation, or the existence of numerous local government units of many different kinds. This situation creates serious problems for metropolitan areas in providing and coordinating public services. Although many metropolises have attempted to create some form of metropolitan government, only a handful have been successful. Many metropolitan areas, meanwhile, have adopted other procedures for coping with this problem, but none of them have provided adequate solutions.

Although the bureaucratic organizational model is intended to facilitate effective and efficient functioning, it frequently produces the opposite results. This management crisis results primarily from two features of the bureaucratic model. One of these is its hierarchy of authority, which is supposed to ensure centralized control over all organizational activities. When all major organizational decisions are made by a few individuals at the apex of the hierarchy, those decisions are often uniformed, unwise, or not in the best interests of the organization.

The second inadequate feature of the bureaucratic model is the commitment to routinization that it tends to foster. Formal operating procedures such as standardized rules and regulations can facilitate rational attainment of organizational goals under routine, unchanging conditions. Whenever organizations face external stresses or internal strains, however, rigid commitment to routinization greatly hinders their ability to respond with flexibility and creativity.

The age-old fact of socioeconomic inequality has been greatly exacerbated by the process of industrialization. Some observers believe that mature industrialization is slowly reversing this condition, as a result of the immense wealth and other benefits presently being created in these societies. That optimistic perspective confuses level of living with equality. Although material and other levels of living have improved greatly for many people in fully industrialized societies during the past fifty years, their relative distributions of income and wealth have remained unchanged during that entire period.

The optimistic argument is invalid because it assumes that unlimited industrial-based economic growth will continue indefinitely. As we approach the limits of economic growth through industrial development, the levels of living of large segments of the population will likely cease rising and may even begin to decline. Although a privileged minority of the people may continue to live comfortably or even affluently, most members of the middle and working classes are likely to sink deeply into debt or experience declining levels of living. This situation could easily become politically explosive.

Much the same pattern could occur on a global scale, with increasing international inequality and a steadily widening gulf between highly industrialized and developing societies. Many developing countries may find it impossible to industrialize fully and attain Western standards of living. Global socioeconomic inequality could be reduced by redistributing technology and wealth among all nations, but this does not appear to be politically realistic at the present time.

SOCIETAL TRANSFORMATION

What fundamental ecological and organizational revolutions have occurred
   throughout human history?

What is a societal transformation, and why are modern societies thought to
   be undergoing such a transformation?

How would existing societies have to change to approximate the model of a
   sustainable society?

How can sociology be applied to society to facilitate social choice making
   and activism?

What is social planning, and how can sociology contribute to it?

SOCIETAL REVOLUTIONS

Fundamental transformations in social life
are frequently described as revolutions.
When sociologists talk of a *societal revolution,* they are not thinking of just a sociopolitical revolution as discussed in Chapter
20. They are speaking in much broader
terms of massive changes in the total organizational structure of a society. And while
such a transformation will inevitably generate much social conflict of all kinds, it need
not involve overthrow of the government or
other kinds of political violence. Total societal revolutions usually transpire over a considerable span of time and consist of countless small changes that may appear to the
people experiencing them as quite unrelated. In the past, it has frequently taken
several hundred years before observers were
able to look back on that process and recognize the interrelated and cumulative nature
of all those separate social changes. In other

words, it takes time for many cumulative alterations *within* a society to result in a total
transformation *of* a society into an entirely
new form. In the modern world, however,
the process of change and our awareness of
its wholistic nature are occurring much more
rapidly than in the past.

Ecological Revolutions

*From an ecological perspective, there have been
two fundamental societal revolutions in human
history,* when societies began relating to the
natural environment in totally new ways.
The first of these was the *agricultural revolution,* which occurred very gradually over
many hundreds of years as people shifted
from hunting and gathering to horticultural
gardening as their principal source of sustenance. The later transition from horticultural to agrarian societies that was discussed
in Part II was a major ecological development but not a fundamental ecological revo-

lution. The second of these ecological revolutions was the shift from agriculture to industry as the ecological/economic foundation of modern societies. This *industrial revolution* began only about two hundred years ago and is nowhere near completion, since three-fourths of humanity still live in predominantly agricultural societies.

Despite the fact that the industrial revolution is an ongoing process that will probably require several hundred more years to be completed—if that ever occurs—*many social scientists argue that highly industrialized societies are already beginning to move into a third fundamental ecological revolution.* This is a shift from industry to information as the ecological/economic base of future societies. It is often described as the *information revolution,* and the societies that will emerge from it are frequently referred to as "information societies."

The basic argument made by these social scientists is that the creation, storage, transmission, manipulation, and utilization of all kinds of information—but especially technological and scientific knowledge—will become the primary features of the economy, polity, and other social institutions in tomorrow's societies. Industry will continue to be an important aspect of those societies, just as agriculture has continued to be important in industrial societies. In future information societies, however, agriculture and industry will be secondary activities within their economies, generating only a minor portion of the total wealth and occupying only a small proportion of the labor force. Most of the wealth will be generated by information-related activities, and a majority of all workers will handle information, not plants and animals or machines. Moreover, a great deal of all agricultural and industrial production will be carried out by automated equipment controlled by computers, so that even in those fields most workers will deal most of the time with information. From this ecological perspective, therefore, the information revolution will be only the third fundamental societal transformation in human history, as shown in Figure 23-1.

FIGURE 23-1 Three fundamental ecological revolutions

Agricultural

Industrial

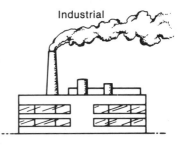

Informational

Organizational Revolutions

Social scientists who take a more organizational perspective on social change view history somewhat differently. They frequently identify at least *four previous fundamental societal revolutions, each marked by the emergence of a new basis of social organization.* The first one has no standard name, but might be designated in sociological terminology as the *differentiation revolution.* It occurred gradually throughout the horticultural and early agrarian eras, as the multitude of social functions that were originally performed by family units were taken over by separate specialized organizations such as community governments, religious bodies, and businesses of all kinds. The family then became only one of many social institutions within societies, and kinship was no longer the primary social bond among people.

The second of these organizational transformations was the *urban revolution,* which occurred as increasing numbers of people lived in urban communities and engaged in nonagricultural occupations. The process of large-scale urbanization is usually described as beginning in advanced agrarian societies, but it is more closely linked with industrialization.

The third organizational revolution was the development of the modern nation-state and hence can be called the *state revolution.* Although the process of state building began in horticultural societies, early political states were rather loosely organized and did not attempt to control most aspects of organized social life. Unified nations with powerful national governments were largely a creation of advanced agrarian societies, and this process did not become fully developed until the late eighteenth and early nineteenth centuries.

The fourth of these organizational transformations is the contemporary *bureaucratic revolution.* It is characterized by the growth of huge, bureaucratically structured organizations within many spheres of social life, and is clearly a product of the twentieth century in modern societies.

These organizational revolutions differ from the ecological revolutions in two major ways. First, they have been less discrete and much more overlapping. Second, they are all continuing today throughout contemporary societies and will undoubtedly constitute major societal trends for a long time to come. However, just as the information revolution has begun while the industrial revolution is still far from complete, *a fifth organizational transformation is now emerging, even while all four of the previous revolutions are still ongoing.*

This latest organizational revolution within modern societies still lacks a common name, but it might best be described as the *interdependence revolution.* Its primary feature is the rapidly expanding interdependence of all dimensions of human existence. No social activity or organization in modern societies can exist independently from the larger social environment, and these functional linkages among all parts of social life are increasing at a very rapid pace. As an example, sociologists used to be able to study communities as distinct social entities, explaining their internal social dynamics entirely in terms of their own particular characteristics. Today, however, no community can be adequately understood without taking into account all of the economic, political, and social influences that impinge upon it from the larger society. Similarly, it has been common in the social sciences to focus attention on only one society (usually one's own) at a time, but we are now coming to realize that all societies throughout the world are becoming highly interrelated and interdependent within the total world system.

These five organizational revolutions are shown in Figure 23-2.

In sum, regardless of whether we prefer an ecological/economic perspective and emphasize the emerging information revolution or take a social organizational perspective and focus on the growing interdependence revolution, it is becoming increasingly evident that *modern societies are presently entering into another fundamental process of transformation.* Moreover, these two current societal revolutions are so thoroughly interwoven that we might more realistically speak of them in combination as the "informational-interdependence revolution." Regardless of the name we give it, however, it is clearly the beginning of a fundamental transformation of human societies.

THE COMING TRANSFORMATION

The underlying thesis of this entire book has been that societies—and all other forms of social organization—have been continually

Differentiation

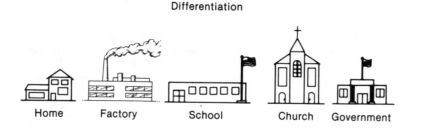

Home Factory School Church Government

Urban

State

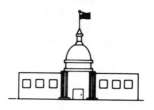

Bureaucratic

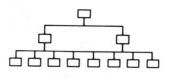

Interdependence

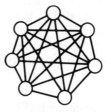

FIGURE 23-2
Five fundamental
organizational revolutions

changing throughout human history. The manner in which people live has gradually but steadily evolved from a simple foraging existence through the successive stages of horticultural and agrarian societies, and during the last two hundred years we have created highly organized and extremely complex industrialized societies.

As a result of this developmental process, it is quite tempting to believe that the forms of social organization existing in contemporary industrial societies represent the apex of human social evolution. If we adopt this belief, we are likely to view the future as simply a continuation and fulfillment of current trends, so that eventually the entire world will come to resemble contemporary Western societies. In addition to the historical and sociological arrogance of this belief, it blindly ignores the fundamental observation that human societies are constantly changing and evolving. If modern industrial societies are just another stage in the ongoing process of societal evolution, however, what does the future hold in store for humanity?

Pressures for Change

The preceding chapters on emerging crises sketched a number of trends and conditions that pervade all industrial societies. Some of these crises are ecological in nature, while others pertain to social organization. Although any one of these crises might be solvable by itself, all of them are impinging on us simultaneously. In combination—and in interaction with one another—they are today creating pressures and tensions in contemporary societies that demand some kind of resolution. If the study of human societies teaches us one inescapable lesson, it is that *whenever societies are beset with a multidimensional set of serious pressures and tensions, those societies will inevitably respond by changing in fundamental ways.* This generalization has held true throughout human history, and there is no reason to think that it does not also apply to contemporary industrial societies. The question is not, "Will present societies change in fundamental ways?". The imperative questions facing us today, rather, ask, "What forms will these changes take?", "When will these changes begin?", "Through what processes will they occur?", "At what rates will they come about?", "What new forms of social organization will emerge from these changes?".

We must also understand that these coming societal changes pertain not just to any single society. Most of the writings dealing with this process have focused on the United States, primarily because the underlying trends are particularly evident in this society at the present time. Nevertheless, these writings make clear that the United States is only a prototype example of emerging postindustrial societies, and that this fundamental process of change is occurring in all modern societies. In particular, Sweden is frequently described as being even further along this route than the United States. In short, we are dealing with a general process of societal change that is likely to affect and transform every industrial nation sooner or later.

In recent years, a number of books dealing with the emergence of postindustrial societies have been written for the general public. Persons interested in exploring this topic in greater depth than can be presented here should find the following works to be thought-provoking: Daniel Bell's *The Coming of Post-Industrial Society* (1973); John Naisbitt's *Megatrends* (1984); Kirkpatrick Sale's *Human Scale* (1980); Alvin Toffler's *The Third Wave* (1980); and Daniel Yankelovich's *New Rules* (1981). These books—as well as numerous more scholarly works on the same theme—deal with differing aspects of the process of societal change and offer different predictions about the future. Nevertheless, *the most striking feature of all these writings is their general agreement that massive pressures for social change are rapidly developing in modern industrial societies.* They also all agree that the changes that eventually result from those pressures will not be minor alterations in existing social patterns but will constitute a major transformation of contemporary societies.

Resistance to Change

If there is a second basic lesson to be learned from studying human societies, it is that *all social change is inevitably resisted.* And the more fundamental that change process, the more voracious the resistance is likely to be.

Perhaps the most common source of this resistance is ignorance of what is occurring. If people are not well-informed about current trends in their society or do not make the effort to think critically and analytically about the meaning and potential consequences of those trends, they will not understand that fundamental social changes are occurring. Caught up on the everyday details of their personal lives, they often pay little or no attention to the broader scene and frequently assert that "everything seems fine to me."

A second source of resistance to change comes from focusing on only a few specific events or problems and failing to see the "big picture." People who do this are aware of specific difficulties in their society—such as acid rain or the national debt or gender discrimination—and often become quite concerned about those topics. However, they tend to view them as separate and relatively unrelated problems, not as interwoven aspects of a much larger societal process. Consequently, they usually assume that if those problems can be solved, society will be improved but not altered in any fundamental way.

A third source of resistance is expressed by people who are aware that at least some basic changes are occurring in society but who believe that those trends are taking us in undesirable directions. They commonly cherish a conception of society that is simpler or more traditional than at present, which they believe existed at some point in the past. They therefore seek to prevent any further movement away from their cherished ideal, and if possible to reverse current trends so as to return their society to past conditions.

There is a fourth source of resistance to social change that is more subtle because it welcomes innovation. People who take this approach may be quite aware that fundamental trends are occurring in society that could have far-reaching consequences, and they want to respond to these trends in ways that will benefit society. However, they commonly hold a technocratic conception of social life. That is, they see the emerging trends—such as shortages of fossil fuels or inadequate decision-making processes—as essentially technical in nature and therefore amenable to technological solutions. If we need more energy, build nuclear reactors. If we need a new method of voting, give everyone access to an interactive computer network. These people thus support technological innovation as a solution for society's ills, but they frequently see changes in social practices and institutions as unnecessary or undesirable.

A fifth source of resistance to change in society comes from established vested interests. These may be business corporations, political parties, special-interest associations, established churches, or elite social classes. Because they are benefiting from existing societal conditions, they do not want them changed. And because they tend to be relatively powerful, they are often able to mount strong opposition to proposed changes. Moreover, if they are sophisticated about the ways in which their society functions, they may adopt the strategy of encouraging some limited changes to cope with pressing problems, while at the same time carefully directing or controlling those changes to their own advantage. Powerful elites and organizations have utilized this manipulative strategy throughout history, often so successfully that most of the population was unaware of what was really happening.

Given all these potential sources of resistance to social change, we can be assured that *whatever societal transformation emerges in the future will not occur without a great deal of conflict throughout all realms of social life.* It will not be a smooth or painless transformation.

SUSTAINABLE SOCIETIES

The coming transformation discussed in the preceding section could eventually produce several different kinds of new societies. This process of change has not progressed far enough, however, to enable us to predict the most likely nature of postindustrial societies. Although this might appear to be unfortunate for us at the present time, it actually offers a great advantage. Because the transformation is just beginning, we can—if we choose—take actions that will push it in the directions we believe are most beneficial for humanity. In other words, we can intentionally design the future in a way that has never before been attempted. To do this, however, we must have a conception of what future societies should be like. That is obviously a highly value-laden issue over which there is already a great deal of controversy.

The Sustainable Society Model

During the past fifteen years, a considerable number of social scientists and other observers of modern societies have begun to formulate a general model of future societies to guide our thinking and discussion about the choices facing us today. Although this model takes account of the emerging informational and interdependence revolutions in contemporary societies, it attempts to go beyond these trands by taking an even broader and longer-term perspective on human societies. The basic assumption underlying the model is that the most fundamental prerequisite of all human societies is to survive on a permanent basis by avoiding the kinds of ecological and organizational crises that could destroy existing patterns of social organization. Only if societies are able to respond to that imperative demand will they survive long enough to complete the information-interdependence revolution. This model of a *permanently sustainable society* is not a prediction of what future societies will be like, but rather *a blueprint for designing societies that can sustain human life indefinitely.*

The basic idea of the model is not at all new. In 1848, when the industrial revolution was just getting underway in England, the political economist John Stuart Mill, in his classic work, *Principles of Economics,* expressed a vision of a very different kind of society from nineteenth-century England:

I confess that I am not charmed with the ideal of life held out by these who think that the normal state of human beings is that of struggling to get on; that the trampling, crushing, elbowing, and treading on each other's heels, which form the existing type of social life, are the most desirable lot of human kind, or anything but the disagreeable symptoms of one of the phases of industrial progress. . . . It is scarcely necessary to remark that a stationary condition of capital and population implies no stationary state of human improvement. There would be as much scope as ever for all kinds of mental, cultural, and moral and social progress; as much room for improving the Art of Living, and much more likelihood of its being improved, when minds ceased to be engrossed by the art of getting on. (Quoted in Sale, 1980:329).

Although Mills was primarily concerned about economic systems, 120 years later, in 1966, economist Kenneth Boulding added an ecological dimension to Mill's vision by introducing the concept of "spaceship earth," (Boulding, 1968). His point was that the entire earth is a closed ecological system (except for the input of sunlight), so that—like a spaceship—it must be self-sustaining if it is to survive for any length of time.

Several names are commonly applied to this model for postindustrial societies, but the term "sustainable society" (Pirages, 1977) is gaining widespread acceptance. *The principal feature of a sustainable society would be its ability to remain in belance with its natural and social environments on a permanent basis.* In other words, the natural and social resources used by the society would not exceed the ability of its environment to provide those resources on a continuing basis, and the activities and waste products of the society would not harm or destroy that environment.

Two other names that are frequently applied to his model are "stable society" and "steady-state society." The former term is usually used in relation to the natural environment, implying that future societies must maintain a stable relationship with the natural world in terms of resource utilization and environmental pollution. Human beings exist within the world ecosystem and must abide by its laws if they are to survive for long. Consequently, we must cooperate with nature to maintain the life-support system of our planet, rather than constantly seeking to exploit it for our own immediate benefit. "Steady-state society" is usually used in respect to economic systems, implying that the goal of continual economic growth is quite unrealistic. As we have seen, there are several ecological, economic, and cultural limitations to continual industrial-based economic growth that cannot be ignored forever. Economic systems must shift from a growth to a steady-state mode of operation if they are to remain viable on a permanent basis.

The model of a sustainable society is usually applied to nation-states, since they are the principal form of social organization in the contemporary world. At the same time, however, the model is fully applicable to the total world system of societies, and as nations become increasingly interdependent in the future, this global perspective on sustainability may likely become imperative. The model can also be applied to many smaller forms of social organization—such as communities, bureaucracies, and governments—although this is less common.

Societal Environments

If societies are to become permanently sustainable, according to this model, they must develop many new kinds of relationships with their natural and social environments. The most frequently mentioned of these relationships are sketched in the following paragraphs.

Natural World. For a society to remain in balance with the world ecosystem, several conditions would have to be satisfied. Ideally, *only renewable resources would be taken from the earth, and only at the rate at which they are replaced by natural or human-assisted processes.* This requirement applies to mineral deposits, soil nutrients, timber, fresh water, petroleum, and all other natural resources. In reality, of course, societies will undoubtedly continue to extract nonrenewable resources—such as fossil fuels—but these extractions would be kept to a bare minimum by substituting renewable resources—such as solar energy—as far as possible. In addition, *all pollutants released into the natural environment would be limited to forms and levels that could readily be absorbed by the earth's ecosystem.*

Population Characteristics. In this realm, an imperative first requirement for sustainability within most existing societies would be to *halt population growth and maintain a stable population size.* (The only exceptions might be those few societies, such as Norway, whose small populations do not yet exceed the carrying capacity of their land. On a world scale, however, no societies would be exempt from this requirement.) Moreover, since the populations of most societies—developed and developing—already exceed the carrying capacity of their land, *most societal populations would have to be reduced in size.* In many countries, an ecologically stable population size might be as small as one-half or even one-fourth of its present size.

Physical and Social Technology. The sustainable society model does not require any limitations on technological development in either the physical or social realms. On the contrary, constant technological advancement could enhance the ability of a society to live within the bonds of its natural and social environments. For example, further development of solar energy technology could greatly reduce demands for fossil fuels, and new forms of international cooperation might significantly reduce the possibility of global war. The requirement of the model is that *technology be used appropriately and wisely. Appropriate use of technology* means that the techniques employed in any situation are suited in scale and complexity to the task at hand. Instead of assuming that larger and more complex technologies are always desirable, our technical tools would be matched to our needs. For example, in the area of transportation the most appropriate technology to use when going to the corner drug store might be a bicycle rather than a car, while a fully automated and highly sophisticated mass transit system might be most appropriate for transporting thousands of workers daily from their homes to their jobs. *Wise use of technology* means that technological tools would be employed to benefit humans individually and collectively, rather than to increase corporate profits or destroy the ecosystem.

Other Societies. The principal types of relationships among societies are economic, political, military, and cultural in nature. All these relationships must remain in relative balance if a society is to approximate the sustainable society model. *Economically,* such a society would not dominate other nations through multinational corporations, foreign trade imbalances, international banking practices, or other procedures. Conversely, it would not be economically dominated by other nations in any of those ways. *Politically,* a sustainable society would be an active participant in international diplomacy and world organizations such as the United Nations, but it would not attempt to impose its political ideology on other nations or control their political activities. At the same time, it would not be a political satellite of any other nation. *Militarily,* such a society would not build military forces that threatened other nations, invade other countries, or engage in international warfare. It might, however, participate in multinational peacekeeping activities. In the *cultural* realm, this kind of society would not seek to impose its values or lifestyles on other people. It would, however, freely exchange scientific, artistic, and other ideas with all other societies.

Societal Change

The sustainable society model allows for great diversity in the social processes and patterns of social ordering that prevail within any particular society. However, most writers who have examined the possibility of creating this kind of society have concluded that the preceding requirements for maintaining balance between a society and its various environments would necessitate a number of major social changes within most contemporary societies. Although observers differ considerably on the exact nature of those changes, the most frequently mentioned ones are sketched in the following paragraphs.

Constrained Economic Growth. This is by far the most hotly debated change that might be necessary to create a sustainable society. The idea of a no-growth economy is emphasized by many writers, although on closer inspection their argument is usually found to focus primarily on industrial growth within heavy manufacturing industries. These include the production of steel and other metals, automobiles, industrial machinery, chemicals, and similar products. It is primarily those industries that seriously deplete natural resources, pollute the environment, and create economic and political imbalances with other societies. *Most manufacturing industries would continue to operate in a sustainable society, but their output would be limited to levels needed to meet genuine human needs.* They would not be allowed to expand indefinitely in quest of unlimited profits. Many other kinds of economic activities, meanwhile, might be encouraged to develop as long as they did not upset ecological or economic balances and they satisfied real individual or societal needs. These economic activities would probably include many kinds of retail and service businesses, public services such as education and health care, cultural and recreational activities, agriculture, and intellectual and artistic pursuits of all kinds. In short, the economy as a whole could continue to grow, but in a steady-state balance with the natural and social environments.

Frugal Personal Consumption. If a society is to reduce its industrial production, *citizens* *must be willing to limit their consumption of material goods.* Consequently, the ideas of "voluntary simplicity" in lifestyles and a "conserver society" are frequently discussed as necessary components of a sustainable society. This argument does not suggest that we must go back to preindustrial lifestyles—washing clothes by hand or driving a horse and buggy—but it does insist that we reject the accumulation and throw-away mentalities of contemporary consumership. Acquiring more and more material goods does not necessarily bring us personal happiness or self-fulfillment, nor do we need to own the latest model sports car to gain social recognition or status. Instead, we should select material goods that are built for durability rather than trendiness, and we should take pride in "keeping the old car going" or in the fact that our ten-year-old wool suit still looks like new. Furthermore, to the extent that individuals and families are able to be frugal in their purchases of material goods, they will have more money available for other purposes, such as education, health care, or recreation.

Power Decentralization. Many of the political and organizational problems that beset modern societies are directly or indirectly caused by excessive concentrations of power within governments and corporations. Power centralization is not necessary to ensure that political and economic systems function effectively, we are discovering, and decentralization of decision-making and operational activities can often enhance organizational flexibility. From the perspective of the sustainable society model, *social institutions and organizations with relatively decentralized power structures are often more capable of operating in relative balance with their environments.* Too often, highly centralized social systems tend to ignore environmental limits, because powerful elites assume that the system can be made to do whatever they wish. As power is decentralized to the component units within a system that are in direct contact with various environments, those units—and hence the entire system—

become more responsible to environmental demands and constraints. For this reason, proponents of the sustainable society model frequently argue that the political and economic systems of modern societies must be decentralized to give more autonomy and decision-making authority to local governments, voluntary citizen associations, work teams, community groups, local chapters of national organizations, and other smaller organizational units.

Social Equality. Severe inequalities of all kinds—socioeconomic, racial, ethnic, and gender—can seriously threaten the stability of a society by creating tensions and conflicts that are not easily resolved. If a society is to approximate the sustainable model, therefore, many writers insist that *all forms of social inequality must be minimized as far as possible.* In particular, such a society must end all racial and ethnic discrimination, gender role inequalities, socioeconomic class exploitation, and other practices that subjugate disadvantaged people to more privileged persons. More positively, such a society would seek to maximize all opportunities for each person to realize his or her fullest individual potential. This might involve providing all persons with such rights as unlimited free education, employment opportunities, a guaranteed minimum income, unrestricted free medical care, legal services when needed, all forms of civil liberties, and opportunities for effective participation in political processes.

Human Scale. This concept, while rather nebulous, incorporates many of the arguments already presented in regard to societal environments and changes necessary to approximate the sustainable society model. The essence of this thesis is that many features of modern societies have become too large and complex for most individuals to comprehend or control. It therefore argues that societies and their component parts should be reorganized on the principle that people matter. In other words, social organization should serve individuals, not vice versa. This principle can be applied to politics, economics, communities, bu-

---

CHARACTERISTICS OF SUSTAINABLE SOCIETIES

1. Environmental resource conservation.
2. Small, stable population size.
3. Appropriate technology.
4. International balance and reciprocity.
5. Constrained economic growth.
6. Frugal personal consumption.
7. Power decentralization.
8. Social and economic equality.
9. Human scale organization.

---

reaucracies, technologies, education, communications, power structures, patterns of inequality, international relations, and all other realms of social life. *All social activities would be organized on a scale that was small and manageable enough so that their participants could understand and control those activities.* Again, this is not an argument for return to primitivism or preindustrial society. Rather, it is an insistence that societies seeking to become sustainable must be organized on a scale that is meaningful to people and must function in a manner that enables individuals to control their personal destinies, satisfy their human needs, and enjoy meaningful lives.

SOCIAL ACTIVISM

In view of the impending transformation of contemporary societies, many sociologists believe that sociology has a moral imperative to use its knowledge to promote social change that will improve future societies.

Applying Sociology

The idea of applying sociology to improve human life is not new. It has pervaded the field—especially in the United States—since its inception. The first book published in this country with the word "sociology" in its title was Lester Ward's *Dynamic Sociology: or Applied Social Science,* which appeared in 1883. Later in his career, in 1906, Ward published another book titled, *Applied Sociology: A Treatise on the Conscious Improvement of Society by Society.* In both these works, he laid out elaborate designs for applying sociology to change society. His contemporaries were apparently quite impressed with these ideas, since they elected him the first president of the American Sociological Association.

A deep concern with the application of sociology was widespread in the field from that time through the 1930s. During the 1940s and the 1950s, however, many sociologists became primarily concerned with making the field more of a science and increasing its respectability in the academic world. Consequently, they largely turned their backs on applied work, focusing instead on basic theorizing and research. Then, during the 1960s and 1970s, a new generation of young sociologists began reasserting the critical importance of applying sociology to the world through action. This renewed concern was strongly influenced by a number of events that were occurring in the United States at that time: the War on Poverty, the civil rights movement, the efforts to create a Great Society, and the Vietnam War. Those events were too critical to be ignored by sociologists, many of whom began asking how sociological knowledge could be used to affect them and shape their outcomes.

This interest in applying sociology became even stronger during the 1980s. Many colleges and universities established graduate programs in applied sociology, several organizations were established to promote the practice of sociology, new journals devoted to applied topics were initiated, and increasing numbers of sociologists began working in nonacademic settings. By the end of this century, the number of sociologists employed in government agencies, community organizations, consulting firms, business corporations, the mass media, and many other applied areas could exceed the number in academia.

Although we often speak of applied sociology as a specialty within the field, more accurately it is an activity that can be carried out by all sociologists, regardless of their focus of specialization. Hence a more appropriate term is "applying sociology." An alternative term that is also becoming widely used by sociologists working outside academia is "sociological practice." Both of these terms refer to *the process of utilizing sociological knowledge and techniques to affect existing social conditions, issues, and problems, with the objective of changing and improving them.*

Sociologists who apply or practice sociology engage in many different kinds of work. They study social problems, explore social change processes, analyze proposed and existing public policies, carry out community needs assessments, determine the social impacts of projects, formulate social plans, develop social programs, act as change agents to implement those programs, administer ongoing programs, and evaluate their outcomes. When sociologists conduct studies of social problems and issues, they are usually called applied social researchers. When they collect and report census or other data sets, they may be classified as data analysts. When they assist families or other groups that are having difficulties, they are often called clinical sociologists. When they work with business firms, government agencies, or other organizations to improve their functioning, they are usually described as doing organizational development. When they work with communities that are experiencing conflicts or other problems, they are commonly described as doing community organization. And when they advise policy makers at the state, national, or international level, they may be termed policy analysts. Regardless of the label given to such work or the setting in which it occurs, applied or practicing sociologists are attempting to change and improve social conditions.

This kind of sociology, as Lester Ward pointed out over a hundred years ago, is always heavily value-involved. It cannot be otherwise, since it presumes that we have an image of what constitutes improvement in social conditions. *Efforts to promote social change to improve society must be directed toward some desired goal, and the selection of that goal is a value decision.* The process of applying or practicing sociology can be done in a rational and objective manner if it follows the rules of the scientific method, but it can never be value-neutral. It is therefore always incumbent on sociologists doing this kind of work to be open and explicit about their value commitments. If they believe that poverty or crime or racism or sexism or war are pragmatically unwise or morally unjust, they must make it clear that their work is intended to change these conditions in specified ways. They can then use the scientific method in their research and action to objectively understand and effectively promote the social goals to which they are committed.

Social Choices

Since the application or practice of sociology is always oriented toward valued goals, the ability to choose those goals in an informed manner is a crucial necessity. This assumes that goal selection is possible within social life. Although we are all born into a social world we did not create and that is largely shaped by pervasive historical trends and social forces that are beyond our control, we are never helpless pawns of society. Because existing patterns of social organization are continually being re-created and changed through social action, they are never totally immutable. We can therefore make meaningful choices about the kind of family, community, work setting, political and economic systems, society, and world in which we live. To do this, however, we must discard the traditional notion that whatever conditions presently exist are necessarily best or right. And we must then create a vision of a different and better set of social conditions. In other words, we must develop an image of the future as we believe it should be.

Organized social life thus presents us with an inescapable paradox. *Although we are always the products of social organization, we are also the creators of it.* As expressed by sociologist Edward Lehman (1977:190), "Inherent in all distinctly sociological perspectives is the assumption that however much human actors are the creatures of society, they can also be its creators. Indeed, once we acknowledge that the ultimate 'stuff' of social life is human interaction . . . then we can see that although we did not make today's world, the consequences of our behaviors, and the behaviors of groups we belong to, function either to sustain, to modify, to weaken, or to overthrow the existing order. Paradoxically, although we did not make the world we live in, we are the world we live in, and hence the creators of tomorrow's world."

If we are to make and carry out meaningful choices concerning our social lives and our societies, there is an additional requirement. *We must be able to exercise some amount of social power within those spheres of social life that concern us.* Choices made in a power vacuum are merely daydreams. Those dreams become viable goals for purposeful social action only to the extent that we can influence individuals and organizations. The ability to exert power in social life provides the route to achieving desired future conditions. If people are powerless, they cannot participate effectively in society or affect it, and hence can only make dreams, rather than meaningful social choices. One imperative goal in all efforts to apply sociology is therefore to empower people so that they can effectively influence the policies and practices that shape their social lives.

Public Activation

The purpose of empowering citizens—and societal leaders—is to enable them to take actions that will guide and improve social life.

Citizen activation occurs as individuals in all walks of life become involved in making public decisions that affect their lives. Representative democratic theory allows citizens to participate in political decision making only sporadically through elections, choosing public officials but not directly deciding public issues. With the advent of public polling in the 1930s, citizens acquired a means of expressing their opinions on current issues, but these preferences are never binding on government officials. The later introduction

of public initiatives and referenda gave citizens a direct role in policy formation, but only on a very limited basis. In recent years, however, the ideal of more direct and extensive involvement of citizens in all forms of collective decision making has gained increasing support in many Western societies.

This conception of *participatory democracy* contains two principal themes (Pateman, 1970). First, the fundamental meaning of democracy is that citizens are entitled to participate in making all collective decisions that affect them. Second, this participation must occur within all realms of social life, including the family, the community, the work place, and the economy, as well as the polity. In short, traditional power structures and decision-making procedures must be considerably broadened throughout society. In the home, decisions must be made jointly by both partners, with input from children. In the community, various kinds of public participation programs must provide many different ways in which citizens can become involved in community decision making. At work, subordinates should be directly involved with managers in formulating policies and operating procedures. Within the economic system, consumers should be able to communicate their needs and preferences to producers, to counter the one-way flow of advertising. In the political system, citizens must become involved in interest associations that represent their particular concerns, and those organizations must be able to exert influence on government decisions.

Leadership activation occurs as public leaders in all spheres of society become aware of, and responsive to, the vital needs and interests of all citizens. Traditionally, public leaders have tended to be concerned about the operational requirements of the political economy, the interests of the dominant class or classes, and their own personal pursuits. They have often given only slight attention to the interests of less advantaged classes, ethnic minorities, women, and other less powerful segments of society. In addition, they have tended to formulate policies and make public decisions that are oriented largely to the present or the near future, and to avoid taking a longer-time perspective on future trends and societal conditions.

Social theorist and activist Amitai Etzioni (1968) has argued that public leadership that provides effective "societal guidance" is simultaneously dynamic and responsible. It is dynamic in that leaders are able to exercise the social power necessary to direct collective activities toward common goals. They are able to effectively manage public resources, communications, policy formation, program development, and administrative procedures. It is responsible in that leaders are always concerned about, and responsive to, the needs and interests of all parts of society. They promote citizen involvement in collective decision-making to the fullest possible extent and continually seek to build public consensus around common values and goals.

When both citizens and leaders become activated in these ways, the outcome is what Etzioni calls an *active society*. This kind of society, he argues, actively and purposefully controls its own functioning and shapes its own future. It is the antithesis of a traditional passive society, which merely drifts along without any attempt to choose valued social goals, formulate rational social plans, or involve citizens and leaders in collective action to improve their society. An active society—like a mature person—is self-directing, self-controlling, and self-actualizing. *An active society acts rationally and purposefully to attain the future goals that its members believe are necessary and desirable.*

SOCIAL PLANNING

Social choices provide meaningful goals for our collective life, and public activation ensures that those choices will be acted upon by citizens and leaders. Without specific objectives and plans for achieving them, however, people are not likely to attain their desired goals. Another contribution that sociology can make to the process of intentional social change, therefore, is to assist people in formulating viable *social plans* that will enable them to take collective action to achieve their collective goals in social life.

The Past

Throughout most of human history, people have rarely engaged in systematic social planning. As long as traditional beliefs and values were seen as sacred commandments to be followed without question, planning was unthinkable. A strong impetus was given to social planning by the rationalists of the enlightenment movement in Europe during the seventeenth and eighteenth centuries. Reacting against the medieval view of the existing social order as preordained and morally prescribed, they argued that social organization is created by humans and hence can and should be altered as people see fit. Their view was nevertheless quite naïve and simplistic, since they believed that, with a minimum of rationality and consensus, any desired change could easily be accomplished.

The romantic movement of the nineteenth century directly challenged this rationalistic conception of society. Numerous philosophers, social theorists, and other writers insisted that the development of social organization is largely beyond human control. Although societies may not be the direct result of divine providence, they are the outcomes of imponderable natural and historical forces that are essentially unalterable. Consequently, rational social planning is futile. The field of sociology was established within this intellectual milieu, with the result that many early sociologists took a very dim view of planning. That view was not shared by all social theorists, however, as seen in the writings of Karl Marx, Herbert Spencer, and Lester Ward.

The Present

Contemporary social science is gradually returning to the view of those early writers. *Purposeful social planning is again being seen as possible and beneficial, although we have come to realize that planning for intentional social change can be enormously complicated.* Historical trends and the weight of established social ordering and cultural ideas severely limit the extent to which we can alter societal functioning or development. We cannot, for example, undo the effects of two centuries of industrialization and urbanization. Nor can we, by political fiat, change basic cultural norms and values, as Prohibition dramatically demonstrated. Within those broad limits, however, we can do much to influence and change—at least slowly and moderately—the social world in which we live.

Present-day criticisms of social planning tend to stress not its futility, but rather the belief that it restricts individual freedom of action. Planning, it is argued, denies the individual control over his or her own life and forces the individual to conform to the dictates of others. There is a kernel of truth in this argument. Consider a few typical examples of social planning. City authorities set aside a plot of land for a park and deny businesses the right to construct a shopping center on it. The federal government institutes an old-age pension program and demands that all workers contribute to it. A law is passed requiring stores to serve all customers regardless of their race. In all these cases, some individuals are denied certain "freedoms" that their ancestors once exercised. But to focus entirely on the negative side of planning misses its central purpose. *Although planning restricts some individual actions, it can greatly expand the opportunities and benefits available to many people.* By surrendering some limited privileges, we can all gain much greater collective social benefits.

This outcome is never inevitable, however. Whether or not the public interest is served by social planning depends on how it is carried out. Planning is just as feasible in totalitarian as in democratic societies, and it can be conducted either autocratically or democratically. Social planning is only a means of rationally and effectively directing the process of social organization toward the attainment of collective goals. It says nothing about the nature or desirability of these goals. We could just as well formulate plans to destroy all humanity as to promote human betterment. *If planning is to be done democratically and directed toward serving human needs, it must combine rational social science knowledge with participatory involvement in decision making.* Only through this kind of participatory planning can we ensure that our collective activities will promote the attainment of social goals that benefit all people.

The Future

The next hundred years—essentially the twenty-first century—may well be one of the most critical turning points in human history. Contemporary industrial societies appear to be entering a process of fundamental transformation that may eventually result in the development of very different new forms of social organization. At this point in time, we cannot foresee the final outcomes of that transformation process. We can, however, influence the course of this transformation by envisioning the kind of society we believe will best serve humanity and then formulating plans and taking actions to change society in those ways. This is the ultimate purpose in studying and applying sociology. *Only as we understand society can we shape its future.*

SUMMARY

From an ecological perspective, there have been two fundamental societal revolutions in human history: the agricultural revolution and the industrial revolution. Many observers believe that modern societies are presently entering a third ecological turning point that is called the information revolution. From an organizational perspective, there have been at least four fundamental societal revolutions: the differentiation revolution, the urban revolution, the state revolution, and the bureaucratic revolution. In addition, an interdependence revolution is presently becoming quite pervasive in the contemporary world. From both the ecological/economic and social organizational perspectives, it is becoming increasingly evident that modern societies are presently entering into another fundamental process of transformation.

Societies and all other forms of social organization have been constantly changing throughout human history, and that process continues today. Contemporary societies are experiencing numerous ecological and organizational crises that are creating massive pressures and tensions that will almost certainly result in fundamental social changes that will transform societies. This process of change will undoubtedly be strongly resisted because of ignorance, limited perspectives, ideological differences, technological orientations, and vested interests. As a result, the coming societal transformation will involve a great deal of conflict throughout all realms of social life.

As a model for creating postindustrial societies, social scientists have recently been developing the concept of sustainable societies. The principal feature of a sustainable society would be its ability to remain in balance on a permanent basis with its natural and social environments.

If societies are to become permanently sustainable, they must develop many new kinds of relationships with their natural and social environments. They must remain within the carrying capacity of the earth's ecosystem, have a relatively stable and limited population, use material and social technologies appropriately and wisely, and maintain relatively balanced economic, political, military, and cultural relationships with all other societies.

To remain in balance with their natural and social environments, existing societies will likely have to undergo a number of major social changes. They will probably have to constrain industrial manufacturing (but not other kinds of economic activities), reduce personal consumption of material goods, decentralize their political and economic power structures, minimize all forms of social inequality, and reorganize many aspects of social life on a more human scale.

Many sociologists argue that sociology has a moral obligation to use its knowledge to promote intentional social change that will improve society, which requires an action perspective. The idea of applying sociology has pervaded the discipline since its inception, and in recent years it has become a pervasive thrust within the field as increasing numbers of sociologists have begun working outside academia.

Sociologists who apply or practice their profession are known as applied researchers, data analysts, clinical sociologists, organization developers, community organizers, or policy analysts. Regardless of the label or setting, they are attempting to change and improve social conditions. This kind of sociology is highly value-involved, since it must be directed toward some desired goal, which necessitates value decisions. Sociologists must therefore be open and explicit about their value positions, but this need not prevent them from doing objective and scientifically respectable work.

Since the application or practice of sociology is always oriented toward valued goals, the ability to choose those goals in an informed manner is crucial. Such choices are possible because existing patterns of social organization are continually being recreated and changed, but making meaningful social choices requires a vision of desired future conditions. While we are always the products of social organization, we are also the creators of it. However, people are able to create new forms of social ordering only if they are able to exercise some amount of social power within their society.

If social choice-making is to be effective, it must be accompanied by efforts to activate citizens and leaders. Citizen activation occurs as individuals in all walks of life become involved in making public decisions that affect their lives. The idea of participatory democracy argues that citizens are entitled to take part in making all collective decisions that affect them, and this participation must occur throughout all spheres of social life. Leadership activation occurs as public leaders become aware of and responsive to the vital needs and interests of all citizens. Public leadership that provides effective societal guidance must be dynamic, in terms of facilitating desired social goals, and responsible, in terms of promoting citizen involvement and building cultural consensus. This kind of active society is able to act rationally and purposefully to attain the collective goals that its members believe are desirable and necessary.

Sociology can assist people in formulating viable social plans that will enable them to take collective action to attain their common goals. Purposeful social planning is possible and can be beneficial, although it is always extremely complicated. We cannot undo the past, but we can formulate plans that provide guidelines for shaping the future. Planning often restricts some actions of some individuals, but it can also greatly expand the opportunities and benefits available to many or all people. However, if planning is to serve the public interest, it must be done democratically through broad citizen participation.

The basic point of this final chapter is that all forms of social organization are created and sustained by people's collective actions and are therefore always open to change. As we come to realize that current social conditions are rife with fundamental crises and are far from ideal, we can act together to change our societies to improve the quality of social life for all people. If we are to be successful in intentionally changing and improving organized social life, however, we must create a vision of the kind of future society we wish to establish. Perhaps the most important reason for studying sociology is to acquire an understanding of societal dynamics and to generate new ideas for improving society. With this knowledge and vision, we can become more effective citizens of our societies and the world and thus take an active part in shaping the future of human civilization.

Theoretical Postlude

ECOLOGICAL-ECONOMIC-EVOLUTIONARY THEORY

The theoretical perspective used throughout this book and sketched here is not a complete theory of social organization or societal development. For simplicity, it largely ignores many crucial aspects of social life, such as the ways in which individuals relate to one another through exchange and symbolic interaction. It also gives insufficient attention to the manner in which cultural beliefs, values, and norms influence social life. These interactional and cultural components of societies must eventually be incorporated into any comprehensive theory of social organization.

In its current initial phase of development, this perspective focuses primarily on the creation and functioning of patterns of social ordering. It draws primarily on three sets of theoretical ideas that are quite pervasive within sociology at the present time but which have never been systematically integrated into a single framework. These are *social ecology, political economy,* and *societal evo-*

lution. A few writers—such as Fred Cottrell (1955), Gerhard Lenski (1966), and Amos Hawley (1984)—have suggested that all these theoretical ideas can and should be integrated, but that task has not yet been achieved.

I do not attempt here to construct a complete or finished version of such an integrated perspective. My present objective is merely to illustrate the general nature of this perspective and some of its major themes. I do this by proposing thirty-three theoretical principles that I suggest must be incorporated within this perspective. Each of these principles could be considerably elaborated, and the list is undoubtedly far from complete. Nevertheless, these principles are basic to the theoretical integration of social ecology, political economy, and societal evolution into a viable sociological perspective on human societies.

This perspective presently has no commonly accepted name. I therefore propose to expand a concept that was initially used by Lenski (1966) into the term *Ecological-Economic-Evolutionary Theory,* or "Triple E Theory," for short.

(1) All human activities are inexorably dependent on the natural environment for life-sustaining conditions and vital resources, so that social ordering is always constrained and influenced by the environment.

(2) Human beings create and use technology (physical and social) to facilitate their efforts to survive in the natural and social environments, so that technology plays a major role in shaping social ordering.

(3) Human populations constantly struggle to survive, satisfy their sustenance needs and improve their level of living, and the characteristics of a population (its size, composition, and distribution) always influence that struggle.

(4) The three basic ecological factors of available environmental resources, level of technological development, and population characteristics continually interact to determine the sociophysical energy flows occurring within a society.

(5) These sociophysical energy flows—which refer to the amount, nature, form, and distribution of all forms of energy that are used to perform necessary and desired work, as well as the exercise of social power derived from energy flows—are affected by numerous physical, chemical, biological, psychological, social, and cultural factors occurring in a society.

(6) Since energy is the fundamental requirement for performing all work, sociophysical energy flows constitute the basic foundation of social ordering, influencing and constraining all aspects of organized social life.

(7) In particular, the flow of sociophysical energy within a society is a crucial—but far from the only—factor affecting the economic production processes through which the members of that society provide for all their material needs and wants.

(8) The nature and effectiveness of the economic production processes within a society directly affect the amount of surplus wealth available to its members that they can use for nonsustenance activities of all kinds.

(9) Other crucial factors that influence economic production and the creation of surplus wealth include political policies and practices, patterns of social and economic inequality, and beliefs and values concerning work and wealth.

(10) In general, the greater the surplus wealth available in a society, the larger its population will become, but the population can grow much faster than the available wealth, which diminishes the amount of wealth per capita.

(11) In general, the greater the surplus wealth available in a society, the larger the amount of social power that can and will be exercised by the members of that society through economic, political, religious, and other institutions.

(12) To maximize the usability of the wealth and power existing in a society, a tiny proportion of the population generally attempts to accumulate as many economic and power resources as possible, thus becoming a dominant elite class.

(13) To acquire extensive amounts of wealth and power, elites utilize whatever techniques are possible and effective, including expropriation, manipulation, coercion, control of economic production, performance of vital functions, socialization, communication, ideology propagation, and religion.

(14) The elite members of a society also create and operate a government that functions to preserve and promote the existing economy that is creating the wealth that underlies their power, so that the economic and political systems of societies tend to become highly interwoven into partially (but rarely fully) unified political economies.

(15) The creation of a relatively unified political economy within a society further concentrates wealth and power, so that whatever set of people controls that political economy is also able to exercise dominant power throughout most (if not all) other sectors of the society.

(16) Elites also use the political system for other purposes, such as protecting the society against external threats, conquering other societies, maintaining internal order within the society, performing necessary functions for the society to ensure its stability and con-

tinued viability, and creating legitimacy for their power and the political system.

(17) The amount of surplus wealth in a society, in conjunction with the structure and functioning of its political system, largely determine its stratification system through which power, privileges, and prestige are distributed.

(18) In general, the larger the surplus wealth and the more effective the government in a society, the greater the socioeconomic inequality among its members, in terms of the per capita distribution of all valued benefits of social life.

(19) In general, the larger the surplus wealth and the more effective the government in a society, the greater its structural complexity, in terms of its functional specialization and the number and kinds of its component parts.

(20) In combination, the greater the socioeconomic inequality and structural complexity within a society, the more likely its stratification system is to contain a number of intermediate class and status levels, although all of these classes and statuses are always dominated by the ruling economic/political elites.

(21) In societies with relatively high levels of economic and political development, intermediate social classes and status groups may (but not inevitably) acquire moderate amounts of power, privilege, and prestige and perform numerous vital functions within the society.

(22) Most generally, this distribution process occurs when nonelites create new sources of wealth and power that are not controlled by the existing elites and thus become able to challenge (either directly or indirectly) the dominance of those elites.

(23) Dominant elites sometimes intentionally promote a limited amount of redistribution of economic wealth and political power to other portions of the population as a means of expanding economic markets (and thus increasing their own wealth) or gaining political legitimacy (and thus increasing their authority).

(24) Regardless of any such distributive trends within a society, wealth and power tend to remain highly concentrated within the dominant elite class and to be quite unequally distributed throughout the rest of the popu-

lation, so that even highly developed societies contain extensive social stratification.

(25) As a consequence of these patterns of economic, political, and social inequality, competition and conflict occur continually in many different forms throughout all sectors of a society.

(26) Political rulers may be (but are not always) relatively effective in preventing, restraining, or controlling social conflict—especially when it threatens their power or positions—so that overt expressions of conflict may be fairly limited or infrequent, but underlying tensions nevertheless continue to exist throughout the society.

(27) Paradoxically, rulers who permit and encourage social conflict to occur in manageable forms are often able to create more stable societies and thus protect the political economy more effectively than can rulers who attempt to suppress all conflict.

(28) Within the limits of the carrying capacity of society's or the world's ecosystem, all the preceding factors tend to (but do not inevitably) move societies toward higher levels of sociocultural development in the long run, although a society may experience numerous short-term periods of stagnation or decline.

(29) If the process of development leads a society (or the world system of societies) to exceed the carrying capacity of its ecosystem, it begins to operate in a condition of ecological overshoot in which it is consuming natural resources and despoiling the natural environment at a faster rate than the ecosystem can endure on a permanent basis.

(30) Societies may continue to exist or even thrive in a condition of ecological overshoot for a considerable period of time by utilizing such coping techniques as takeover, toolmaking, expropriation, conquest, or drawdown, all of which involve taking resources from others in one way or another.

(31) Since all of those coping techniques are only temporary, a society (or the world system) that is operating in a condition of ecological overshoot will sooner or later experience a severe ecological crash if it fails to bring its political economy into balance with the ecosystem.

(32) A severe ecological crash would very likely

result in the death of a large proportion of the population, elimination of most existing forms of social organization, and—if the crash is accompanied by nuclear war— partial or total destruction of the entire ecosystem.

(33) Since human beings are capable of at least limited rational and intentional actions to change their societies, it is conceivable that in the future we will be able to create patterns of social organization that are permanently sustainable within the earth's ecosystem and the increasingly interdependent world system of societies.

GLOSSARY OF KEY CONCEPTS

(Note: All concepts are listed according to their principal word. For example, "social action" is listed as "action, social".)

Accountability, organizational: Assignment of responsibility for organizational activities and decisions to specific positions or offices.

Acculturation: The process in which individuals, usually immigrants or racial or ethnic minorities, become fully familiar with the dominant culture of their society.

Achieved status: A social status acquired on the basis of one's activities or accomplishments.

Action, social: When one social actor acts toward another actor in a meaningful way.

Activation, social: The process of encouraging individuals to become involved in making public decisions that affect their lives, and of ensuring that public leaders become aware of, and responsive to, the vital needs and interests of all citizens.

Active society: A society that acts rationally and purposefully to attain the future goals that its members believe are necessary and/or desirable.

Actor, social: An individual or organization that participates in social interaction.

Adjustment, social: A moderate and unintended social change.

Age composition of a population: The distribution of a population across all ages.

Age, median of a population: The age at which half of a population is younger and half is older.

Aggregate: A temporary type of organization that develops spontaneously as an expression of shared feelings or concerns among a number of people.

Agrarian society: A type of society whose economy is based primarily or entirely on settled agriculture.

Agricultural revolution: The transformation of societies from hunting and gathering to agricultural economies.

Agriculture, settled: Large-scale farming on a permanent basis, using complex tools.

Ancestoralism: The religious belief that one's ancestors are part of an all-powerful sacred presence that exists throughout nature and

585

influences current social conditions and activities.

Animism: The religious belief that numerous spirits inhabit all objects in the world and directly affect human life and natural phenomena.

Apathy, citizen: A political crisis that occurs when large numbers of citizens do not participate in political affairs, even when such opportunities are available.

Applied sociology/applying sociology: The process of utilizing sociological knowledge and techniques to affect existing social conditions, issues, and problems, with the objective of changing and improving them.

Artisan: A skilled worker who makes objects for sale using handicraft techniques.

Artisan class: A class in agrarian societies composed of all kinds of handicraft artisans.

Ascribed status: Status acquired on the basis of one's family origin, ethnicity, sex, age, or race.

Assimilation: The process in which individuals, such as immigrants or racial or ethnic minorities, become fully incorporated into the social life of their society or other organization.

Association: A type of organization that is purposefully created and operated to attain specific goals.

Attraction: Social power based on the personal appeal that an actor has for others.

Authority: Social power based on the legitimate right of an actor to issue commands that others are expected to obey.

Authority, charismatic: Authority whose legitimacy rests on people's beliefs that a person possesses charisma.

Authority, rational-legal: Authority whose legitimacy rests on the fact that a person possesses some kind of expertise in performing a role, plus the fact that he or she occupies an organizational office with which that role is associated.

Authority, traditional: Authority whose legitimacy rests on established, traditional beliefs, values, norms, and customs.

Belief, cultural: A statement or idea that is assumed to express fundamental truths about reality or human social life and that is accepted as true without question.

Belief system: A set of interrelated beliefs that covers a broad area of human activities or conditions.

Birth rate, crude: The number of live births in a year per 1,000 population.

Birth rate, refined: The number of live births in a year per 1,000 women of child-bearing age, between 15 and 45.

Boundaries, organizational: The features of an organization that distinguish it from other organizations in its social environment.

Bureaucracy: An organization whose structure and operations are highly bureaucratized.

Bureaucratic crisis: A condition in which bureaucratized organizations find it difficult or impossible to operate efficiently and effectively to attain their goals.

Bureaucratic model: An ideal type model of a fully bureaucratized organization, emphasizing offices, competence, careers, impersonality, standardization, and hierarchy.

Bureaucratic revolution: The transformation of societies from containing many small, traditionally operated organizations to containing fewer large, bureaucratized organizations.

Bureaucratization: The process of rationalizing and controlling the operations of an organization to increase the efficiency and effectiveness of its goal attainment activities.

Capitalism: An economy in which businesses are privately owned and operate within competitive markets.

Capitalism, free market: A capitalist economy in which the dominant concern is profit making and most or all economic transactions occur within unregulated or free markets.

Capitalism, regulated: A capitalist economy in which most economic activities are regulated, but not totally controlled, by the government to ensure that the economy serves the public interest.

Carrying capacity: The maximum population size of a society or the entire world, given a particular level of living, that the natural environment can sustain on a permanent basis.

Change, cultural: Identifiable significant alterations in cultural ideas over time.

Change, fundamental: Social change that is quite broad in scope and depth, so that it alters most or all parts of a society or other organization.

Change, moderate: Social change that is relatively limited in scope or depth, so that it alters only some parts of a society or other organization.

Change, social: Identifiable significant alterations in patterns of social ordering over time.

Charisma: A perception of a person held by others that he or she has a unique quality or special powers not held by most other people.

Choices, social: Decisions about goals for social action and life that are based on cultural values.

City: As defined by the United Nations, a community with 100,000 or more population.

Civil War: A war between two parts of a society.

Clan: An extended family or larger kinship network that was especially prevalent in horticultural societies, but which continues to exist today in many developing societies.

Class: A type of loosely structured but identifiable organization composed of people with relatively similar amounts of power, privileges, and prestige. (*See also* Socioeconomic class.)

Class bifurcation: A widening gap between an advantaged class and one or more disadvantaged classes.

Class consciousness: Awareness among the members of a class of their common social conditions and interests.

Coercion: (*See* Power, coercive.)

Cohabitation: An unmarried couple living together.

Cohesion, functional: Social cohesion based on task specialization and mutual interdependence among the members and parts of an organization.

Cohesion, normative: Social cohesion based on shared cultural values and norms that are imbedded within the members and parts of an organization.

Cohesion, social: The process through which the members and parts of an organization become bound together into a unified entity.

Cohort: A set of people who experience an important social event, such as birth, socialization, marriage, etc., during the same period of time.

Colonial war: A war in which a society attempts to overthrow a political regime imposed on it by an external colonial power.

Community: A type of organization composed of people who reside in a common geographical area and share a sense of communal belonging, and which is the setting for most of their daily activities.

Complexity, organizational: The existence of numerous distinct and specialized roles and subunits within an organization, arranged both vertically and horizontally, that are highly interdependent.

Concentric zone model of urban spatial patterns: A model of urban land use patterns that consists of several concentric circles extending outward from the city center, each of which tends to contain similar kinds of land uses.

Conflict, ecological: Conflict between or within species for available resources within an ecosystem.

Conflict, economic: Conflict between or within organizations over control of economic production and/or the distribution of economic benefits.

Conflict management: The process of handling and resolving conflicts in ways that benefit an organization or all social life.

Conflict, social: The process in which two or more actors oppose one another in social interaction, exerting power in an effort to attain a common limited goal or incompatible goals.

Control: The exercise of social power whose outcomes are relatively certain or extensive in scope.

Control, external: Affecting a person's actions by imposing positive or negative sanctions.

Control, internal: Shaping one's actions on the basis of expected responses to them by others.

Control, organizational: The utilization of social power by organizational administrators to ensure that the organization operates as intended.

Control, social: The process through which a society or other organization regulates itself to attain its goals and ensures that its members adher to established norms.

Consolidated Metropolitan Area (CMA): As defined by the U.S. Census Bureau, two or more adjoining Primary Metropolitan Statistical Areas with a combined population of at least one million people that form a metropolitan complex, or metropolis.

Corporation: An organization that is chartered by a government, owned by its stockholders, and legally considered to exist independently of any of its members or owners.

Counterculture: A subculture that rejects one or more basic beliefs, values, and/or norms of the dominant societal culture.

Crime: Any intentionally committed action that violates the legal code of the political jurisdiction in which it occurs, either through commission or omission.

Crimes against morality: Crimes that violate established cultural values, such as gambling, prostitution, drug use, and incest.

Crimes against persons: Crimes that harm one or more persons, such as homocide, assault, rape, and robbery.

Crimes against property: Crimes that are directed against physical property, such as larceny-theft, motor vehicle theft, burglary, and arson.

Criminal: A person or organization that has intentionally violated a criminal statute.

Criminal, amateur: A person who has only once or occasionally engaged in illegal activities and for whom crime is not a way of life.

Criminal, corporate: A corporation that has committed an illegal activity in the course of its normal operations.

Criminal, organization: A business that has regularly engaged in illegal activities as its principal activities.

Criminal, professional: A person who has committed numerous illegal activities as a principal way of making a living, and for whom crime is an established way of life.

Criminal, white-collar: A person, usually a respected member of an organization, who has committed an illegal action in the course of work or other activities within that organization.

Cult: A very loosely organized and nonestablished small set of believers in some kind of esoteric religious idea.

Cultural relativity: The assertion that all values and norms are meaningful and relevant only within their own culture.

Cultural universals: Basic themes contained within all societal cultures, which are expressed in countless different ways in specific societies.

Culture: A set of ideas about human social life that is shared by the members of a society or other social organization.

Culture, organizational: The cultural ideas that are associated with a particular organization.

Culture, societal: The dominant, encompassing culture of an entire society.

Death rate, crude: The number of deaths in a year per 1,000 population.

Decision making, organizational: The process through which decisions are made by an organization that guide its functioning.

Decision making, polyarchic: A situation in which organizational decisions are made by many or all of its component parts.

Decision making, unitary: A situation in which all organizational decisions are made by a small set of leaders or elites located at the apex of the organization.

Definition of the situation: The interpretations and meanings that social actors give to a particular social situation and that are true for them.

Degraded class: A class in agrarian societies that is composed of nonagricultural manual laborers and others who perform undesirable work.

Democracy: A polity in which the citizens (however citizens are defined) choose the major political leaders in open and contested elections.

Democracy, classical: The theory that all citizens can and should participate in public decision making and exercise relatively equal amounts of political influence.

Democracy, elitist: The theory that democracy requires only competition for public office and political power among small sets of alternative elites.

Democracy, party: The theory that political parties enact a crucial linking role between citizens and the government in political elections and other activities.

Democracy, participatory: The theory that political activities should be expanded beyond voting to maximize opportunities for citizen involvement in all forms of political and other decision making.

Democracy, pluralist: The theory that democracy depends on a network of private interest organizations throughout the society that mediate between citizens and the government.

Democracy, representative: The theory that all citizens should periodically elect political leaders who will represent their interests and concerns in the legislature.

Democratic principle: The assertion that all the citizens of a nation have the right to influence political decisions that affect them.

Demographic momentum: The tendency for a population whose birth rate is below the replacement level to continue growing for a period of time, as a result of having a relatively large cohort of women in the child-bearing ages.

Demographic transition model: A model that depicts the shift from high birth and death rates to low birth and death rates within a society as it develops economically and socially.

Demography: The scientific study of population characteristics, structures, and trends.

Denomination: A relatively well-established type of religious organization with a large number of members that is only one of many kinds of such organizations within a society.

Dependency ratio of a population: The number of young people (usually age 15 and younger) and old people (usually age 65 and older) in a population per 100 people age 15 to 64.

Deviance: Any action that violates the established norms of a society or other organization and is considered undesirable or unacceptable by most people.

Deviant: A person who commits a deviant action and is labeled as a deviant by others.

Deviant subculture: A subculture whose beliefs, values and/or norms deviate considerably from those of the dominant societal culture, and that is socially defined as deviant.

Differentiation, organizational: Separation of tasks and component parts of an organization on the basis of functional specialization, producing extensive interdependence among those parts.

Differentiation revolution: The transformation of societies from centering on the family to containing numerous specialized organizations.

Diffusion: The transfer of social practices or cultural ideas from one society to another.

Discrimination: Denying people various rights and privileges, or otherwise treating them as socially inferior because of their race, ethnicity, or sex.

Dispossessed class: The lowest socioeconomic class in industrial societies, whose members are unable to participate effectively in the occupational or other spheres of society.

Division of labor: Differentiation of tasks, activities, and roles among the members and/or parts of an organization.

Dominance: Social power based on actors performing their usual social roles or functions.

Dual economies: The existence of two relatively distinct economic systems within a society.

Dual economies in industrial societies: Existence of an industrial economy based on large industries together with an entrepreneural economy based on small businesses.

Dual economies in industrializing societies: Existence of a traditional economy based on agriculture together with a modern economy based on industry and commerce.

Dual stratification systems: The existence in industrializing societies of two structures of socioeconomic stratification, based on agriculture and business.

Ecclesia: A type of religious organization that is closely allied with the prevailing political and economic systems in that society, and to which most members of the society belong, at least nominally.

Ecological crisis: A condition in which a society or the entire world continually exceeds the carrying capacity of the ecosystem.

Ecological-Economic-Evolutionary Theory: A theoretical perspective in sociology that emphasizes and seeks to integrate the ideas of social ecology, political economy, and societal evolution to explain social ordering.

Ecological enhancement techniques: Procedures such as takeover, tool making, expropriation, conquest, and drawdown that are used by a society to enable it to continue functioning even though it is exceeding the carrying capacity of its ecosystem.

Ecological factors: The fundamental factors of environmental resources, technological knowledge, and population characteristics that affect social organization within human ecosystems.

Ecology, social: The study of the ways in which humans relate to the natural environment, and of the patterns of social ordering that populations create as they use technological knowledge to obtain necessary environmental resources.

Economic base: The economic activities that provide the major sources of jobs, income, and wealth in a community or society.

Economy: An interrelated network or system of beliefs, activities, organizations, and relationships that provides the goods and services needed by the members of a society or other organization. Also called an economic system.

Ecosystem: An interdependent web of relationships among all the organisms (plants, animals, and humans) within a geographical area and between them and the natural environment.

Education: The transmission of knowledge, skills, beliefs, and values from one generation to another.

Education, formal: Education that occurs in organized classes within schools.

Education, informal: Education that occurs through interpersonal interaction outside of schools.

Effectiveness, organizational: The extent to which an organization achieves its goals.

Efficiency, organizational: The extent to which an organization minimizes the costs required to achieve its goals.

Elite class: The highest socioeconomic class in industrial societies, whose members are extremely powerful and wealthy.

Elite dominance crisis: A political crisis that occurs when a state is dominated by political and/or economic elites who fail to serve the needs of the entire society and are unconcerned with various forms of social inequality.

Elites: A small set of persons within a society or other organization that exercises extensive power and/or controls a major proportion of its wealth and enjoys very high social prestige.

Elitism theory: The theory that domination of a society or other organization by a small set of elites is inevitable.

Elitist perspective: The argument that domination of a society or other organization by a small set of elites is desirable.

Emigration: The movement of people out of an area.

Energy: The ability to perform work.

Energy, sociophysical: All forms of animate and inanimate energy and social power that flow through, and are utilized by, the individual members and organizational parts of a society.

Environment: Everything that is external to a given society or other type of social organization.

Environment, natural: All aspects of the physical world.

Environment, social: All aspects of social life that are external to a particular society or other organization.

Equity, organizational: The extent to which an organization treats its members fairly and justly and does not discriminate against any categories of people.

Ethicalism: The religious belief that there are sacred principles that should guide all human activities.

Ethnic group: A population of people who have some kind of common ethnicity.

Ethnicity: Identification of a set of people in terms of their cultural or nationality background that is considered inferior by the society in which they live.

Ethnocentrism: Judging the cultural ideas and/or social practices of another society in terms of the values and norms of one's own culture.

Evolutionary trends: Major social and cultural trends that occur within societies as they evolve.

Evolutionary cultural secularization: An increase in the secular, rational, pragmatic nature of cultural beliefs, values, and norms in a society.

Evolutionary functional specialization: An increase in the specialization of activities or functions performed in a society.

Evolutionary structural complexity: An increase in the number and kinds of diverse organizational units in a society.

Evolution, ecological: The process in which evolutionary development of human societies is influenced and shaped by the ecological conditions within which they exist, and by their ability to adapt to and utilize the natural environment.

Evolution, social: A process of long-term social change that moves in an identifiable direction and develops in a cumulative manner.

Evolution, sociocultural: The process in which human societies increase their economic productivity, structural complexity, and cultural knowledge, which is directly dependent on their ability to adapt to and utilize the natural environment.

Exchange interaction: Social interaction in

which actors give and receive benefits among one another in a reciprocal manner.

Expendable class: A class in agrarian societies consisting of persons who survive outside the economic system through begging, thievery, prostitution, and similar activities.

Extended family: A large family unit containing several different kinds of relatives other than parents and children, and which does not usually live together as a single household.

False consciousness: Beliefs among the members of a class that attribute their existing social conditions to factors other than the true causes of those conditions.

Family: A type of organization whose members are linked by kinship ties, who live together at least part of the time, who share economic resources, and who function as a cooperative social unit.

Family functions, universal: Activities or functions that families in all societies perform for their members and/or the larger society.

Fertility rate, total: The average number of children that will likely be produced by each woman in a population during her lifetime.

Fiscal insolvency crisis: A political crisis that occurs when a state finds it impossible to satisfy all the financial demands placed upon it with its available revenues.

Fiscal policies: Public policies that influence economic activities by manipulating governmental income and expenditures.

Foraging society: A type of society whose economy is based on hunting wild animals and gathering wild plants. Also called a hunting and gathering society.

Force: Social power based on the application of pressures by one actor on another to secure compliance with one's directives.

Formality, organizational: The extent to which norms and role expectations are specified in detail and rigidly applied to all relevant situations in an organization.

Functional analysis: Analysis of the functions being performed by social organizations and the outcomes of those functions for those organizations, their members, and other organizations.

Fundamentalism, religious: Religious beliefs that emphasize a traditional conservative theology and personal salvation through faith.

Functional requirements: Basic operational necessities that must be fulfilled in some manner within a society or other organization if it is to survive for long and function effectively.

Functions, organizational: The activities of an organization that serve or accomplish some collective purpose.

Gemeinschaft: A way of life characterized by informal and personal communal relationships, as often occur in small groups and communities.

Gentry class: A class in agrarian societies composed of independent farm owners and professionals with comfortable incomes but who are not titled nobility.

Gesellschaft: A way of life characterized by formal and impersonal associational relationships, as often occur in formal organizations and large cities.

Goal, cultural: A shared objective for collective social action that is contained within the culture of a society or other organization.

Goals, official: The formally specified purposes that an organization is intended to pursue.

Goals, operative: The objectives that are actually being sought by an organization through its daily operating procedures.

Goals, organizational: Shared objectives for collective social action that guide the activities of an organization.

Goal-oriented organization: An organization that is concerned with attaining one or more specific goals.

Government: The set of formal organizations that enact the power of the state and govern a society or one of its political subunits.

Greenhouse effect: Gradual warming of the earth's climate caused by accumulating carbon dioxide in the atmosphere.

Gross National Product (GNP): The total monetary value of all goods and services produced in a society during a year.

Group: A type of small organization whose members identify and interact with one another in a relatively personal matter.

Growth, organizational: An increase in the size of an organization in terms of its members, activities, or subunits.

Guild: An organization in agrarian societies composed of artisans or merchants that controls most aspects of their business activities.

Headman: An informal political leader in foraging and simple horticultural societies.

Hereditary monarchy: A political system ruled by a hereditary monarchy who is legitimized by tradition.

Homogamy: The practice of people marrying those who are similar to themselves in many demographic and social respects.

Horticultural society: A type of society whose economy is based on small-scale gardening and sometimes herding of domesticated animals.

Horticulture: The practice of obtaining food through small-scale gardening, or growing plants on a semipermanent basis using simple hand tools.

Human scale: The organization of all social activities on a scale that is small and manageable enough so that their participants can understand and control them.

Hunting and gathering: The practice of obtaining food by hunting wild animals and gathering wild plants.

Ideal type: An analytical construct of a social process or organization that identifies its most distinctive characteristics and exaggerates them to their maximum conceivable conditions.

Illegitimacy crisis of the state: A political crisis that occurs when the ideological basis of a state contains a fundamental contradiction that cannot easily be resolved.

Immigration: The movement of people into an area.

Industrialization: The widespread application of inanimate energy-driven machinery in factories to accomplish economic production within societies.

Industrial revolution: The transformation of societies from agricultural to a manufacturing economic base.

Industrial society: A type of society whose economy is based primarily on manufacturing and associated commercial activities.

Inequality, social: Established patterns of activities in which categories of people receive greater or fewer benefits than others and are treated as inferior or superior in interpersonal relationships.

Inequality, sociocultural: Patterns of social inequality that rest on cultural beliefs concerning the inferiority of various categories of people.

Inequality, socioeconomic: Patterns of social inequality that rest on unequal distributions of occupational status, wealth, and standards of living.

Infant mortality rate: The number of deaths occurring among infants under age one per 1,000 live births in a society during a year.

Influential class: The second-highest socioeconomic class in industrial societies, whose members exercise influence within organizations, professions, or other realms of society.

Informal social structure: The patterns of personal interactions and relationships that occur among the members of an organization.

Information revolution: The transformation of societies from a manufacturing to an information economic base.

Influence: The exercise of social power in which the outcomes are relatively uncertain and limited in scope.

Inner city: The section of a city located in and immediately around the central business district.

Innovation: The acquisition of new social practices or cultural knowledge through invention, discovery, or diffusion.

Institution, social: A network of interrelated organizational units that all deal with a common functional requirement of a society and hence share similar values, norms, and activities.

Institution, sociocultural: A social institution that is primarily oriented toward preserving and enhancing the shared culture of a society.

Institutionalization: The process of stabilizing and perpetuating established societal patterns of social ordering and cultural ideas within the organizations constituting that society.

Integration cultural: The tendency for the ideas contained in a culture or subculture to constitute a relatively unified whole.

Integration, social: (*See* Cohesion, social.)

Interaction, social: When the actions of one actor affect the actions or ideas of another actor in some way.

Interdependence revolution: The transformation of societies from containing many relatively separate spheres of social activities to complex networks of highly interrelated activities.

Interlocking directorates: The linkages between two or more corporations that occur when individuals sit on the boards of directors of both or all of those corporations.

Intermediate organizations: Private interest organizations that are located in the structure of a society between the citizens and the government.

International bifurcation: A widening gap between fully industrialized and developing nations around the world.

Intragenerational mobility: Changing one's occupational or other socioeconomic status(es) relative to one's first status(es) as an adult. Also called career mobility.

Intergenerational mobility: Changing one's occupational or other socioeconomic status(es) relative to that of one's parents. Also called generational mobility.

Juvenile delinquency: Criminal actions by persons under the legally established age for adult criminals.

Juvenile delinquent: A youth who commits a criminal action and is labeled by the legal system as delinquent.

Kinship: A culturally defined social linkage among individuals based on common ancestry, marriage, birth, or adoption.

Laissez faire: The economic ideology that the state should leave businesses entirely alone, neither supporting nor regulating them.

Latent functions: Activities of an organization whose consequences are either unintended or unrecognized.

Learning, sociocultural: The process of learning the social skills and cultural ideas necessary to participate in a society or other social organization.

Levels of ordering: Vertically arranged levels of organic, personal, social, and symbolic ordering into which the totality of human existence can be divided.

Life expectancy at birth: The number of years that a child born in a given year can expect to live, on the average.

Linguistic construction of reality: The manner in which language shapes our conceptions of physical and social reality and makes conditions and events real to us.

Linkages, organizational: Vertical and horizontal interdependent relationships among all kinds of organizational units.

Management, social: The manipulation of social situations to influence and control actions in desired ways.

Manifest functions: Activities of an organization whose consequences are both intended and recognized.

Market economy: An economy in which goods and services are bought and sold for money and that is not totally controlled by the government.

Marriage: A culturally defined social bond between two or more people that makes them a family unit, establishes shared responsibilities between them, and legitimizes sexual activity between them.

Marriage, commuter: A marriage in which the spouses maintain separate residences in different communities because of their jobs.

Marriage, group: A marriage among three or more adults who consider themselves to be a single marital unit.

Marriage, homosexual: A marriage between two men or two women.

Marriage, monogamous: A marriage between one man and one woman.

Marriage, open: A marriage in which both spouses seek to create new kinds of marital roles and to create close relationships with other persons of the opposite sex.

Matriarchy: The practice of the dominant female in a family making all major decisions and exercising control over family activities.

Matrilocal residence: The practice of a married couple living with the wife's parents or extended family.

Megalopolis: A large area containing many metropolises and other cities, most of which is relatively urbanized.

Mercantilism: The economic theory that business activities should serve the state by increasing its wealth and power, and that the state should protect and support but not regulate businesses.

Merchant class: A class in agrarian societies composed of merchants, traders, and similar kinds of businessmen.

Merger, corporate: The takeover of one corporation by another through buying a majority of its stock.

Metropolis: A large city plus surrounding satellite cities, suburbs, and urbanized areas. (*See also* Consolidated Metropolitan Area, Metropolitan Statistical Area, Primary Metropolitan Statistical Area.)

Metropolitan government: A single government with partial or complete jurisdiction over an entire metropolitan area.

Metropolitan Statistical Area (MSA): As defined by the U.S. Census Bureau, an urbanized area and its entire county, plus any adjacent counties that have close economic and social ties with that urban area.

Middle class: The middle-level socioeconomic class in industrial societies, whose members enact valued roles within communities and organizations.

Migration: The movement of people from one community, region, or society to another.

Migration forces: Social pressures that cause people to migrate into or out of cities or countries. (*See also* Pull forces and Push forces.)

Migration rate, net: The number of immigrants into a society or other area during a year, minus the number of emigrants out of that area during that year.

Military dictatorship: A political system in which military leaders control the government and rule by authoritarian decree.

Minority group: A population of people who are viewed as inferior and are discriminated against by other members of that society.

Minority group treatment policies: Broad explicit or implicit policies followed with a society concerning one or more minority groups.

Minority group assimilation: The policy of encouraging or forcing a minority group to give up its separate identity and join the dominant majority.

Minority group expulsion: The policy of physically removing the members of a minority group from membership in the society.

Minority group extermination: The policy of deliberately killing most or all the members of a minority group.

Minority group legal equity: The dual policy of establishing legal constraints against discrimination by organizations toward minority groups, while accepting informal discrimina-

tion in interpersonal relations with minority individuals.

Minority group pluralism: The policy of encouraging the retention of ethnic and racial differences within the society and treating all categories of people equally.

Minority group subjugation: The policy of organizing a society to promote and maintain the social inequality of minority people through legal discrimination, segregation, and other practices.

Mobility, social: Acquiring a higher or lower status on one or more dimensions of stratification.

Mobility, structural: Social mobility that is forced upon people by changes in the economic system that push them into different occupational or other socioeconomic statuses.

Mobilization, sociopolitical: The process in which individuals are mobilized for political participation through involvement in all kinds of social activities.

Monetary policies: Governmental policies that control the amount and flow of money in an economy.

Monogamy: Marriage between one man and one woman.

Monogamy, serial: Having a series of monogamous marriages during one's lifetime.

Monotheism: The religious belief that there is a single diety who is all-knowing and all-powerful.

Movement, social: A broad effort by a large number of people to change their society in some critical way.

Movement, expressive: A social movement that attempts to change society by modifying the psychological and emotional states of its members.

Movement, reactionary: A social movement that desires to recreate some social conditions that it believes existed in the past.

Movement, reform: A social movement that seeks to improve some specific aspect of the society.

Movement, revolutionary: A social movement that attempts to create an entirely new kind of social, political, and/or economic system, and thus a totally new society.

Movement, utopian: A social movement that seeks to create some imagined and desired future social conditions.

Multinational corporation: A corporation that operates in two or more countries.

Multiple-nuclei model of urban spatial patterns: A model of urban land use consisting of numerous local areas throughout an urban community, each of which tends to contain similar kinds of land uses.

Mutually Assured Destruction (MAD): The avoidance of international war based on the realization that it would destroy all its participants.

Nation: A society in which the state and its government are coterminous with the total society. Also called a nation-state.

Nationalism: A belief system that emphasizes the importance of the nation-state and its unique social and cultural characteristics above all other forms of social organization.

Nobility: Members of the ruling class in agrarian societies who own large tracts of land and are titled.

Norm, cultural: A shared cultural agreement concerning actions that are considered socially or morally desirable and undesirable.

Nuclear family: A small family unit normally consisting of a couple or a single parent and one or more preadult children, which lives together as a single household.

Nuclear winter: The likely effect of a global nuclear war in which dust and ashes in the atmosphere would block out so much sunlight that plants could not grow and animals and humans could not survive.

Oligarchic democracy: The existence of oligarchy within democratic polities.

Oligarchy: Rule by a few over the many, so that a small set of elites controls a society or other organization.

Oligopoly: Domination of an industry by a few giant corporations.

Organization: A bounded social unit that is relatively stable and enduring and that contains patterns of social ordering and a distinctive organizational culture.

Overpopulation: When the population of a society or the entire world exceeds the level that can be sustained on a permanent basis.

Overshoot: When the population of a society with a given level of living exceeds the carrying capacity of its ecosystem.

Patriarchy: The practice of the dominant male in a family making all major decisions and exercising control over family activities.

Patrilocal residence: The practice of a married couple living with the husband's parents or extended family.

Peasant class: A class in agrarian societies composed of small independent farmers, tenant farmers, serfs, and farm workers.

Planning, social: The process of formulating viable social plans for taking collective action to attain common goals.

Pluralism, sociopolitical: Existence of a large number of autonomous interest associations throughout a society that mediate political influence between the citizens and the government.

Political activists: Persons who engage in organized political activities within private organizations or political parties.

Political citizens: Persons who perform the expected minimal activities of citizens, primarily voting.

Political communicators: Persons who communicate political information, interests, beliefs, or values to others.

Political economy: A relatively integrated system consisting of the economy and the polity of a society or other organization, both parts of which are partially distinct but highly interwoven.

Political isolates: Persons who rarely or never participate in any political activities.

Political leaders: Persons who are directly involved in governmental affairs.

Political marginals: Persons who have only minimal and sporadic contacts with the political system.

Political participation: All activities through which individuals take part in political activities within their society or other organization.

Political participation roles: Identified roles that individuals enact within a political system.

Political party: An association of persons with similar political ideologies and opinions that seeks to have its candidates elected to public offices and to influence governmental affairs.

Polity: An interrelated network or system of beliefs, activities, organizations, and relationships that directs and regulates the collective functioning of a society or other organization. Also called a political system.

Polity, elitist democratic: A democratic political system that is dominated by a small set of powerful elites. (*See also* Democracy, elitist.)

Polity, one-party dominant: A political system in which one political party is considerably larger and stronger than any of the other parties and consistently wins national elections.

Polity, participatory democratic: A political system in which opportunities for citizen involvement in political decision-making are maximized. *See also* Democracy, participatory.

Polity, pluralist democratic: A political system in which citizens act through special interest organizations to influence the government. (See also Democracy, pluralist.)

Polity, single-party: A political system that contains only one party that totally controls the polity.

Polyandry: Marriage in which one woman has two or more cohusbands.

Polygamy: Marriage involving three or more persons.

Polygyny: Marriage in which one man has two or more cowives.

Polytheism: The religious belief that there are a number of gods who rule the world and must be respected and placated.

Population: A set of individuals who are defined as having one or more characteristics in common.

Population density: The number of people per square unit of land.

Population policies and programs: Public policies and programs intended to affect population structures and processes in desired ways.

Population processes: The processes of fertility, mortality, and migration, and their effects on populations.

Population replacement level: The total fertility rate at which births equal deaths in a population.

Population structures: Population sizes, rates of change, distributions, and compositions.

Position, social: A location within a social organization with which one or more roles are associated.

Positivism: The belief that the scientific method provides the most effective and valid means of acquiring knowledge.

Positivism, sociological: The belief that social organization is a real, natural phenomenon that can be studied scientifically.

Postindustrial society: A type of emerging society whose economy is based primarily on activities other than agriculture or manufacturing, and in which knowledge plays a central role.

Poverty: The condition of having very little income and wealth and living in a very deprived manner.

Poverty line: The level of annual income set by the U.S. government that officially defines those persons and families who are considered to be poor.

Power centralization: Concentration of social power within a society or other organization in one or a few positions at the top of a hierarchy of authority or control.

Power, coercive: Exercise of social power based on the application of punishments.

Power decentralization: Dispersion of social power to the lower-level units within a society or other organization that are performing goal-oriented tasks.

Power distribution: *See* "Power structure."

Power, normative: Exercise of social power based on identification by individuals with an organization and its values and norms.

Power, remunerative: Exercise of social power based on the application of rewards.

Power resource: Anything that can be drawn upon as a basis for exercising social power.

Power resource, finite: A type of power resource that is inherently limited and hence becomes depleted with use.

Power resource, infinite: A type of power resource that is unlimited and hence does not become depleted with use.

Power, social: The ability to affect the actions or ideas of others despite resistance, or to accomplish collective activities.

Power structure: The distribution of power resources and the patterns of power exertion within a society or other organization, including the degree of power centralization/decentralization and the number of levels of authority.

Preindustrial societies: All types of societies whose economies are not based on manufacturing, including foraging, horticultural, and agrarian societies.

Prejudice: A negative prejudgement about a category of people that is based on false assumptions or stereotypes about them.

Priestly class: A class in agrarian societies composed of the religious leaders, especially the high priests and others associated with the established church.

Primary group: A small group characterized by face-to-face interaction in which much sociocultural learning and socialization occurs.

Primary Metropolitan Statistical Area (PMSA): As defined by the U.S. Census Bureau, two adjacent Metropolitan Statistical Areas that are functionally interrelated.

Primary relationship: An interpersonal relationship characterized by relatively informal, personal, and close bonds.

Proprietary conception of the state: A belief among political elites that the polity is their personal property, to be used as they desire for their own benefit.

Protestant ethic: A set of beliefs and values emphasizing hard work, thrift, and self-discipline that Max Weber argued was necessary for industrialization, and that he claimed originated in Calvinist Protestantism.

Pull forces: Conditions within an area that cause people to immigrate to that area.

Push forces: Conditions within an area that cause people to emigrate to other areas.

Race, biological: A minor subcategory of a biological species, the members of which have one or more common physical characteristics.

Race, sociocultural: A sociocultural categorization, based on a few minor physical characteristics, that differentiates people in terms of status and/or culture.

Racism: Patterns of sociocultural inequality that systematically discriminate against one or more sociocultural racial categories of people.

Rationality, organizational: The extent to which the norms, rules, and social technologies within a society or other organization are designed to obtain collective goals as efficiently and effectively as possible.

Redistribution of income and/or wealth: Shifting income and/or wealth from financially advantaged to financially disadvantaged portions of a population.

Reference group: A group or other organization with which an individual strongly identifies, and whose beliefs, values, and norms that person accepts.

Reform, social: A moderate and intended social change.

Regulation, organizational: Coordination and direction of the activities of an organization and its subunits by organizational leaders.

Relationship, social: A set of social interactions between two or more social actors that becomes relatively stable and enduring, and with which those actors identify.

Relationship to the means of production: Social arrangements that determine who owns or controls the major means of economic production in a society.

Relative deprivation: A perception held by a number of people that they are not as well off as they believe they should be or that they think others actually are.

Religion: A set of shared cultural beliefs that are viewed as sacred and that are expressed through symbols and rituals.

Retainer class: A class in agrarian societies composed of persons who personally serve the ruling elites in various ways.

Revolutionary war: A war in which a large proportion of the population seeks to overthrow the established government.

Revolution of rising expectations: A condition in which people's expectations for future improvements in their standard of living or other conditions far exceed the actual rate of improvement.

Revolution, social: A fundamental intended social change.

Revolution, societal: A massive change in the basic organizational structure or culture of a society, resulting in a total transformation of that society.

Revolution, sociopolitical: A sociopolitical movement that makes fundamental changes in the structure or functioning of the government or political system of a society.

Role conflict: Incongruencies within the expectations or actions of a role, or between the expectations or performances of two or more roles.

Role partner: A person with whom one normally enacts a particular role and who enacts a corresponding reciprocal role.

Role, social: A set of expectations and actions that is part of a social relationship or organization and is defined as appropriate for a particular social setting or position.

Ruling class: The dominant class in a society that is usually composed of political, economic, religious, military, or other elites, and that influences or controls much of what occurs in that society.

Sacred: Beliefs and values that are believed to emanate from or reflect the supernatural.

Sanctions: Rewards and punishments that are applied to social actors to encourage desired actions or discourage undesired actions.

Satellite city: A smaller city located near a larger city and closely linked with it, but having its own economic base.

Sect: A relatively less established type of religious organization with fewer members and a more informal structure than a denomination.

Sector model of urban spatial patterns: A model of urban land use patterns that consists of several wedge-shaped areas defined in terms of transportation routes extending outward from the city center, each of which tends to contain similar kinds of land use.

Secular: Beliefs and values that are created by humans and reflect human concerns.

Segregation: Legal and/or social prohibitions against certain actions by minority group members, such as living in particular neighborhoods, using facilities reserved for the dominant population, or holding more desirable kinds of jobs.

Self-fulfilling prophecy: A self-image, based on what others think and expect of one, which guide one's actions so that they eventually fulfill those expectations.

Sex ratio of a population: The number of males per 100 females in a population.

Sexism: The belief that women are biologically inferior to men, together with established role expectations and practices that restrict the activities in which women participate and the roles they enact.

Shaman: A religious leader in foraging and simple horticultural societies who was believed to intervene with the spirits on the behalf of humans.

Socialism: A political economy in which the major means of economic production are owned by the state and political democracy is promoted by empowering all citizens and eliminating government repression.

Socialist economy: An economy in which major or all businesses are owned by the state and operate within state-controlled markets.

Socialization: The process of learning to be a functioning human being.

Social ordering: The process in which social relationships become interwoven into patterns that are relatively stable and enduring.

Social movement organization: An organization that seeks to promote a particular social movement.

Social organization: The process in which social relationships become interwoven into patterns of social ordering that are infused with shared cultural meanings; the process of creating social ordering and cultural meaning in social life.

Social structure: A static representation of dynamic patterns of social ordering.

Social system: A general analytical model emphasizing wholism, interrelationships among its parts, and dynamic activities, which can be applied to any instance of social organization.

Socioeconomic class: An organization of people who hold similar statuses on one or more dimensions of socioeconomic stratification, and which displays boundaries, internal ordering, and a unique subculture.

Socioeconomic base of democracy: Social and economic conditions that must exist in a society if it is to sustain a stable and effective democratic polity.

Society: The most inclusive type of social organization, exercising functional and cultural dominance over all other social units within it.

Sociological practice: Applied sociological work done outside of academia.

Sociology: The scientific study of the process of social organization and all its various forms.

Specialization, organizational: The process in which organizations and their component parts perform increasingly specialized activities, and thus become highly interdependent.

Stability, organizational: The ability of an organization to cope with external stresses and internal strains and to preserve its existence and cohesion.

State: The arrangement of political authority and other forms of political power within a society.

State building: The process of creating societal-wide political systems, so that societies are also political states.

State revolution: The transformation of societies from loosely linked political fiefdoms into unified nation-states.

Status attainment: The factors and processes that determine the status positions and social mobility of individuals during the course of their lives.

Status, social: An identified position or rank on a dimension of stratification.

Stereotype: A cultural image of the members of a minority group that depicts them as having undesirable personal characteristics.

Stratum, social: An arbitrarily defined set of individuals who hold similar statuses on a dimension of stratification.

Strain, social: A social tension originating inside an organization that may produce social change.

Stratification, social: The process through which social benefits are distributed unequally among actors, creating patterns of social inequality that are perpetuated across generations.

Stress, social: A social tension originating outside an organization that may produce social change.

Subculture: A set of cultural beliefs, values, and norms associated with particular organizations or populations within a society.

Suburb: A smaller city located near a large central city that is politically autonomous but economically dependent on that city, since it contains primarily residences and lacks an economic base of its own.

Suburbanization: Growth of numerous suburbs around central cities.

Supernaturalism: The religious belief that some kind of supernatural force or power pervades and influences all existence.

Sustainable economy: An economy that remains in balance with its ecosystem and hence can operate indefinitely.

Sustainable society: A model of a society that remains in balance with its natural and social environments on a permanent basis and hence is ecologically stable.

Symbolic interaction: When actors reciprocally communicate common ideas and meanings through language and other symbols.

Taking the role of the other: Viewing a situation or oneself from the perspective of another person, usually a role partner.

Technology: Knowledge that can be used to obtain desired objectives.

Technology, material: Knowledge about physical objects and processes and how to use them.

Technology, social: Knowledge about social practices and processes and how to use them.

Tensions, organizational: Tensions experienced by a society or other social organization as a result of stresses and strains acting upon it, or from its simultaneous efforts to establish relationships with other organizations without becoming dependent on them.

Traditions: Well-established cultural beliefs, values, and norms and related social practices within a society that are accepted without question as true and appropriate.

Transformation, societal: A fundamental unintended social change that usually affects an entire society.

Tribe: A network of interpersonal relationships and social obligations based on extended kinship ties, but often including more than one kinship unit and also unrelated individuals, which occurred primarily in horticultural societies but continue to exist today in many developing societies.

Urban: Anything pertaining to cities or their residents.

Urban economy: The economic system of an urban community.

Urban economy, export sector: Goods and services that are produced within the community but are marketed largely outside it.

Urban economy, local sector: Goods and services that are produced and consumed within that community.

Urbanized area: As defined by the U.S. Census Bureau, a city or contiguous cities with a population of at least 50,000, plus the immediately surrounding densely settled areas.

Urban gentrification: Renovating existing residences in inner city areas to turn them into desirable and prestigious housing, using private funding.

Urbanism: The way of life practiced by residents of urban communities.

Urbanization: A process of societal change in which an increasing proportion of the population resides in relatively large and dense communities.

Urbanized: The proportion of a nation's population living in urban communities, however they are defined by that country.

Urban locality: As defined by the United Nations, a community with 20,000 or more inhabitants.

Urban rehabilitation: Renovation of old buildings in inner-city areas to attract new, higher-status activities and people, primarily using public funding.

Urban renewal: Large-scale replacement of old buildings, activities, and people in inner-city areas with new buildings and higher-status activities and people, primarily using public funding.

Urban revolution: The transformation of societies from rural to urban living.

Value, cultural: A shared cultural conception of what is desirable and undesirable in social life.

War: Organized violent conflict between socio-political units for the purpose of defeating or destroying the enemy.

Welfarism: A type of economy based on the assumption that society has an obligation to ensure that all its members receive minimal necessary economic benefits and which contains programs intended to attain that goal.

Wholism: The belief that social organization is always a unified process that is more than the sum of its component parts.

Working class: The socioeconomic class of ordinary people, whose members perform routine jobs and roles within society and other organizations.

World system: A theoretical perspective that views all societies as constituting a single functional system of economic and political interdependencies.

Worldview: A belief system and its associated values that pertains to most aspects of social life and is held by most members of a society.

World war: A war between nations or coalitions of nations.

REFERENCES

ABRAHAMSSON, BENGT. 1977. *Bureaucracy or Participation: The Logic of Organization.* Beverly Hills, Calif.: Sage Publications.

ACUNA, RODOLFO. 1980. *Occupied America: A History of Chicanos.* New York: Harper and Row.

ADAMS, RICHARD N. 1975. *Energy and Structure: A Theory of Social Power.* Austin: University of Texas Press.

———. 1982. *Paradoxical Harvest: Energy and Explanation in British History 1870–1914.* Cambridge: Cambridge University Press.

AIKEN, MICHAEL. 1970. "The Distribution of Community Power: Structural Bases and Social Consequences," In Michael Aiken and Paul E. Mott, eds., *The Structure of Community Power.* New York: Random House, pp. 487–525.

AIKEN, MICHAEL, and PAUL E. MOTT, eds. 1970. *The Structure of Community Power.* New York: Random House.

AKERS, RONALD L. 1977. *Deviant Behavior: Social Learning Approach,* 2nd ed. Belmont, Calif.: Wadsworth Pub. Co.

ALDRICH, HOWARD E. 1972. "Technology and Organizational Structure: A Reexamination of the Findings of the Aston Group," *Administrative Science Quarterly,* 17 (March), 26–43.

———. 1979. *Organizations and Environments.* Englewood Cliffs, N.J.: Prentice–Hall, Inc.

ALLEN, MICHAEL PATRICK. 1974. "The Structure of Interorganizational Elite Cooperation: Interlocking Corporate Directorates," *American Sociological Review,* 39 (June), 393–406.

ANGELL, ROBERT C. 1968. "Social Integration." In David L. Sills, ed., *The Encyclopedia of the Social Sciences.* New York: Crowell-Collier and Macmillan, pp. 380–86.

ARGYRIS, CHRIS. 1972. *The Applicability of Organizational Sociology.* Cambridge: Cambridge University Press.

BACHARACH, SAMUEL B., and EDWARD J. LAWLER. 1980. *Power and Politics in Organizations.* San Francisco: Jossey-Bass.

BACHRACH, PETER. 1966. *The Theory of Democratic Elitism: A Critique.* Boston: Little, Brown and Co.

BALES, ROBERT F. 1949. *Interaction Process Analysis.* Reading, Mass.: Addison-Wesley.

BANE, MARY JO. 1976. *Here to Stay: American Families in the Twentieth Century.* New York: Basic Books.

BANFIELD, EDWARD. 1961. *Political Influence.* New York: Free Press.

BARRY, HERBERT III, IRVING L. CHILD, and MARGARET K. BACON. 1959. "Relation of Child Training to Subsistence Economy," *American Anthropologist,* 61, 263.

BEAVER, S. E. 1975. *Demographic Transition Theory Reinterpreted.* Lexington, Mass.: Lexington Books.

BECKER, HOWARD S. 1963. *Principles of Criminology.* Philadelphia: Lippincott.

BEEGHLEY, LEONARD. 1978. *Social Stratification in America: A Critical Analysis of Theory and Research.* Santa Monica, Calif.: Goodyear Publishing Co.

BELL, DANIEL. 1973. *The Coming of Post-Industrial Society.* New York: Basic Books.

BELLAH, ROBERT. 1964. "Religious Evolution," *American Sociological Review,* 29 (June), 358–74.

————. 1975. *The Broken Covenant: American Civil Religion in Time of Trial.* New York: Seabury Press.

BENELLO, C. GEORGE and DIMITRIOS ROUSSOPOULUS, eds. 1971. *The Case for Participatory Democracy: Some Prospects for a Radical Society.* New York: Viking Press.

BENNETT, H. S. 1960. *Life on the English Manor: A Study of Peasant Conditions, 1150–1400.* London: Cambridge University Press.

BENNETT J. W. 1976. *The Ecological Transition: Cultural Anthropology and Human Adaptation.* New York: Pergamin Press.

BENNIS, WARREN G. 1970. *American Bureaucracy.* Chicago: Transaction Books.

BERELSON, BERNARD, PAUL F. LAZARSFELD, and WILLIAM N. MCPHEE. 1954. *Voting.* Chicago: University of Chicago Press.

BERGER, PETER L. 1969. *A Rumor of Angels: Modern Society and the Rediscovery of the Supernatural.* New York: Doubleday.

BERRY, DAVID. 1970. *The Sociology of Grass Roots Politics.* London: Macmillan and Co.

BIERSTEDT, ROBERT. 1950. "An Analysis of Social Power," *American Sociological Review,* 15 (December), 730–38.

————. 1963. *The Social Order.* New York: McGraw-Hill.

BIRDSELL, JOSEPH. 1968. "Some Predictions for the Pleistocene Based on Equilibrium Systems Among Recent Hunter-Gatherers." In Richard B. Lee and Irven DeVore, eds. *Man the Hunter.* Chicago: Aldine, pp. 229–40.

BLAU, PETER. 1964. *Exchange and Power in Social Life.* New York: John Wiley.

————. 1970. "A Formal Theory of Differentiation in Organizations," *American Sociological Review,* 35 (April), 201–18.

————. 1971. *The Structure of Organizations.* New York: Basic Books.

————, and OTIS DUDLEY DUNCAN. 1967. *The American Occupational Structure.* New York: John Wiley & Sons.

————, and MARSHALL M. MEYER. 1971. *Bureaucracy in Modern Society,* 2nd ed. New York: Random House.

————, and RICHARD C. SCOTT. 1963. *Formal Organizations.* San Francisco: Chandler Publishing Co.

BLOOD, ROBERT O., and DONALD M. WOLFE. 1965. *Husbands and Wives.* New York: Free Press.

BLUMBERG, PAUL. 1969. *Industrial Democracy: The Sociology of Participation.* New York: Schocken Books.

————. 1980. *Inequality in an Age of Decline.* New York: Oxford University Press.

BLUMBERG, PHILLIP I. 1975. *The Megacorporation in American Society.* Englewood Cliffs, N.J.: Prentice-Hall, Inc.

BOLLEN, KENNETH. 1983. "World System Position, Dependency, and Democracy: The Cross-National Evidence," *American Sociological Review,* 48 (August): 468–79.

BOLLENS, JOHN C. and HENRY J. SCHMADT. 1982. *The Metropolis: Its People, Politics, and Economic Life* (4th ed.). New York: Harper and Row.

BOLLIER, DAVID. 1982. *Liberty and Justice for Some.* New York: Frederick Ungar Publishing Co.

BOULDING, KENNETH. 1968. "The Economics of the Coming Spaceship Earth," In Kenneth Boulding, *Beyond Economics: Essays on Society, Religion, and Ethnics.* Ann Arbor: The University of Michigan Press, pp. 275–87.

BRITAIN, CRANE. 1952. *Anatomy of a Revolution.* New York: Vintage Books.

BROWN, LESTER R. 1981. *Building a Sustainable Society.* New York: W. W. Horton Co.

———, et al. 1988. *State of the World 1989.* New York: W. W. Norton and Co.

BURNS, TOM R., LARS ERIK KARLSSON, and VELJKO RUS, eds. 1979. *Work and Power: The Liberation of Work and the Centralization of Political Power.* London: Sage Publications, Ltd.

BUTTEL, FREDERICK H. 1979. "Social Welfare and Energy Intensity: A Comparative Analysis of the Developed Market Economies." In Charles Unseld, et al., eds., *Sociopolitical Effects of Energy Use and Policy,* Washington D.C.: National Academy of Sciences, pp. 297–327.

CANAN, PENELOPE, and GEORGE W. PRING. 1986. "The Role of the Courts in Laws that 'Chill' Public-Interest Advocacy." Presented at the 1986 annual meeting of the Law and Society Association.

CARMICHAEL, STOKLEY and CHARLES W. HAMILTON, 1967. *Black Power: The Politics of Liberation in America.* New York: Vintage Press.

CATTON, WILLIAM R., JR. 1980. *Overshoot: The Ecological Basis of Revolutionary Change.* Urbana, Ill.: University of Illinois Press.

CHAMBLIS, WILLIAM J. 1973. "The Saints and the Roughnecks," *Society,* 4 (December 11), 24–31.

CHANDLER, TERTIUS, and GERALD FOX. 1974. *3000 Years of Urban Growth.* New York: Academic Press.

CHILDE, V. GORDON. 1949. *Man Makes Himself.* New York: Mentor Books.

———. 1964. *What Happened in History.* Baltimore: Penguin Books.

CLARK, GRAHAME, and STUART PIGGOT. 1965. *Prehistoric Societies.* New York: Knopf.

CLARK, TERRY N. 1968. *Community Structure and Decision Making: Comparative Analysis.* San Francisco: Chandler Publishing Co.

CLARK-STEWART, ALISON. 1977. *Child Care in the Family.* New York: Academic Press.

CLOWARD, RICHARD A., and LLOYD E. OHLIN. 1960. *Delinquency and Opportunity,* NewYork: Free Press.

COCH, LESTER, and JOHN R. P. FRENCH, JR. 1958. "Overcoming Resistance to Change." In Eleanor E. Maccoby, et al., eds., *Readings in Social Psychology,* 3rd ed. New York: Holt, Rinehart and Winston, pp. 233–50.

COHEN, ALBERT K. 1955. *Delinquent Boys: The Culture of the Gang.* New York: Free Press.

COHEN, MARK. 1977. *The Food Crisis in Prehistory: Overpopulation and the Origin of Agriculture.* New Haven: Yale University Press.

COLEMAN, JAMES. 1957. *Community Conflict.* New York: Free Press.

———, et al. 1966. *Equality of Educational Opportunity.* Washington, D.C.: U.S. Government Printing Office.

CONSTANTINE, LARRY L. and JOAN M. CONSTANTINE. 1974. *Group Marriage.* New York: Macmillan Co.

COOLEY, CHARLES HORTON. 1956. *Human Nature and the Social Order.* Glencoe, Ill.: The Free Press.

———. 1956. *Social Organization.* Glencoe, Ill.: The Free Press.

COON, CARLTON S. 1971. *The Hunting Peoples.* Boston: Little, Brown.

CORWIN, RONALD G. 1973. *Reform and Organizational Survival: The Teacher Corps as an Instrument of Educational Change.* New York: John Wiley and Sons.

COSER, LEWIS A. 1956a. *The Functions of Social Conflict.* New York: Free Press.

———. 1956b. "Social Conflict and the Theory of Social Change," *British Journal of Sociology,* 8 (September), 197–207.

COTTRELL, FRED. 1955. *Energy and Society.* New York: McGraw-Hill Book Co.

COULTER, PHILIP. 1975. *Social Mobilization and Political Democracy.* Lexington, Mass.: Lexington Books.

COUNCIL ON ENVIRONMENTAL QUALITY AND THE DEPARTMENT OF STATE. 1974. *The Good News About Energy.* Washington, D.C.: U.S. Government Printing Office.

———. 1980. *The Global 2000 Report to the President.* Washington, D.C.: U.S. Government Printing Office, three volumes.

DAHL, ROBERT. 1961. *Who Governs?* New Haven: Yale University Press.

DAHL, ROBERT, and CHARLES E. LINDBLOM. 1957. *Politics, Economics, and Welfare.* New York: Harper and Row.

DAHRENDORF, RALF. 1958. "Out of Utopia: Toward a Reorientation of Sociological Analysis," *American Journal of Sociology,* 64 (September), 115–27.

———. 1959. *Class and Class Conflict in Industrial Society.* Stanford, Calif.: Stanford University Press.

DALPHIN, JOHN. 1981. *The Persistence of Social Inequality in America.* Cambridge, Mass.: Schenkman Pub. Co.

DALTON, MELVILLE. 1969. "Conflict Between Staff and Line Managerial Officers." In Amitai Etzioni, ed., *A Sociological Reader on Complex Organizations,* 2nd ed. New York: Holt, Rinehart and Winston, pp. 266–74.

DALY, HERMAN. 1977. *Steady State Economics.* San Francisco: W. H. Freeman and Co.

DANIELS, ROGER. 1974. "The Japanese-American Experience: 1890–1945." In Rudolph Gomez, et al., eds., *The Social Reality of Ethnic America.* Lexington, Mass.: D.C. Health Co.

DAVIDSON, BASIN, with F. K. BUAH. 1966. *A History of West Africa: To The Nineteenth Century.* Garden City, N.Y.: Doubleday Anchor Books.

DAVIES, JAMES C. 1962. "Toward a Theory of Revolution," *American Sociological Review,* 27 (February): 5–19.

DAVIS, KINGSLEY. 1955. "The Origin and Growth of World Urbanism," *American Journal of Sociology,* 60:429–37.

———. 1972. "World Urbanization 1950–70: The Urban Situation in the World as a Whole." *World Urbanization, Population Monography Series No. 9.* Berkeley, Cal.: University of California.

——— and WILBERT E. MOORE. 1945. "Some Principles of Stratification," *American Sociological Review,* 10:242–49.

DeFRONZO, JAMES. 1973. "Embourgeoisement in Indianapolis," *Social Problems,* 21 (Fall), 269–83.

DOBYNS, HENRY F. 1966. "Estimating Aboriginal American Population," *Current Anthropology,* 7 (October), 395–416.

DOLESCHAL, EUGENE and NORMAL KLAPMUTS. 1973. *Toward a New Criminology.* Hackensack, N.J.: National Council on Crime and Delinquency.

DOMHOFF, G. WILLIAM. 1967. *Who Rules America?* Englewood Cliffs, N.J.: Prentice-Hall, Inc.

———. 1990. *The Power Elite and the State.* Hawthorne, New York: Aldine de Gruyter.

DRUCKER, PETER F. 1972. "School Around the Bend," *Psychology Today,* 6 (June), 49.

DUBERMAN, LUCILLE. 1975. *The Reconstructed Family: A Study of Remarried Couples and Their Children.* Chicago: Nelson-Hall.

DUBOS, RENE. 1968. *So Human An Animal.* New York: Scribners.

DUMOND, DON. 1975. "The Limitations of Human Population: A Natural History," *Science,* 187 (Feb. 28):715.

DUNCAN, OTIS DUDLEY. 1964. "Social Organization and the Ecosystem." In Robert E. L. Faris, ed., *Handbook of Modern Sociology.* Chicago: Rand McNally & Co., pp. 36–82.

DURANT, WILL. 1965. Quoted in *Time Magazine,* August 13, p. 48.

DURKHEIM, ÉMILE. 1915. *The Elementary Forms of the Religious Life.* London: George Allen and Unwin.

———. 1933. *The Rules of Sociological Method,* trans. by Sarah A. Solovay and John H. Mueller. New York: Free Press.

———. 1947. The Division of Labor in Society, trans. by George Simpson. New York: Free Press. [Originally published in 1893.]

———. 1951. *Suicide,* trans. by John Spaulding and George Simpson. New York: Free Press. [Originally published in 1897.]

———. 1961. Moral Education. New York: The Free Press. [Originally published in 1925.]

———. 1964. *Suicide.* Glencoe, Ill.: Free Press. [Originally published in 1893].

DYE, THOMAS R. 1983. *Who's Running America? The Reagan Years,* 3rd ed. Englewood Cliffs, N.J.: Prentice-Hall, Inc.

——— and L. HARMON ZEIGLER. 1978. *The Irony of Democracy,* 4th ed. North Scituate, Mass.: Duxbury.

EASTON DAVID. 1965. *A Systems Analysis of Political Life.* New York: John Wiley.

EHRLICH, PAUL R., ANNE H. EHRLICH, and JOHN P. HOLDREN. 1977. *Ecoscience: Population, Resources, Environment.* San Francisco: W. W. Freeman Co.

EMERSON, RICHARD M. 1962. "Power-Dependence Relations," *American Sociological Review* 27 (February), 31–41.

ERASMUS, CHARLES J. 1977. *In Search of the Common Good. Utopian Experiments Past and Future.* New York: Free Press.

ESTER, PETER, et al. 1984. *Consumer Behavior and Energy Policy.* Amsterdam: North-Holland.

ETZIONI, AMITAI. 1961. *A Comparative Analysis of Complex Organizations.* New York: Free Press.

EWENS, WILLIAM. 1984. *Becoming Free: The Struggle for Human Development.* Wilmington, Del.: Scholarly Resources, Inc.

FARMER, B. H. 1968. "Agriculture: Comparative Technology." In David L. Sills, ed., *International Encyclopedia of the Social Sciences,* Vol. I. New York: Macmillan, 204–05.

FEAGIN, JOE R. 1975. *Subordinating the Poor: Welfare and American Beliefs.* Englewood Cliffs, N.J.: Prentice-Hall.

FEDERAL BUREAU OF INVESTIGATION. 1975. *Uniform Crime Reports.* Washington, D.C.: U.S. Government Printing Office.

FILLEY, ALAN C., and ROBERT P. HOUSE. 1969. *Managerial Processes and Organizational Behavior.* Glencoe, Ill.: Scott, Foresman and Co.

FLEISHER, FREDERIC. 1967. *The New Sweden: The Challenge of a Disciplined Democracy.* New York: David McKay Co.

FORBES. 1977. "The Forbes 500s," 119 (May 15), 156–290.

FORRESTER, JAY. 1977. "New Perspectives on Economic Growth." In Dennis L. Meadows, ed., *Alternatives to Growth I: A Search for Sustainable Futures.* Cambridge, Mass.: Ballinger Pub. Co., Ch. 5.

FREEMAN, LINTON, WALTER BLOOMBERG, JR., and MORRIS H. O. SUNSHINE. 1963. "Locating Leaders in Local Communities: A Comparison of Some Alternative Approaches." *American Sociological Review,* 28 (October), 791–98.

FREITAG, PETER J. 1975. "The Cabinet and Big Business: A Study of Interlocks." *Social Problems,* 23 (December), 137–52.

FRIEDEL, ERNESTINE. 1975. *Women and Men: An Anthropologist's View.* New York: Holt, Rinehart & Winston.

FROMM, ERICH. 1963. *Marx's Concept of Man.* New York: Frederick Ungar Pub. Co.

The Futurist. 1982. "The New Megalopolises," 16 (October), 62–63.

GAGNON, JOHN J. 1977. *Human Sexualities.* Glenview, Ill.: Scott, Foresman, Co.

GALBRAITH, JOHN KENNETH. 1958. *The Affluent Society.* Boston: Beacon Press.

———. 1967. *The New Industrial State.* Boston: Houghton Mifflin Co.

GALLUP REPORT. 1982. Nos. 201–02.

———. 1983. No. 216.

GAMSON, WILLIAM A. 1974. "Violence and Political Power: The Meek Don't Make It," *Psychology Today,* 8 (July), 35–41.

———. 1975. *The Sociology of Social Protest.* Homewood, Ill.: Dorsey Press.

GANS, HERBERT J. 1962. *The Urban Villagers.* Glencoe, Ill.: Free Press.

———. 1968. "Planning, Social: II. Regional and Urban Planning." In David Sills, ed., *International Encyclopedia of the Social Sciences,* Vol. 12. New York: Macmillan Co., pp. 129–37.

GARDNER, DAVID. 1983. *A Nation at Risk: The Imperative for Educational Reform. Report of the National Commission on Excellence in Education.* Washington, D.C.: U.S. Government Printing Office.

GARFINKEL, HAROLD. 1956. "Conditions of Successful Degradation Ceremonies," *American Journal of Sociology,* 61 (March), 420–24.

GILBERT, K., G. HANSEN, and B. DAVIS. 1981. "Perceptions of Parental Responsibilities: Difference Between Mothers and Fathers," *Family Relations,* 31 (Spring), 267–77.

GLICK, PAUL C. 1979. *The Future of the American Family.* Current Population Reports, Bureau of the Census, Special Studies, Series P-23, No. 78. Washington, D.C.: U.S. Government Printing Office.

———, and ARTHUR J. NORTON. 1977. "Marriage, Divorce, and Living Happily Together," *Population Bulletin,* 32 (5):1–40.

GOFFMAN, ERVINE. 1963. *Stigma: Notes on the Management of Spoiled Identity.* Englewood Cliffs, N.J.: Prentice-Hall, Inc.

GOLD, DAVID, and GEOFF QUIFF. 1981. "Misguided Expenditure: An Analysis of the Proposed MX System," *Council of Economic Priorities Newsletter,* p. 6.

GOLDTHORPE, JOHN H., et al. 1969. *The Affluent Worker and the Class Structure.* Cambridge, England: Cambridge University Press.

GOODE, WILLIAM J. 1959. "The Theoretical Importance of Love." American Sociological Review, 24 (1):38–47.

———. 1963. *World Revolution and Family Patterns.* New York: Free Press.

GOULDNER, ALVIN W. 1960. "The Norm of Reciprocity," *American Sociological Review,* 25 (April), 161–78.

GREELEY, ANDREW M. 1977. *The American Catholic: A Social Portrait.* New York: Basic Books.

GREEN, MARK. 1972. *The Closed Enterprise System.* New York: Grossman.

GREER, SCOTT. 1962. *The Emerging City: Myth and Reality.* New York: Free Press.

———, DENNIS L. McELVATH, DAVID M. MINAR, and PETER ORLEANS, eds. 1969. *The New Urbanization.* New York: St. Martin's Press.

GRONBJERG, KIRSTEN, et al. 1978. *Poverty and Social Change.* Chicago: University of Chicago Press.

GRUSKY, DAVID B., and ROBERT M. HAUSER. 1984. "Comparative Social Mobility Revisited: Models of Convergence and Divergence in 16 Countries," *American Sociological Review* 49 (February), 19–38.

HACKER, ANDREW, ed. 1983. *A Statistical Portrait of the American People*. New York: The Viking Press.

HAGE, JERALD. 1970. *Social Change in Complex Organizations*. New York: Random House.

———, and MICHAEL AIKEN. 1967. "Relationship of Centralization to Other Structure Properties," *Administration Science Quarterly*, 12 (June), 72–92.

HALL, RICHARD H. 1982. *Organizations: Structure and Process*, 3rd ed. Englewood Cliffs, N.J.: Prentice-Hall, Inc.

HAMMOND, MASON. 1972. *The City in the Ancient World*. Cambridge, Mass.: Harvard University Press.

HARDIN, GARRETT. 1968. "The Tragedy of the Commons," *Science*, 64 (December 13), 1243–48.

HARRINGTON, MICHAEL. 1963. *The Other America: Poverty in the U.S.* Baltimore: Penguin Books.

HARRIS, CHAUNCY, and EDWARD ULLMAN. 1945. "The Nature of the Cities," *The Annals of the American Academy of Political and Social Sciences*, 252:7–17.

HARRIS, MARVIN. 1968. *The Rise of Anthropological Theory*. New York: Thomas Crowell & Co.

———. 1974. *Cows, Pigs and Witches: The Riddle of Culture*. New York: Random House.

HARTLEY, EUGENE. 1946. *Problems in Prejudice*. New York: Crown Press.

HAUSER, PHILIP and LEO SCHNORE, eds. 1965. *The Study of Urbanization*. New York: John Wiley.

HAUSER, ROBERT M., PETER J. DICKINSON, HARRY P. TRAVIS, and JOHN N. KOFFEL. 1975. "Structural Changes in Occupational Mobility Among Men in the United States," *American Sociological Review*, 40 (October), 585–98.

HAUSER, ROBERT M. and DAVID L. FEATHERMAN. 1978. *Opportunity and Change*. New York: Academic Press.

HAWLEY, AMOS H. 1963. "Community Power and Urban Renewal Success," *The American Journal of Sociology*, 68 (January), 422–31.

———. 1964. "World Urbanization," In Ronald Friedman, ed. *Population: the Vital Revolution*, Garden City, N.Y.: Doubleday and Co., Ch. 5.

———. 1971. *Urban Society: An Ecological Approach*. New York: Ronald Press.

———. 1984. "Human Ecological and Marxian Theories," *American Journal of Sociology*, 89 (January), 904–17.

———. 1986. *Human Ecology: A Theoretical Essay*. Chicago: The University of Chicago Press.

HAYES, DENNIS. 1977. *Rays of Hope: The Transition to a Post-Petroleum World*. New York: W. W. Norton and Co.

HEILBRONER, ROBERT L. 1976. *Business Civilization in Decline*. New York: W. W. Norton and Co.

HENDERSON, HAZEL. 1978. *Creating Alternative Futures*. New York: Berkeley Pub. Co.

HERBERG, WILL. 1960. *Protestant-Catholic-Jew*. Garden City, N.Y.: Doubleday.

HERNENDEZ, CAROL A., et al., eds. 1976. *Chicanos: Social and Psychological Perspectives*. 2nd ed. St. Louis: Mosby.

HIRSCHI, TRAVIS. 1971. *Causes of Delinquency*. Berkeley, Calif.: University of California Press.

HOBBES, THOMAS. 1881. *Leviathan*. Oxford: James Thorton. [Originally published in 1651.]

HODGE, ROBERT W., PAUL M. SIEGEL, and PETER H. ROSSI. 1964. "Occupational Prestige in the United States: 1925–1963," *American Journal of Sociology*, 70 (November), 286–302.

HOEBEL, E. ADAMSON, 1956. *Anthropology*, 3rd ed. New York: McGraw-Hill Book Co.

HOUGH, JERRY F. 1977. *The Soviet Union and Social Science Theory*. Cambridge, Mass.: Harvard University Press.

HOUT, MICHAEL. 1984. "Occupational Mobility of Black Men: 1962 to 1973," *American Sociological Review*, 49 (June), 308–22.

HOYTE, HOMER. 1939. "The Structure and Growth of Residential Neighborhoods in American Cities." Washington, D.C.: United States Federal Housing Administration.

HSU, CHO-YUN. 1965. *Ancient China in Transition*. Stanford, Cal.: Stanford University Press.

HUMPHREY, CRAIG R., and FREDERICK R. BUTTEL. 1982. *Environment, Energy, and Society*. Belmont, Cal.: Wadsworth Pub. Co.

HUNTER, FLOYD. 1953. *Community Power Structure*. Chapel Hill, N.C.: The University of North Carolina Press.

———. 1959. *Top Leadership U.S.A.* Chapel Hill, N.C.: University of North Carolina Press.

INDEPENDENT COMMISSION ON INTERNATIONAL DEVELOPMENT IMPASSES. 1980. *North-South: A Program for Survival.* Cambridge, Mass.: MIT Press.

INSTITUTE OF SOCIAL SCIENCES, BELGRADE. 1962. *Review: Yugoslav Monthly Magazine*, 2 (May), 14.

JACKMAN, ROBERT W. 1975. *Politics and Social Equality: A Comparative Analysis.* New York: John Wiley and Sons.

JANOWITZ, MORRIS. 1975. "Sociological Theory and Social Control," *American Journal of Sociology*, 81 (July), 82–108.

JENCKS, CHRISTOPHER, et al. 1972. *Inequality: A Reassessment of the Effects of Family and Schooling in America.* New York: Basic Books.

JOHNSON, CHALMERS. 1964. *Revolution and the Social System.* Stanford Calif.: Stanford University, The Hoover Institution.

JOHNSTONE, RONALD L. 1975. *Religion and Society in Interaction: The Sociology of Religion.* Englewood Cliffs, N.J.: Prentice-Hall, Inc.

KANTER, ROSABETH MOSS. 1977. *Men and Women of the Corporation.* New York: Basic Books.

KARSADA, JOHN D., and GEORGE REDFEARN. 1975. "Differential Patterns of Urban and Suburban Growth in the United States," *Journal of Urban History*, 2 (November), 43–66.

KELLER, SUZANNE. 1963. *Beyond the Ruling Class.* New York: Random House.

KEYNES, JOHN MAYNARD. 1936. *General Theory of Employment, Interest, and Money.* New York: Harcourt, Brace & Co.

KOLKO, GABRIEL. 1962 *Wealth and Power in America.* New York: Praeger.

KORNHAUSER, WILLIAM. 1959. *The Politics of Mass Society.* Glencoe, Ill.: Free Press.

KUHN, THOMAS S. 1970. *The Structure of Scientific Revolutions,* rev. ed. Chicago: University of Chicago Press.

LANDECKER, WERNER S. 1981. *Class Crystallization.* New Brunswick, N.J.: Rutgers University Press.

LANDSBERG, HANS H., et al. 1979. *Energy: The Next Twenty Years.* Cambridge, Mass.: Ballanger Pub. Co.

LEHMAN, EDWARD E. 1977. *A Macrosociology of Politics.* New York: Columbia University Press.

LEE, GARY R. 1977. "Age at Marriage and Marital Satisfaction: A Multivariate Analysis with Implications for Marital Stability," *Journal of Marriage and the Family*, 39 (August), 493–504.

LEMERT, EDWIN M. 1967. *Human Deviance, Social Problems, and Social Control.* Englewood Cliffs, N.J.: Prentice-Hall, Inc.

LENSKI, GERHARD E. 1954. "Status Crystallization: A Non-Vertical Dimension of Social Status." *American Sociological Review*, 19 (August), 405–13.

———. 1966. *Power and Privilege: A Theory of Social Stratification.* New York: McGraw-Hill.

———. 1961. *The Religious Factor.* Garden City, N.Y.: Doubleday and Co.

———. 1976. "History and Social Change," *American Journal of Sociology*, 82 (November), 548–64.

———, and JEAN LENSKI. 1982. *Human Societies: An Introduction to Macrosociology,* 4th ed. New York: McGraw-Hill Book Co.

LENSKI, GERHARD, and PATRICK D. NOLAN. 1984. "Trajectories of Development: A Test of Ecological-Evolutionary Theory," *Social Forces*, 63 (September), 1–23.

LEWIS, MICHAEL. 1978. *The Culture of Inequality.* New York: New American Library.

LIAZOS, ALEXANDER. 1972. "The Poverty of Sociology Deviance: Nuts, Sluts, and Perverts," *Social Problems*, 20 (Summer), 103–20.

LIKERT, RENSIS. 1961. *New Patterns of Management.* New York: McGraw-Hill.

LIND, ALDEN. 1975. "The Future of Citizen Participation," *The Futurist*, 9:316–28.

LINTON, RALPH. 1933. "The One Hundred Percent American," *The American Mercury*, 40:427–29.

LIPSET, SEYMOUR MARTIN. 1959. *Political Man.* Garden City, N.Y.: Doubleday and Co.

———, and REINHARD BENDIX. 1959. *Social Mobility in Industrial Society.* Berkeley Calif.: University of California Press.

LITWAK, EUGENE. 1961. "Models of Organizations Which Permit Conflict," *American Journal of Sociology*, 76 (September), 177–84.

LLOYD, JEAN, RAYMOND W. MACK, and JOHN PEASE. 1979. *Sociology and Social Life,* 6th ed. New York: D. Van Nostrand Co.

LOCKSLEY, ANNE. 1980. "On the Effects of Wife's Employment on Marital Adjustment and Companionship," *Journal of Marriage and the Family*, 42 (May), 337–46.

LOUIS HARRIS and ASSOCIATES, INC. 1978. "A Study of Attitudes Toward Racial and Religious Minorities and Toward Women." New

York: National Conference of Christians and Jews.

LOWIE, ROBERT. 1948. "The Tropical Forests: An Introduction." In Julian Stewart, ed., *Handbook of South American Indians*, Vol. III. Washington, D.C.: Smithsonian Institution Bureau of American Ethnology, pp. 1–56.

LYMAN, STANFORD M. 1974. *Chinese Americans*. New York: Random House.

LYONS, STEPHEN, ed. 1978. *Sun: A Handbook for the Solar Decade*. San Francisco: Friends of the Earth.

MACCOBY, MICHAEL. 1976. *The Gamesman: The New Corporate Leaders*. New York: Simon and Schuster.

MAIR, LUCY. 1962. *Primitive Government*. Baltimore: Penguin Books.

MALTHUS, THOMAS R. 1960. "An Essay on the Principle of Population," In Gertrude Himmelfard, ed., *On Population*. New York: Modern Library. [Originally published in 1798.]

MANNHEIM, KARL. 1936. *Ideology and Utopia*. New York: Harcourt, Brace and World.

———. 1940. *Man and Society in an Age of Reconstruction*. London: Routledge and Kegan Paul.

MARGER, MARTIN N. 1981. *Elites and Masses: An Introduction to Political Sociology*. New York: Wadsworth Publishing Co.

MARX, KARL. 1936. *Capital*. New York: The Modern Library. [Originally published in 1867.]

———. 1956. *Selected Writings in Sociology and Social Philosophy*, T. B. Bottomore and Maxmillian Rubel, eds. Baltimore, Md.: Penguin.

——— and FREDERICH ENGELS. 1948. *The Manifesto of the Communist Party*. London: George Allen & Unwin. [Originally published in 1848.]

MCCARTHY, JOHN D., and MAYER N. ZALD. 1977. "Resource Mobilization and Social Movements: A Partial Theory," *American Journal of Sociology*, 82 (May), 1212–41.

MCCLENDON, MCKEE J. 1977. "Structural and Exchange Components of Vertical Mobility," *American Sociological Review*, 42 (February), 56–74.

MCNEILL, WILLIAM. 1963. *The Rise of the West: A History of the Human Community*. New York: Mentor Books.

MEAD, GEORGE HERBERT. 1934. *Mind, Self, and Society*. Chicago: University of Chicago Press.

MEADOWS, DENNIS, et al. 1974. *The Dynamics of Growth in a Finite World*. Cambridge: Wright-Allen.

MEADOWS, DONELLA H., DENNIS L. MEADOWS, JORGEN RANDERS, and WILLIAM W. BEHRENS III. 1972. *The Limits to Growth*. London: Earth Island Ltd.

MEARS, WALTER. 1977. "Ending the Welfare Myths," *New York Post*, (May 27), p. 36.

MEEKER JOSEPH W. 1974. *The Comedy of Survival: Studies in Literary Ecology*. New York: Harper and Row.

MELLART, JAMES. 1965. *Earliest Civilizations of the Near East:* London: Thames and Hudson.

MERTON, ROBERT. 1957. *Social Theory and Social Structure*. Glencoe, Ill.: The Free Press.

MEYER, MARSHALL W., WILLIAM STEVENSON, and STEPHEN WEBSTER. 1985. *Limits to Bureaucratic Growth*. Hawthorne, N.Y.: Water de Gruyter, Inc.

MEYERSON, MARTIN, and EDWARD C. BANFIELD. 1955. *Politics, Planning and the Public Interest*. Chicago: Free Press.

MICHELS, ROBERT. 1962. *Political Parties*, trans. by Eden and Cedar Paul. New York: The Free Press. [Originally published in 1911.]

MILBRATH, LESTER. 1965. *Political Participation*. Chicago: Rand, McNally and Co.

MILIBAND, RALPH. 1969. *The State in Capitalist Society*. New York: Basic Books.

MILLER, BRENT. 1976. "A Multivariate Development Model of Marital Satisfaction," *Journal of Marriage and the Family*, 38 (November), 643–57.

MILLS, C. WRIGHT. 1956. *The Power Elite*. New York: Oxford University Press.

———. 1956. *White Collar: The American Middle Classes*. New York: Oxford University Press.

———. 1959. *The Sociological Imagination*. New York: Oxford University Press.

MINTZ, BETH, and MICHAEL SCHWARTZ. 1981. "Interlocking Directorates and Interest Group Formation," *American Sociological Review*, 46 (December), 851–69.

MOORE, GWEN. 1979. "The Structure of a National Elite Network," *American Sociological Review*, 44 (October), 673–92.

MORSE, NANCY C., and EVERETT REIMER. 1956. "The Experimental Change of a Major Organizational Variable," *Journal of Abnormal and Social Psychology*, 52 (January), 120–29.

MOSCA, GAETANO. 1939. *The Ruling Class.* New York: McGraw-Hill Book Co. [Originally published in 1896.]

MOTT, PAUL E. 1965. *The Organization of Society.* Englewood Cliffs, N.J.: Prentice–Hall, Inc.

MUMFORD, LEWIS. 1934. *Technics and Civilization.* New York: Harcourt Brace Co.

———. 1967, 1970. *The Myth of the Machine,* 2 vols. New York: Harcourt Brace Co.

MURDOCK, GEORGE PETER. 1935. "Comparative Data and the Division of Labor by Sex," *Social Forces,* 15 (May), 551–55.

———. 1949. *Social Structure.* New York: Free Press.

———. 1954. "The Common Denominator of Cultures," in Ralph Linton, ed., The Science of Man in the World Crisis. New York: Columbia University Press, pp. 123–142.

———. 1959. *Africa: Its People and Their Culture History.* New York: McGraw-Hill.

MURRAY, MARGARET. 1949. *The Splendor That Was Egypt.* London: Sidgwick and Jackson.

NAISBITT, JOHN. 1984. *Megatrends.* New York: Warner Books.

NATIONAL ACADEMY OF SCIENCES. 1979. *Energy in Transition: 1985–2010. Final Report of the Committee on Nuclear and Alternative Energy Systems.* San Francisco: W. H. Freeman Co.

NATIONAL INSTITUTE OF MENTAL HEALTH. 1974. "National Conference on Child Abuse: A Summary Report." Rockville, Md.: NIHM.

New York Times. 1974. "Wide Disparities in Crime Totals Found in Sampling of 8 Cities," (January 27), p. 34.

NISBET, ROBERT. 1962. *Community and Power.* New York: Oxford University Press.

OBSERSCHALL, ANTHONY. 1973. *Social Conflict and Social Movements.* Englewood Cliffs, N.J.: Prentice-Hall, Inc.

O'CONNOR, JAMES. 1973. *The Fiscal Crisis of the State.* New York: St. Martin's Press.

OGBURN, WILLIAM F., and MEYER F. NIMKOFF. 1950. *Social Change.* New York: Viking Press.

OLSEN, MARVIN E. 1965. "Durkheim's Two Concepts of Anomie," *Sociological Quarterly,* 6 (April), 37–44.

———. 1968. "Multivariate Analysis of National Political Development," *American Sociological Review,* 33 (October), 699–712.

———. 1973. "A Model of Political Participation Stratification," *Journal of Political and Military Sociology,* 1 (Fall), 183–200.

———. 1979. "Interest Association, Participation and Political Activity in the U.S. and Sweden." In George A. Kouvetaris and Betty Dobratz, eds., *Political Sociology: Readings in Research and Theory.* New Brunswick, N.J.: Transaction Books, pp. 291–307.

———. 1982a. "Linkages Between Socioeconomic Modernization and National Political Development," *Journal of Military and Political Sociology,* 10, 41–69.

———. 1982b. *Participatory Pluralism: Political Participation and Influence in the United States and Sweden.* Chicago: Nelson-Hall.

———. 1990. "The Energy Consumption Turnaround and Socioeconomic Well-Being in Industrial Societies in the 1980s." Presented at the World Congress of Sociology of the International Sociological Association.

———, and MARY ANNA HOVEY. 1974. "Legitimacy of Social Protest Actions in the U.S. and Sweden," *Journal of Political and Military Sociology,* 2 (Fall), 173–89.

OLSON, MANCUR, and HANS H. LANDSBURG. 1973. *The No-Growth Society.* New York: W. W. Norton and Co.

O'NEIL, NENA, and GEORGE O'NEIL. 1972. *Open Marriage: A New Life Style for Couples.* New York: M. Evans and Co.

OPHULS, WILLIAM. 1977. *Ecology and the Politics of Scarcity.* San Francisco: W. H. Freeman Co.

PALEN, JOHN. 1981. *The Urban World,* 3rd ed. New York: McGraw-Hill Book Co.

PARETO, VILFREDO. 1935. *The Mind and Society,* trans. by A. Bongiorno and A. Livingston, ed. by A. Livingston, 4 vols. New York: Harcourt, Brace and Co. [Originally published in 1916.]

PARK, ROBERT E., and ERNEST W. BURGESS. 1925. *The City.* Chicago: University of Chicago Press.

PARKIN, FRANK. 1971. *Glass Inequality and the Social Order.* London: McGibbon and Kee.

PARKINSON, C. NORTHCOTE. 1957. *Parkinson's Law.* Boston: Houghton Mifflin Co.

PATEMAN, CAROLE. 1970. *Participation and Democratic Theory.* Cambridge, England: Cambridge University Press.

PBTAICOV, LEONARD. 1967. *Strangers to the City: Urban Man in Jos, Nigeria.* Pittsburgh: University of Pittsburgh Press.

PERROW, CHARLES. 1961. "The Analysis of Goals in Complex Organizations," *American Sociological Review*, 26 (December), 845–66.

PETER, LAWRENCE, and RAYMOND HULL. 1969. *The Peter Principle*. New York: William Morrow.

PETERSEN, JOHN E., CATHERINE L. SPAIN, and Martharose F. Laffey. 1978. *State and Local Government Finance and Financial Management*. Washington, D.C.: Government Finance Research Center.

PETERSEN, WILLIAM. 1975. *Population*, 3rd ed. New York: Macmillan Co.

PILIAVIN, IRVING, and SCOTT BRIAR. 1964. "Police Encounters with Juveniles," *American Journal of Sociology*, 70 (September), 206–14.

PIRAGES, DENNIS CLARK, ed. 1977. *The Sustainable Society*. New York: Praeger Publishers.

PLECK, JOSEPH L., G. L. STAINES, and L. LAING. 1980. "Conflicts Between Work and Family Life," *Monthly Labor Review*, 40 (March), 29–32.

POPULATION REFERENCE BUREAU. 1987. *World Population Data Sheet*. Washington, D.C.: Population Reference Bureau, Inc.

PRESIDENT'S COMMISSION ON LAW ENFORCEMENT AND THE ADMINISTRATION OF JUSTICE. 1967. *The Challenge of Crime in a Free Society*. Washington, D.C.: U.S. Government Printing Office.

PRESTHUS, ROBERT. 1965. *The Organizational Society*. New York: Knopf.

QUINNEY, RICHARD, ed. 1974. *Criminal Justice in the United States*. Boston: Little Brown and Co.

RASMUSSEN, DAVID W. 1973. *Urban Economics*. New York: Harper and Row.

RECKLESS, WALTER C. 1961. *The Crime Problem*. New York: Appleton-Century-Crofts.

REDFORD, EMMETTE S. 1969. *Democracy in the Administrative State*. New York: Oxford University Press.

REISMAN, DAVID, NATHAN GLAZER, and REUEL DENNY. 1954. *The Lonely Crowd*. New York: Doubleday and Co.

REISS, ALBERT J., JR. 1959. "Rural-Urban Status Differences in Interpersonal Contacts," *American Journal of Sociology*, 65 (September), 182–95.

RICCI, DAVID. 1971. *Community Power and Democratic Theory: The Logic of Political Analysis*. New York: Random House.

RICHARDSON, HARRY W. 1977. *The New Urban Economics and Alternatives*. London: Pion.

ROBERTS, BRYAN R. 1973. *Organizing Strangers: Poor Families in Guatemala City*. Austin: University of Texas, Austin.

ROBERTSON, IAN. 1981. *Sociology*, 2nd ed. New York: Worth Publishers.

ROETHLISENGBER, FRITZ J., and WILLIAM J. DICKINSON. 1939. *Management and the Worker*. Cambridge, Mass.: Harvard University Press.

ROGERS, H. R., JR. 1978. "Hiding Versus Ending Poverty," *Politics and Society*, 8:254–55.

ROOSIDES, DANIEL W. 1976. *The American Class System*. Boston: Houghton Mifflin Co.

ROSA, EUGENE, ALEN E. RADZIK, and KENNETH M. KEATING. 1980. "Energy, Economic Growth, and Societal Well-Being: A Cross-National Trend Analysis." Presented at the annual meeting of the American Sociological Association.

ROSTOW, W. W. 1960. *The Stages of Economic Growth: A Non-Communist Manifesto*. Cambridge: Cambridge University Press.

RUBINSON, RICHARD and DAN QUINLAN. 1977. "Democracy and Social Inequality: A Reanalysis," *American Sociological Review*, 42 (August), 611–23.

RUSSELL, J. C. 1958. *Late Ancient and Medieval Population*. Philadelphia: American Philosophical Society.

RYBCZYNSKI, WITOLD. 1983. *Taming the Tiger: The Struggle to Control Technology*. New York: Penguin Books.

RYTINA, JOAN H., et al. 1970. "Income and Stratification Ideology: Beliefs About the American Opportunity Structure," *American Journal of Sociology*, 75 (January), 703–16.

SALE, KIRKPATRICK. 1980. *Human Scale*. New York: Coward, McCann & Geoghegan, 1980.

SAWHILL, JOHN C. 1979. *Energy Conservation and Public Policy*. Englewood Cliffs, N.J.: Prentice-Hill, Inc.

SCHAPERA, I. 1956. *Government and Politics in Tribal Societies*. London: Watts.

SCHNAIBERG, ALLAN. 1980. *The Environment: From Surplus to Scarcity*. New York: Oxford University Press.

SCHNEIDER, DAVID, and DATHLENE GOUGH, eds. 1961. *Matrilineal Kinship*. Berkeley: University of California Press.

SCHUMACHER, E. F. 1973. *Small Is Beautiful.* New York: Harper and Row.

SCHUMPETER, JOSEPH. 1943. *Capitalism, Socialism, and Democracy.* London: George Allen and Unwin.

SCHUR, EDWIN M. 1965. *Crimes Without Victims: Deviant Behavior and Public Policy.* Englewood Cliffs, N.J.: Prentice-Hall, Inc.

SCHURR, SAM H., et al. 1979. *Energy in America's Future: The Choices Before Us.* Baltimore: The Johns Hopkins University Press.

SCOTT, W. RICHARD. 1981. *Organizations: Rational, Natural, and Open Systems.* Englewood Cliffs, N.J.: Prentice-Hall, Inc.

SEEMAN, MELVIN. 1981. "Intergroup Relations," in Morris Rosenberg and Ralph H. Turner, eds. *Social Psychology: Sociological Perspectives.* New York: Basic Books.

SELZNICK, PHILLIP. 1966. *TVA and the Grass Roots.* New York: Harper Torchbooks.

SEMENOV, S. A. 1964. *Prehistoric Technology,* trans. by M. S. Thompson. New York: Barnes and Noble.

SERVICE, ELMAN. 1962. *Primitive Social Organization: An Evolutionary Perspective.* New York: Random House.

———. 1966. *The Hunters.* Englewood Cliffs, N.J.: Prentice-Hall, Inc.

———. 1975. *Origins of the State and Civilization: The Process of Cultural Evolution.* New York: W. W. Norton.

SEWELL, WILLIAM H., ROBERT M. HAUSER, and WENDY C. WOLF. 1980. "Sex, Schooling, and Occupational Status," *American Journal of Sociology,* 86 (November), 551–80.

SILLS, DAVID L. 1957. *The Volunteers.* New York: The Free Press.

SIMON, HERBERT. 1957. *Models of Man, Social and Rational.* New York: John Wiley and Sons.

SIMPSON, GEORGE E., and J. MILTON YINGER. 1972. *Racial and Cultural Minorities.* New York: Harper and Row.

SIMPSON, RICHARD. 1956. "A Modification of the Functional Theory of Stratification," *Social Forces* (December), 132–37.

SINGLEMAN, PETER. 1972. "Exchange as Symbolic Interaction: Convergences Between Two Theoretical Perspectives," *American Sociological Review,* 37 (August), 414–24.

SJOBERG, GIDEON. 1960. *The Preindustrial City.* New York: Free Press.

SKOCKPOL, THEDA. 1979. *States and Social Revolutions.* Cambridge: Cambridge University Press.

SLATER, PHILIP. 1970. *The Pursuit of Loneliness.* Boston: Beacon Press.

SLOMCZYNSKI, KAZIMIERZ M., and TADEUSZ K. KRAUZE. 1987. "Cross-National Similarity in Social Mobility Patterns: A Direct Test of the Featherman-Jones-Hauser Hypothesis," *American Sociological Review,* 52 (October), 598–611.

SMELSER, NEIL J. 1962. *Theory of Collective Behavior.* New York: Free Press.

———. 1963. *The Sociology of Economic Life.* Englewood Cliffs, N.J.: Prentice-Hall, Inc.

SMITH, ADAM. 1937. *Inquiry Into the Nature and Causes of the Wealth of Nations.* New York: The Modern Library. [Originally published in 1776.]

SORENSON, ANNEMETTE, KARL E. TAUEBER, and LESLIE J. HOLLINGSWORTH, JR., "Indexes of Racial Residential and Segregation for 109 Cities in the United States, 1940 to 1970," *Sociological Focus,* 8 (April), 125–42.

SOROKIN, PITIRIM. 1962. *Social and Cultural Dynamics,* vol. III. New York: Bedminister Press.

SPENCER, HERBERT. 1862. *First Principles.* New York: A. L. Burt.

———. 1873. *The Study of Sociology.* New York: D. Appleton.

SPIRO, THOMAS G., and WILLIAM M. STIGLIANI. 1980. *Environmental Science in Perspective.* Albany, N.Y.: State University of New York Press.

STARK, RODNEY, and WILLIAM S. BAINBRIDGE. 1981. "American-Born Sects: Initial Findings," *Journal for the Scientific Study of Religion,* 20 (2):139–49.

———. 1985. *The Future of Religion: Secularization, Revival, and Cult Formation.* Berkeley, Calif.: University of California Press.

STEWARD, JULIAN, and LOUIS FARON. 1959. *Native Peoples of South America.* New York: McGraw-Hill Book Co.

STOBAUGH, ROBERT, and DANIEL YERGIN, eds. 1979. *Energy Futures: Report of the Energy Project of the Harvard Business School.* New York: Random House.

STOCKMAN, WILLIAM. 1978. "Going Home: The Puerto Rican's New Migration," *New York Times,* (May 12) pp. 20–22, 88–93.

STUEVER, STUART. 1971. *Prehistoric Agriculture.* Garden City, N.Y.: Natural History Press.

SUMNER, WILLIAM GRAHAM. 1940. *Folkways.* New York: Ginn and Co. [Originally published in 1906.]

SUTHERLAND, EDWIN H. 1939. *Principles of Criminology.* Philadelphia: Lippincott.

———. 1961. *White Collar Crime.* New York: Holt, Rinehart & Winston.

SUTTLES, GERALD. 1978. *The Social Construction of Communities.* Chicago: University of Chicago Press.

TALLMAN, IRVING, and ROMONA MORGNER. 1970. "Life Style Differences Among Urban and Suburban Blue Collar Families," *Social Forces,* 48 (March), 334–48.

TAUEBER, KARL K., and ALMA F. TAUEBER. 1965. *Negroes in Cities: Residential Segregation and Neighborhood Change.* Chicago: Aldine Publishing Co.

TAYLOR, FREDERICK W. 1911. *The Principles of Scientific Management.* New York: Harper and Brothers.

THOMPSON, ANTHONY P. 1983. "Extramarital Sex: A Review of the Research Literature," *The Journal of Sex Research,* 19 (February), 1–21.

THOMPSON, JAMES D. 1967. *Organizations in Action.* New York: McGraw-Hill.

TILLY, CHARLES. 1975. "Revolution and Collective Violence." In Fred I. Greenstein and Nelson W. Polsby, eds. *Handbook of Political Science,* Vol. 3, *Macropolitical Theory.* Reading, Mass.: Addison-Wesley, pp. 483–556.

Time Magazine. June 15, 1987.

TITTLE, CHARLES K., et al. 1978. "The Myth of Social Class and Criminality: An Empirical Assessment of the Empirical Evidence," *American Sociological Review,* 43 (October), 643–56.

TOCQUEVILLE, ALEXIS DE. 1961. *Democracy in America.* Vol. 2, trans. by Henry Reeve. New York: Schocken Books. [Originally published in 1840.]

TOENNIES, GERDINAND. 1957. *Community and Society.* East Lansing, Michigan: Michigan State University Press. [Originally published in 1887.]

TOFFLER, ALVIN. 1980. *The Third Wave.* New York: William Morrow and Co.

TOMASSON, RICHARD F. 1970. *Sweden: Prototype of Modern Society.* New York: Random House.

TOMEH, AIDA. 1964. "Informal Group Participation and Residential Patterns," *American Journal of Sociology,* 70 (July), 28–35.

TRIEMAN, DONALD J. 1977. *Occupational Prestige in Comparative Perspective.* New York: Academic Press.

TROELTSCH, ERNST. 1931. *The Social Teaching of the Christian Churches.* New York: Macmillan.

TROUNSTINE, PHILIP J. and TERRY CHRISTENSEN. 1982. *Movers and Shakers: The Study of Community Power.* New York: St. Martin's Press.

TROW, MARTIN. 1961. "The Second Transformation of American Secondary Education," *International Journal of Comparative Sociology,* 2:144–65.

TURNER, JONATHAN H., and CHARLES E. STARNES. 1976. *Inequality: Privilege and Poverty in America.* Pacific Palisades, Calif.: Goodyear Publishing Co.

TURNER, RALPH. 1946. *The Great Cultural Transformations: The Foundations of Civilization,* Vol. I. New York: McGraw-Hill Book Co.

———. 1962. "Role Taking: Process Versus Conformity," in Arnold Rose, ed., *Human Behavior and Social Processes.* Boston: Houghton Mifflin Co., pp. 20–40.

UNITED NATIONS. 1986. *World Population Prospects: Estimates and Projections as Assessed in 1984.* New York: Department of International Economic and Social Affairs.

———. 1987. *U.N. Demographic Yearbook 1985.* New York: Department of International Economic and Social Affairs.

UNITED NATIONS DEPARTMENT OF ECONOMIC AND SOCIAL AFFAIRS. 1980. "Patterns of Urban and Rural Population Growth," No. 68.

UNITED STATES BUREAU OF THE CENSUS. 1960. *Historical Statistics of the United States.* Washington, D.C.: U.S. Government Printing Office.

———. 1975. *Historical Statistics of the United States: Colonial Times to 1970.* Washington, D.C.: U.S. Government Printing Office.

———. 1981. *Social Indicators, III.* Washington, D.C.: U.S. Government Printing Office.

———. 1981, 1982, 1984 and 1987. *Statistical Abstract of the United States.* Washington, D.C.: U.S. Government Printing Office.

———. 1987. *"Population Profile of the United States,"* Current Population Reports P-23, No. 150. Washington, D.C.: United States Government Printing Office.

UNITED STATES DEPARTMENT OF HEALTH, EDUCATION AND WELFARE. 1972. *Welfare: Myths vs. Facts.* Washington, D.C.: U.S. Government Printing Office.

UNITED STATES SENATE. 1974. "Disclosure of Corporate Ownership," Subcommittee on Intergovernmental Relations, Budgeting, Management, and Expenditures, of the Committee on Government Operation. 93rd Congress, 2nd session.

VAN DEN BURGHE, PIERRE. 1978. *Race and Racism,* 2nd ed. New York: John Wiley & Co.

VANEK JOANN. 1980. "Household Work, Wage Work, and Sexual Equality." In Sarah Fenstermaher Berk ed., *Women and Household Labor.* Berkeley Hills, Cal.: Sage Publications, pp. 275–291.

VANNEMAN, REEVE. 1977. "The Occupational Composition of American Classes: Results from Cluster Analysis," *American Journal of Sociology,* 82 (January), 783–807.

VAN VALEY, THOMAS, WADE CLARK ROOF, and JEROME E. WILCOX. 1977. "Trends in Residential Segregation, 1960–1970," *American Journal of Sociology,* 82 (January), 826–44.

VATTER, HAROLD. 1976. *The Drive to Industrial Maturity: The U.S. Economy, 1860–1914.* Westport, Conn.: Greenwood Press.

VERBA, SYDNEY, and NORMAL NIE. 1972. *Participation in America: Political Democracy and Social Equality.* New York: Harper and Row.

VERNON, RAYMOND. 1977. *Storm Over the Multinationals.* Cambridge, Mass.: Harvard University Press.

WALLERSTEIN, IMMANUAL. 1974 and 1980. *The Modern World System,* 2 vols. New York: Academic Press.

WARD, LESTER F. 1883. *Dynamic Sociology: Or Applied Social Science.* New York: D. Appleton and Co.

———. 1906. *Applied Sociology: A Treatise on the Conscious Improvement of Society by Society.* New York: Ginn and Co.

WATSON, WILLIAM. 1961. *China: Before the Han Dynasty.* New York: Praeger Publishers.

WEBER, MAX. 1947. *The Theory of Social and Economic Organization,* trans. by A. M. Henderson and Talcott Parsons. New York: Free Press.

———. 1958. "Class, Status and Party." From *Max Weber: Essays in Sociology,* trans. and ed. by H. H. Gerth and C. Wright Mills. New York: Oxford University Press, pp. 180–95. [Originally published in 1922.]

———. 1958. *The Protestant Ethic and the Spirit of Capitalism,* trans. by Talcott Parsons. New York: Charles Scribner's Sons.

———. 1970. "Religion." From *Max Weber: Essays in Sociology,* trans. and ed. by H. H. Gerth and C. Wright Mills. New York: Oxford University Press, 267–359. [Originally published in 1922].

WELCH, CHARLES E. III, and PAUL C. GLICK. 1981. "The Incidence of Polygamy in Contemporary Africa: A Research Note," *Journal of Marriage and the Family,* 43 (February), 191–94.

WENDORF, F., et al. 1979. "Use of Barley in the Egyptian Paleolithic," *Science,* 205:1341–47.

WHITE, LESLIE A. 1949. *Energy and the Evolution of Culture: The Development of Civilization to the Fall of Rome.* New York: McGraw-Hill.

———. 1975. *The Concept of Cultural Systems: A Key to Understanding Tribes and Nations.* New York: Columbia University Press.

WHITEHEAD, ALFRED NORTH. 1929. *Process and Reality.* New York: Macmillan.

WHYTE, WILLIAM H. JR. 1956. *The Organization Man.* New York: Simon and Schuster.

WILENSKY, HAROLD L. 1966. "A Second Look at the Traditional View of Urbanism," In Ronald Warren, ed., *Perspectives on the Urban Community.* Chicago: Rand McNally.

WILLIAMS, ROBIN. 1970. *American Society: A Sociological Interpretation,* 3rd ed. New York: Alfred Knopf.

———. 1977. *Mutual Accommodation: Ethical Conflict and Cooperation.* Minneapolis: University of Minnesota Press.

WILSON, ROBERT A., and BILL HOSOKAWA. 1980. *East to America: A History of the Japanese in the United States.* New York: W. W. Morrow.

WILSON, WILLIAM JULIUS. 1984. *The Truly Disadvantaged. The Inner City, the Underclass, and Public Policy.* Chicago: University of Chicago Press.

WIRTH, LOUIS. 1938. "Urbanism as a Way of Life," *American Journal of Sociology,* 44 (July), 8–20.

WOLFE, ALAN. 1973. *The Seamy Side of Democracy: Repression in America.* New York: David McKay.

———. 1977. *The Limits of Legitimacy: Political Contradictions of Contemporary Capitalism.* New York: Basic Books.

WOODWARD, C. VANN. 1974. *The Strange Career of Jim Crow*, 3rd ed. New York: Oxford University Press.

WOODWARD, JOAN. 1965. *Industrial Organization: Theory and Practice*. London: Oxford University Press.

YANKELOVICH, DANIEL. 1981. *New Rules*. New York: Random House.

YINGER, J. MILTON. 1970. *The Scientific Study of Religion*. New York: Crowell-Collier and Maxmillan.

ZALD, MAYER. 1970. *Organizational Change: The Political Economy of the YMCA*. Chicago: University of Chicago Press.

———. 1970. *Power in Organizations*. Nashville, Tenn.: Vanderbilt University Press.

———. 1970. "Political Economy: A Framework for Comparative Analysis," In Mayer N. Zald, ed., *Power in Organizations*. Nashville, Tenn.: Vanderbilt University Press, pp. 221–261.

ZALTMAN, GERALD, ROBERT DUNCAN, and JENNY HOLBECK. 1973. *Innovations and Organizations*, 2nd ed. New York: John Wiley and Sons.

ZIM, MARVIN. 1978. "The Inflation Isn't Over in TV Advertising Rates," *Fortune*, 98 (November 6), 52–55.

INDEX